THE MAKING OF
FDR

Linda Lotridge Levin

THE MAKING OF

FDR

The Story of Stephen T. Early, America's First Modern Press Secretary

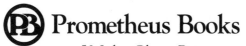

Prometheus Books

59 John Glenn Drive
Amherst, New York 14228–2119

Published 2008 by Prometheus Books

Inquiries should be addressed to
Prometheus Books
59 John Glenn Drive
Amherst, New York 14228–2119
VOICE: 716–691–0133, ext. 210
FAX: 716–691–0137
WWW.PROMETHEUSBOOKS.COM

12 11 10 09 08   5 4 3 2 1

Library of Congress Cataloging-in-Publication Data

Levin, Linda Lotridge, 1940–
   The making of FDR : the story of Stephen T. Early, America's first modern press seccretary / by Linda Lotridge Levin.
        p. cm.
   Includes bibliographical references and index.
   ISBN 978–1–59102–577–1
   1. Early, Stephen T. (Stephen Tyree), 1882–1951. 2. Presidential press secretaries—United States—Biography. 3. Journalists—United States—Biography. 4. Roosevelt, Franklin D. (Franklin Delano), 1888–1945—Friends and associates. 5. United States—Politics and government—1933–1945. 6. Government and the press—United States—History. I. Title.

E748.E13L48 2007
352.23'2748092—dc22
[B]   2007038275

Printed in the United States of America on acid-free paper

For My Three Muses—Len, Rachel, and Sara

And for Mike Hamilburg, Who Believed

CONTENTS

PREFACE

There won't be a book, he told his friends just before he left the White House. In fact, he said, he had destroyed all his notes and papers. Perhaps he intended to, or he did discard some, but happily for historians, enough of Stephen T. Early's papers—his White House diaries during the 1930s, a treasure trove of personal letters, White House memos, scrapbooks, and personal memorabilia—did survive, and in 1969, seventeen years after his death, his widow, Helen, appropriately turned them over to the Franklin D. Roosevelt Library in Hyde Park, New York, where they were carefully catalogued and today are open to researchers and anyone else interested in the life of this first, and longest-serving, modern presidential press secretary.

Had there been no Franklin D. Roosevelt, Steve Early would have toiled in semiobscurity overseeing the production of newsreels for the Hollywood movie moguls, eventually perhaps moving into a fancy public relations office in New York or Washington. His name would have meant nothing to the average person. He would have died a well-to-do—although probably not wealthy—man, admired by his colleagues for his forthrightness and dedication to both his job and his family.

Had there been no Steve Early, it is possible that Franklin Roosevelt would have been a one-term president. For without the publicity machine developed by Early with the president's blessing and encouragement during his first term in office, the charismatic Roosevelt might have found the hostility of most of the nation's newspaper publishers too much of an obstacle to overcome when it came time for the 1936 election. Louis Howe, often credited with successfully steering Franklin into politics after he was felled by polio and then became his closest adviser in the White House, had died that spring. When it appeared that ennui had settled over the White House, its chief occupant doing little to promote his own campaign for reelection, First Lady Eleanor Roosevelt and press secretary Steve Early stepped in and set the campaign publicity in motion. Early ironed out the kinks, dividing his time between campaign headquarters in New York and his office in the White House, where he continued to hold his press conference each morning. He worked diligently to solidify the relationship between the president and the reporters who regularly covered him, ensuring that in spite of the publishers' Republican voices on the nation's editorial pages, the news pages would be filled with positive news about the president.

When Franklin Roosevelt hired Steve Early as his full-time press secretary, it was the first time a White House secretary would exclusively handle the press. Theodore Roosevelt had been the first president to understand the press could be of value to him. He could see the reporters in the cold winters and the steamy summers huddled outside against the iron fence in front of the White House. So he decided they should have their own room inside the newly built Executive Office Building. However, Roosevelt played favorites, giving favored reporters news tips and interviews. He held press conferences, but much of what he said was "off the record." During Woodrow Wilson's first term as president, he held regular press conferences, but reporters were never quite clear what information they could use and whether they could attribute it to the president. Unlike Teddy Roosevelt, Wilson always seemed uncomfortable with the reporters. By his second term, he was too busy with the war to bother with meetings with the press. President Herbert Hoover, FDR's predecessor, did not much care for reporters, so he requested that they submit their questions in writing, and often as not, his replies, when they did come, were in writing.

Franklin Roosevelt was like a breath of fresh air to the reporters who covered the White House. He told them he would hold twice-weekly press conferences. Steve Early said he would hold his own press conference every morning, and he did. Roosevelt's decision then was not only a radical departure from past practices; in many ways it would prove to be a hallmark of his presidency. At last, the White House was opening its doors to the press on a daily basis, and until the United States entered World War II, the news flowed freely from the president and his press secretary through the press to the public. In her book *FDR and the News Media*, Betty Houchin Winfield calls the Roosevelt presidency "*the* historical yardstick for measuring how well contemporary presidents communicate and mold public opinion."[1]

The lives of Stephen T. Early, a native Virginian and the son of a railroad clerk, and Franklin Delano Roosevelt, a New York patrician and a politician, were inextricably bound from the day they met at the 1912 Democratic National Convention in Baltimore. Their lives continued to intersect, their friendship deepening, right up to the day Roosevelt was elected president. Early, a reporter for the wire service United Press, was covering the convention, and Roosevelt, a Wilson supporter, was there as a delegate from New York. The twenty-three-year-old reporter and the thirty-year-old politician struck up a friendship, and later, when Wilson named Roosevelt assistant secretary of the navy, Early was covering the navy as part of his beat for the Associated Press. Soon after the United States entered World War I in 1917, Early enlisted in the army infantry and left for France.

When he eventually returned, his friend Franklin Roosevelt was the vice presidential candidate on the Democratic ticket. He desperately needed a campaign staff, so he turned to his friend Steve and asked him to be his advance man, traveling around the country a train ride ahead of the candidate, setting up meetings with the local press and politicians in cities and towns. The Republican ticket, headed by Senator Warren G. Harding, won the election, and Early went back to the Associated Press, where, ironically, he got the scoop on Harding's death in a San Francisco hotel. (All the other reporters covering Harding's visit had gone out to dinner when the president, already ill, suddenly died.) Roosevelt returned to New York and, in a story that has been told and retold, he contracted polio, recovered—although paralyzed—and was elected governor of New York. By the late 1920s, after an outstanding career with the AP, Early left to oversee production of Paramount Pictures newsreels in Washington.

The two men continued to correspond and occasionally socialize, so it seemed natural that when Roosevelt was elected president, he would ask his friend Steve to handle the press as one of his three secretaries. (Louis Howe was Roosevelt's confidential secretary and Marvin McIntyre was his appointments secretary.) Early agreed, but said he would stay for only two years. Less than two weeks after Roosevelt was sworn in for his first term, the *New York News* said Early had "taken Washington by storm." Together, he and Roosevelt were launching a breathtaking reorganization of the way the government informed the public. They utilized press conferences in ways no previous president had, with Roosevelt holding two of them a week, open to all accredited White House correspondents with no favoritism allowed, as had been the hallmark of so many earlier presidencies. With Howe's death in 1936, Early stepped in to fill the void.

Early held his own press conference every morning, and within a short time the secretary was being quoted regularly in the newspapers. Early and Roosevelt established the wildly popular and effective Fireside Chats. Early set about restructuring and expanding the press offices in the federal agencies and departments by tapping into the roster of contacts he had made as an AP reporter, bringing journalists from newspapers around the country to Washington who, in their new jobs, would act as spokesmen for the New Deal. Through his contacts at Paramount, he ensured that the Roosevelt image appeared regularly on the movie screens of America. And throughout it all, Early managed to keep the photographers—still and moving—from revealing the crippled president as anything but healthy, a feat that in today's news media would be impossible because of the sheer breadth of sources of news, printed and visual, and the intense competition to get that news to the public.

Early's loyalty to "the Boss," as he called Roosevelt, kept him at his post year after year. Occasionally he would ask to be released from what he sometimes described to friends as his prison. Despite the fact that Early desperately needed to earn more money to support his family, the president time and again rejected his request—and he stayed. By the late 1930s, stories about the press secretary were legendary, repeated in radio and newspaper interviews and recorded by Early himself in letters to friends and acquaintances asking about his scoop as an Associated Press reporter on Harding's death, about how he met FDR, and what it was like to work so closely with the president.

Early was the first presidential press secretary to have the luxury and the frustrations of dealing with both broadcast and print media on a daily basis. Members of the White House press corps wrote about his "towering temper," but they respected him and trusted him to be honest with them. When Early became involved in a racial incident just weeks before the 1940 election, the White House reporters immediately came to his defense. By this time, newspapers were saying that he had become the principal link between the White House and the public. His capable handling of critical news in the hours and days after Pearl Harbor drew the applause of the White House press corps.

Early's first official contact of the day was with Roosevelt, while the president was still in bed. The press secretary and two or three other close advisers would meet each morning with FDR to discuss the day's events. These men were more than his aides; they were his cronies, his counselors on policies, sharers of state secrets, companions on fishing trips, and targets of the banter he used to lighten his workload.

Because Early served Roosevelt longer than any other close aide, the two men found themselves weathering the frustrations of the New Deal. Then they survived the intensity of the war years, even though on occasion the two men did not always see eye to eye on Early's relationship with the press. Roosevelt found newspapers an irritant and often chastised reporters in public, leaving Early to calm his former colleagues. In 1944, when Early asked Roosevelt to make a statement on freedom of the press, the president replied, "Quite frankly I regard Freedom of the Press as one of the world's most microscopic problems."[2] Working for a charismatic but controversial president, Early was often left to play the role of the "squarer," where he would end up at the Press Club for a drink with some enraged journalist who planned to blow the lid off one of the president's pet projects, or take an angry businessman out for a couple of hours of golf to cool him down. During Roosevelt's rough-and-tumble press conferences, especially during the New Deal years, Early would stand behind the president's desk, steering him over the worst of the shoals.

The two men shared a fondness for practical jokes, so much so that when Roosevelt called Early on the Sunday that the Japanese bombed Pearl Harbor and asked him if he had a pencil handy, Early thought the Boss was pulling a prank. They enjoyed fishing, and Early accompanied the president and other close aides on Roosevelt's winter cruises in the Caribbean. When he had time, Roosevelt would play poker with Secretary of the Interior Harold Ickes, Works Progress Administration head and FDR adviser Harry Hopkins, Early, and other White House friends, an activity that often found Early on the losing end and the Boss kidding him about it. Roosevelt also got a kick out of poking fun at Early's penchant for betting on the horses, but he was always interested in whether his press secretary, whom he sometimes affectionately called "Old Stevie," had won or lost at the track the previous day.

As the war progressed and Roosevelt periodically left the country for wartime conferences or was holed up for long weekends at his home in Hyde Park, Early sat at his desk in the White House serving as the liaison between the public and the president. These were difficult years for the press secretary, who resisted censorship and tried to be as honest as he could with the reporters. Presidential travels were conducted in secret. Even when reporters knew the president's destination, Early would plead with them not to publish or broadcast it. Astonishingly, the media went along with these and other requests. Reporters always knew where they stood with Early. If they asked a question about a military secret, for instance, he would deny knowing anything about it and then tell them the information was "off the record" and give them the background.

So knowledgeable about White House policies and politics was the press secretary that in 1944 a publisher in Georgia suggested in an editorial that he should be Roosevelt's vice presidential candidate that year. The president was amused, but went ahead and chose a United States senator from Missouri named Harry Truman.

When Roosevelt decided to run for a fourth term, the rumors were rampant that he was in poor health, probably dying. It was left to Early and the somewhat ineffectual Ross McIntire, the president's longtime naval aide and physician, to attempt to convince the press that the chief executive was fit enough to carry on if reelected. He won, but he died less than three months after he was inaugurated. Eleanor Roosevelt asked Early to announce the death of his friend and boss to the world. Then he agreed to stay on for a brief time to help the new president deal with the press. Early left to become a vice president of the Pullman Railroad Company and at last earn the money he needed to support his family. But Truman called him back to the government in April 1949 as assistant secretary of defense and that August promoted him to deputy secretary of defense, a position he left in 1951 to return to Pullman in another attempt to bolster his depleted savings account. It was a short-lived career. He died suddenly a few months later.

When Early left the White House soon after FDR's death, the *Nashville Tennessean* said, "Mr. Early has been the presidential buffer at that sparking point where the capitol newsgatherers meet the nation's most important news source. When the chief executive himself was not available for [an] interview, it has been the press secretary's part to release White House statements, to confirm or deny reports brought to be tested at headquarters, and generally to handle relations of the presidential office with what is undoubtedly the keenest group of inquisitors on earth."[3]

This consummate newsman, a loyal presidential aide and friend, might have been embarrassed, but probably not surprised, at the wide press coverage his death received. He would have appreciated the journalistic reporting that went into the long, detailed obituaries in newspapers throughout the country. To underscore his importance, his death was announced by the White House, little more than seven years after he himself had announced Franklin Roosevelt's death to the world.

The former press secretary's funeral in Washington attracted a who's who of Washington officialdom. Honorary pallbearers included the secretaries of defense, army and navy, the chief justice, and Vice President Alben Barkley. President Truman was there to pay respects to his former aide. Early was eulogized in the House of Representatives by Representative John McCormack of Massachusetts. Condolence letters and telegrams to his widow, Helen, ran into the hundreds. Some were written by people who had only read about Early as FDR's press secretary; others came from prominent Americans such as J. Edgar Hoover, who sent a kind but formal telegram from San Diego saying he was unable to get away for the funeral but was pleased to be an honorary pallbearer. He expressed his sympathy for her loss and his respect for Early, ending with: "The memory of Steve's friendship will live with me forever." It was signed John Edgar Hoover.

Harold Ickes, who considered Steve Early a friend and a loyal and respected press secretary, wrote a two-page letter to Mrs. Early, saying her husband's death "has left me almost speechless." He went on, "I was devoted to him and admired his human qualities and his instinct for leadership." Of Early's relationship with Roosevelt, Ickes said, "I do not believe that President Roosevelt ever had anyone on his staff with such sound judgment as to how the country would feel about some particular act or expression."

Early's death was announced over the Voice of America. David Sarnoff, founder and head of NBC, sent a telegram. Eleanor Roosevelt sent condolences to Mrs. Early in a letter after the funeral and in a telegram: "It was with great sadness that I read of Steve's death. I shall always be grateful for his devotion to my husband."

President Truman called him "honest, honorable, forthright— irascible sometimes but never vindictive and always just—he had vision as well as courage and a rare faculty of seeing all things in due proportion and through to their logical sequence."

Truman said Early gave the best years of his life to public service. It was a most fitting tribute. Perhaps Early's real legacy was opening up the business of the White House to the public and ensuring that it would remain an important news source throughout the Roosevelt presidency. Although today presidential press secretaries are often mere mouthpieces for administration policy and would-be manipulators of public opinion, for the most part they recognize the importance of some kind of continuing dialogue between the press and the White House.

THE JOURNALIST
MEETS THE POLITICIAN

S oon after he went to the White House with Franklin D. Roosevelt, Steve Early wrote to a woman who had inquired about his Early family origins: "As far as I know, my ancestors landed in Virginia and remained there." Indeed the family had settled on the eastern shore of Virginia in the early 1660s, probably arriving directly from England. Over the next 130 years, descendants of those first Earlys slowly made their way west across the state until they reached the Rivanna River, near Charlottesville, not far from the site where Thomas Jefferson chose to create his exquisite Monticello. The area became home to two more presidents. James Monroe lived nearby at his estate, Ash Lawn. Up the road from Ash Lawn was Montpelier, the home of James and Dolley Madison.[1]

Thomas Joseph Early and Ida Virginia Wood Early, parents of Stephen Tyree Early, lived far less sumptuously. The young couple married in 1888 and settled in Crozet, a village ten miles west of Charlottesville in the rolling foothills of the Shenandoah Mountains. Crozet was a stop of the Chesapeake and Ohio Railway. Thomas Joseph worked for the railroad as a postal clerk. Stephen was their first child, born on August 27, 1889. His birth was followed three years later by a brother, Felix, who later studied law at Georgetown University and spent his life with the Interstate Commerce Commission.

Their next sibling, Mary Catherine, who was born in 1894, eventually married George Holmes, head of the International News Service (INS) bureau in Washington, DC. In 1897 Virginia, who later married Magnien McArdle, a well-known Washington lawyer, was born.[2]

When Steve Early was born, Benjamin Harrison was president. George Eastman had just perfected the Kodak hand camera, allowing amateur photographers to snap away, and the modern bicycle, with two equal-sized tires and a saddle seat in between, was being mass produced, making it a popular mode of transportation. On November 14, Nellie Bly, the fearless reporter for Joseph Pulitzer's newspaper the *World* in New York, began her around-the-world trip, which ended successfully seventy-two days later.

None of this probably had much effect on a lad growing up in the middle of one of the most fiercely proud of the old Confederate states, where tales recounted by old men must have left him dreaming of the adventures of a war that had affected his own family. The records show that at least one of his great-uncles, on his mother's side, was killed in the Civil War, and his grandfather was a captain in the Confederate cavalry. After Steve Early went to the White House, the *Washington Post* said that he was brought up in an atmosphere "of confidence in the old American tradition and respect for constituted authority," an apt description of Thomas and Ida's first child.[3]

The ancestor whose war exploits so fascinated Steve—as a youth and as an adult—was Lt. Gen. Jubal A. Early, who marched his Confederate troops to within five miles of Washington in 1864. During Steve Early's years in the White House as Roosevelt's press secretary, his ancestry was often recounted, especially in Washington and Southern newspapers, and he was asked by reporters and interested citizens—some of them with the surname Early—about his relationship to the crusty and eccentric old general. His explanations varied depending on his state of mind. If relaxed and playful, he would refer to himself as the "grandson of that famous bachelor general, Jubal Early, confederacy's shining star." In serious moments, he would painstakingly write back to anyone who inquired that he was indeed a kin of Jubal Early and then explain as best he knew the details of that relationship.

Just what was Steve Early's relationship to the Confederate general? He definitely was a collateral descendant—a lineage that went back, he once told someone, to 1728 and an ancestor named Jeremiah Early Sr., whose great-great-great-grandson was Thomas Joseph, Early's father. In 1937 Steve asked a friend in the Department of State who dabbled in genealogy to look into the relationship. The friend turned to the Library of Congress, whose genealogists informed him that the general and the presidential press secretary probably were third cousins twice removed.[4]

The Early family moved to Washington in 1899 when Thomas was transferred by the railroad. Steve was only ten years old, but he remained rooted psychologically and emotionally in Virginia throughout his adult life. His two sons attended military school there, and his older son was a student at the University of Virginia. Steve and Helen often vacationed in the state. He corresponded with cousins and other relatives who remained in Virginia, and when he enlisted in World War I, it was with a Virginia regiment.

Washington must have been quite a change for the young lad who had roamed the rolling countryside around Crozet. With the move to Washington, the Early family had traded the relative tranquility of rural life for an urban setting a few blocks north of the United States Capitol, a building that in its awesome splendor must have captivated the imagination of young Steve. The family lived in a large, boxy house at 1228 North Carolina Avenue, a working-class neighborhood where Steve Early grew to manhood.[5]

After the family arrived on North Carolina Avenue, Ida Early gave birth to five more children over the next eleven years. Julia Lee was born in 1899; she later married a lawyer. Rachel, born two years later, died when she was three. Oma, who married Barry Faris, the general manager of the International News Service, came along in 1903. Elisha, who as a child contracted polio and remained crippled, was born in 1906; and Thomas Joseph Jr. was born in 1910. This youngest son and namesake of his father was injured in a childhood fall from a tree and spent most of his adult life at home until he was placed in a nursing home in 1947. As the oldest child and son, Steve remained close to his brothers and sisters all his life, coming to their emotional and financial aid during all the years he served in the White House, despite his and Helen's own—often severe—budget constraints.[6]

North Carolina Avenue is a broad, undistinguished street; the houses are close enough for next-door neighbors to converse out their windows. It was far from a glamorous neighborhood, but in those unendurably humid summers, the Early children could play in the park a few blocks away at Lincoln Square, where a bronze figure of President Abraham Lincoln holds a copy of the Emancipation Proclamation in his right hand, his left hand resting on the shoulder of a crouching black man whose shackles had been broken. Unveiled in 1876, it was a gift from emancipated slaves. It is unlikely, though, that the Earlys ever attended a social function at the White House or had any reason to interact with those with surnames of Riggs, Mays, Beale, or Blair—the city's social elite, with whom Steve Early would be at ease at the dinner table or on the golf course thirty years later.

It must have been a cash-strapped family in which the eight surviving Earlys grew up, especially since two of them had infirmities. As soon as he was old enough, young Steve delivered the *Washington Post* in the neighborhood, adding his own small earnings to the family's budget. There probably was little left over for a scrappy boy moving into his teenage years to spend on himself, but if he did, he may have attended a baseball game, where he would see the great Walter Johnson pitch for the Nationals (or the Senators, as Washington's hometown team also was called). It would have been difficult for a railway mail clerk to take a family of ten very far on his salary, since the six-day workweek was the norm, and the two-week summer holiday was just becoming popular.

The Early family probably read the *Post* and maybe the *Washington Star*, the two largest newspapers in town. Like so many journalists, Steve could trace his fascination with the profession to a childhood where reading newspapers was part of the family's daily routine. What Steve read while he was growing up may have planted the seeds of his choice of career: Richard Harding Davis, the most famous journalist of his time, was at the height of his career, having covered the brief but sensational Spanish-American War. In September 1901 President William McKinley was felled by an assassin's bullet, and Teddy Roosevelt succeeded to the presidency.

Steve Early attended the Peabody and Edmonds schools, both public, and moved on to Business High School, since stenography and typing were considered necessary for young men or women who did not plan to attend college. It is likely that the Early family budget would not have allowed him that luxury; his brother Felix later worked his way through Georgetown University as a law student. Steve liked to point out that he did not attend college, but the truth was that he did take a few college-level courses at George Washington University while he was in high school.[7]

In August 1907, just out of high school and a week shy of his eighteenth birthday, Steve Early took a job as a messenger boy with the Government Printing Office. His salary was $360 a year, and since he was still living at home—and would continue to do so until his marriage, years later—the extra money helped pay some of the family's bills. In December 1908 he wrote to the head of the office, pointing out that he had been performing the same duties as a $900 a year man and requesting a similar salary. He was now nineteen, he wrote, "and therefore within the age required by the Civil Service Commission." The reply came back: "I recommend that Mr. Early be promoted from messenger boy at 15 cents per hour to messenger at 25 cents per hour. Civil Service bars him from going higher on account of his age." On October 9, 1909, less than a year after he received the requested raise, he resigned. The reason on his official resignation form: "Has a better position."[8]

When young Steve Early went to work right out of high school for the Government Printing Office, Washington was emerging as the news capital of the country, "one of the notable journalistic phenomena in the first decade of the 20th century." The city had become a symbol of united democracy following the Spanish-American War, and, perhaps more important, with Theodore Roosevelt as a vigorous president the city had become the center of issues, reforms, and legislation that were significantly changing the social and economic fabric of the country, not unlike the changes that were to come during Franklin Roosevelt's presidency.[9]

It was not unusual for a young man to go directly from high school into a newsroom. If the job was at a metropolitan daily newspaper or a wire service, he would be a copy clerk or typist. If the young man wanted to, he could learn the basics of news reporting by tagging along with a veteran on news assignments. Eventually the apprentice might draw an assignment of his own. Years later, Early told an interviewer, "There was no college for me, unless you regard the Fourth Estate [journalism] as an educational institution."[10]

When he left the Government Printing Office, Early was hired by the fledgling United Press wire service office in Washington to take dictation over the telephone from reporters in the field, one of the lowliest—but most important—jobs in the newsroom. Working for a wire service was faster paced and far more hectic than working for a newspaper, which might have several deadlines during a twenty-four-hour period. Deadlines for wire service employees were around the clock. Early was energetic and ambitious, and the work gave him the opportunity to discover how a journalist crafted a news story. He was a neophyte lacking any journalism skills when he joined United Press, so it is unlikely he was sent out on any stories during the first year he was there. After a while, he probably was allowed to cover the occasional police or fire story before he was finally promoted to reporter and assigned to cover the State, War, and Navy beat. Years later, he was remembered as having "something ingratiating about him that always opened doors for him."[11]

United Press was founded in 1907 by E. W. Scripps, owner of a chain of newspapers in the Midwest. Instead of joining the Associated Press, which was a cooperative supported by its member newspapers, Scripps established his own press association. By 1908, when Early was hired, United Press had a dozen bureaus, but except in a few key cities, these "offices" consisted of one newsman, a young assistant, and as many telegraph operators as needed operating out of the corner of the newsroom of a client newspaper. News stories in smaller bureaus came from the bureau's single reporter and were supplemented with stories brought in by low-paid stringers or reporters at the client newspaper. In larger cities like Washington, the bureau was independent of any local newspaper and thus had its own staff of reporters, clerks, dictationists, and telegraphers, all overseen by a bureau chief. In contrast, the much older Associated Press had bureaus in all major cities and many smaller ones, as well as access to stories produced by European news agencies.[12]

The United Press bureau in Washington at the time Early went to work there was run by a crusty newsman named Ed J. Keen, who had covered the Spanish-American War in Cuba for the Scripps-McRae Press Association, one of the forerunners of United Press.

Keen was responsible for establishing the reputation of the Washington bureau of United Press. He came up with a clever time-saving method of transmitting stories over the wire to client newspapers. The Phillips Code, a system for abbreviating words going out over the wires, saved both time and money. Phrases such as "Supreme Court of the United States" were shortened to "scotus"; "of the" became "f"; and "that" became "tt." Keen decided that if everyone on the staff learned the code, reporters could use it as a form of shorthand and when they telephoned a story to the office man on the desk, he could take it down in longhand using the code and give it to the telegrapher for instant transmission. This resulted in saving as much as five minutes on short stories and much more time on longer ones. It meant that the under-staffed bureau could get stories out to client newspapers more quickly than other wire services in a business where time was of the essence. Today many journalists use their own version of Keen's code.[13]

As members of an underdog organization, United Press reporters were eager to best the Associated Press. When Early joined up, the Washington bureau was operating on a budget of $1,000 a month, including staff salaries. (The Boston bureau, in contrast, was given $300 a month.) Salaries at United Press were probably in line with, or slightly lower than, those at daily newspapers. Early's pay was $50.[14]

For an aspiring young journalist like Early, the Washington office of the United Press must have been an exciting place to hang his hat every day. Fires and police stories were the routine fodder of all journalists in cities big or small, but in a place like Washington, if you worked hard and kept on the good side of the bureau chief, you could land some better-than-average assignments. His tenacity must have paid off, because within a year after he arrived he was sent out to cover the State, War, and Navy beats. During his four years with United Press, Early covered Atlantic fleet battle maneuvers, where he forged a friendship with Herbert Bayard Swope, an influential reporter and editor for Pulitzer's New York World, among other journalists in Washington.[15]

Washington was a swamp in those hot, steamy summers, but for Early lodging was cheap, since he lived at home. And he was a single man working at one of the more exciting jobs in the city. Not that it was all glamour: Early recalled years later that when Theodore Roosevelt was in office, newsmen used to wait outside the White House gates "whether it rained or shined, waiting for Teddy Roosevelt to call in a favorite reporter and give him a story. There wasn't a comfortable press and radio room [inside the White House]."[16]

In late June of 1912, United Press sent Early as part of the news team to cover the Democratic National Convention in Baltimore. It was there that he met Franklin Delano Roosevelt, a progressive young state senator from New York who had come to support the nomination of the governor of New Jersey, Woodrow Wilson. Roosevelt was the leader of his state's Wilson Conference, a rather weak organization of about 150 independent Democrats in the state. He and his wife, Eleanor, had left their children with his mother at her home in Hyde Park, New York, about seventy miles up the Hudson River from New York City. Unfortunately, Eleanor did not appreciate the noisy demonstrations and outbursts that permeated the convention, nor could she tolerate the oppressive and humid heat, so after a few days she returned to Hyde Park to collect the children and journey on to Campobello Island, New Brunswick, where the family had a summer home.[17]

Amid the convention hoopla in Baltimore, the twenty-three-year-old wire service reporter and the thirty-year-old Harvard-educated politician from a wealthy old upstate New York family struck up a friendship. Later recalling what became a significant meeting for both men, Early said that he got to know Roosevelt "because I liked him as a personality and for the additional reason that he always was 'good copy' for a newspaper reporter." By 1913 Steve Early was ready to jump ship and move to United Press's richer, better-known rival the Associated Press, where he continued to cover the State, War, and Navy departments. Better pay and more prestige were undoubtedly the lure. It was a good move for him. Many years later in a letter to Kent Cooper, general manager of the AP, Early wrote, "Those years I spent with the Associated Press were the happiest of my life."[18]

Early's arrival at the AP coincided with the arrival in Washington of the young New York politician he had met at the Democratic convention in Baltimore. Woodrow Wilson won the election, and as a reward for Roosevelt's support at the convention, Wilson named him assistant secretary of the navy, to work under another Wilson supporter, Josephus Daniels, a small-town North Carolina newspaper editor/publisher. One of the first stories Early covered for his new employer was the March 17 swearing-in of Roosevelt, the youngest in a long succession of assistant secretaries of the navy. Writing to his mother after his first day in office, Roosevelt had this to say about his new post: "[I] am baptized, confirmed, sworn in, vaccinated—and somewhat at sea." He added that he "would have to work like a turbine to master this job."[19]

Early's years with the big wire service before and after World War I allowed him to develop relationships—both with people he worked with and those he covered—that helped him as Roosevelt's advance man in the unsuccessful 1920 campaign for vice president and later, when he moved into the White House as FDR's press secretary, gave him tremendous clout and prestige with the media. But what the young reporter for the Associated Press saw in the new assistant secretary was not "a likely occupant of the White House." Rather, Early said soon after Roosevelt was elected to his first term as president, "I only saw a fine young Democratic progressive, handsome and possessing a most pleasing personality." As assistant secretary of the navy, Roosevelt proved be to "a veritable news oasis" for the eager journalist. The coincidence that Theodore Roosevelt, a distant cousin of Franklin, had been assistant secretary of the navy in 1898 when war broke out between the United States and Spain was not lost on the media of the day. They speculated on whether war with Germany would be declared during Roosevelt's tenure as assistant secretary.[20]

So it was in Roosevelt's office that Early renewed his acquaintance with the playful, good-looking New Yorker. It was also here that he hooked up with two other men, both former journalists. Years later the three would become the most visible and influential members of Roosevelt's personal staff when he went to the White House. They were Louis Howe, a former reporter who had covered Roosevelt in Albany, and Marvin McIntyre, a former reporter and editor now doing government press work for the navy.

Howe was born in Indianapolis, but at the age of seven he had been taken to Saratoga Springs, New York, where his father purchased the *Saratoga Sun* newspaper. Young Howe got his start in journalism there, covering among other stories the famous politicians who came to enjoy the spring waters at Saratoga. His father was the local correspondent for the *New York Herald*, and occasionally his son filled in for him until he became the Albany correspondent for the *Herald*. He was covering the state legislature when Roosevelt was a senator. Howe was barely five feet tall, weighing less than one hundred pounds and thin to the point of emaciation. His face was scarred from a childhood accident; even he referred to himself as "one of the four ugliest men in New York." If he had one redeeming facial feature, it was his large, expressive brown eyes. As he grew older—certainly by the time he went to the White House with Roosevelt—he had a wizened face, a bulbous nose, and lips that had become a mere line across the lower part of his face. Soon after Roosevelt accepted the chairmanship of the New York State Wilson Conference, he hired Howe to handle the publicity for the conference. In the summer of 1912, Roosevelt came down with typhoid fever, and he asked Howe to run his campaign for reelection to the state senate. Except for short periods, Howe worked steadily for Roosevelt from then until Howe's death in 1936. Roosevelt narrowly won his senate race, and when Wilson appointed him assistant secretary of the navy, Roosevelt brought Howe with him as a kind of administrative aide and troubleshooter.[21]

Marvin H. McIntyre, son of a Methodist preacher and a native of Kentucky, had briefly attended Vanderbilt University. He then tried his hand at a variety of jobs before joining the *Louisville Times* as a reporter. He worked there for two years before moving to Washington, DC, to work at the *Washington Times* (later the *Times-Herald*), where he worked his way up from reporter to acting managing editor. McIntyre eventually had disagreements with the publisher of the *Times* and took a government press agent job soon after Roosevelt became assistant secretary of the navy.[22]

Early had garnered a plum beat when he was sent to cover State, War, and Navy. Roosevelt and Howe gave him plenty of news to write about. In fact, Roosevelt often held his own press conferences. As a result, the three men grew closer in the years before the United States entered World War I. Roosevelt was at the forefront of those in the country who strongly advocated preparedness for war. His news stories were "hot," so Early spent a lot of time in the assistant secretary's office; he checked in at least once a day and sometimes more frequently. "The Boss and Louis gave me many exclusive first-page news stories," Early later recalled. This is the way Harry Butcher, later an aide to Gen. Dwight Eisenhower and a longtime friend of Early's, once described the reporter's friendship with the assistant secretary: "Roosevelt was enough of a politician to want particularly a man on the AP to be a good contact. And Steve was a good newsman; he wanted a man who was close to the throne as a news contact. But there was a friendship deeper than just business."[23]

Franklin Roosevelt was described in those days as "tall and handsome" and very social, joining exclusive Washington clubs, frequently attending parties at the homes of the political, business, and social elite of the city. He, Eleanor, and their children lived in an exclusive residential section of Washington called Kalorama, favored by high-ranking government officials. Woodrow Wilson lived in the neighborhood for three years before his death, and Warren G. Harding lived there while he was a United States senator. In contrast, Early continued to live with his parents in their modest home on North Carolina Avenue. He probably worked long hours, including weekend shifts, at least when he first came to the Associated Press as a junior man. When the AP assigned Early to cover the War, State, and Navy departments, Early and Roosevelt found they shared a love of practical jokes and games, which undoubtedly was one of the strengths of their long friendship.[24]

The friendship no doubt helped Roosevelt get publicity. He certainly missed few opportunities to get his name in the news. He scheduled numerous formal inspections of navy yards and ships—and he produced headlines. He found fleet reviews and target practice "among the most thrilling of all spectacles." He even designed a flag for himself that could be run up the mast of the ship he was inspecting. The fact was that most cabinet underlings garnered little more publicity than state senators. Not so for Roosevelt. He realized when he accepted the assistant secretary's job that he was following in the footsteps of his wife's uncle and his own distant relative, who had sat at the same desk in the Navy Department and then ascended to the presidency. Comparisons were inevitable, and Franklin Roosevelt made the most of them. Although the power of the assistant secretary was limited to some extent, he reveled in being acting secretary of the navy when Daniels was away. In those days the government was small enough that the president could take a personal interest in a variety of details throughout government. Some of Roosevelt's duties took him on frequent errands to—or meetings in—President Wilson's office.[25]

Though reporters for the AP had no bylines on their stories in those years, one of the bigger Navy Department stories Early probably covered for the AP during those years was the abolition of the wine mess aboard all ships and in navy yards or stations, bringing the service's regulations into line with those of the army, an order issued by Secretary Daniels on April 4, 1914. Others included Howe and Roosevelt's campaign to save the navy money, such as the new bidding procedures for coal and other naval supplies. As early as December 1913, Roosevelt was publicly pressing for a bigger, stronger navy, and after 1914 he frequently criticized the relative inaction of the government to prepare for the eventuality of war. All this made for good headlines. Early was a sympathetic reporter, and he too believed that a strong defense establishment was necessary.[26]

Soon after Early went to the White House, he told a radio interviewer that covering State, War, and Navy provided him with some big scoops, such as the fact that Gen. John J. Pershing was to be sent to Mexico to bring back the famous bandit Pancho Villa, dead or alive. And when something went wrong with the Punitive Expedition schedule, Early scored another beat with the first news that Pershing had been ordered to withdraw and leave Villa alone. During the years he was with the AP before World War I, he also traveled on occasion with President Wilson, to Princeton and New York City in 1913.[27]

Early was involved in a story that resulted in the Associated Press getting a scoop that sealed America's entry into World War I—and it happened on Early's beat. In January 1917, a few months before the United States entered the war, the decoding experts in the state department had discovered through a telegram sent by Dr. Arthur Zimmerman, Kaiser Wilhelm II of Germany's foreign secretary, to Count Johann Heinrich von Bernstorff, German ambassador in Washington, that Germany was proposing to Mexico that it ally itself with Germany and go to war against the United States if that country relinquished its neutrality and joined the Allies in Europe. Germany would supply financial aid to Mexico. Its reward would be Texas, New Mexico, and Arizona, territory it had lost in 1848. If Mexico agreed, Germany would attempt to persuade Japan to leave the Allies and join Germany against the United States. In addition, Germany announced that it intended to resume unrestricted submarine warfare against its enemies. This occurred at an especially tense and sensitive time when President Wilson was appealing to Germany to cease fighting.

AP reporter Edwin M. Hood was the recipient of a news leak from Secretary of State Robert Lansing. If the AP wanted the story, Lansing told him, Hood could not disclose the source, nor could he quote any administration official. Unfortunately, this violated AP policy, and it meant the wire service would have to carry the story based solely on its own authority, with no sources to back it up. AP officials debated the issue and finally decided to go with the story. Lionel C. Probert, the Washington Bureau's news editor, realized that if he assigned Hood to the story, Hood's close connection to the State Department as the primary reporter covering that beat would be a giveaway as to the story's source when it was published. He looked around the office. Byron Price, who would later serve as director of the Office of Censorship during World War II, was needed on the desk. It was a busy news night, with reporters covering a late session of Congress. Probert spied Early. "You're to go to Secretary Lansing's home on Eighteenth Street and bring back whatever Lansing gives you," Probert told his young reporter. "Then you're to forget that you ever saw the secretary tonight. That's all. No questions." It's easy to picture the slender, five-foot-ten-inch Early, eager to get a beat on the competition, tearing out the door of the bureau and hurrying over to the secretary's house. A servant took him inside, and shortly after Lansing, in his dressing gown, came down the stairs and handed a large, unmarked envelope to Early. He quickly took it to the office, where Probert wrote the story. A month later, Congress declared war on Germany and its allies.[28]

Ironically, the Zimmerman telegram, which cast the die that plunged the United States war, also put Early into uniform. Just as his journalistic star was ascending at the Associated Press, he found himself faced with deciding whether to continue to serve his employer or to serve his country. He chose the latter, leaving the biggest scoops of his career as a reporter until after the war.

2

MR. EARLY GOES TO WAR

In the dawn of a summer morning in London in 1914, British foreign minister Sir Edward Grey stood in his office beside his secretary, the Hon. Arthur C. Murray. Parliament had just approved a declaration of war against Germany. Grey turned to his aide and said, "The lights are going out all over Europe; I wonder if we shall see them lighted again in our lifetime." Murray later described the scene in a letter to his distant American cousin and close friend since boyhood, Franklin D. Roosevelt.[1]

When Wilson was reelected president in 1916, the country was deeply divided over whether or not to enter the European war. Days after the Zimmerman telegram was intercepted, Wilson was telling Congress he still believed a negotiated peace could be achieved, thereby avoiding sending American soldiers to fight on foreign soil. At the end of February 1917, he again appeared before Congress asking for the arming of all American merchant ships, a move that would signal an unofficial declaration of war. Events moved quickly.

Wilson recalled Gen. John J. Pershing from Mexico, where he was busy chasing the Mexican guerrilla leader Poncho Villa, to head the American Expeditionary Forces (AEF) in France. On March 9 Wilson gave the order to arm the ships; nine days later the cabinet unanimously supported a declaration of war, and on April 6 Congress declared war on Germany. On May 28, 1917, General Pershing left for Europe. Registration Day was June 5, and within a few days of that, more than 9.5 million young men between the ages of twenty-one and thirty-one had signed up for the draft.[2]

Early had beat the draft by enlisting in May, one of the first dozen or so men to do so in the capital. He was twenty-seven years old, still living with his parents on North Carolina Avenue, and engaged to a young woman, somewhat against his better judgment. He once told his son that they had decided against marriage before he enlisted: "I felt it would not be fair to her to marry her; to live with her only a very brief time before being ordered away for service overseas; then to come home, after the war, only to face a very uncertain future; maybe to have her nurse and take care of me or possibly be dependent on her for support because of my inability to provide for her."[3]

Within days after war was declared, the Associated Press began to lose staff to enlistment. The Washington bureau lost three of its best reporters when Early, Byron Price, and W. F. Caldwell, later news editor of the AP's Southern Division, joined up. Years later, Early would tell interviewers that he was the first Washington correspondent to enlist, which probably was true.[4]

There is no mention in Early's papers or in any of the many articles written about him and by him during his White House years to indicate whether he may have wanted to cover the war for the Associated Press. Since his beat included the State, War, and Navy departments, he certainly had the journalistic background for such an assignment, but in the end he may have realized he was too far down the wire service's pecking order.

The war already was a big story, and once the United States joined the Allies it became the biggest story to cover. Until the US became involved in World War I, members of the Associated Press European bureaus were considered sufficient enough staff to cover it. Once America sent in troops, the AP assigned some of its best domestic men to reinforce the European staff, including the day cable editor from New York and five members of domestic bureaus.[5]

The real reason Early may have opted for military service can be credited to his friendship with a young major, Douglas MacArthur, who in 1916 was acting as liaison between Secretary of War Newton Baker and the general staff of the army. He became a friendly adviser to the Associated Press reporter and suggested to Early that if he had the proper training, he could, when the time came, join the army as an officer. Since Early lacked both a college education and military training, MacArthur served as his tutor, providing him with an intensive course of study that led to Early's joining the army's reserve corps and becoming one of the first to enroll when the first officers' camp opened.[6]

In May 1917 Early was vaccinated for typhoid and smallpox and successfully passed a tuberculosis test. His first choice had been the cavalry, so he was sent to the Officers Training Camp at Fort Myer, Virginia, just outside Washington, as a second lieutenant in the 80th Division's first cavalry school there. The photo of Second Lieutenant Early on his army identity card shows a serious soldier with just a hint of a smile and a full head of dark, wavy hair. His regiment, the 317th Infantry, was part of the 80th Division, which at full strength numbered twenty-three thousand soldiers and included troops from Virginia, West Virginia, and Pennsylvania. Nicknamed the "Blue Ridge Division," its insignia bore a shield of olive drab cloth with three blue hills representing the three states and the Blue Ridge Mountains, all outlined in white, superimposed in the center.

Life at Fort Myer that summer, as Early many years later recalled, was blazing sun above and baked red clay underfoot. The regiment dug trenches in the hard clay, marched under the hot sun, and practiced using their newly acquired bayonets.[7]

Early's commanding officer at Fort Myer wrote the following letter to Major MacArthur about the progress of his protégé: "I look upon him as one of my most promising candidates and shall certainly recommend him for a commission in the Officers' Reserve Corps." MacArthur passed along the glowing affirmation with this handwritten note at the bottom: "My Dear Steve, The above is self explanatory. I have also seen Babcock [his commanding officer] within the week and he gives a bully account of you. Cordially yours, MacArthur."[8]

While the cavalry had been Early's first choice, German tactics changed that, and he was trained as a machine gunner. By early August, after a five-day leave—presumably to spend time with his family—Early was sent off to Machine Gun School at Fort Sill, Oklahoma. It was here he trained in the use of automatic weapons.

If the heat at Fort Myer had been overwhelming, the heat in Oklahoma that summer was downright debilitating. The mercury in the thermometers jumped to 105 and higher. The heavy machine guns, tripods, and sand bags used in the training exercises only added to the men's discomfort. A month later Early returned to Virginia and, until he was shipped overseas the following May, he trained at Camp Lee, where, as an officer, he also served as an instructor, teaching rookies how to handle automatic weapons.[9]

Life in the military camps could never be termed pleasant, but Camp Lee, for a time, must have been one of the least attractive. Home to Early's 80th Division, the camp's plumbing system left a lot to be desired. In addition to the heat that suffused the camp, a single creek carried the latrine waste to a nearby marsh, and engineers decided to clear the marsh by dredging a channel. In doing so, they had to dam the creek. The result was a "semi-solid mass of sewage 600 feet long and alive with fly larvae." The latrines themselves had square holes, apparently easier to cut than oval ones.[10]

Toward the end of May, the 80th Division left camp to sail for France. Early kept a diary, which began with his company's march from Camp Lee to an unnamed nearby port, probably Newport News, Virginia, where the troops boarded small boats to take them to the large transport ships that were to carry them to France and the war. The march was severe; the men were carrying their full equipment and packs weighing about sixty-five pounds under unfavorable weather conditions, the southern heat and humidity of midsummer. He wrote that the troops were given enthusiastic greetings and farewells by people along the route of the march. As they passed by, they were showered with fruits, candies, and other delicacies.

His story of his trip across the Atlantic was both detailed and carefully crafted with fine writing, giving the reader an intimate account of a group of modestly trained young men headed to the slaughter fields of France to defend a country that most had seen little of outside their own hometowns.

That first night at sea, he wrote, he realized that probably 80 percent of the men on board had never even seen a ship. They were from the mountains of Virginia and the mines of Pennsylvania and West Virginia. Probably many had never seen a railroad train or an automobile. But he noted that they were not long on board when they were climbing all over the ship, hanging out over the water, oblivious to fear.

His account of the Atlantic voyage ended with his desire to obtain permission to mail his diary on the first steamer back to the States.

Whether he mailed it immediately or carried it with him until an opportunity arose to send it home is not known. But today a typed copy of the diary resides in one of his scrapbooks in the Franklin D. Roosevelt Library in Hyde Park, New York.[11]

On June 8, Early and the troops landed in France. From then until mid-August, the 80th Division trained with the British Third Army. For years the United States had been supplying France and Great Britain with small arms, but the factories that made them were not equipped to produce large weapons, and this meant that American soldiers had to be trained in France to operate the big European machine guns, tanks, and artillery before they could be sent into battle.[12]

Thus it was not until toward the end of July that Early and his regiment saw any fighting. They were sent in to the Picardy sector, which included the great cathedral city of Rheims, to assist British and French troops in repelling the last major German offensive. The Americans may have been inexperienced in battle, but they proved to be brave and resourceful soldiers. The fighting lasted until the middle of August, and by the end of the month Early had been promoted to first lieutenant. His next assignment was a month of additional training in automatic rifles at the Third Corps School, of which the 80th Division was a part.[13]

In late September he was back with the 80th Division in the midst of battle, this time in the Meuse-Argone area of France, where, shortly after midnight on September 26, troops from the United States, Great Britain, and France assembled to push ahead with the final offensive of the war.

Their instructors in camp had not prepared the novice Americans for what they would experience that night and for the next several days. The noise was deafening, the terror numbing. Gen. George C. Marshall, who was commanding the troops, later said, "The troops were tired when they went into the fight. They had been held in the woods in wet clothes and wet feet for a week or more, made a long march the night before going in, without any sleep." Not only were the men faced with flames and noise of the artillery, but a heavy fog shrouded the troops, making it difficult for the troops to remain intact and forcing them to form their own ad hoc units. Many simply became marooned, targets for enemy fire. When the fog finally lifted, one young soldier saw this scene: "Many dead are lying around and many who have been buried are tossed out of their graves. The stench is terrible."[14]

For a genteel son of Virginia this must have been horrifying, which may explain why, years later, Early's daughter said he never talked about his war experiences. It also helps to explain the close relationship he had with his eldest son and namesake, who served in World War II.[15]

After twenty-four hours of combat, many divisions were disorganized and disoriented, cold and tired, having spent the night in muddy holes under the blaze of gunfire. On the evening of September 29, General Pershing admitted failure and suspended the offensive. The reasons for its failure are too numerous to list, but certainly the inexperience of the American troops was high on the list.[16]

The American attack in the Meuse-Argonne was resumed on October 4, and again Early's division took part. Again, the troops met serious resistance from the Germans, who poured their most experienced men into the battle. At first the Allies achieved little in this second offensive, but by October 10 the Americans had overrun the obstacle of the Argonne.[17]

Unfortunately the force of the American troops declined because, in addition to the casualties, an influenza virus was spreading among the men, who were still in their summer clothes without overcoats or blankets. Its impact was not felt only on the battlefields of France; as it moved across the United States, it felled workers in factories producing war materials.

When the second Meuse-Argonne offensive ended on October 12, Early was detailed to the division's grenade school as an instructor until he rejoined his unit for the final Meuse-Argonne offensive, which began on November 1 and lasted for six days.

The Allies had carefully laid the groundwork for this last battle by running bombing raids over the German lines during the previous days. When the big Allied guns opened fire on November 1, it was a coordinated blanket of fire. The day proved a success, and the Americans captured 3,602 prisoners, sixty-three guns, and hundreds of machine guns. In Early's scrapbook is a 2nd Class Iron Cross, taken, he wrote, in the Argonne from a prisoner in trade for tobacco.[18]

A veteran of the final Meuse-Argonne offensive wrote a letter to President Roosevelt some years later relating the following story: "I was seriously wounded in action on November 1, 1918, in the battle of the Argonne, and it may be of interest to recall that your own secretary, Stephen T. Early, a splendid officer, was fighting only a few feet from me at the time and picked me up and placed me in a shell hole."[19]

The German line was shattered, and this final Allied thrust effectively brought the war to a close. On November 11 at 11 a.m., hostilities ceased. An armistice was signed, and the Allies had won the war. Even as hostilities ceased, Early remained the consummate journalist, recognizing a good story when he saw it. In his scrapbook is a half sheet of official-looking paper that says: "American Official Communique, November 11, 1918, Morning. No. 197. In accordance with the terms of the armistice, hostilities on the fronts of the American Armies were suspended at 11:00 o'clock this morning."

On the back of the paper Early typed, "Dear Mother: This is today's official American Communique—the best-one I have seen since arriving in France. Save it as an official document of historic value, announcing the greatest event in the world's history."[20]

First Lieutenant Early was not yet allowed to deliver this historic piece of paper to his mother in person. Although he had been one of the lucky ones, surviving intact, he had been reassigned to General Headquarters, where he was given one final assignment in France— one that led him into one of the finest adventures of his life to date. On January 7, 1918, Early, formerly of the Associated Press, reported to the Paris office of the great army newspaper *Stars and Stripes*, to be the assistant officer in charge.

Early was taken from his artillery regiment and sent to the army's weekly newspaper because, according to Brig. Gen. Dennis E. Nolan, chief of intelligence for the AEF, his services were "badly needed." In an official memorandum, Nolan pointed out that "in addition to being one of the ablest newspapermen on the staff of the Associated Press, he is a fine soldier and we about broke his heart by taking him away from his Regiment."[21]

His broken heart healed quickly, though, once he arrived at the *Stars and Stripes* offices, an operation edited by a group of dedicated former newsmen thrown together by the vagaries and harshness of war, many of whom would be leaders in their profession after the war.

For instance, the managing editor was Pvt. Harold W. Ross, who had been working as a journalist in San Francisco when war broke out.

He enlisted in the 18th Engineers, but because he had recruited some of his colleagues and he had an old typewriter, they started a regimental newspaper during training in the state of Washington. It didn't last long, because he was shipped overseas. Soon after he landed in France, he saw an advertisement in an English-language daily published in Paris that a new troop newspaper was being started for the American Expeditionary Forces, and it needed journalists. He reached Paris just after the first edition of the weekly was published on February 8, 1918, and joined the staff as a reporter. After the war, Private Ross founded his own magazine in New York City and called it the *New Yorker*.

Ross was part of an illustrious crew of journalists, including Early, who came through the newsroom of *Stars and Stripes*. Sgt. Alexander Woollcott, drama critic for the *New York Times* before the war and later an acclaimed playwright and radio commentator, became the amusement editor of *Stars and Stripes* and also did some of the best reporting of his career covering stories of the battlegrounds at Chateau Thierry, St. Mihiel, and the Argonne; Lt. Grantland Rice, who, during the 1920s and 1930s, was America's most famous sports writer, naturally was the sports editor for many issues until he was recalled to the front; and Capt. Franklin P. Adams, whose column, "F.P.A.," was a popular read in the *New York Tribune*, was detailed from the Army's Intelligence Section to write poems and editorials. Other staffers included Pvt. John T. Winterich, a copy editor for the *Springfield* (Massachusetts) *Republican*, the first managing editor of *Stars and Stripes* (later succeeded by Ross); Lt. Adolph S. Ochs Jr. of the *Chattanooga Times*, whose father owned the *New York Times*; Sgt. Major Philip Von Blon of the *Cleveland Plain Dealer*; Jack S. Connolly of the *Boston Herald*; and Robert Snadjir and John Black of the *Brooklyn Eagle*.

The newspaper was the brainchild of Gen. John J. Pershing, commander of the American Expeditionary Forces in France, who was concerned that the morale of the troops should be kept at a higher pitch, fearing that because many of the men were being trained by the British and brigaded with the French, they would lose their sense of unity. As an aid in this direction, it seemed to Pershing that a publication of some sort, available to all troops, would be useful.[22]

About the time Pershing and his associates were wrestling with a solution to maintain esprit de corps, Guy T. Viskniskki, a second lieutenant in the infantry and a partner in McClure's Syndicate, an agency that peddled feature stories to newspapers, showed up for censorship duty at press headquarters. Viskniskki, married and in his mid-thirties, had organized and been the editor of a weekly newspaper for the troops at Camp Lee, Virginia, before he was sent overseas. Now he proposed such a venture to General Pershing's staff, and one member, the same General Nolan who later requested Early's services at *Stars and Stripes*, realized that this might be the answer to the morale problem. Pershing liked it, and Viskniskki was named editor, confident that he could make a success of such a publication and that eventually it would be self-supporting.

Viskniskki's idea succeeded beyond anyone's wildest dreams. But the newspaper's amazing success was not easily achieved and, in a bizarre way, led to its editor's fall from grace.

When it began, *Stars and Stripes* needed to overcome a host of obstacles, one of which was an effective distribution system, since the goal was to ensure that all members of the AEF had access to the paper every week. It also needed a staff—both editorial and business—an office, and a printing facility. It required funding. And not the least, once a staff was in place the members wanted assurance that this would be a real newspaper, not a propaganda sheet for the US Armed Forces. Little by little, the problems were solved, sometimes easily and successfully, sometimes not for many months and then not necessarily to the satisfaction of the men who ran it.[23]

The goal of the newspaper was to cover any and all stories of interest to the enlisted men, written in a style easily understood by them but without resorting to coarseness and vulgarity. The latter two goals were relatively easy to achieve, but the first ran counter to army traditions and regulations. Viskniskki decided that the paper would tell the men everything that was safe for them to know.[24]

The first issue was dated February 8, 1918; the last was June 1919. The paper appeared every Friday. The front page featured a variety of stories: "Tooth Yanking Car Is Touring France," about a Red Cross vehicle carrying dentists to work on soldiers; "Army Men Build an Overseas Pittsburgh," about the army engineers' construction of railroad tracks, buildings, and warehouses for the war in France; and "Huns Starve and Ridicule U.S. Captives," about conditions under which prisoners of war were living. They were informative, like the one titled "How You May Win Our Army's Decoration," detailing each of the major medals awarded for service. The style of writing was breezy and easy to read. Even eighty years later, *Stars and Stripes'* writing has an au courant flavor, and, though dated, the stories invite reading. In the center of each page one was a photo or cartoon, some humorous, some maudlin, such as the May 5, 1918, issue's drawing of a mother holding two young children. The caption reminded the solders "What We're Fighting For."[25]

For the first few weeks, the paper was written largely at field press headquarters and in a small office in Paris in a local army headquarters on Rue Ste. Anne. Eventually the staff settled into a commodious suite in a modern building at 1 Rue des Italiens. From February 1919 on, the issues were prepared in the Credit Moblier building at 32 Rue Taitbout, also occupied by the American Chamber of Commerce, which played a significant role in Early's immediate postwar life.

A French firm supplied paper, and typography and printing were done at the plant of the continental edition of the *London Daily Mail*, which continued to print *Stars and Stripes* until August 1918, when circulation became too great. From then on, the paper was put together at the *Daily Mail* plant but was printed at *Le Journal*, a Paris daily. The result was a very cosmopolitan-looking newspaper that today still looks fresh and modern.

The paper was always sold for 50 centimes, or 10 cents, to avoid the suspicion in the minds of the soldiers that if the paper was free, it must be full of propaganda. The only exception was that free copies were distributed to the sick and wounded in hospitals.[26]

Now to the story of how Lieutenant Early, the former Associated Press reporter in Washington, DC, ended his military career as the assistant officer in charge of the army's popular and highly successful weekly troop newspaper. By December 1918 it was apparent to the staff that Viskniskki was not cut out to be the leader of a pack of disparate soldiers cum journalists, or vice versa. Indeed they must have tried his patience more than once. When displeased with a staff member, Viskniskki would yell, "You're under arrest!" Most of the time the men ignored him, chalking his outbursts up to mental fatigue. But one night, shortly before Viskniskki left as editor, he passed by Harold Ross, sitting listlessly at his desk. Viskniskki asked, "Why, Private Ross, you still here?" Ross replied in mock humility, "I'm under arrest, Sir."

The editor looked at Ross, puzzled. "But Harold, old man, that's ridiculous. I wasn't serious when I spoke harshly to you this afternoon. You were justified in defending the way you handled the story. I didn't agree, but I forgot our difference immediately." Ross replied, "Then I am released?" Viskniskki stammered, "Of course, of course."[27]

It was not too long before the staff moved toward outright mutiny against the editor. Ross drew up an indictment of what he and the newsroom crew thought were Viskniskki's inept and cruel management techniques and circulated it among the men. Two staff members took the petition to the high command, where news of it quickly reached General Nolan. The upshot was that as much as Nolan appreciated Viskniskki's efforts in creating and publishing the paper, he had to go. He was given a promotion to major and sent home to rest. He was later given the Distinguished Service Medal for his work at *Stars and Stripes*.[28]

Once Viskniskki was gone, Capt. Mark Watson of the army's press section was named the senior officer in charge, and Lieutenant Early became assistant officer in charge. Watson had been a reporter for the *Chicago Tribune* before the war and had been in regular touch with *Stars and Stripes* from the AEF headquarters. It was a credit to their journalistic professionalism and their confidence in the newsmen who had been putting out the paper that Watson and Early took over the running of the paper so seamlessly that virtually no one on the outside was aware of the change in leadership. The men were encouraged to get the paper out in their own way, and aside from a touch of army discipline, the newsroom staff continued in its casual manner.[29]

Meanwhile, Watson and Early busied themselves with two aspects of the newspaper's operation: its continued circulation growth and the eventual wrapping up of publication, as gradually the enlisted men boarded ships for their return home. During the war, the newspaper's job was to keep up the soldiers' morale; once the armistice was signed, the goal was to ensure decent patriotic behavior among the nearly two million men until they were officially discharged.

In addition, Watson and Early solved a riddle that had plagued the newspaper's staff since the beginning: If not a squad, a platoon, or a company, what exactly were the men who put out *Stars and Stripes*? After some cajoling, Watson and Early persuaded General Nolan to create a special military company for the newspaper's personnel. Nolan had always viewed the newspaper as a civilian auxiliary to the army, and accordingly the soldiers on the paper had been relieved of military duties. They set their own working hours and were free in their spare time to do as they pleased and to live where they wanted, just as if they were working on a regular newspaper.

The result was a band of hard-drinking, poker-playing journalists—who just happened to be soldiers—roaming the streets of Paris at all hours, dining and sleeping wherever they chose. Unfortunately for the *Stars and Stripes* men, the US commanding general for Paris wanted control over all the men in his jurisdiction. So early in 1919 the *Stars and Stripes* crew had to face the fact they were in the army, and they were forced to give up their furnished rooms and favorite restaurants and live and eat in barracks under military discipline, except when on duty at the newspaper.

But the solution created more problems than the command had anticipated. Newspaper employees never work regular hours, and when circulation department men were supposed to be preparing bundles of papers for shipment, an officer detained them at the barracks for a personal inspection—leaving twenty-five thousand copies of *Stars and Stripes* in piles, unbundled and unlabeled. The problems mounted until the high command agreed to give the newspaper staff a special designation: Censor and Press Companies 1 and 2, once again giving them the freedom they required to put out the paper.[30]

It may have broken Steve Early's heart to leave the battlefield, but while little has been documented of his stay at the army newspaper, he must have been consoled to find a newsroom full of dedicated journalists who also loved a good poker game.

Saturday was the news staff's regular day off, and they took full advantage of their freedom from the office. Along with a random assortment of foreign correspondents—sometimes including Richard Oulihan of the *New York Times*; Walter Duranty, then on the staff of the *London Daily Mail* and later Moscow correspondent for the *New York Times*; and Heywood Broun from the *New York Tribune*—the *Stars and Stripes* gang gathered at The Cornille, known simply as Nini's, a tiny restaurant in the narrow Place du Tertre on top of Montmartre, in the shadow of the magnificent Sacre Coeur cathedral and some distance north of the newspaper office. They usually made a day and a night of it: drinking, talking, and playing craps or, more often, poker, risking their paychecks and anything else negotiable week after week.

Jane Grant, who later married Harold Ross, had been a young reporter at the *New York Times* in New York before the war. She ended up working in Paris, where she met up with her old friend Alexander Woollcott, who one Saturday took her to Nini's to meet the guys from *Stars and Stripes*. She recalled entering the little bistro during the height of an intense poker game. So passionate was the game that Woollcott did not even bother to introduce her, she wrote in her memoir, until "Captain Early, the victor and ranking member of the group, gave me a friendly nod as he triumphantly showed his third king in the hole and raked in the winnings. Captain Early then rose and led me to a vacant chair near the end of the table."

She did not join the game. She was told that unless Early, who was still a lieutenant, or Lieutenant Ochs or one of the other officers invited her, she must remain a spectator. It was obvious that Early had considerable status at the game, and not just because of his frequent winnings. Grant wrote that when Privates Winterich and Ross appeared in Nini's doorway that day, Early said, severely, "It's about time you fellows showed up."[31]

Early in April 1919 Early was invited by General Pershing to join about two hundred other soldier-newspapermen and publicity men for a tour in a private train, visiting battlefields, ports, and other war-related sites. They were guests of the US government, a public relations effort to ensure that when they returned to their civilian occupation of reporting and writing, they would be able to inform their readers with some accuracy about the scope of the war.

The train carrying the journalists and public relations men visited the seaports of Brest, St. Nazaire, and Bordeaux, and then moved across to Chaumont, headquarters of the American Expeditionary Forces, where the generals showed off the operations and machinery of the war. Pershing was absent, but Secretary of the Navy Josephus Daniels, an old friend of Early's from his Associated Press days, was there to greet the men.

After Chaumont, the train headed to the battlefields, Chateau-Thierry, St. Mihel, the Meuse-Argonne, Varennes, and Verdun, among others. Because this was after the armistice, the men were able to visit the German cities of Cologne and Coblenz. A memory one member of the group carried with him for years was leaving the rail-road station in Coblenz on the foggy Easter morning, and, as the fog lifted, across the Rhine River, he saw a massive American flag whipping in the breeze.[32]

Two weeks later, the men returned to Paris, and Early went back to *Stars and Stripes* to begin overseeing, with Captain Watson, the wrap-up of the army's newspaper. Already men were going home, leaving the office understaffed—or, worse, some of those that had replaced them were what Harold Ross called "incompetent."

Ross believed that the newspaper had fulfilled its purpose and it was "no longer needed." He wrote Watson a four-page letter, dated March 26, saying the staff had seen the publication "grow into probably the most powerful newspaper in the world." His concern was that this great paper should "go out on the high tide." Ross told Watson he thought the paper should fold, perhaps by late April. Watson and Early apparently thought otherwise, and *Stars and Stripes*' last issue was June 13, 1919.[33]

In May General Nolan recommended Early for promotion to captain "in recognition of the work he did with his regiment in the Argonne and for the splendid way he has cooperated in helping to maintain the high standard of *The Stars and Stripes* during the critical period of the demobilization of our Army." The general had more kind words for Captain Early: "Your previous experience in the newspaper business has made your work valuable and at all times while on this duty you have had an important share in the editorial policy and management of this paper." On June 1, 1919, he accepted a commission as captain, infantry, US Army.[34]

Letters of commendation also came from General Pershing to the *Stars and Stripes* staff, and to Captain Early in particular. In addition, the general awarded Early a silver citation for "exceptional and meritorious service" to the newspaper.

Before he left Paris, Early had time to attend the horse races at Longchamps, the famed track on the western edge of Paris, which undoubtedly was a thrill for the young captain who throughout the coming years would always find time, even in critical moments as press secretary to President Roosevelt, to head off to a late afternoon race—or at least place a bet.

On June 21, 1919, Early went to Brest and sailed for home aboard the SS *von Steuben*. He immediately went to Military Intelligence in Washington, DC, where he was debriefed and discharged on July 3.[35]

THE 1920 CAMPAIGN

Captain Early returned to the States to find himself unemployed for the first time since he was a teenager and his girlfriend married to another man. The good news was he was in good physical shape, unlike the thousands of soldiers who had come home missing limbs, their sight lost, or their minds in disarray.[1]

His social life could be put on hold; finding a job could not. The logical place for him to turn was his former employer, the Associated Press, but he did not return until December 1920. He may have wanted to, but like the economy in general, which was seeing a downward turn as the United States moved from a wartime to a peacetime industrial nation, jobs at the news agency may have been scarce as returning newsmen clamored for their old positions.

What were available, however, were well-paying publicist jobs with the Chamber of Commerce. It is easy to speculate that while Early was working at *Stars and Stripes* in the same building that housed the American Chamber's Paris headquarters, he made contacts that led him to what became his first postwar job. Or on his return he may have reconnected with some employees he knew at the Chamber in Washington, the organization having been created in 1912 as a national clearinghouse of business opinion. As the popularity of the new heroes—American capitalists—increased after the war, the National Association of Manufacturers and local chambers of commerce across the country hired hundreds of highly paid publicists to proclaim the virtues of capitalism and at the same time denounce opponents as unpatriotic.[2]

As soon as the thirty-year-old Early returned home, he moved back to his parents' house on North Carolina Avenue and went to work for the Chamber's national headquarters in Washington to study the readjustment of industry from war to peace conditions. It was a job that sent him traveling coast to coast, a task that must have not only been welcome but may have proved somewhat of a culture shock to the soldier returning from the bloody battlefields of France.[3]

Meanwhile, Franklin Roosevelt had been in training for a high political office for several years. Whether he would run for governor of New York, the United States Senate, or on the Democratic national ticket, he had been astutely paving the way. His frequent speeches and press conferences on the need for navy preparedness before the war, his fact-finding missions to Europe during the war, and his continuing campaign for efficient government all had brought him into the spotlight, sometimes at the expense of his navy boss, Josephus Daniels. It was no secret that at times Secretary Daniels found his brash young assistant irritating. However, this never seemed to put a damper on Roosevelt's enthusiasm and outspokenness for whatever project he happened to be promoting at the time.

When he was covering the Navy Department for the Associated Press, Early—young and no doubt impressed by the attention the ebullient and self-assured Roosevelt paid him—probably unwittingly at times acted as an important cog in the assistant secretary's publicity machine. And no doubt once Early left for the war, another equally impressionable reporter took his place, willing to give Roosevelt plenty of ink.

So while Early was traversing the country on behalf of the Chamber of Commerce, his old friend and useful source at the Navy Department was collecting the political currency necessary to run for a high office. In June of that summer, the Republicans had nominated an undistinguished senator and small-town newspaper publisher from Ohio named Warren Gamaliel Harding to head their national ticket. His running mate was a diffident Yankee, Calvin Coolidge. The two would run on an anti–League of Nations platform.

The following month, a very ill President Wilson remained in Washington while members of his party headed to their national convention in San Francisco. After a struggle among various factions, the party finally nominated Governor James M. Cox, a progressive from Ohio. Several party faithful were being considered for his running mate, including Edwin T. Meredith, Wilson's secretary of agriculture, and Edward L. Doheny, a wealthy California oilman. But it was Franklin D. Roosevelt of Hyde Park, New York, and Washington, DC, who was nominated by acclamation. But for some reason, when his name was about to be placed in nomination, the candidate left the convention hall, and Josephus Daniels, probably the most personally popular member of Wilson's cabinet, was called upon to speak on behalf of his assistant.

Putting aside their enmity and attempting to allay any hints of bad feeling between the two men, Daniels told the delegates, "I wish to say that to me and to the five hundred thousand men in the American Navy and to five million men in the Army, it is a matter of peculiar gratification that this Convention unanimously has chosen as candidate for Vice President that clear-headed and able executive and patriotic citizen of New York, the Assistant Secretary of the Navy, Franklin D. Roosevelt."[4]

The Cox-Roosevelt platform would include a pro-League plank —certainly in deference to Wilson—and ultimately that was their downfall. But Roosevelt especially made a valiant attempt to sell that message to the American public, and selling himself and his ideas was what Franklin Roosevelt did best. From the beginning he had no illusions about the outcome, telling his confidant and aide in the Navy Department, Louis Howe, "The votes will be cast for Harding and not for Coolidge, for Cox and not for me." Howe agreed. Before he set out on the campaign trail, no matter how uphill, Roosevelt required a staff. He did not realize it at the time, but the men he selected to run his vice presidential campaign, a "small group, utterly distinct from the party national campaign organization," would follow him twelve years later as his core White House advisers.[5]

Early claimed years later that the vice presidential nomination had come as a surprise to him. After all, he had been outside the intimate Roosevelt political circle since he left Washington to join the army. It is not clear whether Early was in the convention hall in San Francisco that summer, although later he indicated he had been. He told a journalist, "The picture that kept coming back to mind was of the day at

San Francisco when young Roosevelt from his back row seat as an upstate leader in an otherwise largely anti-Wilson New York state delegation ripped the state standard up and carried it into the Wilson demonstration parade through the aisles. He marched along with two or three anti-Wilsonites clinging to him; but with his face upthrust in that characteristic way so familiar to everybody now, and the joyous Roosevelt smile greeting the din with which the Wilson demonstrators hailed him. A big, young, wide-shouldered, powerful figure, he shook off interferers without deigning to notice them."[6]

One thing is certain: Early as well as many others in the party realized that it would be a difficult—if not impossible—battle to beat the Republicans that year. Early later described the convention as the "gayest and happiest of national conventions at San Francisco, despite the certainty of defeat." Throughout campaign, Early felt that Roosevelt was making an uphill fight, in spite of the enthusiasm for him personally. For instance, during the campaign, Early wired Howe from South Dakota, "The bitterness toward Wilson is evident everywhere and deeply rooted. He hasn't a friend."[7]

If Early was in San Francisco during the convention, Roosevelt may have approached him as soon as he captured the nomination to ask him to join the campaign. What is known is that Roosevelt needed a campaign staff that consisted of men he knew and could trust, and with whom he felt comfortable. Howe, his political alter ego, would of course be his chief confidant, eventually traveling around the country at his side. For the time being, though, he remained in Washington, filling in as acting assistant secretary of the navy.[8]

Roosevelt drafted Marvin McIntyre, the former newsman who had done publicity work for the navy, as his speechwriter. During the war, McIntyre had worked for George Creel's Committee on Public Information, a government propaganda agency established a week after the country went to war. McIntyre stayed on in the navy now to work for the Creel Committee, as it was known. Described as affable, McIntyre was forty-one at the time of the campaign, three years older than Roosevelt. Tom Lynch, a Dutchess County friend who had helped launch Roosevelt's earlier political career in Albany, would handle campaign funds and travel part of the time with the candidate. Remaining in the campaign headquarters in New York City was Charles McCarthy, Roosevelt's former secretary.[9]

The advance man for the campaign would be the "brilliant and brittle newspaperman" Steve Early. Roosevelt described him as "the ideal man for me." He added, "I cannot think of anyone else who exactly meets the qualifications I require." This meant that Early would leave his job with the Chamber of Commerce, a project that probably was coming to an end anyway, and travel ahead of the candidate and his staff, relaying information about the political climate in each community soon to be visited by Roosevelt.[10]

Early would ensure transportation was available in the community and make arrangements for meals and accommodations. It undoubtedly was a lonely job at times. Moving from city to city, never enjoying the camaraderie of the campaign staff, his job was to keep "the Boss" alerted to what to expect when his train rolled into town. It was not glamorous work, but it allowed Early, who was "hardboiled and highly efficient," to build an astonishing network of media contacts that would eventually follow him and Roosevelt into the White House.

Early's inside knowledge of how the media worked, such as deadline requirements, and his understanding of the kind of information newsmen needed to write a story enhanced his ability to get the job done well. In addition, no doubt the contacts he made during his tour of the country for the Chamber of Commerce gave him a foot in the door in some cities and towns. The advance man contacted reporters, politicians, and businessmen, the goal being to keep the candidate well informed on local issues and on the attitudes of the voters on such topics as the League of Nations, the economy, and prohibition, among others. This in turn helped Roosevelt and McIntyre formulate effective speeches.

It was Early who in essence set the itinerary and topics to be addressed by Roosevelt when he arrived in town. The election may have been lost, but the teamwork proved to be excellent.[11]

Once he had secured the nomination, Roosevelt returned to his home in Hyde Park. It was July 13 and time for the candidate to make plans to hit the campaign trail. He and Howe already had mapped out rough itineraries of speaking trips he would make across the country and had begun securing a staff. Final itineraries and precise speeches would not be possible until Early had laid the groundwork along the way.

Roosevelt submitted his resignation to Wilson as assistant secretary of the navy on August 6, the same date on which he drafted a letter of introduction for Early to use as he traveled around the country during the campaign. It said: "To Whom It May Concern: This is to introduce Mr. Stephen T. Early, member of my personal staff. Any favors or courtesies extended to Mr. Early will be greatly appreciated by me. F. D. Roosevelt." Early left Washington on August 7, returning on August 31.[12]

The thirty-eight-year-old vice presidential candidate had planned an arduous campaign. Between early August and Election Day, Roosevelt engaged in two long speaking tours of the Midwest and the West and a two-week tour of New York and New England. Roosevelt traveled well in excess of ten thousand miles coast to coast, averaging ten speeches a day. Some years later Early told Harold Ickes that Roosevelt seemed to have a "playboy" approach to life during the campaign and that he did not take it seriously enough, "treating it as though it were a great lark. He couldn't be made to prepare his speeches in advance, preferring to play cards instead." Franklin D. Roosevelt Jr. told one of Roosevelt's biographers, "Up until 1921, Father was a rich playboy, living off his cousin's name and his mother's money."[13]

The facts tell a somewhat different story: By the end of the campaign, Roosevelt had traveled to almost every state outside the South and given hundreds of speeches as well as numerous impromptu talks and countless interviews with journalists.

None of the members of Roosevelt's staff for the 1920 campaign ever wrote an account of his experiences, so it is only through extant telegrams, letters, and memos in the papers of the candidate himself, Howe, and Early that the details of the campaign trips can be gleaned.

Once Early had obtained a leave of absence from the Chamber and had his letter of introduction from Roosevelt, he was ready to roll. The campaign train was headed west, its destination San Francisco, by way of Chicago, Minneapolis, Bismarck and Fargo, North Dakota, with stops in Montana and Washington, and then on to Portland. This meant that Early had to arrive at least a day or more ahead of the train. It also meant he had to relay to the candidate, Howe, or McIntyre the necessary details to ensure a successful Roosevelt visit. To accomplish this and to make sure key strategic information on issues would not be intercepted by someone in the Republican Party, the men devised an ingenious code. It was quite simple, reflecting the major issues of the campaign, and it could be easily incorporated into brief telegrams and quickly decoded by the recipient.

It is uncertain just who came up with the idea. It could have been any one of the three—Roosevelt, Howe, or McIntyre—all of whom had been working so long in the Navy Department, or Early, just back from military service and aware of the need for secret codes and the use of cryptology in the military. Using a code with short words replacing phrases was also economical since it avoided long, costly telegrams. It also meant that a telegraph operator would be unable to pass on Roosevelt's campaign strategy to the Republicans in a town.

The use of codes to communicate information in telegrams was not new to political campaigning.[14] The staff came up with a color code for prohibition. For instance, if the word "black" was used in a telegram about a particular state or community, it meant the area was against prohibition. "White" meant sentiment was divided on the issue, and "blue" meant the state or town favored prohibition. The word "red" was a warning for Roosevelt not to mention the topic at all.

They also implemented a numbers code. For instance, the number one next to a person's name told Roosevelt he should make a special effort to seek out the person, who could help the campaign. "Two" next to a name meant he should not bother to see the person. "Four" referred to Democrats in a town or state, "five" was for Republicans, and "six" meant nonpartisans. The League of Nations was number ten. So if Early wanted to let Roosevelt know that the sentiment in a town favored the establishment of the League of Nations, he would write, "Ten paramount."[15]

It is difficult to piece together Early's precise itinerary for this or any of the campaign trips that summer and fall, but it appears that he met up in Minneapolis with Roosevelt, who a day or so earlier had left Chicago, where he had given a rousing speech on August 11. While Roosevelt spoke in Minneapolis, Early circulated through the audience to get comments, and later he informed Howe, "Without exception they were excellent for the Boss. He is speaking easier, going good and will be a finished product of oratory before we see New York again."[16]

Earlier telegrams did not feature the code, but they were informative. From Chicago Early had wired Howe that, as he saw it there, "the educated classes favored the League, hence were sympathetic to FDR, but that these classes were in the minority and that the majority were opposed to the League or indifferent because they did not understand it."[17]

One of the earliest existing telegrams using the code was sent by Early on August 14 from Fargo, North Dakota, to Roosevelt and McIntyre aboard a train due to arrive at St. Paul, Minnesota, at 8:30 a.m. the following day. Early had set up a time and place for a speech Roosevelt would make in Fargo; then he would move on with stops in Valley City, Jamestown, and Bismarck, which Early noted was "four," that is, Democratic.

When he reached Fargo, Early said, Roosevelt should "let six alone," because they "are pounding five national ticket with criticism and slurs and leaning to four ticket but final move uncertain." Early points out that "blue prevails," and that "eleven were solid for Teddy," a reference to former president Theodore Roosevelt. Early ended with the suggestion that the candidate should "mention front porch comma full dinner pail slogan and ten cartoon." What he was telling the candidate in code was he should not bother with the nonpartisans because they apparently were doing a good job of "pounding" the Republicans there and leaning toward the Democrats. The area was dry, and the farmers were fans of Teddy Roosevelt. The last part of the telegram refers to a cartoon on "ten," the League of Nations.[18]

By August 15 Early had reached Billings, Montana, and was reporting back via telegram to McIntyre: "Ten paramount." He said it was a "blue state" and "six vicious on fives national ticket." He noted, "Some six newspapers openly endorse four." And he told Roosevelt, "Red on six." According to the staff's code, this meant the League of Nations (ten) was paramount. The sentiment in the state was decidedly dry (blue), and the nonpartisans (six) were vicious on the Republican ticket there (five). Some of the nonpartisan (six) newspapers in the state were openly endorsing Democratic candidates there (four). "Red on six" told Roosevelt not to support or make public reference to the nonpartisans.[19]

There were letters, too, long and full of details, suggestions for topics the candidate should touch upon in his speeches, and predictions about the way the political winds were blowing—sometimes accurate, sometimes not. From Butte, Montana, Early wrote Howe a two-page typed letter that begins,

> From the mountain tops of Butte, I today proclaim Montana for the Democracy. Butte is the most optimistic city I've struck. Butte is

quite enthusiastic but feels less secure because of the big Irish element. This demands the Freedom of Ireland. The leaders say Uncle
Sam should never have brought his army home until Ireland had
been established a Republic. They won't be argued with—just a
fight for them and they will be satisfied. Nothing less will do.[20]

By the time Roosevelt spoke in Deer Lodge, about thirty miles
north of Butte, he told the audience he was the author of the Haitian
constitution, and in a later speech in San Francisco, he claimed he had
been "running Haiti and Santo Domingo" for the past seven years. As
assistant secretary of the navy, Roosevelt had ordered a navy gunboat
to Haiti, but, as one recent FDR biographer wrote, claiming he wrote
Haiti's constitution was akin to Vice President Al Gore saying, when
he ran for president in 2000, that he had invented the Internet. The
reporters had a field day with Roosevelt's claim, which the candidate
later denied. His hyperbole probably cost him the election in Montana, which went solidly Republican in November.[21]

These coded telegrams allowed Early to suggest timely topics for
Roosevelt to address, sometimes with a dash of Early's cynical brand of
humor thrown in, which was probably not lost on the candidate's own
sense of levity. For instance, in the Billings telegram, Early explained to
Roosevelt, "This is undeveloped section nation. Stop. Feeling apparent
that federal government should give special recognition to its need and
development and its resources. Stop. Suggest something on irrigation
figuratively moving Montana nearer coasts."[22]

Early skipped no details in his reports. From Spokane, Washington,
Early sent McIntyre a two-page letter written on *Spokane Daily Chronicle* stationery. He told him that the itinerary for the city "was badly confused. It is now corrected and newspapers understand." The campaign
train was on its way to meet with the Coeur d'Alene Democratic delegation in the nearby small town of Rathdrum and then would stop so
Roosevelt could give a brief speech in Coeur d'Alene at 6 p.m. "in the
park—open air." He urged Roosevelt to skip dinner in Coeur d'Alene
so he would arrive in Spokane no later than 8:30 p.m. since "it will be
difficult to hold the crowd after that hour." He asked that McIntyre
have a copy of Roosevelt's Coeur d'Alene speech ready to be filed with
the Associated Press and the local press from Rathdrum.

No code was necessary in the letter. Early reported that Washington State "is dry." Voters were interested in land reclamation and "destruction of Non-Partisan League." He suggested that McIntyre refer to a speech Wilson had given in Seattle the previous summer, "copy of which you have in Senate Document I gave you for something along this line, if any statement is given on the subject. Advise strongly that you do not hit the NPL directly. Lumber is the big industry. Wheat is the big crop. Agricultural development is the aim of all. State is strong Republican." He noted, "[L]ess than ten percent of the people are familiar with the issue [the League]. Impression here is that President Wilson failed to stimulate interest. I am leaving tonight for Seattle. Regards Early."[23]

On August 18, Early sent an equally detailed letter from Seattle to Howe, this time written on stationery provided by the Democratic State Central Committee. In it he vented his frustration at the state of the press in the city: "There is nothing approaching a Democratic newspaper in Seattle. The Times says today that it will print Governor Cox's speech of acceptance in full in *next* Sunday's paper. It has not been printed here."

He went on:

And to illustrate the trend of sentiment: The Times has heretofore been known as an independent newspaper. It was in 1916. Now, it won't even print the acceptance speech of Cox until it is compelled to by the demands made upon it by its subscribers.

·   The Post-Intelligencer is and always has been a republican paper of the staunchest sort. As a matter of fact if the Democrats get their issues before the people here they will have to get themselves a newspaper. One of the directors of a bank here who I met last year and called upon today told me that the P I could be bought and was a good proposition commercially without regard to its political value in the campaign. The Star is the other paper here. It is Scripps and caters to the working classes, murders, sobs and sensations. It doesn't touch politics.

He lamented that he had not seen Roosevelt since Minnesota: "Rapid traveling has made it impossible for me to follow him by the press. Then, too, not a local Seattle paper today had a story of his speeches yesterday. Neither did the final afternoons carry a word of his big speech at Butte at ten o'clock this morning."

Early told Howe he was leaving Seattle that night, but not without a promise from the *Times* and the *Post-Intelligencer* that they would carry stories on Roosevelt's arrival in Seattle. "I was desperate. The only advertisement the meeting [Roosevelt and the local Democrats] had been given was by paid advertisements in the papers. There has been a lot of this done and paid for by the Democrats here. And the *Times* charges $5.40 an inch for political advertising. It doesn't want any from the Dems. Of course, none is necessary for the Republicans. They get theirs in the news columns." He reported that he was more optimistic about his next stop, Portland, Oregon.[24]

From Portland, he told Roosevelt the progressive sentiment was "overwhelming." And he found the high cost of living "a knotty problem." He added, "Suffrage same old thing here." He was leaving Portland that night for San Francisco, where he would be at the St. Francis Hotel.[25]

All of Early's traveling from town to town and city to city, all his frustrations and meetings with local politicians, laid an intricate groundwork for the candidate who made twenty-six speeches in two days in the state of Washington.[26]

The campaign had continuous difficulties with newspaper coverage in the West. When Roosevelt spoke in Butte, Montana, he veered from the text of his speech to reply to a charge that while the British Empire would have six votes in the League of Nations Assembly, the United States would have only one. Not true, he said. The United States would in fact have a dozen votes because "does anyone suppose that the votes of Cuba, Haiti, Santa Domingo, Panama, Nicaragua, and of other Central American States would be cast differently from the vote of the United States?" According to an Associated Press dispatch, he added, "I have something to do with the running of a couple of little Republics. Until last week, I had two of these votes in my pocket. Now Secretary Daniels has them. One of them was Haiti." Again, he told the audience, "I know, for I wrote Haiti's Constitution, and if I do say it, I think it was a pretty good little Constitution."[27]

Roosevelt's claim was false and incited outbursts from a variety of factions, since the *Nation* magazine was publishing a series of articles on American military exploitation in Haiti and Santa Domingo. Liberals were incensed at Roosevelt's remarks, blacks were outraged, and even Harding got into the fray, saying that he would never allow an assistant secretary of the navy to draft a constitution "for helpless neighbors in the West Indies and jam it down their throats at the point of bayonets borne by United States Marines." Roosevelt's speech containing his misguided assertion was run in both Democratic and Republican newspapers in Montana, and when he denied he had made the Haiti comment, more than a score of reporters signed a statement swearing that he had.[28]

This proved to be an advance man's worst nightmare. Early followed the party line and asserted that Roosevelt had been misquoted. What he really thought about the affair, however, he related to Louis Howe in a letter that began, "This is strictly confidential." Dated September 8 from Washington, DC, it is a revealing document, for it shows the depth of pain and conflict Early the reporter must have felt at times as he found himself the public relations man with journalists covering the campaign.

Early wrote that he had spent all of the previous day with Lionel C. Probert, who had been news editor of the Washington Bureau of the Associated Press when Early worked there. Now he was chief of the bureau and superintendent of the Southern Division of the AP. Early told Howe that he went to Probert to "talk personally, not as a representative of Mr. Roosevelt, but strictly as an ex-Associated Press man, who still has the interests of the organization at heart." His complaint? He had seen no AP reporters covering Roosevelt from the time he left Chicago until he returned there at the end of his campaign swing through the West.

The problem issue, Early explained to Probert, was that the coverage that *did* go out over the AP wires was done by local reporters (even today not an uncommon method of newsgathering for wire services outside the major cities). Since the press in that section of the country was "hostile" toward the Democratic Party, it meant that the AP was sending biased stories to its member newspapers in the United States.

Harking back to the Butte speech, Early told Probert that the wire service "had unintentionally misquoted Mr. Roosevelt and sent out over its name reports that were not justified from what Mr. Roosevelt said." He then dropped his real reason for the visit to Probert: Would the AP assign a staff man to cover the rest of the campaign "in order that it might not be placed in the position of misrepresenting Mr. Roosevelt"? Early said, "I played on the pride of the organization, which as you know holds a high regard for the impartiality and authenticity of its dispatches."

Probert's answer? At first he told Early that vice presidential candidates did not rate their own AP staff correspondent. "Expenses were too much of a burden as compared with the news matter involved," he explained. But he did tell Early he would take the matter up with the New York office of the Associated Press and recommend that a staff man travel with the Roosevelt party on the next trip, "and also with Mr. Coolidge, in case he decided to leave the 'front porch.'"

Early ended his letter to Howe optimistically, saying that Probert's letter had been sent to New York and that the chief of the news department there "regards Probert's suggestions and I have never known him to fail to comply with one." Early was certain that an Associated Press staff correspondent would join the campaign party in the East and continue on to the South and West until the end. Early had prevailed. The AP sent Stanley W. Prenosil of the New York bureau to accompany Roosevelt. Prenosil, who had been in the Boston bureau before the war, had sailed to Europe aboard one of the early transports to cover the landing of the American troops in France. At the end of the war, back in New York, he met returning ships in New York harbor to interview the soldiers.[29]

Newspaper coverage was not the only serious problem Early encountered on that tour of the West. Temperamental party bosses nearly cost the Roosevelt campaign the services of its advance man. Early sent a six-page, typed letter to Howe written after he arrived in San Francisco from Portland, Oregon. It was obvious that Early was frustrated by the meddling of local politicians in the candidate's itinerary, and at one point he told Howe he was moving on to Reno, Nevada, and suggested, "If they [the politicians] continue to conflict, I shall probably credit Reno's record with another divorce."

The letter, written on stationery of the Palace Hotel in San Francisco and dated Sunday, August 22, outlines the turf wars between the Democrats in Washington and Oregon. It seemed that the bosses in Washington decided that the party there had a better chance of taking the state in the November election than the Oregon Democrats did. Therefore, they informed Early that Roosevelt should spend more time campaigning in Washington. When the Democrats in Oregon heard about this, they demanded equal time, claiming that "Oregon had as much of a chance to go Democratic in November as Washington did, etc." The outraged Oregonians were bitter and resented the "hogging" of Roosevelt by Washington, Early wrote. He also noted that Wilson had "few friends" in Oregon. The Democrats there told him Wilson "gave every war office contract and commission to the Republicans of that State, and excluded loyal Democrats from every favor he had to give."

The upshot was that Early was caught in the middle. He sent numerous telegrams to the Roosevelt train, explaining the situation and asking what the candidate preferred to do. Evidently no one replied to the telegrams, which further angered Early. "If the train has been getting my messages, it has failed to acknowledge them or to send word to me. I have not received a word since I left the crowd in St. Paul, Aug. 13," he told Howe, who was still in Washington, DC.

Later that Sunday, Early said, he planned to head north in hopes of meeting up with Roosevelt's train before it reached San Francisco. He lamented, "He has probably been given another and revised itinerary." Roosevelt was scheduled to bypass Sacramento, as planned, and travel south to Los Angeles, spending two days campaigning in California instead of one. "I hope I will be able to straighten these things out before I go on to Reno," he told Howe. He attempted optimism: "I am certain, however, that I will be able to get a correct itinerary from the train and go East without the trouble I have found everywhere on the Pacific Coast." He ended his letter with the hope that "my next letter will be less complaining than this."[30]

The remainder of that campaign trip was without major incidents, returning east by the first of September via Salt Lake City, Indianapolis, and Chicago and on to New York City when Early submitted an accounting of his expenses thus far: 74 meals, $119.25; rail transportation, $354.07; taxicabs and hotel buses, $26.15; hotel rooms, $43.50; telegrams, $47.53; local and long distance telephone calls, $11.10; public stenographers, $8; and incidentals which included tips, $12.15. Typed at the bottom of the bill is "RECEIVED PAYMENT FROM FRANKLIN D. ROOSEVELT." Early notes at the top of his bill that he began the trip by converting $900 cash into traveler's checks. There is no record that Roosevelt paid Early a salary in addition to his expenses. The campaign was chronically short of funds; Roosevelt put up $5,000 of his money, his mother another $3,000.[31]

Apparently Early was doing a satisfactory job as the advance man, because on August 23 McIntyre, presumably at Roosevelt's behest, sent a telegram to Howe from Oakland Pier, California, asking that he "get in touch with Early's employer and arrange for an extension of his leave of absence which expires September First." With Early still on the road for the campaign, Howe then got in touch with Early's sister, Virginia.[32]

His leave was extended and soon he was in western Massachusetts and upstate New York, where he reported that both areas were "hopelessly lost territory." But FDR "barged in gaily anyway" even though the farmers and others in upstate were apathetic toward the candidate. They often found only thirty or forty people at a train stop. Things were so dull on that trip that Howe decided to have some fun. He had the men aboard the train place bets on where they would find the smallest crowds of the day. The loser had to wear an enormous bow tie in a hideous color that Howe had dug up from somewhere, then go out on the platform and stroll up and down while the natives gaped in astonishment. It is not clear whether Early was along on that trip, but had he been, no doubt he would have enjoyed the merriment.[33]

In a long letter Early wrote from Boston to McIntyre, he discussed "the Irish question," since that city was heavily populated with Irish immigrants. He said it was "the only split and troublesome issue of importance." But the sentiment was "overwhelmingly in favor of the League," he wrote. He told McIntyre that there were "hundreds of Republicans" in Boston who disliked Harding at the head of their ticket. He urged Roosevelt to appeal to the Republicans and those Irish Democrats who were having problems accepting the League of Nations "to act like the independent voters of the West, think for themselves after studying the treaty, the platforms and the heads of the tickets." A reference to the winning of the war under a Democratic president was suggested. Coolidge was charging that the administration spent too much money to win the war, so Early wrote: "Admit that money was spent and BOAST that it did the trick; accomplished what the world believed to be impossible—the transporting of 2,000,000 men across thousands of miles of water, through submarine zones, without the loss of a man and doing the trick."

His final appeal? "Boston wants to see the Boss in his FIGHTING togs. More boasts and not the apologetic tones used by some democratic speakers with weak knees," he wrote.[34]

By October the campaign had resumed the frenetic pace of

August. According to the *New York Times*, Roosevelt gave speeches in Charleston, West Virginia, on October 1; in western Kentucky on October 3; in Kansas City, which he flew to on an airplane, on October 10; in Canton, Ohio, on October 12; and in western Indiana from October 14 to October 16. He moved on to Grand Rapids, Michigan; Cleveland; and eventually, by October 24, to the New York City area. By October 30 he had given five speeches in the city. But the campaign was a lost cause. As much as Roosevelt and Cox wanted to educate wider swaths of the electorate on the benefits of the League of Nations, they were failing to accomplish this in any significant manner, and even Roosevelt was beginning to wonder whether the issue should be a centerpiece of the Democrats' campaign.[35]

Roosevelt may have seen the League of Nations as a lesser campaign issue, but in the telegrams from Early to Roosevelt and McIntyre, the code word "ten" shows up prominently in most. A telegram from Early in Marion, Indiana, to Roosevelt in Cincinnati dated October 15 shows the campaign was still using the code. Early wrote that race was an issue, with six Negroes on the state ticket, but they were "black" (sentiment decidedly wet). However, the German were the most influential and anti-"ten" (League of Nations). The "four" (Democrats), he added, were "strong and friendly."[36]

The campaign drew to a close and Roosevelt headed to his home in Hyde Park to await the results. Early probably returned to Washington. There were no surprises: Cox and Roosevelt lost to Harding and Coolidge 16 million to 9 million, with the Harding ticket taking 61 percent of the popular vote. The electoral vote was 404 to 127, with the Republican ticket carrying thirty-seven states. Even Roosevelt's home state of New York went Republican.

Roosevelt's mother, Sara, wrote in her journal on Election Day, November 2, "Franklin rather relieved not to be elected Vice President." Roosevelt told a friend that "[t]he campaign had been a darned good sail." And in a letter to another he wrote, "Franklin D. Roosevelt, Ex. V.P., Canned. Erroneously reported dead."[37]

Early sent Roosevelt a brief letter dated November 8. Roosevelt was in Hyde Park. The letter begins, "My dear Boss:—The days of 'normalcy' returned this morning." He said he was in Washington but had not yet decided what his future there would be, because it turned out the Chamber of Commerce project had been terminated.[38]

Two days later Early sent Roosevelt a longer letter and a bill for his expenses, beginning on September 8 and ending November 4. The total was $979.40. An earlier bill, for expenses from August 7 to August 31, was $636.25, making the "grand total" $1,615.65. Early was reimbursed by Roosevelt for all but $115.65. Early said he would like to consider that his contribution to the campaign: "I hope it will be accepted in that way and my only regret is that I am not able to give more."

In that same letter, Early tried to cheer up Roosevelt. He wrote that he was convinced that "we can be better prepared for the next campaign and, being prepared, we shall win. That is my firm conviction, for the people will demand a 'change' in '24 after four years of the Syndicate Government, and will return the Democrats to power with a greater majority than they were ousted in '20. Then, too, I confidently expect you to HEAD the ticket and pledge myself meanwhile to do all in my power to accomplish that end."

Early told Roosevelt that he had enjoyed working for him:

> The crying shame of it all, as I review the time we spent together on the road, is that this country is too big and the machinery too inadequate to establish personal contact and relations with all the people of all the states in the brief time allowed for a campaign. If we had been able to do that, there would have been no Republican victory, particularly with the Democratic ticket headed by two such men as Cox and yourself. Also people would have come to know you as the man you are rather than as the Candidate you were. And, knowing you in that light, as we who were with you had the good fortune to do, the voters would have loved and supported you as we do and always shall. I sincerely trust that I shall be able in the next years to come, to see you often and keep fresh always the memories of the past. As always, please believe me Yours most sincerely, Stephen T. Early.[39]

Roosevelt and Cox indeed suffered a huge election loss, yet many of Early's telegrams and letters written to Roosevelt, McIntyre, and Howe are optimistic. And FDR is described by his biographers as being "buoyant," throughout the campaign. Were Early's advance dispatches giving the candidate false hope as he moved along the campaign trail? Perhaps on occasion they did, but reading his words recalling those weeks many years later, it is easy to understand why Early may truly have believed the "Boss had at least a glimmer of a chance.

"The zest for political adventure was on us—that, and the Roosevelt spell," he wrote. "To know Franklin Roosevelt intimately at all is to become virtually a member of his family." Early noted that even Stan Prenosil, the Associated Press reporter who covered the campaign, "must have had a hard time maintaining that requirement of neutrality for the great news organization, for he was soon just another member of the happy family."

We see Early the newsman's fascination with Roosevelt when he writes:

> The most significant thing I noted in the early days of that campaign was the unfailing ability of Mr. Roosevelt himself to unravel the intricacies of each new local political situation into which he was projected. He made it his business to make friends with party leaders everywhere, to steer clear of factional disputes. Once he met a man along the road who wielded any political influence whatever, he never forgot him. And he never forgot the particular circumstance in party relationships or what-not in which that man stood. He made friends and kept them. That was to prove a far more important part of his campaigning than what he said in his speeches on the issues of 1920. It opened the road to the White House for him.[40]

The same could be said for any good journalist: He makes it his business to meet everyone, to remain nonpartisan, and to never forget a source.

On November 30, less than a month after the election, Roosevelt ordered five sets of gold cuff links from Tiffany & Co. in New York. On one side of each link were the initials FDR and on the other side were those of the recipient. They were a gift to Howe, Early, McIntyre, Tom Lynch, and Charles McCarthy. The cost, including engraving, was $142. They were not just a souvenir of the campaign; they bound together an unusually talented group of men who would come together years later to run another—this time successful—campaign. Meanwhile, "a unique and highly personal campaign organization went on furlough."[41]

McIntyre said he, Early, and Howe liked to think of themselves as the "Unholy Trinity," who, after the 1920 campaign, "were thoroughly convinced that Franklin D. Roosevelt's days were yet to come."[42]

4

BACK TO THE
ASSOCIATED PRESS

"It is awfully nice to hear of your new work—one of us at least has landed in the Senate Chamber—though I think your job will be more interesting than the one I was after," Roosevelt wrote to Early a few days before Christmas in 1920.

Roosevelt was referring to Early's return to the Associated Press, where he had worked before the war. His job at the Chamber of Commerce had been terminated, presumably because the project itself was completed, and it was not until December that Early was notified he would be hired back at the AP. Now he would be covering the Senate, a body that Roosevelt called "that Den of Thieves" in his letter to Early, which continued, "I have often thought how lucky you were in [the] campaign to avoid all or at least most of my perorations—perhaps in this life things have to be evened up in the end—at least you will have nice 'chatty' times with V.P. Coolidge."

Roosevelt passed along some family news—a move to 47 East 65th Street in New York, where they would live during the week, the weekends being spent at Hyde Park with his mother. He asked Early to visit him in the city. "If you can get off for a Sunday come up here and spend it with us—very quiet but plenty to eat and wash it down," a suggestion that must have appealed to the bachelor Early. He also said he wanted to arrange a reunion of the campaign gang in New York. "I told Louis H. to get everyone to choose the same date for an evening in the 'big city.' Also I want to have a talk with you about the situation in general—You were so perfectly fine in the way you helped in the campaign, and I value your judgment so much that I look to you for many things in the days to come. Thank the Lord we are both comparatively youthful."

Early replied to Roosevelt on Christmas Day, reminding him that "if there is any chore you want done in Washington I shall be delighted to attend to it." He said if Roosevelt needed any information from the capital, "please let me get it for you." This was pure Early, the always thoughtful, even sentimental man with a tinge of the sycophant—characteristics he exhibited toward his powerful friends and acquaintances on numerous occasions during his life. "There are not many things I can do for my friends and when they want something I have, or can get, it is a real pleasure for me to give it. And this desire to serve applies to none quite as much as yourself."

He then turned to affairs of state: "I can not quite realize yet what we lost in November. I suppose the arrival of Coolidge will be the bitter awakening. It could not be otherwise when I think how different it might have been. But, I am confident in the future and find the confidence increasing with each day's observations of the Senate and House Republicans. You were always mild in your condemnation of them."[1]

While Early had returned to his old employer, Roosevelt had taken temporary leave of politics to enter the business world. In early January he accepted an offer on Wall Street as a vice president of the Fidelity & Deposit Company of Maryland, the fourth largest surety bonding concern in the country. He was paid $25,000 a year, or five times what he had earned as assistant secretary of the navy. On the side he practiced law.[2]

The Associated Press Early returned to was not the same operation he had left, nor was he by any stretch of the imagination that still-wet-behind-the ears young reporter who had resigned from the wire service less than four years earlier to join the army. Bloody battles on the fields of France, a stint running the army's newspaper in Paris, and the long and sometimes lonely campaign of 1920 had left their imprint. If he was eager and energetic in pursuit of a story before the war, during his second tour with the wire service he was downright daring and sometimes reckless as he moved through the 1920s covering some of the major events of the decade.[3]

While Early was away from the AP, the board of directors, in a bold move for the times, had set up a comprehensive system of employees' insurance, pensions, and disability and sick benefits. Until then, only commercial and industrial concerns with large financial resources had put similar plans in place. Such a system in the field of journalism was indeed unusual. It meant employees could retire with more than just the meager savings they had cobbled together from relatively low pay; sickness or disability would no longer mean financial devastation for a wire service reporter's family.[4] Early probably was earning about $4,000 or possibly more, since the Washington Bureau staffers were among the elite of the Associated Press reporters.

Apparently Early's advance-man duties for Roosevelt had not imperiled his chances of returning to the business of reporting. Even today it is difficult, although not impossible, for journalists to move back and forth between public relations (particularly that involving politics) and journalism. The assumption is that once a journalist has left the profession to work for a politician, he or she becomes tainted and cannot return to the profession with any impartiality. Perhaps Early's contributions to the Washington Bureau of the AP before the war and his experience with *Stars and Stripes* overrode his association with Roosevelt. Or maybe the AP simply needed experienced newsmen.

Whatever the reasons, Early was back with his colleagues in the Washington Bureau by the beginning of 1921, a year that would be— for both him and his friend Franklin Roosevelt—memorable personally and professionally. By the end of the year, Early would be a married man and well on his way to becoming one of the AP's finest reporters. And Roosevelt would be fighting the physical battle of his life.

Early began in earnest to court the lovely, dark-haired Helen Wrenn, the daughter of Augustus C. Wrenn, chief clerk in the Bureau of Engineering in the Navy Department. The Wrenn and Early families had been neighbors on North Carolina Avenue when Helen and Steve were growing up, and, according to their daughter, Helen Elam, they had known each other for years. Miss Wrenn, however, was seven years younger than Steve Early, so it is probable that when he was in high school she was nothing more than "the little neighbor girl." After he came back from Europe and discovered his prewar girl-friend had left him for someone else, he and Helen Wrenn recon-nected and began dating.

Then Miss Wrenn was sent to San Francisco as a stenographer for the navy, and, for a while at least, the romance became a long-distance one. It was difficult for the couple to carry on a courtship from oppo-site sides of the country, so after regular telephone calls between Washington and California, Steve said, "Why don't you come back here?" She did, and they were married later that year. He was thirty-two; she was twenty-five.[5]

Meanwhile, he was keeping busy covering the United States Senate for his employer. Indeed it was a busy year in the Capitol. In May Congress passed the Quota Act, a law to limit immigration that put a cap of 357,000 on annual immigration. The following month it approved the Budget and Accounting Act, which created the Bureau of Budget and provided for an annual submission to Congress of a federal budget for the coming year. Charles Dawes—who, as vice president of the United States a few years later, would assist Early in his career path—was named the director of the budget. In July Con-gress, in a joint resolution, declared an end to World War I, and in August it approved an act to eliminate price manipulation and monopolies in the meat-packing industry. On August 16 the Depart-ment of Labor announced that unemployment had risen to 5 million, bringing an end to the wartime boom.

With the emergence of Margaret Sanger and her American Birth Control League in New York City, 1921 heralded a sexual and cul-tural revolution that would become better known as the Roaring Twenties. Women were seen wearing dresses with short skirts and plunging necklines, their faces painted with lipstick, rouge, and eye shadow. Young men and women engaged in nearly sexually explicit dances in public. And F. Scott Fitzgerald, recently of Princeton Uni-versity, was capturing it in his novels, the first of which was *This Side of Paradise*. It is unlikely that the rigorous, almost around-the-clock schedule wire service reporters were expected to follow gave Early much time to devote to the blossoming social culture. When he and Helen did get together for an evening, they probably spent it at a play or at the homes of their parents, where each still lived.

In July Early once again came to the aid of his friend Franklin

Roosevelt in one of the politically dark moments in the life of the future president. The story, which eventually included a Senate investigation, dated to 1917, when Roosevelt was assistant secretary of the navy. For more than two years the navy, and in particular Secretary Daniels, had been concerned about the flourishing prostitution business in Newport, Rhode Island, one of the large bases of the navy's Atlantic fleet and home to the Naval War College. For a time it appeared the problem had diminished, even disappeared, but in 1919 Daniels was again hearing complaints from residents and clergymen in Rhode Island. He also heard rumors of widespread homosexuality among the seamen in Newport, so he ordered the command there to appoint a court of inquiry and "clean the place up." Then he sailed for Europe in March, leaving the problem to his assistant, Roosevelt.[6]

Soon after Daniels left the country, Roosevelt asked the attorney general to use his office to help with the "cleanup." Later Roosevelt said he was not aware until the next September of the details of the methods used by the navy investigators, which included assigning newly enlisted sailors to entrap homosexual sailors. Some of these sailors, who were performing fellatio in their pursuit of the homosexuals, were among those arrested and eventually court-martialed. Then more sailors were recruited for the investigation, and more arrests were made. One of those arrested was the Episcopal chaplain of the naval hospital in Newport and a highly respected cleric among the city's elite.

About the same time the "cleanup" in Newport was underway, Roosevelt signed an order restoring to active duty ten navy men who had served sentences in the naval prison in Portsmouth, New Hampshire. This seemed in keeping with Daniels's long-standing belief that the navy should rehabilitate its lawbreakers. Eventually the two seemingly unrelated reforms erupted into a scandal. It didn't help either Roosevelt or Daniels that the *Providence Journal*, Rhode Island's largest and most powerful newspaper, which once had endorsed the Newport "cleanup," now was calling for a full-scale investigation of both the Newport affair and the reforms at Portsmouth. The editor of the Republican newspaper, John R. Rathom, relentlessly attacked Roosevelt in the news pages.

It was not until the summer of 1921, after Roosevelt had unsuccessfully run for the vice presidency and now was a respected member of the business community, that an investigation of the incidents by a subcommittee of the Senate Naval Affairs Committee, consisting of two Republicans and one Democrat, was about to be announced. In spite of a promise to allow Roosevelt to explain his role in both the Newport "cleanup" and the reforms in the Portsmouth prison, the committee proceeded without his statements, saying it was unnecessary for him to appear since he had told his side of the story to the navy board that earlier had held its own investigation.

The Senate subcommittee members did allow him a few hours to examine the fifteen volumes and six thousand pages of testimony and submit his statement. It indeed was damaging. If he had not known about the methods used in the "cleanup," then he was "derelict in the performance of his duty" as assistant secretary of the navy. Roosevelt, who had rushed to a hot, sticky July Washington from his summer retreat on Campobello Island, was determined not to allow a negative report to impinge on any future political plans he might have.

Once again he turned to Early for assistance. Roosevelt asked his former advance man and friend if the Associated Press could spare him. Without hesitation, Early agreed to help out. Loaned an empty office in the Navy Department for the day, Roosevelt asked Early and Marguerite A. LeHand, who had served efficiently as his secretary during his 1920 campaign and later would become his personal secretary in the White House, to help him draft a reply to the subcommittee's report. It was unusual for a journalist—especially one who was covering the federal government, as Early was—to step away from his job, if even for a day, to do work for a politician who one day might again be an important source. But the Roosevelt-Early relationship was too solid for Early to have considered declining the request, and the AP must have allowed him the leave.

Working in a stuffy room in the Navy Department in Washington, the three came up with a reply as best they could, considering the circumstances. According to one Roosevelt biographer, Geoffrey Ward, as they began to work, Roosevelt turned to Early and said, "Damn it, Steve, this whole business is nothing but dirty politics. That's the point we have to emphasize." Roosevelt labored "in his shirtsleeves, clenched his teeth, angrily penciling point after point on a lined yellow pad, then passing the pages to be typed up by Missy."[7]

When they finished, Early and Roosevelt had drafted a four-page typed statement, which was released to the press for publication in the following day's afternoon newspapers. Referring to the "cleanup" operation, they said, "No one other than partisan politicians could ever, in their wildest dreams, assume or charge that the squad was under the 'direct supervision' of the Acting Secretary of the Navy." In fact, the statement said, after Roosevelt learned what was going on in Newport, he gave orders to halt the activities of the investigators. They ended the statement with, "This business of using the navy as a football of politics is going to stop. People everywhere are tired of partisan discussion of dead history." They asked only for "fair play."

Naturally the story made headlines, but, as Roosevelt feared, his denials were buried. Ward in his biography of Roosevelt calls the headline in the July 20 *New York Times* "all the more damaging for its genteel opacity":

LAY NAVY SCANDAL
TO F.D. ROOSEVELT
SENATE NAVAL SUB-COMMITTEE
ACCUSES HIM AND DANIELS
IN NEWPORT INQUIRY
DETAILS ARE UNPRINTABLE

Page one of the *Providence Journal* that day was devoted almost entirely to the conclusion of the naval inquiry, which now had been in the news for the last year and a half. The good news was that the headline did not include Roosevelt by name:

SENATE NAVY COMMITTEE REPORT SUSTAINS
CHARGES MADE BY PROVIDENCE JOURNAL
BEFORE U.S. SENATE[8]

Ten days after releasing the statement, Roosevelt left for Campobello, where he intended to pass a leisurely summer sailing and playing with his young family; Early went back to "having nice chatty times" with Vice President Coolidge and colleagues in Congress.

For Early, it proved to be a busy summer and fall. He was working long and sometimes erratic hours for the Associated Press, but he took time out of his diligent reporting schedule to marry Helen Wrenn on September 17. Their first home was at 409 Quincy NW, where her parents now were living. By 1923 the young couple was renting a home at 409 Rock Creek Church Road NW. And two years later they had moved to 2042 Pierce Mill Road, where their only daughter, Helen (known in the family as Sis) was born.

However, for Roosevelt that summer and fall proved to be the defining moment in his personal and professional life. On August 9, toward the end of a day spent fishing under the hot sun with friends, he slipped and tumbled overboard into the freezing Bay of Fundy. That night he felt unusually tired, and his legs ached. It signaled the beginning of polio and his long, dark struggle to regain the use of his legs—as well as his political career.

It is probable that Early learned of his friend's catastrophic illness either in the newspaper or, more likely, from Louis Howe, but when he did, he later recalled, "The shock of that was crushing." All his life Early was a sensitive man who felt deeply the pain of friends and family, so this news must have affected him greatly. He said he kept recalling the day in San Francisco at the Democratic convention when the wide-shouldered and powerful Roosevelt had ripped the New York State standard up and carried it into the Wilson demonstration: "And now he was stricken, doomed, it must be, to look out from a wheel chair on the rush and hurry of political life he loved above all things. It brought a queer, tense feeling in my throat to think about it."[9]

The public read about Roosevelt's affliction for the first time in a story on page one of the September 16 issue of the *New York Times.* The headline told it all:

F.D. ROOSEVELT ILL
OF POLIOMYELITIS
Brought on Special Car from Campobello,
Bay of Fundy, to Hospital Here
RECOVERING, DOCTOR SAYS
Patient stricken by Infantile Paralysis
A Month Ago, and Use of Legs Affected[10]

In a poignant letter dated September 16, Early wrote to his old friend: "My Dear Boss, Is there a mite for me to give or do? I feel there is not, but I can not refrain from extending the offer. Please know our love goes out to you and yours in distress and nothing would give me greater joy than to be used, if use for me can be found. It's unnecessary to say, I hope and pray for your rapid and complete recovery." It was signed, "Affectionately, Stephen."[11]

But it was not until the following January, on Roosevelt's fortieth birthday, that Early saw him for the first time when he and other members of the Cuff Links Gang, those who worked in his 1920 campaign to whom he had earlier given the gold cuff links, went to New York City to fete their old boss and friend. Howe, of course, had been with Roosevelt when he was stricken and had remained with him, faithfully nurturing and encouraging him in the battle to use his legs.

Early recounted that first meeting:

All of us who had not seen "the Boss" since his physical disaster went with trepidation I think. I know I did. I wondered what change I would find in that gay, happy-hearted man I had known when the inner assurance of high political preferment was before his eyes.

We mobilized. And we found him, as high of heart, as gay in humor, and more overwhelmingly interested in politics—national, State, international—than he had ever been. It was dumbfounding. Men of courage are no rarity, but a man who could face such a cruel stroke of fortune so blithely with so utterly an unchanged demeanor, with an outlook on the world and its affairs so unaffected with such utter absence of repining—this was beyond anything I had ever known. I think we were all a bit dazed—and, if possible more ardently the friends of Franklin Roosevelt than we had ever seen.

We discovered another thing, too. Not for a moment had his determination to have a share in great party affairs and national political life abated. Whether he then foresaw the possibility that despite the physical handicap he himself could again seek high public office, I do not know. That was not discussed. But the good of the Democratic party, stiff, groggy from its 1920 defeat, was. And it developed that out of the card-index memory of F.D.R.'s had come the beginnings of perhaps the most vast and unusual political mailing list I had ever heard.[12]

By November Washington was the site of two important events: the burial of the country's Unknown Soldier from the war and an armament conference that brought together nine nations from around the world.

This was a time of isolationism for the United States. By electing Warren Harding and Calvin Coolidge, the voters had in effect left the League of Nations to a future generation. It was to be a decade of gratuitous self-indulgence, with little interest in the outside world unless it directly affected the United States. At his inauguration the previous March, Harding had told his audience, "We seek no part in directing the destinies of the world." And yet ten months later, representatives of nine nations were meeting to reduce naval armaments and consider the problems endemic to East Asia.

While the country wanted nothing more than to move forward, leaving the ashes of the war forever scattered on the battlefields of France, it had to deal with the aftermath. As the arms conference was preparing to open, on November 5 Harding declared November 11 to be Armistice Day, a national holiday, and the country buried its Unknown Soldier in Arlington National Cemetery. A simple black coffin, draped with an American flag, contained the body of the unknown American soldier brought back from France and stood in the rotunda of the Capitol, where it was viewed by thousands of men, women, and children on the day before it was taken to Arlington for interment.[13]

As poignant as the lying in state was, the burial on an unusually chilly and windy day for a Washington fall served as a historic moment in modern technology. The *New York Times* wrote that at the formal address before hundreds of guests at Friday's ceremony at the cemetery, Harding's voice, "multiplied billions of times by the inventions of brilliant electrical engineers," was heard on both coasts. Radio was still in its infancy, and it had been just one year since the first scheduled broadcast emanated from a station in Pittsburgh, sending out the results of the Harding-Cox election. The station, KDKA, claimed it was "the world's first scheduled broadcast." The writer for the *New York Times* was almost breathless in his fascination with this new phenomenon as he explained to his readers how the country would hear the president's words at the Arlington ceremony:

> At the start, the President's voice will enter several receivers as the ordinary speaker's voice enters the telephone mouthpiece, the sound waves being translated into electrical waves. This current of electricity carrying the impression of the President's voice is passed into a vacuum tube. Another current 1,000 times as great is passed through the tube at the same time.

The President's words will travel more than 3,500 miles in its simultaneous trips from Washington to California to New York and will be louder at the end of the journeys than at the beginning. His audiences are expected to number more than a quarter of a million.[14]

The crowds at Arlington heard Harding's talk over telephone amplifiers, which the *Times* described as carrying "the crisp notes of the bugle, the playing band and the singing quartet. . . . And except for the slight blurring of deep sounds and the occasional re-echoing of the rolled 'r,' the voices were reproduced with sharpness and clearness."[15]

The day following the dramatic burial, the Conference on the Limitation of Armament and Far East Questions, called by Secretary of State Charles Evans Hughes, officially opened. It was to have started on November 11, but it was delayed a day because of the new national holiday. Its telegraphic facilities were equipped to handle up to 2 million words a day for ten hours. It also had two direct cable circuits to Nova Scotia and two to San Francisco.[16]

All of this use of new technology was not lost on Early, who must have been fascinated with it as he covered the conference, unaware that the miracles of airwaves and technology would play a paramount role later in his professional life.

Reporters covering the arms conference were given working space in the Navy Building on Constitution Avenue side of the Mall at Eighteenth Street. A temporary but solid structure built during the war, it was large enough to house all the administrative bureaus of the navy. By placing all the correspondents in the same building—they came from across the United States as well as from numerous foreign countries, including those taking part in the conference—it was the hope of the conference planners that a good feeling and understanding among the journalists might result from their coming together daily. It was an interesting public relations ploy, and apparently stemmed from the fact that during the Paris Peace Conference in 1919, reporters from the participating countries had scarcely come into contact with each other.[17]

The arms conference sessions themselves were held in the Hall of the Americas in the Pan American Building, a block from the Navy Building and across the street from the White House. Built at the turn of the century, the white marble Pan American Building, with its

broad lawns set with shrubbery and trees, was one of the most beautiful in a city of magnificent buildings. The Hall of the Americas, with
its all-white interior, was on the second floor. It was here that Early
and eleven other Associated Press men—including the Rome, Paris,
and Tokyo bureau chiefs—joined the other journalists for the daily
sessions of the conference, which was scheduled to end by Christmas.
It did not conclude its business until February 6, 1922.

Day in and day out throughout the coldest winter the city had
seen so far in the century, the AP reporters trudged to the conference,
writing about the intricacies of the daily meetings. A January blizzard,
in fact, dumped twenty-nine inches of snow on Washington. A photo
of the staff reporters in the Service Bulletin of the Associated Press
shows the group of men, mostly in their thirties—a few were older—
who covered the conference. They included colleagues who also had
worked with Early in the Washington office before the war: Byron
Price; L. C. Probert, who also covered Roosevelt's 1920 campaign;
and Edwin M. Hood.[18]

The conference made diplomatic history when Hughes proposed
a ten-year naval holiday and the scraping of sixty-six capital ships in
the interests of world peace. Essentially he wanted the world
powers—the United States, Great Britain, and Japan—to freeze their
navies at the ratio of their existing strengths to each other. For several
days, the journalists covering the conference struggled with ways to
explain to their readers in a clear and understandable manner a for-
mula that provided for fleet equality between the United States and
Great Britain and a Japanese navy of 40 percent less strength. After
flailing with complex phrases, the Associated Press reporters decided
to call it the "5–5–3 ratio," and the expression was used by most news
reporters after that.[18] In the end, the nations agreed to limit their
navies, and nine countries, including the United States, reaffirmed the
Chinese Open Door Policy set after the turn of the century to avoid
monopolies in China by any foreign country.[19]

It is unlikely that Early spent every day at the arms conference;
rather, he would have been needed to head over to the Capitol to
cover Congress or pick up the odd story at his other regular beat,
State, War, and Navy, and even the White House. Meanwhile, his
reporting on the big stories was not lost on his colleagues. By the end
of 1921 he had been elected to the board of governors of the National

Press Club, joining on the board of that notable organization a handful of elite Washington journalists.[20]

Early continued to find stories—big and small—for the wire service, although his primary beats were Congress and the White House. He did not know it, but one of the defining moments of his journalistic career was a year and a half away.

In early 1923 President Harding, whose political fortunes were rapidly declining, began plotting a Voyage of Understanding, a cross-country train trip designed to take him as far as the country's northernmost territory, Alaska, where no president had ever set foot. His goal was to encounter the ordinary Americans. It was an ambitious undertaking, even for a younger man; Harding already was fifty-seven years old, in less than perfect health, and weary from the bubblings of the scandals that later would leave such a black mark on his presidency.

Harding's biographer said that by the spring before the trip west, Harding was overweight and flabby, his blood pressure was high, he had trouble sleeping at night because his breathing was labored, and he was growing haggard.[21] The Veterans' Bureau had been mismanaged by his longtime friend and poker companion Col. Charles Forbes and his assistant, Charles Cramer. Both men were forced to resign after Congress threatened an investigation. Soon after, Cramer committed suicide, and soon after that another poker crony, Jess Smith, took his own life; although no scandal was attached to his name, he later was found to have been part of the widespread corruption that tainted the White House during Harding's tenure.

Nonetheless, Harding forged ahead with plans for the two-month trip, and on June 20 at 2 o'clock on a hot, humid Washington afternoon, the presidential train pulled out of Union Station carrying sixty-five people, including President and Mrs. Harding, General Pershing, other guests, Secret Service men, stenographers, a nurse, photographers, newsreel cameramen, several telephone technicians to install amplifiers and arrange for long-distance playing of the president's speeches, and twenty-two Washington correspondents representing large newspapers across the country and the wire services. Two of these reporters were Steve Early and his colleague E. Ross Bartley, who normally covered the White House. But because L. C. Probert, now in charge of the Washington AP office, knew the trip would require twenty-four-hour coverage, he selected Early to travel with Bartley.[22] When they returned to Washington, Early would be a journalistic hero.

The White House published a large program detailing the itinerary of the entourage and listing the names and affiliations of those traveling with the president. The names of the two AP correspondents, Bartley and Early, appeared at the top of the press list. George Holmes, a reporter for Hearst's International News Service, was part of the contingent. A few years later he would become Early's brother-in-law and one of his closest friends. The big newspapers represented included five New York papers—the *Times*, the *Tribune*, the *World*, the *Herald*, and the *Evening Post*—along with the *Chicago Tribune*, the *Los Angeles Times*, the *Denver Post*, the *Detroit News*, and the *Baltimore Sun*.

But before Early packed his bags and headed into the biggest scoop of his career, he became a first-time father when Helen gave birth to a son, whom they named Stephen Tyree Early Jr. The father, who throughout his life had an almost zealous attachment to his family, must have found it wrenching to leave his young wife and new baby behind for the wilds of a most unfamiliar Alaska.

And it certainly was a trip with its share of adventures for Early. The first one came when the presidential train stopped in St. Louis. Despite all his press credentials, Early was arrested as a Communist agitator while he was trying to push through the crowd to reach the president and his party. It was a short-lived arrest, for it was not long before the Secret Service explained the error and the St. Louis police released the wire service reporter to continue the trip. (When Early returned to Washington, the Associated Press began preparing a suit for false arrest against the police, but the attorney for the AP decided that no jury would ever believe that Early's professional standing had been damaged by the arrest since he had been given a monetary bonus for the journalistic coup he scored later in the trip.)[23]

Certainly the news reporters must have been aware for months that the president's health was deteriorating. During the first part of the trip, Harding appeared listless; his audiences were polite but apathetic. When the train pulled into Kansas City, William Allen White, the influential publisher of the *Emporia* (Kansas) *Gazette*, noticed that the president's eyes were puffy and his hands seemed stiff when White shook them.

These same reporters probably knew about Harding's sexual escapades in the White House, but that facet of a chief executive's life simply was not considered appropriate grist for the journalists. Unlike the political scandals of the Harding administration, his extramarital activities were not made public until years after his death. For, despite his general ineptitude as president, the reporters had developed a genuine fondness for Harding and frequently protected him. Without this affection, his administration and his personal life might have been punctured long before they were.[24]

It was not just an arduous trip for an ailing chief executive; it also proved exhausting for those with him. The train headed west to Denver, north to Cheyenne, and on to Salt Lake City, with a brief detour south to Cedar City and Zion National Park, then north to Butte, west to Portland, up to Seattle, and finally via ship through Puget Sound and into the Pacific to Alaska, which they reached on July 5. The train made numerous sightseeing stops, and of course Harding spoke to the citizens of many of the communities along the way, as had been his original plan. As he moved west, people seemed more enthusiastic about and sympathetic toward his talks. Somewhere along the way, a photographer snapped a picture of the members of the press corps with the president and Mrs. Harding. There, standing at the end of the second row in a white suit, wearing a broad grin and holding a Panama hat, is Steve Early.[25]

After they had seen their first totem pole, were greeted by blanketed Indians in war canoes, and had made their way past glaciers and through small wooden villages, the party sailed back to Vancouver on July 26. Back on board the train, they moved south again through Seattle and Portland, arriving in San Francisco on Tuesday, July 31. They were scheduled to leave for Los Angeles at 11 that night, arriving the following noon. On Saturday, August 4, the party was to sail from San Diego and eventually travel through the Panama Canal. But all that changed when they got to San Francisco.

By the time he reached San Francisco, Harding had been showing signs of exhaustion for several days. He nearly collapsed during a speech in Seattle, and a major speech in Portland was canceled, the official line being that he was suffering from indigestion from tainted crabmeat. What he had was a serious heart problem.[26] How much of this the reporters accompanying him suspected can only be guessed at. Those like Early, who came in contact with the president in Washington more or less regularly, no doubt had watched his physical decline.

Early later recalled in a letter that the reporters "did not learn of the President's illness until he had left Seattle. . . . As a matter of fact, the President attended a dinner in Seattle which was given in his honor by the press club there. We went from dinner to the train and headed for the Grand Canyon. The next morning, when I woke up, my sense of direction seemed to tell me that something was wrong. Upon inquiry I discovered that the train had turned around and was heading for San Francisco. Further inquiry developed the fact that the Secretary of the Interior, a member of the President's official party, had announced that the President had eaten something that had disagreed with him and was being taken to San Francisco for rest and treatment."[27]

When he arrived at the Palace Hotel in San Francisco, Harding immediately went to bed in his suite, Room 8064 on the eighth floor. He sent word that he was merely resting and had every intention of keeping to his schedule the next day. But he did not, even though the official medical bulletins were optimistic: "The President is out of danger and on the road to recovery." The Associated Press, however, continued to keep a twenty-four-hour watch in the corridors outside Harding's suite. The wire service's telegraph operators also were at their posts around the clock, always alert for an emergency flash.

In the afternoon on Thursday, August 2, the president was allowed to sit up in bed. He seemed to be improving. Early recalled that his doctors issued a bulletin under their signatures "saying that at no time since the President's illness had his condition be[en] so satisfactory."[28]

By dinnertime that day, most of the reporters had written their stories and had left the hotel for dinner and a night on the town, so Early, who already had eaten, told Bartley to go out for dinner. Early would remain on duty in the hotel. "A few minutes later, as I was standing in the corridor talking to some of the Secret Service men, the door of the President's bedroom was opened suddenly. Mrs. Harding stood there. She seemed greatly excited. She called to us saying: 'Get the doctors quick.' All of us sensed something unusual. The Secret Service men scattered, running to find one of the doctors. None was on duty at the time. I ran down the stairway to my room," Early recalled. His news instincts told him the president was dead.[29]

The AP had left a telegrapher on duty in the room Early and Bartley shared, so Early had the man cut into the AP's trunk transcontinental line so he could dictate a series of bulletins, which he slugged

"E.O.S." In the AP, this meant "Extra Ordinary Service," meaning member newspapers could use the story anytime. He related Mrs. Harding's sudden appearance and her cry for the doctors, ending with the alert that an official statement would soon follow.

Early then returned to the corridor outside Harding's suite, where he met Herbert Hoover, then secretary of commerce, who refused to make a statement. Neither would any of the doctors Early stopped. When one of the president's secretaries and a stenographer went into a nearby room to draft an official statement, Early said he heard them putting together the announcement of Harding's death: "It was not until then that I flashed the tragic news over the AP wire system."[30] The president had died not of indigestion, but of either a cerebral hemorrhage or a heart attack. Mrs. Harding would not allow an autopsy.

Early later wrote, "This was not a gamble. I had been trained by the old school masters—to report facts, never to speculate or gamble with the facts." It is probably not surprising that Early scored a beat on Harding's death. A contemporary labeled him a "fast, crack spot-news man."[31]

How did Early know that Harding had died rather than just suffering a relapse of the indigestion? Despite the reassuring bulletins, the San Francisco AP bureau chief was not satisfied with the official explanation, so he consulted two local doctors, who told him that a patient with the symptoms Harding apparently had was not out of danger. The result was that the AP made certain a reporter and a telegrapher were on duty every minute, day and night. The reporting success also could be traced to the ability of Early and Bartley to work as a well-synchronized team, their intimate acquaintance with the members of the presidential party and their confidential news sources, together with the fact they were talented newsmen "of the highest type."[32]

When the black-streamered train, once the presidential train and now a funeral train, pulled out of San Francisco and headed east to Washington, Early and Bartley were on board to take up the threads of the dramatic story. Harding was the first president to die in office since William McKinley's assassination in 1901, and, despite the rumblings of scandal in his administration, he remained a very popular president. The spontaneous outpouring of public sorrow along the way was massive. Mrs. Harding insisted that the train run slowly at every point where people had gathered to pay their respects.

But the reporters aboard the train found it difficult, if not impossible at times, to relay news dispatches. The orderly procedure of the trip from Washington to Alaska and then to San Francisco had been turned into a catch-as-catch-can operation on the return trip to the capital. The continuous movement of the train, under orders to stop only where necessary for provisions and changing of locomotives, meant little contact between newsmen and the commercial telegraph. So the AP devised some unusual methods to ensure communication of its dispatches. They were filed in duplicate, with the first copy, addressed to the nearest AP bureau, often thrown on the station platform as the train passed; while the second one was filed at the next stop, where, thanks to the foresight of the San Francisco office, staff from the local bureau would meet the train.

This well-oiled operation meant that none of their reports failed to reach the AP promptly, and at no time during the five-day trip was the wire service out of communication with Early and Bartley for more than an hour or so.

On the evening of August 7, the train arrived in Washington, DC, where the body lay briefly in the East Room of the White House. The next day it was taken, in a long and formal procession of dignitaries, to the Capitol for a service. From there, the casket returned to Union Station for its final trip to Marion, Ohio, Harding's home, for burial. Again, Early and Bartley accompanied the president, according to a personal request from Mrs. Harding.

When Early and Bartley returned to Washington, the accolades descended. The general manager of the AP, Frederick Roy Martin, called their reporting "a magnificent manifestation of newspaper work." The official bulletin of the Associated Press hailed them for their "preparedness and watchfulness." Even the *New York Times* wrote about the coup. Because it was not the AP's policy to use reporters' bylines, the *Times* referred to Early as simply "the reporter," noting that "he grasped the situation instantly and rushed to the Associated Press wire, close by, and dictated a bulletin of the startling news of the President's collapse." And from Probert, the AP chief in Washington, came this message: "Thanks for the best example of sane accurate and yet colorful reporting I have ever known. The profession and the service owe you both a debt."[33]

After this remarkable assignment, Early went back to what was known as the "uptown beat," covering War, State, Navy, and the White House. There is no record that he returned to cover "the Den of Thieves."

Getting news out of the White House during the Coolidge administration proved frustrating for reporters, since, unlike the former newsman Harding, who regarded the press corps as his friends, Coolidge was reluctant to even give out his official engagements for the coming week. A quiet and extremely private man, Coolidge irritated the Washington correspondents by not answering all of their written questions, and he rarely answered them from the floor at press conferences. He also implemented a rule that he could not be quoted directly; rather his remarks were attributed to "the White House spokesman." In spite of his restrictions, Coolidge did meet with the reporters twice a week, but it was obvious he managed the news in his press conferences.[34]

Early's next big assignment was twofold. In the summer of 1924 he joined eight other Washington Bureau men to cover the Democratic and Republican national conventions.

The Republican convention in June was one of relatively quiet deliberations, the presidential candidacy a foregone conclusion. The Republicans would stick with Coolidge. His choice of running mate proved to be about the only excitement the convention could generate, and even that did not last long. After what the Associated Press described as "a brief and spectacular fight," Gen. Charles Dawes received the necessary votes. Dawes was the founder and head of the largest bank in Chicago, a lawyer, author, and at the time comptroller of the national treasury; he had served as head of the Dawes Commission that had dealt with German reparations after the war and then as director of the US budget.[35]

In contrast, the Democratic convention held in New York City in late June and early July proved to be anything but quiet. It was the lengthiest in the party's history, a two-week marathon of contentious bickering and full-blown battles. Appropriately, it was held in Madison Square Garden. For the journalists covering it, however, the convention was a theme park of news stories.

At the beginning of the convention, the headlines read: "Bewilderment Hangs Like Storm Cloud Over Democratic Delegates," as it appeared Governor Al Smith of New York and William G. McAdoo,

Wilson's son-in-law and secretary of the treasury during the war, would be seeking the nomination. Smith was a progressive and a Catholic, and, as such, an enemy of the Ku Klux Klan; McAdoo, a wealthy Georgia-born corporate lawyer in New York who had moved to California, enjoyed the support of the Southern and Western democrats as well as the Klan.[36] He had been tainted by the Harding administration scandals because of his legal work for Edward L. Doheny, the California multimillionaire who was one of the two major beneficiaries of Harding's secretary of the interior Albert Fall's dishonesty. McAdoo was a dry and Smith a wet, which further split the delegates.

Then the headlines read: "Wave of Confusion and Disorder Engulfs Democratic Convention." The lead on the AP story for June 26 read: "The deep, swift currents of Democratic rivalry and dissention burst their dykes today in Madison Square Garden and engulfed the party's national convention with a bellowing wave of confusion and disorder." An anti-Klan demonstration had resulted in some fistfights among the delegates. That day McAdoo's nomination was followed by a raucous hourlong demonstration. The following day, the McAdoo supporters engaged in yet another demonstration. Then, when Smith was nominated later in the day, the result was "a noisy hour and a half of rooting" for the candidate.[37]

As part of his and Howe's strategically orchestrated political comeback, Franklin Roosevelt, in a dramatic appearance at the convention, placed Smith's name in nomination. "The delegates cheered for three minutes as he swung on crutches to the speaker's stand—his first important public appearance since the polio attack." In fact the long speech, in which he called Smith "the Happy Warrior," and his appearance on crutches made him a star of the convention.[38]

The following day's Associated Press lead story in newspapers across the country read: "After four days of oratorical flourish and colorful demonstrations, the Democratic national convention is ready for its final showdown on nominees and policies." On Sunday, June 29, the headline for the Saturday session was: "Democrats in Scenes of Wild Disorder Beat Klan Plank by One Vote; Reject Wilsonian League Issue." The Smith faction of the party had insisted that the Ku Klux Klan be denounced by name in the platform, while the McAdoo supporters obviously opposed such a move. But after the voting, the platform neither contained a Wilsonian plank supporting the League of Nations nor did it single out the KKK by name.[39] Now it appeared that neither McAdoo nor Smith would get the nomination.

"Deadlock" became the convention byword for the next nine days and 103 ballots. During that time, a major tornado killed more than one hundred people in northern Ohio, and the sixteen-year-old son of President Coolidge died after a brief battle with blood poisoning. In the end it was a dark horse, John W. Davis of West Virginia, who captured the nomination. An outstanding constitutional lawyer and a former ambassador to Great Britain, Davis ultimately stood no chance against the popular Coolidge. The country was simply too content with the status quo.

It had indeed been a long and contentious convention, and no doubt Early, while he loved a good news story, was not unhappy at the prospect of returning to his beloved Washington and his wife and young son. However, this was short lived. About three weeks into the campaign, the Associated Press man covering Davis took ill, and Early took off once again on a campaign trail.[40]

Once the election was over and Coolidge was assured of another four years in the White House, Early went back to covering the government. One of his last big assignments for the wire service during his second tour of duty was the court-martial of Col. William ("Billy") Mitchell of the Army Air Service.

For years Colonel Mitchell had been advocating an independent air force. He even accused the army and the navy of hindering the development of a strong air force, calling the two military departments "incompetent." Soon after the war, he had urged the navy to develop some defense against aircraft; battleships alone could not defend themselves against enemy aircraft, he argued. Assistant Secretary of the Navy Franklin Roosevelt had dismissed his views as "pernicious" and publicly questioned why Mitchell believed aviation should be separate from the navy. Eventually, Mitchell's attacks became so ferocious and so controversial they resulted in his court-martial on charges of insubordination.

It opened on October 28, 1925, in Washington, DC, in a khaki-painted room in an old army warehouse. Early was dispatched to cover the trial, which was predicted to last three or four days. It did not conclude until December 17. Some of the people who had played important roles in Early's life—or would in the future—were a part of the highly publicized court-martial. Douglas MacArthur, now a gen-

eral, was one of the judges. Joseph E. Davies, future ambassador to
Russia, who had been Mitchell's best man at his wedding a few years
earlier and would later become one of Early's close friends, served as
one of the defense counsel.

At 3:40 in the afternoon of December 19, nine generals and their
legal counsel filed solemnly from the room to a chamber next door to
determine the verdict and sentence. Early wrote a description of the
scene for the Associated Press Service Bulletin:

> The accused and the prosecution and defense counsel, not to men-
> tion the newspaper reporters and spectators anticipated a verdict of
> guilty. Interest and speculation, keyed to a high pitch, revolved
> chiefly about the question of sentence and court procedure. A mili-
> tary guard was posted outside the room while the court officials
> deliberated. In the courtroom, Colonel Mitchell chatted with
> friends; newspapermen kept alert, and spectators gossiped. Thirty
> one minutes passed in this fashion before the generals marched into
> the courtroom. Their president asked the senior trial judge if there
> was any further evidence he desired to place before the court. Then,
> at precisely 4:12 p.m., the court marched out again.[41]

Early immediately transmitted to the AP a bulletin, which went
on the wire to member newspapers, saying, "A step prescribed by regulations to accompany a finding of 'Guilty' was taken late today by the
court-martial trying Col. William Mitchell. Soon after the court was
closed to consider a verdict, it returned to open session to ask if the
prosecution had any further evidence to place before it." The bulletin
went on to explain that this was not a guilty verdict, rather under law
this question had to be asked when a verdict of guilty has been found
and is not customarily asked when the accused is to be found not
guilty. Other news services construed the court's action to mean
Mitchell had indeed been found guilty and flashed a verdict on their
wires. The Associated Press did not, preferring to wait until the verdict was announced. Difficult as it must have been, Early was forced
to watch his colleagues racing to telephones to transmit the news to
their offices. It was not until 6:34 p.m. that the sentence and the verdict were announced. Mitchell was guilty.[42]

It wasn't until the following fall that Early picked up an assignment that was more of the daring and reckless reporting he seemed to

so enjoy. On September 18 a hurricane roared up the East Coast, first and most seriously smashing into Florida, leaving behind a trail of destruction and flooding—and a great news story. It is not clear whether Early volunteered to travel to Florida to cover the story or whether the AP, understanding his need for adventure and his ability to get a story under difficult conditions, selected him. Staffers in the Florida AP bureaus were swamped with work, and they were finding it impossible to adequately cover all the stories resulting from the hurricane. So Early went from Washington to Jacksonville, where he was sent to Moore Haven, a small city on the western edge of the huge Lake Okeechobee. The city had been one of the hardest hit by the devastating winds and rains; 110 residents had been killed there.

Early traveled to Sebring, about one hundred miles south and slightly west of Orlando, and there he hooked up with A. R. Bird, an AP staffer from the Orlando Bureau. The two men commandeered a car from a *Tampa Times* reporter and headed seventy miles south to Moore Haven. It proved to be a nightmare. Here is Early's account of their adventure: "The first 65 miles were easy, although it [was] filled with swampy detours. But when we reached the National Guard outpost five miles or so from Moorehaven, the road vanished under water. It was a sea-going job then with only stakes along the road edges to keep you out of ten-foot drainage ditches on both sides. The whole business was covered with slimy black, sting water."

Their car stalled in the water, so they abandoned it and hitched a ride in a passing truck. "We bumped and slushed along and in the early dark of night made our way into town. When we pulled up the water level had subsided to about two feet and we went mucking about in that to get the story. When we were ready to return the wind had come up and the water in the streets and and over the road was rising." Then the truck stalled, and the two reporters had to climb into the murky water and wade for four miles, their goal being the abandoned car. "I decided to save my clothes and bundled them up, taking [to] the road in B.V.D.'s and shirt-tail. Before we pushed off, someone handed us some creosote and coal oil and we smeared ourselves against the swarms of insects and foul waters. I had not gone far before I lost the clothes. It was stiff plugging with that water surging almost to our waists. We did our four miles and about 3 o'clock in the morning made the Guardsmen's outpost."

There the two reporters found the car they had abandoned. The balky engine started, and they drove back to Sebring, where the wire facilities had been restored, and got their story out. When the final figures were tallied, the hurricane had left 372 dead, 6,281 injured, and 17,884 families homeless.[43]

For his professionalism in covering the Florida hurricane, Early's peers elected him chairman of the board of governors of the National Press Club in Washington. He had been a board member since 1921.[44]

By the following spring, Early was wrestling with a somewhat painful professional decision. He now had a wife and two young children. A reporter for a wire service often has erratic hours and assignments, as Early knew firsthand, that could take him away from home for days, even weeks, at a time. In addition, he had met most of the major challenges that could be thrown at an eager and talented reporter: He had gotten the scoop on the death of a president, he had covered political conventions and campaigns, he had been on the front lines as a reporter covering the White House and Congress, and, most recently, he had risked his life—and the future of his growing family—to cover a hurricane.

It was time for a change.

5

PREPARING FOR THE WHITE HOUSE

On May 6, 1927, Early submitted his resignation from the AP to his bureau chief, Byron Price. A month earlier E. Ross Bartley, Early's reporting partner for the Harding death story and now secretary to Vice President Dawes, had introduced his friend to Emanuel Cohen, the head of Paramount Famous Lasky Corporation, the newsreel component of Paramount Pictures. Cohen then began a quest to hire Early away from the AP to set up Paramount's newsreel operations in the capital. A month later, Early agreed. Because of his many news sources in Congress, the White House, and numerous government agencies, he was an ideal choice.

There is no written record of the specific reason Early had for leaving the wire service and the world of words for one of moving pictures. His letter of resignation to Price suggests that he had already given Price his reasons orally and notes it "was necessary for me to resign." Perhaps Early believed that this new job would keep him anchored to the capital city, leaving him more time for his growing family. Years later, newspapers were reporting that his salary at Paramount had been $20,000 a year, although that may have been somewhat exaggerated. No doubt the higher salary was an inducement. Garrison Elliott, assistant general manager for the AP in New York City, wrote to Early saying he understood it was "necessary for you to go on another payroll," and noted that Early had made with Paramount "an honorable, pleasant and profitable connection."[1]

Without doubt this was a heady time to become associated with the newsreel business. Early recalled that it was vastly competitive; people all over the world wanted to watch the short newsreels that accompanied motion pictures in the movie theaters, and they wanted them fresh, "with all the savor of something that happened today or yesterday and that still was on the world's tongue."[2]

By the mid-1920s more than twenty thousand movie houses were scattered across the country, and weekly attendance averaged 46 million; it would hit 90 million by 1930. The addition of soundtracks to movies and newsreels accounted in large part for this dramatic increase, and almost all the movies were produced by six companies: Fox, Metro-Goldwyn-Mayer, Paramount, Warner Brothers, Columbia, and Universal. When the big makers of movies showed the short—usually ten minutes long—newsreels along with the regular feature, they were eagerly anticipated by the audience as a window to events as far away as the Arctic when the newsreels covered Adm. Richard Byrd's flight over the North Pole in 1926.[3]

Newsreels in fact had been around since 1911. In the early days audiences discovered the time to leave was when the newsreel flashed on the screen. The theater's orchestra silently filed out of sight below the pit, leaving the pianist alone "vamping his way through the low spot of the show." With the advent of World War I, the newsreels became a "living contact between people at war and their sons in battle 3,000 miles away." They became "instantly the high spot of the show."[4]

Early recalled those war newsreels in a radio interview in 1930. The flickering images on the screen were accompanied by the theater orchestra "playing fervent marches." The audience would rise to its feet "to cheer the marching columns, the files of prisoners returning, the decoration ceremonies for our heroes." As the movie companies in Hollywood grew, so did the newsreels. "The standard of news[reels] now was on par with the front page make-up of great metropolitan dailies," Early noted.[5]

This novel way to give the public its news was not lost on the AP reporter Early as he trolled the political halls of Washington for stories that would run, sans his byline, in newspapers across the country. Although he was highly respected by his AP colleagues because of his remarkable reporting on a variety of major news events, he now had worked for wire services since 1912, a long time in a job famous for its fast pace, long hours, and relative anonymity

His enthusiasm for the newsreels made it obvious that he had made the right decision when he left the Associated Press for the talkies, although as it turned out his lifestyle changed little from that of the intrepid wire service reporter sent out to follow a president across the country or to cover a hurricane in Florida. Early said, "I have no idea where I may be when that day's sun sets—perhaps at home, eating with my family at my own table—but perhaps speeding by air or rail a thousand or two miles West, South or North—to be home again, who knows when? But it IS a great game. The newsreel brings to a modern world a truer picture of itself, and of its people than any other agency heretofore known to mankind."[6]

When Paramount hired Early, it had acquired not just a talented newsman whose antennae were trained to detect a good story, but a man whose news sources numbered just about everyone who was anyone in the Washington political milieu. It made him a valuable property for both the motion picture business as well as the fledgling newsreel business in the capital. As a result, Early continued to be in intimate contact with all phases of the government because Hollywood often sought the assistance of high government officials in movie making. He also arranged many newsreel interviews with the power brokers in Washington and had dealings with numerous congressional committees. He is credited with producing the first "talkie" of Gen. John J. Pershing, and he obtained the only exclusive sound newsreel with Herbert Hoover when, through the White House secretary's efforts, he had Hoover congratulating Adolph Zukor, the founder of Paramount Pictures, on the inauguration of sound in motion pictures.[7]

In 1927, the year Early joined Paramount, Franklin Roosevelt was coming to grips with the fact he would never again walk, and he reluctantly ran for governor of New York and was elected. He agreed to the nomination as a favor to Al Smith, who was again running for president and needed the Democratic vote in his home state. However, it had not been part of Louis Howe's grand plan for Roosevelt to seek the governorship; his timetable had Roosevelt running for president in either 1932 or 1936.[8]

The politician Roosevelt and the publicist Howe used the four years in Albany to give the governor a national voice, keeping his image in the public venue until Roosevelt was ready to make a run for the presidency. For instance, Howe established a publicity bureau in Albany and then had Roosevelt give talks over the radio at least once a month. For the reelection race in 1930, Howe made a propaganda film, *The Roosevelt Record*, which included newsreel footage of the governor during the last two years.[9]

Roosevelt, long aware of the importance of photography, also received coaching from experts on how to look and act in front of the cameras, always making certain his disability was not apparent, according to Howe's orders.[10] When newspaper and newsreel photographers attempted to take Roosevelt's picture as he was getting out of his car at Hyde Park to vote in the 1928 governor's race, he asked them to wait. "No movies of me getting out of this machine, boys," he requested. They turned away until he had alighted, adjusted his braces, and was standing upright.[11]

Roosevelt's fascination with the new medium of radio was evident during the 1928 Democratic National Convention in Houston, when Roosevelt nominated Al Smith as the party's candidate for president. Four years earlier, when Governor Roosevelt had given a speech in Madison Square Garden that had been broadcast over the relatively new medium, it had been a novelty. Now, improved technologies had made radio a viable means of speaking to the nation, and Roosevelt, with Howe's prompting, seized that opportunity in Houston. Sensing not only the popularity of radio but also the importance of this nominating speech to his own future political career, Roosevelt directed it not just at the convention delegates, but at the radio listeners across the country. "He was enormously successful."[12]

While Howe was busy in Albany preening his candidate for the White House, Early was acting as Roosevelt's "eyes and ears in Washington," a role he had relished throughout his years at Paramount. He kept Roosevelt attuned to the political happenings in the capital. Early's contacts in the radio business proved useful, especially in 1927 when Paramount purchased enough of the fledgling Columbia Broadcasting

System network's stock to aid in its financial development. This allowed Early the use of CBS radio crews for some newsreel work.

After Roosevelt became governor of New York, he often asked Early to send him the latest movies to watch with family and friends in Albany. For instance, when Early was doing what he called "a European run-a-round for Paramount"—that is, traveling on the Continent with a camera crew—Roosevelt asked him to send "talking pictures of the crowned heads, lesser royalty, etc." Apparently it took a while, but Early got them and shipped them to Albany. Roosevelt wrote, "I went to see your pictures of the crowned heads, big and little."[13]

Since Paramount obtained some of its news from the Associated Press, the newsreel company gave the wire service organization exclusive rights to stills from its newsreel footage. When it came time for the 1932 Democratic Convention in Chicago that July, Early was especially helpful to Roosevelt in ensuring that photographs of the governor and then presidential candidate frequently got into the news. Roosevelt repaid Early when the newsreels had problems with the Democratic National Committee over who should pay for special camera lights at the convention by intervening in the dispute and persuading the committee to pay for the lights.[14]

And so it seemed not only logical but most politically astute that once Franklin Roosevelt was declared the victor at the polls that November, he should turn to his longtime friend and ally Steve Early to join him in the White House as his secretary in charge of all press relations.

6

LAUNCHING THE JUGGERNAUT

"It was much like the bugle call I heard in 1917 when I resigned from the AP to go into the Army. So I resigned from Paramount. I reported to FDR for duty in the Mayflower Hotel on the evening of March 3, 1933, the eve of his first inaugural. I went into the White House with the understanding that I would serve two years and then be permitted to return to private life."[1]

Early claimed that Roosevelt's request for him to handle press relations for the White House came as a surprise. Perhaps it did. But in reality, while Early had no official ties to the president-elect, he had kept in touch with Roosevelt over the years, apprising him of political gossip in Washington when he was with the Associated Press and Paramount, attending the annual Cuff Links dinners to celebrate FDR's birthday, and, on request, shipping the latest films from Paramount to the governor's mansion in Albany.[2]

It is hard to believe that as Election Day grew closer and it became apparent that his old friend Franklin Roosevelt would be elected president of the United States, Early did not speculate on what role, if any, he might be playing in the new administration, especially since he had seen Paramount reduce salaries and lay off employees over the last three years. Soon after Roosevelt was nominated, he telephoned Early and asked him to help run his campaign. Early replied, "You don't need me, and after all, in 1920 I helped you to be the worst defeated candidate in Democratic history."[3]

Nonetheless, in December, Roosevelt called Early to Warm Springs, Georgia, where Roosevelt stayed frequently to enjoy the baths that soothed his crippled legs, and the president-elect asked Early to become one of his three secretaries to handle the press. The two old friends discussed the job offer. But first they undoubtedly reminisced about cronies from the Navy Department, about the ill-fated 1920 campaign, about the Newport navy affair, about their respective families, about the recent campaign, and probably about the health of Louis Howe, which by now was rapidly declining. They may even have harked back to their first meeting, at the Democratic National Convention in 1912. Roosevelt may have thanked Early again for being his eyes and ears in the nation's capital. Certainly their conversation must have touched on the condition of the economy, especially the massive unemployment and the bank closures.

However the conversation went, Roosevelt asked Early to come with him to the White House to handle the press. Early then gave Roosevelt an ultimatum: He would stay with him for only two years. It's easy to imagine that Roosevelt told him that two years would be fine, but secretly he knew he would be able to persuade Early, his loyal friend of so many years, to remain longer when the time came.

In the final analysis, the two men recognized they played well off each other's strengths and weaknesses. They nurtured each other professionally and even socially. FDR had once wanted to be a journalist, but found he was a far better politician; Early wanted to be part of the power structure and had found his way there by being a successful journalist. Both appreciated a good joke, verbal or practical; they enjoyed the sweet success of winning a bet—or, in Early's case, a winning horse. As adults, they knew each other better than some siblings do.

As newspaper stories about Early throughout his years in the White House never failed to mention, the two men traced their friendship to 1912. In fact, until he died Early kept on the wall of his den at home a photograph of a young and stern-faced Franklin Roosevelt, inscribed, "To Steve Early with more warmth and informality than this picture would indicate." It was dated 1914.

Roosevelt was never considered an intellectual, nor was he a man who dealt in the abstract. Pondering the ramifications of an idea for any length of time, looking at the philosophical structure of a plan of action, did not in the least interest him. Neither did Early, the newsman who was used to racing out to cover an event and then hurrying back to the office to write an account of it before moving on to the next story, care to look too deeply into the issues of the moment. Thus, the professional marriage of Franklin D. Roosevelt and Stephen T. Early, after years of friendship, was consummated the moment Early agreed to sign on as the presidential secretary in charge of press matters.

Early later may have wondered what he was in for when he agreed to work for Roosevelt. On the evening of February 15, 1933, Roosevelt embarked from Vincent Astor's yacht, *Nourmahal*, in Miami after an eleven-day cruise. He then spoke to a waiting crowd, and just as he finished, an assassin fired a pistol at him. Roosevelt was not hurt, but Anton Cermak, the mayor of Chicago, was seriously injured and several other people nearby were wounded. Cermak died on March 6, two days after Roosevelt was inaugurated.

James Roosevelt, the president's eldest son and for a time in the late 1930s one of his White House aides, wrote years later that Early's appointment was not a casual, passing one; rather, he was meant to stay—and he did: "Father believed he was the best man for the job." James Roosevelt called Early and his father "pals," and once in the White House, he said, Early became a "part of inner-circle, high-level discussions."[4]

This is what Roosevelt had in mind, he told Early: Longtime intimate friend and adviser Louis Howe would be chief secretary; Marvin McIntyre, another friend from his Navy Department days and the 1920 campaign and his press officer during the 1932 campaign, would be the appointments secretary and have the office next to FDR's to announce and keep track of visitors. Early would handle press relations and, for the time being, the president's travel arrangements.

Only Howe would hold the title of secretary; the other two men would be assistant secretaries, and the three would be referred to in the press, at least until Howe died, as "The Secretariat." A less-flattering soubriquet bestowed by presidential critics was "The Praetorian Guard," referring to those Roman soldiers who were the elite bodyguard of their emperor.

Howe's salary would be $10,000; Early and McIntyre would each be paid $9,500 a year. (The president's salary in 1933 was $50,000 annually.) While there was not a great deal of difference in the salaries of the three men, making Howe the chief secretary was Roosevelt's way of honoring him for his years of devotion. Early would be earning less than he had been making at Paramount, but in the current economic climate perhaps he felt that a guaranteed government salary was better than a volatile one in the movie business. James Roosevelt wrote in his *My Parents: A Differing View* that Howe wanted desperately to be his father's first presidential press secretary, but Roosevelt felt him unfit for that public position, never offered it to him, and, to the best of James Roosevelt's knowledge never had the heart to tell him why.[5]

Early said he was flattered to be offered the job with Roosevelt, "but it was like sticking one's hand into the lion's mouth to accept it. The job has been the graveyard of more than one luckless man." Early may have been thinking of Presidents Coolidge and Hoover, who wanted little or nothing to do with reporters, often against the advice of their press secretaries, leaving the secretaries unable to do their jobs effectively. Early understood that the extraordinary responsibility of serving a president as dynamic as Roosevelt, in particular at such a turbulent time, would leave him little time for a normal family life.[6]

James Roosevelt thought the press secretary's job was one of the most difficult in Washington: "The press secretary is on the firing line; he is the link between the president and the public. He is subjected to questions he may not be able to answer. He sometimes is an apologist, covering up problems that the press is determined to uncover. The resulting friction between the presidential press secretary and the press often causes sparks and touches off fires on both sides."[7]

With the appointments of Howe, Early, and McIntyre, the furlough from the 1920 campaign of the Cuff Links Gang was over. As Early put it, "We are back on duty again." The Gang had never doubted that one day Roosevelt would be president of the United States. Now they were together. Roosevelt was fifty-one years old; Howe was sixty-two; McIntyre was fifty-four, and Early, who would outlive them all, was forty-three.[8]

A lot of thought had gone into Roosevelt's placement of the three men on his staff. Howe was his closest confidant and had been so for years, as long as anyone in politics could remember. Howe and Roosevelt's relationship predated their navy days. After Roosevelt was struck down with polio, when his life seemed its bleakest, Howe had moved in with the family in New York City and had taken control of Roosevelt's political future, an oft-told story, and became, with Eleanor's blessing, a kind of Svengali. But Howe also was a deeply sensitive man whom Roosevelt knew would be wounded if all three men were of equal rank.

Roosevelt recognized that Howe was suffering from a variety of ailments. He also understood that he needed Howe's wisdom and counsel for as long as he was able to offer them. Howe could talk with Roosevelt about anything, and he was, Roosevelt knew, his most skillful critic. So his job was tailored to his strengths and his limitations.[9]

As for McIntyre, Roosevelt felt his years of loyalty deserved a reward. Known around Washington as "an affable Southerner," McIntyre, or "Mac," as he was called by his friends, had little interest in or understanding of the complex political and economic issues that were facing the president when he took office, nor did he especially care to learn more about them. As an appointments secretary, however, he was perfect. He ingratiated himself with visitors, often joking with them, extracting some Washington gossip, and generally keeping them pleasantly occupied until the president could see them.[10]

While FDR has been given credit by most historians of the era for establishing an unprecedented working relationship between the presidency and the press, it is unlikely that, for all his interest in the workings of the media and his desire to communicate effectively with the newsmen, he would have been nearly as successful had he not had the talents, assistance, and advice of Steve Early.

Unlike any previous presidential press aide, Early was privileged to have been born at the right time. He had come of age when wire services were developing into behemoth news-gathering agencies, their tentacles reaching around the world. From his earliest years as a journalist, first with United Press and then with the Associated Press, he moved seamlessly into the world of news and then into moving pictures, the technology having been born at almost the moment Early had.

It did not hurt that Early personally knew almost every Washington reporter and newsreel and still cameraman, or that two of his brothers-in-law were prominent journalists. George Holmes, husband of Early's sister Mary, was manager of the Washington office of the International News Service, and Early's sister Oma was married to Barry Faris, the general manager of INS.

Early and Roosevelt had been witness to the chaos, the unfairness, and the consequent frustrations earlier presidential secretaries who dealt with the press had wrought upon the newsmen attempting to gather and disseminate news, from the White Houses of Theodore Roosevelt on through Herbert Hoover. The two men had the advantage of being able to study the mistakes made. Firsthand, Early the reporter had watched Woodrow Wilson establish regular semiweekly press conferences open to all reporters on equal terms, promising to take them into his confidence and conversely asking them to keep him apprised of public opinion. But the president then proceeded to use his press conferences as classroom lectures, looking down at the journalists. The upshot was that they sometimes misquoted or criticized him, and gradually the unusually sensitive Wilson held fewer and fewer press conferences, finally canceling them after the sinking of the *Lusitania* in 1915.

His successor, Warren G. Harding, a former newspaperman himself, should have developed the ideal working relationship with the press. Unfortunately, he was too often less than informed on foreign affairs, and after he blundered once too often at his twice-weekly press conferences, his staff persuaded him to require all questions in writing and submitted well in advance of press conferences. Harding's successor, Calvin Coolidge, continued the written questions policy and ordered the newsmen never to quote him, directly or indirectly, instead opting for a fictitious character known as "the White House spokesman" to get information to the public.[11]

Then came Herbert Hoover, who promised improvements in the way the White House communicated information to the public. As secretary of commerce under Harding, Hoover had always been a good source of news, but once he moved into the White House he followed his predecessors' rule of requiring written questions, and of these he often ignored any he did not want to discuss. Early later wrote that during those years pertinent questions were so rarely answered that "many of the correspondents gave up the idea of submitting them." For the last two years of his administration, Hoover held few press conferences, resulting in little information from the White House. "Toward the end of the Hoover administration, there was scarcely any direct link between the President of the United

States and the public, so far as the majority members of the correspondence corps were concerned," Early wrote.[12]

Early and Roosevelt were determined not to repeat history, so Early set out to develop what would become the seminal study of the successful White House press secretary. They wanted to ensure a free flow of news from the White House to the reporters covering it, and they decided the most effective way to achieve this would be for Roosevelt to hold regular press conferences where reporters could both ask questions and receive answers. This free flow of information allowed Roosevelt and to communicate the New Deal agenda to the public.

Early told one reporter a few days before the inauguration, "I may even take the door of the office off so anybody can walk in at any time." He did not, but he and Roosevelt did decide to abolish the practice of written questions. The president would take direct questions from the reporters and answer them right there. The two men wanted an open exchange between reporters and the president during the press conferences.

Early recommended Wednesday press conferences at 10 a.m. to accommodate the deadlines of afternoon dailies and Friday afternoon press conferences at 4 p.m. for the morning newspapers, in particular the Sunday papers, much of whose news content was often decided on Friday. Knowing his boss, Early expected that Roosevelt would frequently call in reporters at other times when he had something to tell the press. Early believed he would be able to more successfully control the White House message if he could speak to the reporters, most of whom he already knew, and be quoted directly. This latter request was the reason that throughout the Roosevelt presidency, Early became probably the one member of the White House staff best known to the public—a personage in his own right, regularly holding his own press conferences.

Because Early the journalist understood the nature of newspaper deadlines, the days and times of the president's press conferences were changed periodically to accommodate the deadlines of morning and afternoon dailies. For instance, in November of 1935, the press conference schedule was changed to Tuesdays at 4 p.m. and Fridays at 10:30 a.m.[13]

Early said he wanted "to make the White House assignment an important one for the reporters, not just a watchdog affair, one that would require the very best correspondents to swing." He recalled that during previous administrations, presidents often played favorites, taking certain reporters into their confidence and ignoring the others. As the years passed, Roosevelt did indeed on occasion play favorites. But it was not Early's original intention that this practice should continue.[14]

In spite of his desire to open up the office of the president to the press, probably at Roosevelt's request Early did restrict the press conferences to background or unattributed information from the president unless Roosevelt himself wanted something quoted directly. In this case Early would mimeograph the quote—not the whole transcript of the press conference—and give it to the reporters. Apparently Early was concerned that foreign journalists who attended the press conferences might mistranslate information given orally. In reality it gave Roosevelt and Early a sort of final say about what the press could publish from the White House, or at least from press conferences.

Attendance at the press conferences was limited to the working press, primarily to those men assigned to cover the White House, mostly representing daily newspapers and the wire services. Since newspapers owned and edited by blacks for black readers in those days were weeklies, no black reporters were accredited to the White House. Neither were women reporters until later in the 1930s, so throughout her husband's presidency Eleanor Roosevelt held her own press conferences. Early decided that editors and other visitors would be received separately and, if they asked, given special permission to attend Roosevelt's press conference on a one-time basis. Radio reporters and microphones were excluded until after Pearl Harbor.[15]

Photographers, too, were restricted and came under the watchful eye of the press secretary. Despite Roosevelt and Early's insistence that censorship not be tolerated, the reality was that they carefully managed the news and in particular the visual portrayal of the president. A lot has been written over the decades about the White House's refusal to allow the president to be photographed in a way that would show or accentuate his disability. That was one reason Early banned photographers from the press conferences and restricted their presence at many White House events; the other was to avoid over saturation of the president's image.

It must have been a fascinating study in understated diplomacy as

Roosevelt and Early jockeyed to come to an agreement on details for the press conferences, with Early the newsman, who had for so many years himself attempted to obtain news from previous presidents, urging the current office holder to allow reporters frequent access to the inner workings of the White House by letting them quote him freely and ask any questions they wanted during the press conferences. But Roosevelt, the consummate politician—however much he had enjoyed a repartee with the press in Albany during his years as governor—would brook no such latitude. He insisted on controls. In addition to the strictures on direct quotations, anything the president said at a press conference was for those present only and could not be shared with other correspondents. And, of course, microphones and cameras were forbidden.[16]

If twice-weekly press conferences were to be held regularly, as Early promised the reporters, these rules—while restrictive by today's standards, where cameras and microphones pick up, often live over the air, anything and everything the president says—the reporters covering the White House knew that they would be much better off than with Roosevelt's predecessors.

When Early told Theodore G. Joslin, secretary in charge of press relations for President Hoover, how Roosevelt intended to handle his press conferences, Joslin, who had in fact had been the first newspaperman to hold that position in the White House, was horrified. He told Early that the president could not allow reporters to question him directly. Suppose the president made a mistake, he said—then he would have to take the blame for it himself. "A President can not do that. That is what the Presidential secretaries are for—to take the rap when it is necessary to ease the President out of a tight spot," Early, quoting Joslin, later recalled.[17]

Inauguration Day—March 4, 1933—was the beginning of the rest of Stephen T. Early's professional life. Despite a short-lived foray into the private sector near the end of his life, he would remain in government service until his death, first with Roosevelt and then with President Harry Truman.

On the evening of Thursday, March 2, a train rolled into Washington from Hyde Park, New York, the president's home. Aboard were Early, McIntyre, and, of course, Howe, along with a panoply of Roosevelt family members, advisers dubbed the "Brain Trust," a group of academic advisers Roosevelt gathered to help him develop aspects of the New Deal, and several cabinet members. These were the players, the cast of characters Early would be working with, and sometimes answering to, day in and day out for the next few months as what became known as the New Deal took shape.

Franklin and Eleanor were driven to the Mayflower Hotel, where the incoming president conferred well into the night with his advisers. Steve probably stopped off at home to check on Helen and the children before returning to the Mayflower ready to serve the Boss should he need his aide before he headed to the White House early that morning for his inauguration. Early's plan had been to be ready to take from Roosevelt the final draft of his inaugural address, which he would mimeograph for the reporters. Apparently this plan went awry, because when he arrived at the White House that morning he found the Hoover staff uncooperative, refusing to allow him to make copies of the speech.[18]

Interestingly, Roosevelt had no better luck in establishing a working relationship with Hoover himself. According to Grace Tully, who served for many years as one of Roosevelt's secretaries, the president-elect paid the customary preinaugural social call at the White House on March 3, only to be faced with a strained atmosphere and desultory conversation. Hoover, who had been so sorely defeated the previous November by Roosevelt, carrying only six states, had no intention of discussing anything of substance with his successor.[19]

The following day, amid more pomp and circumstance than some of his advisers thought necessary considering the depressed economy, Roosevelt was sworn in on a cold, windy afternoon outside the White House as "mile after mile of parade passed before him." According to one biographer, the new president always enjoyed a parade and public ceremony. As the day came to a close, he moved into the White House to oversee, at least briefly, a reception for thousands of guests. His family attended the inaugural ball that evening. Roosevelt chose to end this remarkable day with the little man who had been at his side through so much during the last decade: his longtime confidant Louis Howe.[20]

Franklin D. Roosevelt came into the office of the presidency at what historians have called one of the lowest points in American history, and he immediately found himself grappling with some of the most intricate and difficult decisions any president, outside wartime, had ever faced. After the cheering and the festivities died down, the real work of the new chief executive—and his press secretary—began on Sunday. The opening weeks of the Hundred Days, as the time immediately following the inauguration has been dubbed, were a trial by fire for Early.[21]

Unfortunately Early did not begin keeping a diary—both personal and of his White House work—until early the following year, so there is no record that the new press secretary returned to his family that night, but if he did, it must have been very late, and he must have had little sleep, coming back to the White House early the next day and forgoing his favorite Sunday morning ritual of reading the newspapers in a comfortable chair in his den.

The new president began his day by attending church services and then meeting with his cabinet to map out what became the first stages of his recovery plan for the nation. Early had his own pressing duties at the White House, besieged by reporters wondering what Roosevelt had in mind and when the president would be announcing these plans.

So as Roosevelt met with his cabinet, Early was placating eager reporters and arranging a meeting with representatives of the four major press associations. By 9:30 that night, the four men were ready to meet with the president: Kenneth Clark of Universal News Service, Raymond Clapper of United Press, Early's old friend and colleague Byron Price of the Associated Press, and George Holmes from the International News Service.

In his diary, Clapper described the meeting: "Went to the White House at 9:30. Steve Early took us up to study on second floor. Roosevelt in good humor. Shook hands said he remembered me and others, etc. Said he wanted to explain to us what he was doing."

What the president then read was a proclamation declaring a national bank holiday to begin the following day and to end on Thursday, calling Congress into immediate session. By this time almost half of all banks in the country had failed or suspended payments, especially in small cities and rural areas. Most states had either closed banks or placed restrictions on them. Roosevelt told the reporters they were the first to hear his proclamation. Clapper wrote that the president had one request: "[I]n handling this we call it a modified bank holiday or partial holiday—didn't want it called a moratorium." He then explained "step by step details of the proclamation."

When Roosevelt had finished, Early directed the reporters to nearby telephones—Clapper wrote that he used one "in the north corridor with a direct view into Roosevelt's study." They were told by Early they could dictate a lead for their story, based on the meeting, but they were to tell their editors that the information could not leave the newsroom just yet. Clapper said that it was not long before Early gave them a text of their meeting with Roosevelt. He then released it in the pressroom for all the journalists. Only then could the wire service men finish dictating their stories. What Early and Roosevelt had given the four men was a slight beat on the journalists from the daily newspapers. Clapper said he was on the telephone for "about an hour straight until 11:30."[22]

The next morning, one of the reporters described to his readers Roosevelt's demeanor as he outlined his New Deal plans this way: "Sturdy-shouldered, smiling, calm, talking pleasantly with an occasional humorous sally, he was a picture of ease and confidence. As he talked, he deliberately inserted a fresh cigarette in an ivory holder. It was as if he was considering (nothing more important than) a bill for a bridge in some . . . rural county."[23]

At 11:30 that night, Roosevelt made a brief radio speech specifically addressed to members of the American Legion, asking the public to make sacrifices for their country and saying he hoped that "the efforts I am giving in these first days of my Administration may be crowned with success and that we may achieve a lasting restoration of national well-being." To his frustration, Early had discovered earlier in the day that the White House had no radio facilities, and the broadcast almost did not get on the air. But thanks to his old friend Harry Butcher, the manager of CBS's Washington office, the two set up a makeshift studio in the president's study. As it came time for Roosevelt to go on the air, all appeared quiet and pleasant. Standing by for moral support were Eleanor and the president's mother, Sara. The only distraction apparently was Scottie, the First Dog, which was "hopping about." The brief radio address went off without a hitch.[24]

The Roosevelt-Early media juggernaut had been launched.

Monday, March 6, was just as busy. Early accompanied the president to the funeral of Senator Thomas Walsh, who was to have been the attorney general in the new cabinet, but who had died hours before the inauguration. Early prepared several press releases, including one on the death of Mayor Cermak; one announcing the

appointment of Rexford Tugwell, the Columbia University economics professor and one of the famous Brain Trust advisers to Roosevelt, as assistant secretary of agriculture; and another listing the
presidential nominations that would require Senate approval. He also
spent time answering reporters' questions on the banking proclamation. Not surprisingly, he soon found that reporters knew less about
economics than he did, so he went to Secretary of the Treasury
William H. Woodin for some clarification. For some reason, perhaps
because he was tied up with his own work on the banking problems,
the secretary refused to help, so Early went to Roosevelt and the two
put together a clearer statement for the press.[25]

Eventually, at Early's suggestion, Roosevelt would hold "semi-
nars" with the reporters—his "pupils"—to explain his budget or some
other complex issue. These sessions proved extremely popular and
helpful to the correspondents.

As the complexities of the New Deal and the resulting Supreme
Court decisions tumbled forth in the next few years, Early himself
would hold tutorials with the reporters, almost always off the record.
Early's intent was to explain the technicalities of some issue, perhaps
a presidential budget message; as a result, when the message was made
public the reporters were prepared to release their stories immediately and had been spared hours of laborious research.[26]

Tuesday brought the Governors Conference to the White
House, and Early was in charge of collecting and distributing statements from those attending the conference along with Roosevelt's
replies to the media.[27]

As he began to sort out the responsibilities of his new job, Early
found the mundane intruded that first week. For one thing, the staff
needed offices, and Roosevelt gave them some latitude in selecting
headquarters most suitable for their particular jobs. For instance,
Howe, for all practical purposes the number-one secretary, would
have an office across from the cabinet meeting room and just down
the hall from Roosevelt's. McIntyre set up shop right next door to the
Executive Office, as it was known then (now the Oval Office), since he
was the secretary charged with ushering visitors in to see the
president. This had once been home to Hoover's press man, Joslin.
Early, however, apparently was torn between working physically close
to Roosevelt and being easily accessible to the press, and since the

pressroom was on the other side of the West Wing from the president's office, in the end it seemed more convenient and probably more appropriate for Early to move in next door to the pressroom. It also allowed him to give out breaking news easily.[28]

Reporters hanging around waiting for news often would congregate in the large waiting room across the hall from Early's office. Joseph C. Harsch, then a young reporter for the *Christian Science Monitor*, described the scene in the waiting room, where, he said, "Reporters spent a lot of time sitting there in the big, black leather chairs." It was a perfect spot, too, for the press to see who was going in to meet with Roosevelt. "Most people seeing the President had to pass through this room, and we would talk to them," he recalled. Harsch also talked about the ease of access to Early: "It seemed we could go in there [Early's office] any time. We didn't even need a pass to get into his office." Apparently his "open door" policy was successful. Early also made frequent forays into the waiting room to shoot the breeze with the journalists, even when he had no news for them, Harsch said.[29]

Roosevelt and Early's first official press conference began a little after 10 o'clock on Wednesday morning, four days after the inauguration. A photo of that historic meeting shows a grinning Roosevelt, with McIntyre prominent behind his chair. Early is conspicuously out of range of the camera. Newsmen ring the president's desk. All are men. All are white. Roosevelt said he preferred to have these meetings with the press in his small office rather than in a larger room, which would have been more comfortable for the newsmen. Roosevelt felt the small room lent a coziness and informality.[30]

At the appointed time, Early opened the door to the president's office and whispered something to the veteran doorkeeper, Patrick McKenna, who clapped his hands twice, the signal to the reporters that the meeting was about to begin. Nearly 125 newsmen were in attendance. It was a somewhat casual affair, just as Roosevelt and Early had planned. The president talked off the record about the banking problems. The reporters crowded around his desk, all smiles. Roosevelt appeared at ease in a comfortable cloth chair. Clapper wrote in his diary that Mrs. Roosevelt came in and whispered something to the president, and that their son Elliott, off to "ranch it awhile" in Arizona, stopped by to tell his father good-bye.[31]

The new president was informal, joking at times and stern as a schoolmaster at others, when he reminded the correspondents when information was "off the record" or "background information." He kept his answers fairly short, talking in a folksy and frank manner with the reporters. Occasionally he turned the tables and asked them a question about a bill before the Senate.[32]

Roosevelt's first official press conference as chief executive of the country ended at 10:45 a.m., and the newsmen broke into a spontaneous applause, something that had never happened at the conclusion of a Coolidge or Hoover press conference and an act that must have both stunned and pleased Early, who himself had been part of more than one presidential news conference in his reporting career. Although Roosevelt had in fact told them almost nothing they could attribute to him, they "had a heady sense of being welcomed into the sanctum sanctorum of the new administration and there being entrusted with state secrets."[33]

Their euphoria may have been short lived. As they left, Early warned them ominously that he would "make an example of anyone who violated the President's confidence."

And he could, too, since it wasn't long before he had Teletype machines installed in his office, thereby allowing him to keep tabs on what the reporters were writing about the new administration.[34]

During the course of his presidency, Roosevelt made press conferences an important instrument in his endeavor to acquaint the country with his policies. He was to hold nearly one thousand of them on topics as diverse as bank closings, cabinet resignations and appointments, and facets of the war that so occupied the country during his last full term. In addition, Early himself met almost daily with the press, just as he had promised he would.

Most of Early's dealings with the press over the years were agreeable, often enjoyable both for the press secretary and the press. Early respected the journalists, and they in turn respected him. He would reason with them: "Look, you're trying to put me on the spot, but I can't help you out in this case. There is something here and it's going to develop, and when it does I'll tell you all about it, but I simply can't talk about it now and that's that." He tried to avoid being evasive with them unless it was absolutely necessary. But most of the time, he leveled with them and kept his promises. Of course, it helped that Roosevelt leveled with him.

Early was known for his temper, and the infrequent times he lost it with the press corps were when they had been drinking together, James Roosevelt recalled. In fact, Early's hot temper and "towering profanity" were legendary during his years in the White House, and occasionally they landed him in hot water.[35]

Charles Hurd, a reporter for the *New York Times* who covered the White House, gave this picture of a Roosevelt-and-Early-produced press conference:

> Newspaper readers are of course aware of the White House confer-
> ences, but it is doubtful whether the reports of them convey a dis-
> tinct picture, for a relatively few persons have ever seen the Presi-
> dent in contact with the press. One who attends a conference for the
> first time never forgets the experience. Even the sophisticated is
> impressed when he sees the President of the United States dis-
> cussing momentous affairs and perhaps has the opportunity to shake
> hands with him afterward and receive one of his laughing sallies.
>
> In the few minutes before a conference opens, the lobby of the
> Executive Office becomes crowded with men, and a few women,
> representing all the press associations and the more important news-
> papers in the country.

In spite of the off-the-record rule imposed by Roosevelt and Early, what Hurd appreciated about the press conferences, he wrote, was two-fold: They had the advantage of personal contact between the newsmen and the president, and they gave a direct indication of the president's reaction to what was going on, allowing reporters some "understanding of underlying motives and ideas behind administration action."[36]

The rest of that first week found Early writing and distributing more press releases on myriad subjects: Congress convened on Thursday; Friday it was releases on the president's order to close banks; and Saturday, an earthquake hit Los Angeles and FDR issued a number of releases.[37]

Leo Rosten, writing in the *Public Opinion Quarterly* in 1937, said that Roosevelt's impact upon the Washington correspondents was "galvanic." Precedents were brushed aside, formalities ignored, and the hocus-pocus of presidential aloofness was forgotten.

"In the days after he had taken office, Roosevelt was lifted to the stature of savior by the public and a political wizard by the news-papermen."[38]

7

THE HONEYMOON

Early and the Boss had taken on the Washington press corps with aplomb; now it was time to charm the American public. Although he was not the first president to use the radio to address the nation, Roosevelt was fortunate to have arrived in the White House at a time when the technology had improved sufficiently to send a relatively clean signal to homes around the country. Unlike Hoover, who was not an especially effective speaker, Roosevelt had discovered when he was governor of New York that he was as comfortable seated in front of microphones as he was in front of a roomful of reporters. As a result, he was able to direct that genial, homey approach to disseminating information toward his radio audience. It was not surprising, then, that after he and Early held their first press conference in the White House, they set up the president's first major radio talk to the nation, the earlier address to the American Legion having been brief and formal.

So on Sunday night, four days after his successful meeting with the reporters, Roosevelt took to the airways to "meet" with the public. It was the first of what would become the famous Fireside Chats, which eventually turned into a long-running soap opera of sorts, set in the White House. One newspaper called these Fireside Chats Early's "biggest of promotional coups for which he has received credit."[1]

The Sunday night time slot was probably selected for several reasons. First, some of radio's most popular programs were on then, thus assuring the president an audience. Second, it was the one night when people were most apt to be at home and relaxed as they prepared to begin another workweek. And finally, from Roosevelt's and Early's perspective, it would be the conclusion of their first week in the White House, a hectic and news-filled seven days. The time chosen was 10 p.m. in Washington, after the audience's favorite programs had concluded in the East and just as Western listeners were ready to begin their evening with the radio. Forty million Americans tuned to listen to their new president talk to them.[2]

Upon hearing the trademark opening words, "My friends . . . ," the audience immediately became convinced that this indeed was a friend—their friend—in the White House. The listeners were mesmerized. And when the president asked them to write to him with their problems, they did. Letters poured into the White House, each receiving a reply over Roosevelt's signature. What was even more remarkable was that this effect was caused by voice alone. No one could see the speaker until the newsreels taken at a later Fireside Chat were processed and rushed into the theaters.[3]

This first Fireside Chat became the prototype of the style of radio address that would help Roosevelt achieve a kind of celebrity status among ordinary people. There was the intimacy the president created with these informal, yet carefully prepared and orchestrated talks, and there was the quality of his voice, which listeners praised as "beautiful" and filled with "magnetism." Despite his East Coast origins, his radio speech seemed "untainted with any regional dialect," a voice the average American could comfortably relate to. The *New York Times* decided that his use of the modern medium of radio was comparable to his cousin Theodore's "Big Stick."[4]

Radiomen liked to handle FDR's radio broadcasts, despite the fact that anything could go wrong at any moment. He had an excellent radio voice: rich, melodious, seductive. It was warm, intimate, and friendly—and most importantly—it inspired confidence.[5]

But it should be noted that these Fireside Chats "were as much the result of the efforts of Steve Early and a team of ghost writers and radio technicians as they were of the President's creativity" and personality. It was the shrewd manipulations and careful preparations by Early that ensured a wide audience for the radio talks.[6]

Early and Harry Butcher, a longtime friend and at the time manager of the Washington Bureau of CBS, worked through the day that
Sunday to arrange the technical aspects of the broadcast while Roosevelt and his speechwriters put finishing touches on his talk. The
focus would be the banking crisis, but just how it would be introduced
became a subject of debate.

It had been agreed that the president would be introduced by the
newsman Robert Trout of CBS's Washington Bureau. But how to set
the stage for this first—and obviously important—talk? Two intro-
ductions were prepared, a formal one by Trout and a folksy one by
Butcher. Then Early told Butcher that the president "likes to think of
the audience as being a few people around his fireside." Butcher then
incorporated that word into Trout's script, and when he went on the
air, he told listeners that "the President wants to come into your home
and sit at your fireside for a little fireside chat." And with that, a
phrase was coined that soon would become a household word.[7]

Roosevelt's Fireside Chats became memorable in part because there
were so few of them. Throughout his presidency there were only thirty,
although he spoke more often than that over the radio. In the crisis year
of 1933, for instance, there were four Fireside Chats in addition to the
more than twenty other broadcast addresses he made. During his first
two terms in office, however, there were only sixteen Fireside Chats.[8]

The president used radio throughout the critical Depression year
of 1933 to allay fears, weld a new faith in government, and lay the
basis of the New Deal programs. In general, one magazine reported,
"the inhabitants of the White House" liked to listen to the radio.
Roosevelt apparently was fond of the humorist Will Rogers and the
singer Rudy Vallee.

Early liked radio, he once said, because of its directness and speed:
"It cannot misrepresent nor misquote. It is far reaching and simultaneous in releasing messages given it for transmission to the nation or
for international consumption."[9]

The president could have any air time he wanted. An hour's notice
was sufficient to clear the channels. But Early usually gave the networks a week's or ten days' notice. He would call and say, "Hello,
Studio. This is Steve. The president would like to make a broadcast—
oh, about ten days from now. Or maybe two weeks. See what you can
do, will you?"

It was a quid pro quo. The presidential broadcasts did much to sell radio to the people. So when Early called the two big broadcast companies, CBS and NBC, would get together to decide upon a day and hour that suited them both. They would tell Early, who would relay the information to the president. He almost always approved. Then the two companies would get busy shifting contracts with sponsors. On the day of the broadcast, all the circuits were cleared and independent stations were notified so they could carry the broadcast. In the afternoon before the evening broadcast, heavy curtains draped the oval room in front of the desk where the president would sit with microphones in front of him. It was a $41 table brought in by the radiomen because none of the White House furniture was adaptable for this use. Wires were everywhere.

About an hour before the broadcast, the movie men came in and set up. Then the guests would come in—maybe the secretary of the treasury or the director of the budget. Mrs. Roosevelt usually showed up with her knitting. A few minutes before the broadcast, usually at 10 p.m., the president would enter, accompanied by Early or McIntyre. Roosevelt would nod or smile at the radio and movie men, often calling out to some by name.[10]

For all their appearance of spontaneity and simplicity, these broadcasts were meticulously planned, from the angle of the microphone Roosevelt spoke into to the addition of a false tooth to close the space between his front two lower teeth so he would not whistle on certain words.[11]

Because the president received fifty or more requests daily to speak or appear at some function or other, it would have been easy for him to rely almost solely on the radio. But he and Early realized soon enough that to be really effective he should go on the air only when he had something truly important to say.[12]

Early gave the Fireside Chats special attention, announcing them sometimes as much as three weeks before they were scheduled, but usually not releasing the topic to be discussed. Again, it was the Early-Roosevelt genius at work. The mystery of the topic gave columnists fodder for speculation, and the White House benefited from the publicity. Gradually, as the talk neared, Early parceled out hints about the talk until just before the president was set to speak; then Early distributed the transcript to the reporters, sometimes even marking a passage where he thought the journalists could find their lead.[13]

Roosevelt's radio talks were always prepared ahead of time, carefully timed to the word, although no one would ever have cut the president off the air. The announcers then told the audience the president of the United States was about to address the nation, and Roosevelt went on the air. Sometimes he began with a folksy story or two, and his listeners loved them.[14]

Early's journalist's eye for detail and drama comes through in this letter he wrote to his friend Joseph Davies in 1940 describing the preparations for a Fireside Chat:

> This is Saturday morning in the White House. Unusual for the day, is a strange but subdued excitement. The cabinet room, for example, ordinarily a cold and deserted chamber, is much alive. The big table is covered with newspaper clippings, reference books and typewriter sheets of paper. Some of these are marked first draft—second draft—insert A—while others have been edited by hand so that some 250 words have been cut to 30 or 40 words.
>
> Editing, redrafting, checking and double checking, etc. will go on through the day—probably through the evening and maybe into the morning hours. And there won't be church services for any of these workers tomorrow morning—nor any golf—because tomorrow at 9:30 in the evening, the President goes on the air. And that is why this Saturday is the day it is for us.[15]

Sometimes Early took to the airwaves himself. For instance, in a September 17, 1933, radio interview he talked a bit about what it was like to work for the president and assured the listeners that their president was never out of touch with the White House when he took a vacation away from Washington.

His interviewer, a local radio man named Walter Trumbull, introduced Early this way: "Since the fourth of March [inauguration day], you have trailed the President pretty much everywhere he has been and at times you must have felt like the second man in a 100 yard dash." He explained that Roosevelt was known for his fourteen- to eighteen-hour workdays.

Early said Mrs. Roosevelt had awakened the president in the night recently to tell him about the earthquake that had hit the Long Beach, California, area. Then she called Early and said the president wanted him to instruct the army, the navy, and the Red Cross "to place every facility they had at the command of Long Beach and all other munici-palities affected. And I should like to say that within the next hour I was able to advise the President that the Navy already had landed men at Long Beach, that the regional director of the Red Cross was actively at work and that the Army had men moving in to prevent looting," Early said.

He talked about the logistics required to reach the president when he occasionally did get to leave Washington and spend a weekend on the *Sequoia*, the presidential houseboat Roosevelt used to cruise on the Potomac. Rather than the escort ship *Cuyahoga* coding and decoding messages, and because the *Sequoia* was always near a landing, Early said, a system of automobile and launch communication had been devised for emergencies. That way, if Roosevelt needed to get back to the White House in a hurry, he could return by car from a dock.

Early was careful to tell the audience that the president was rarely out of touch with the White House. For instance, he said, when Roo-sevelt went driving in a car, for security reasons they preferred not to communicate with him by two-way radio. Instead, he said, "We know in advance where he is going; the route he will take; the approximate speed he will travel and all available telephones along the way."[16]

Those first weeks of the Hundred Days proved a "trial by fire" for Early, with the White House a command post for the duration of the economic crisis. The new press secretary spent eighteen-hour days "struggling to keep pace with the chain of events unleashed by the President." Early told a radio interviewer in May that things had been moving so fast at the White House that it had been "kind of dizzy trying to keep up."[17]

The *New York World-Telegram* noted on March 8 that Early "has made a good start during these night and day vigils on the banking crisis. Almost every correspondent—and they are notoriously hard to satisfy—patted him on the back and extended congratulations."

The reporter continued: "[A]s a former newspaperman quick on the trigger, Steve knew what the public wanted through the press, and he got it. The indecision and long waits which have marked coverage of pre-vious 'great stories' at the White House were missing. The statements all through the emergency have been crisp, pertinent and prompt."[18]

A week after the new administration had moved into the White House, the *New York Times* wrote, "There is no more resemblance between the citadel of aloofness which Mr. Hoover built and the friendly, welcoming air of the Executive Offices now than there would (have been) between a formal embassy tea and old-home week at Hyde Park." It noted that Early and the other secretaries could walk into and out of Roosevelt's office at will. "They are a united family."

"Now when one walks into the Executive Offices, it is not with the expectation of encountering a hostile atmosphere, but knowing that one is welcome," the *New York Times* said. "Those who are known can walk into one of the secretaries' offices (i.e., Early, etc.) any time and ask a question. And because of the informal atmosphere and because the three secretaries are long-time friends of the President, they can walk into his office at any time. To say they are devoted to their chief is to put it mildly. They would literally do anything for him, and he knows it."[19]

In short, the press reaction to the new team in the White House was just short of ecstatic. And praise for Early, one of their own, was effusive.

Two weeks after the first press conference, Raymond Clapper, one of the reporters and a friend of Early's, wrote to him: "I think you are doing a simply magnificent job. This feeling, as you undoubtedly know, is general among Washington correspondents. I expect eventually to find something to complain about and herewith reserve all rights but up to now the performance from our point of view is one hundred percent."[20]

It may have been for Early yet another job with long hours and a lot of headaches, but the White House never lacked for news in those early New Deal days—news that would satisfy the cravings of the most demanding reporter, and Steve Early was there to ensure their fix. Covering the news in Washington in 1933 was a journalist's theme park, and almost as soon as he took office, Roosevelt's press conferences became one of the best shows in town. They lasted from twenty to thirty minutes and were open to only the hundred-plus reporters assigned by their news organizations to cover the White House.[21]

One writer concluded that "few Presidents had received as eulogistic a press as Franklin D. Roosevelt." In fact, this writer noted, not even Theodore Roosevelt, for all his brash exhibitionism, had created as sympathetic a rapport with the Washington press corps—or profited so markedly from it.[22]

A year after Theodore Joslin, Hoover's secretary, had expressed horror that Early would allow reporters to directly question the president, Joslin himself attended some of the press conferences and described them this way: "There is a rush to the door. The surge into the president's office when important news is anticipated is more like the drive for unreserved bleacher seats at a world series baseball game than a procession into the private office of the nation's Chief Executive."

He went on: "The tide sweeps up against the President's desk. The President exchanges pleasantries with those nearest to him as the late comers continue to crowd in. When all have assembled and there is a semblance of quiet, the President addresses the correspondents." Once the news conference was over, the reporters dashed for the door in a rush to the telephones. "Seconds, let alone minutes are vital in this day of the keenest possible competition. Newspapers somewhere in the world are going to press every minute of the day and night. A few ticks of the clock may mean the making or losing an edition somewhere," he noted.

The man who thought Early and Roosevelt were crazy to believe they could be frank with the reporters admitted that these same journalists "almost never make an error." He attributed this to "their keen understanding of the momentous subjects with which they must deal every day and their skill in writing. At one minute they are kidding each other, seemingly without a care in the world; the next minute they are with the President, and a minute later they are dictating cryptic sentences over the telephone about the latest momentous happening in this troubled world of ours."[23]

Throughout the spring and early summer of 1933, the president and Congress were busy creating those alphabet soup agencies that became the heart of the New Deal: the Civilian Conservation Corps (CCC), which by 1942 had employed about 3 million men; the Federal Emergency Relief Administration (FERA), headed by Harry Hopkins; the Agricultural Adjustment Administration (AAA), which provided financial aid to farmers and attempted to reduce crop surpluses; the Tennessee Valley Authority (TVA), set up to coordinate and develop all aspects of resources of the Tennessee River Valley, which covered seven states; the Home Owners' Loan Corporation (HOLC) to help nonfarm homeowners by refinancing mortgages and providing loans for taxes and repairs; and the Farm Credit Administration (FCA), created to refinance farm mortgages.

In June the National Recovery Administration (NRA) was established to help reduce unemployment and stimulate business; the National Labor Relations Board (NLRB) was set up to guarantee the right of labor to bargain collectively; and the Public Works Administration (PWA) provided government funds for construction of public projects. This agency came under the leadership of Harold L. Ickes, also secretary of the interior.

There also were the lesser problems. Right after Roosevelt took office, Joseph Patterson, the publisher of the *New York Daily News*, decided that what this once athletic president required to ensure his good health and fitness was a swimming pool in the White House.

When a reporter from the newspaper suggested the pool idea to Eleanor Roosevelt, she told the journalist, a woman named Grace Robinson, to "see Steve Early." He liked the idea; in fact, Robinson recalled, "I believe that his shrewd journalist's mind immediately saw the possibilities of favorable reaction to a Presidential pool, financed by public subscription." The idea was to have the *Daily News* get the ball rolling, and other newspapers around the country take up the cause by raising money from their readers.

Apparently McIntyre was opposed to a pool; Howe thought a pool "politically inexpedient." Early met with Robinson several times to give her progress reports, none of which were optimistic. Then one day he called her and said, "It's all arranged. I've just had dinner with the [Roosevelt] family. They want the pool."[24]

And throughout it all, Early prepared press releases on a host of topics, he arranged the twice-weekly press conferences, and he held his own daily briefings for the press. At the same time he was becoming something of a celebrity, at least in the local media and occasionally in the New York newspapers, eventually being quoted in his own right on White House affairs.

These were heady days for Early, who until now had been behind a camera or with a pencil and pad in hand, covering the greats and near greats of Washington. Now he was one of them: His photo, along with those of Howe and McIntyre, appeared regularly in the Washington and New York newspapers as well as in magazines and other newspapers. His life became a matter of public record, his movements captured in ink for everyone to read. "Steady Steve" Early had taken Washington by storm, one New York columnist wrote two weeks after Roosevelt moved into the White House.[25]

On March 28 Roosevelt, Early, McIntyre, and Howe were honored at a National Press Club dinner, an event thoroughly covered by the Washington papers. The previous week, when Mrs. Roosevelt took a Sunday sightseeing trip into Virginia's Blue Ridge Mountain country, Early and Howe accompanied her, and the trip was detailed in the newspapers. And when Mrs. Roosevelt attended a children's theater performance of *Pinocchio* at the National Theater in Washington, her two young guests were Buddy and Sis Early.[26]

The following month a formal portrait of the Early family appeared in the pictorial section of a Washington newspaper. There was daughter Sis, now seven and wearing a frilly dress with a fetching ribbon band in her hair; Buddy, nine, in a white shirt and tie; and Helen, her hair freshly waved and a coy smile on her face, sitting in an overstuffed chair holding Tommy, two. Steve, looking appropriately serious and wearing a dark suit, sat on the arm of the chair.[27]

The publicity continued. One newspaper columnist reported that around Easter time Roosevelt had asked his secretariat if they had bought new hats "for the season of rejoicing and remodeling." When they told him they had been too busy to think about new clothes, he gave them each a new hat.[28]

In June rumors were flying that Roosevelt would be heading to London to put in an appearance at the World Economic Conference, but then the newspapers denied the rumor on the word of Roosevelt's press secretary, who, one paper reported, "is in a position to know what he is talking about."[29]

Instead Roosevelt sent Secretary of State Cordell Hull and a delegation to the conference, and the president took a vacation away from the affairs of the New Deal, chartering a yacht called *The Amberjack II* and heading up the New England coast to his summer home on Campobello Island. This meant leaving Early in the White House to handle the day-to-day affairs.[30]

By August Roosevelt was in Hyde Park, and so was his press secretary. A photo in his scrapbook shows Early at a desk with a birthday cake loaded with candles in front of him. He was forty-four. He is surrounded by staff members—secretaries, Secret Service, and others. Under the photo, he wrote, "My birthday party at Hyde Park, 8-27-33." Attached are wishes from Sara Roosevelt, Eleanor, and one from the president addressed to "Steve—Unreconstructed Rebel from the

G.A.R." This referred to the Grand Army of the Republic, a fraternal organization composed of veterans of the Union Army who had served in the American Civil War. The party was held at Nelson House, Poughkeepsie's leading hotel, where the president's staff stayed when he was at his Hyde Park home.[31]

On October 5 Roosevelt threw out the ball for the first game of the World Series played in Washington between the Senators and the New York Giants. And seated next to him was Helen Early, along with Marvin McIntyre, Roosevelt's personal secretary Missy LeHand, and Steve.[32]

A year after Early took over the press job in the White House, the media generally gave him high marks. The *Washington Post* described him as "an efficient type of Southern gentleman, the type that has supplied the Army and Navy with some of its best officers for generations." It went on to call him "friendly but disciplined and his words are precise and close clipped." It praised him as "the most efficient press representative the White House has ever had." It noted that press releases were handed out promptly and that he was available to answer questions, although he neither inspired stories nor indulged in propaganda. "In spite of his loyalty to 'the boss,' he still retains the newspaperman's objective attitude."

The example the *Post* cited to highlight Early's efficiency was this: "The announcement of Russian recognition in Moscow and Washington; the President's message to the heads of all nations on May 17, 1933, concerning peace and disarmament, which required practically simultaneous release in all the world capitals—that is easy meat for Early." The article called him "an intelligent, candid and attractive gentleman." It concluded that the press secretary "knows his job and does it well, with unswerving devotion to FDR."

Even the once-hostile Theodore Joslin, Herbert Hoover's secretary, had to admit that Early was "discharging his exacting duties with extraordinary ability."[33]

Although still popular with and respected by his former colleagues, Steve Early was becoming well known for his temper. Faith Baldwin, a novelist and syndicated columnist, described him as "the Cardiac Menace over and in the White House." She referred to "his tanned face, ready laughter, white teeth and a sense of humor as long as your arm. Charm, lots of it. I wouldn't enjoy seeing him angry though."[34]

Not all publications were effusive in their praise of Early. *Time* magazine, known for its dislike of Roosevelt and his New Deal policies, called the press secretary a "big, fat-jowled fellow." It said that his job was "to jolly the Press along, see that the 'boys' (reporters) obey the White House rules on quoting and not quoting the President, (and) bark out his angry displeasure at those who do not play his game." However, the magazine grudgingly gave him credit for conceiving the president's "fireside" broadcasts and "arranging them at such intervals as to maintain the maximum amount of public interest."[35]

There were the more mundane but pleasurable moments in his job in 1933. When Joseph M. Schenck, president of United Artists Company, visited the president at Warm Springs on November 21, Early joined them, with Roosevelt at the wheel of the little specially equipped car he kept there while the three men and a Secret Service agent spent two hours talking and driving around the area.[36]

But the skies were beginning to cloud. In mid-December, a disgruntled member of the Civilian Conservation Corps sent Early a threatening letter saying the government, the president, and the country were "no good"—and threatened to blow up public works around the country. Publishers were beginning to complain that the president had hypnotized their reporters with his charm and misled them with "propaganda." By the beginning of 1934, the New Deal and Franklin Roosevelt were under attack. The honeymoon was over.[37]

8

HOBGOBLINS

"Just a routine high pressure day," Early wrote in his diary on April 18, 1934. It was a day that ran the gamut of meetings and conferences with reporters, dinner with a friend, and then back to the White House for more meetings, first with visiting newspaper editors and then with the president.

By the beginning of Roosevelt's second year in office, his press secretary had settled into his job quite nicely, but his days were anything but routine. There were frustrations, to be sure, but overall he seemed to be enjoying the intensity of life in the White House under a demanding, high-powered, and creative boss.

An important crisis that Early handled came along in February: the airmail controversy involving Charles Lindbergh, who had drafted a telegram to the president protesting the government's cancellation of domestic airmail contracts on grounds of price fixing among the privately operated airlines. But the flier's lawyer released the telegram to the press before it reached the White House, something the Roosevelt administration did not appreciate. In fact, the president saw it purely as a publicity stunt. The upshot was that he avoided replying to the telegram by having Early handle it, turning it into an occasion for a sharp rebuke of Lindbergh's tactics. It wasn't every day that the White House rebuked an American hero. The story went out across the country. Early took the rap, and Roosevelt backed him up.[1]

Not everyone felt Early and the White House had been fair with Colonel Lindbergh. A letter in one of Early's scrapbooks from Elmendorf Carr of New York City was highly sarcastic and critical of the White House's—and specifically Early's—handling of the Lindbergh telegram. He called the incident "an example of the insolence of office."

Referring to one of the news stories on the affair, Carr wrote: "I had to read several columns down to find out who under the suffering heavens Stephen T. Early might be. Now I know, and can die happy. When the great silence settles over our generation, and the bones of the heroes of our times are dust, Lindbergh will be forgotten, along with Byrd and Scott and the Wrights and Peary and other seekers after publicity safely acquired, but the name of Stephen T. Early will ring down the ages as an inspiration to our children's children unto the tenth generation—Stephen T. Early, the man who, from the White House roof's protection, told Lindbergh where to get off. Truly, our descendants will sigh enviously, there were giants in those days."[2]

Early began keeping a diary on January 1, 1934. His daughter said he dictated the day's events to his secretary faithfully the following morning. These diaries, which stop at the end of 1939, chronicle his work in the White House and, somewhat more briefly, his private life. They contain lists of visitors he met with, as well as an accounting of the almost daily morning meetings he had with Roosevelt in his bedroom in the White House, his press conferences and often the topics covered, and brief descriptions of the more personal and mundane parts of his day, like the outings to the golf course and the racetrack, complete with scores or winnings.

In keeping with a desire to not reveal secrets of the inner workings of the White House, Early's diary is circumspect, only occasionally offering insight into the background of an event or situation. When it does, it is written with the precision and flair that made his stories for the Associated Press so readable.

To fill in the gaps, though, the diary requires supplemental readings of newspaper stories of the time and books of memoirs written by those men and women who were intimate players in the administration—Grace Tully, who was Roosevelt's secretary; Robert E. Sherwood, a speechwriter for Roosevelt; and Harold L. Ickes, longtime secretary of the Interior Department—to uncover Early's involvement in many of the seminal moments of the Roosevelt presidency.[3]

In November of 1934 Early was called in by Roosevelt, as he would be so often over the years, to repair a temporary schism between two warring parties in the administration: Ickes, who had announced his backing of a public housing program under the New Deal, and James A. Moffett, a wealthy Democrat and a director of Standard Oil, who was the federal housing administrator. Moffett told the press he was dead set against a public housing program. The dispute made the headlines.

With Roosevelt in Warm Springs for his annual Thanksgiving vacation, it was left to Early to separate the adversaries. So he called them in to his office, listened to both sides, and then conferred with Howe, who was in the White House, and Roosevelt, still in Warm Springs. The president suggested the two men release a joint statement, which eventually they did. In a a bit of an understatement, Early noted in his diary for Thursday, November 22, that his office was "the go-between for Warm Springs and all the Departments."[4]

It was not always warring parties that needed Early's expertise. In January 1934 Harry Woodring, assistant secretary of war, announced that the Civilian Conservation Corps should be a part of the army. The CCC was an independent agency developed to put unemployed men to work and was one of Roosevelt's favorite creations. The Labor Department selected the men and the army transported them to camps, from which they were sent to jobs. Now the army wanted to take over the CCC. It caused such an uproar that Early was forced to summon Woodring to his office; then Early told the press that the assistant secretary had not expressed his views clearly. "What Woodring intended was that the army would oversee the CCC equipment." The CCC remained independent, and it remained one of the most popular parts of the New Deal until its termination in 1942.[5]

Minor but irritating problems with members of the press corps cropped up now and then, such as the incident late in 1934 when Early called in Leon Dure, who covered the White House for the *Washington Post*, to dislodge from him the name of the reporter for the United Press whose story that day had made liberal use of direct quotes from Roosevelt's press conference the previous day. The reporter had violated the rule that no quotes could be published except with Early or Roosevelt's approval.

Early took care of the matter, which probably aggravated Roosevelt more than it did Early. Writing in his diary, he said, "After talking with Lyle Wilson, head of the Washington office of the U.P., it was unnecessary for me to take any disciplinary steps as he will handle it in the U.P. office."[6]

A few days later, one of the reporters remained behind after Early's usual morning press conference; she said she was doing a story on a new set of china recently purchased for the White House and asked whether he would help her arrange for a photo of it. Early said, "I decided against this, as we have so many requests from newspapers and the spreading of such stories would not do any good." Evidently the idea of the White House buying new china at the height of the Depression was not something Early wanted publicized.

Maybe Early was simply in a bad mood that week, but that same day he turned down a request from well-known radio commentator H. V. Kaltenborn to attend one of the presidential press conferences, noting, "I explained how necessary it was to hold to minimum exceptions" to the rule that banned microphones in the press conferences.[7]

He did not turn down every journalist's request. Right after Christmas that year, he wrote, "Allowed myself to be interviewed by a Yale student who wants to be editor of his college paper."[8]

Then there were the minuscule crises for Secretary Early to handle. One day the Chamber of Commerce suggested that a peanut vendor named Steve who had been stationed on the street in front of the White House for twenty-eight years should move to make way for automobiles and new traffic regulations. The president had never been a customer, but Eleanor Roosevelt had bought peanuts from him. So she sent Early a note: "Must this man go?" The answer was no, and the peanut man stayed. The newspapers loved the story of the First Lady and the president's press secretary standing up for the little guy.[9]

Another little crisis involved Louis Howe's wife, Grace, who mostly lived in Massachusetts with the couple's children. She publicly criticized the state's governor, James Curley, for being more concerned about his political friends than about attending to affairs of state. A story about Mrs. Howe's comments ran in a Boston newspaper, and word got back to Roosevelt that she was chastising another Democrat. So Steve was asked to "handle it." Roosevelt wrote: "Would you tell her politely that it would be a good idea for her to keep quiet."[10]

No matter how seemingly insignificant the information, the news media were hungry for any scraps about the Roosevelt White House.

In her book *FDR and the News Media*, Betty Houchin Winfield writes that so much news was coming out of the White House and the government offices that by 1934 the United Press wires were carrying three times more Washington news than in 1930, and one-quarter of all Associated Press news was originating in the capital. "The public's demand for news in the dramatic days of 1933 was literally insatiable."[11]

So popular with the public was anything from, by, and about the Roosevelts that Eleanor Roosevelt began holding her own news conferences, writing magazine and newspaper columns, and eventually writing books. Her own press conferences followed the rules Early had established for the president's. Louis Howe was looking to movies that could be made to promote the New Deal, and the heads of government agencies were frantically churning out information about their activities in an effort to reach the public's eyes and ears.

Soon after Roosevelt was elected to office, it became obvious to him—and then to Early when he was brought aboard—that if the New Deal was to be broadly publicized and sold to the public, it would be necessary to overhaul the way government information was distributed to the media, in part because the system itself was antiquated and because the ever-increasing flow of publicity and its distribution were becoming unwieldy. Something had to be done. And so again Roosevelt asked Early, who rapidly was becoming the director and the producer of the publicity machine for both the president and the New Deal, to solve the problem.

Now that he had modernized the president's press conferences and made Roosevelt's radio addresses a must-hear for the public, Early tackled the quagmire of publicity operations in the various government departments. What he accomplished became the benchmark for the way the vast government bureaucracy even today informs the public about its work.

Federal agencies had had publicity arms since the Department of Agriculture created the first news bureau in 1889, eventually becoming the largest in the government. In the ensuing years, publicity components had, in some form, been a part of various agencies. But most of the employees had little or no experience in journalism, resulting in a kind of hopscotch approach to news reaching the media. Those agencies with large and active publicity offices saw their work publicized; those with no office or nonprofessional employees got little or no coverage.[12]

Early studied the publicity departments in both the departments, such as interior and agriculture, as well as the newly created agencies under the New Deal, went over the records of each press officer, and finally decided the most efficient way to make their agencies more accessible to the press and the public was to replace many of the agents with more energy and imagination drawn from the ranks of working journalists around the country. In all, he hired more than one hundred, many of them to publicize the new agencies that popped up to oversee the programs of the New Deal. They came from large newspapers like the *Chicago Tribune*, the *Washington Post*, and the *Louisville Courier-Journal*, and from smaller, lesser known publications. "Do your job just like you were working for a newspaper," Early advised the newly minted press agents. In other words, their releases were to be fair and accurate.[13]

He told a Washington newspaper reporter, "All information must be made available promptly to the press and if the official publicity men don't know the answers to questions off-hand, they are supposed to find them out." The reporter wrote, "Early is the executor of Roosevelt's thesis that the workings of the government are the public's business."

Delbert Clark, a *New York Times* reporter who covered Washington, said that as a result of Early's reorganization of government publicity, with a few exceptions, cabinet officers and heads of independent offices now discussed with the press the affairs of state "with a freedom and frankness having no parallel here or elsewhere. The results were spectacular."[14]

But by 1935, critics were calling Early's restructuring efforts nothing more than "the wholesale hiring" of Washington correspondents and editors and publishers by government agencies to spread the propaganda of the New Deal. Others called the changes a form of government censorship because they saw the positive news about the New Deal coming from the agencies and assumed it was the result of White House directives.

Early explained in a magazine article he wrote later that year to countermand criticism of the changes he had made in the publicity departments that his and Roosevelt's goal had been to "turn on the light" of government, to "acquaint the public through the newspapers with the business of the Government." No questions were asked, he wrote, about the politics or past affiliations of the new publicity men and women.[15]

In her book, Winfield concludes that in spite of Early and Roosevelt's attempt to "turn on the light" by hiring the journalists to be publicity agents and by helping the working press get news quickly, they "maximized positive results for the administration." She believes that the president and his press secretary indeed created nothing more than a huge publicity bureau for the New Deal.[16]

One of Early's harshest critics was none other than Theodore Joslin, Hoover's former press secretary. He called the hiring of the press agents scandalous and said it would gravely threaten freedom of the press. Early replied that Joslin was "reveling in Bunk."

The *Chicago Tribune*, never a supporter of Roosevelt, in a headline called Early "the counterpart of Nazi Goebbels," saying he was "the minister of propaganda for the New Deal."[17]

Generally, though, the changes and improvements Early made were appreciated by the journalists covering the federal government. The *Washington Star* dubbed the publicity agents "The Fifth Estate" and said their job was "to make life easy for the Fourth Estate." They were the newspapermen and women from the city rooms of newspapers around the country who had forsaken the city room, the press gallery, and the beat-the-edition business and had graduated to an office, a secretary, and several assistants. And the pay often was better—especially for those men and women who had come from smaller newspapers—and the hours were more regular, with fewer late night shifts.

This is how the reporter from the *Star* saw the publicity agents: "Some of them are as difficult to see as a member of the Cabinet himself; some of them are as accessible as a police station is for a drunk. Some of them have offices as ornate as a Hollywood hotel lobby; others carry with them the aroma of printer's ink and newsprint into their offices, which look like miniature city rooms—blue with tobacco smoke, cigarette stubs on the floor, tickers clacking, telephones ringing and feet on the desk. Usually the press rooms, themselves just as unkempt and littered, are close by."[18]

But without the agents, reporters would have been forced to spend too much time hunting down a story source only to learn there was no story, and department and agency heads then would have been besieged by harried reporters all trying to get a scoop. Government information was to be made available promptly to the press, and if the official publicity people did not know the answers offhand, they were supposed to find out and get back to the reporters.

The job of the press agents was not just to aid the reporters, but they also served as a clearinghouse for hundreds of requests from citizens and organizations needing information about the bureaus and agencies, and they wrote speeches for the bureau heads.

The individual agents operated "miniature news operations" based on the format Early had developed for the White House. The agents attended the president's press conferences so they could pass on to their own bosses "the tack" Roosevelt had taken on important issues. Not surprisingly, the president's own style of open, regular meetings with the press was adapted by many of the cabinet members and agency chiefs, "each suited to the official's own personality." For instance, Secretary of State Cordell Hull held dignified press conferences, while Postmaster General James Farley, known for his jovial personality, was much more informal with the press.[19]

Roosevelt believed that it was necessary for Early to keep tabs on the flow of information from the various departments and agencies, so in the summer of 1933 they chose to set up the Division of Press Intelligence within the National Recovery Administration to maintain a press clipping service of all articles in magazines and newspapers relating to public reaction to the New Deal. The NRA was established under the National Industrial Recovery Act of 1933 to coordinate economic recovery. Early also would feed congressmen friendly to the administration information about New Deal activities and have them place it in the *Congressional Record*, which then was mailed by their offices to their constituents.[20]

In 1937 Early requested from the government publicity agents two copies of brief summaries of their achievements in their departments. The summaries "should be factual and prepared with such care that they will not be vulnerable to political attack," he told them. He also asked that a copy of each summary be sent to all senators so that the Democratic senators could use them as part of a series of pro-administration speeches being made as Congress readied to adjourn.[21]

By the end of Roosevelt's first term, Early was not only the president's "troubleshooter," but he was regularly reviewing and editing speeches, radio addresses, and important announcements of officials in the administration, "always with an eye to their effect on public relations." Sam Rosenman, a Roosevelt speechwriter, made several references in his autobiography to Roosevelt calling on Early to look over the draft of a speech or a radio address and make suggestions.[22]

With Roosevelt's blessing, Early had the NRA send a weekly clip sheet and special articles in mat form, ready for the printer, to the weekly newspapers and smaller newspapers around the country that did not have correspondents stationed in Washington.[23]

By July 1936, five thousand government recordings made to publicize the work of the many federal agencies were in circulation, and Early urged the agency heads to cooperate with the newsreel companies to produce motion pictures about the agencies. Wire services alone were carrying an average of 250 releases every week.[24]

This may have been the motivation behind a movement to replace the big three privately owned wire services—the Associated Press, the United Press, and the International News Service—with a national press service that would have exclusive use of all government news, and, as Early interpreted the idea, it would "give its service only to those newspapers loyal to the Roosevelt dictatorship."

Early said that Roosevelt was "so utterly opposed" to putting the existing wire services out of business that he sent word to the senator whose idea it was, Thomas D. Schall, a Republican from Minnesota, promising to put a stop to any such movement.[25]

Why? For one thing, Early was a product of two wire services— the United Press and the Associated Press—with many friends still working in those services and the others, including some who were top editors, including two of his brothers-in-law. Early and Roosevelt knew that these connections throughout the wire service organizations that distributed news stories to the country's newspapers and radio stations were vital to the success of the New Deal. They also were acutely aware, as Early had noted, that a single wire service freely using government news and handouts would confirm those charges that Roosevelt was nothing more than a dictator.

There may have been a third reason Early especially was opposed to a single wire service. Steven E. Schoenherr, in his unpublished doctoral dissertation "Selling the New Deal: Stephen T. Early's Role as Press Secretary to President Franklin D. Roosevelt," concludes that Early's middle-class background made him more sympathetic to the traditional values of "individualism, patriotism, duty and free enterprise capitalism," and it may have been these values that kept him from supporting any form of centralized news bureau or agency.[26]

With the opposition of the White House, the issue died quickly, but it again showed the importance of Early's media savvy in the administration. And as the months and years rolled on, Roosevelt's reliance on Early went beyond that of a super press secretary and overseer of publicity for the administration. Early gradually assumed the status of what in private business would probably be known as "assistant to the president." He became the funnel through which virtually everything in the way of White House business—except presidential appointments (and even then he kept himself informed of those appointments and for the most part knew what they were about)—flowed daily. By 1935 Early was being referred to as Howe's successor. In his syndicated "Broadway" newspaper column, Ed Sullivan wrote: "Steve Early has taken Louis Howe's spot in the inner White House circle."[27]

One reason for Early's rising star was Howe's declining health and diminishing influence. Another was that with the institution of the wildly popular press conferences, the hugely successful Fireside Chats, and the efficient reorganization of the publicity offices throughout the government, Early had now proven how valuable he was to Roosevelt and to the success of the New Deal with the public.

At times he served as the president's legs, like the day in March of 1934 when Roosevelt sent him to the War Department to confer with the secretary of war on a proposal to increase the army appropriations bill and the findings of a recent grand jury investigation into the purchase of army supplies.[28]

Early became, to a considerable extent, the president's eyes and ears, making a point of keeping in close contact with key members of Congress as well as Executive Branch officials. It was clear that Roosevelt trusted him and relied heavily on his judgment.[29]

Because of his extensive network of journalist friends, Early had connections he could use to gather information for the president, such as the time he called a reporter friend on the West Coast to inquire about a threatened longshoremen's strike there. Early learned that such a strike would be a "crushing blow" to the area's revived economy. He relayed the conversation to Roosevelt, who sent a telegraph to the president of the union, asking that in the public interest a strike order be suspended. The journalist reported back that the longshoremen would comply with the president's request.[30]

Sometimes these requests from the Boss came out of the intimate morning conferences Early had in Roosevelt's bedroom while he was still in bed or while he was shaving; others came in the form of a memo, while still others were simply verbal requests made while Early was meeting with Roosevelt in his office. Many of these requests are mentioned and occasionally detailed in Early's diary. They become the basis for some inside looks at how the White House was coping with the New Deal.

Although there were few "typical" diary entries, the one Early wrote on May 28, 1935, the day after the Supreme Court invalidated the National Recovery Administration, which had been set up soon after Roosevelt took office to develop a code of self-regulation in industry with agreed upon fair trade codes, illuminates succinctly one of Early's days in the White House:

> After seeing the President this morning, I returned [to his/Early's office] and made a number of telephone calls for him asking the heads of various government agencies not to make any statement with respect to the Supreme Court decisions of yesterday. Met with the press and told them not to expect any statements on that subject from here until the latter part of the week.
>
> Talked by long distance telephone to Ray Moley [Columbia University professor and an original member of the Brain Trust] and Bernard Baruch [financier and advisor to Roosevelt] both of whom called me from New York City.
>
> Took up with the President the draft of suggested remarks prepared by the State Department for his use tomorrow night when he opens the California Pacific International Exposition at San Diego by telephone.
>
> Spent most of the afternoon talking with various newspaper men; also put out a notice that the President's press conference this week, for his convenience, would be changed as follows: Wednesday at 4:00 P.M.–Friday 10:30 A.M. Worked late on the mechanics of preparing an advance on the telephone message for tomorrow night. I sent a copy to (Commerce) Secretary Roper's office to be wired in confidence to him tonight.[31]

The president did indeed hold a press conference later that week to discuss the ramifications of the Court's decision. However, he needed time to prepare his remarks, so it temporarily fell to Early to fend off the press. The court case itself involved the Schechter brothers in New York, who were selling diseased poultry and failing to observe the wage and hour regulations of the NRA code. The Court ruled that because the Schechters were not engaged in interstate commerce, the federal government had no power to set working conditions. The day the Court handed down the decision was known as Black Monday in the White House because not only did it invalidate major portions of the New Deal legislation, but it questioned the extent of the federal government's powers to help the unemployed. The president decided he needed some time to digest all this before he talked to the newspapermen.

But when the press conference was held, it was not Roosevelt's carefully prepared remarks or analysis of the decision that made the headlines; rather, it was something Early had told him off-handedly.

Early had come to the White House that morning and as usual had gone to Roosevelt's bedroom while he was dressing to confer with him about the press conference and other affairs. In the course of the conversation, Early mentioned that he had driven in to work with his brother-in-law George Holmes, and they had talked about the Court's decision.

Casually, Early added, "George says that those boys up there think that this is still the horse-and-buggy age."

The president never said a word as he slipped into his coat and motioned that he was ready to be wheeled over to his office. But he immediately recognized a phrase that everyone could understand. So in the middle of his speech to the reporters, he said, "The whole tendency over these years has been to view the interstate commerce clause in the light of present-day civilization. The country was in the horse-and-buggy age when that clause was written. . . ."

Because everything said by the president during a press conference was considered "background" information and therefore could be quoted only if Early or Roosevelt gave the okay, the reporters asked if they could quote Roosevelt's "horse and buggy" reference. Early's reply: "Just the phrase."

So it was the "horse-and-buggy age" that made the headlines. It was the phrase that people used most in discussions at the time and in arguing about the Court's decision, and it is the phrase that has become most closely associated with Roosevelt's fight with the Court.[32]

9

ON BEHALF OF THE PRESIDENT

During his first term, Roosevelt was away from the office fairly frequently—sometimes on official business, at other times for a relaxing weekend cruise on the Potomac River or a visit to Hyde Park. When he traveled, he took either Early or Marvin McIntyre to handle the press that always accompanied him. But more often than not, it was Early who was left behind to mind the store at the White House.

When the entourage was at Hyde Park, the biweekly press conference was held at Roosevelt's home; temporary offices were set up in Nelson House, a hotel in nearby Poughkeepsie, where Early said "a daily flow of telegraphic memoranda was exchanged between there and Washington." The *New York Times* reported that Roosevelt's system of communications "enables him to steer the ship of state wherever he may sojourn."[1]

What this really meant was that whoever wanted to communicate with the president was forced first to go through Early. This did not mean that while he was in the White House Roosevelt was any more accessible; it did mean that Early would send the request or the information to Roosevelt, sometimes giving it his own spin or suggesting that the president reply one way or the other.

For instance, on April 9, 1934, Early wrote in his diary that he "dealt with Speaker [of the House] Rainey on Congressional matters," then relayed the information to Roosevelt who was vacationing in Florida. This time, Roosevelt had gone to Miami for a ten-day fishing trip aboard Vincent Astor's *Nourmahal* off the Bahama Islands, a repeat of the cruise he had taken the previous year when the attempt on his life had been made in Miami, and it was a vacation he would repeat the following year amid some serious criticism.[2]

Early wrote that before Roosevelt left for Florida, Early had spent two days cleaning off his desk, and as the president's car pulled away from the White House Roosevelt told his press secretary, "Close up shop. Get away and get a good rest." So Early canceled a dinner engagement with some old friends, ate at home, "and early to bed."[3]

While he did get in some golf on Thursday afternoon and Sunday morning at his favorite club, Burning Tree in Maryland, and made a Monday afternoon visit to the horse races at Bowie, also in Maryland, with Mrs. Early and the youngest Roosevelt son, John, he simply was unable to follow "Doctor Roosevelt's" prescription. He worked until 2 p.m. in his office that first Saturday and then attended a Democratic dinner at the Willard Hotel, making a stop on the way home at the White House photographers' dinner dance at the Shoreham Hotel.[4]

Later on Sunday, James Roosevelt, the president's oldest son, asked Early to postpone the date of the annual Gridiron Dinner in Washington, an event of newspapermen that Roosevelt enjoyed attending, so his father could extend his cruise another week. After some telephone calls and negotiations the following day, the Gridiron club's board agreed to change the dinner date to the night after Roosevelt returned from his fishing trip.

In his diary, Early wrote: "I spent several hours explaining to newspapermen that the Gridiron Dinner had been postponed as a courtesy to the President and not because he was ill or had suffered any accident." He noted that these rumors were "prevalent."[5]

He also met with Howe on Monday to talk about the charges of Communism among members of the Brain Trust and the administration being made by Dr. William A. Wirt, superintendent of schools in Gary, Indiana. In his book *FDR: The New Deal Years*, Kenneth S. Davis calls Wirt "an excessively loquacious gentleman, elderly, and possessed of an excessively dramatic and conspiratorial imagination," who in the summer of 1933 had attended a dinner party in Washington where his table companions had included some members of the Brain Trust. Wirt claimed the dinner talk had been "a Communist conspiracy to overthrow the existing order," with the Brain Trust guests involved in the conspiracy. Roosevelt was their alleged leader.

When a manuscript by Wirt containing the charges came to the attention of a House committee, the press got hold of it, and some sensational stories resulted. Roosevelt left for Florida in the midst of this brouhaha, and it fell to Howe and mostly to Early the next week to meet with House Speaker Henry T. Rainey about appointing a congressional committee to look into the charges.[6]

That same day, Early wrote, he met with Vice Admiral Ross McIntire, personal physician to Roosevelt throughout his years in the White House. They talked about Louis Howe's health, which had been steadily deteriorating. Early gave no details on their conversation.

He did manage to get in a few more rounds of golf before, in typical Early press agent fashion, he set to work arranging a congressional reception for Roosevelt on his return to Union Station on Friday, April 13. When the president's train pulled in, he learned that two hundred members of the Senate and House, led by Vice President John Nance Garner and Speaker Rainey, had marched from the Capitol to the station to give him a welcome home. Early said it was the first time Congress had ever paraded in a body. The Marine Band, in brilliant red uniforms, added a touch of color. "The legislators put on a genuine parade, the like of which could not be found within the memory of the oldest inhabitant," Early wrote.

Roosevelt appeared at the rear of the train and addressed the legislators, saying he could not truthfully say he was glad to return and added that it seemed to him "both Houses of Congress have been having a wonderful time in my absence." Referring to his fishing experiences in Florida, he said, "I have come back with all sorts of new lessons which I learned from barracuda and sharks. I am a tough guy. So if you will come down [to the White House] and see me as often as you possibly can, I will teach you some of the stunts I learned."

The rousing reception at Union Station was followed by a press conference at the White House. Early decided that the newspaper reporters who attended came less in hopes of getting any news "but more to see the President and satisfy their curiosity as to the rumors concerning his health."[7]

The next day, after his daily meeting with Roosevelt in the president's bedroom and his press conference with the reporters, Early put together a speech for the president to make that night at the Gridiron Dinner, incorporating material sent to him by Charles Michelson, director of publicity for the Democratic National Committee.

Roosevelt received "a tremendous ovation" when he arrived at the dinner, and after the club members tossed their usual sharp but witty barbs at the president, Roosevelt announced that even though Early and Michelson had labored over a speech for him, he preferred to speak extemporaneously. And he stole the show.[8]

One quick trip Roosevelt made in May was to New York City to attend the funeral of William Woodin, his first secretary of the treasury. It was a trip fraught with complexities, pitting the president's single-mindedness against Early's zeal to maintain good public relations for the White House.

A gentle man of elfin appearance, Woodin had been a tough and shrewd businessman before he came to Washington, and his role in the banking crisis of the Hundred Days had been incalculable. Also a composer, it was Woodin who wrote the "Franklin D. Roosevelt Inaugural March," which the marching bands played during the inauguration parade.

Woodin had been seriously ill for some time, and while his death was not unexpected, when he learned of it on May 4, it dampened Roosevelt's enthusiasm over the positive treatment some newspapers were giving a speech he had made the previous night in which he called on big business "to stop crying 'wolf'" and assist in the economic recovery. Early expected the president to put aside his duties for a day and attend the funeral. However, Roosevelt asked Eleanor to take his place. Early would accompany her. The Silver Conference then in session, the need to prepare two messages to Congress, and other business kept Roosevelt from going to New York, he claimed. And at his press conference that afternoon, Roosevelt explained to the reporters why he could not attend the funeral.

But Early thought he should change his mind and go. In his diary, Early said that he urged Roosevelt several times that day to make the trip. Then that evening, while Roosevelt was in the swimming pool, Early wrote, "I went to him again to urge that he reconsider the New York decision and permit us to arrange his engagements so that he would literally move his office on Saturday from the White House to the train. I pointed out that he could keep his Silver Conference engagement with the senators, having them meet him at the Union Station and go as far as Baltimore; that he could have a stenographer with the Sugar and Revenue Bills and other correspondence with him on the train."

Then Early appealed to Eleanor. He told her that he "had a deep feeling that the president should go to the Woodin funeral. I found that she shared my conviction. Mrs. Roosevelt promised to talk to the President when he came to the House from the pool." The First Lady prevailed, for by the time Early was back in his office, Roosevelt was calling him on the telephone from the family's living quarters in the White House to say he would attend the funeral.

Early and McIntyre then shifted into high gear, making the arrangements, notifying the Secret Service, and telephoning the pastor of the church where the funeral was to be held to inform him that the president of the United States would be in attendance. They called Mrs. Woodin to alert her and made sure the senators would be at Union Station for the conference aboard the train—and, of course, they let the press know the change of plans.

The statement released to the reporters was pure Early—loyal to the Boss, informative to the press, and in no way hinting at the struggle that had taken place to ensure Roosevelt's attendance: "The President had feared that his engagements for tomorrow would prevent his going to New York, but found late today that it would be possible for him to so arrange his appointments that he could make the trip." The statement concluded with a sentence on the arrangements at Union Station. The last line of Early's two-page typed diary entry that day was: "Dined at home late."[9]

The next day was Saturday, and a party including the president, Early, Mrs. Roosevelt, several members of the cabinet, the vice president, and several members of Congress took the train to New York—but not until Roosevelt and the senators had their conference at the station.

Early and McIntyre's last-minute arrangements worked. Thousands of people lined the sidewalks as the president's car drove to the church on Fifth Avenue. When they arrived, Mrs. Woodin told Roosevelt, "I am glad you have come. Will knows you are here."

Early described the service as "simple but impressive," and said,

"The President kept his eyes upon the casket of his friend and helper, the late Secretary of the Treasury, throughout the services."

They were back on board the train in less than two hours and arrived in Washington at 8:10 p.m., in time for the president to stop off at the White House and change his clothes so he, Early, and some others from the funeral party could make an overnight and Sunday cruise on the Potomac.[10]

Early finally took a vacation in early July when he and Mrs. Early spent a few days at a resort on the New Jersey shore with his sisters Mary and Oma and their husbands. They were joined by Arthur Sinnott, managing editor of the *Newark News*. They had dinner one night with Joseph Tumulty, secretary to the late president Woodrow Wilson, and his wife.

Another day, clad in a bathrobe and shorts, Early was interviewed by a reporter from the nearby *Asbury Park Press*. The press secretary's enthusiasm for the Boss bubbled over. He called Roosevelt "Just one grand man." But Early admitted to the reporter that his job of "keeping the press in line" may have contributed to his graying hair.

Apparently the fame of Stephen T. Early, son of the Confederacy, had eluded this reporter, because he kept referring to Early's "New England background."

But it wasn't all play. After a few days, with Helen remaining in New Jersey, Early and Holmes drove back to Washington so George could interview him in an NBC radio broadcast over a national hookup. But the vacation resumed when, the following morning, George and Steve flew to Toledo, where they joined Harold Boeschenstein, vice president of Owens-Illinois Glass Company, for a week-long cruise on the Great Lakes.[11]

That was the summer the executive offices in the White House were remodeled, so the president and his staff found it more convenient to be away for long periods of time. It also gave Roosevelt an opportunity to make an official tour of the West after he returned from a holiday cruise to Hawaii.

Early and Howe headed West to meet the presidential party in San Francisco. And in what must have reminded all three men of that cross-country campaign tour in 1920, they traveled by train north to Portland, Oregon, and to Spokane, Washington, and then by car to view the Grand Coulee Dam. There Roosevelt addressed a crowd of more than twenty thousand, some of whom had driven two to three hundred miles to hear him.

From there, the party moved east by train, stopping at Belton, Montana, to visit Glacier Park. A long drive through the park took them to Two Medicine Chalet, where Roosevelt, thanks to Early's careful planning, was able to give a radio address to the nation.

What they saw as they traversed the north-central part of the country through the summer heat was a drought-stricken land, blighted for hundreds and hundreds of miles. When the train stopped at Devils Lake, North Dakota, another large crowd greeted him, this time with a crudely lettered sign that read: "You gave us beer, now give us water." Roosevelt told them, "The beer part was easy," but water was out of his control, despite the array of New Deal programs aimed at helping those very same victims of the drought. Even the great Franklin D. Roosevelt could not come up with a way to force open the heavens and send the people the rain they so desperately needed.

The presidential party reached Washington at noon on Friday, August 10, and Early wrote that Helen had met him at Union Station to take him home "to get some much needed rest." Normally he went into his office on Saturdays, but not that week. He said he planned to stay away until Monday.[12]

Other than his usual visits to Hyde Park and Warm Springs, Roosevelt took no more long trips until the following March, when he planned to make his spring fishing jaunt with Vincent Astor off the coast of Florida, but a complication arose.

By the beginning of the year, Louis Howe was seriously ill, his condition steadily deteriorating, so that on March 20, Early was forced to issue a bulletin to the press saying, "Secretary Howe is extremely critical." He wrote in his diary that day "Louis is expected to pass away at any time."[13]

This also meant that Roosevelt would have to either cancel or postpone his fishing trip. Early thought he should cancel. After all, Howe was the president's closest friend and longtime adviser.

Howe had been ill for so long and always seemed to rally at a critical moment, so at first Roosevelt's fishing trip remained on his agenda. But this time, Howe was so sick that Eleanor canceled all her plans that would take her out of the city; the president put off his vacation. On March 22 Early told the press that Howe was "still clinging to life." But four days later, Howe was sitting up in his bed drinking coffee and eating Cream of Wheat. Roosevelt then boarded the train for Florida, and soon received a wire from Early telling him that Howe was "generally brighter."[14]

Meanwhile, Marvin McIntyre, who was with the president in Florida, and Early, who was minding the store in Washington, were faced with a dilemma. Recognizing that the Boss needed the rest and relaxation he was afforded on this annual fishing trip, the two pondered whether to tell Roosevelt if Howe were to die while he was away or simply go ahead with the funeral and not tell the president until he returned.

But the tough little former newspaperman held on, and Early and McIntyre did not have to break up the Boss's vacation. On April 6 Early wrote in his diary that Howe asked him to have McIntyre issue a statement to the newspapermen in Florida as if it were coming directly from Roosevelt that the president had received reports that "Howe is out of danger and it is expected that he will be able to resume his former activities."[15]

A busy late spring and summer of 1935 meant that Early could only take a week off in late June, spending it with Helen and George and Mary Holmes in Spring Lake, New Jersey. Then, in late July, he found time for a few days of fishing at Shadyside, Maryland, where Helen and the children were staying for a month.[16]

If the spring had been hectic, with Howe at death's door and Roosevelt and McIntyre away, the fall brought with it yet another presidential vacation, this time aboard the USS *Houston* for a month-long cruise from San Diego through the Panama Canal and back to Washington via Charleston, South Carolina.

Once again Early was minding the store. He made little mention in his diaries about his feelings concerning these long presidential voyages at sea, where communication could be complicated and he acted as the liaison between the government and the president. Early's diaries and the newspaper stories in his scrapbooks don't indicate any concern from the reporters about the president's absences. Early continued to hold his own press conferences and passed along any news he received from Roosevelt as he traveled. Thus, the reporters were getting news for their stories.

For long trips, through Early the president would inform the press corps of his itinerary, but for briefer forays he sometimes didn't. Once Early chastised the president for leaving the White House and not letting the regular White House reporters know of his plans. Evidently Roosevelt and a small party of friends and staff had driven outside the city for a picnic the night before and did not allow Early to tell the newspapermen until after they had gone. "I left memorandum for the President protesting this practice," Early wrote. His protest must have been effective, for he was able to assure the reporters that "such a happening would not occur again."[17]

As 1935 drew to a close, attached to his increasing responsibilities was the need for Early not only to act as press secretary to Roosevelt, but to advise him when it appeared the president's judgment had gone astray. Grace Tully, another of Roosevelt's secretaries, recalled that Steve's greatest problem with the Boss arose whenever Roosevelt tore out from a newspaper a column that enraged him and said, "It's a damn lie from start to finish."

Tully recalled, "Steve knew the press was in for a dressing down at the next press conference. He tried to dissuade the Boss from this course of action but, failing this, he tried to tell Roosevelt to direct his remarks to the writer of the article and not to the press as a whole. Early assured him that most of the reporters would agree with him about the few who violated the rules of decency from time to time, but when the president took the whole group to task for the sins of a few, he made every man in the room sore. Steve explained this to the Boss time and again, but there were many occasions when the press secretary felt his advice had gone in one ear and out the other."[18]

The leaking of the contents of presidential speeches was another problem for Early. They did occur and often involved one point in a speech—and the leak could often be traced back to Roosevelt himself. The leak could end up in a newspaper column or from the mouth of some radio commentator. The job of checking back to find out where the leak came from fell to Early, and he discovered after a while it was best to start with the Boss himself.

"Boss, have you talked with anybody outside the White House about this speech?" he would ask.

"Now Steve, don't look at me that way. I'm not guilty this time. I may have mentioned the paragraph on flood control to Congressman Joe Doakes when he was in yesterday, but he's on that committee and he knows a lot about the problem. You know he wouldn't tell any-body."

"Of course not, Mr. President," Steve would nod with a wry face—and the inquiry would be closed.[19]

This may be why by 1936 Early, who had come into the White House with a thick head of dark hair, was showing patches of white hair at his temples.

THE 1936 CAMPAIGN:
TO STAY OR LEAVE

"New Year's Day, 1936: The beginning of what promises to be a very interesting year."

W hen Early wrote this in his diary, he had no way of knowing that it indeed was to be a watershed year for both him and the Boss. For Early the year brought professional frustrations and personal decisions about his future. For Roosevelt it saw the loss of his longtime friend and mentor Louis Howe, as well as the death of his bodyguard and valet, Gus Gennerich, who had been with him since his days in the New York governor's mansion in Albany. And not only for Roosevelt, but for everyone in the White House, 1936 heralded a presidential election year and the uncertainties connected with it.

On the international front, this was the year Britain's King George V died in mid-January, and his popular son, the Prince of Wales, became King Edward VIII. But within the year, the new king had abdicated the throne to marry the twice-divorced American Wallis Warfield Simpson. It was the year that Roosevelt appointed Early's close friend Joseph Davies the second person to be ambassador to the Soviet Union.

On the domestic front, by January 3 the White House was gearing up for the president's annual State of the Union address, delivered in person before an evening joint session of Congress. The speech, forty minutes in length, was broadcast over both NBC and CBS radio networks to a nationwide audience, and, Early noted in his diary, the evening event angered the Republican minority in Congress because Roosevelt was "abandoning the age-old custom of regular day-time conclaves." Normally, the address would have occurred during the day, but the press secretary had realized that a far wider audience would be assured for an evening address.[1]

While he had scored a publicity coup and reached a national audience with his evening speech, three days later Roosevelt saw the Supreme Court declare unconstitutional important parts of the Agricultural Adjustment Act of 1933, which had guaranteed farmers financial aid, and Early was swamped with calls both from members of Congress and from newsmen seeking comment from the president.[2]

In addition to holding his daily press briefings and dealing with questions from journalists and others who insisted on knowing what Roosevelt was doing or thinking that day, Early was serving as a clearinghouse for all speeches made by members of the administration, especially those touching upon the Supreme Court and the Constitution.[3]

One reason for Early's increased workload was the continuing illness of Howe, who in the past would have shouldered much of the nonpress-related burden that Early now was forced to carry. Howe had turned sixty-five on January 14, but it was hardly a cause for celebration. At the end of the month, the Cuff Links Gang, those who were with Roosevelt in the 1920 campaign, resumed their annual reunion and celebration of the president's birthday, which had been called off the previous year because Howe was at death's door. But the 1936 party lacked the usual boisterous horseplay and humorous stunts that had been choreographed by Howe, in consultation with Eleanor, Early, and Marvin McIntyre.[4]

The fact was that Howe had given the White House palpitations for more than a year with weeks of his being near death and then his unexpected remissions. Most of the time he remained in his room in the White House, or, when his condition was deemed serious enough, he was taken to the hospital. Howe's health had been precarious for so long that despite his poor physical state in mid-March, Roosevelt nonetheless took off for Florida for his annual fishing cruise. Then, in early April, Early himself headed to Florida for a brief vacation. Did they realize Howe was at death's door? Perhaps, but the feisty gnome had cheated death so often in the past that they undoubtedly thought he would pull through once again.[5]

Then on April 18, while Roosevelt and Early were at the annual Gridiron Dinner for the Washington press corps at the Willard Hotel, and Eleanor was at the White House entertaining the "widows" of the newsmen, Howe died quietly in his sleep at the Naval Hospital in Washington. The president and his secretary learned of the death when they came back from the dinner, and Early made the announcement to the press shortly after midnight, saying Howe had died of "heart and chest complications."[6]

Howe's biographer, Alfred Rollins, concluded that "Louis would have been appalled and pleased with Franklin's last token to his 'great little' friend—the state funeral in the East Room of the White House, the flags at half-staff, the solemn funeral train pulling up the East Coast to Fall River." Both the president and Mrs. Roosevelt, accompanied by Early and McIntyre and others from the White House staff, were aboard the overnight train. Then they attended the Episcopal service and the burial on a cold day in a snow-covered plot in Fall River's Oak Grove Cemetery. Early supported on his arm Margaret ("Rabbit") Durand, Howe's personal secretary.

Apparently it was a big event in the old mill city on the road to Cape Cod. The *New York Herald-Tribune* reported, "The townspeople were out in great numbers, enclosing the plaza around the railroad station and lining the streets of this black mill town as the funeral cortege made its way to the cemetery. A chill wind stirred the still bare limbs of the trees in the cemetery."[7]

Early's diary entries on Howe's last illness and death were terse, and there was no mention of Roosevelt's or his own feelings about the loss. However, Jim Farley, postmaster general and chairman of the Democratic National Committee, wrote in his memoirs that shortly after Howe's death, the president told Farley that he felt bad about the passing of his faithful friend, "[b]ut in view of the circumstances, it must be considered a blessing in disguise, because Louis had been getting to the point where he gave a lot of orders that were annoying and likely to cause a lot of trouble."[8]

Even from his hospital bed, Howe had continued to plan the strategy for the upcoming campaign, and often would call the White

House with ideas or suggestions until finally the president ordered that Howe's direct line be available only from 10:00 a.m. to 4:30 p.m. But he did request that the White House staff treat Howe with respect and courtesy no matter what he asked for over the telephone.[9]

Now who would replace the wizened little former newsman, the genius who had been at Roosevelt's side for more than two decades and who had been the architect of the president's political career? The newspapers began speculating. No one could fill Howe's shoes as the president's closest confidant, the *Washington Star* concluded. That certainly was true. But the *Washington Times* called Early "the man of the hour," the one person in the White House upon whom Roosevelt relied to handle sensitive information, just as he once had with Howe.[10]

Now, for the first time, Louis Howe would not be the point man for a Roosevelt campaign, and according to the *New York Times*, Roosevelt was "at the lowest point of his political force since he entered the White House," and his entering the campaign for reelection was not a sure thing. Even before Howe died, Early had been unofficially acting as Roosevelt's liaison with campaign headquarters in New York City in addition to fulfilling his press secretary duties. One fallout of this dual role was that Early was publicly criticized by the cantankerous Drew Pearson, the *Washington Herald*'s syndicated political gossip columnist, who in February wrote that Early was leaving many of his press contacts "to a corps of snippy young stenographers with the result that White House press relations have suffered."[11]

It was Early who had made the White House and its chief occupant accessible to the press and had changed the atmosphere, in Early's own words, to one in which the correspondents would be "welcomed, as gentlemen, not suspected as spies." Early himself was available day or night to the press; he anticipated their questions, and if he didn't know the answer, he quickly sought out the appropriate official and got the information. It was no wonder they were complaining about his absences.[12]

Early now was forced to serve both masters: the president and the press. Although he did manage to sneak away for a few days of rest with his family that summer, his days were "hectic and tiresome." By September he was writing in his diary that his weeks were "strenuous and nerve wracking."[13]

Early told his friend Joe Davies that because Roosevelt expected to be away from Washington frequently that summer and, with Early's own trips to New York, "[a]ll of this means that, except for the striped uniform, the ball and chain and number, it makes me a prisoner by duty. I hope to get a pardon in November. There seems to be no possibility of a parole at this time." Early was telling Davies that he hoped to be able to leave his White House job after the election that fall.[14]

And it seemed the headaches were coming from all directions. Even the small ones caused him a degree of frustration, like the March afternoon when Early was working in his office and a police captain walked in to tell him that the president's car was caught in a traffic jam in Rosslyn, just over the Potomac in Virginia. Apparently when Roosevelt had left the White House earlier in the afternoon, he said he planned to stay on the Washington side of the river to inspect recent flood damage, but for some reason he had changed his mind and crossed over the Memorial Bridge, expecting to return by the Key Bridge. Then he was stranded in traffic. The police eventually extricated him from the jam, and Early wrote in his diary that he met the president as his car drove up to the gate at the west entrance of the White House, near his office. While still sitting in the car, Roosevelt stopped long enough to sign a bill and then headed out again to continue his inspection.[15]

In early June Roosevelt, accompanied by Early, left Washington by train on what ostensibly was a series of presidential visits in Arkansas, Texas, and Indiana. In reality, any foray outside the capital by a president during an election year is suspect: Is he campaigning or simply fulfilling his duties as the chief executive? Early detailed his preparations for that trip in his diary: "Mac [MacIntyre] and I went over to the White House to see the President and he gave me several speeches which he intends to make on the trip to Texas. After returning to my office, I saw the press and then proceeded to revise and go over these drafts. Spent most of the day at this; getting the President's final approval; stenciling and mimeographing. Made arrangements to have them put up in packages of 100 to take along on the trip to be given out just prior to their delivery. Stayed until late in the evening, cleaning my desk or paper work and leaving last minute instructions to be carried out in my absence."[16]

Later that month, to no one's surprise, Roosevelt was renominated by acclamation at the Democratic Convention in Philadelphia.

His Republican opponent would be Alfred M. Landon, the governor of Kansas. From then on, Early claimed that any trips the president undertook were for the reason of fulfilling his duties as chief executive, that Roosevelt was "not campaigning." In fact, Early made a point of telling reporters that the president would not be endorsing local candidates. Newspapers published editorials denouncing that stance. And by August reporters were wondering if indeed there even was a political campaign in progress. One evening that month, on the pretext of visiting a friend in the hospital, Roosevelt drove out to the Maryland country home of Sumner Welles, assistant secretary of state, to give a pep talk to Maryland Democrats, and the next day, Early told the press, "The President said it was a social call, and I'm going to stick to that."[17]

In his unpublished dissertation on Early and the media, Steven E. Schoenherr concludes, "To a large degree Roosevelt's campaigns were personal crusades, in which he viewed himself as a leader of the people, not of the Democratic Party. As the personal representative of the President, Early's role in these campaigns was a broad and difficult one."[18]

All in all, the summer of 1936 was one long headache for Early, with Roosevelt insisting he was not campaigning and Early's frequent trips to Democratic Headquarters in New York and occasional visits to Hyde Park when the president was in residence there. With no Howe to offer his sage counsel, the press secretary was on his own to deal with a host of charges by the media: Roosevelt was quietly accepting support from "alien organizations," interpreted by the public to mean Communists, a charge Early said was "conceived in malice and born of political spite"; and there were the innuendos about the president's health. "Is Roosevelt a Well Man Today?" ran one magazine headline in late July.

An odd rumor that persisted during the campaign was that Roosevelt was forcing the government to pay his mother, Sara Delano Roosevelt, between $17,000 and $100,000 a year, depending on who was spreading the rumor, for the use of her home at Hyde Park as a summer White House. It was untrue. Until her death in 1941, Sara Roosevelt owned the house, and there is no evidence to show that the government paid her rent.[19]

Another rumor that dogged Roosevelt for years regarded his alleged

Jewish ancestry, and this time it found its way to Early's desk via a letter from Philip Slomovitz, editor of the *Detroit Jewish Chronicle*. Slomovitz wrote that a former governor of Michigan had written an article for a local publication referring to the "Jewish origin" of the president. The writer theorized that Roosevelt was a descendant of the Rossacampo family, which had been expelled from Spain in 1620; fled to Germany, Holland, and other countries; and changed their name to Rosenberg, Rosenblum, and Rosenvelt. Slomovitz said it was not the first time he had seen Roosevelt's name "coupled with the Jews." Although he said he doubted whether the Jewish community "may hope to feel so deeply honored with the truth of your lineage," he did ask that someday the president would find the occasion to comment on the rumor.[20]

Roosevelt replied to Slomovitz explaining that he did not know the early geneology of his family: "All I know about the origin of the Roosevelt family in this country is that all branches bearing the name are apparently descended from Claes Martenssen Van Roosevelt, who came from Holland sometime before 1648—even the year is uncertain. Where he came from in Holland I do not know, nor do I know who his parents were."

He ended by telling the Jewish editor, "In the dim distant past they may have been Jews or Catholics or Protestants. What I am more interested in is whether they were good citizens and believers in God. I hope they were both."[21]

That ended the discussion, and, as far as the curators of the Roosevelt Library in Hyde Park know, that was the president's only public statement on the issue, although rumors continued to surface, perhaps in part because some of Roosevelt's closest advisers throughout his presidency were Jewish: Henry Morgenthau, secretary of the treasury; Felix Frankfurter, a Harvard Law School professor, then a Supreme Court justice; Bernard Baruch, a financier who served informally as an adviser; and Benjamin Cohen, a brilliant lawyer and adviser during the New Deal years.

Shortly after the election in November, Rep. Samuel Dickstein of New York wrote to Early telling him of the many "vicious documents" about Roosevelt that he had picked up during his own campaign. Dickstein said these documents, most of them hate mail by businessmen trying to discredit FDR's administration, were sent "by the millions" through the mail.[22]

Rumors aside, Early had bigger headaches as the campaign pro-gressed into the summer. And temporarily one of them was Eleanor Roosevelt. He and Mrs. Roosevelt had always maintained an amiable and even warmly cordial relationship in spite of some very obvious dif-ferences. Her support of Negro rights, her magazine columns and press conferences, and generally her outspoken views on myriad sub-jects did not always sit well with Early. For instance, when she held a garden party at the White House for mostly Negroes from a girls' reformatory school in the District of Columbia, Early was furious, but he said nothing to her, although he apparently made his views known to others, including the president. But in the summer of the 1936 cam-paign, a telegram from the White House staff, signed by Early, was sent to Mrs. Roosevelt on her fifty-second birthday. It said, "This is to assure a gracious lady who fills her days with good deeds on behalf of others that the home folk appreciate all of her kindness to them."[23]

While Steve was quietly pondering his future and considering leaving the administration after the election, Eleanor was deeply com-mitted to reelecting her husband and ensuring a continued life in the White House. By July 16 she was urging Early and the rest of the pres-ident's reelection team—Jim Farley; Charlie Michelson, a former news-paper reporter and the director of publicity for the Democratic National Committee since 1929; and Stanley High, who had been a radio publicist—to move more quickly to develop an effective reelec-tion organization. Her impression, she wrote in a memo to them, was that the women's group was "further along in their organization and more ready to go than any other unit as yet." She then put together a three-page typed memo full of questions and suggestions: Would Early and the rest of the committee, whose tasks would include radio, speeches, movies, pamphlets, fliers, news releases, and whatever other news needed to get to the public, immediately begin defining the duties of each member? Who was responsible for studying news reports and suggesting answers to charges, and who would oversee arrangements for the radio campaign? Who would handle the research, especially regarding information on the New Deal and its programs?

The memo was quite extensive, with a total of twelve highly detailed questions. She concluded by reminding them that reports were indicating "this is a close election and that we need very excel-lent organization."[24]

Early fired back a four-page typed and very frank reply almost immediately, attempting to detail the problems the Roosevelt campaign was facing. But he admitted, "I find myself in a position where it is impossible for me, at the present time, to give definite answers to the questions you ask." Why? The president was out of town, he replied, and "I have been tied by drouth [sic], inter-departmental squabbles, callers and telephoners to the office here ever since. It has not been possible to get away. However, I plan to return to New York and spend two days there this week."

He admitted that the Republicans were already well organized: "We knew all of this and yet it was decided, principally because of financial and other reasons known to you, to postpone our organization." The problem, it seemed, was quite simply lack of funds, and Early told Mrs. Roosevelt that he realized the campaign was "at a disadvantage." He also noted that during the day he had spent recently at Democratic Headquarters, he had witnessed "apparent confusion all over the place." He wasn't surprised, though, since almost all the employees were new, and no one knew who anyone else was or exactly what they were supposed to be doing.

To compound his headache, he told her that those who were running the campaign "are laboring without competent staffs and consequently are personally overloaded. Under the circumstances, in my opinion, those now on the job are doing surprisingly well." About the same time, Early told Harold Ickes that there were no campaign plans and no budget.[25]

One of the frustrations of the campaign's organization centered on Farley, who was less interested in the campaign issues—especially those of the New Deal—and more eager to play the dealmaker. His insistence that he make campaign speeches led him into hot water when he called Landon "governor of a typical prairie state." Not only had he violated Roosevelt's dictum that the campaign not mention Landon in any way, but Farley's bombastic remark was fodder for the Republicans, who reminded voters that Abraham Lincoln had come from a prairie state.[26]

But Farley wasn't the only headache at campaign headquarters. Michelson, the publicity director, apparently had wanted to handle publicity and other campaign activities in his own way, "to play a lone hand," Early told Mrs. Roosevelt. In fact, Early had doubted

Michelson's loyalty and had wanted him replaced. And while Early wanted to emphasize the positive accomplishments of Roosevelt's administration, Michelson wanted to go on the attack against the Republicans. So the president and Early talked with Michelson, and by now, apparently, he was willing to be a team player.[27]

That did not mean that Roosevelt and Early entirely trusted Michelson. One way they circumvented him was for Early, with the president's approval, to bring in outsiders such as Edward Rodden, a reporter who covered the White House for the International News Service and who moved to New York to do public relations work for the campaign. Stanley High also became an important player, working closely with the Good Neighbor League, which had been developed by Howe to pull in such groups as blacks and the clergy. While Early was less interested in the Negroes, in large part because of his own upbringing and background in the South, he was concerned that Roosevelt may have alienated the clergy with his lackadaisical approach to keeping the Sabbath, a day he often found more conducive to hosting picnics and baseball games when he was at Hyde Park. And, of course, his Fireside Chats often were on Sunday nights, which the clergy claimed contributed to a decline in attendance at evening church services.[28]

As for his own role, Early told Mrs. Roosevelt that unless he left Washington when Roosevelt was out of town and let McIntyre carry the burden in the White House, "certainly too heavy for one man to shoulder," he would continue to divide his time between Washington and New York. When the president was away, either Mac or Steve remained behind. "I have found by experience on many occasions, it is absolutely necessary for one secretary to be on the job. Otherwise the telegraph wires and radio facilities would be taxed to capacity, carrying problems and work to the President. There would be little rest for him."

He then told her that he hoped she would not interpret what he was saying as indicating an unwillingness on his part to do anything needed in the campaign. He said he would divide his time between New York if necessary, or remain solely in Washington, but "I do believe, however, that divided time and divided jobs do not give the best results." If he did go to New York and remain there until November, Early said, he would resign his job in the White House because, he explained, "it would provide the opposition with a legitimate criticism if men working in the New York headquarters regularly remain on the Government's payroll."

Even Ickes, who was a good friend and great supporter of Early, had to admit that Howe had supplied most of the political strategy that had resulted in the nomination and election of Roosevelt in 1932: "Howe was the only one who dared talk to him [Roosevelt] frankly and fearlessly."[29]

Actually, confusion and dissension on campaign personnel and tactics had surfaced as early as January that year. It seemed everyone close to Roosevelt had his own idea on how to proceed: discount or counteract speeches by the Republicans, or do nothing; come out fighting, or soft-pedal criticism by the opposition; let the president run a one-man show, or allow other high-placed Democrats in the administration to campaign.[30]

Not surprisingly, Jim Farley, who was on leave as postmaster general while working as campaign chairman, had a far less pessimistic view of the brouhaha. When he wrote his memoirs more than a decade later, he considered in hindsight that the reelection victory was due in part to "magnificent teamwork" and called the campaign "the campaign without a mistake."[31]

A week after Early sent his long response to Mrs. Roosevelt, he told the president he had spent three days at the headquarters, and he reported "a thousand percent improvement" from two weeks earlier. Any confusion that remained he attributed to the fact that most of the personnel were new.[32]

By August the *Washington Times* told readers that Early "is now recognized as the President's spokesman at Democratic headquarters . . . which gives the glamorous touch."

With Roosevelt away half the time, the *Times* said, "you will see Mr. Early constantly in the East, never with the President on the campaign trains. Instead he will be the man who stays at the White House to take care of the myriad details which are now keeping the wires hot; and in between time he will be in New York using his eyes and ears for the President's political use." When in Washington, telephone callers tried to reach the president, but instead they got Early.[33]

There was one big headache that plagued Early and Roosevelt throughout the campaign, and that was the press. In spite of Early's personal and professional newspaper and wire service connections and in spite of his and Roosevelt's courting of publishers, editors, and reporters with informal parties and with receptions at the White House for such organizations as the American Newspaper Publishers Association and the American Society of Newspaper Editors, outings at Hyde Park, and one-on-one meetings with various working journalists and newspaper owners, when reelection time rolled around garnering their support proved an uphill fight. It was not unexpected. Roosevelt and Early were aware that most publishers were conservatives, and as businessmen they found Roosevelt's policies anathema.[34]

In addition, Roosevelt's relationship with the White House press corps had been slowly eroding since those heady days of 1933, largely the result of his own actions during press conferences, when he would renege on statements or, worse, deny information he had earlier given to government officials. As long as the president supplied them with page one stories and "a good show," the reporters were willing to overlook the restrictions on "off-the-record" comments and his occasional lecturing of them on a headline or story he did not like. Roosevelt's reliance on charm to evade questions he did not feel like answering or worse for which he had no answer was wearing thin with the press corps, and on more than one occasion Roosevelt became so annoyed that he ordered Early to tell those reporters responsible for the annoyance that they were "cowards" or "cads." Early usually did not, understanding the importance of remaining on good terms with the reporters. But gradually the reporters perceived they were being given fewer big stories and more Rooseveltian showmanship, and attendance at the press conferences began dropping off. Each day there were new complaints from the White House reporters, making Early wonder if he should not simply resign.[35]

However, often the reporters got their real news stories from Early during his daily meetings with the press or through the reporters' contacts in other government agencies. For instance, Early noted in his diary on September 15 that Roosevelt asked him to tell newsmen what the president would be discussing later that day with representatives of insurance companies.[36]

In and of itself, this deterioration of interest in the president's press conferences did not mean they were not heavily attended by reporters hungrily in search of a story, nor did it mean that publishers were turning against Roosevelt in droves. Many never had liked him or what they saw as his anticapitalist programs, and throughout the campaign they did not hesitate to unleash their venom on the editorial pages of their newspapers. On the other hand, the White House reporters for many of the anti-Roosevelt newspapers continued to write neutral or positive stories about the president, in large part because of the successful rapport Early had with the reporters.

The Democrats' New York campaign office, under Michelson, was churning out pamphlets, bulletins, and news releases on behalf of the candidate, but newspapers published only 40 percent of what they printed during the 1932 campaign. However, they were using Early's press releases because these apparently tended to reach an editor's desk via legitimate wire service reports, while the Democrats' releases were mailed to the editors and appeared to them to be just what they were: political propaganda.[37]

Not all the newspapers were Roosevelt haters, but some of the most influential and powerful ones—and their publishers—were. One of those voices was that of the very conservative Col. Robert McCormick, whose *Chicago Daily Tribune* carried some of the most scurrilous and vituperative headlines and columns about Roosevelt even before the campaign, and certainly throughout it. After the Democratic convention in June, the newspaper went so far as to inform its readers that it would attempt impartiality, but that lasted about as long as it took the ink on the page to dry. From September 1 until Election Day, the newspaper ran a box on page one that counted down the number of days that remained for voters "to save your country." Then it asked, "What are you doing to save it?" Certainly, the *Tribune* hoped, the answer wouldn't be "Voting for Roosevelt." The newspaper's telephone operators were told to answer incoming calls with "Good Morning" or "Good Afternoon" and then give the caller the daily countdown.[38]

The day after the president's October 14 campaign visit to Chicago, the *Tribune* published a photo of a ragpicker gathering Roosevelt campaign buttons that littered the street. The caption speculated that the buttons had been dropped by people along the parade route because they did not want them. The *Tribune*'s competition, the *Daily Times*, did a little investigating and learned from the ragpicker that he had been paid to pose by the buttons, which a *Tribune* photographer had tossed around the street.[39]

The *Tribune* not only told its readers that, if reelected, Roosevelt planned to place around the neck of each American worker a dog tag bearing the worker's Social Security number, it insisted that the president was the preferred candidate of Communists, Jews, and Catholics. One headline read: "MOSCOW ORDERS REDS IN U.S. TO BACK ROOSEVELT."[40]

Roosevelt's other major media nemesis was William Randolph Hearst, who owned a vast empire of big-city newspapers, magazines, and radio stations. A friend of sorts of the president during his first years in office, Hearst stayed in the White House when he came to visit FDR in October 1934. But Hearst gradually became disenchanted with what he saw as the New Deal's relentless hammering away at the nation's big businessmen, an act he considered "a bastard product of Communism."[41]

As early as the summer of 1935, Edmund B. Coblentz, Hearst's *New York American* newspaper editor, was instructed by his boss to send a memo to other Hearst editors and wire service bureaus: "The chief instructs that the phrase 'soak the successful' be used in all reference to the administration's tax program instead of the phrase 'soak the thrifty' hitherto used; also he wants the words 'raw deal' used instead of 'new deal.'" The White House retaliated with a statement that "a minority of editors or owners . . . engage in what is known as the deliberate coloring of so-called news stories."[42]

As the election of 1936 approached, Hearst decided he considered Roosevelt "dangerous," and his newspapers were not shy about informing their readers that the president was being backed by Moscow. Headlines linked Roosevelt to the Soviet Communist Party as well as the American Communist Party. One headline said simply, "THE ENEMIES OF AMERICA WANT ROOSEVELT."

The fact that Roosevelt had been the first president to resume diplomatic relations with the USSR must have made some readers wonder if there was indeed any truth in such headlines. Other influential newspapers that opposed Roosevelt's reelection included the *New York Herald-Tribune*, the *New York Sun*, the *Detroit Free Press*, the *Los Angeles Times*, and the large and influential Midwestern Scripps-Howard chain. Other very respectable newspapers, such as the *St. Louis Post-Dispatch*, the *Washington Post*, and the *Kansas City Star*, also opposed Roosevelt, but they chose to stick to the issues and cover the campaign fairly objectively.

That the press was anti-Roosevelt is more than mere allegation. It can be shown through the statistics: More than 80 of the 150 daily newspapers with circulations over fifty thousand gave Landon their endorsement, 55 supported Roosevelt, and 15 remained neutral, more or less, since some of them backed Landon without officially endorsing him. And the larger the newspaper, the more likely it was to support the Republican candidate. The campaign fared better with the newsreels and radio, over which Early had more control, where Roosevelt continued to be a dominating force.[43]

Because Roosevelt continued whenever possible to claim he was not a candidate but rather a president speaking in his official capacity, he could have free radio airtime—and he needed it since the Democratic campaign coffers lacked the sustenance of the Republicans'. In the 1932 campaign, the networks each donated three free hours of airtime each week for political broadcasts. By 1936 the Federal Communications Commission (FCC) required candidates to buy airtime. For instance, a candidate was forced to spend a minimum of $5,208 for fifteen minutes during the evening on CBS, and one hour over a coast-to-coast hookup of some two hundred stations could cost $52,000.[44]

That fall, at the height of the campaign, when Early scheduled a Fireside Chat—always broadcast free because it was the president at the microphone—two Los Angeles radio stations said the Democrats should pay for the airtime because of the FCC rule requiring political parties to pay for candidates to speak on air. Early turned to the FCC and was told the stations were within their legal rights. An angry Early said, "As far as I am able to ascertain, these are the only two, of all the stations in the United States, that refused to carry the President's 'fireside' chat." He then told Michelson to bypass the two stations, both owned by the same person, whenever handing out paid advertising during the campaign.[45]

Early also was able to rein in the movie men when they came knocking at the White House for footage of the president. In early October he allowed them to film an informal Roosevelt and his family at Hyde Park, but he then required them to sign an agreement that they would not release any of the films until October 23, no doubt a clever ploy to ensure that the films were shown as close as possible to election day.

His oversight of the wire service and newspaper photographers was just as controlled. On October 6 he wrote in his diary, "Put out notice that still pictures could be made at 11:00 this morning when the President received Commander Bernard W. Kerney of the Veterans of Foreign Wars." Schoenherr, in his dissertation, noted that because Early was "well aware that editors used only a small portion of the photographs actually shot, he insured that all of the stills and motion pictures of Roosevelt showed the President at his best." Early also understood that the high quality and broad distribution of the photography of newsreels and wire services assured the Democrats of the publicity that the campaign budget simply could not pay for. As Election Day neared, Early's diary entries became more terse. "Nerves unsteady," he confided on October 20.[46]

Roosevelt may have remained confident, but the results of a poll published by the *Literary Digest* in October could not have helped steady Early's nerves. It showed Landon defeating Roosevelt by about 1.3 million to just under 1 million. The magazine claimed its poll represented "the most extensive straw ballot in the field," and in its twenty-five years of polling, the results had always been correct.[47]

The weekend before the election, the president and many of the White House staff left for Hyde Park. They assumed this would be the last election. In fact, Missy LeHand, Roosevelt's personal secretary, said she almost cried as the entourage left the White House. She thought it seemed as if they were leaving for good. They even speculated about Roosevelt's life after the presidency. His staff thought he should retire to be "Squire of Hyde Park."

Early headed to Democratic headquarters in New York that Monday to make final preparations for election results to be transmitted to Hyde Park. He asked the three big wire services to install printers in the smoking room off the dining room at the president's home. He wanted the printers as opposed to telegraph wires with operators "to keep the number of people about the President that evening down to an absolute minimum." Roosevelt requested a telegraph wire and a private telephone line to connect the Hyde Park house to the New York headquarters.

Election night saw the president sitting in his dining room checking and double-checking election returns as they came in. Early told journalist Raymond Clapper that Roosevelt spent the night working over the figures, but rather impersonally, not as though he were the one involved.[48]

When the votes were tallied, Roosevelt had defeated Landon with 523 electoral votes to his opponent's 8, carrying every state except Maine and Vermont. And both the House and the Senate would be about 80 percent Democratic. Newspapers may have waged a fierce war, but the victory was Roosevelt's. After it was all over, the *New Republic* called the campaign "one of the most slanderous campaigns in the entire history of American journalism."[49]

Early told Clapper, "Roosevelt elected himself." As for the overwhelming majority of Democrats in Congress, Early was less enthusiastic. He said the president did not want such a large majority "because the job is going to be vetoing." It was "crackpots who rode in" with Roosevelt who would "try to shove through bad stuff," Early said. The president feared "the left getting out of hand rather than the rightist opposition."

Early told Clapper that this blisteringly hectic campaign was his last. He was in debt and needed money, but he would stay another year.[50]

When he wrote to his friend Joseph Davies in August, Early described his White House years as "long and difficult." He said, "I must continue to serve for the remainder of the first term. There are less than three months to go. Then I must go and none of those who obtained their freedom at the hands of Abraham Lincoln could have welcomed their emancipation with more happiness and joy than will I give vent to in November." He went on, "So until November— and until I find a place to go from here—I shall move along in accordance with orders—just hoping that my good conduct will gain me a new freedom and assurance that the wife and children may face the future without fear."[51]

When the election was over, the newspapers again speculated about Early's role. Would he leave the White House, perhaps to return to Paramount or to take a job with a New York public relations firm?

Newspaper columns pasted in Early's scrapbook in late 1936 and 1937 tell of the media's fascination with the press secretary's future. One writer suggested that Early remained with Roosevelt because he placed "loyalty above personal desire." Another told readers that Early had been offered a job with Carl Byoir & Associates, a New York public relations firm that had done work for the Democratic National Committee, but that Early would stay in Washington probably until 1940. The same journalist wrote, "His tie of loyalty keeps him at his desk. But a family and a graying thatch are reminders of his economic needs. Otherwise it is doubtful if he would ever change bosses."

The *Washington Herald* reported that Early had told friends that he would like to begin new work as soon as the president would release him. A *Chicago Tribune* headline read: "Stephen Early, Aide to President, May Leave White House." A *New York Times* headline on Wednesday, November 18, 1937, said: "Early's Resignation Rumored in Capital." That day's speculation? He would take a job with Paramount Pictures effective January 1. The *Times* story concluded: "It is said that Mr. Early's loyalty to the President is such that if the latter urgently requested him to stay he would do so regardless of what other situation was offered him."[52]

In the end, he stayed. But it proved to be a decision fraught with frustration.

11

COURT PACKING AND OTHER PROBLEMS

I n the early afternoon of January 6, 1937, a confident—perhaps even cocky—Franklin Roosevelt, his son Jimmy, Steve Early, and Marvin McIntyre, all clad in silk top hats, rode in the back of a black open car to the Capitol. Leaning on the arm of his son, the president entered the House of Representatives to an enthusiastic reception. Then he delivered his annual State of the Union address to the joint session of Congress amid cheers from the members as well as spectators seated in the gallery.[1]

Essentially it was a message aimed at the Supreme Court, even though its members had chosen not to attend, maybe having been tipped off earlier about what the president planned to say. He chastised the Court for declaring unconstitutional portions of his New Deal program during his first term. He believed, probably rightly so, that the Court had every intention of continuing to obliterate portions of the reforms, many enacted by Congress. Harold Ickes, the secretary of the interior, thought this was perhaps the first time since Andrew Jackson that a president had publicly taken issue with the Court, and he concluded that the country was on the eve of an era where the powers of the Court might begin to be more strictly limited.[2]

When the group returned to the White House, McIntyre, always in a party mood, persuaded the president to "convene" the usual cronies for a poker game in his office to celebrate the event. So out came the poker table, and over "liquid refreshments," caviar, and cheese, Roosevelt, McIntyre, Early, Henry Morgenthau, Ickes, Harry Hopkins, Pa Watson, and Jimmy Roosevelt played "a friendly game of poker," with the president keeping track of wins and losses with a sheet balanced to the penny. Hopkins was the big winner, followed by Watson and, in what proved to be one of his few wins that year, the president. Everyone else lost, with Ickes reporting that he was out $8.75. (The balance sheet for this impromptu game today resides in one of Early's scrapbooks at the FDR Library.)[3]

Less than a week later, Early was hard at work preparing for the press a statement on the proposed reorganization of the federal government, a five-point plan put together by the President's Committee on Administrative Management, also known as the Brownlow Committee, after its chairman, a journalist and public administrator. Its goals were to give the president six high-grade executive assistants to help him deal with the various departments and agencies of government; consolidate the more than one hundred separate departments, boards, agencies, and commissions in the executive branch into twelve departments (the Department of the Interior would be renamed the Department of Conservation); overhaul an ineffective civil service system; place the Treasury Department's Budget Bureau, an opponent of New Deal monetary spending, under the control of the president; and strengthen the budget, research, and planning services of the government to allow them to become effective managerial arms for the president. On the surface, the plan appeared to be an economic measure to improve the efficiency of a federal government that had gradually been growing unwieldy. In fact, it was a device for expanding the president's control over the bureaucracies of government.[4]

When Early arrived the morning of the day the plan was released, one of Roosevelt's secretaries, Grace Tully, was waiting for him in his office with a draft of the message to Congress. She asked him to read it over, suggest any changes, and then return it to the Boss for final approval when Early went to Roosevelt's bedroom later that morning for his daily meeting. So Early spent the better part of the morning checking and double-checking each page of the message. At 12:25 p.m. the message went to the Capitol and was distributed to the reporters.[5]

One reporter called it a "breath-taking," almost revolutionary, plan for modernizing the Executive Branch. But much of it did not make members of Congress happy, not even those in the president's own party. Consolidating government agencies, they believed, would curtail some of their own power. Their real fear, however, was that a Roosevelt fresh from his November victory was becoming the dictator that some Republican newspapers had for several years been claiming he was.[6]

No matter: congressional and press reaction did not dampen Roosevelt's high spirits as he prepared for his second inauguration. On Thursday, January 14, two days after he released his reorganization plan, Roosevelt, who loved a practical joke, was kidding around with his friend Adm. Cary Grayson, who as chairman of the inaugural ceremonies extended the official invitation requesting the president's attendance and participation. It was meant as a souvenir, but Roosevelt decided to make a pencil notation on it asking that his social secretary send regrets "because of the rush of official business." Later, in a jesting mood, he wrote at the bottom of the beautifully engraved "regrets" card: "I have rearranged my engagements and work and *think* I may be able to go. Will know definitely Jan. 19th. FDR." Early called in the photographers and told them they could make a picture of the "invitation regretted." Later he and Grayson "had a good laugh" over the president's little joke.[7]

Finally inauguration day arrived, and, of course, Franklin D. Roosevelt found time to attend. "We were confronted with a chilling downpour of rain that sluiced down in torrents during the entire Inaugural ceremonies," Early wrote. It was the first inauguration on the new date, January 20, but it really didn't matter. It was still the middle of the winter, and if it had not been rain it would have been snow. Under the Twenty-first Amendment, approved in 1933, the inauguration was moved to January to reduce the time between the election of Congress and the president and the beginning of their terms.[8]

As he had four years earlier, the president, accompanied by Eleanor and other family members—and this time Early and McIntyre—attended church services before heading through the steady rain to the Capitol, where the president would take his second oath of office and give his inaugural address, an event that saw thousands of chilled citizens standing for hours in the driving rain just to see and hear the president of the United States.[9]

Early was pleased to report that the White House denizens had survived the inauguration "without a sniffle." He had been felled by the flu over the previous holidays, leaving him "a little weak in the legs," and Roosevelt, who was susceptible to upper respiratory infections, had recently recovered from a nasty head cold that had kept him confined to his bed for a few days.[10]

Early thought the most dramatic moment of that rain-soaked ceremony was when Chief Justice Charles Evans Hughes administered the oath of office. He stood facing the president and asked him "with steadily mounting emphasis" whether he would "preserve, protect and defend the Constitution of the United States." And, Early said, "[w]ith equal emphasis and with his voice rising in volume as he spoke, the President replied that he would 'defend the Constitution of the United States, so help me God.'" Early decided the scene was even more significant in light of Roosevelt's State of the Union Address two weeks earlier.[11]

The presidential party, including Helen and Steve Early, returned to the White House for a lunch before the president and Vice President Garner reviewed the inaugural parade again in the soaking rain, since Roosevelt had instructed the engineers to remove the bullet-proof glass from around the alcove where they stood. A reception and tea for three thousand guests followed, with the president and first lady "facing the ordeal of greeting" their guests.[12]

After what Early called "a very strenuous but exciting day," he telephoned Roosevelt from his home about 9:30 that evening to advise him of the press reaction to the inaugural address. "I was able to give him a favorable report," he wrote. He asked Roosevelt if he would like to hear himself deliver the address, and when Roosevelt said he would, Early told him to turn on his radio in about ten minutes. Radio companies had recorded the ceremonies and were rebroadcasting them. Roosevelt said he had eaten a nice family dinner and everyone had finally left him alone. "You can't guess what I'm doing," he asked Early.

"Playing with your stamps," Early replied. (Stamp collecting was one of FDR's prime hobbies, begun when he was a boy.)

"That's right," Roosevelt said, laughing. "Rather a nice contrast to the Inaugural evening four years ago." The reference, of course, was to the financial panic. Early recalled, "I saw the ghost of ole Will Woodin (the secretary of the treasury); I saw the expressions of concern as they were written on the face of the President's other financial advisers that evening of March 4, 1933. And I decided it was a rather nice contrast. He had brought about such changed conditions that he could sit here alone Wednesday evening, with nothing more to worry about than toy with his stamp collection. Thus a very historic day ended."[13]

But the euphoria would be short lived. When he took his second oath of office, Franklin Roosevelt had the country by its proverbial tail. He was riding high. He had been elected by 60 percent of the popular vote, a landslide that he believed validated his New Deal reforms. Then he made a tactical error.

On February 5 the president's press conference was unusually large, reporters having been tipped off that something important was on the agenda. Early had stayed at the White House until one that morning working on what was to be another of Roosevelt's messages to Congress, the details of it being "held in the strictest confidence." Early had learned of the contents of the message only a few days earlier. With a few hours of sleep under his belt, Early was back in his office at 7:00 a.m., and Roosevelt informed him that he planned to have a cabinet meeting at 10:00, just before he held a special late-morning press conference. Usually he met with reporters on Tuesdays and Fridays.[14]

What Roosevelt sent to Congress that day was a proposal that would reorganize the Supreme Court and the lower federal courts. Ostensibly Roosevelt's intent was to enhance the efficiency of the court system, which he felt had too few judges for the volume of cases it must handle. To corroborate this, he had Attorney General Homer Cummings, the only member of his cabinet to whom Roosevelt had confided his proposal, compile statistical tables to prove his contention. The tables were attached to the message to Congress. What the president really was aiming for was a way to increase the membership on the Supreme Court, thus allowing him to appoint up to six new justices—enough to ensure survival of what remained of the New Deal as well as future programs. It was a plan, Early said, that he had begun work on almost immediately after the election, and he told Raymond Clapper that in all only five people knew of the plan before it was announced. He refused to divulge the names but did note that none were members of Congress. He said Roosevelt feared a leak that would lead to "a hostile buildup before the plan got out."[15]

Once the message had been delivered to Congress, Ickes concluded, "There will be reverberations for days and weeks to come." He was correct. Early noted in his diary that by the end of the day the president had "received a great number of telegrams endorsing his proposal." But as time went on, it was apparent not everyone was pleased with the plan.[16]

One of Roosevelt's biographers, Kenneth S. Davis, believes that the president's victory the previous fall "was now corrupted by a heady sense of limitless power." He was convinced that the overwhelming vote was a popular mandate, perhaps even "divine," to proceed with the New Deal, and if ensuring its continuation and its ultimate success meant tampering with the sanctity of one of the three branches of the federal government, so be it.[17]

"The fight is on," Early told Joe Davies, a fight he predicted would be "the greatest fight of [Roosevelt's] career." Party lines had failed to hold because of the widespread opposition to the court plan, which the newspapers had almost immediately dubbed "court packing."

Even the defection of some of his own party members did not deter Roosevelt's determination to see his plan enacted by Congress; in fact, it seemed to energize him. "Our Commander-in-Chief loves a fight. I have never seen him happier than he is now. He is extremely confident of the final outcome," Early told Davies, who now was in Moscow as ambassador to the Soviet Union.[18]

On February 18 Early told Davies that "definite progress is being made." He and Roosevelt were convinced the House would pass the bill Roosevelt wanted. "There is no doubt about that," Early wrote. He predicted it would not be a fight easily won when it went before the Senate, where he saw a "prolonged discussion." The progressive bloc there already was divided, and some of the Democratic senators who previously had supported New Deal legislation "have pitched their tents with the opposition forces." In fact, Early thought that in some respects, the situation revived memories of the League of Nations controversy. "But, when the final roll is called, the President will have the votes," he believed.[19]

Throughout the spring and summer, he turned to Davies and a few close friends to explain his feelings on the highly charged Court plan. He told Davies, "The issue is not whether there are nine or fifteen members of the Supreme Court. Stripped of its embroidery, the issue is whether the President and his New Deal, moving forward step in step with the legislative branch of the government, is able within the Constitution to rid itself of the veto power previously exercised by a judicial oligarchy of five or six judges. In other words, shall the government be able, if it chooses, to set up substitutes for the A.A.A., future relief of agriculture, or, in the light of experience gained by the N.R.A., be able to assist legitimate business and rout the chiseler?" By late May Early was telling Clapper that he wanted Roosevelt to drop the Court plan.[20]

If he really felt that way, Early was forced to keep his counsel to himself, since Roosevelt remained optimistic that Congress would see fit to approve his plan. For a while, it appeared that his optimism might be rewarded. Many members of the Democratic-controlled Congress were unhappy that the Supreme Court seemed to be carefully dismantling the very New Deal measures they had considered and passed. Thus, they were willing to consider the need to expand the Court's membership, giving Roosevelt an opportunity to make his own appointments—with Senate approval—and quite possibly preserve the remainder of the New Deal.

Then later that spring, the Court unexpectedly upheld the validity of the Social Security Law and the Wagner Act, which established the National Labor Relations Board, and then Justice Willis Van Devanter retired, thus taking some of the steam out of Roosevelt's Court reform plan. Roosevelt eventually decided it would be politically prudent, if he wanted any reform at all, to accept a modified plan whereby he would be allowed to appoint an additional justice at the rate of one every year for each Supreme Court justice over the age of seventy. Within the next three years, he could appoint three. The compromise went to the Senate floor, where it had a fighting chance of passing. But on July 6 Joseph Robinson, the Senate majority leader, who was leading the fight for the bill, died suddenly of a heart attack. That very day, no doubt before he had heard of the senator's untimely death, Early told Davies, "Unless I am sadly mistaken, I expect to see the Boss prove his mastery again." Two weeks later the bill was sent to committee, where it died, a major defeat for the president.[21]

Ickes wrote that by this time, it was evident Roosevelt was "tired and nervous," the events of the previous months having taken their toll on him. On July 20 Ickes was having lunch with the president at the White House when Early came in to explain that the United Press wire service had garbled something Roosevelt had said about the Court situation. Ickes said the president "was quite put out and made no endeavor to conceal it." He then told Early that no statement should have gone out from the White House. "Poor Steve had to take it on the chin," Ickes wrote.[22]

At the end of July, Early told Davies that Roosevelt had accepted "at least temporarily" the apparent loss of his controversial plan "without showing so much as a frown of displeasure, without even the most petty sign of annoyance and with his usual good grace, and in accordance with his high standards of sportsmanship."

Early explained why. "Back in the dark days of '33 he said he did not expect to make a home run every time he came to bat. As an observer of things close on the inside, it seems to me that he has accepted the Senate's decision in the sense of that old statement."[23]

All in all, it had not been an easy fight. Political fires had to be extinguished, or at least brought under control; rumors needed to be squelched—like the one in early May that Steve had to deal with. It had Roosevelt lying on his desk, face down, in a coma, and claiming he had "a rash on the back of his neck," implying syphilis, both of which led him, so the rumors went on, to be hustled off to the Gulf of Mexico on an alleged fishing trip and put aboard a navy vessel where he was surrounded by guards who kept reporters at bay, thus making verification of the president's health impossible. None of it was true. What was true was that after the Court had handed down the Wagner Law decision, Roosevelt felt he needed a vacation, so at the end of April he left Washington, quite healthy, for a two-week fishing trip in the gulf, although when he met with reporters on the train to Texas, he told them the trip was not about fishing: "I don't give a continental damn whether I catch a fish or not. The chief objective is to get a perspective on the scene which I cannot get in Washington any more than you boys can." Early stayed behind in Washington writing letters to editors and publishers in the McClure's Syndicate who had seen fit to publish the obviously unsubstantiated rumors.[24]

Out of the brouhaha over the plan to expand the makeup of the Supreme Court came a change in the way reporters could attribute news to the president. It arose out of a press conference at which Roosevelt was asked for a comment on the status of the court plan. He said he had none but would discuss background off the record, which he then proceeded to do for half an hour. Uncertain how to label the remarks, some reporters used variations of the "White House spokesman" for attribution. But it proved clumsy and confusing to readers, so, at Early's suggestion, at his next press conference, Roosevelt told the reporters that when he spoke for background purposes, they could attribute the information to him, but without quotation marks so that it appeared as if he were speaking offhand and could not be held to an exact phraseology.[25]

Whether or not it had anything to do with the court-packing problems, it was at about this time that electric push buttons were installed on the mahogany desks of Early, McIntyre, Jimmy Roosevelt, and Missy LeHand. They were connected to the desk of the White House police in the lobby of the executive office. It is not clear who made the decision to use the buttons, but someone—probably not Early—decided that the press secretary especially needed this extra precaution in the event the press became unruly during one of his meetings with reporters. In addition, Early's door was equipped with an electric switch that made it impossible for anyone to barge in uninvited. To enter his office, he would push a hidden button near the door. The irony was that the press got onto the story of the new push buttons and reported on it, complete with the information about the "hidden" button.[26]

The Court fight consumed most of Early's energies at the White House during the first half of the year, although he did manage to get in his regular golf games at Burning Tree, often with Jimmy Roosevelt, and when Joe Davies returned for a few weeks in April, the two resumed to their habit of lunch and golf whenever Steve could get away. He also managed to slip out of town for golf with friends in Florida for a week in March while Roosevelt was in Warm Springs, Georgia, where he could relax in the warm waters that soothed his crippled legs. White House associates often accompanied him so he could tend to affairs of state.[27]

In June Steve accompanied Eleanor and Franklin to Wilmington, Delaware, for the wedding of Franklin Jr. and Ethel du Pont, daughter of Pierre S. du Pont, a rabid Roosevelt/New Deal hater. It was one of the most publicized weddings of the century, generating not only stories about the prominence of the bride and bridegroom but critical articles about the money spent on the wedding by the bride's family. Roosevelt himself seemed to get a kick out of the coupling of the two families. Early was left to explain to the press that "Franklin Junior was only the bridegroom," implying that it was not his family that had opened its bank accounts to pay for the occasion.[28]

That month he also found himself handling rumors about why Vice President John Nance Garner had suddenly left Washington for his home in Texas at the height of Roosevelt's fight with Congress over his Court plan. It was a national story, and headlines gave a number of reasons. The *Los Angeles Times* headline was "Roosevelt and Garner Rift Reported"; the *Nashville Banner*'s story led with "Texan Seen as Avoiding Court Fight"; the *Indianapolis Star* wrote "Jack Garner's Fishing Trip Really Walkout on New Deal, Insiders Say"; and the *Philadelphia Bulletin* told readers "Garner's Walk Mystifies."

Early's official explanation to the press was that Mrs. Garner's health demanded that the couple leave the capital. However, he told Raymond Clapper that the real reason Garner left was that he "was cracking up." His wife "was in tears about it" and decided she had to take him back to Texas. Early said that at a recent cabinet meeting, Garner brought up the relief program, saying that New York was not contributing enough of its share. The president had Harry Hopkins get the figures. At the next cabinet meeting, Garner brought up the same issue, and again Roosevelt pulled the figures for New York. Garner said, "All right, boss. You're right." Then five minutes later he brought up the matter again as if it had never been mentioned. Early said Mrs. Garner was "taking the rap to cover up for Jack." According to Harold Ickes, Garner was reputed to be "a heavy and constant drinker."[29]

Twice on one day in August, Early managed to extricate himself from potential credibility snafus. On August 12, a Thursday, he arrived at his office, ready to hold his daily press conference—unaware that the president had just sent to the Senate the nominee to replace Justice Van Devanter. So Early proceeded to tell the reporters that Roosevelt was at the moment contemplating about sixty or seventy names of possible successors, adding that an appointment was unlikely anytime soon. Just before noon, he called the reporters back to his office and started to hand them mimeographs of the long list of names under consideration. Just then a call came. "See FDR immediately." He soon returned breathless and told the reporters, "Get your

offices on the wire and tell them a nomination was being made."
However, he said, he could not release the name. That name, Sen.
Hugo L. Black of Alabama, was made public by the Senate later in the
day, when it received the nomination. Roosevelt had chosen not to
inform any of his staff—even his closest confidants in the White
House—of his decision, and Early was left with egg on his face before
the White House press corps, which promptly turned it into a news
story. (Black was confirmed by the Senate, but shortly afterward, a
brief public controversy erupted over his membership in the Ku Klux
Klan for two years in the 1920s.)[30]

Unfortunately for Early his day did not get better. After he had
lunch with Pa Watson at Becks, one of their favorite restaurants, Early
returned to his office to discover there existed a phonographic
recording of a telephone conversation implicating him in a scandal
involving a low-level operative from Democratic National Committee
named Myles Lasker and a New York oilman named J. Edward Jones,
who was under indictment on charges brought by the Securities and
Exchange Commission. It seems the committee employee told Jones
he could help him get the charges dismissed. He supposedly said he
would go to Washington and talk with Early, and Early "would go the
way I want him to." The recording was damaging enough, but it had
been entered into evidence before the House Rules Committee.

A steamed Steve Early immediately issued a statement: "Luckily
for him, Mr. Lasker never came to see me on behalf of J. Edward
Jones. In all my life it has never before been my fate to be mentioned
in an obviously libelous and scandalous effort to sell my name." And
because Lasker had implicated Eleanor Roosevelt in his conversation
by claiming to be her agent for her radio addresses, Early was forced
to call her in Hyde Park to inform her and then release a statement on
her behalf noting that Lasker had represented her for only a brief time
before she dismissed him. Early ended his diary that day with this: "I
waited for the President to go for a swim at 6:00 and left for home."[31]

By September 1 Early, who was still hoping to leave for another
job, told Joe Davies, "Congress has gone; the President is at Hyde
Park; so is Mac [McIntyre]; Jimmy is at Rye Beach in Massachusetts,
and I am sitting on the lid here in Washington. This business of running a clearinghouse single-handed, presuming to act on as many
things as possible so as to save worry and trouble for others and

deciding what should be forwarded to them for consideration, keeps a fellow close to the job every hour around the clock and permits little diversion."

In fact, Roosevelt was away from the White House, sailing or visiting members of his family in other parts of the country, for most of the month. In spite of that, Early did get in the occasional game of golf, and he told Davies he planned to get away for two weeks beginning September 15: "I have no plans and don't know where I will go. I want only to get away from telephones and telegraph wires and find a quiet, restful retreat."[32]

He did get away. He and his favorite brother-in-law, the journalist George Holmes, flew to Toledo on September 14, where they joined a wealthy mutual friend for ten days on his sailboat.[33]

There were the little moments that fall of 1937 that added another gray hair or two to Early's mane. One morning, Jimmy Roosevelt called and asked Steve to find someone to play golf with his wife, Betsy, of whom Early was especially fond. So he got on the phone and called several women he thought might want to join her on the links. Finally he found one. Then he sent his official car for them to use. However, a new chauffeur was at the wheel, and he mistook the Chevy Chase Club for the Columbia Club, where the women were supposed to play. Apparently they never did get in their golf game, but Early said, "I had plenty of explaining to do in order to get things straightened out."[34]

On November 15 Congress was meeting in a special session called by Roosevelt with the hope of seeing passed additional New Deal legislation involving farmers, labor, conservation, and government reorganization. Early, who was in his office by 6:30 that morning working to prepare press copies of the president's address to Congress, called it "an extra session to expedite work that will need to be done in January when it [Congress] convenes." But little was accomplished during the five weeks Congress worked, primarily because Southern Democrats had allied themselves with Republicans in opposing most of the administration's policies.[35]

A year that had seen Franklin Roosevelt suffer defeat and frustration came to an especially painful close. The day after he addressed Congress, he was suffering with an infected tooth, his jaw was swollen, and he was unable to fulfill a speaking engagement. The following day his tooth was still infected, and he had an intestinal disorder. Five days later Early told the press that Roosevelt's gum was sore and still draining. That year the president remained at home for Thanksgiving, the first time he had not traveled to Warm Springs since he took office. Right after the holiday he left for Florida for a vacation, returning via Warm Springs, but he returned early to have the abscessed tooth removed. Early had hoped to get in some duck hunting while Roosevelt was out of town, but the tooth problem forced his early return as well, and he found himself once again giving the press reports on the state of the president's jaw. The dentist decided the bone around the tooth had no infection and would not need scraping, so Early went back to his duck-hunting vacation.[36]

Again it proved to be short lived. He returned in time to prepare a statement on the sinking of the USS *Panay*, a gunboat that had been bombed by Japanese planes and sunk in Chinese waters near Nanking. Two members of the boat's crew were killed and ten were injured. It was an aggressive and probably premeditated act on the part of Japan. The United States demanded a formal apology from Japan and a guarantee that such an attack would never occur again. Two days later Japan sent an apology and a guarantee.[37]

12

GOOD FRIENDS AND JOB OFFERS

Early did indeed stay with the Boss, but the odds are that if the press aide and friend to the president of the United States had wanted to leave the pressure cooker of the White House for employment outside government, he would have been amply rewarded with a job of his choice and no doubt with a salary high enough to more than adequately support his young family. His diaries, which veer off into intimate details about his friends' lives, can be maddeningly circumspect about his own feelings, so there remains little in his own words other than some letters to his friend Joe Davies to explain his decision to stay on with Roosevelt.

Aside from his connections with the highest and mightiest in the federal government, Early had amassed an intriguing résumé. He was a longtime wire service reporter who was knowledgeable about the world of movie newsreels, and he had excellent organizational skills gained from his restructuring of the federal agencies' publicity machines. But he was an equally adept and loyal lieutenant who faithfully carried out orders of his commander in chief.

On the negative side were his towering temper, which on more than one occasion had loosed itself on some overeager reporter looking for a White House scoop; his ability to work under duress, which was sometimes taxed almost to the breaking point, leaving him to complain that he was overworked or his nerves were shot; and his lack of a degree beyond that of high school, a credential that may or may not have mattered much at this point in his life.

Aside from his White House connections, Early had plenty of friends in high places, many garnered during his days as a reporter and as a newsreel executive. He might have considered returning to Paramount, but only in an executive position, and that might have necessitated a move to the West Coast. He could have sought the editorship of a metropolitan newspaper or a management job at one of the wire services, where the salary certainly would have been more than his government pay, but the long hours on the job would have differed little from those at the White House, and the stress would have been equal or perhaps worse. One job in which his credentials as a White House insider would have been applauded and where he could have earned at least two or three times his government salary would be in public relations. But shilling for an oil company or a department store chain would have quickly led to boredom for a man who had once been a top-flight journalist and a secretary to the president of the United States.

Early faced a dilemma: He had "steadily increasing economic needs"; on the other hand, he was "tied heart and hand by loyalty and affection" to Roosevelt. He told Davies, "These necessities and ties stand in direct contrast to one another, pulling and sawing in opposite ways. I frankly do not know what the final result will be."[1]

There are no extant letters or memos between Early and Roosevelt dealing with the press secretary's desire to extricate himself from the pressures of the White House, but it is easy to picture the president using his immense charm to inveigle his friend and aide into staying "just through this, my last, term." An "I need you here, Steve" or a "We've still got a lot to accomplish" would have gone a long way to play on Early's sense of loyalty. And without Lewis Howe and longtime friend and valet Gus Gennerich around, Roosevelt needed Early more than ever—as a friend and often as a sounding board about important issues, but even more so to handle the day-to-day problems. In fact, in the summer of 1937 Early told Davies that Roosevelt was "determined to forestall any conversation with me regarding a possible [job] change."[2]

It was not just Early's economic worries that preyed on his mind as he considered a career move. The inner circle around the president had shrunk through death and illness, and Early more and more found himself doing what he called managing "two-thirds of this three-ring circus." This also became a running complaint in his diaries for the next several years. One person he did confide in regularly was Joe Davies, and it was to him that Early would relate the struggle to nail down his future.[3]

On the surface, these two men seemed an odd match to be close friends. Joseph E. Davies was born in Watertown, Wisconsin, on November 29, 1876, of Welsh immigrant parents. His father was an alcoholic who died when Joe was ten, and his mother was an ordained minister of the Welsh Congregational Church. Thanks to the help of a well-off uncle, Joe received undergraduate and law degrees from the University of Wisconsin. He married and practiced law in the state and became active in Democratic politics. By 1912 he was chairman of the party's western headquarters in Chicago, where he campaigned for Woodrow Wilson. It was likely during this time that he met Franklin Roosevelt and probably Early, who covered that year's Democratic convention in San Francisco. Like Roosevelt, Davies was "devoted to the Progressive cause in the Democratic Party."

Davies had offers to serve in several different capacities in the Wilson administration, including chairmanship of the new Federal Trade Commission, a position which he accepted and held for two years. He then returned to his home state to run for a United States Senate seat, but he lost by a narrow margin and returned to Washington as an economic adviser to Wilson at the Versailles Conference. By the 1930s Davies was a highly successful and wealthy Washington attorney representing a variety of foreign governments, such as Peru, Mexico, and the Dominican Republic, and cultivating friendships in the White House. In December of 1935 he became the third husband of one of the wealthiest women in the world, Marjorie Merriweather Post Close Hutton, the only child of cereal magnate C. W. Post. However, Davies required one more achievement to cap his career— and he needed Roosevelt, via Early, to ensure success.[4]

Any friendship is layered with complex nuances and often can be difficult, if not impossible, to dissect. Although Davies was thirteen years older than Early, the two men frequently played golf together at Burning Tree during Roosevelt's first term, and in 1935 Early won the

Davies Trophy at a tournament there. Steve and Helen attended Joe and Marjorie's lavish wedding in her Manhattan apartment, and it is likely that Early and Davies drew even closer during the reelection, when Davies was tapped to serve as chairman of the executive committee of the Democratic National Committee. In addition, he and Marjorie contributed "a generous sum" (estimated to be between $17,500 and $100,000) to the campaign.[5]

Joe and Marjorie had homes in New York, Washington, and Palm Beach and an oceangoing yacht that eventually took them to Russia. The Earlys lived in a modest home in not-quite-fashionable northeast Washington. The Early children called Davies "Uncle Joe," and he lavished the family with frequent gifts. He never forgot Steve and his family at Christmas and once sent young Buddy Early tuition money for his education at Staunton Military Academy, a gesture that Steve wrote he appreciated but could not accept. While Early's finances did not allow him to reciprocate in kind, he did on occasion use his influence to repay the Davies' generosity.[6]

Sometime after their marriage, Joe and Marjorie had decided he should become an ambassador, or, as Early put it, they "got the diplomatic bug." He told Davies he would have to be prepared to "take a hard beating in the press if they went into the diplomatic corps." Apparently that was not a deterrent, although Moscow was not high on their list of priorities primarily because Davies knew little or nothing about Russia. Press speculation had them headed to a more glamorous post in France or Great Britain, which is exactly where the Davies could see themselves.[7]

On August 26, 1936, Davies, who was vacationing with Marjorie at her retreat, Topridge, in the Adirondacks, got a call from "dear old Steve Early" saying the president wanted to see him. Over lunch in the White House, Roosevelt offered his old friend Davies the ambassadorship to the Soviet Union.[8]

Even before Roosevelt appointed Davies his ambassador to Russia, Early was relaying messages between the two men. "Tell Joe I will write him soon," FDR told Early one morning in January of 1936. That August Early hinted to Davies that the ambassador's job was in the works. Early said, "I am confident that the delay is in no way significant. I know the regard and the trust, the friendship and the readiness to act when conditions permit." Referring to the president, Early told Davies, "I want you to know, however, that he has you very much in mind." A few days later, Davies thanked Early for "the personal matter, which you so generously submitted to the 'big boss.'"9

Throughout the years of their friendship, which lasted until Early's death, Early would intervene on Davies's behalf. Once Early asked journalist Raymond Clapper "to write a piece giving Joe Davies a break." Early told Clapper that Davies "had received a raw deal from the press." He was referring to the gossip columns.10

From the beginning, Davies's relationship with the fabulously wealthy Marjorie had been fodder for the gossip columnists. He had been married to the same woman for thirty-three years, and they had three grown daughters when he met Marjorie. It was a whirlwind courtship. He quickly divorced his wife; when Marjorie's second divorce was completed, they married in a small but lavish ceremony in her Fifth Avenue apartment. Rumors ran through society that he had married her for her money, probably not true since his law practice was enormously successful. Then the gossipmongers focused on his sudden desire for a diplomatic post, and when he won the ambassadorship—albeit not the one he apparently coveted—they heckled Roosevelt for sending the world's richest woman and her spouse to represent the United States in one of the most backward and isolated countries in the world and chided the Davies for seeking a more glamorous posting. Clapper considered it a "touch of Rooseveltian humor." Two years later, as promised by Roosevelt, Davies was named ambassador to Belgium, a more suitable place for the couple.11

According to one of Marjorie's biographers, the reason behind the Moscow assignment may have been simply that Roosevelt wanted someone he could trust as only the second ambassador to Russia to restore strained relations between the two countries. The president's charge to Davies was to "make the Soviets as appealing to the American public as possible."12

Indeed Davies succeeded. In his final briefing to the State Department before he left Moscow for Brussels, Davies wrote that the "Good Neighbor Policy" between the two countries remained "consistent with the best traditions of our diplomatic history." In fact, he concluded, he had no doubt of the "sincerity and friendliness" of the Soviet Union toward the United States. Tucked into that report appear brief mentions of the courts-martial and mass executions of the Stalinist regime during Davies's years there, but that was not what Roosevelt wanted to hear, and Davies knew to downplay these horrors.[13]

Throughout his stay in Moscow and then in Brussels, Davies was a sounding board for Early's agonizing decision to stay or leave. A few weeks after Roosevelt was inaugurated for a second term, Early told Davies that sooner or later he must leave. "But I shall not make a move until I have counseled with you and obtained your approval. You make me very happy by saying in your letter that you are very glad that I am staying on and going through," Early wrote.

In a telling reference to his relationship with Roosevelt, Early said, "As you say, he [Roosevelt] does punish himself and 'with what gallantry.' As long as he does punish himself, I cannot find it within myself to leave him when, by remaining in his service, I can lighten the burden that otherwise would be heavier for him."[14]

In June 1937 Early had some good news for Davies. Now that FDR's oldest son, James, had moved into the secretarial slot vacated by Howe's death, Early and McIntyre were promoted from "assistant secretary" to "secretary to the president," thus making all three men of equal rank. Their salary also increased from $9,500 to $10,000 annually, equivalent to $118,888 in the year 2000.[15]

Even that did not stem his desire to leave the White House. He told Davies that Carl Byoir, whose New York agency had handled the publicity for the Democrats in the 1936 election, might offer him not just a job with the agency but a partnership and $50,000 a year, probably in September, although apparently no definite proposal was on the table. "I am sitting tight, marking time and feel contented, largely because of your advice and friendship, to bide the time," Early told Davies.[16]

The following month he said it was still "a status quo situation." However, he had had an intriguing proposal from a New York Congressman named William Sirovich, who offered him the presidency of the Brunelli Company, an aviation engineering outfit that designed airplanes, with an annual salary of $25,000 and a block of stock.

But Early was skeptical, so he asked his friend Bernard Baruch, the financier who had been both an official and an unofficial adviser to presidents beginning with Woodrow Wilson, to check out the financial status of Brunelli. He also asked some other friends, including a colonel in charge of the finance division of the Air Corps, to advise him on the company, and the result, he told Davies, was that "I am not disposed to regard the Sirovich proposal with favor." It seems he was still holding out hope that the Byoir job would materialize.[17]

Baruch also was on the lookout for a suitable job for his friend. In June another possibility apparently loomed. "My dear Steve," Baruch wrote. "I have not forgotten what you told me to look out for but I have not seen anything worth while until now. It is a pretty good prospect, but I do not want to talk to you about it, until it develops further."[18]

Baruch, a self-made millionaire, primarily as a Wall Street speculator of 1929, was not an active supporter of Roosevelt's, but since he had proved a heavy financial contributor to the Democratic Party in 1932, FDR could hardly ignore him. Although never a member of the president's inner circle of advisers, his advice was sought somewhat reluctantly on an ad hoc basis throughout Roosevelt's tenure in office, and toward the end of war he called on the financier more and more for help on management of the economy.

It is probable that Early first met Baruch when he was working for the Associated Press, and the friendship ripened when Early went to work in the White House and Baruch was dropping by to visit the president—or more likely Eleanor, with whom he retained a longtime warm and comfortable friendship. During his years in the White House, Early made vacation visits to Baruch's estate, Hobcaw Barony in South Carolina, and when in New York he dined with the older man. In 1940 Baruch purchased for Early a lifetime membership in the exclusive shooting and fishing club for high-placed Democrats, the Jefferson Island Club in Virginia.[19]

A few weeks later, he told Steve what that mysterious prospect was. The radio industry was "looking for a Will Hays or Judge Landis," and Baruch, who remained a good friend of Early's until the latter's death, had put the press secretary's name in the hat. Will Hays was president of the Motion Picture Producers and Distributors and had developed a censorship code for the movies; Kenesaw Mountain Landis was commissioner of baseball. Early's longtime friend Harry Butcher was on the committee to select a radio czar, and he had inquired about Steve's availability. The *Philadelphia Ledger* speculated that night that Early would become "czar of the bewildered and befuddled radio industry." He was interested, but he would for the time being remain an inactive candidate. He told Davies that when he received a definite offer, then he would give the committee a definite answer. Meanwhile, he said, he was "not turning a hand to seek the position."[20]

It didn't matter, because a month later, it seems, the committee had abandoned the idea of a radio czar. About the same time, when David Sarnoff, the pioneer in radio and television broadcasting and at this time the president of the Radio Corporation of America (RCA), the parent company of NBC, told Roosevelt he had a place at RCA for Early, the president replied, "Not until 1940."[21]

So the waiting game continued through the fall, with the newspapers occasionally speculating about Early's future and Roosevelt determined to retain his lieutenant unless the president himself selected the job.[22]

And Roosevelt indeed had a job in mind for Early. Since it had its genesis in Jimmy Roosevelt, as a way of ensuring a steady future for his somewhat less than professionally stable son, it is necessary first to explain who Jimmy was and how his father decided his and Early's futures should be intertwined.

Roosevelt had hoped his firstborn son would attend his alma mater, Harvard, although Jimmy had his heart set on a smaller, less snobbish school. To please his father, he headed north to Harvard, where he joined some of the same clubs to which his father had belonged. He also spent time working with the poor in settlement houses in Boston. But by his own admission, he was spoiled.

He also did not graduate from Harvard, lacking one language credit, which kept him from entering the university's law school. Instead, he married the Boston socialite Betsy Cushing and then entered Boston University Law School. In a move to be independent of his grandmother's money and to support his new wife, he left law school after a year and found a job in the insurance business in Boston, and he even worked briefly in politics with the city's notorious Democratic boss, James Michael Curley.

But problems arose. Eventually Jimmy accepted the presidency of a grain and yeast firm in New Jersey that had been suspected of making bootleg alcohol. All this led to newspaper attacks on the president by his political opponents. It did not, however, stop him from offering his son a job. While it eased Early's burdens somewhat, eventually it only added to Jimmy's.[23]

Franklin hoped that installing Jimmy in the White House would somehow serve as kind of replacement for his late friend, Louis Howe. At the most, Jimmy would be the protégé, with his father tutoring him in the expediencies of politics. At the very least, Jimmy would provide his father with some pleasant and intimate companionship. But Eleanor did not approve. She saw it as another reason for her husband's enemies to attack him. She also may have feared for her son's physical ability to handle such a high-pressure job. And events proved her absolutely correct.[23]

When he joined the White House secretariat at the end of 1936, the tall, slender, and balding Jimmy Roosevelt, who more closely resembled his mother than his father, was twenty-nine years old, married, and the father of two young daughters. His job? He would serve as a kind of "intermediary and clearinghouse" for his father, primarily overseeing the eighteen independent government agencies, such as the Works Progress Administration headed by Harry Hopkins, the Federal Maritime Commission chaired by Joseph P. Kennedy, and the Securities and Exchange Commission, chaired by future Supreme Court justice William O. Douglas. If any of the heads of the commissions and agencies had a problem, they first had to meet with Jimmy, who would transmit what he considered pertinent information to the president. The plan was to ensure closer cooperation among the agencies and attempt to prevent overlapping duties and jurisdictions.[25]

As his mother had predicted, the media were rough on him, questioning his ability at such a young age, with little or no political experience, to handle the egos of the men of these powerful agencies and deal with their complex problems. The media looked at this appointment as nepotism, and some newspapers began to refer to Jimmy as "the crown prince" while others called him "the clown prince" and charged that he was feathering his insurance business with golden eggs obtained through his father's office, a charge Jimmy and FDR denied. The media also speculated on whether Early and McIntyre would end up playing subordinate roles in the secretariat.[26]

In fact, Jimmy Roosevelt and Steve Early quickly became friends, golfing together and dining together with their wives. Years later, Jimmy told Early's grandson, Bill Elam, that his grandfather was "not only a kind person to me but a wise tutor."[27]

Betsy Roosevelt, who was a favorite of her father-in-law although not of her mother-in-law, often was the hostess for White House functions when the First Lady was absent, and she, too, quickly became a favorite of Early's. In short, the young Roosevelts seemed to fit into the White House.[28]

Then, a little more than a year later, the president's dream of his eldest son at his side came to a crashing halt. Jimmy had suffered from chronic stomach problems since childhood, and, as Eleanor had predicted, the pressures of his new job—not to mention his jealousy of his beautiful and vivacious wife because of her closeness to the president and his mother's animosity toward her—compounded to bring on a series of ulcer attacks. By late May 1938, the attacks were so severe he was rushed to the Mayo Clinic in Rochester, Minnesota, and treated for a gastric ulcer. He spent the summer on Campobello Island relaxing, but by September he was back at the Mayo Clinic where doctors operated on his stomach, fearing cancer. It was benign, but it signaled the end of his career in the White House.[29]

What would Jimmy do now? The president had what he thought would be the perfect solution. His eldest son and his trusted friend and press secretary could go into the insurance business together.

It was an odd solution to both Early's and Roosevelt's dilemmas. With no background as a businessman and having shown no interest in so mundane an occupation (at least for him) as an insurance executive, Early could only have reacted with surprise when his friend and employer put the proposition to him. And why would Roosevelt want to rid himself of the man who was one of his oldest and closest confidants as well as a key behind-the-scenes player in the reelection campaign? Was Roosevelt so sure of his ability to continue to deal with the media in light of his stunning reelection that he could cavalierly toss aside the man whose personal friendships with the reporters covering the president had smoothed the way during some of the most difficult days of the New Deal?

Early's reaction? "I do not want to do that," he emphatically told Joe Davies. "I have tried to analyze the situation and have come to this conclusion. Jimmy is young and ambitious. I am older and perhaps my judgment on things is more mature than Jimmy's. Whatever the President's motive may be in making this request to me, I do not feel that I should be Jimmy Roosevelt's Louis Howe," he explained.[30]

Early appeared to be trapped. He had no intention of agreeing to be a mentor to the president's son. At the same time the prospect of a job with the Byoir agency, on which he had pinned many of his future hopes, was withering. Byoir had made yet another offer to Early, but apparently the agency had handled the publicity for Roosevelt's annual birthday balls—events held around the country on FDR's birthday to raise money for the Georgia Warm Springs Foundation— and for the first time someone from the foundation had alleged that, as Early described it, there had been "some poisoning of Carl Byoir's well," and the agency lost the publicity contract. Although Roosevelt had not been responsible, Early decided he could not take a job with Byoir without "a break" from his old friend the president. "I cannot break," he told Davies. So there was nothing he could do "in the way of moving toward a solution of my very own economic problems."

Even if there had been no "poisoning of the well," Early told Davies that when he did take up the Byoir offer with Roosevelt, he got nowhere with him: "Quite confidentially, the President does not want me to go with Byoir."[31]

It remains speculation only as to how Roosevelt really felt about Early's job searches, about his desire to leave the president after the two of them had built up the most successful publicity machine in the history of the White House. Roosevelt, who demanded and expected loyalty from his advisers and confidants, must have wondered just how loyal Early was if he was regularly on the prowl for another job, even if he, Roosevelt, did understand and sympathize with his press secretary's need for a bigger income.

By early September 1938, despite the three-man secretariat being reduced by one, Early was telling Davies, "Work has not been too strenuous this summer and I believe I am in better physical condition that I have known for the past several years. The old nerves have calmed down."[32]

Interestingly, Early had expected Jimmy to return to his White House duties, and his resignation that fall "was a sad blow" to Early, who had hoped that Jimmy's return "would provide the way for my going." He said the president was still hoping his son would rejoin the staff, perhaps in the spring. But Early had no reason, he said, to believe that would happen. So once again Steve asked the Boss to release him. "The answer was the same."[33]

13

MOVING TOWARD WORLD CHAOS

T he last two years of the decade saw Early absorbed in personal and professional crises. His firstborn son and namesake
was in military school as the country was slipping and sliding toward
inevitable war. Early remained wracked with a desire to leave the
crushing stress of the White House for what he was convinced would
be a more lucrative and tranquil life in the private sector. He continued to define and strengthen his role as the president's press secretary and confidant, but he often found himself at the helm of a one-
man show, holding together with a fragile strength the offices of
McIntyre, Jimmy Roosevelt, and, at times, the office of the commander in chief himself.

The year 1938 opened with the president giving his annual message to Congress, an event once again attended by Early. Roosevelt's
speech ran about forty-five minutes. He touched on world peace,
stressing that the policy of the United States had been to live at peace
with other nations. In addition, Early wrote in his diary, Roosevelt
reminded his audience that the country had been among the leaders
in advocating conciliation and pacifism in international differences, a
position that Roosevelt would cling to for the next two years.
According to Early, the speech was "broadcast to the four corners of
the earth" and translated into seven languages.[1]

As they had the previous year after the congressional address, the usual poker-playing suspects changed into their everyday clothes and assembled in the president's study for a game and libations, both liquid and solid. When a newspaper editor and his family from Chicago unexpectedly stopped by the White House to see the president, Roosevelt told his secretary to tell them he was having dinner in bed. "Of course, I won't," he added. And the gang continued its poker game.[2]

After a busy week of newsmen demanding details and explanations regarding Roosevelt's message to Congress; the crash of a Northwest Airlines plane in the mountains of Montana, killing all ten persons on board; and an afternoon away from his office with a stomach disorder, Early returned to work to announce the president's nomination of Stanley Reed, a former solicitor general, to be an associate justice of the Supreme Court, replacing George Sutherland, who had retired. In all, Roosevelt appointed eight justices to the court during his presidency.[3]

He managed the occasional game of golf at Burning Tree on the milder days that winter and spring and got away from Washington in February for a week of quail shooting at Bernard Baruch's retreat in South Carolina, quite possibly a vacation he felt he sorely needed. Earlier in the week, Early's and Roosevelt's good friend Cary Grayson, chairman of the American Red Cross and onetime physician to President Woodrow Wilson, had died suddenly at the age of fifty-nine. After Steve and Helen attended the funeral and then the burial in Arlington Cemetery, Early confided in his diary, "I felt so low."[4]

Although he was felled several times that winter with stomach and teeth problems, Early managed to spend nearly two weeks playing golf and attending the horse races in Florida in mid-March, a chance for him to get "some real rest," he told Joe Davies. It was just as well that he took that vacation, because when he returned to Washington, he learned just how fragile the infrastructure of the White House inner circle was proving to be.[5]

As was his custom, Early's day began with a visit to Roosevelt's bedroom for an informal meeting in which the two men, sometimes joined by Harry Hopkins—and Marvin McIntyre and Jimmy Roosevelt when they were not ill—talked over the day's events and appointments. Now all this was in flux.[6]

By early April 1938 McIntyre had become edgy and physically

exhausted, no doubt because of what later was diagnosed as tuberculosis. Roosevelt and Dr. McIntire ordered Mac to the Naval Hospital, where their old friend Louis Howe had died two years earlier. He remained there for most of the month, leaving Early, as was so often the case lately, "to manage two jobs at once." Even after he returned to work, Mac showed up only for the mornings, which may have temporarily but only slightly relieved Early's burden. Early said he was "feeling very much worn out." Jimmy Roosevelt left for the Mayo Clinic for treatment of a gastric ulcer. He returned to work briefly but was back at Mayo by the end of September, leaving Early holding the fort on his own.[7] It shocked his family and friends, caused an upheaval in the White House offices, and played havoc with Early's desire to leave the White House for private employment.

That spring also brought with it the usual headaches, such as the editorial criticism over what would happen to the profits from the five published volumes of Roosevelt's speeches and papers, carefully collected and edited by his friend and speechwriter Sam Rosenman. Early was called on to advise Rosenman on the most effective way to announce publication of the volumes and then to deal with the press about why the speeches had been edited into book form and who was profiting from their sale. He explained that the books were the best solution to the large number of requests from libraries, schools, colleges, and researchers for the president's public papers. Early finally quelled widespread rumors that Roosevelt was making money from their sale by announcing that the president had decided to give the proceeds to charity. The announcement garnered this brief memo from Roosevelt for Early's adroit handling of the tempest: "Well done . . . FDR."[8]

Another "little problem" Early handled in an informal announcement to the reporters during one of his press conferences was the case of the "various and sundry things" that had been missing from the White House offices. It seems that one of the employees had taken to rifling through offices, taking trinkets, money, and even clothing. The hapless employee was caught when he decided to lift some marked dollar bills. He was taken to the district's 12th Precinct and charged with petty larceny, so, Early told the reporters, "Any news would have to come from the district attorney's office as this case was going to be handled in the same fashion as though it were 'John Smith' from one of the (government) departments."[9]

But, for Early at least, that same day in May ended on a more pleasant note. His good friend Harold Ickes, secretary of the interior and a widower, was married to Jane Dahlman in a secret ceremony in Ireland. "It came as a great surprise to all in official circles," Early wrote in his diary. It seems that Ickes had confided his plans to FDR, who enjoyed keeping such secrets, telling no one, not even Secretary of State Cordell Hull, who became upset when he heard Ickes was planning a trip abroad. He thought the president was sending his interior secretary on a secret diplomatic mission.[10]

Some of Early's days that year were simply long and tedious. He arranged for newsreel and still photographers to make silent movies and pictures when the president laid a wreath at the Lincoln Memorial marking the slain president's birthday; he set up another Fireside Chat, held his daily meetings with the press, and fielded the usual multitude of complaints and questions from politicians, journalists, and those citizens important enough to reach the inner sanctum of the White House either in person or by telephone.[11]

Memorial Day weekend saw Early working in the office and relaxing at home. Roosevelt, on the other hand, decided to get some rest and a change of scenery at his beloved home in Hyde Park. Alas, the house was overrun with family and guests. Early told Joe Davies, "I take it that they talked him to death . . . from early morning until late at night."[12]

Early made several memorable trips during his years with Roosevelt. The one he took that summer of 1938 was one he described as "a perfect joy from start to finish." It began on July 9 with a ten-day train trek across the continent to San Diego with the usual entourage of White House staff and newsmen covering the commander in chief. The presidential train made stops along the way at which Roosevelt displayed the charm he had so often exhibited during a political campaign. Early thought it all "a continuous triumph." The fact that some of his closest journalist friends—his brother-in-law George Holmes among them—were on board certainly raised Early's spirits. The train proved a "madhouse with the animals [the reporters] in their respective cages roaring and bellowing," he told Davies.

One highlight of the cross-country trip occurred late one night when a group of friends, including Early, were socializing—and no doubt drinking—in the dining car. Loudspeakers had been placed on the rear end of the president's private car and had been connected to two amplifiers in the dining car, so that when Roosevelt spoke from the platform at the end of his car, reporters could gather in the dining room to listen. This eliminated the need for them to jump off at each stop, run around to the end of the car, make their notes, and then run back before the train pulled out of the station.

The train had passed through the Royal Gorge on the Arkansas River in south-central Colorado and stopped for the night. In the spirit of fun, Early said, he left the dining car and went to the microphone on the rear platform. The loudspeakers were disconnected, but the wires to the amplifiers connected to the dining car remained in place. Imitating the president's voice, Early began to speak. He said he was told there was an instantaneous hush in the dining car, and the press people present, believing the president was about to make a speech, quickly grabbed pencils and pads. After "the president" had spoken for a minute or two regarding the appointment of one of the men in the dining car to a judgeship, it slowly dawned on them that the speaker was none other than the president's press secretary playing a prank.[13]

It should be noted that when the Roosevelt traveled by train, security precautions involved an advance check by the railroad company of the train tracks, overpasses, and junctions that would be guarded by police. A pilot locomotive traveled about a mile ahead, and no train was allowed to immediately follow the presidential train. Daytime train speeds were rarely above thirty miles an hour, since anything faster forced the president to brace himself with extra care, a procedure that could be tiring and painful for his weakened legs. At night, speeds increased to seventy miles per hour.[14]

Once the party arrived in San Diego, six of the president's closest friends, including Early, Dr. McIntire, and Pa Watson, boarded the USS *Houston* for a leisurely fishing cruise in the Pacific, a stop in the Galapagos Islands and then through the Panama Canal and up the Gulf of Mexico to Pensacola, Florida, then on to Warm Springs, and then home. With no journalists on board, Early filed dispatches twice daily, which were sent out on the ship's radio to newspaper and wire service offices in Washington. The morning dispatch was for the afternoon papers, and the late afternoon dispatch was for the next morning's newspapers. However, one day as the *Houston* anchored off the Galapagos Islands, Roosevelt decided to play journalist and wrote the dispatch himself, and the newspapers that ran it carried this byline: By F. D. Roosevelt, Special Correspondent Pro Tem. Now this was not because Early was abdicating his position as press secretary; he was unable to do his job that day, according to correspondent Roosevelt.

It seems the previous night had seen a series of high jinks and partying aboard the ship related to a "shellback"—the crossing of the equator—and they lasted well into the morning. Roosevelt, the senior shellback, dubbed Early the king of the pollywogs, or those on board who had never crossed the equator. It was up to the shellbacks, the veterans, to initiate the pollywogs. And it all had proved too much for the press secretary. It did provide the president with a delicious diversion, if only temporarily, and his journalism endeavor proved a light, chatty piece about fishing and the weather that day, written in the third person.

Several pages of photos taken on the cruise, now in one of Early's scrapbooks in the FDR Library at Hyde Park, show the crew and the guests frolicking in a variety of shipboard costumes. Another shows a grinning Roosevelt in a floppy-brimmed soft hat, wearing a short sleeved shirt open at the neck and white cotton pants, seated next to what Early said was a three-hundred-pound man-eating tigerhead shark that the president landed using only a rod and reel. It took him two and a half hours. The "friendly and jolly good fellows" aboard the *Houston* found the fishing "marvelous," as they got "a tremendous kick" out of battling "sharks, wahoos, marlin, and barracudas."

Eventually they docked in the Panama Canal, where they met some of the journalists who had traveled across country on the train. They spent a day and a half in the Canal Zone, including a night ashore in Balboa, where, Early said, they found the night life "unrestricted, unrefined, and unending."[15]

The travelers were back by the end of August in time for Early to celebrate his forty-ninth birthday. The good times had ended. Even his birthday saw Early busy at the office most of the day before he left for the Naval Hospital for an x-ray treatment of a stubborn fungus growth.[16]

At this time, Early was attempting to enroll his son, Stephen Junior, known in the family as Buddy, in Staunton Military Academy, a prestigious prep school in Virginia. Although he did not attend

Staunton, Early said that as a Virginian he had "a decided sentimental attachment" to the school. He said he knew sending Buddy to Staunton would stretch the family budget, one already drained by the social and other expenses associated with his White House job. Buddy was accepted for the fall semester.[17]

Right after Labor Day, news arrived that Jimmy Roosevelt would be undergoing surgery for his ulcer. It was quite a shock to the whole family as well as his extended White House "family," since they thought he was at the Mayo Clinic just for a checkup. So once again the presidential train steamed west out of Washington carrying Early, Roosevelt, and a small staff, this time to Minnesota so Roosevelt could visit with his eldest son before he went into the operating room for stomach surgery, which lasted nearly two hours. Eleanor and Jimmy's wife, Betsy, had arrived a few days earlier. The president and Early stayed only three days, with plans to stop at Hyde Park on the way back to the capital. But that was scrapped when the president decided the European situation was "too critical."

Adolf Hitler, already having annexed Austria, was moving into Czechoslovakia, poised to grab the Sudetenland (the part of Czecho-slovakia that borders Germany) by force if necessary. The day Roosevelt and Early arrived back in Washington, Early noted in his diary that Great Britain's prime minister, Neville Chamberlain, had flown to Germany to make a personal plea to Hitler in an attempt to avert war in Europe. The plea failed, and the following day the newspapers announced that Hitler had told Chamberlain the annexation of the Sudetenland would have to be the price of peace.

Thus, it must have been with a heavy heart that Early watched his wife leave that same day to drive Buddy to Staunton Military Academy, where he would spend the next four years as a military student while his father watched firsthand as the country entered its second major war of the century. But on that day in mid-September, as Buddy left for a future that most certainly would include military combat on foreign soil, the best his father could reassure him was that he would "hope things shape up" in the White House so he could go to Staunton one Saturday to visit his son.[18]

Yet events in Europe seemed so distinctly separate from events at home—the balancing of the budget, continuing welfare relief, the reorganization of the federal government, and the makeup of the

Supreme Court. As the president kept vigil over the country from his headquarters in the White House, Hitler was rapidly becoming the dominant force in Europe, promising one thing and accomplishing another as he solved the problems he saw facing Europe. In a letter to Davies that fall, Early summed up the domestic and world situations in his usual succinct way: "With the international crisis and home problems, the pressure is great."[19]

Meanwhile, a week after Jimmy's surgery, on September 22, the president was felled by a cold, and Dr. McIntire ordered him to remain in bed. Early arrived at work earlier than usual that day and, as was his practice, went to see the president. Little was happening in the White House, but the great hurricane of 1938 was sweeping its way up the Atlantic coast, leaving hundreds dead and millions of dollars in damage from Long Island to Massachusetts, including the devastation of the splendid old trees on Jimmy Roosevelt's estate on Long Island. Nonetheless, it didn't stop Early and his wife from having lunch at Burning Tree, followed by a round of golf. In spite of the hurricane further north, he decided "this is the first decent day we have had for ten days."[20]

By the fall of 1938, Early was being quoted in his own right and was now and again the subject of a cartoon on a newspaper's editorial page. Even his golf scores made their way into print. His name appeared in headlines in both large and small newspapers, even showing up occasionally in the popular comic strip "Joe Palooka."

On September 23 the newspapers noted that Early made New Deal history when he conducted FDR's press conference because the president was still suffering from his cold. Apparently he had only ten minutes' notice to prepare before he was peppered with questions and speculations about government appointments and resignations. He cheerfully deflected those questions he could not—or would not—answer. When the press conference began, Doris Fleeson, a syndicated columnist and a regular in and out of Early's office, was grousing, "Do you mean to say I got up early to come over and talk to Steve Early?" By the end of the meeting, the reporters were joking among themselves about who was the oldest.

The next day the *Washington Times* headline read: "Early Conducts Press Conclave for the President," and then noted in the story that "it was the first time such a thing had occurred."[21]

On September 27 Roosevelt sent what Early termed "a final plea to Hitler in an effort to avert war" and called for a meeting of all interested nations in a neutral location. The next morning, Early noted, the United Press ticker in his office revealed that Hitler would meet the following day in Munich with Chamberlain, Italy's Benito Mussolini, and Edouard Daladier, French premier and war minister. Early wrote in his diary that day, "We shall await, with great anxiety, the outcome of this conference." They did not have to wait long. That conference determined the fate of Czechoslovakia. Hitler got what he wanted, and the world marched one step closer to war.[22]

Two days before Christmas, Roosevelt nominated his close friend Harry Hopkins to be secretary of commerce. A tense, brilliant Midwesterner and former social worker who first worked with Roosevelt when he was governor of New York, Hopkins went on to administer several New Deal programs, including the Works Progress Administration. For Early the year ended on a quiet note as he spent the holidays with his family. But the final year in this tumultuous decade was to be one of peaks and valleys for the overworked presidential press secretary. It was to be a year, he wrote in his diary that "seems to be bringing us many busy days."[23]

On January 12, 1939, he prepared for release to the reporters Roosevelt's annual message, which the president delivered to Congress later that day. Most of it was devoted to warning of danger to international peace and democracy by the aggressors in Europe. Early called it "a minimum statement of national needs as found by the President after consultation and long and much advice with the army, navy, and marine corps." Earlier that month, Roosevelt's budget for 1940 asked Congress for $1.3 billion for defense. Now he was requesting that $510 million be made available immediately, with much of it going to the army for planes. However, Early noted that the president "was painstaking in avoiding any hysteria of war."[24]

While Hitler and Hermann Goering began the year quietly plotting the elimination of Europe's Jews, on the other side of the Atlantic January plodded on, gray and snowy. Early left his office for lunch with friends at the elite Metropolitan Club now and again, a luxury for which his wealthy friends no doubt footed the bill, since Early was finding Buddy's military school education a severe strain on the family budget. Sometimes that month he had news "for the boys," the newsmen and women who waited not always so patiently for the big page one story from the White House. Other times, he told them, "No news today." One day the Boss did not even bother to come over to his office. Instead, he stayed in his study and went over his mail.[25]

January ended on a tragic note when a major earthquake wiped out several towns in Chile, killing thousands. February brought with it a personal tragedy for Early, a "shock" that he said hit him "two-fold": His close friend and favorite brother-in-law, George Holmes, died suddenly of a heart attack at home early on Sunday morning, February 12. His wife, Mary Catherine, was visiting friends in northwestern New York state at the time, so, although he was in bed with a cold, it was left to Steve to break the "terrible news" to her. Holmes's death, however, may not have proved as much of a shock to his brother-in-law as it did to those who knew him less well. Just a few months before he died, Early had told Joe Davies "some unpleasant news" about Holmes. He had neuritis in both legs, his blood pressure was high, and "his heart is not what it should be." He did note that Holmes had been to the doctor and had gone "on the wagon," and his health seemed to be improving.

Holmes was only forty-four years old, the father of two young daughters, and, according to the many press reports of his death, "one of the outstanding newsmen of the nation." He had been twenty-four years old when he was named Washington Bureau chief for International News Service, the Hearst-owned wire service, and in recent years, in addition to his position at INS, he was host of a national weekly news analysis program on NBC radio. Early and Holmes had been reporters and friends since 1912. Early described their friendship as "close and intimate." He liked to tell people they became friends even before Holmes knew Early had a sister. In recent years, because Holmes and his family lived on Massachusetts Avenue, on the way to the Early home on Morningside Drive in the Shepard Park area of northeast Washington, Early and his driver would pick up Holmes so the two friends could talk on their way to work.

Holmes had covered the burial of the first soldier at the Tomb of the Unknown Soldier in Arlington Cemetery, a story for which he had won an honorable mention in the Pulitzer Prize competition that year. Less than a week after Holmes died, Early told Joe Davies: "George was buried Tuesday. He lies today on the brow of a hill in

Arlington Cemetery, within a few hundred yards of the Tomb of the Unknown Soldier, where he can look down upon the old Capital of this U.S.A.—across the river and almost see his old I.N.S. carrying on." Twelve years later, Early himself would be buried nearby. Early's diary gives no hints as to the depth of his feelings about Holmes's passing, but he no doubt mourned his loss for a long time.[26]

But for now he had more pressing problems to deal with. Marvin McIntyre, whose primary job was handling political appointments for the president, was back in the hospital, and the president boarded his special train for Key West, Florida, where he embarked on his favorite cruise ship, the USS *Houston*, for two weeks of rest in the sunny, warm Caribbean.

While the Boss was relaxing, Early was again facing a staff shortage in the White House. And perhaps still reflecting on the early death of his hard-working brother-in-law, he fired off a letter to FDR marked "STRICTLY PERSONAL" and dated February 23, 1939. It began: "Dear Boss, This concerns a problem in regard to your secretariat—a problem about which I have given much thought because I believe it is more important to you than you perhaps realize."

The problem was that once again Early was left to handle the press, greet politicians and attempt to solve their problems, and meet with other important visitors to the White House. He confided in his diary that he was being hit from all sides, with Mac's illness, the necessity of helping his sister Mary at the moment, and with his wife and younger son, Tommy, home in bed with the flu (a malady that in those days before antibiotics could become serious), Roosevelt was on another fishing trip off Florida.

His two-page typed letter to Roosevelt enumerated the reasons why Early felt the situation was important: He said he believed that Mac's condition "makes it extremely doubtful" that he would be able to continue his job in the future unless he were "given rest periods from time to time." He added that Dr. McIntire would confirm this. Then Early reminded the president that with Jimmy Roosevelt's resignation, the position he had held, for the most part, was nonfunctioning.

He explained: "No one of three secretaries to the President (assuming there were three) can single-handedly and efficiently carry on the work of these three offices. However, able, industrious and willing this one secretary may be, the load is too heavy for him to carry. He can answer some of the telephone calls; he can see some of the visitors; he can attend to some part of the inner office work, the paper work and routine, but he cannot answer all of the telephone calls, see all of the callers and keep pace with the other demands up on him."

The upshot, Early added, was "disappointments on the part of those who call and are not seen; who telephone and cannot talk; who write and are not answered, etc. These disappointments add up in terms of dissatisfaction. Unfortunately, they reflect upon you. Frankly, I feel the time for action has come."

Early said that he disliked the idea of "presenting problems to someone, particularly to you, unless, at the same time, I can offer something constructive in the way of a solution." So, here's what he suggested: Col. Edwin M. "Pa" Watson, another Virginian with the southern prejudices and views of Early and McIntyre and an occasional military aide to the president, should move into Jimmy Roosevelt's office. Early and Watson had been lunching together on and off for some time, so no doubt they had discussed this arrangement; Early told Roosevelt that Watson did not intend to stay in the army much longer and would be interested in working in the White House.

So Early, the public relations man, went to work on the president, probably less a hard sell than was actually needed, because the colonel often went on fishing trips with Roosevelt and at that very moment was aboard the USS *Houston* with him. Nonetheless, Early felt compelled to point out that the large, burly Watson was "well known and well liked." He said that "most Senators and members of Congress love him," and that he "makes friends and keeps friendships." And if that weren't enough to get his friend the appointment, Early added, "His appearance is imposing and his personality is happy and pleasing." Another plus was that, at six feet tall, he could bear the weight of the president when he chose to be photographed standing.[27]

It is not known whether Early, who described himself as "an eight ulcer man on four ulcer pay," had been verbally hounding Roosevelt for some relief in his job as secretary, but the carefully worded letter did the trick. Two weeks later at his press conference, Early announced that Watson would be promoted to brigadier general on March 31, and a few days later he would retire from the army after thirty years and move into Jimmy's old office. In an understatement, Early told the journalists, "I, of course, am extremely happy over the appointment of Colonel Watson as he will make a great working pal."[28]

All had not ended well just yet. A week later, Early asked Dr. McIntire to join his press conference that day so he could give the journalists the latest on Mac's health. He had left the hospital and was en route to Asheville, North Carolina, for "a long rest." The doctor told the newsmen it was a "severe gastric intestinal upset that had floored him." Then, five days later, Early told the boys at his press conference there was a "snag" with Watson's appointment. Watson's nomination had been confirmed by the Senate; then someone, perhaps a Republican, unearthed an old law that said no officer holding a rank above that of colonel could be retired, except for disability, until he had served at least one year at that rank. But Roosevelt did not want "Pa" to blemish his record by retiring for disability nor did he want his friend to lose his rank of general. A solution was reached: The army would detail Watson to the White House for a year to be assigned to Jimmy Roosevelt's office. He moved in immediately.

It didn't take long for the jovial Watson to become part of the White House staff. On March 17 the staff asked him in all seriousness what he thought of the president crossing a picket line at a Washington hotel to attend a St. Patrick's Day dinner. Waiters were on strike all over the city, so the playful White House staff suggested the strikers be forced to wear green uniforms and the "scab" waiters wear orange. They asked Watson how he thought this would go over with the public. Watson's answer? "Ah, I don't think that would be such a good idea." In his diary for that day, Early wrote, "It was quite a while before he realized we were 'pulling his leg.'"

For all his bonhomie and sense of humor, "Pa," who had picked up his nickname on the football team at West Point to distinguish him from another Watson, proved a discerning and intelligent appointments secretary with an uncanny ability to distinguish between those seeking favors and those desiring to see the president because of a genuine interest in the affairs of the country. He was not especially interested in the process of government, but he was a loyal and companionable aide to Roosevelt throughout the war years.[29]

The recent staff shortages and turmoil may explain the ambiguous answer Early gave reporters at a press conference late that March. When they asked if the president still planned to head for Warm Springs the following week, his press secretary replied, "I hoped there will be no cancellation as I want him to get away from here." Whether Early wanted Roosevelt out of town because Roosevelt was sorely in need of a vacation at the Georgia retreat, or because it gave Early a much-needed break from the daily problems and hassles created by a boss whose tendency was to strategize, order his associates to carry out the strategy, and then leave them to deal with the fallout, is not known.[30]

But more and more Early was standing in for the president on the day-today activities and at times acting as a go-between for Roosevelt and congressmen or members of the administration on affairs of state, occasionally taking the brunt of political wrath that should have been more correctly directed at Roosevelt. For instance, that same month, while Harry Truman, then a senator from Missouri, was in his home state dealing with some local political problems, he got a call from Early urging him to return at once to Washington to vote on the reorganization bill in the Senate. Truman arrived back in time for the vote, but not without traveling through a dangerous snowstorm.

Angry at the way he thought Early had treated him and how apparently he had treated him several times previously, Truman phoned him, and said, "Well, I'm here, and I damned near got killed getting here by airplane in time to vote, as I did on another occasion. I don't think the bill amounts to a tinker's damn, and I expect to be kicked in the ass just as I have in the past in return for my services," referring to those times he believed FDR had treated him with disdain.

"Well Senator, what is it you want?" Early replied.

"I don't want a God-damned thing. My vote is not for sale. I vote my convictions just as I always have, but I think the president ought to have the decency to treat me like the Senator from Missouri and not like a God-damned office boy, and you can tell him what I said. If he wants me to, I'll come down and tell him myself."

The following day FDR did invite Truman to the White House to thank him for his crucial vote.[31]

As Roosevelt hesitated and procrastinated, such as waiting six months until early 1939 to finally replace Supreme Court Justice Benjamin Cardozo, one of FDR's biographers called this "indirection" and "the secretive deviousness" that he had practiced intermittently in more prosperous times, often for the sheer fun of dramatic surprise and role-playing. Now he practiced it almost continuously out of some "grim-felt necessity."[32]

This game playing, this vacillation, could only have contributed to the frustrations of his press secretary and set off his "towering temper." It may have explained why Early was eager for the Boss to depart for Warm Springs.

The president did leave, but after he returned Roosevelt was back in bed with a cold, which Early described as "just a cold, nothing serious, but it certainly can make a fellow miserable." He added that everyone in the executive offices had sinus and neck colds from the cooling system.[33]

By the beginning of the summer, a nation intent on staying out of war was watching as the Japanese military moved on Russian troops, Germany and Italy forged an official alliance, and Germany made plans to invade Poland. Britain was nervous, afraid of a full-scale war against its old enemy Germany and even more fearful that this time its friend on the other side of the Atlantic would decide not to come to its aid.

Roosevelt, meanwhile, recognized the inevitability of war and realized steps had to be taken to prepare the country for such a conflict, but he was forced to deal gingerly with an isolationist Congress that reflected sentiments shared by much of the American public. It seemed quite fitting that when he learned the British king and queen were coming to Canada in June he should orchestrate a royal visit to Washington and perhaps in the process solidify in the public's mind, if not that of Congress, the bond between the two countries. It would be the first time a reigning British monarch had set foot in this country. Late in 1938 Roosevelt sent a personal invitation to the king and queen; the king replied, "[T]he visit is a definite possibility."

And indeed their majesties did come to Washington, in the heat and humidity of early June 1939. It must have been a memorable moment for Early, the son of a railroad clerk, when he joined the Roosevelts and other White House staffers to greet the king and queen as they arrived at Union Station that Thursday morning. Like a teenager recounting a meeting with a famous star, Early's diary for Thursday, June 8, describes in detail the historic arrival and procession to the White House.

Early was part of the small White House delegation, including the president, Mrs. Roosevelt, and "Pa" Watson, who greeted the royal couple at Union Station. Early wrote that it was understood that the president's first words to King George were, "Well, at last I greet you." The king replied, "Mr. President, it is indeed a pleasure for her majesty and me to meet you." He and his wife, Elizabeth, greeted Mrs. Roosevelt, and the two couples chatted for a minute or so in the train station's reception room. As they stepped out of the room, they were met with a twenty-one-gun salute and a band playing "God Save the King," Early wrote. As the procession moved toward the Capitol, crowds estimated at more than four hundred thousand packed the sidewalks and jammed the buildings and hotel windows.

Because the temperature rose above 90 degrees, once he returned to his office, Early changed his wet clothes immediately. He then left for the Willard Hotel, where he was attending a lunch put on by the Overseas Writers. Back in his office in the afternoon, he met with the chief press liaison officer of the king. That evening, he and Helen attended the state dinner at the White House, which was followed by a receiving line and a musicale.

Then it was back to work. The following morning, he tried to ensure that the additional newsmen who had been sent to Washington by their respective newspapers were accommodated for the president's press conference that day. Since Mrs. Roosevelt was still meeting separately with the women reporters, Early paid special attention to her press conference at 9:30 a.m., because she planned to introduce the queen to the women journalists. He advised the still picture syndicates and the newsreel men as to what pictures could be taken when the royals visited George Washington's tomb at Mount Vernon and, on their way back to the city, the Navy Yard.

When the entourage boarded the train and moved north that evening for a weekend of less formal receptions and picnics at the president's estate in Hyde Park, Early was there. However, it was mostly business, as he handled the demands of the huge press contingent there to record the historic visit. As was the rule in the Early press department, still and motion photographers and radiomen worked under highly controlled conditions when their cameras were aimed at the president. Early told them they could not broadcast services at St. James Church in Hyde Park, and photographers and the press were barred from the picnic.[34]

Stringent as these regulations may seem by today's standards, apparently the cameramen in those days found them not unusual. So the following Thursday the White House News Photographers Association surprised Early with an honorary White House Photographers Badge. Later that day, he confided in his diary: "I did not feel so very well today, undoubtedly the reaction from the last two weeks of strain, so I took a nap in the afternoon."[35]

One of the strains that plagued him that June was the reaction to an article he wrote that appeared in the *Saturday Evening Post*, titled "Below the Belt." Critical of what he called "below-the-belt blows" to the president, Early disputed a number of rumors that had been circulating, some of which were mentioned earlier in chapter 10. Extrapolated from letters to the president and stories published in newspapers and magazines in recent years, the rumors included speculation that Roosevelt's health was too poor to be an effective president. The letter writers criticized Roosevelt's selection of Jews for positions in his cabinet and on the Supreme Court, one calling Felix Frankfurter and Bernard Baruch "more dangerous to American traditions and ideals that all the Communists that could find their way into Union Square."[36]

In the magazine article, Early dismissed what he called "a fantastic tale" about what one unidentified news outlet reported was the president's role in the kidnapping of the Lindbergh baby. Calling the story "strange and striking and unbelievable," Early said it claimed that foreign agents under the direction of leading bankers and lawyers had taken the baby. Then these millionaires "were shielded and protected from exposure and prosecution by Franklin Delano Roosevelt's Department of Justice."

Early's defense of the president against the gossipmongers in the article was, "Franklin Roosevelt has been my friend for more than a quarter of a century. My service to him has been that of a devoted friend. It has afforded me opportunities for observation and inside knowledge that go, very naturally, with such long and intimate associations between men. Out of that knowledge, association and friendship comes the license to say: 'He can take it.'"

Why did Early choose to write an article that proved to be so controversial? The ending may explain. "Certain it is that with the approach of 1940, as it has been every four years since this democratic form of government was adopted by the people of the United States, new rumors, whisperings, variations of truth and untruth will mix with the old." It was a preemptive strike. Was Roosevelt planning to run for a third term? The president was not talking, but that did not stop his left hand from perhaps signaling his intention. It may also have been another avenue for Early, the public relations man in the White House, to build support for the president's European interventionist policies.[37]

After the article was published, Early seemed surprised that he received what he described as "a great number of criticism letters," not only from his friends but from many readers of the magazine. Newspapers wrote editorials questioning why he would choose to write about rumors and innuendos. Others applauded him for making the rumors public.[38]

He left behind any lingering controversy in late June when he joined a group of about fifty prominent Americans and British citizens and a handful of newsmen on the Pan American World Airways *Yankee Clipper*'s first mail and passenger trip, taking the Great Circle Route up over Newfoundland to London and back. In some White House joviality, Early bet three other men who had been invited, including Pa Watson, that either their wives would not let them take the trip or for some other reason they could not go. Mrs. Watson apparently vetoed Pa's trip, and the other two men were unable to get away from work. So Early took $300 in spending money with him "compliments" of the three losers. The plane hit bad weather on the way over and was delayed overnight in New Brunswick, so the White House sent him a telegram that read: "You're no lone eagle. You're Sitting Bull."[38]

Early returned to spend a relatively quiet and somewhat cooler than normal summer for Washington, one that saw the radio press galleries officially opened with a nationwide broadcast from the Capitol, the first time radio had been given an equal footing with the print press there. He traveled to Atlantic City to address the National Association of Broadcasters; he dined with friends and colleagues, including his sister Mary, Joe and Marjorie Davies, and Henry and Eleanor Morgenthau; he served as a pallbearer for a friend's wife; and one day in mid-July he complained that he was working sixteen-hour days.[39]

Then came a relaxing four-day weekend with Roosevelt, Watson, Dr. McIntire, and Harry Hopkins aboard the *Potomac*. The men left from Quantico, Virginia, the navy base near Washington, and then headed down the Potomac River and out into the Atlantic off Virginia

Capes. The marlin were running, and Early hoped for some prosperous action at the poker table. "In my hands, these men are so much putty. If they venture into any games of chance, as I suspect they will, I will mould as I please and bring them back home all in the red and, I don't mean sunburned," a brash Early told his wife, who was vacationing with their three children at the home of friends in New York's Adirondack Mountains. Apparently his luck on both the fishing and the gambling fronts failed him, but he said he did "catch a lot of sleep."[40]

In mid-August Roosevelt was off on another cruise, this time up the Atlantic coast to his home on Campobello Island, leaving Early behind in the White House pressure cooker to hold things together. He told Joe Davies what life in his office was like when the president was relaxing on board a ship:

> Very naturally, we do our utmost when the President is away on a cruise to keep all possible work and worry from reaching or disturbing him. At such times, my desk becomes the clearing house through which all things from the outside world either stop or pass on to the Boss. The things we stop require action by us here in the executive offices or by those appropriately referred. The things that pass on are in the nature of affairs either too personal or too important and which, in our judgment, the President alone can dispose of. They go out of here by wireless or by pouch and, it so happens, that the job runs continuously on and requires the clearing house to keep open around the clock, each and every day.[41]

On August 24 Early's leave for a vacation with Helen to visit friends in North Carolina was approved by the Boss, despite the fact that Europe was in crisis and Roosevelt was canceling all "run-of-the mill" appointments to keep himself available for officials of the War, Navy, and State departments. Early said he fully expected to be called back, and after a week he was—but not before Europe was immersed in a series of diplomatic and military crises that consumed the occupants of the White House and filled the pages of the last diary Early ever kept.[42]

14

FATAL DAYS IN EUROPE, DECISIONS AT HOME

"The seven days I was away in the mountains of North Carolina on a 'hoped for two weeks vacation' were eventful and fatal days in the history of Europe and the world," Early confided in his diary.

Pa Watson phoned him in North Carolina at 6:00 a.m. on September 1 to tell him the Boss wanted him back in Washington immediately. An army plane was waiting at the Greenville, South Carolina, airport. "It was what I would term a 'record-breaking trip from Heaven to Hell,'" Early wrote. When he arrived in the capital, he said, he found "the feeling tense." He wrote, "The tension grew when we received word that the French civilians, urged by the Government, were leaving Paris five hundred thousand strong; that the Mayor of Warsaw was helping his fellow citizens dig air-raid trenches; that the German cafes and restaurants were deserted while the German men joined their regiments."

Roosevelt had received a telephone call at 2:50 a.m. the day Early arrived back in Washington. It was from William Bullitt, American ambassador to France, reporting that Germany was invading Poland and four cities were being bombed. As he did on his voyage to France to fight in World War I, Early kept a meticulous and factual account of events in Europe for that September, as far as those in the White

House could ascertain. For a man who had fought in one war and whose son would probably see action in another, Early remained the dispassionate newsman, even when he came to the end of his account:

> The war had begun. Guns boomed along the Polish Frontier. Twenty five cities were air-raided.
>
> [Prime Minister] Chamberlain on that day (September 1) addressed a crowded House of Commons [in Parliament] and denounced the Fuehrer. He told the British people of an ultimatum sent to Germany demanding recall of troops from Polish soil.

A similar ultimatum was sent by France. Italy remained neutral.[1]

As events began to explode slowly, like a Fourth of July fireworks display, Roosevelt was in close touch with the American ambassadors in the European capitals. The State Department and the White House worked overtime, with officials from State "having the right-of-way and are free to come and go [to meet with the President] without scheduled appointments," Early wrote.[2] And reporters were demanding answers that Roosevelt and Early could not always supply. One answer Roosevelt did have for the press when they asked him at his September 1 press conference was whether the United States would stay out of a European war: "I not only sincerely hope so, but I believe we can and every effort will be made by the Administration to so do."[3]

The next day, Saturday, Early found himself before the reporters at his own press conference giving a most simplistic explanation of the Neutrality Act. Among other things, it "requires the President to issue a neutrality proclamation when war is declared." Then he pointed out, "So far, no war has been declared." He decided to give the reporters a hypothetical: "Suppose the English Parliament and the French Deputies today vote to authorize their governments to carry out their agreements with Poland. The question there, is that a declaration of war? There are many questions involved—very deep ones."[4]

Apparently the reporters were still hounding him about the Neutrality Act, so on Monday, sounding a lot like "Professor" Roosevelt at his press conferences, Early suggested the reporters take on "the following homework": Pick up a copy of the act and read through it. He then gave them a detailed explanation of the terms of the act. Whether the reporters completed their "homework" is not recorded in his diary. There is no doubt that for some time Early had believed that the president should speak out publicly on the need to revise the act, but Roosevelt refused, instead preferring that any publicity be generated by members of the public to keep it from appearing to be government propaganda.[5]

The Neutrality Act was a series of complex laws passed piecemeal by Congress beginning in 1935 with the basic aim of keeping the country out of a foreign war. For the most part, Roosevelt had supported the laws, since they tended to give him a wide latitude on such issues as defining "implements of war," determining when an embargo could go into effect, deciding when to prohibit American war vessels from carrying war materials to belligerent nations, and withholding protection from Americans traveling on ships of belligerent nations. A later act gave the president discretionary power to make the sale of non-embargoed goods on a "cash-and-carry" basis and to prohibit belligerent ships from using American ports. However, by January 1939 Roosevelt had concluded that the neutrality law "may actually give aid to an aggressor and deny it to a victim." The problem was that efforts to repeal the embargo were falling on too many deaf ears in Congress.

That fall, Early sparred regularly with the reporters at his press conferences, sometimes deflecting sensitive questions and other times lying to them outright. He repeatedly cautioned them not to include departure and arrival times of the presidential train when it carried Roosevelt because, he told them, the Secret Service was "getting pretty cautious." Another time, he told the reporters that Roosevelt was leaving for Hyde Park during the day when he in fact was leaving that evening.

On September 20, the day before Roosevelt had decided it was time to ask Congress to repeal—or at least amend—the Neutrality Act, Early told the reporters at his press conference that they would not be given an advance copy of the president's speech to what was being called an "extraordinary session," since Congress had adjourned and would not normally reconvene until the following January. The reporters could sense his anger bubbling beneath the surface when Early told them, "I do not want the people on the Hill to start calling up this office saying that they have seen advance copies brought up by newspapermen. That is bad business." If they planned to run to Congress, text in hand, to get reaction statements beforehand, Early said, they would not receive a copy of it until "very late." He solved the problem by distributing copies of the speech to the press just one hour before Roosevelt spoke to Congress.[6]

Perhaps Early was still stinging from the rebuke Roosevelt had given him a few days earlier for something Steve had said at his press conference that made the newspapers. In Hyde Park with the president, Early held a Sunday press conference during which he commented on a press release dealing with the organization of the White House staff. In response to a question with respect to Tommy Corcoran and Ben Cohen, two of the remaining members of the so-called Brain Trust, Early offhandedly replied that the "Brain Trust was out of the window," a comment that apparently hurt both Cohen and Corcoran, of whom, according to Harold Ickes, Early had been "pretty jealous." The aggressive, outgoing member of the team, Corcoran was a fervent New Dealer, almost slavishly devoted to Roosevelt and his programs for getting the country out of the Depression. Although there is no record of any specific instances, perhaps Corcoran stepped on Early's toes now and again as he moved freely and exuberantly in and out of offices in Washington.

Despite an attempt by Early to square things with Corcoran, Ickes thought that Roosevelt "gave Steve quite a spanking because Steve appeared to be very contrite." Corcoran was convinced that the press secretary had the question about the Brain Trust planted with a reporter at the press conference to take a whack at the two men. Ickes chalked the incident up to Early's "rough clumsy way of handling things," describing Early as "a little Gargantuan in his humor, given to playing practical jokes even if the object of his humor is hurt in doing so."[7]

It was about this same time that Early told his son Buddy, now away at military school, "It is but the simple truth to say that I have never before in the almost eight years I have spent in the White House seen either such volume of work to be done or so much of such great importance. All of it seems to be pressing. All of it seems to have a time element tied into it—a time element that compels you to give it immediate attention rather than let it wait and take its turn." He continued, "The war in Europe, the new crisis in the Far East, trips I have to make with the President when he travels away from Washington, all combine to make the sum and total almost impossible. I am quite sure you understand my problems. I am quite sure also that I have your sympathy."[8]

By October 14 Early appeared more than exasperated with the reporters. No doubt when he met earlier that morning with Roosevelt in his bedroom after the president had read the day's newspapers he had received an earful from the Boss about a story in the *New York Times*. By the time Early held his press conference, he was in a bad mood. He lashed out at the reporters, saying that the story "exemplifies a situation that we run up against quite often." This chastising of the press no doubt was the result of another verbal "spanking" from Papa Roosevelt, although in this case, it was not Early's indiscretion that made the president see red. Early told the reporters:

> There is one thing I would like to point out to you this morning. In a newspaper that has one ear announcing every day that it publishes "all the news that's fit to print," they give five columns on the first page today to a headline which says that the "U.S. Ignores Nazi Mediation Plea." That headline, in spite of repeated declarations by the President, by White House officials, by the Secretary of State and State Department officials that there is no Nazi mediation plea before this government. None has been received.
>
> Down in the story over which the head I just read appears, there is a paragraph which says: "Always reluctant to discuss international affairs at his press conferences, the President was even more so today. That he was aware of the gravity of the European picture since last midnight, when a German Government spokesman announced after conferring with Chancellor Hitler that President Roosevelt was the only one who could head off another 'blood bath' on the continent, was taken for granted by his press conference." Now this is a late edition of this newspaper and over on page three, in small type, single column, sub-head, there is an A.P. dispatch from Berlin I would like to read to you. "An official statement issued today by the Deutsche Nachrichtenburo read: 'In connection with The Associated Press report from Berlin that the Reich Press Chief, Dr. Dietrich, made a statement according to which only intervention by President Roosevelt could halt the war in the west, which has been interpreted in various quarters abroad as an appeal to President Roosevelt to intervene, we announce that no such appeal was made at all or intended. This is apparently due to a misunderstanding of the meaning of a private conversation which does not permit this interpretation.'"

Then Early said, "Now, gentlemen, I submit, that is not printing the news. It puts the President and this government in the position of sulking in their tents—which they are not doing."[9]

Later that fall he again took to task the newspaper with one ear announcing that it publishes "all the news that's fit to print." This time the *Times* had published a story that claimed the resignation of Joe Davies, now ambassador to Belgium, was on Roosevelt's desk. Early said he had already denied the story, "but apparently the *Times* thought they knew something neither the State Department nor the White House knew."[10]

On November 2 Congress amended the Neutrality Act to combine the "cash-and-carry" clause with repeal of the arms embargo, which meant US manufacturers could not sell arms to belligerent nations if the goods were shipped under the flag of a foreign country. It also gave the president latitude in proclaiming combat zones. Strange as it may seem today in reflecting on the magnitude and horror of World War II and its impact on the United States military and citizens alike, the years preceding the war were filled with bitter arguments about the need for the country to remain neutral.

Now with the immediate crisis with Congress safely navigated, Roosevelt and Early could leave Washington for some relaxation. Roosevelt spent the weekend of November 17 in Hyde Park, participating in the laying of the cornerstone of his beloved presidential library on the grounds of his estate. The contractor who was then constructing the handsome Jefferson Memorial in Washington, DC, also was overseeing the building of the library, and Roosevelt was keeping an eye on both projects. He returned to Washington on Monday and the following day headed south to Warm Springs to celebrate Thanksgiving, as he had done for so many years. On the way home, he stopped in Asheville, North Carolina, to visit Marvin McIntyre, whom Early told friends would not ever return full time to the White House. Meanwhile, Early spent four days playing in a golf tournament with friends in Pinehurst, North Carolina, and while Roosevelt was in Warm Springs, Early went duck hunting on the Maryland shore for five days, where he and five male friends lived in a hunting cabin and killed enough ducks and geese to feed themselves. Early said they were "away from telephones and other connections that might bring us troubles from the outside world."[11]

By the end of the month, play time was over and Watson, Roosevelt, and Early were back at work in the White House, or, as Early wrote in his diary on November 30, "The family is reunited. Now we must go to work. The old pressure is on." They returned in time to learn that the fragile diplomatic negotiations between the Soviet Union and Finland had irrevocably broken down, and on December 1 Russian troops were invading Finland. At his press conference three days later, Early held an off-the-record discussion with the journalists on the question of the United States breaking off relations with Russia. Increasingly he was using his press conferences as a venue to explain both domestic and foreign events, perhaps at Roosevelt's request. Sometimes these comments were off the record; other times Early would "straighten the boys out" on a story they had previously reported, leaving the decision to publish his scolding or not. As often as not, only the Washington papers, always eager to scoop their competition, would allude to one or another of Early's little lectures.[12]

Early's comments at the December 4 press conference showed his self-assurance in sharing his own opinions on the complicated and fragmented geopolitical events in eastern Europe:

> From what I see of the spreading idea to break off diplomatic relations with Russia, I have come to the conclusion that those who are considering it or would be responsible for the action are not looking ahead. For example, with friendly relations existing there are many advantages possible which would automatically be lost. Information, reports, intelligence reports and things like that now have a regular channel to come through and that channel is very valuable. Then if you go further into the future and assume that some day the world will become more rational and there will be another peace, it is natural to assume that the U.S. and the other nations—North and Central America—will have real need and value in what they may be able to contribute to the restoration of peace in the world.[13]

Long days and late nights of handling the press and acting as a go-between for the president and various members of the cabinet, Senators, and other important White House visitors who passed through the press secretary's office began to take its toll on Early, for a week later, he wrote, "Mrs Early came to the office with the car at three-thirty and I went home with her as I felt the need for a few hours rest."[14]

Indeed he did get away again, albeit for only two days, when he went duck hunting at the Maryland shore with his old friend Raymond Beebe, a Washington lawyer, returning just in time to announce to the press the scuttling of the German passenger liner *Columbus* about 450 miles off the shore of Cape May, New Jersey. The ship had been followed by the American cruiser *Tuscaloosa*, the same ship that would take Roosevelt north to his vacation home on Campobello Island and which was reporting its progress via radio to nearby ships from the time it left Vera Cruz, Mexico. Apparently the captain of the *Columbus* realized ultimately his ship would be seized or sunk, so he scuttled it. Although the action left some diplomats wondering just how neutral the United States really was, Germany did not protest, fearing it could further antagonize America.

The story from the White House, as relayed by Early to the newsmen at his press conference, was that the *Tuscaloosa* was "on routine neutrality patrol" when it found the German liner sinking. It proceeded to pick up survivors and brought them to either Norfolk, Virginia, or Ellis Island. Early said he was stressing that when the *Tuscaloosa* arrived, the *Columbus* already was sinking, adding that nearby was a British warship, which he believed had caused the German crew to scuttle its ship. He did admit that the *Tuscaloosa* "may have been trailing the *Columbus* waiting for it to get beyond the neutrality limits."[15]

The end of 1939 saw Early lunching frequently with his friend Joe Davies, who by now had resigned as ambassador to Belgium to return to Washington, and being on call to Roosevelt, who spent the last few days of December virtually incommunicado while preparing his annual message to Congress, which now had reassembled for its regular session. Still attempting to remain neutral but finding it more and more difficult as events played out in Europe, Roosevelt warned Congress of the effects of a Nazi victory. The following day in his budget message, he remained "equally cautious," calling for $1.8 billion for national defense, only a modest increase over previous years, and for substantially lower budgets than in the past for agriculture, public works, and various assistance programs. No one was pleased, in particular the army.[16]

As winter drifted slowly into spring that year, Britain instituted food rationing; Russian troops continued to hammer away at neighboring Finland, finally halting by mutual agreement on March 12; and once the Japanese had installed puppet governments in China, the US fleet left West Coast ports for maneuvers in the Pacific. In early May Hitler's armies marched west, and on May 10 they invaded Belgium, the Netherlands, and Luxembourg. When Roosevelt was informed that night, he called Early to the White House to monitor incoming messages on the invasion; Early remained until 3:00 a.m., arriving back at his office at his usual time to join Pa Watson in Roosevelt's bedroom. The geopolitical situation was so serious Roosevelt asked Early to delay the president's press conference by an hour.

That same day, Chamberlain resigned as the British prime minister, to be succeeded by Winston Churchill, heading a coalition government. Churchill's first speech to the House of Commons three days later, one that since has been recited by schoolchildren and quoted by scholars alike, began, "I have nothing to offer but blood, toil, tears, and sweat." He explained his foreign policy in true Churchillian prose: "It is to wage war by sea, land, and air, with all our might and with all the strength that God can give us: to wage war against a monstrous tyranny, never surpassed in the dark, lamentable catalogue of human crime."[17]

As mesmerizing as the expanding war in Europe was to both Republicans and Democrats in Congress as well as to those in the Executive Branch, what intrigued them even more were the political plans of the sitting president of the United States. One reporter called it "the No. 1 enigma of 1940." Now coming to the end of his second term in office, would he choose to run for an unprecedented third term or would he retire quietly to his home in Hyde Park, where he would oversee the remainder of the construction of his presidential library, write his memoirs, and perhaps, if called to do so, act as a wise sage to his successor? The rumors were rampant. Would he or would he not? Should he or should he not? The president kept his own counsel.[18]

A year and a half earlier, in the fall of 1938, Early had told Joe Davies that Roosevelt would not seek a third term. "Personally, I am certain in my conviction that the President does not want to be a candidate in '40." Early explained that Roosevelt would "do everything humanly possible to advance the cause of liberalism," ensuring that a liberal Democrat would win in 1940, adding that the president "does not believe a victory for the Democratic Party in 1940 is possible if the conservative Democrats take over the controls."

A man who has put in six years of killing and tireless effort to promote liberalism in government, very naturally, does not want to see all that he has done and will do in the next two years go promptly into the discard, should his Administration fail to be succeeded by one of the same sort. He knows, of course, that a conservative (Democratic or Republican) government would wreck everything he has done as certainly as the seas destroy a ship on the rocks.

As one who, for six years, has been privileged on the inside to view a picture as the artist worked on his production—this, as clearly as I can produce it in words, is precisely what I see and why I see it as I do.

Of course, no one had foreseen the tumultuous events in Europe throughout the spring and early summer of 1940. Either Early was not being candid with Davies or he was not being candid with himself, but years later, after Roosevelt's death, he told Jimmy Roosevelt that he had hoped the president would not run for a third term.[19]

In Miami Beach that spring for some golf, apparently to replace the late summer vacation cut short by events in Europe, Early reluctantly agreed to leave the greens long enough for an interview with the *Miami Herald*, but when the reporter asked him about Roosevelt's future, he replied, "Why should I say anything about it when the President doesn't mention it?" He did talk about Roosevelt's famous press conferences, noting, "Third term or no third term, succeeding administrations will find it difficult to establish the same relationship between the press and the government."[20]

Even Washington cabbies got in on the speculation. In early June a Diamond cab driver picked up Early and Roosevelt's son from the airport to take them to the White House. During the ride, young Roosevelt said his father "positively would run again." The driver repeated the remark to a friend whose brother worked for the *Washington News*, so of course the comment made the newspapers.[21]

Not unexpectedly the newsmen at Early's daily press conferences got into the guessing game. One day in mid-June, as talk expanded beyond a presidential third term to the choice of vice president, one reporter noted that Count Rene de Chambrun was in Flanders and had escaped, now working as a liaison for the French and British. As the great-grandson of Lafayette and therefore an American citizen, the reporter said, "As an American citizen, he would be eligible as vice president." Early quickly retorted, "That is a good idea. He is an American citizen-at-large. Which is perfect from a geographical light."[22]

As spring blossomed into summer, speculation focused on four possible successors to Roosevelt: Harry Hopkins; Henry Wallace, secretary of agriculture; Cordell Hull, the elderly and respected secretary of state; and Jim Farley, postmaster general and chairman of the Democratic National Committee. Each had his strengths and weaknesses, but none of them was Franklin Roosevelt.

Hopkins, close to the president since the inception of the New Deal and now secretary of commerce, was ailing; Wallace, both intelligent and moral but seen as sometimes too idealistic, had until 1928 been a Republican; Hull, who had been overseeing the State Department since the beginning of Roosevelt's presidency, already was sixty-eight years old and in the sunset of his career; and Farley, an old upstate friend of Roosevelt's, was a shrewd politician but a Catholic, and Democrats vividly recalled the defeat of Al Smith, the last Catholic who ran for president, in 1928.

On the periphery but still in the picture was the current vice president, John Nance Garner, whose relationship with Roosevelt had deteriorated to tenuous at best. In fact, one day in December 1939, the president said jokingly at a cabinet meeting, "I see that the vice president has thrown his bottle—I mean his hat—into the ring." Then he added, according to Ickes, that Thomas E. Dewey, the energetic young prosecutor who was ridding New York of racketeers, "has thrown his diaper into the ring." Roosevelt confided to Early that if neither of them could be connected with it, he wished a cartoonist would draw a picture of Baby Dewey throwing his diaper and Baby Garner throwing a bottle of "red eye" into the ring. Ickes said he passed the suggestion on to several people, but nothing came of it.

By April Ickes wrote in his diary: "All of us are inclined to believe that the President, as a result of the force of circumstances, will have to run again, and we believe that he will be elected, although we look for a hard fight."[23]

Early knew Roosevelt as well as anyone and better and longer than most of those around the president, so as the two men watched the events in Europe unfold, Early must have gleaned hints from the Boss as to what the latter was thinking. Would he dare walk away from a war? Could he seriously consider turning over the running of the country to anyone else at this pivotal point in history? Was it his destiny to see the United States through the inevitable war? Even Eleanor Roosevelt, who did not want her husband to seek reelection, was uncertain of his plans. She believed new leadership was needed, that Franklin should retire, and that only an international crisis would require his continued leadership.[24]

Those "circumstances" that Ickes had referred to somewhat obliquely in his diary came down to one word: war. By the end of May, Roosevelt had increased his budget request for defense appropriations: he was proposing production of fifty thousand planes a year, and he ordered the navy to recommission thirty-five destroyers. On May 28 the Belgian army surrendered, stranding English and French troops in Belgium and forcing more than 340,000 men to withdraw across the English Channel from Dunkirk, France. Then, on June 5, the Battle of France commenced when the German army crossed the Somme River. Nine days later, the troops reached Paris. Italy had now declared war on Britain and France and moved into France from the south.[25]

Early compared the spread of the European war to "a conflagration heading this way." He told the press, "The feeling here is that if there is a four-alarm fire up the street and the wind is sweeping it in the direction of your home, the issue at once becomes the protection of your home. What you want to do is keep it from reaching your home." But, he added, Roosevelt would leave it up to Congress to decide how to finance any acceleration of defense.[26]

If Early had ever wanted to jump out of the pressure cooker, it probably was now. For almost three weeks that March, Roosevelt was felled by a nasty flu, and Early was forced to look after business in the executive office as well as in his own office. It meant long meetings with the president in his bedroom so that Early could answer all the questions posed by the reporters at his daily press conferences, since Roosevelt was holding none of his own.[27]

In April he apologized to Buddy, who was away at military school, for not writing. He said he had failed to attend to many other personal duties, "the sort that could be put off temporarily and which did not have to be done immediately," because, he explained, "the fact is that we have been so busy at the office, lately, that we have had to sidetrack all but the most important and pressing affairs." Another time that spring, he told Buddy, "I find myself day after day 'out of time.'" He said the president had returned from his annual cruise off Florida and "is in fine fettle." Early wrote, "I thought I was busy while he was away—sitting on the lid and holding it tight so that he could enjoy himself. I had no idea then how busy a fellow really could be. I have been that busy since he got back—busier than I thought I could be." His words to his son may sound like an overworked press secretary but not one who would walk out on the Boss any time soon, third term or no third term.[28]

That spring and summer, work kept him tied to the White House often until late into the evening, like the night of June 10, when he was there until midnight to inform the press that Roosevelt would make an important announcement on the war the following day when he spoke at Franklin Junior's graduation from the University of Virginia. Not only did Early accompany the president to Charlottesville, but he oversaw arrangements for the speech to be broadcast live on all the radio networks.[29]

Nonetheless, Early apparently was still anxious to leave public life. That summer, he told Harold Ross, his old friend from *Stars and Stripes* and now the editor of the *New Yorker*, that he planned to leave the White House. "One thing is certain. I will not be here another four years," he said. And one night around the same time before one of the gang's poker games, he told Ickes that his savings were used up, his children needed educating, and still Roosevelt would not let him go. He seemed never to be home. No doubt like everyone else, Early was waiting for an announcement from Roosevelt.[30]

As it appeared more and more likely that the United States would be forced to enter the war to defend her longtime allies in western Europe, Roosevelt announced two cabinet appointments that left little doubt as to his increasing concern about events in Europe as well as in the Far East. He replaced Secretary of War Harry Woodring and Acting Secretary of the Navy Charles Edison, the son of the famous inventor, with two men who advocated military buildup and held far more international views than their predecessors. Frank Knox, publisher of the *Chicago Daily News* and a Republican vice presidential candidate in 1936, would take over the War Department, and Henry L. Stimson, an elder statesman who had served in the Taft and Hoover administrations, would become secretary of the navy.[31]

When the Republicans convened in Philadelphia in late June to nominate a presidential candidate, the party remained united in its defense of big business, but it now was split on foreign affairs. Of the viable candidates, Sen. Robert A. Taft of Ohio and Sen. Arthur H. Vandenberg of Michigan were isolationists, and Thomas E. Dewey was unwilling or unable to take a strong stand on foreign affairs. Only the outgoing, bearlike Wendell Willkie, who until 1938 had been a registered Democrat and had never held public office, appealed to a broad spectrum of the party, with his call for aid to the Allies but without war. Thus, on June 28, he was nominated to run against whomever the Democrats selected the following month. The ball was now in Roosevelt's court.[32]

Sam Rosenman, Roosevelt's friend and speechwriter, believed that if France had withstood Hitler's attack that May and if the war had then developed into a long stalemate, as World War I did between 1915 and 1917, Roosevelt would have allowed a liberal Democrat to be nominated, one who stood a fair chance of winning the election.[33]

Roosevelt's longtime secretary Grace Tully concluded that if the world had been at peace, Roosevelt would not have run for a third term; instead he would have retired to Hyde Park. In her memoirs, Tully said that no one really knew the exact date that Roosevelt decided to run again, although she speculates that it may have been on that hot Sunday, July 7, when Jim Farley, who by now represented the only potentially serious competition to Roosevelt if he were to run again, visited the president at his home in Hyde Park.[34]

A week earlier Early had telephoned Farley's office, indicating that the president would like to meet with him sometime the following weekend. Farley said he recognized this as a command and telephoned Early, whom he considered a good friend, saying he would drive from his home in Westchester to Hyde Park on Sunday. According to his memoirs, Farley said he planned to tell Roosevelt he would allow his name to be placed in nomination at the Democratic convention in Chicago in less than two weeks. After a somewhat friendly family lunch with Hopkins, Early, Missy LeHand, Eleanor, and the president's mother, Roosevelt and Farley excused themselves and moved into the president's study for a two-hour private conference.

Farley told the president that he personally was opposed to a third term. He said that at first Roosevelt told him he would not run for reelection and he would tell the convention so, but before the meeting ended, the president had said, "Jim, if nominated and elected, I could not in these times refuse to take the inaugural oath, even if I knew I would be dead within thirty days." Farley recalled that there were times during their meeting when he thought Roosevelt appeared to be in doubt about a third term, but the longer the two men talked, Farley believed that Roosevelt was convincing himself of the feasibility of running again.

Later that day, as he had promised, Early drove Farley to Nelson House in nearby Poughkeepsie, where the White House press corps was waiting to hear about his meeting with the president. First, however, he had to spend more than an hour driving an angry Farley around the area trying to cool him down. Early described Farley as "the maddest white man" he had ever seen. When they finally arrived at Nelson House and Farley met with the reporters, he was calmer but still not smiling, and he refused to reveal any of the president's plans or hints about his future.[35]

The press did not have long to wait. On July 11 Roosevelt asked Congress for another $4.8 billion for defense. The following day, two labor unions endorsed him for a third term, and seventy-seven members of the House signed a petition urging him to run again. By the weekend, Roosevelt was on an overnight cruise on the *Potomac*, away from the political and meteorological heat of the capital. Meanwhile, Hopkins and Sen. James Byrnes, the jaunty Irishman from South Carolina and Capitol Hill friend of the president, were in Chicago uniting Democrats for "a draft Roosevelt" movement at the convention. Still Roosevelt remained coy.[36]

Farley also had gone to Chicago, and Early told the media that Roosevelt and Farley were keeping in touch by telephone, the president preferring to remain in the White House, orchestrating the show from his office rather than from inside a smoke-filled hotel room in Chicago. It was all a part of his plan, one that he had been preparing for perhaps several months or more. If he could force the convention to draft him, something that he had hinted at during his meeting with Farley, he reasoned that he would be well positioned to select a vice presidential candidate of his choice, and the convention would have no option but to approve his man. A draft also meant that Roosevelt would be leaving the issue of a third term to the convention delegates, rather than his being forced to make the announcement that he sought to run again.[37]

All of this meant long days and nights that week for Early in his dual role as go-between for the president and the press and as confidant to Roosevelt. Early told the press that although the president was remaining in Washington, he was keeping his daily appointments, listening to the convention on the radio, and being available to talk by telephone with Hopkins and others of his key men in Chicago. By the second day of the convention he also was working on his acceptance speech, although this piece of information was carefully concealed from the press for the time being.[38]

That same evening Roosevelt's message releasing those delegates pledged to him was read to the convention. This now allowed them to vote for any candidate they wished, the White House plan being that they would choose the president. And they did: Farley received 72 votes; Garner, 61; and Roosevelt, 946.

The next night, Wednesday, July 17, 1940, the convention was set to select a vice presidential candidate, an act that it turned out was fraught with tension and acrimony. Early, Watson, Dr. McIntire, Rosenman, Missy LeHand, Grace Tully, and several others of the White House family gathered around the radio in the oppressively hot Oval Office. Perspiring, their clothing soaked since air conditioning was forbidden because of Roosevelt's sinus problems, they listened to the convention roll call. The president sat quietly nearby at a card table playing solitaire. His face was grim. As it appeared that his candidate, Henry Wallace, might just be defeated, Roosevelt picked up a pad and pencil and drafted a speech declining the nomination, obviously intended to be delivered if Wallace lost.

The tension in the room mounted as the vote was taken. It was close, but Wallace had won. Roosevelt, quietly relieved at the outcome, was wheeled into his bedroom where he bathed, changed his clothes, combed his hair, and returned a short time later at 12:15 a.m. to face a battery of microphones and tell the nation he would accept the nomination and run for a third term. According to Sam Rosenman, the president was smiling, "looking his usual jaunty, imperturbable self." As Early stood there in the wee hours of that Friday morning listening to the Boss accept the nomination for a third term, he realized that he would again be bound to the White House for four more years, and if the country indeed went to war he would never be allowed a release from his duties. The pressure was on.[39]

Roosevelt himself did little campaigning that summer, so when the National Association of Broadcasters invited Early to represent the president at its annual convention in San Francisco in early August, Early shipped the invitation over to the Boss, who returned it with this message: "Steve Go FDR." He headed west, played some golf, gave a speech at the convention, and created a little controversy along the way. It was a trip that he parlayed into a week, stopping in various cities on his way back to bring the president's campaign message. His stops were covered in all the local newspapers, even when his plane landed for a few minutes at the Butte, Montana, airport. Both local newspapers noted his presence. One ran this headline: "Stephen T. Early Passes Here on Eastbound Plane."

He fanned the flames of the already tension-filled Democratic politics in California when he met privately for forty-five minutes with Democratic Party leaders. His speech before the convention focused on freedom of the press in a democracy, saying that in spite of pending rumors that controls would be placed on radio because of defense plans, "radio is as free as the press." A photo of him that ran in the *San Francisco News* shows a consummate newsman wearing a white fedora hat, white shirt, and polka-dotted necktie with a cigarette dangling from his lips. He is squinting, looking off to the side with a cynical frown. Another newspaper photo portrays a pensive Early, same hat and tie, clutching a folded newspaper in his hands. When he arrived in Seattle, the *Star* showed him in the same hat, this time smiling, and noted, "Steve Early, presidential secretary, looks more like his boss every day (even the hat)."[40]

As Hitler moved into Romania and Italy invaded Greece that fall, Roosevelt and Early for the most part were tied to the White House, and when the candidate did venture out, he preferred to call them "inspection trips." Democrats were beginning to worry that their candidate would lose the election for lack of campaigning and in his stead was allowing cabinet members and others to handle his speaking duties. Early and Ickes both urged him to give up these trips and begin making outright political speeches, saying the "inspection trips" were deceptive. Early said he had been "pounding away without result," and the very day that he had made an especially intense effort, Roosevelt turned around and announced to his press conference that he would be making yet another such "inspection trip" the following week.[41]

The Boss might not leave the White House often, but the press secretary could engage in his own brand of campaigning, the kind he did best. He wrote a two-part series of articles on Roosevelt, titled "Inside the White House with Europe at War," for the August and September issues of *Cosmopolitan* magazine. They were unabashedly paeans to his employer.

Just as he did in the article "Below the Belt," which he wrote during the 1936 campaign, Early began by warning the reader to discount any rumors and skeletons rattled and to consider instead the difficult tasks he called "grilling ordeals of long and sustained labor that Roosevelt had been dealing with during the last eight years." He said that "a peep into" the president's regular schedule of duties would show that his day sometimes runs from midnight to midnight, although Early went on to tell readers that Roosevelt ordinarily did not wake until 8:00 a.m. He noted that the president always ate lunch in his office, often dining with one or two visitors who were there to discuss state business.

He talked about Roosevelt's health, but limited his comments to a recent bout with the flu, noting that the president, in a playful mood, had dashed off this jingle:

> Twinkle, twinkle, little nose.
> You remind me of a hose.
> Way above my mouth so high.
> Like a spigot in the sky.

He ended the first article with the poem and this piece of campaign puffery: "After all, Roosevelt long ago learned that few things in life are to be taken seriously and that nothing is ever to be taken tragically."

No doubt the president ran his eyes over the two articles before they were published. If so, it may have been his impish sense of humor that allowed Early to keep such comments as the one referring to Roosevelt's retinue of daily visitors to whom he was forced to listen "with interest, if possible, but always with patience." He added, "Not all of them are saints!"

Apparently the president enjoyed his twice-weekly press conferences where the correspondents engaged in "rough-and-tumble questioning" of the chief executive. Early noted that these conferences gave Roosevelt "a welcome interlude in a schedule that is often heavy with dead and uninteresting routine and the droning of dull visitors." However, Early said the president did not mind his workday interrupted by visitors bringing gifts, such as a newly baked cherry pie, the first salmon of the season, a huge cheese, or even a Homburg hat or a bedspread.

Early described the articles as "a simple straightforward recital of the events that make up the President's day, together with a sketch of the background against which he works and moves and has his being." They were filled with homilies and vignettes, aimed at the middle-class female reader who was curious about the president's life, both professional and personal, such as his habit of reviewing the events of his day when he retired for the night. And "if he concluded, as he usually did, that he had done the best he could, he was able to get to sleep without counting his sheep." Or how when he was at his home in Hyde Park he could sleep late in the morning. In neither article is there a mention of Eleanor Roosevelt.[42]

Until about a month before the election, Roosevelt relied more on radio than on public appearances. For instance, in mid-September he addressed the International Brotherhood of Teamsters, Chauffeurs, Stablemen and Helpers via radio from Hyde Park. A few days later, he and Early and other staffers headed to Alabama for the funeral of House Speaker William B. Bankhead, a three-day train trip.[43]

The *Washington Star* reported that fall that the White House continued to dominate the news, no matter what Wendell Willkie did. It was, the paper said, typical of the well-established White House system of blanketing opponents with bigger news than they can create," a system that was "originated and largely perfected by the president's secretary, Steve Early." In short, the paper went on, it was simply a matter of timing presidential actions and utterances so as to take the lion's share of the front page. And with a war on the system had been easier than ever to operate.[44]

As the election drew near, the president did roll up his shirtsleeves and headed out on the campaign trail, although most stops were limited to the East Coast.

Then, a week before the election, when Roosevelt and his entourage, including Early, traveled to New York City for some last-minute campaigning, all hell broke loose—and Steve Early almost lost his job and the candidate almost lost the traditionally Democratic Negro vote.

15

THE SLOAN AFFAIR

W hile there is no evidence that Steve Early ever was a member of the Ku Klux Klan, there is plenty of evidence to show his inborn southern prejudice against Negroes. Early was, in many ways, a man of his times.

A man who still considered himself a son of Virginia, Early lived in a city that was "rigidly and thoroughly segregated." When he went to the movies or the theater, he would find no blacks in the audience. When he dined at a restaurant, he would see no blacks eating there. Hotels, libraries, and taxis refused to serve blacks, and even retail stores in black neighborhoods defiantly refused to hire black clerks. Of course, there were Negroes in professions and businesses, but they usually served only those of their own race. The remainder found menial jobs that barely kept their families fed and clothed.[1]

In recounting a day in the life of President Roosevelt in 1941, a *Life* magazine reporter told of the meetings with his aides each morning in his bedroom, noting that they often began with a quip or a joke, such as this, typical of one from the president: "A couple of Negroes were walking along Pennsylvania Avenue when they were startled by the scream of police sirens and the roar of eight motorcycles preceding a long black car. In wonderment, one of the Negroes, impressed with the number of police, asks his companion who it was.

'Why, you ignoramus,' says the second Negro, 'Dat's the president of the United States.' Whereupon the first Negro said, 'What he done?'" Even Eleanor Roosevelt still used terms like "pickaninny," and "darky," a word she once included in one of her syndicated columns.[2]

One biographer of Eleanor Roosevelt has labeled the president's three closest male aides, Early, McIntyre, and Watson, "good old boys of the South," adding that they were "dedicated to all the trappings of race etiquette, the customs and traditions of servility, segregation, and discrimination." When the First Lady asked Early if she could have black women reporters at her press conferences, he said no because the president had none at his and doing so would create "a terrible precedent." Apparently she repeated her request a number of times, and the answer was always the same. Early's policy, from the beginning, had been to exclude newsmen from the Negro newspapers, his argument being that most of the black papers were weeklies and only dailies and the wire services were allowed to have representatives at either his or the president's press conferences.[3]

Another of Eleanor Roosevelt's biographers, Joseph P. Lash, claimed that although Roosevelt wanted to improve the conditions of the Negroes, as he did with all disadvantaged groups, he never considered himself a second emancipator. However, he did understand the need to protect his white support in the South, so he preferred to leave issues relating to race to Eleanor. And sometimes it was left to Early to handle the First Lady.[4]

Thus, there were times when the southern white man and the liberal northern woman collided head-on over matters of race. In the summer of 1935, Early told Eleanor's secretary that Walter White, the head of the National Association for the Advancement of Colored People (NAACP), had been "bombarding the President with telegrams and letters" demanding passage of an antilynching bill before Congress. Early said that White recently had entered a restaurant in the Capitol and expected to be served, "apparently deliberately creating a troublesome scene," which Early said some believed was for publicity purposes and "to arouse Negroes around the country." Early also said he had been told that even before Roosevelt came into the White House White had been "one of the worst and most continuous troublemakers."[5]

Mrs. Roosevelt, in her genteel but firm fashion, defended her friend White in a reply to Early: "If you ever talked to him and knew him, I think you would feel as I do. He really is a very fine person with the sorrows of his people close to his heart." She admitted that White had "an obsession" with the lynching issue and that he had been "a great nuisance with his telegrams and letters, both now and in previous administrations." But, she noted, "[I]f I were colored, I think I should have the same obsession that he has."[6]

The following summer, during the 1940 campaign, Roosevelt's more conservative advisers, including Early, were especially concerned that Eleanor's championing of Negroes could hurt the president's reelection chances and felt she should remain in the background for the duration of the campaign. The result was that she tended to keep a low profile, unlike the more aggressive role she had played during the summer of the 1936 campaign.[7]

In September 1940, at Eleanor's urging, Negro leaders (including Walter White), the secretary of the navy, and the assistant secretary of war met to discuss participation of Negroes in the armed services. The president also attended and promised to get back to the Negro group. Several days passed and there was no word from the White House. Then Early issued a statement that the Negroes had approved the policy of segregation. They had not, and they demanded a retraction. They asked Eleanor to intervene. Whether or not Early had deliberately issued an incorrect statement or whether it was simply a miscommunication between the president and his press secretary, Early wrote to White expressing regret that the wording in the statement had upset the Negroes. However, no one in the White House was prepared for the fallout from a chaotic moment involving Early and a black policeman that occurred just one week before the 1940 election.[8]

On Sunday, October 27, the presidential party—including Early, Pa Watson, Dr. McIntire, Missy LeHand, Grace Tully, and half a dozen other aides—plus twenty-four newspaper reporters and wire correspondents and eleven radiomen, newsreel people, and photographers, took an overnight train to Newark, where the president would greet mayors of northern New Jersey. From there they headed to Penn Station in Manhattan so that Roosevelt could attend some meetings and ceremonies. It was a hectic trip; the party made eight stops during the day, leaving Penn Station that night at 11:00 p.m. with an arrival time back in Washington at 8:30 the following morning.

That Monday night, with Roosevelt already in his private Pullman car, the entourage descended the stairway in the station to begin boarding the train for the return trip. But according to Early, when he tried to go down the stairs, his way was blocked by two policemen, who, he said, started shoving him and blocking his path to the train. "They [the police] wouldn't listen when I showed my credentials and told them I had an important message for the President," he later told reporters. When a third policeman, a Negro, joined the fracas, Early said that in an effort to protect himself, his knee came up against the man's lower abdomen. Eyewitness accounts pointed to the confusion resulting from members of the White House staff and journalists all showing credentials in an effort to board the train. The police finally decided not to allow anyone through no matter who they were, even Secretary of the Treasury Henry Morgenthau and his wife.[9]

The incident set off a firestorm and made headlines around the country. Negroes and northern liberals were shocked that the president's aide would injure a Negro who also was a policeman. Republican politicians recognized it as delicious election fodder. Republican newspapers made mincemeat of Early and Roosevelt. One headline said, "Power Always Corrupts." Another headline called Early "Often the Mouthpiece of the Third Term Candidate."

Harold Ickes called for his friend's resignation, fearing that if the president kept Early in his administration, Roosevelt's election chances could be seriously damaged. New York's district attorney, devoted Republican Thomas E. Dewey, opened what one publication called "an intensive investigation." Even J. Edgar Hoover, head of the FBI, got on the case, except that he set out to dig up dirt on those in the Negro community who had spoken out against Early. The boxer Joe Louis jumped into the verbal ring and declared Early's allegedly kneeing the policeman was "the foulest blow in the campaign."

Eleanor deplored the press secretary's loss of temper but said rather cavalierly, "He would have behaved in exactly the same way no matter who the person was. He has a hot temper." The president's first reaction was one of annoyance, but he did not show it to Early.[10]

The Negro policeman was James Sloan. He was forty-two years old and had undergone surgery for a hernia the previous July. After the incident at Penn Station, he complained of pain in his abdomen and took to his bed, which created more headlines. Republicans wasted no time in producing a five-by-seven-inch flyer with a photograph showing Sloan at home in his bed with his young daughters, looking solicitous, at his side. "Negro Kicked in Groin by President's Secretary" was in large type, and the copy on the flyer noted, inaccurately, that Early was a grandson of Jubal Early, the Confederate army general. It concluded with this: "Negroes—If you want your President to be surrounded by Southern influences of this kind, vote for Roosevelt. If you want to be treated with respect, vote for Wendell Willkie."[11]

What did Early have to say about the incident? He said he was simply performing his official duty, attempting to obtain permission for the newspapermen and women and others to board the train. Some of the reporters on the scene said the police refused to look at anyone's credentials. One reporter said that after Early identified himself to the police, "they came at him, pushing him backwards, almost off his feet. Early then raised his knee and caught Sloan in the stomach."[12]

One eyewitness who was standing next to Early, Thomas F. Reynolds, a United Press correspondent and president of the White House Correspondents Association, said that Sloan shoved Early so violently that he would have fallen had Reynolds not caught him. As he fell, Reynolds said, Early's leg was flung into the air and struck the policeman.[13]

Reporters said the officers had been brusque and unwilling to do anything to help the group get on the train. In fact, Early's intervention was at the request of the journalists, a request that one reporter described as "in a completely calm tone of voice." Another eyewitness said that even the Secret Service could not make the police understand who the party was.[14]

Early did apologize, saying he was sorry if a policeman was hurt. He admitted that in the midst of the shoving his knee "came up against his [Sloan's] body." But, he added, "I do not think I did anything wrong." He also sent a copy of his official statement and apology, dated October 31, to Patrolman Sloan. One publication suggested that if Early had indeed struck the policeman in the groin with the force he was alleged to have used, Sloan would not immediately have run up the stairs in the train station but instead would have doubled up and collapsed on the floor.[15]

Harold Ickes called the apology "very trifling and grudging" and suggested Early go to Sloan's home in New York and apologize in person, but Harry Hopkins, a former administrator for several New Deal agencies and now a White House adviser to Roosevelt, pointed out that if he did a warrant, no doubt for assault, would be served by Dewey, and Early would be arrested. Ickes decided that might be a positive political move because "the country would know that Dewey was playing cheap politics and would react in our favor." But Early did not go to New York. He was afraid of a lawsuit, and after the election he had the Democratic National Committee pay an agent in New York to gather information about Sloan to prevent any legal action. No legal action came about from Sloan or New York City.[16]

It was in part testimony to the kind of generally good working relationship the press secretary enjoyed with the reporters and photographers who covered the White House that many of them who were on hand when the fracas occurred wrote stories for their publications supporting Early. *Editor & Publisher*, a weekly trade magazine for journalists, published an account of the incident two weeks after the election.

An editorial in the *New Republic*, a liberal magazine, questioned *Editor & Publisher*'s publication of the story after the election, rather than right after the incident occurred. The *New Republic* wrote, "How does it happen that this version [Early's version] of the affair was given so little publicity before the election? Why did most newspapers go on printing sob stories about the heroic policeman writhing on his bed of pain, when they must have known better? Is it possible that the publishers of the country were negligent about correcting a falsehood against Mr. Early because they hoped the story would help to defeat the presidential candidate whom they opposed?"[17]

When *Time* magazine's account of the incident differed sharply from those of the other reporters on the scene, the White House Correspondents Association sent a letter to *Time*, no fan of the Roosevelt administration, calling the magazine's story inaccurate. The story, titled "Early's Temper," chastised the press secretary's behavior and said he "jerked up his knee into the Negro policeman's groin." The following week Manfred Gottfried, *Time*'s managing editor, grudgingly admitted that the original story was inaccurate since the magazine's reporter had not witnessed the event. In fact, an office staffer had written the story. But *Time* had to get in the last word: Gottfried wrote, "[M]aybe we do Steve Early an injustice, but when the cops were pigheaded, Early lost his head."[18]

Early decided that the whole affair ended "satisfactorily." He was especially impressed with the support from the news media, but he admitted that the incident would not soon be forgotten. "It did leave its scars," he said, noting some of his old friends, no doubt Ickes included, had disappointed him. On the other hand, he said, others of whom he expected little or nothing went out of their way to help.[19]

Politically the story had a happy ending. Patrolman Sloan ended up endorsing Roosevelt and said he would vote for him. Roosevelt won the election 27,308,000 to Willkie's 22,321,000. The electoral vote was Roosevelt, 449, and Willkie, 82. After the election Sloan sent Early a letter saying he regretted the incident and thanked him for his earlier apology, calling it all "an accident void of all malice." He said he waited to write so his words "would not be seized upon for purely political purposes." Early replied, telling the policeman that if he ever got to Washington, "please come see me."[20]

Early was right. The Sloan affair, as it often was called, was not soon forgotten. It would dog him throughout the rest of his professional life and long after his death. In fact, when a policeman was beaten up by a soldier during World War II, New York and Washington newspapers covered the story, and every one of them noted that the victim was the same policeman who was injured in a "scuffle" or a "fracas" with Early in 1940. Most historians of the Roosevelt era who choose to include the Sloan story in their books place at least half or more of the blame on the press secretary, citing his legendary temper as the reason for the alleged assault. It also has become a touchstone for assuming that Early was a racist.

It was too true that Steve Early could "turn the air blue with expletives," sometimes erupting "every hour on the hour like an active young volcano." Merriman Smith, a White House correspondent for United Press, concluded that it was this low boiling point that probably saved Early from ulcers during the twelve years in a difficult job. The press secretary was available to reporters who had his unlisted telephone number, but he hated to be awakened at odd hours, and when he was, Smith recalled, "he had the early morning or midnight temper of a mountain lion freshly trapped by only one leg."[21]

Robert Sherwood, the playwright and a Roosevelt speech writer, agreed that Early was quick tempered, and "being intolerant of the arts of diplomacy, [he] felt no great need to hide his emotions," a fact that Sherwood concluded no doubt was another reason for his survival in the White House. Early suffered acutely from Roosevelt's tendency to snap back at a hostile press, but since there was nothing much he could do about it, his occasional outbursts at members of the press often assuaged that frustration, and the reporters seemed to understand it.[22]

Long before he was elected president, Roosevelt had determined, more or less accurately, that most newspapers were owned or controlled by Republicans, and as honest and forthright as Early tried to be with the reporters covering the White House, there was little he could do to quell his boss's outbursts directed at the press. He did try. For instance, when Roosevelt ripped out of the newspaper a column or story that offended him and yelled, "It's a damn lie from start to finish," Early would try to dissuade Roosevelt from railing against the reporters at his next press conference. He would attempt to explain to the president that when he took the whole group to task for the sins of a few, he ran the risk of alienating all of them. Sometimes Roosevelt listened; sometimes he did not. No doubt this latter course of action contributed to the press secretary's own outbursts.[23]

Early's temper became so legendary around the White House that during the war when he flew to London to make a radio address that was beamed to the United States, someone asked one of the White House switchboard operators if she had heard the talk.

"Did he start off 'Jesus Christ on a mountaintop, hell and damnation?'" the woman asked. When told that he had not, she emphatically announced, "It wasn't Mr. Early then."

Jonathan Daniels, son of Josephus Daniels, Roosevelt's old boss at the navy, was an assistant to Early beginning in the early 1940s and eventually replaced Early as press secretary near the end of the war. Daniels called Early "efficient in handling the press," its members finding him "trustworthy." But they recognized his explosive irascibility, Daniels said: "As a man with a low boiling point, he engaged in almost poetic profanity."[24]

Right after Early's death in 1951, Marquis Childs, a reporter for the *Washington Post* and one of the most highly respected political analysts, recalled that the press secretary "served two temperamental masters." Childs wrote that while President Roosevelt "invariably presented a genial exterior, his very geniality, his whimsicality, often must have made Early's task almost unbearably difficult. Of the many virtues that made up FDR's greatness, precision was not one."

Early's other taskmaster, Childs wrote, was the corps of working newspapermen and women and the broadcasters, and behind them was the whole powerful complex of the information industry. In the early years of Roosevelt's administration, the relationship with the working press was excellent. It deteriorated as the years wore on, and Early often was forced into the role of arbiter between "the Boss" and the journalists who demanded the news.[25]

Perhaps, then, what made the press corps' defense of Early remarkable was that six weeks before the episode at Penn Station, the White House photographers, angry at yet another Early press rule, had held a sit-down strike and refused to take pictures of Roosevelt swearing in Frank Walker, Jim Farley's successor as postmaster general.

Apparently relations between the photographers and Early had been strained on and off recently, so when Early decided that only one photographer, from the Associated Press, would be allowed into the executive office to take pictures of the ceremony and the pictures would become pool photos for everyone else, the cameramen rebelled, though they said they had nothing against the president. "We just refuse to be shoved around by Steve Early." Roosevelt was so amused by the incident that he ordered Early to take the picture of Walker, himself and the lone cameraman. The feud ended two days later when an angry Early, clearly forced to compromise, allowed the photographers en masse into the Cabinet Room to photograph Gen. John J. Pershing when he came by to receive the Distinguished Service Cross from the president. The new laissez-faire system of everyone shooting the event would apply, he said grudgingly, "whenever the presence of the photographers does not detract from the dignity of the occasion."[26]

Despite his reputation for candor in dealing with the press and for his appreciation of the right of the press to full and accurate information, Early and the press did not always see eye to eye. One of those periods was during the late spring and early summer of 1940. The reporters were complaining that the press secretary was reviving the old Coolidge policy of the "unofficial spokesman," where nothing could be attributed to the president, a situation that in part may have arisen because Roosevelt was playing his plans for reelection close to the vest, making it nearly impossible for his press secretary to be as candid with the reporters as he would have preferred. Foreign policy in Europe, with its overtones of secrecy and intrigue, may have contributed to tying Early's hands now and again at his press conferences.

One newspaper called Roosevelt "the silent occupant of the White House," pointing out that Early no doubt was speaking on behalf of the president, but "if his utterances go unchecked, so much to the good. If he puts his foot in it, he was speaking on his own and without the consent or authority of the President." This way, the newspaper said, the president "got credit for all the hits but never assumed the liability of any errors."[27]

It was indeed placing the press secretary between a rock and a hard place, but for the most part he handled these difficult situations with aplomb—although now and again with a burst of ire. For example, there was the day in June that year when Early took to task the *Chicago Tribune*, Roosevelt's constant nemesis and a newspaper the president regularly read in spite of how much he detested it for a story it published. Early told his press conference: "I am lacking in decent language to deny that story." His famous temper barely in check, he added, "This leads me to wonder whether all the news published in the United States is published from an American patriotic point of view or from a foreign point of view." The story said that the State Department had been informed that France was considering a separate peace treaty with Germany, which was more or less true. After Early's outburst, the *Tribune* had the last word: "Mr. Early showed that an official denial from Washington is to be regarded as conclusive evidence on this point." Walter Trohan, the newspaper's longtime White House correspondent, who broke the story on the peace treaty for his paper, told his readers with tongue in cheek, "A good deal of experience with politics and politicians suggests the wisdom of placing something less than complete confidence in such denials."[28]

In his book *Washington Goes to War*, the journalist/author David Brinkley says that while Roosevelt could ignore or even joke about attacks by his political opponents, attacks in McCormick's *Tribune*, the Hearst newspapers, and in the *Washington Times-Herald*, owned by McCormick's cousin, the flamboyant Cissy Patterson, "made him see red." In general, Early and Roosevelt agreed that they shared two pet aversions: editorializing columnists and irresponsible gossip writers, the worst of the latter being Drew Pearson, son-in-law of Cissy Patterson. Pearson was the chief purveyor of not only gossip but salacious scandal that focused on politicians in the capital. It also may have irked Roosevelt that Pearson earned around $250,000 a year, more than double the presidential salary.[29]

When occasionally the famous Early wrath did descend upon a newsman for a story he wrote or a question he asked during a press conference, the reporter nursed no grudges, probably because the next time the newsman who had set off Early's temper ran into the press secretary, he would find him in a jolly mood, the incident totally forgotten. One reporter said Early pulled no punches with the reporters, although he sometimes "raises his voice in a sharp, icy reply to a reporter's question." But the reporter concluded that in spite of his periodic outbursts, Early was one of the main reasons why the president got along so well with the press in Washington: "He treats all newsmen alike, regardless of whether the papers they represent are anti–New Deal or pro–New Deal. His attitude is that reporters are entitled to honest, forthright replies to important questions. If he becomes nettled occasionally, it is because he thinks a question is trivial or that a newsman is trying to press him to say more than he wants to say."[30]

But as we have seen, Early's problems with photographers were more complex than the intermittent skirmishes with reporters at his press conferences. When Early came on board as press secretary to a president who had no use of his legs and spent his waking hours in a wheelchair, he was faced with a public relations problem the likes of which no aide to a chief executive had ever had to deal. As Jimmy Roosevelt said, Steve Early's job "was one of the most difficult in Washington," and dealing with the cameramen who covered the president certainly made the job no easier. Early once pointedly told the press regarding Roosevelt's handicap: "It's not a story." But it was, and every journalist in Washington—and especially those covering the White House—knew it was. Early kept close tabs on rumors about the president's health, and he and others on the White House staff would go to great lengths to deny or put a lid on the myriad rumors that seemed to pop up with great regularity.[31]

From the beginning, with Roosevelt's blessing, Early had complete control over where photographs, both still and moving, could be taken. For instance, no photos were allowed in the White House without Early's permission, and these generally were limited to official occasions and then only in the areas of the building normally open to the public. Photos also were forbidden in the living areas of the president's home at Hyde Park, in his private quarters at Warm Springs, and aboard the presidential railroad car and yacht. In rare instances when a photographer did penetrate these forbidden areas and capture the president on film, Early would immediately call for an investigation to learn how the photographer was able to get the picture. In addition, newsreel coverage was carefully planned to avoid oversaturation. Although Early did not prohibit members of the White House staff from taking informal shots, he did require they remain private and not be published.[32]

The most famous of the Early rules, of course, was his ban on all photographs depicting the president's handicap. From the time he had returned to politics, Roosevelt's advisers had been astutely aware that if images of his immobility were to be widely disseminated, they could undermine his political strength. Thus, when Roosevelt was elected president, Early simply continued that ban.

In his dissertation, "Selling the Presidency," Steven Schoenherr writes, "Most Americans knew that Roosevelt had suffered from infantile paralysis, and most probably knew that as a result he had some trouble walking, but few realized he was totally crippled because they never saw photos showing his handicap." Newsreels and newspaper and magazine photos portrayed him from the waist up, "the ever moving head, the powerful arms and chest, the gestures and facial expressions of what had to be a dynamic personality."[33]

In fact, when J. B. West began working as an assistant usher in the White House in 1941, he said he was surprised when he first saw Roosevelt. "We all knew he was supposed to be 'crippled' or something, that he walked with a limp or something, but when standing on the back platform of the campaign train, he looked strong, a barrel chest, as he stood well over six feet tall." West said he had seen the president once when he had visited his Midwestern hometown: "I don't remember a word of his speech, but there was something in his manner. He was truly dynamic, I thought." Then, the first time he saw Roosevelt in the White House, he said, "The door opened, and the Secret Service guard wheeled in the President of the United States. Startled, I looked down at him. It was only then that I realized that Franklin D. Roosevelt was really paralyzed."[34]

Early's ban apparently had been a success.

Even John Gunther, the author and chronicler of Roosevelt, said that because news stories almost never mentioned the president's disability and the fact that he used a wheelchair was never published in stories, coupled with Early's ban on photos of the crippled Roosevelt, the vast majority of Americans were simply unaware that their leader was running the country from a wheelchair. Gunther said that correspondents newly assigned to the White House were disconcerted to see the president wheeled into the room. And when Roosevelt was taken from a car or off a ship, out of public view, he was carried, a sight that even Gunther, who knew he was paralyzed and had no use of his legs, found unsettling. He said that at those times Roosevelt "seemed so small."[35]

Schoenherr points out that photographers obeyed the Early rule "in part out of respect for the office of the president and in part out of respect for the suffering of the man himself." He noted that once when a Republican newspaper assigned a photographer to get a picture of Roosevelt being carried, the White House photographers blocked his view and moved his camera to prevent him from getting the shot.[36]

On the other hand, the movie newsreels proved even easier to control and were treated well by Early, in part because he had worked for Paramount and in part because as a form of entertainment the newsreels preferred to show positive images of the president. The cameramen in general never challenged Early's rules. Early remained close to Robert Denton, his handpicked successor at Paramount, with whom he also socialized. In fact, Early's daughter Helen said that she and her siblings called him "Uncle Bob." Early even referred to Denton's camera crew as "the President's own," and the company was the only one to give the White House a copy of every presidential story used in its newsreels.[37]

One of the still photographers, a man named Sammy Schulman, became a friend of Roosevelt's, and Jimmy Roosevelt once asked Schulman why he and his fellow photographers were so ready to adhere to Early's dictum. He told Jimmy that the president "treated us well, so we treated him well. There never was a public figure who was so accessible to the press, who was so responsive to them [the reporters and photographers] and easy with them, who treated them as equals and would joke with them. He was a decent human being, we genuinely liked him, and we didn't want to embarrass him."[38]

Of course, today it is impossible to imagine a president of the United States—or for that matter any other man or woman in the public eye—keeping such a disability under wraps.

16

"JUST BETWEEN US 'GIRLS'"

By 1941 the *New York Times* told its readers that Early was "the only Presidential secretary to be regularly quoted in his own right in the newspapers" and was "almost as much of a fixture in the administration as the president himself." It noted that to the press correspondents in Washington and, to a lesser degree, the American people, Early was an "authentic public figure—almost an assistant to the President." About the same time, *U.S. News* wrote, "His importance and influence in the Administration are greater than is generally realized."[1]

That same year, when Early traveled to St. Paul, Minnesota, to speak in place of the president at the dedication of the new plant for the city's newspaper, the *Pioneer Press*, that paper called him "the best-informed man in Washington, next to the president himself, on Administration policies." In a nationally broadcast speech, Early warned the American public of "the dangers of totalitarianism" and stressed the government's—that is, Roosevelt's—commitment to "a policy of all-out defense." This talk was all part of a continuing plan by Early and the president to prepare the country for war, to make the public understand the necessity of defense mobilization that had been in motion since 1938 when Hitler marched into Czechoslovakia.[2]

More and more, Roosevelt was encouraging Early to take the lead in pushing the White House agenda. By now Early had three stenographers at his own press conferences taking down his remarks to the newsmen, since what he was saying could be quoted and attributed to him. The *St. Louis Post-Dispatch* called him "the acknowledged White House spokesman," noting that he used extreme caution in his phrasing and his demeanor, aware that the tone of his voice as well as the words themselves were news and had the potential to cause an international incident or a domestic quarrel.[3]

More than a secretary and friend to the President, Early was a close personal adviser, certainly when it came to handling the media, and nowhere was this more in evidence than at Roosevelt's press conferences. Early usually stood a few feet behind the Boss's chair, always at the ready. If, for instance, an announcement to be read by the president came to his attention just as the reporters walked in, Roosevelt would turn his head slightly and call out, "Steve," who would step forward. The two men would huddle, and then the president would comment. Or a reporter might ask a question involving a matter Roosevelt was unfamiliar with, and again he would call on Steve for the information. Sometimes it was simply to clarify a presidential remark that he recognized as being misunderstood by the reporters. If he thought the president's remarks were injudicious for one reason or another, Early would interrupt, sometimes quite sharply, and tell the reporters, "Make that off the record." According to Walter Trohan, the *Chicago Tribune's* White House man, Early saved the president "from many a blunder."[4]

Because the relationship between the two men was so intimate and of such long standing, Early would sometimes simply step forward without being called and whisper something in the president's ear. Roosevelt might nod and continue, or he might grin in amusement at what Early had whispered and head off on a different tack.[5]

At a Roosevelt press conference early in 1942, as the president was discussing the ramifications of wartime blackouts in Washington, he attempted to read a memo from James M. Landis, who had left Harvard to head the Office of Civil Defense, regarding instructions for blacking out office windows. It said: "Such obscuration may be obtained either by blackout construction or by terminating the illumination." Reporters, recognizing bureaucratic jargon, began laughing. One said, "That isn't the one you said Steve wrote, is it?" Roosevelt replied, "No, Steve did not write that. The dean of the Harvard Law School wrote this." Again the reporters laughed. The president handed the memo to Early, who as an Associated Press reporter had often had the syllables knocked out of him: "Rewrite that for me, will you? Tell them the buildings that have to keep their work going, put something over the windows. In the buildings that can afford it, so that work can be stopped for a while, turn out the lights." The newspapers loved the story.[6]

The Roosevelt-Early banter at FDR's press conferences one day in March 1941 led to an amusing exchange at Early's expense. It seems the president was a half hour late. When the reporters called him on his tardiness, his excuse was that he was using a clock given to him by Steve Early, and, he explained, it told "Early time." It may have been late nights at the bridge or poker tables or simply that his boss was not an early morning riser, but Early rarely showed up at his office before 9:15 a.m., a practice he carried through the war years, although he often stayed late into the night when a hot story was brewing and reporters needed it to meet deadlines for the morning editions.[7]

According to *Editor & Publisher*, throughout the entire Roosevelt administration the press received most of its White House news from Early during his own daily press conferences. The reasons were several: From 1941 until his death, Roosevelt made at least forty separate trips, often on weekends, to his home in Hyde Park, New York; he undertook a half dozen missions for the war effort, including those to Casablanca, Tehran, and Yalta; and he took to his bed with various minor and not-so-minor ailments during those years.[8]

In the 1930s Early often accompanied the president on his trips to his New York home. However, after Pearl Harbor, Roosevelt needed Early to keep the lid on in Washington, and anyway the press secretary preferred to stay in the capital, where he could get home every night and hit the golf course or the racetrack in his spare time. Thus, the quiet, bookish William D. Hassett, Early's assistant, took Early's place dealing with the press on the weekend trips to Hyde Park, which by then were conducted in extreme wartime secrecy and with careful press censorship.[9]

If a reporter newly assigned to cover the White House showed up one morning in the late spring of 1941 to check in with the president's press secretary, here's what he would find: A fifty-two-year-old man of 170 pounds, 5 feet 10 inches in height, with thick, wavy brown hair, parted on the left and with patches of gray at the temples. His handshake is warm and firm and creates an impression in the reporter's mind that he is welcome. As they talk, the reporter won't be surprised that the press secretary calls him by his first name, since he is on a first-name basis with every newsman and woman who covers the White House.

Still Mr. Early to the new man in the press corps, he might take off his horn-rimmed glasses and twirl them in his right hand as he gestures and speaks in a slightly discernible southern drawl. In his relaxed mood today he may be puffing on his pipe, although he often smokes a cigarette. He is wearing a dark blue suit with double-breasted jacket, white handkerchief in pocket, and a vest. He sits behind his desk, which, like the president's own, is cluttered with knickknacks and memorabilia, including a plaque with these words from Mark Twain: "Always do right. This will gratify some people and astonish the rest." On a narrow shelf behind his chair is a wooden sign that reads: "We Ain't Mad with Nobody." Several photographs of the president decorate his walls.

The new man has heard that Steve Early is considered "hard boiled" with a "towering temper," and that the press secretary can be quick to castigate a reporter, even wounding the sensibilities of the person against whom the words are directed. When he gets angry, his lips seem to disappear. Most often he is angry with a reporter who asks a stupid question at a press conference, although he doesn't stay mad for very long. Reporters describe him as "a tough guy with a big heart." They consider his loyalty to the president one of his outstanding characteristics, and it also keeps him close to the telephone night after night, even after a losing night at the bridge table, to answer inquiries from those same reporters.

Today, the press secretary is almost mellow, in spite of the deepening diplomatic and military crisis in Europe, a side of him that Roosevelt's secretary Grace Tully calls "soft as putty." The new reporter is in the company of a man with slightly hooded expressive blue-gray eyes that crinkle at the corners when he laughs—and he can laugh heartily, closing his eyes and enjoying the moment. Early's real charm comes through in personal meetings. It is then that he instantly relaxes and turns on a smile that lights up his features and for a moment softens the thin lips, the double chin, and the heavy jowls.

Handsome he is not. He never will be taken for a film star, a fact of which he is acutely aware. During the meeting, he points to a photograph of himself taken recently in the office of John S. Knight, publisher of the *Miami Herald*, and calls it "the best informal picture ever made of me," adding matter-of-factly, "I'm the type that doesn't photograph well." A couple of years earlier, in a brief letter to his friend Joe Davies during a transcontinental trip with the president, Early noted that some of the press photographers had just shown him a photo of himself. He told Davies, "Sometimes it is difficult to believe that the camera lens can see and register such queer objects. I refer particularly to my face."[10]

A *Philadelphia Bulletin* reporter around the same time saw a man plagued with sinus infections, overworked for days on end and deprived of exercise and time to relax, and occasionally angered by tactless probing into the president's affairs. On the whole, though, the reporter decided Early was doing his best to keep the country informed, at the same time protecting Roosevelt and the administration as a whole against "half-baked or totally unwarranted publicity." This reporter concluded, "American newspapers would not be as well informed on what the president is thinking, saying and doing if there were no press secretary and if that press secretary were not Steve Early."[11]

What the new reporter at the White House may not know is that soon after Early returned from St. Paul earlier that winter of 1940–1941, he was felled by a cold. Roosevelt, who himself was recovering from the flu, chose to play doctor to his press aide, writing him this note: "For your own comfort you had better stay in bed, too." Then, thinking this might cheer up the patient, he told Early that Pa Watson was planning to refurbish his office while he was out sick. It had the opposite effect. Early jumped out of bed the following day and hurried to the White House to discover that Watson indeed had replaced some of his furniture. Early held his press conference that morning and when a reporter said he understood that the press secretary had thrown out the new furniture, Early replied sarcastically, "Very quickly. Did you see it?" Apparently the reporters had seen it, and one of them replied, "Don't blame you."[12]

No doubt the two weeks Early spent fishing off Florida in March 1941 with Roosevelt, Pa Watson, Harold Ickes, Attorney General Robert H. Jackson, and Harry Hopkins relieved some of that stress and kept the sinus infections at bay. Of course, with a war imminent, this was not the usual presidential March outing. The party boarded the president's special train late on Wednesday, March 19, for Florida, where the yacht *Potomac* awaited. On the way, they stopped to inspect the Naval War Station at Jacksonville. But high seas kept the ship in port for the first thirty-six hours of the trip, just two hundred yards from a German warship that had been seized fifteen months earlier. Flying a swastika, the "enemy" ship had forty-four sailors interned on board, who watched as the president of the United States and his party, wearing suits and hats, sat on their afterdeck before dinner and sipped cocktails.[13]

As the conversation continues between the new man and the press secretary, the reporter begins to understand why Early is such a success in his job. Other than the president, Early probably knows more about what is going on in this country and perhaps around the world than any other living person. As an old war horse in the Fourth Estate, he understands the problems of those with whom he holds daily press conferences. From his newspaper training and his many years at the White House, he has the ability to visualize a story from the spoken word, to predict what will be emphasized, even what the headline probably will be, and gauge the immediate and long-term reaction to the story. He is direct, concise, and well informed. The reporter decides he could write a first-rate lead for any type of story.[14]

The reporter no doubt will attend Early's daily press conference that morning. In fact, he may find himself giving up his Saturdays soon, since Early usually holds a press conference on that morning, too. On this day, Tuesday, May 6, he will join a couple of dozen other reporters in an informal group around Early's desk. Most correspondents are men, although recently a woman showed up. As always, unless Early is traveling with Roosevelt or, on rare occasions now, on vacation himself, the press conference begins with an announcement. Today it is that the president is laid up in bed with a fever of a degree and a half. He tells the reporters that the president's doctor, Ross McIntire, thinks he ate "something that disagreed with him; he thinks he knows what it is and that the situation will soon be cleared up." Dr. McIntire, who is standing next to Early, adds, "Slight gastro-intestinal upset; we will have to give him a little time to straighten out."

At least for now, the give-and-take at these press conferences is easy and informal, with first names employed. Early announced when he arrived at the White House that he would have no favorites, and most reporters agree that he has kept that promise. If the reporter stays on his beat long enough, eventually he will find a far more tense, even wary, press secretary addressing reporters on such somber issues as censorship and insisting more and more that the information remain off the record. But today's announcement about the president's health is followed by a bit of banter between Early and the reporters. *Was it something Pa Watson fed him?* they ask. Early replies, "You'll ruin Pa if you say that." Then Dr. McIntire goes off the record. "For your information," he says, "we have a nice 'stomach rolling' and we have to give it a few hours to get cleared up."

Apparently Roosevelt had met that morning with Henry Stimson, secretary of war, and by noon was not feeling well. The reporters now ask if Early can tell them what transpired at the meeting between the president and the secretary. "No," Early answers. Remarkably, they do not pursue it. A stenographer is always present so that a transcript of the conference is made and then typed and later handed out to the reporters in their pressroom across the corridor from the executive offices.[15]

The following day, the president, apparently ill with more than food poisoning or something more serious, again remains in his private quarters, his temperature slightly lower, Early tells the reporters, but he is holding several meetings, including one with Harry Hopkins. The reporters tell him about rumors coming out of Tokyo that the United States is going to close the Panama Canal. "Do you know anything about that?" they ask.

Early's ire is beginning to seep through when he replies, "Why don't you wait until those rumors come to Washington; that is about the fifteenth report—not from that source—but the same old rumor. We were supposed to be closing the Panama Canal when the President proclaimed a limited emergency—remember all the rumors we had at that time? They have been continuous ever since." The reporters turn to a different topic, and ten minutes later the conference comes to an amiable close.[16]

On Thursday Early opens his press conference with these words: "I haven't a thing in the world for you today," a phrase the new man will find the press secretary and the president employ more and more after the country is at war. Early tells the reporters the patient is improving and eager to get back to his office, but the doctor has said,

"No, stay where you are, Mr. President." Then the press secretary says, "That is exactly the situation. No appointments today [for the president]. You can put the lid on right now, if you want to; I'm leaving here about noon." He then expands on the president's activities: He is in bed in his room, taking care of his mail and conferring by telephone. But he won't be back at his desk the rest of the week. Surprisingly, no one questions the original diagnosis of food poisoning.[17]

The last medical update of the week comes the following day, Friday, at Early's press conference. The president is improving; his temperature is nearly normal, but it fluctuates: "Sometimes it is normal; sometimes within a degree." He is probably not going to Hyde Park for the weekend, Early says. "Just between us 'girls'—you would not want to be moved around much if you were in his condition, would you, without his legs and with his stomach disorder? After taking the medicine that he has taken to clean out his stomach, you would not feel much like traveling; you would feel a little weak, wouldn't you? This just gives you the picture *confidentially*." There is some back-and-forth discussion about military information and a speech the president will make the following week.

But the reporters are curious about the president's health. "Steve, these usual rumors that always begin whenever he gets a cold are going around." One rumor, via ticker from Rome, has Roosevelt "extremely ill and in a sanitarium." Not to worry, one reporter says, American reporters had Mussolini in a sanitarium several times, too. There are more questions about what the president's work activities are, and the conference ends.[18]

Roosevelt remains in bed over the weekend. By Monday he is able to spend much of the day meeting with Harry Hopkins. Busy in his office, the president skips his usual Tuesday press conference that first week back on the job because, according to Early, Dr. McIntire thinks it best to keep him in a quiet atmosphere for another day.[19]

Kenneth S. Davis, one of Roosevelt's biographers, claims that Roosevelt was plagued with bad health during most of the spring of 1941, and those closest to the president were beginning to suspect he was malingering, the result either of a flu that refused to go away or because of the intensifying events in Europe, which at times left him feeling politically impotent. Or perhaps both. His alleged ill health was beginning to exasperate people like Early.[20]

It is not until May 16 that the new reporter comes face to face with the chief executive—but not his press secretary, who has escaped to a golf tournament in North Carolina. At the start of the presidential press conference, reporters ask Roosevelt how he is feeling. "Coming along all right. Still feel a little weak, but otherwise I am coming along all right." He is told he looked "swell," to which he replies, "Complexion is better, and everything else. It's a good thing."

After a bit more banter about his health and Early's leaving town, Roosevelt tells the reporters, "I don't think that I have any news." He then fields some hypothetical questions, which the reporters loved to throw at him in thinly disguised efforts to uncover a page one story. Then "Professor" Roosevelt takes over briefly as he lectures them about the German government's extension of combat zones to the Red Sea area. Then he talks about soil conservation and parity for farmers. The ball is tossed back and forth, the reporters pressing him for news, the president tantalizing and teasing them, a typical Roosevelt ploy to avoid answering questions. "You'll have to ask the State Department." Or "I have no news on that." Or one of his favorite responses: "Never heard of it." In fact, he ends the press conference with this thrust and parry: A reporter asks, "There are still reports, new reports, going about that the government will go into the steel business. Have you any comment, please?"

Roosevelt says, "Where?"

The reporter replies, "Birmingham, Alabama, for example."

The president answers, "Never heard of it."

And another press conference is concluded.[21]

For a year now, Roosevelt and Early were opposing mandatory censorship of any information related to a possible war. Early hoped that voluntary censorship would work, but gradually Roosevelt believed that some kind of mandatory curb must be placed on the flow of information. In May 1941 the Associated Press criticized the president for his "one-man direction of all the national defense activities." It was producing a "tired and weary executive" who was showing the effects of the nervous and physical strain.[22]

And more and more Roosevelt was sick or indisposed, leaving the unpleasant tasks to his press secretary. For instance, in April, when Gen. Hugh S. Johnson, onetime head of the National Recovery Administration and now a Roosevelt-bashing syndicated columnist, asked to have his army reserve commission renewed, Roosevelt refused but asked Early to handle the announcement. The press secretary put a positive spin on it: As a civilian, Johnson would have greater freedom of expression than if he were in the reserve. Editorial writers around the country criticized Roosevelt's action, claiming he had lobbed the ball to Early to handle. Two days later Johnson wrote in his column that the president was within his rights, and he defended Early, calling him "one of the most forthright, honest and courageous officials in Washington."[23]

That same month Early, speaking on behalf of the president, denied that American warships were escorting British vessels, calling such information in the press "a deliberate lie." He also said exactly what was on his mind and no doubt Roosevelt's when Charles Lindbergh returned his commission as a colonel in the army to the secretary of war. Early asked the reporters at his daily press conference if this meant the famed flier would return the Order of the German Eagle conferred on him four years earlier by Hitler. The next day, the *Washington Star* headline read: "Early Wonders If Lindbergh Will Return Nazi Decoration."[24]

Early continued to advise the president, and because Roosevelt seemed more and more "indisposed," sometimes Early found himself making decisions that at one time Roosevelt might have argued over or at least added his own thoughts. In late May, to ensure that the president's war plans had solid backing, Early suggested that Alfred Smith, John W. Davis, and James M. Cox, three former Democratic candidates for president, go on the air after the upcoming Fireside Chat. "I feel that recently there has been a little too much of Knox and Stimson," he told Roosevelt. William F. Knox was secretary of the navy, and Henry L. Stimson was secretary of war; both men had been outspoken proponents of preparing for war. Their speeches would precede those of Wendell Willkie and several Republican senators, but, he added, not former president Hoover. He also wanted Bernard Baruch to make the arrangements so they were done outside Washington. Roosevelt's handwritten reply at the bottom of Early's memo to him on all this is a terse: "S.T.E. OK F.D.R." The three Democrats spoke, and Willkie issued a statement in support of the president's war plans.[25]

In mid-June Steve and Helen Early, Grace Tully, and several other White House staff members spent the weekend on the *Potomac* with the president. Absent was Missy LeHand, Roosevelt's dear friend and private secretary, who lived in the White House. She had suffered a stroke earlier that spring and would never return to work. That Monday Roosevelt was sick in bed with another cold. All engagements were canceled. At the end of the month, however, he was well enough to travel to Hyde Park for the dedication of his presidential library, which he had meticulously planned and watched over as this lovely little stone building rose near his beloved home.[26]

In early August Roosevelt left Washington for what was described as a sailing trip off the New England coast. But contrary to past practice, no reporters were allowed to accompany him and none of his ports of call would be announced. In fact, from the time the yacht left the port of New London, Connecticut, Early, who remained in Washington, refused to release any details on the trip—because even he did not know its real purpose. But he did decree all movements of the presidential yacht to be a confidential naval operation. Newsmen were given bulletins along the way, and only a few of the very alert reporters eventually figured out where the president was headed.[27] Soon the press was speculating that Roosevelt was holding an at-sea conference with Prime Minister Winston Churchill. This kept Early busy firing off radiograms to keep the president informed about what press reports were saying and what was going on back in Washington.[28]

One of these radiograms that shows up in one of Early's scrapbooks at the FDR Library is labeled "secret," but that word has been scratched out and the message is stamped January 11, 1973, the date it was declassified. It says:

> London is leaking. An official photograph of you and Churchill is being offered to American photographic agencies. Have talked to Lord Halifax [the British ambassador to the United States] who is advising that a photograph is as revealing as the written word and should be subject to the same safeguards until hour of release. Would be most unfortunate if American people got their first news from London, written or photographic, and so told Halifax. Our press now is in a state of complete jitters on account photographic offering.[29]

No doubt Steve Early, too, was in a state of jitters.

What the press was slowly realizing was that President Roosevelt was indeed holding what would become one of numerous wartime meetings with the British prime minister, and on orders of the president—and while there is no record of this, probably against the advice of his press secretary—the meeting was being kept secret. It was this secrecy that was giving Early the jitters. Grace Tully, Roosevelt's long-time secretary, claims that Early was not told the real nature of the yacht voyage, so when the story about the meeting broke out of London, Early "blew his top, threatened to quit and otherwise raised a fine ruckus around 1600 Pennsylvania Avenue." After that, he was told about such conferences in advance. Early's fear, he told Roosevelt, was that "Americans are getting too much information from British news sources." He added that one news commentator had gone so far as to conclude that as a result of all the secrecy, "Americans are losing some of their freedoms." Early urged Roosevelt to hold a press conference as soon as his yacht returned to dock in Portland, Maine.[30]

Roosevelt's reply: He would hold a press conference the following day, but he disagreed on the loss of freedoms. The commentator, he said, "is either senile or an ass. The same happy thought applies to press queries as to whether principles of civilization apply today or next week or a year hence. Tell the boys I said so off the record."[31]

Early may have been angry, but outwardly he appeared relaxed when he held a press conference that day where, with his left leg crossed over his right knee and pipe in hand, he leaned back in his chair in his office and read the joint statement Churchill and Roosevelt had formulated during their secret meeting on board naval vessels anchored off Placentia Bay, Newfoundland, from August 9 through August 12. The meeting accomplished two goals: It showed, after a fashion, a public display of Anglo-American cooperation, and it produced the Atlantic Charter, with its eight-point program for world peace once the two countries had destroyed the common enemy, the Nazi tyranny. A split second after Early completed the announcement, the reporters made a mad dash to the telephones to relay the story to the world. A month later, all anti-Axis countries had endorsed the Atlantic Charter.[32]

By August 26 Early again was forced to handle the delicate task of protecting activities of American troops in military zones and taking care of the reporters hungry for news. At the beginning of July, an agreement was reached with Iceland that allowed US Marines to occupy Iceland to relieve British troops there and prevent Germany's use of that country's military bases. Roosevelt refused to allow American journalists and photographers to go there to cover the story, claiming the military needed time for adjustment and organization. After an outcry from the newsmen, Roosevelt allowed Early to lift the ban, and applications for permission to go to Iceland were accepted, in keeping with the regular rules and regulations of censorship in military zones.[33]

When Early celebrated his fifty-second birthday on August 27, he told his press conference that morning that the new ornament on his desk, a rod and reel with a clock in the reel, was a gift from Roosevelt, perhaps a hint to his press secretary to show up earlier at work. Early told the reporters the gift had been on his desk when he arrived that morning.[34]

This may have been one of the few bright notes for Early and Roosevelt that late summer and fall of 1941. On September 7, Sara Delano Roosevelt, the president's devoted and beloved mother, died at the age of eighty-six. A strong, often domineering woman, Sara Roosevelt took a negative view of both politics and her son's choice of a wife, but she supported Franklin's political ambitions and his accomplishments. As for Eleanor, she admitted she could not feel "any real grief" when her mother-in-law died. For the year following, the president wore a black armband. Then, less than two weeks after Sara died, Eleanor's younger brother, Hall Roosevelt, died of chronic liver disease after a long bout with alcoholism. Six years older than Hall, Eleanor had, with great love and deep grief, watched him drink his life away. Early, who had made some of the arrangements while Hall was hospitalized in Washington, received this note from the First Lady: "Dear Steve, You were so good and so helpful about Hall, and I am very appreciative of your kindness in coming to the services and for the beautiful flowers. The kindness of my friends means so much to me at this time, Very sincerely yours, Eleanor Roosevelt."[35]

That same month, Mary Catherine Holmes, Early's favorite niece and the daughter of his late brother-in-law George Holmes, created a minor scandal. When she had married Dr. Dana Coman, a chemist, explorer, and physician, just a year earlier, Early had given the bride away in a lavish wedding attended by a bevy of powerful politicians and journalists in the nation's capital. Unfortunately, after the honeymoon, the bride discovered that the bridegroom had lied to her about the size of his income, and now she was asking for an annulment. The newspapers covered it with such headlines as "Annulment Is Requested by Early's Niece."[36]

It's no wonder that on October 10, Early sent Roosevelt this handwritten note: "May I have permission to make a very important *business* trip to nearby Maryland this afternoon—Please! SE" The business, as the president well knew, was a visit to the racetrack in Laurel. This was his reply: "Yes—but for God's sake don't let this *business* sell you a Gold Brick. FDR."[37]

It may have given Early a much-needed moment of relief from the stress in the White House, but not enough. Columnists now were speculating that he might leave the White House. One even told readers that fall that the press secretary was on the verge of becoming a top executive with the Pittsburgh Glass Company, whose president was a friend of Early's. On November 3 he sent a telegram to his assistant Bill Hassett, who was with Roosevelt in Hyde Park, asking Hassett to give the president this message: "My nerves have gotten to the point where I must either get away or explode sooner or later if I stay here. I would like to go over to the hunting shack on the Eastern Shore for the remainder of this week and then go to Pinehurst for a week of golf, sleep and sunshine." Roosevelt concurred: "This seems as good a time as any. Have a grand rest but don't shoot a wood duck." Early sent this reply: "Many, many, many thanks."[38]

That fall, Roosevelt—and Early, through his own press conferences—continued to fight the isolationists in Congress and aviation hero Lindbergh and his America Firsters as the president sought ways to ensure that the United States could stay out of a war and that the nation's allies, in particular Britain, would not be destroyed by the German machine. When he gave another Fireside Chat on September 11, Early promised the media it would be "all covering and leave no unanswered questions." Later he claimed the talk was heard by the second-largest American radio audience on record. The Columbia Broadcasting System, which aired it, said its listenership survey showed 67 percent of the potential listening audience of 60 million tuned in. Early told the press that only 150 of the 1,600 messages received overnight at the White House disagreed with Roosevelt.[39]

In part what prompted this particular Fireside Chat was the attack a week earlier by a German submarine on the *Greer*, an American destroyer, 175 miles southwest of Iceland. The *Greer* was headed toward Iceland to deliver mail to US troops stationed there. As much as Roosevelt had wanted to aid the Allies, especially Britain, without actually entering a war, he was finding it more and more difficult to remain neutral, and he realized it was imperative that he speak to the American public. The death of his mother intervened, so it was not until September 11 that he finally went on the air to discuss it, without releasing many details about the *Greer* incident. He called it "piracy." The Nazi submarines, he said, were "raiders and rattlesnakes of the Atlantic." Then he came to the point of his talk and announced what he acknowledged was a grave step: The naval and air patrols now had the authority to do whatever was necessary to protect American ships. The following morning, newspaper headlines told readers that the undeclared war in the Atlantic had now, on orders of the commander in chief, become "a shooting war."[40]

If the newspapers needed any more 72-point headlines that week, they got them when Lindbergh delivered a scathing attack on Roosevelt, the Jews, and the British at an America First rally in Des Moines, Iowa. It, too, was broadcast nationwide. He accused the three groups of leading the United States into a war against Germany. As an uproar broke out over Lindbergh's pronouncements, Roosevelt may have fretted privately about this thorn in his side, but publicly he chose, as he often did in the midst of crisis, to stay out of the fray. But not his press secretary, who again was no doubt expressing the president's own thoughts when he railed against the aviator and the Nazi propaganda machine at his press conference the next morning. He told reporters, "You have seen the outpourings of Berlin in the last few days. You saw Lindbergh's statement last night. I think there is a striking similarity between the two."[41]

At his press conference the day before Thanksgiving, Early announced, "I am in the position to say that this office will not be open at any time tomorrow for the transaction of any business whatsoever. That means exactly what I said. I am not going to be here."[42] He did return for his press conference on Saturday. Threats of a strike by coal miners, which would be disastrous to the precarious war preparedness, and State Department hints that Hitler might be planning to hold a conference of some of the Axis nations and possibly some neutral countries the following month had brought him back to work.[43]

Roosevelt did go to Warm Springs the day after Thanksgiving, with his usual retinue of press, Secret Service, and staff, including Early, for some rest and relaxation. They were planning to return to Washington on Tuesday. However, a phone call from Secretary of State Cordell Hull Saturday night forced Roosevelt to summon Early from his nearby cottage to arrange for a hasty return to Washington the next day to deal with the real possibility of war in the Pacific. Japan had announced that it would purge American and British influences from East Asia "with a vengeance." American troops and warplanes already were on a war footing, and the American fleet in the Pacific—most of the country's naval power—had been on alert for several weeks in case hostilities were to break out.

The United States had been seeking clarification from Japan since early October on whether it planned to withdraw troops from China and Indochina. On November 20, 1941, Japan assured the United States that no expansion in the Pacific was planned and demanded that the United States would not aid China and would allow the Japanese a free hand in China and Indochina. On November 26 the United States sent a counterproposal: Japan would withdraw from the two countries and sign a nonaggression pact in return for the resumption of trading with the United States.[44]

The issue of press censorship continued to plague the White House when, on December 4, the *Chicago Tribune* published a story detailing a confidential government report prepared by the joint army and navy high command. It was a blueprint for a world war with the resources that would be required to wage an unprecedented global war, including the need for an American expeditionary force of 5 or 6 million men to lead an offensive against Germany. The report angered the president, but Early danced around the story and its accuracy. He told his press conference that he had not talked with the president about any of this, but later in the day he recanted—sort of— and said Roosevelt and War Secretary Stimson were looking into the matter. Whether "the matter" was the leak of the report or the *Tribune*'s story was unclear. But the following day, *P.M.*, a newspaper in New York, interpreted Early's remarks to mean he was refraining from criticizing the Chicago paper for what quite possibly was a violation of the Espionage Act. Early said that no action would be taken against the newspaper for publishing the information: "Your right to print the news is, I think, unchallenged and unquestioned. It depends entirely on the decision of the publisher and editor whether publication is patriotic or treasonable." One newspaper translated this statement to mean that since there was no press censorship in the United States, it was up to the government to keep its secrets, not up to the press to refrain from publishing them if they could get them.[45]

Thus far Early and Roosevelt had avoided any serious consideration of censorship, recognizing that any attempts by the government to stifle the media would only incur the journalists' outrage against the White House at a time when the president was seeking to build national unity in the event of a war.[46]

Despite a week of on-again, off-again irritation at the press, when Steve Early walked into his Saturday press conference on December 6, 1941, he was in a jocular mood, telling the assembled reporters, "I can't see any news for pads or pencils or even minds this morning. I think the President decided you fellows have been so busy lately and Christmas is coming so close that he would give you a day off to do some shopping."

This nonchalance did not deter one reporter from asking, "I suppose he is over at the house writing a declaration of war, isn't he?" Early's answer: "He is over at the house. He is not writing. At the present time, he is shaving." Still prying, another reporter asked: "I hope it isn't one of those nervous-lid days—on again—off again."

Early replied: "No, I can only give you the lid right now. The only appointment he has is the budget director at 11:15. That is to sign some papers—routine. He will stay over at the house this morning, and is not coming to the office. No appointments for today and none for tomorrow, and I don't assume there will be."[47]

Perhaps no less accurate forecast had ever come from the press secretary's mouth.

17

PEARL HARBOR

I t was the first Sunday in December 1941—the seventh. Steve Early, the temperamental press secretary to the longest-serving president of the United States, was sitting comfortably in his favorite easy chair in solitude in his study at the back of the family home on Morningside Drive in northeast Washington, immersed in the Sunday newspapers. He had probably hoped to play a round or two of golf at Burning Tree, but the mild and sunny weather of the past two weeks had turned chilly and windy. Early liked Sundays. He could relax in his shirtsleeves away from the demanding reporters, the clacking teletypes, and the ringing telephones at the White House.

Then his telephone rang—the private line that connected the press secretary's home to the president of the United States. Early put down his newspaper, reached over, and picked up the phone. It was the Boss. "Have you got a pencil handy?" he said. Aware of Roosevelt's puckish sense of humor, Early replied, "Do I need it?" He suspected the fun-loving president was probably up to his usual jesting. But the president was serious. "Yes," Roosevelt said, "I have a very important statement. It ought to go out verbatim."

From the tone of the president's voice, Early knew he was not joking. He called out to his wife, Helen, the former secretary, to take down the message. She grabbed a pencil and two nearby scraps of paper, and as Roosevelt read the statement to Early, he repeated the words to her.

The first piece of paper, three by five inches from a lined notebook, now in one of Early's scrapbooks at the FDR Library, says: "So far as known now, 4 attacks on Hon + Manil wr md wholly wot warning when both nations at peace, were delivered at least an hr before + Jap." and continues in cryptic notes, which, translated say: "As soon as information of the attacks was received by the War and Navy Departments, the President issued directives to the Army and Navy to execute all previously prepared orders looking to the defense of the United States."

The second page is from a 5-by-7 lined notebook and says: "A prelim rpt from Haw ex t + belief th damage has been heavy +th tr has been heavy (put in over the word "great," which has a line through it) loss of life. No info yet avail from M."

When he finished dictating, Roosevelt couldn't resist asking his press secretary, "Have you any news?" a question years later Early still thought was very funny. The press secretary replied, "None to compare to what you have just given me, sir."

With the newsman's understanding of immediacy, Early called the White House operator and asked her to set up a three-way hookup into the offices of the wire services—the Associated Press, the United Press, and the International News Service. It was 2:22 p.m. Washington time. The attack had occurred at dawn in Hawaii. As a seasoned newsman, Early spoke in clear low tones, with ice-cold composure, as he read the statement over the telephone to the wire services: "The Japanese have attacked Pearl Harbor from the air and all naval and military activities on the island of Oahu, the principal American base in the Hawaiian Islands." He asked the White House switchboard to repeat the message to the radio networks, the British Press Service, all New York and Washington daily papers, the *Chicago Tribune*, the *Baltimore Sun*, and the *Philadelphia Record*. Five minutes later, he called with a follow-up announcement: "A second air attack is reported. This one has been made on Army and Navy bases in Manila." When he finished his announcement to the wire services, he asked the switchboard operator to repeat the message to the eleven newspapers, including the New York and Washington papers, and the four radio networks on the White House list.

Within a matter of minutes, the news of the Japanese attack on Pearl Harbor and other United States and British territories spread around the world. Eventually, when the damage to the American fleet was tallied, US losses at Pearl Harbor were twenty-three hundred soldiers and sailors dead and thirteen hundred wounded; nineteen ships sunk or disabled, including eight battleships and three destroyers; and about 140 planes destroyed.[1]

Within twenty-four hours Congress had declared war on Japan. On December 11, Germany and Italy declared war on the United States, an action that led Congress to adopt a resolution recognizing a state of war with the Axis countries. By the end of the month, labor and business had agreed on a no-lockout policy for war industries. So began a massive changeover from domestic production to munitions manufacturing and the eventual rationing of butter, sugar, rubber, and other everyday products that Americans took for granted. Millions of men would be drafted and sent thousands of miles from home to fight and possibly to die. The United States was officially at war.

After he telephoned the switchboard with his announcements to the press, Steve Early left the comfort of his newspapers and easy chair, grabbed his coat and hat, and arrived at the White House in less than thirty minutes. He was about to face the most intense press scrutiny since those first days of the Roosevelt administration. Grace Tully, the president's secretary, called the news "shattering" and said she hoped she would never again experience the anguish and near hysteria of that afternoon.[2]

When he arrived at the White House, Early met briefly with Roosevelt, who was working in his study off his bedroom. Then the press secretary called in a dozen or so reporters who had rushed there from their Sunday dinners. For the first time, he even allowed NBC and CBS radio to broadcast live his announcements that day. At 3:10, standing on the leather chair in his office, he told them he had little more information than what he had flashed to their offices earlier. He said both attacks—on Hawaii and Manila—were made without warning and were delivered within an hour or so before the Japanese ambassador had gone to the State Department and handed Secretary of State Cordell Hull a reply to the earlier negotiations with Japan over its occupation of China and Indochina. Early said that as soon as the information of the attacks was received by the War and Navy departments, it was flashed immediately to the president at the White House. At this moment, Early said, Roosevelt was meeting with Secretary of War Henry Stimson and Secretary of the Navy William Knox, and steps were being taken to advise congressional leaders.[3]

Five minutes later he made another—and confusing—announcement: "So far as the President's information goes and so far as we know at the moment, the attacks are still in progress. We don't know, in other words, that the Japanese have bombed and left. In other words, both of the attacks are still in progress as far as we know."[4]

Then Early, Hopkins, and others went to the president's study, where Roosevelt told them he had decided to call a special meeting of his cabinet that night and then bring in a group of congressional leaders to join the cabinet meeting. He asked Early to contact the congressmen, including Speaker of the House Joe Martin and House Minority Leader Sol Bloom. These and other names show up on a list written by Hopkins on a three-by-five-inch sheet of paper ripped from the bottom of some government publication and given to Early. At the bottom of the list of eleven names, written in red ink, is the name of Hiram Johnson, the senator from California and one of the Senate's leading isolationists.

Early rushed back to his office. At 4:00 p.m. he again called in the reporters and told them he would try to bring them up to date. The president was still huddled with Stimson and Knox and would meet with the cabinet at 8:30 that night. At 9:00 p.m. congressional leaders from both parties would join them. He said this was the same group Roosevelt had been meeting with regularly: "That means you can give it the inference of an international discussion rather than a military one, because he has not as yet called the chairmen of the Military Affairs Committees of the House or the Senate." He told the reporters they could write or broadcast that the president was assembling all of the facts as rapidly as possible and that in all probability he would, as quickly as possible, make a full informative report to Congress, probably in the form of a formal message. At 4:10 p.m. Early made a brief addition to his earlier announcement: He told reporters that Hiram Johnson had been invited to the conference that evening.[5]

As new developments popped up, Early called press conferences. A Secret Service man would stroll across the hall from Early's office to where the reporters were working in the press room and announce:

"Press conference," setting off a stampede for Early's office. As the day wore on, more than 150 reporters were at the White House waiting for the latest news.[6]

Outside the White House people began gathering in groups, sometimes ten deep, along the sidewalks, looking through the iron gates and waiting for news. Inside, Steve Early held a 4:30 press conference at which he now allowed the hungry newsmen to ask questions—not that he had a lot of fresh information for them. He said the president was in his study dictating a first draft of his message for Congress to Grace Tully and reassured the reporters that he would keep in touch with Roosevelt and pass on whatever he could to the journalists, "development by development, as reports are received." What he could tell them was that a preliminary report from the navy in Hawaii was that there appeared to be heavy damage and heavy loss of life. No information, he added, was available on the damage in Manila. He told a reporter he could call it "a dawn attack."

They wanted to know if the secretary of state had known about the attack when he met with the Japanese representatives that morning. Early said no. Still trying to establish a timeframe for the events, another reporter asked, "They [the Japanese] attacked first and then came to the meeting." Early explained, "They attacked within an hour [before] of the meeting." Any truth to the radio reports of a heavy naval engagement off Hawaii? they asked. "I can't confirm it," Early said. Any likelihood of Congress being called into session that night? "No, it couldn't be." Anything happening over at the Japanese Embassy? "I know nothing that has happened over at the Japanese Embassy.

Before leaving the press conference, Early asked if any of them were reporting for Japanese news agencies. "If there are," he said, "I am giving you no information, and I have asked the Secret Service to take up the credentials of Japanese correspondents." As to whether they would be arrested or not, he replied, "That is an activity of the Department of Justice."[7]

At 5:55 p.m. Early held a brief press conference telling the reporters that the War and Navy departments had been endeavoring to get confirmation or subsequent reports from Manila but so far had been unable to reach authorities there, including the army and navy commanders. He said Roosevelt was "disposed now to believe and is hopeful that that report at least may be erroneous." He was, of course, referring to the attack on Manila. The reporters asked him to repeat that, which he did, adding that the president had just talked on the telephone with the governor of Hawaii, who confirmed previous reports of heavy damage and casualties, and he said that as the governor was talking to Roosevelt a second wave of planes was just coming over the area. This had occurred within the half hour, Early said, adding that a navy report just received said that a squadron of unidentified planes had just been sighted over Guam.[8]

From then on that night, Early made only three announcements, all of them brief. At 6:10 p.m. he repeated the navy report about the sighting over Guam. At 6:22 p.m. he said the president now had navy confirmation that Guam had been attacked. And at 7:40 p.m. he told the reporters that a preliminary report from the War Department showed that losses in the army only on the island of Oahu in the Hawaiian Islands were about 104 dead and more than 300 wounded. Later, reporters agreed that Early's handling of the events of that day had been "one of his finest performances" as press secretary to the president.[9] James MacGregor Burns, a Roosevelt biographer, believes that the attacks in the Pacific at first left Roosevelt with a "sense of relief that the uncertainty was over at last," then a "growing alarm and agony about the extent of the losses," and finally "a calm acceptance of the fact of war."[10]

A fatigued Early did not return home to Morningside Drive until very late that Sunday night, only to arrive back at work Monday morning well in advance of his usual press conference. Grace Tully said that by the time she reached the White House that morning, there already was a sense of "normality." She said the grounds were being guarded by a special detachment of military police, and the White House police were assisted by men from the Metropolitan Police and the Secret Service. Blackout curtains were being hung at windows, and a bomb shelter was under consideration, although Roosevelt was against it. Tully said Treasury Secretary Henry Morgenthau and the Secret Service wanted it, and eventually it was built and equipped with an office for the president along with beds and telephone facilities, much like the one constructed for Winston Churchill. Merriman Smith, then a young United Press correspondent covering the White House, later recalled that one day, early in the war, reporters saw steam shovels "chewing a deep path toward the Treasury." He said Early confirmed their suspicions. The government was building a tunnel from the White House basement to the lower vaults of the Treasury Building next door, which the president would use as his air raid refuge.[11]

When Early got to his office, the pressroom had a network of new telephones and radio facilities, and reporters were eager for facts. When Early met with them, he said: "I scarcely know where to begin, except maybe this way." He told them the reaction of the country, as expressed in hundreds of telegrams received the previous afternoon and overnight, was one of horror and pledges of loyalty, aid, and support to the president and the government, some of which he read to the reporters. He said they came from governors, mayors, leaders of civic organizations, labor leaders, newspaper editors, radio broadcasters, and clergymen. He mentioned some by name. In one telegram, Alf Landon, Roosevelt's Republican opponent in 1936, said, "Japanese attack leaves no choice. Nothing must be permitted to interrupt our victory over a foreign foe." Early said David Sarnoff, chairman of the Radio Corporation of America, simply said: "We await your commands."

Early said the Reverend Daniel A. Poling, editor of the *Christian Herald*, "and you can quote him, if you wish to," told the president: "Complete American unity in defense of world freedom and to win the peace is now a fact." One of the first messages, a telephone call to the White House within a few minutes after the attack was announced, came from a Washington, DC, man who drove a taxi, which he had just finished paying for. He offered to drive free of charge any government official who needed transportation. He left his telephone number so they could call him when they needed his services. Early called this gesture "rather sweet."

Once he had completed his task as public relations man for the White House, he got down to business and gave the reporters a statement he said was approved by Roosevelt. The latest information on Pearl Harbor—or at least as much as the president was willing to make public—was this: American operations against the Japanese in the Hawaiian Islands were continuing, and a number of Japanese planes and submarines had been destroyed. The damage to the American forces in Oahu appeared more serious than first thought. One destroyer was blown up; several small ships were seriously hit; army and navy fields were bombed, resulting in the destruction of several hangars; and a large number of planes were put out of commission. In Pearl Harbor itself, the statement said, one "old battleship" had capsized and several other ships had been damaged. American bombers from San Francisco had arrived while the bombing was underway, and reinforcement planes were being rushed to Hawaii. Total casualties were still unknown, but they probably would mount to three thousand, with more than half of those fatalities. Early confirmed that Wake Island, the Midway Islands, and Hong Kong had been attacked, but he had no details about them. Two hundred marines in China— all that remained—had been interned by the Japanese.

A reporter asked if there was any official explanation as to how the Japanese were able to get beyond the Americans' outer defense at Oahu. Early replied, "I don't know that there is any official explanation. The consensus of the experts is that probably most, if not all, of the planes that attacked came from carriers. Apparently these planes were dive bombers, of that type. The attack came at daybreak or dawn. The carriers naturally would have all night under the cover of darkness to approach. The planes would take off naturally and gain a high altitude and come in from the darkness. That is the consensus." It was a clear and logical explanation of the logistics of the attack, one the reporters no doubt would have figured out on their own. But Early's explanation gave them a White House official to quote.[12]

The real story was that the eight battleships at Pearl Harbor were out of commission, a fact that, according to one Roosevelt biographer, was known to the president by late that Monday morning, probably by the time Early met with the press corps. Did Roosevelt know in advance of the attacks? Not unlike the attacks of September 11, 2001, on New York City and the Pentagon, no clear-cut answer emerged as to who knew what and when, but as far as the Pacific attacks were concerned, it is obvious from the failures of ongoing diplomatic relations between Japan and the United States that some kind of Japanese military aggression was not unexpected. (Congressional investigations in late December 1941 and in 1945 provided no real answers.)[13]

Grace Tully believed that Early and Roosevelt were telling the press as much as could safely be disclosed as quickly as possible and that there was no censorship, voluntary or mandated. But, she explained, "[T]here had to be a careful sifting at the source to protect security while keeping a free people and their press responsibly and intelligently informed." What happened in those first twenty-four hours, she noted, demonstrated how quickly the free press and radio of the country readjusted to a mutual and satisfactory working arrangement. She decided it was a fitting climax "to the more than eight years of frank and honest dissemination of public information which had become the pattern of White House dealings with the press."[14]

While no immediate and visible censorship emanated from the White House that Monday morning, Early did fire off a memo to be read over the telephone to the War, Navy, and State departments informing them that for the time being—"it will be just temporary"— the president wanted all the news to come out of the White House. Representatives from these departments should attend all the press conferences at the White House to ensure that they knew what was going on. Early said he would let the departments know when he was about to announce something that came under their jurisdiction, "but when that announcement is given out, they had better have a man here to get it."[15]

Shortly before noon that Monday, December 8, six black limousines pulled up to the White House. The president, on the arm of his son James, now a captain in the marines, was helped into the first one. Into the others went Eleanor Roosevelt, Mrs. James Roosevelt, Helen Early, Grace Tully, Early's secretary Dorothy Brady, and General Watson. From there, the procession moved to the Capitol. When they arrived, they went into the House, where Roosevelt was to address a joint session of Congress. He received an ovation that, according to the *New York Times*, was unmatched in his years as president. Then he denounced Japanese aggression, in what was the shortest of all the messages he had personally delivered there. He began: "Yesterday, December 7, 1941—a date which will live in infamy—the United States of America was suddenly and deliberately attacked by naval and air forces of the Empire of Japan." In staccato rhythms, he quickly described the attacks. Then he asked Congress to declare a state of war with Japan. Thirty-three minutes later, Congress formally declared war on Japan.[16]

Later on Monday Early held a rare evening press conference, its objective being to announce that Roosevelt would give a half-hour radio address to the nation at 10:00 the following night to "give a more complete documentary report of the Japanese attack on Americans in Hawaii, the Philippines and other areas than has yet been possible." He told the reporters that nothing had come in during the day "of a news character" to add to what he had told them that morning. "I am going to put the lid on and in case of any emergency the switchboard will call you."

But the journalists were not going to let him get away that easily. They pounded him with questions. He gave few answers. The United Press reporter asked, "Our lines to Hawaii have been down for the last 18 hours. Is that a result of censorship or war conditions?" Early said he would have to take the question to the Navy Department. Another reporter asked, "Is there anything to the Rome report that they [Italy] are declaring war on us?" Early was vague. He had heard it was in the offing: "I heard it from some newspaperman or I saw it in the paper today that Italy didn't feel that it was necessary that they should follow Japan."

A reporter asked him whether the battleship *Pennsylvania* had been sunk at Pearl Harbor. Early told the reporter no and added that he did not think Roosevelt would be giving out any description of what was sunk there: "That is military information. There are a lot of folks not in the United States who would like very much to know what was sunk, etc. That is military information on military operations." (The battleship, which was in dry dock on the Oahu mainland, suffered serious damage but was repaired within a few weeks.)

From another reporter: "Is there censorship on the Philippines?" He had heard that an aircraft hangar there had been hit. Early had an answer: "I saw a complete story in the papers of the attack on Manila. It doesn't look like any censorship to me."

And the biggest question of all: "When will censorship be put on?" The Early temper barely in check, he replied, "When the Army and Navy folks see a reason to put it on. If you are anxious, I will make a recommendation that they put it on at once." Then he added, "This government isn't disposed to put a censorship on anything that there isn't a real military need for censoring."

The reporters returned to the problem of United Press, wondering why the wire service had not been able to contact its reporter in Hawaii. Was there still a bottleneck of radio and wire messages in San Francisco? "That's strictly Navy," Early replied. "I don't know anything about it. That's up to the Navy Department to clear up." (Almost immediately after the attacks, the army and navy had taken control of all cable and radio messages addressed from abroad and originating in the United States, which explained the complaints from United Press.)

What would the president be up to that evening? Working on his radio address, Early said. Then Early stonewalled the last question as the reporters returned to the attack on Pearl Harbor: Was there any truth to the rumor that the Japanese had sunk four battleships? "Is there anything that can be said here?" they asked. "Nothing that will be said here," Early replied. And the conference ended.[17]

David Brinkley, who later became the NBC evening news anchor, was a young reporter in Washington at this time. He said that the public received few details about what happened at Pearl Harbor quite simply because Roosevelt and the military establishment were fearful that the Japanese would find out just how seriously damaged the American naval fleet in the Pacific was and they might attempt an amphibious attack on Hawaii.[18]

By the end of the year, a cloak of secrecy—previously unknown in the Roosevelt presidency—would shroud the White House, and no longer was Early able to freely share with the reporters intimate details of the president's health, his travels, and certainly not the military's plans. It proved a difficult time for Early, as the former newsman was forced continually to sidestep questions thrown at him during his press conferences. By telling the reporters that "you know as much as I do," or prefacing comments with "I think," he tried to retain his reputation for openness and candor. After Pearl Harbor he chose to become "uninquisitive about matters requiring secrecy." He felt that if he did not know about something, he could speak honestly to the reporters. How much Early really knew about the details of the attacks and the American military plans in those days after Pearl Harbor remains a mystery. Frankly, he was simply too busy gathering information he could hand the reporters day after day.[19]

His Tuesday, December 9, press conference was a boilerplate for so many he would hold in the war years. On this day, the reporters were determined to learn more than Early could give them. In fact, he told them, "the president has just concluded a careful reading of all dispatches, and comparing those dispatches to the Press dispatches, we find that there is no news to give you. You have it. You have about as much as we have—exactly as much." This was hardly an accurate statement, since obviously the president had access to top-secret military dispatches.

A disbelieving reporter asked for more. He wasn't going to get it from Early, who said the president was insisting that rumors and reports be given to the press as they were received, but then he immediately backtracked, adding that these rumors and reports had to be "sifted to find the truth." He said, "We are in the sifting process now." As the reporters continued to mine for answers, Early was forced to give such replies as "There is no answer to that," or "The picture is much bigger," but with no description of that picture. He even suggested they take their questions to the military, knowing full well that if they did, they would learn little or nothing.

In all fairness to Early, there simply was too much going on for him to be aware of all of it. For instance, the reporters wanted comments on Roosevelt's views on the attitude of Central and South American countries toward Japan. Early had nothing to give them. All he could say was that they should talk to the State Department.[20]

While Early was fending off questions from the press that day, Roosevelt was closeted with his speechwriters preparing to address the nation via radio that evening. In fact, Early told his press conference that morning that he had "darned little news" for them. He pointed to the typewritten pages on his desk and noted that this was the third draft of the speech, and he now was on the fifth. When Roosevelt finally spoke that night at 10:00 p.m. Eastern Standard Time (7:00 p.m. on the West Coast), he was heard by more than 60 million Americans, eager for reassurance from their leader that war was the only route, the best route to protect democracy, and that the United States could win the war. It proved to be another rousing Roosevelt radio talk.[21]

When Early met the press in his office the next morning, he was ready with his usual package of statistics for them: The radio audience was the largest in history, with 92.4 percent of American families listening—virtually every adult in the country. The president had received six hundred telegrams before he went to bed and they had been coming in steadily since then. He told reporters that war news now would emanate from individual departments, such as the one from General MacArthur that would be released by the War Department. But there remained concern about censorship: Would there not be a central source of information? one reporter asked. "No. And I hope there never will be," Early said. In fact, he said, if a reporter came across any unreasonable delays in the release of information from the various government departments, he or she was to come to Early. "Tell him to ring the alarm; sound the sirens," Early said.

That same morning Early held another press conference, this one notable for its brevity, at which he announced that "the long expected is now a reality." Germany had declared war on the United States. Italy, he said, had "goose-stepped." Roosevelt then asked Congress to "recognize a state of war between the United States and Germany, and between the United States and Italy." By midafternoon, December 10, 1941, Congress did so.[22]

Now it was time for the Republicans to throw off the cloak of isolationism and to join forces with the Democrats. The country was at war and a united political front was imperative for success. On December 11 Early told his press briefing that Ed Flynn, chairman of the Democratic National Committee, and Speaker of the House Joe Martin, his Republican counterpart, had agreed that "politics stood adjourned." Roosevelt, who despised Congress almost as much as he hated newspaper columnists, would now have the support of that august body.[23]

The spokesman for the president of the United States came into his office on Saturday, December 13, to give reporters a statement, but they were not allowed to release it until 7:00 a.m. EST the following Tuesday. When the newsmen looked it over, what they found was nothing urgent, no news that would call out: "Hold the presses!" It was Early, the publicity man, ensuring that through the reporter's pens and microphones, the citizens of the United States would be reminded that their commander in chief was indeed worthy of his job.

The statement began by saying that Roosevelt was bringing "to the grim responsibilities of being wartime President a temperament and physique suited to his exacting task." It outlined his workday, emphasizing that he wasted neither time nor energy and worked late into the night; it reassured the people that his doctor considered him physically fit and only alluded to "a period of broken health" in the 1920s, and it carefully outlined Roosevelt's achievements as undersecretary of the navy. Lest the voters have any lingering doubts, the statement ended with: "The hardening experiences of these past thirty years are the factors which enable him to do his job 'in his stride—on the alert.'" It was sheer puffery. There is no indication who initiated this statement, nor does the author's name appear on it. But it has Steve Early's verbal fingerprints all over it.[24]

On December 15 Early told the press that he would be handing them what he called "a chronology message," a detailed account put together by the president and his advisers that outlined the history and negotiations leading up to December 7. That's about all they gleaned from the press secretary, since the rest of his press conference that morning was a jumble of "Don't know's," "Haven't seen it's," "Don't think so's," and "It may be's." Obviously if he knew anything about the activities of the moment, he was not about to discuss them. And if he did not, he was being honest with them.[25]

It had become almost painfully apparent to both the journalists and the White House that some kind of machinery needed to be put into place to deal with the release of military and related information. No one, least of all the media, wanted voluntary censorship—and certainly not compulsory censorship. Too many journalists, including Early, remembered the Committee on Public Information (CPI), headed by a former muckraking newsman, George Creel, and set up at President Woodrow Wilson's behest when the United States entered World War I in 1917. The CPI was an effort to keep war information centralized in the White House. As a system of voluntary self-censorship codes, it ended up mostly being a propaganda bureau, and some liberal newspaper editors got into trouble with the CPI for publishing information considered by the committee to offer aid to the enemy.[26]

Later during the winter of 1941, when reporters asked about plans for better coordination of press services in the federal government, Early told them that he was "principally concerned about one thing, that there not be set up anything comparable to the old Creel committee. Also, that they not broaden the Office of Censorship on anything but strictly censorship duties. In other words, you can't have an office there to censor news, which is a negative action, and at the same time have another department, or a part of a staff, operating for the manufacture or the production of news, which is affirmative." He added that such a plan "can't be, and I don't think it will be. It won't be, if I can help it."[27]

Throughout the fall of 1941, Early had been reassuring the press that should war break out, the Roosevelt administration would avoid mandated censorship at all costs. The previous June, Early had addressed the issue of freedom of the press in an article he distributed to newspapers titled "No Iron Heel Here—Your Press Is Free," in which he declared that no freedom in the United States is more important than freedom of the press. He said that as totalitarian nations around the world were obliterating any semblance of a free press, journalists in the United States continued to enjoy a free press. Early quoted Roosevelt as saying, "As far as I am concerned there will be no government control of news unless it be of vital military information."

Some months before Pearl Harbor, Early had said that during his tenure as press secretary his office had given "facts only" to the correspondents covering the White House and "has yet to write a story for the reporters. They are free, entirely free, when given the facts, to write the story; to interpret the facts as they please. That is their job—their right—their freedom." Of course, that did not mean that Early's boss always appreciated the way the correspondents interpreted facts.[28]

But now the country was officially at war. In his first press conference after Pearl Harbor, Roosevelt told the reporters that there would be two primary rules of censorship of war news: The news released must be true, and it must pass a test to see that it does not give aid and comfort to the enemy. Reporters complained that they were still getting the runaround from officials at the War and Navy departments. Roosevelt told them to be patient, since only "very high ranking officials" could release the news.[29]

By the middle of December, using the First War Powers Act, Roosevelt, with Early's advice and assistance, created the Office of Censorship. At the behest of Early, the president turned to a respected Associated Press newsman, a former colleague of Early's dating to before World War I, to head the new office. Byron Price, the executive news editor of the Associated Press, turned out to be the perfect choice for this sensitive position. Early called him "the ideal man for the job." After the war, Early told Price, "You made voluntary censorship a success. Had you failed, in all probability there would have been compulsory censorship."[30]

Price brought with him a cadre of seasoned newsmen and women, their primary job being the censoring of mail, cables, and radio communications between the United States and other countries. He established a censorship code that in effect allowed for voluntary censorship, although it warned the media against publication of news relating to shipping, planes, troops, fortifications, war production, and armaments. In addition, radio networks and stations were asked to omit all references to weather because of the possibility of instantaneous reception by the enemy. Newspapers and magazines were permitted limited use of weather reports. Information handed out by a government agency generally would not need to be cleared with the censor, but if a reporter got "an exclusive," for instance, that information would have to pass by the censor. Early insisted that Price's office would not be a news production office. "You get your news where you have always been getting it," he said.

On December 17 Early spent considerable time at his press conference explaining the reasons for the creation of a censorship office. The real problem, he said, was that the public relations departments he had so carefully set up soon after Roosevelt took office had not functioned in time of war, and Early believed they now needed guidance on what information was suitable for release. Price's office would be there for them. Early assured the reporters the system was "completely decentralized." He told them, "News has value, and I think the great factor or great value in news is getting it from the source to the readers in a minimum of time. This plan is designed to bring that about."[31]

Overall, the news media were not unhappy with the new censorship code. The *New York Times* called it "intelligent censorship machinery." The *Decatur Herald and Review* in Illinois told its readers, "Americans can be happy in the knowledge that the important posts of secretary to the president and official censor are held by former newspapermen of such ability as Steve Early and Byron Price." At the end of the month, Early told his old friend Kent Cooper, general manager of the Associated Press, that he found it "an amazing fact to see the press and radio asking for [guidance on censorship] rather than standing solidly against such a thing as censorship."[32]

Early and Roosevelt may have resisted compulsory censorship, but neither was hesitant to play dumb when the reporters asked questions that neither man wanted to answer. At his December 22 press conference, Early was confronted by reporters about ongoing conferences in Washington, presumably relating to war plans. "This thing [rumors of conferences] has been bubbling all over town but there's no place to put your finger on it," one reporter said. Early's retort: "I think it will have to bubble."

Then the reporters badgered him about reports that Winston Churchill was coming to town to confer with Roosevelt. It would be the British prime minister's first visit to Washington during the Roosevelt administration. "That's another bubble that will have to bubble and that I don't know anything about," Early told them. Then he reminded them that if Churchill were on his way, "I would not be in a position to tell you anything about it and neither would you be able to publish anything about it." He may or may not have been aware of the pending visit, but if he was—and he probably did know—he recognized that when the press got wind of the visit, it would be a hectic time for him and his staff as the reporters and photographers would be demanding a continual stream of news about the meetings, news that under the circumstances might be difficult for him to release to the hungry journalists. According to *Roosevelt and Churchill: Men of Secrets* by David Stafford, the British prime minister came to Washington to find out what Roosevelt planned to do about the war that was raging in Europe.[33]

As Early was playing cat-and-mouse with the press, the prime minister was sailing across the Atlantic aboard the *Duke of York*. It arrived at Hampton Roads, Virginia, on Monday, December 22. That night he and his entourage of more than eighty, including Lord Beaverbrook, the Canadian-born newspaper magnate and now minister of aircraft production in Churchill's cabinet, flew into National Airport in Washington, where Roosevelt met him. Roosevelt biographer Kenneth S. Davis writes that Early allowed a small crowd of reporters and photographers to wait outside the White House when the two leaders arrived. Following custom, no photos were taken of the president emerging from his car. But as Roosevelt "walked" into the White House on the arm of a naval aide alongside Churchill, cameras flashed away. The next day newspapers carried photos of the tall and upright Roosevelt "walking" next to the short, pudgy prime minister. Once again, the Early publicity machine managed to make a crippled president look healthy.[34]

Early called a press conference for 6:55 that night to inform the same journalists who had badgered him two days earlier that

Churchill now was with Roosevelt in the White House. But before he made the announcement, Early asked his two secretaries to make sure no one left his office until he said, "Go." He wanted to avoid having one news organization scoop another one on this momentous story.

The press conference was pretty much chaos. When he told the reporters he had copies of a statement for them on his desk that outlined the objectives of the conference between the two leaders, the journalists made a mad dash for them, disrupting objects on the desk and even pushing the desk back. Early's comment when they had settled down was a sarcastic, "This is a nice demonstration of what adults can do." In fact, he told May Craig, the only woman reporter in the group, after most of the men had left, "I rather apologize for that performance."[35]

His press conference the next morning found Early sounding harassed, sometimes short with the reporters. They demanded information, yet he had not much to give. How late did the prime minister and the president meet the previous evening? Until about one o'clock, Early said. Where were they talking? In the old Lincoln study, now the Oval Room study, he answered. Did the two men shake hands at the airport? It was too dark for anyone to see. What room was Churchill occupying in the White House? "Do you think it will make a great deal of difference to your readers? It does to the Secret Service," Early replied. Will Churchill attend Roosevelt's press conference later that day? "You know the size of the President's office," he answered. "You know what would happen if I told you." Any details on the arrival Prime Minister Mackenzie King of Canada? "I haven't heard when he will arrive," Early said.

Off the record, at least for now, he told them, the president and Churchill would attend church on Christmas Day. But where? the reporters asked. Early refused to say which church or what time. "I make that at the request of the Secret Service." The reporters weren't satisfied. Could he at least tell them the denomination of the church? "Inter-denominational," Early said. Still mining for details, they asked, "High or Low Church?" Early's answer: "I haven't had time to go to church. I don't know the difference between a High or a Low."[36]

Early met with the reporters again that day. Shortly after noon, he called them into his office to tell them that Roosevelt would hold a press conference at 5:00 p.m. In attendance would be the secretaries of war and navy, four United States admirals and generals, Harry

Hopkins, three high-ranking British military men, and, yes, Winston Churchill. Early referred to the group as "the War Council." When a reporter asked if the names had been released earlier, perhaps by Churchill's staff, the by now much-put-upon press secretary snapped, "You read your papers as well as I do. I could only look in the papers to answer that."[37]

After the mad scramble in his office the night before, Early was taking no chances of a repeat. He made certain that when Roosevelt held his own press conference later that day—with Churchill at his side—no more than three reporters from any one press association and no more than two from each newspaper were allowed to attend. For once, Roosevelt was not the star of the press conference. The reporters peppered the prime minister with questions about British military strategy and the joint war effort with the United States, all of which he "fielded . . . with adroit evasiveness."[38]

On Christmas Eve, the two leaders watched from the South Portico of the White House for the annual lighting of the nation's Christmas tree, placed this year, for security reasons, on the White House grounds instead of in Lafayette Park across the street. A "few hundred" invited guests were on the mansion grounds. Outside, however, several thousand cheered and applauded the two men when each spoke briefly.[39]

Christmas Day saw no members of the Roosevelt clan at the White House. The sons were all serving in the armed forces, and Anna was with her family in Seattle. Only Eleanor and Franklin, the White House staff, Churchill and his closest aides, and Harry Hopkins and his nine-year-old daughter, Diana, who had been living on and off in the executive mansion since Hopkins's wife died in 1938, remained. Churchill and Roosevelt attended services at the Foundry Methodist Church and then turned their attentions back to preparing the address the prime minister would make to Congress the following day. In fact it was not until the morning after Christmas that Roosevelt and his devoted little Scots Terrier, Fala, spent an hour together opening their gifts. Early told reporters that morning that Fala even had her own stocking.[40]

Meanwhile, Early was busy preparing copies of Churchill's historic half-hour speech to Congress to hand out to the press. While the prime minister was at the Capitol, Mackenzie King was arriving in Washington. At 2:00 p.m. Roosevelt was holding his regular cabinet meeting, and at 3:30 the president would meet with what Early referred to as his "Supply Group," which included Harry Hopkins and William S. Knudson, president of General Motors and now codirector of the Office of War Production. That would be followed by a conference with military leaders, including the secretaries of war and navy. The country was in the midst of a war, and the White House was bursting with meetings and overnight guests. When he was asked by a reporter if Prime Minister King would be staying there, Early replied, "No. I think not. I think the White House has reached the point where there is 'standing room only.'"[41]

It proved a logistics headache for everyone working in the White House, especially so for Early. The reporters working at the Capitol also wanted copies of Churchill's speech to meet afternoon deadlines, but it was a close call. Early promised he would send over copies by motorcycle messenger, but by 12:30 p.m., when Churchill was set to start his address, Early had not been able to finish making the copies for the reporters. He met the reporters in his office and apologized. But in pure public relations fashion, he followed his apology with some juicy "just for your information" announcements about meetings Roosevelt had scheduled the next day with representatives of China, Australia, and New Zealand. He said they could use this, but only if they did not pin it on him.[42]

It must have been something of a relief to Early, who by now was suffering from a cold, when Churchill left Washington the following Monday, December 29, for Ottawa, where he addressed the Canadian Parliament. Churchill, with his late-night work habits, his prodigious drinking and eating, and the continual parade of visitors and meetings, had kept the White House running at full tilt. Grace Tully, FDR's secretary, says that Churchill stayed irregularly at the White House until January 14, when he finally returned to London.[43]

At his press conference the day Churchill left the city, Early complimented the reporters on their coverage of the events of the last week. It was not off the record, he told them, that Roosevelt "has been delighted, and has commented several times on the fact that while it was more or less an open secret to you gentlemen, no newspaper or radio comment was made" until Churchill arrived at the White House, nor had they published or broadcast that the prime minister had left Washington, despite the fact that the Canadian press reported the previous day that he would be arriving in Ottawa. The president "asked me to give you a well-deserved though somewhat belated 'orchid.'"[44]

On the last day of the year, Early confirmed to the reporters at his press conference—but "for your guidance," meaning "off the record" —that Churchill would be returning to Washington on January 1. What Churchill and Roosevelt and their advisers had been so diligently crafting during the Christmas holidays was a kind of follow-up to the Atlantic Charter. It was known as the Arcadia Conference, and it produced the Declaration by United Nations, its signatories constituting an alliance against Hitler, thus forming the basis for what eventually became the United Nations. Each country pledged maximum war effort and agreed not to sign a separate armistice or peace treaty with Germany. After much compromising and numerous cables among the twenty-six countries involved, on the night of January 1 Churchill and Roosevelt signed the declaration, along with representatives of the Soviet Union and China. Other leaders sent their consent via cables.[45]

At 1:30 p.m. on January 3, Early called the reporters into his office and gave them a statement announcing the historic agreement but warned them not to put it on their wires until 2:00: "You can prepare your pieces and have them ready to go at two, but nothing on your wires until two." It was scheduled for release around the world at that time, Early told them. But when the reporters demanded background on the statement, he said simply, "It speaks for itself." It was another chaotic meeting between press secretary and press, with the reporters wanting more and the secretary giving away nothing. As the press conference drew to a close, one reporter eager for more news asked Early, "Anything more coming up Steve, today?"

Mr. Early's reply: "Lunch, in a few minutes."[46]

18

"SERVE IN SILENCE"

By the beginning of 1942, Steve Early had replaced the "We Ain't Mad With Nobody" sign behind the bookcase in his office with one that said, "Serve in Silence. Do not reveal military information." It was a dictum that would plague him throughout the war, as he wrestled with his desire to keep the news flowing and at the same time bow to the wishes of the Boss and the military establishment who insisted on informing the public on a strictly need-to-know basis, if that.[1]

One newspaper told its readers that it was not as if Roosevelt wanted to abandon the free flow of news, but that the war had deemed so many questions improper that the president was forced not to answer them. The ban on information was expanding day by day, and nowhere was this more evident than during Early's daily press conferences, for as the winter dragged into spring, he was sharing less and less with the reporters who crowded his office, sometimes twice a day, to find out what Roosevelt was doing, how the war was progressing, or what foreign notable was on the way to Washington. A frequently agitated Early beat around the bush; he changed the topic, and still they persisted but to no avail; he even scolded them sometimes about printing rumors.

Early in January, he assured them that when the president was going away from Washington, they would get the full story. "But you won't get it until it is announced. You can also be sure that you can't say where he is, if you know, until he returns and it is announced," he said. Merriman Smith of the United Press later wrote that as the war continued, Roosevelt did virtually what he pleased, in public and in private, secure in the knowledge that it would not appear on the radio or in the newspapers.[2]

And while Early's daily press conferences seemed to contain less news for publication than before Pearl Harbor, he said he tried hard to dig up as much news as he could every day that he could give the reporters. "But news is not always available. We don't go out and man-ufacture it. We go over countless reports and documents in search of news—factual news," he told one journalist. More often than not, what the reporters wanted, he was, for security reasons, unable to supply. This did not mean that they came away from his or Roosevelt's press conferences with blank pads. Both men had a habit of handing the reporters tasty morsels not necessarily anything worth a banner head-line, such as the day in May 1942 when Early told the reporters, "This might make a story for you." Gold Star Mothers, those whose sons had died in the war, had asked the president to allow them and each member of their families to wear a black armband with a gold star on it. Roosevelt thought it a good idea, so Early said he would advise the national president of the Gold Star Mothers later that day.[3]

Later in the war, Early told a radio interviewer that his job might be compared to that of a fireman or a doctor: "When the phone rings at home, as it often does, and there is a news story in the making at the White House, my job is to see that it is released so that every paper and radio station gets it, as quickly as the machinery permits, and, simulta-neously, if possible." He also explained that when the president trav-eled, the censorship office looked to him to indicate when the news could be released so as to not endanger the president's life. "It's never necessary to make these things too official. I simply explain the facts as best I can and let the reporters take care of the rest," he said.[4]

Robert Sherwood, a playwright and one of Roosevelt's speech-writers, recalled that Early had hoped to remain rigorously uninquisitive about White House secrets during the war and wanted to be told of no military plans. He had told the Boss he didn't want to know any secrets lest he inadvertently reveal them to the press. Gradually, however, he changed his mind and believed he should know about all the president's secret travels. This may have stemmed from the frustration and embarrassment he had suffered the previous August when Roosevelt and Churchill met secretly in the Atlantic, leaving an ignorant Early behind to deal with a curious and sometimes hostile group of reporters.[5]

If 1942 could have been described in one word, that word would have been "bleak." For the first six months, the Allies were being pummeled on all fronts. Congress, with the blessing of the White House, had instituted controls to curb rising prices. By the end of January, civilian passenger car production was halted. The first nuclear chain reaction was set off at the University of Chicago, a discovery that would forever change the world but was known about at this time by only a very select few.[6]

In March of that year the United States government, in one of the most disgraceful moments in its history, saw fit to remove 110,000 Japanese, more than half of them American-born citizens, from their homes on the West Coast and place them in camps hundreds of miles inland. It was perhaps an odd action for a president who often spoke of the importance of individual liberties. Just a week after Pearl Harbor he had proclaimed Bill of Rights Day on the 150th anniversary of the ratification of that document. His biographer, James MacGregor Burns, points out that in a few short months, the climate of the country—in particular California, home to large numbers of Japanese Americans—had turned to "fear, suspicion, intolerance" as the Japanese military seemed to be moving closer and closer to the West Coast of the United States. While Roosevelt never officially approved of the internment plan, Burns says, he remained coldly indifferent to it all—as did his press secretary. There is no mention in either Early's press conferences or his letters of the internments.[7]

Even Major League Baseball was in jeopardy. Would the teams play in wartime? When the commissioner of baseball, Judge Kenesaw Mountain Landis, asked Roosevelt for guidance in early January 1942, the president said that although the final decision rested with the owners of the teams, he honestly thought it would be best for the country to keep baseball going. Early told reporters the president had decided that with fewer people unemployed and everyone working longer hours, they needed recreation to take their minds off work. A baseball game might be just the ticket. Players of draft age should, of course, serve in the military, he said. Then Early said Roosevelt had looked at the question of baseball during war from a different perspective: If three hundred teams use five to six thousand players, these players are a definite recreational asset to at least 20 million people, and, in the president's judgment, "that was thoroughly worthwhile."[8]

In early February, Daylight Saving Time went into effect across the country. It was first observed during World War I, and when the war ended, it became optional. Now Congress and the president felt it again was needed. But railroads, some government agencies, and industries wanted a term for the new time, so Roosevelt dubbed it "War Time": Eastern War Time, Central War Time, and so forth.[9]

Washington's winter that year was unusually cold. By mid-January, it had hit 7 degrees below zero, drawing skaters to the Reflecting Pool, where their bonfires partially impaired the blackout imposed on the Washington Monument. Inside the Senate Office Building, boxes of sand and shovels cluttered the doorways, ready for clerical workers to smother incendiary bombs if necessary. Later that winter, eighteen inches of snow fell overnight on the city. District of Columbia engineers were doubling the amount of chlorine in the drinking water supply to guard against enemy plots to pollute water mains with bacteria. All were pitching in to do their part for the "war effort." Even the sedate and impeccably attired Charles Hurd, one of the White House correspondents for the *New York Times*, decided to save wear and tear on the tires of the family car, so he gave his wife a bicycle, complete with a wire basket for marketing.[10]

On January 6 President Roosevelt traveled up Pennsylvania Avenue to deliver his annual State of the Union message to Congress. About an hour earlier, Early had called the reporters into his office, not to give them a copy of the message, as was the custom, but to ask that they refrain from printing or reporting on the radio or in movie newsreels any future movements of Roosevelt and Churchill. Since mid-1939 Early had asked reporters not to publish in advance the exact travel times of the president. Now, Early said, their travels should be treated by the press "on a basis exactly similar to the manner in which the press now treats ship movements and movements of our armed forces." He said the safety of the prime minister and the president was "more or less at stake." The reporters could, however, write about these travels once they were complete.

If photographers, for instance, were to catch Roosevelt going into the Capitol or some other public place, could they take his picture? one reporter asked. Early had a simple answer: "Well, there won't be any objection to that, because it isn't going to happen."

What prompted this request, which he said was "off the record" and should be passed along to the reporters' offices "in confidence," was the fact that Churchill had left Washington the day before for "a hideout and a rest for a day or two," and some alert reporters had discovered his whereabouts in Florida. Early said that his request came in an effort to ensure Churchill's safety because the government was aware of enemy spies in the United States not yet apprehended and shortwave radio transmissions that the government had been unable to suppress.[11]

Roosevelt's speech to Congress on January 6 was a militant one as he raced through an impressive list of war production goals. Perhaps the dynamism of that talk came in part, according to Robert Sherwood, because the president's aides—and Early in particular—were concerned that the oratorical skills of the British prime minister were eclipsing those of the president of the United States. Sherwood calls Early "fiercely loyal and jealous of his Chief's prestige." Early kept flow charts of the sizes of Roosevelt's radio audiences, and he did not welcome the competition from the other side of the Atlantic. Sherwood said that Roosevelt never seemed bothered by the possibility of Churchill's upstaging him; instead, he seemed to go to the opposite extreme, searching for the shortest and most succinct way to get his message across. Roosevelt actually was "greatly amused" by Early's concern. Churchill, who originally had planned to stay only a week in the White House and then go on to Canada for two days before returning to England, instead came back to Washington after his vacation in Florida for a few days before he went home.[12] The president found Churchill a delightful companion and enjoyed their meetings, which were many during the war years.

The day after Roosevelt's address to Congress, the reporters were still concerned about what they were allowed to tell the public and what they could not. Early, who had spent another late night in his office, was a bit edgy and at the same time exhibiting that fierce loyalty to the Boss, who was leaving for a few days' break to a destination Early could not share with the reporters. (He went to his home in Hyde Park, New York.) This is what he told them:

You can be sure that any one of you who has been through what *he* [Roosevelt] has since the seventh of December—the beginning of the war—the arrival of the Prime Minister—the preparation of his annual Message yesterday—and the Budget Message today—the conferences that have gone on well into the night—when it has reached the point that January 7 arrives and he hasn't had a chance to open his Christmas packages, he is entitled to two or three days away without anyone bothering him. And nothing is going to bother him, or disturb him, until he returns here, except business that is most important to the conduct of the war. And you can be sure, gentlemen, that if you all know where he is, as I assume many of you do, there would be many others who would know where he is, as I assume many of you do. And it is the "many others" that prevents you, on this occasion, from knowing more than you do.

Then one of the reporters asked him if this constituted an announcement that Roosevelt was away or was it "off the record"? Fumbling a bit, Early said it was "something to think about. I am quite certain that it would be on [the record], that it is his usual—that it does not constitute an announcement that he is away." But wouldn't that contradict what he had just told them? Early thought about it for a couple of seconds, then said, "Yes, it would be. It would be, so consider the whole thing off the record, and confidential." It was painfully obvious that both reporters and press secretary were continuing to confront the issue of censorship almost on a daily basis.[13]

Throughout the war on occasion a reporter would inadvertently —or perhaps on purpose—disclose to readers or listeners Roosevelt's location when he was out of town. And each time, the reporter incurred Early's wrath, usually during one of his press conferences. In fact, the whole White House staff was trying to get a grip on the need for secrecy in time of war. For example, it was customary to fly the flag over the White House when the president was in residence. Soon after Pearl Harbor, Roosevelt slipped away for the weekend, and the staff followed the usual routine of not raising the flag. At his press conference that morning, Early fielded a question from an alert newsman who asked where the president had gone. After that the flag flew every day throughout the war.[14]

So it was that during the January 7 press conference, as Early tap-danced around the problems of security and secrecy, a reporter asked him, somewhat jocularly, if this meant the flag would be flying from the White House. This and other details, which Early said had been left to him to handle, indicated the president had left town. He told them that "any blind man, just released from any institution where they put people with mental disorders, would know at once. It is so obvious it's silly, but it can't be helped, fellows." Someone suggested that if the Secret Service were smart, it would plant a couple of decoys. Early agreed. One of those "other details" he alluded to was the president's daily appointments list given out by Pa Watson, his appointments secretary. The wire services carried the list for papers to publish if they cared to. One of the wire service reporters asked, "Now what would happen when Roosevelt was away?" He said that if they were even fifteen minutes late getting the list on the wire, newspapers began asking where it was. Early decided he would solve the problem by having Watson issue a "no appointments list" on days the president was away. It was a sham, and everyone knew it, but for the most part, the media complied with this and other similar requests during the war.

Impatient, they asked if Early had anything they *could* print. So he handed them a few crumbs, some minor nominations the president was sending to the Senate. Then Early the journalist, understanding their need for news, dropped another news nugget, but again it was off the record: "Still in the strictest of confidence, I think I ought to tell you fellows—although I don't suppose I expected to—I think you are entitled to know—I think the president will be back here this weekend. And, very much in the same confidence, Churchill will be back here this weekend. And they will be publicly together before there is any return to the off the record. We are going on and off the record, but I think you ought to know that. At least that is the plan as of today. But please keep it to yourselves."[15]

Churchill did make it back to Washington to briefly bid goodbye to Roosevelt, and by the end of the week he had returned to London, but at his Saturday press conference Early was reluctant to confirm the prime minister's arrival home. When the reporters told him the news had been announced from London, Early cautiously said he wanted to wait until it was definite that he was there. But the reporters had heard it first. Early blamed his own delay on "the censor," adding, "I just want to see that it is correct before I make any move on it." The reporters were not happy. They were afraid their British colleagues would beat them to the punch on a story about the results of Churchill's meetings with Roosevelt. So was a White House announcement imminent? they asked. Early understood their dilemma, but he could not tell them. All he would say was that Roosevelt was "working on staff matters, and when he arrives at the point to make an announcement" they would then know.

Even Early had gotten his news of this from the radio, saying, "I have been hearing some radio reports, which I suppose would be traceable back to you fellows, about grand strategy, and that sort of stuff. I wouldn't get too far out on a limb on that. It's FOR YOUR GUIDANCE, right now." They also asked him if they now could tell the public that Churchill had vacationed in Florida. "Everybody's kept hands off," they complained. Early said he would see what he could eventually give them: "For the time being, don't mention anything." They thanked him, and another press conference ended in frustration for the press and for the press secretary. By the end of the month, Early probably was wishing he would never hear the name Winston Churchill again. But the Roosevelt-Churchill collaboration continued throughout the war, and if Early thought this winter's meetings were giving him headaches with the press, the worst was yet to come.[16]

James MacGregor Burns says that gradually, after the beginning of 1942, the White House turned into a military command post, with soldiers and heavy chains at the gates, listening devices around the grounds, and manned antiaircraft guns on the roof. The Secret Service banned tour groups from inside the White House, visitors had to be carefully vetted, and employees were forced to carry passes that were inspected when they came to work.[17]

For more than a week in the middle of January Early's sinuses again were bothering him, so when the reporters spilled into his office on Monday, January 19, one reporter asked, "Feel any better, Mr. Early?" The answer was, "I'm not boasting." He called the day "a blue Monday," and had little to offer them in the way of news. That did not stop them, however, from harking back to the Churchill story. They pressed for more details on what the prime minister did when he was last in Washington. Early stood firm. He could give them "nothing more than I did Saturday morning."[18]

A week later the press conference topic again was Churchill, and it could not have helped Early's sinus headache. The prime minister would address Parliament, and the American reporters wanted a copy of the speech. Early told them he was putting together some materials relating to the talk, which would discuss Churchill's activities in the United States. The reporters could have the materials that night, but they would be marked "Hold for Release, Confidential" until the prime minister actually had begun his speech the next day, maybe at noon, London time. Early did not know the exact hour. Even then the reporters would have to get the okay from the British Ministry of Information to release the story. The reason the story could not break until the speech was in progress, Early explained, was that the British had stopped announcing the hours that Parliament was in session.

The reporters wanted to know whether the talk would be broadcast from London. Early did not know. He said he had read in the newspapers that the British did not broadcast live from Parliament, so if it was aired, it would be recorded and then broadcast without applause. He added, "The Laborites objected to the broadcasting because it would not have their heckling in it. So I am just tied up in a good sailor's knot."[19]

Churchill did address Parliament at noon the next day, London time, and all but one American news outlet had respected the "Hold for Release." The exception was the *New York Times*. During his press conference that morning, Early was told by one of the reporters that both the Associated Press and the United Press wire services had called the *Times* the night before to remind them the story was not to be released until Churchill started speaking. The reporter said that the *Times* had told him last night that Early had given the newspaper permission to release the story ahead of time. "It isn't true," Early replied and said he would demand a written report from the *Times* on the incident.

Early was angry. He told the assembled reporters, "As you know I took a great deal of time last night to work out that release." He had telephoned London twice, and at first was told that Churchill might not give the speech because he had a severe cold. During the second call, Early said, he was told the talk was on, so he had put together the release he gave to the American reporters. When the *Times* jumped the gun, the story, which included the time Parliament was meeting, got out in Britain and Canada. "I put my neck in the noose on that," he said, adding, "I did it knowing that I could give it to you in confidence and that it wouldn't get out of this country." One reporter spoke up, "The *Times* did apparently a very good job tightening the noose."

Early was not the only one upset because the *Times* jumped the embargo. Wire service reporters were in hot water overnight with their offices because the *Times* was "scooping them." One reporter said the *Times* should be charged with violating the "censorship law." To the amusement of his colleagues, Early suggested a penalty of ten years and ten thousand dollars. "It will be taken up with the *Times*," Early assured him. There is no record that it was, but the offending reporter, Frank Kluckhohn, no doubt received a blistering, profanity-filled tongue-lashing from the angry press secretary.[20]

Censorship continued to be the major theme of Early's press conferences. On February 2 he asked the reporters, "off the record entirely," to recall the "certain situation" two weeks ago in respect to the whereabouts of the president. "A similar situation again is present, and all I can do is turn to the sign and say, 'We will Serve in Silence for the duration.'"[21]

Later that week the reporters were checking out another rumor. This one was that Early had ordered that all speeches of federal officials, including cabinet members, be cleared through the Office of Facts and Figures, headed by Archibald MacLeish, the librarian of Congress, and his assistant, Robert Sherwood.

Not exactly, Early answered. Then he proceeded to patiently explain that for the last nine years his office had been held responsible by the president for clearing speeches of the cabinet and other high-ranking officials in the executive branch. Gradually it became "a burden of work" that his office could no longer perform without additional help. And with the entry of the United States into the war, it became more important than ever for these speeches to be cleared by the White House to keep policy statements uniform. When MacLeish took over the Office of Facts and Figures, which had "a sizeable staff," Early said, he asked him to help to clear the speeches. Their biggest problem, Early said, was that an official would give him a speech in the afternoon that he needed to deliver that night. Would Mr. Early have any objections to giving the reporters a copy of this memo? "Yes. I am not going to give you a copy. You have the substance of everything that is in it," he said.

Mr. Early may not have played favorites, but he could hold a grudge when a reporter crossed him. The reporter who asked for a copy of the memorandum was none other than Frank Kluckhohn, the

New York Times man who had broken the embargo on the Churchill story the previous week.[22]

Early continued to have little publishable information from the White House for the reporters for the next couple of weeks. His sinuses continued to bother him, and again Roosevelt was under the weather with a cold, a story that resulted in a headline in the *Washington Post* that said, "President Kept to Rooms by Coed." The editor laying out the page inadvertently placed the headline below a story about a local businessman who was on trial for assaulting a nineteen-year-old government girl. The incident amused Early so much he ordered a dozen copies of the paper. When Roosevelt read it, he had "a belly laugh."[23]

It could have been the nasty Washington weather that sapped the presidential energy that February of 1942, or it might well have been the depressing war news from abroad. One by one, Japanese troops were gobbling up islands throughout the western Pacific, tightening the noose around Singapore, even attacking Darwin, Australia, and reaching north to the Aleutian Islands. British troops were forced by the Japanese to withdraw from Burma; Moscow was barely staving off invasion by the Germans; Leningrad was under siege, one that lasted nine hundred days; all Allied shipping in the Mediterranean was halted because of severe losses; and on February 19 and 20, Dutch and American warships were unable to halt a Japanese invasion of Bali. It was obvious that the president of the United States needed to take to the airwaves.

By February 23 Roosevelt was well enough to give a Fireside Chat, a talk that focused on the progress of the war. In fact, Early had been publicizing the conference for three weeks and, announcing that the president would refer to a map of the world during the talk, and in an ingenious attempt to engage the audience in a complex topic, Early the publicist inadvertently caused an increase in map sales. When he did take to the airwaves, Roosevelt asked listeners to spread out their world maps and follow his talk. He called the war "a different kind of war," not just in methods and weapons but also in geography: "It is warfare in terms of every continent, every island, every sea, every air-lane in the world." However, Early's efforts to build an audience for this talk also attracted a Japanese submarine that surfaced to shell a ranch near Santa Barbara, California, during the radio broadcast. In his dissertation, "Selling the New Deal," Steven E. Schoenherr says that after this incident, Early gave only bare publicity before a Roosevelt speech.[24]

A few days later, Early got a much-needed respite from the clamoring reporters when he and Helen headed to Florida for a two-week vacation as guests of a local businessman. While he was away, either Bill Hassett or Marvin McIntyre filled in at his press conferences. Mac's meetings with the reporters were far more informal than those gently bantering but thoroughly businesslike sessions of Early's. Mac frequently offered his personal opinions on people and issues and appeared far less informed on topics than Early. On March 9 Hassett, who sometimes was a victim of Early's temper, gave the reporters little news, but when they asked when Steve was returning, Hassett told them that if they missed him so much they could feel free to hurry over to Union Station at 11:10 that morning and meet his train coming in from Florida.[25]

To the relief of the reporters, a rested Early was back on the job the next day. Later that month Roosevelt was off on another of his "off the record" weekends, or what Grace Tully called "invisible traveling." As it was so often, this was another visit to Hyde Park, and Early was left behind to mind the shop. Hassett, who had once worked with Early at the Associated Press and had been a White House aide, mostly for Early, since the mid-1930s, now accompanied Roosevelt on his jaunts to Hyde Park, acting as a kind of intellectual valet.[26]

The night before the presidential entourage left town, Early dined with Roosevelt, Hopkins, and Lord Beaverbrook, minister of aircraft production in Churchill's cabinet, at the White House, but when asked by reporters the following morning, he refused to share with them the details of meetings between the president and Beaverbrook.[27]

Early told his press conference on Thursday, March 26, that he would be in his office the next morning, but from then on, he would be "weekending myself, or afternooning, or something." A reporter noted wryly, "Too bad Bowie doesn't open until the first of the month," referring to one of the nearby horse racing tracks Early frequented. He confided to the reporters that the president had given him permission to go to Florida again, but he was not going: "I can't afford it."[28]

It is fascinating to read transcripts of Early's press conferences, because he often opened them by telling the reporters he had no news for them, then proceeded to answer their questions in great detail, unless, of course, they veered into the realm of censored information. One morning in mid-March he opened by saying, "I went into all the pantries and closets in the building and all over the House in search of news, and I find that yesterday pretty well emptied the shelf. I can give you a little bit of the canned variety." The reporters laughed, then he listed the president's appointments for the day and read a brief citation Roosevelt would deliver to a retiring admiral. This was followed by a give and take with a reporter over a military appropriation the president was asking from Congress. Early confirmed that Gen. Douglas MacArthur, at the behest of Roosevelt, was on his way to take command of the Southwest Pacific Allied Forces. Another day that spring he told the reporters, "Well, gentlemen, if you are looking for news today, you can draw a circle around the White House and find nothing in it."[29]

On the day before Easter, Early began his press conference by telling the reporters "off the record" that the president would be attending church services the next morning. He said the reporters could attend the services for their stories, but "I don't want anything published on it until after the services." They respected the temporary ban.[30]

In 1941 Merriman Smith joined "the regulars," those dozen or so correspondents who traveled with the president and who spent eight to ten hours a day at the White House waiting for stories to break. These few reporters were classed practically as members of the White House family. They represented the major daily newspapers and the three wire services. Smith described the pressroom during the war years as large, 18 by 40 feet, with tall windows on two sides and close to forty telephones crammed on ten desks, which themselves were jammed against each other. The room also held a line of private phone booths for the wire service reporters. He said that when all the phones, all with different toned rings, rang at the same time, it sounded like a concert by a swarm of drunken Swiss bell ringers.[31]

Early's easy banter with the press corps at the beginning of his daily press conferences, and the trust the reporters had in him as one of their own, allowed him to give them information "off the record." He was confident they would respect his requests, and they knew that if they broke that trust, they might find news less forthcoming from the White House. This is a practice that would be impossible in today's competitive multimedia climate, but it had worked comfortably, for the most part, beginning with the very first meetings Early and Roosevelt held with the press. The voluntary censorship was working, and as long as no military information was disclosed, Early and Byron Price, head of the office of censorship, allowed reporters as much freedom to write their stories as they had before the war. However, Early remained wary that in some way he might accidentally blurt out something that the president did not want in the hands of the reporters—in particular the columnists, whom he continued to mistrust to write accurate accounts.

Then, two weeks later, that fragile connection of trust between press and press secretary snapped. At his April 17 press conference, on a Friday morning, opening pleasantries were replaced with a curt "Good Morning." Abruptly the Early "towering temper" exploded. What precipitated his blast were rumors that had been published or broadcast overnight and that morning.

His voice "vibrant with anger," Early attempted to explain to the reporters why he was so furious:

> Gentlemen, there are just a few words I want to say to you. For nine years this office has been trying to cooperate with you. It has not been playing favorites. The whole desire was to do away with the favorite few that have been dealt with in previous—and by previous administrations and to help all of you to get the news and to work with you in getting it. Yesterday, for example, I told you as a matter of personal convenience that there would be an unimportant statement to be released at 10:30 this morning. I also told you, for your own convenience, that there would be no [Roosevelt] Press Conference today. Now that was in continuation of the desire to work with you and to make your work here as convenient as possible and, at the same time, protect you so that you would get the news. Now out it goes on the radio, and on the front pages, and there is much speculation about this word of a statement today—on the basis of merely a confidential tip to you here at 10:30 this morning—despite the fact there would be no Press Conference . . .

He went on,

> I thought if I told you that there would be no Press Conference some of you might not be here to get the news. I couldn't tell you

what the news was, although I told you that it was not important. It was—it was an arrangement between the United States Government and that of Canada—a simultaneous release to be issued in Ottawa and in Washington, this morning, at 10:30. That was what I wanted you to get, and that's what I thought you wanted to get—so that you would have it on time, particularly the wire services, and those who have Canadian papers . . .

He wasn't finished.

And I want to tell you right now that after the experience with you last night and today—ringing the gong like there was a four-alarm fire somewhere, like we were going to have some astounding, amazing new headlined world announcement to make on Vichy or half a dozen other subjects that I read this morning that came from your fertile imaginations—that I am putting out the news from now on as it comes and when it comes without any cooperation on the basis of the old understandings with you whatever. If you can't cooperate, then you will get nothing in advance or for your guidance.[32]

So why had Roosevelt forgone his usual Friday press conference? The night before he had headed north on his usual overnight train ride to Hyde Park, where he spent the weekend poring over a pile of work he had brought from Washington and dining with friends before returning Monday morning. During the first six months of 1942, Roosevelt was at his home in New York nine times, mostly over weekends, with several visits lasting as long as five or six days. All were off-the-record trips, meaning reporters were forbidden, under censorship regulations, to report on them. Merriman Smith, the White House correspondent for United Press, concluded that Roosevelt simply did not want anyone outside his "official family" to know just how much time he was spending at his home in Hyde Park.

It is astonishing the breadth of confidential or off-the-record information that Early did share with the reporters when they stood around his desk every morning during his press conferences, even though he suspected some of them were indirectly feeding information to other journalists who were not present. In May, holding back the usual anger he would exhibit when the reporters had betrayed his trust, he warned them that the more they discussed confidential information with colleagues in Washington, the more likely some of them would pass some of this on to the gossip columnists who had no problem publishing it. "They know I take you into my confidence," he told them. "They tell others and the thing mushrooms. There it goes. And so the columnist gets it. I don't tell them about it. I tell you fellows about it, but they are the ones who sting you, and they sting you because you fellows tell them."[33]

What prompted this was an announcement to various newspaper and radio offices the previous day from Byron Price's censorship office that a Russian was scheduled to arrive at the White House later that month. But as usual, the White House and the State Department wanted no mention of the visit until it was concluded. And, as usual, the reporters were on to the story.[34]

Early confirmed the visit "entirely off the record," adding that they did not know who the visitor would be or when he would arrive, but that it probably would be by the end of the week. But mum was the word. They were to tell no one. "I am telling you fellows about it because you will be worrying about it, and expecting a release that won't be coming. And you will be thinking he is probably going to get here this week or over the weekend. If he comes, he will be here for a week or so." He chastised the Censorship Office for a premature announcement. Then he retracted and decided that if the media had not given some hint, reporters might have begun speculating. The announcement "makes it less possible for anyone to break the story through innocence or indiscretion," he said.

When a reporter asked, amid gales of laughter, if he could tell his editor, Early replied, "If you want to tell your desk [editor], why don't you ask me if you may?" The reporter said he planned to tell the editor anyway, to which Early responded, "I haven't any objections if you tell your desk, if your desk then in turn doesn't tell somebody else and get . . . the endless chain in operation . . . then some columnist gets it." Later, Merriman Smith admitted that most of the reporters had no idea who the visitor was. If they did, he said, they were just speculating. He found out quite by accident from an old army friend over lunch the day after the "secret" visitor arrived.[35]

The visitor was V. M. Molotov, the Soviet minister of foreign affairs, who arrived on a Friday at the end of May straight from talks in London with Churchill, and he stayed in the White House, a pistol, a roll of sausage, and a chunk of black bread in his suitcase. During his visit, Molotov's code name was "Mr. Brown," and, according to Robert Sherwood, the Russian's presence in the capital imposed a real strain on Early because Joseph Stalin had requested that "Mr. Brown's" visit not be made public. Alas, the rumor mill and the intrepid Washington press corps eventually led to Early's decision to give reporters some latitude in telling their editors about the visit. Smith said he ran into Early at a cocktail party soon after Molotov arrived in Washington. Smith said he asked Early, "How's Molotov?" guessing that was the "visitor." He said Early almost choked on his highball and wanted to know what the hell he was talking about. Once Smith convinced him he was not on a fishing expedition, Early took him aside and confirmed the foreign minister's presence in Washington. However, nothing of that visit was published or broadcast in the United States until Molotov was safely back in Moscow.

The Germans already were blitzing their way across western Russia, and, convinced that Hitler's troops were prepared to launch a major offensive that the Russian army could not defend, Molotov had come to ask Roosevelt for military supplies and that the United States join the British in launching a second front in Europe by the end of the summer, a request to which the president offered only a vague agreement, his mind perhaps on burgeoning secret plans for a second front not in eastern Europe and Russia, but rather in North Africa. As soon as the Soviet minister left, Roosevelt boarded his train to spend most of the week in Hyde Park, leaving the beleaguered Early to again fend off reporters' questions about the president's whereabouts.[36]

Even as Molotov left Washington to fly home to Moscow, reporters were in the dark over who the "important visitor" had been, although the infamous rumor mill undoubtedly had already supplied most of them with a name. At Early's press conference that day, one reporter told him, "Several reporters, and more alleged reporters, are skirting around a subject which we are forbidden to write about. I might call attention to a columnist on the *New York Daily News*, who remarks this morning that something big is going on in Washington which may change the shape of the world." Did that mean the reporters now could write about it? Early said they could not. Nothing would be announced, he added, "pertaining to a visit of a certain official" until the official had returned safely home. The

Captain Stephen Early in France after the Armistice.
(Stephen T. Early Collection, FDR Library)

During the 1920 Campaign. *From left*: unidentified man, FDR, Eleanor Roosevelt, Stephen Early, and Stanley Prenosil of the Associated Press.
(Stephen T. Early Collection, FDR Library)

Early (left) and FDR on the back of the train during FDR's visit to the west.
(Eisenhower Library)

FDR's three secretaries in March 1933. *From left*: Louis Howe, Stephen Early, and Marvin McIntyre.
(Stephen T. Early Collection, FDR Library)

Eleanor Roosevelt and Stephen Early in Fort Worth, Texas, in October 1935.
(Stephen T. Early Collection, FDR Library)

FDR with Early in October 1936.
(The March of Time, Time Magazine)

En route to the Capitol for a message to Congress on January 1, 1937. *From left*: FDR, Marvin McIntyre, Stephen Early, and James Roosevelt. *(Stephen T. Early Collection, FDR Library)*

Stephen Early at his White House desk in the summer of 1939.
(Stephen T. Early Collection, FDR Library)

The Early family at home in January 1941. *From left*: Helen, "Sis" Helen, Stephen, Buddy, and Tommy seated on the floor with the family Boxer, Heine.
(Stephen T. Early Collection, FDR Library)

Stephen Early and "the Boss" in the White House, January 1941.
(Stephen T. Early Collection, FDR Library)

AT BREAKFAST THE PRESIDENT HOLDS HIS BEDSIDE CONFERENCE WITH DR. McINTIRE (LEFT), "PA" WATSON (TELLING JOKE), STEVE EARLY, HARRY HOPKINS (SEATED)

ROOSEVELT FROM BREAKFAST IN BED TO WISECRACKS AT MOVIES, PRESIDENT RETAINS HIS BOUNCE AFTER EIGHT YEARS
by GEOFFREY HELLMAN

In January 1941 *Life* magazine depicted FDR in his bedroom at his morning conference with his close aides. *From left*: Dr. Ross McIntire, FDR, Edwin M. "Pa" Watson, and Stephen Early. Seated is Harry Hopkins. *(Life magazine, box 30, "Press and Radio/Misc.," FDR Library accession number 9786.)*

Stephen Early with FDR and the president's secretaries, Grace Tully, left, and Marguerite "Missy" Le Hand, right, in May 1941. *(Stephen T. Early Collection, FDR Library)*

President Harry S. Truman awards Stephen Early the Distinguished Service Medal, May 31, 1941. *(Life Photo by George Skadding, Life Picture Service, New York)*

Eager reporters crowd around Stephen Early's desk on December 22, 1941, to get a press release on Prime Minister Winston Churchill's arrival at the White House.
(Stephen T. Early Collection, FDR Library)

Prime Minister Winston Churchill and President Roosevelt at their joint press conference in the White House on December 23, 1941. Stephen Early is in the background between Churchill and FDR. *(Stephen T. Early Collection, FDR Library)*

Stephen Early, left, with golf buddies at Burning Tree Country Club in Bethesda, Maryland, in February 1942. *From left:* George Allen, a District of Columbia commissioner; Early; Joseph Davies, former ambassador to the Soviet Union; and Senator Millard Tydings of Maryland.
(Stephen T. Early Collection, FDR Library)

FDR shares a light moment with aides Edwin M. "Pa" Watson, left, and Stephen Early, center.
(Stephen T. Early Collection, FDR Library)

reporters were concerned that they were missing a big story. Get a ruling from the censorship office on what they could write and when they could release it, he told them.[37]

Three weeks later another foreign dignitary, this one well known to the occupants of the White House, came to town, and again the reporters were kept in the dark until he had arrived in the city. Then "the lid blew to pieces." It all began on June 19, when the British government announced that Churchill would be going to the United States again. A newspaper on Fleet Street, home to the offices of the major British newspapers, tipped off the New York office of the Associated Press to be on the lookout for a story of "momentous importance."

Churchill arrived at Bolling Air Field in Washington on the evening of June 18; Roosevelt had left for Hyde Park the night before to prepare for a visit from the British prime minister, who was only stopping overnight in Washington and then flying north to spend the weekend with Roosevelt to discuss the opening of a second front.

The night Churchill's plane landed in Washington—about 8:00 p.m. on Thursday—Early called the members of the White House press corps at home and told them to hurry over to his office. Associated Press reporter Doug Cornell showed up in his bedroom slippers. Another reporter said he drove so fast he was lucky not to have gotten a speeding ticket. One reporter told Early the next day that he was upset because he had gone out to dinner and had forgotten to leave his phone number with the White House operator, so he never got the message and missed the big news.

So once the barely dressed newsmen arrived at the White House what could Early tell them beyond confirming the rumor that Churchill indeed was in Washington? Not much. He told them "for their guidance" that the two men would be meeting out of town but he could not reveal the exact location. "Certainly might be a lot of places," he commented. Who would be joining the prime minister and the president? No reply. What else could he tell them? Nothing.

But Early, being Early, could not keep the reporters completely in the dark: "Now I will put my neck in the 'noose.' Just FOR YOUR GUIDANCE AND NOT FOR PUBLICATION, just trying to make the coverage as easy in your mind as possible, under the circumstances that we have to function under, I wouldn't expect anything here to take place before Sunday afternoon. Now don't take that out of the room, will you? I am just trying to give you something, and I don't anticipate another word on the subject before then. I will help you to that extent, and I am not supposed to do that. So please protect that. If you don't do it, I might not be here much longer to protect you." The reporters laughed, and one assured him, "We think we know what you mean."

It was obvious he was frustrated that he could give them so little, so he tried to explain his position to them: He called the two heads of state his battleships "to protect for the duration, and their movements and whereabouts, and their operations are just as secret as would be the movement of two men-of-war, in times like this." When Tom Reynolds of the United Press insisted on knowing who would be joining Roosevelt and Churchill for their meetings, Early looked over at the reporter and pleaded, "Tom, I told you all I know, and there is no reason for you to keep asking questions. I would answer them if I could. I can't. It's no fun for me either." Of course he knew more, a lot more, and how tempting it must have been to hand the reporters, some of them his former colleagues, a platter rich with answers to their questions. Churchill, clad in his famous siren suit and accompanied by a retinue of five military aides, arrived at the Roosevelt home in Hyde Park a few hours later.[38]

As the war progressed, the White House found itself knee-deep in rumors, no doubt in large part because of the ban on news about the president's travels until they were completed. In a city where rumors are its lifeblood, the very essence of daily life, the rumor mill was playing havoc with the White House's efforts to keep a lid on almost anything and everything that a journalist would desire to make a news story. Early told one reporter, "I wish I could tell you the many amazing rumors, entirely false, which I've exploded to the satisfaction of the Press and Radio newsmen."[39]

It got so bad by the middle of 1942 that Early suggested that *Life*, the widely circulated and highly regarded weekly magazine of photography, do a photo essay on wartime rumors—and it did. The layout of photos of people in various walks of life—bus driver, gas station attendant, dentist, and so forth—illustrated the passage of a rumor through a community. The credits say: "Suggested by Stephen Early, Directed by Alfred Hitchcock, and Photographed by Eliot Elisofon." The essay ends: "Moral: Keep your mouth shut." Steve could not have said it better.[40]

However, occasionally the rumor came directly from the lips of the president of the United States. In March Early called Roosevelt "a rumor factory" after the president told his press conference that he had entertained an elderly woman at a White House dinner recently with a story about General MacArthur escaping from the Bataan Peninsula to Australia disguised as a Filipino fisherman rowing a boat the whole 2,200 miles. A bit of Rooseveltian humor it may have been, but it annoyed Early so much that he felt the need to pass it on to the reporters. The truth was that on orders from the president, MacArthur had arrived earlier that week in Australia from the Philippines to take command of the Southwest Pacific Allied Forces. Roosevelt just decided to embellish the truth a bit to amuse himself at a staid and culinary-deprived White House dinner.[41]

At another press conference, the president regaled the reporters with his itinerary for a recent trip to Hyde Park, giving them precise details. Sitting by his side, Early nudged the garrulous Roosevelt, but he just kept on talking. Finally beside himself, Early suggested that all this should be off the record. But the president refused, saying the trip was completed, so let it remain on the record.[42]

Leaks, especially those springing from the White House, could get Early's dander up. In one case, it was a false report, but the whole matter occupied an entire Early press conference one morning that August. It seems that a surprise blackout in the city was announced ahead of time, and the media reported that according to the chief air raid warden for Washington, the leak had come directly from the White House. Early decided to get to the bottom of the story, so he asked the Secret Service to investigate. The results? "It was found that no definite information regarding the origin of the report could be determined." After the press conference, a relieved Early told a *Washington Post* reporter, "There is every disposition at the White House to keep secrets. People working here are not given to loose talk—or else they wouldn't be here."[43]

All the depressing military news from abroad and the swirling rumors at home had persistent reporters crowding White House press conferences for nuggets worthy of a page one story. It was not until late May that Early was able to escape the fishbowl for the annual Homer Cummings Golf Tournament in Pinehurst, North Carolina, an event he often had attended in the past. In an effort to spring the overworked press secretary from his duties, William Stanley, a Washington attorney and golf crony of Early's, wrote Roosevelt: "The tournament is to be held at the end of this week and in view of Hitler and the Japs may be the last one we hold for some time. Please, Sir, if not too inconvenient to you, let Steve attend this one. He is a very necessary evil to a pleasant occasion to forty or more not too righteous souls."[44]

Steve went to Pinehurst, and shortly after he returned to Washington, Roosevelt wrote Stanley, "I operated on Steve's conscience. He went. I hope you enjoyed him. At least he came back most unexpectedly with money in his pocket and a tall tale about how somebody's ball knocked his ball in a cup. We still think he was in his cups. The FBI is investigating. I am glad to have done you a service—even though it probably cost you money. My motto is 'service always with a smile.'"[45]

Late in May Early again left Washington, this time on business; he represented the president at the dedication of the American Propeller Corporation plant, owned by Aviation Corporation, a company headed by Early's friend Victor Emanuel, the New York industrialist who a few years before had offered to help Early find a job in the private sector.[46]

In mid-July Harry Hopkins; Gen. George Marshall, the army's chief of staff; and Adm. Ernest J. King, the commander in chief of the US fleet, went to London to hold strategy discussions with British officials, including Churchill. Joining them aboard a four-engine transport plane was Steve Early, who was being dispatched by Roosevelt to make a study of the British Information Services and cement relations with his British counterpart, Churchill's protégé, Brendan Bracken. The party landed at Prestwick Airport, near Glasgow, Scotland, but the bad weather over England would not allow them to fly south to London. Instead, Churchill provided a special train that carried them directly to London. One of those meeting the plane at Prestwick was Early's old friend Harry C. Butcher, head of CBS's Washington Bureau when Early ran Paramount's office there. Butcher became a vice president of CBS, and when the war began in Europe in 1939, he was commissioned a lieutenant commander in the naval reserve. Shortly before Early arrived in England, Gen. Dwight D. Eisenhower had requested Butcher as his personal naval aide, a position he retained for the remainder of the war.

Obviously Early was delighted to see his old friend when they landed in Scotland, and for the next nine days, in between work, they managed to dine and drink often with Eisenhower, a bridge-playing friend of Early's from the general's days in Washington. Early and Butcher toured some of the bombed-out areas of London; Early lunched with Churchill and attended a late-night party on July 25 at Claridge's Hotel, where the American delegation was staying. The revelers included Hopkins, Mrs. Randolph Churchill, Averell Harriman (soon to be named United States ambassador to Moscow), his daughter Kathleen, and Eisenhower. The Americans left London the following morning via train to eventually fly home. Butcher wrote in his memoirs: "Poured Steve on the train and he poured me off."[47]

Details of the trip were not released until weeks later, even though the men and their entourage stayed in London's very public and posh Claridge's Hotel, around the corner from the American Embassy, and were wined and dined by the ambassador and other British and American officials and military personnel. Early must have heartily enjoyed this, despite its being a working visit. During the day he conferred with Bracken, the minister of public information and a former magazine editor who at Churchill's behest had taken up his post in 1941 to organize British propaganda and oversee wartime censorship of the press. It may have been the first time Early had met with the self-promoting Bracken, but it would not be the last, for a year later the two would find themselves dealing with a voracious and unruly press during the Quebec City meeting between their respective bosses.

Early's trip across the Atlantic took him away from the office until the end of July. At his first press conference after his return, the reporters called out to him as he opened the meeting, "The lost is found." They no doubt knew where he had been, but censorship had kept them from reporting his whereabouts.[48]

On August 27, 1942, Steve Early turned fifty-three; he spent the day at his desk. One newspaper reported that he was "the only man in history to have worked as a secretary to a President of the United States for more than nine years consecutively." It was indeed a long nine years, and when the reporter asked Early if he had learned to deal with the "hellish pressure" of White House work, the press secretary replied that although his disposition and temperament were "not as calm and even as they could be"—indeed an understatement—he had learned from Roosevelt to say to himself when things go tough, "Calm down now, and take things in your stride and do the best you can."

Early may have been hard at work in his office that hot summer day, but the ever fun-loving Roosevelt stopped by to wish him felicitations, then ordered a surprised Early to drape himself over the president's knees while the Boss proceeded to give him fifty-three resounding whacks. When Early recovered enough to look up, he discovered the entire White House clerical staff standing in the doorway. Loud guffaws shook the White House rafters before they all settled back down to work.[49]

This was a brief moment of levity in an otherwise busy summer and fall. James MacGregor Burns says that by late that summer, Roosevelt had a desire to once again "go to the country, an urge as powerful in some politicians as the migratory instinct in the wild goose." The fact that this was a year without a presidential election gave the trip an underlying political theme, even though the president announced that if politicians wanted to join him, they would represent both political parties. He would travel coast to coast, and the entire trip would be off the record until he returned—not an easy accomplishment even in these days of strict censorship. Burns said the president declared there would be no speeches, no parades, and no publicity, despite the fact that, as they always did, a reporter from each of the three wire services and eight photographers would accompany him, along with a dozen members of the White House staff, including Early.[50]

The reality was that it probably would not make much difference to the White House press corps if Roosevelt were out of town and holding no meetings with them. Betty Houchin Winfield, who wrote *FDR and the News Media*, says that with the war going badly, Roosevelt's press conferences had been generally unproductive or not held at all. In 1941 he held eighty-nine press conferences and in 1942 he held seventy-four. (In 1943 he met fifty-eight times with the reporters, and in 1944, an election year, there were fifty-five.) After one Roosevelt press conference in 1942, a frustrated reporter complained to Early, "Not much of a meeting."[51]

On Thursday, September 17, a train carrying Roosevelt and his entourage, including Early, left the soupy humidity of Washington behind as they embarked on a "confidential" inspection trip of war production, from coast to coast, border to border. How secret the trip actually was is speculative, since, after pressure from Early, Roosevelt had decided to allow the wire service reporters to come along because every newspaper and broadcast news agency in the country was served by at least one of the wire services. Early explained that "the Boss" had decided that allowing all the thirty or forty reporters who usually accompanied the president to come along on this trip would mean more sleeping cars on the train, and as such would attract too much attention and make it impossible to maintain the secrecy Roosevelt demanded.

It was the first time the Big Three, as Early referred to them at his press conferences, were allowed to accompany the president on one of his out-of-town trips since Pearl Harbor, when the White House threw a blanket of censorship over his travels. Even though they were ride-alongs on this trip, the three reporters were forbidden to file a single word of copy with their offices until the party was safely back in the capital. The day before the presidential party was to leave for the "confidential" inspection trip that September, Early called them into his office and locked the door. He told them about the trip, giving them few details and noting that they alone would represent the media, but then, as part of the president's demand for secrecy, Early handed them credentials as Secret Service agents, complete with each reporter's photo and the silver badge of authority. All they knew was that the first stop on the trip would be a Chrysler plant in Detroit, and Early admonished them not to tell their bosses (or their families) anything other than to say they would be gone for more than two weeks. On top of that, the reporters were annoyed to learn that the president intended to review every word they wrote.

It was an odd kind of secrecy that Roosevelt practiced on this trip. For instance, at the Puget Sound in Bremerton, Washington, riding in an open car, Roosevelt leaned over the side, microphone in hand, and told the assembled workers that "I am not really here. You haven't seen me." In Seattle he waved to cheering crowds, all off the record, he told the reporters. In Portland, Oregon, he appeared before a crowd of twenty thousand, on the record and in full view of a phalanx of cameras. Yet Roosevelt told them he was not supposed to be there that day. The crowd laughed, and Roosevelt joined in. Merriman Smith, the United Press reporter who accompanied the presidential party on this trip, said, "Damned if I saw anything to laugh about. Here was the president of the United States making an important public appearance in front of twenty thousand people, yet the newspapers and radio stations had to play like they knew nothing about it."[52]

In his book *FDR, The War President*, Kenneth Davis says the ban on filing any copy and the president's requirement that he read every word led to the reporters to produce much more copy than they might actually have written and to speculate that the issue was not at all about secrecy; rather, it was Roosevelt's odd sense of humor and his desire at the conclusion of the trip to have "a flood of publicity favorable to the administration" released to the public, just weeks before the elections. Merriman Smith said there was not much the reporters could do about the president's ban on coverage of his trips, and Early could do nothing about it because both Roosevelt and the Secret Service liked the secrecy.[53]

In all, they traveled 8,754 miles and inspected army and navy bases; shipyards; tanks; airplanes; shell-producing plants; army, navy, and marine training centers; supply depots; and ports of embarkation. It may have been an exhausting itinerary, but it seemed to reenergize Roosevelt.[54]

When he returned—much to the frustration of both Early and the press—Roosevelt seemed in no rush to hold a press conference, to officially give a firsthand account of the trip to the public. Eventually he did meet the reporters, but not until nearly two weeks after he got back to Washington. As he always did before a press conference, he asked Early about questions he might expect from the reporters and how he could handle those that annoyed him. Early told him he could expect some angry reporters. David Brinkley, a young reporter in Washington at the time, relates that as Early and Roosevelt talked, the time for the press conference came and passed, so the reporters began pounding on the president's office door. When the door finally opened, the reporters spilled in. It was a hot and smoky affair. He explained the trip's "secrecy" by saying that it had been done solely for his safety, which none of the reporters really believed. He then gave the reporters a rundown on what he had seen and heard on the trip. Then he thanked the press, the radio and newsreel people, and the photographers in attendance for "the fine way in which they had cooperated in delaying the publication of news about the trip until it was over . . . until I got back to Washington." He went on to assure them that there "was no suppression of news on the trip, only this confidential stuff, mostly photographs."[55]

The president may have believed that censorship during the trip had been kept to a minimum, but the newsmen and women felt quite differently. That same day thirty-five angry reporters sent a formal protest to Roosevelt claiming they were not allowed to accompany him and were given no explanation. They believed that complete suppression of the news of the trip while he was away was neither wise nor necessary. Roosevelt countered, telling them that taking them along would have required two or three additional trains.

What really upset the journalists was that Roosevelt continued to keep them in the dark by waiting so long to hold his first posttrip press conference. While he was away, they said, all news about the trip had come from the White House, which must have been little to none, since Early was with Roosevelt. There is nothing to indicate that Early pleaded with Roosevelt to meet with the press immediately upon his return, but it is likely that he confronted the Boss over his decision, perhaps predicting just what Roosevelt would confront: an angry press corps. Merriman Smith recalled that in response to a plea from the reporters to write about one censored presidential trip to Hyde Park, Roosevelt sent the following message to the correspondents through Early: "What do you want to do—watch me take a bath or go with me to the toilet?"[56]

As he had for so many years, Roosevelt was simply using the press for his own ends, giving reporters dollops of news when it suited him, when he needed or desired publicity. In the case of his cross-country trip, the public relations value after the fact was minimal. War censorship had kept the lid on news stories at the exact time he most needed their publication: that is, during the trip. The time was past, and no matter how angry Early became, his words sometimes drifted away unheeded. Late in the war, Roosevelt sent a brief memo to Early in which he said, "Quite frankly I regard Freedom of the Press as one of the world's most microscopic problems."[57]

Early's fuse continued to burn as fall moved into winter. When he heard that the Allied troops had at last invaded North Africa, he barked, "Jesus Christ, why couldn't the Army have done this before the election?" Why was he so steamed? When voters went to the polls for midterm elections four days earlier, they ousted forty-six Democrats in the House and nine in the Senate. Although this still left both chambers with a Democratic majority, Early must have concluded that the arduous, cross-country trip that had taken him away from home for two weeks and then had forced the press corps to cry censorship foul had done nothing to induce voters to keep Democrats in office.[58]

But in fact, Roosevelt seemed energized later that fall. He still had a majority in Congress despite the election losses, and now that the war was looking up, with plans well under way for the British and American invasion of North Africa, an operation whose code word was TORCH and which, if successful, would keep the Germans out of the western coast of the continent and give the Allies a crucial base of operations against southern Europe. It also spelled the end of the Vichy government, which was allied with Hitler after the Germans overthrew the French government.

If the media suspected any such massive operation was about to be implemented, they kept it off the front pages and the airwaves. So it was 7:00 p.m. on Saturday night, November 7, 1942, that a warning went out from the White House switchboard to the press corps. An important announcement from Early was imminent. The men and women gathered outside his office door, and at 8:54 he called them inside and asked his secretary to lock the door and not allow anyone to leave until 9:00. Early spent the next six minutes reading the high points of a presidential statement on the invasion. At the same moment, he said, War Department officials were giving reporters there the details of Operation TORCH, led by General Eisenhower and British admiral Sir Andrew Cunningham, now underway.[59]

Three weeks later, after a Thanksgiving service in the East Room of the White House, the president left from the rail siding at the Bureau of Engraving and Printing for Hyde Park, and again Early remained behind, holding press conferences on the holiday and again on Friday, with nothing of consequence to hand the reporters. Roosevelt returned to the capital early on Monday and a week later was felled by a minor cold. He did manage to hold a press conference on December 1, although it generated no major news story. Mostly it proved to be a cat-and-mouse game full of banter doled out by the president and the press secretary, full of ambiguities and generalities designed to tantalize and tease the reporters. Even when pickings around the White House were slim, Early and Roosevelt managed to entertain:

Roosevelt: "What have you got?"

Early: "Can't find anything that's useful, sir. You haven't got anything that I know that you are ready to talk about."

Roosevelt: "Well, it's terrible."

Early: "Maybe questions [from the reporters] will bring out something."

Roosevelt: "I don't think so."

Early: "Well, that's what I thought. There's nothing around here."

Roosevelt: "Steve says there's nothing ready to serve. Quite a lot—quite a lot of food that's on the range, but it isn't cooked yet."

Reporters: "Nothing on the fire?"

Roosevelt: "Yes."

Reporters: "Maybe it has been cooked, Mr. President?"

Roosevelt: "It isn't cooked."

More back and forth about whether the story on the range was cooked.

Then Roosevelt said: "The first thing I know somebody will start singing 'Home on the Range,'" which happened to be one of his favorite songs.[60]

Late on Friday, December 15, the president again left Early to hold down the fort in Washington while he headed to Hyde Park, where he spent time resting and going over State Department documents and planning a holiday party for the soldiers who served as his guards, the people who worked on his estate, and the staff of his presidential library. Bill Hassett, who had accompanied him to Hyde Park, called it a "grand party" with a large, brightly decorated Christmas tree and a Virginia Reel organized by Eleanor with the president calling the turns. Two days before Christmas, Roosevelt was back at the White House, working on the annual State of the Union message that he would deliver to the new Congress on January 6.[61]

Early's last press conference of 1942 was on the final day of the year, and he told the reporters that the most serious discussion he had had earlier that morning with the president had been whether or not to "impose" a Roosevelt press conference on them at 10:30 the next morning—Friday, the day the president normally met with them— which also happened to be New Year's Day. To the sound of "boos" and laughter, Early told them there would be a press conference, although it might be in the afternoon rather than in the morning. They had not yet decided. Roosevelt did meet the press, but only for a few minutes, at 10:30 a.m. When they came into his office, he said he had "a little dispensary" available for them.[62]

Two weeks later, at his own press conference, Early was asked if there would be a presidential press conference that day, with one reporter pointing out, "If we don't want a press conference, we don't have to have one." To which Early replied, "You tried that New Year's, and you found out." Then Early detailed the thinking that went into the decision to hold a January 1 meeting: "So we took it up on New Year's Day, and the President reasoned something like this: that while it would be, possibly, a little on the cruel, brutal and inhuman side, that after all it was a work-day, that if we didn't hold a press confer- ence at 10:30, it would be a bad precedent to begin the New Year with." Early said they decided that if they moved it to 12:30 p.m. "to give the boys time to clear up, he would give them time to begin another celebration so that if we made it an afternoon instead of a morning press conference, by that time they would be extremely 'tight.' We held it at 10:30 for your own good."[63]

It was another one of those delectable ripostes between the pres- ident and his press secretary.

19

"THE TRAVELINGEST PRESIDENT"

If 1942 had found Steve Early holding down the fort more and more as Roosevelt was either traveling to conferences or seeking solace at his home in Hyde Park from the blackness of a depressingly deepening war, the following year saw him standing in the guard tower of the White House, manning the battlements in an effort to keep at bay a press insistently and incessantly curious about the many presidential travels, monitoring White House visitors demanding an audience with the chief executive—whether or not he was in residence—and privately agonizing about the fate of his eldest son, now at the precipice of combat in Europe.

The year opened on a grim note. At the end of December, French admiral Jean François Darlan, a Vichy collaborator with Hitler who was trying to negotiate deals with the Allies, was assassinated in Algiers; FDR called it "murder in the first degree." The complicated situation with the French in northern Africa rapidly made it apparent to Roosevelt and Churchill that a face-to-face meeting with the French generals Charles de Gaulle and Henri Giraud, who was de Gaulle's choice to succeed Darlan, was necessary to plot future Allied strategy. Stalin was invited to join them, but he pleaded that the fighting in Russia made it impossible for him to leave. The site chosen was Casablanca, the capital of French Morocco. For such a meeting to take place required the president, in the interest of time and military secrecy, to board a plane and fly across the Atlantic, an arduous journey for someone whose idea of comfortable traveling was in a slow-moving train on American soil where he could watch the countryside drift by.[1]

The trip proved to be a series of "firsts." It was the first time Roosevelt had flown while in office, the first time any US president had visited Africa while in office, the first time a president had flown during wartime, and the first time a president had left the continental United States during wartime. It was the first time since Woodrow Wilson that a chief executive had crossed the Atlantic, and it was the first time since Lincoln that a president had visited troops in a battle zone. This historic trip saw Roosevelt away from the White House twenty-two days, traveling 16,965 miles, which included stops on his return trip in Liberia and Brazil. The *New York Times* called him the "travelingest" president in history, with a total of 200,000 miles. In spite of his distaste for flying, Roosevelt seemed to enjoy the Casablanca trip. Afterward, when asked by reporters what sort of "air sailor" the president had been, Early replied, "Perfect. He didn't get sick."[2]

Few people in the White House knew the president would be traveling, and fewer still knew his destination. He did discuss his plans with Early, since he knew he would need someone to handle the press at Casablanca, but he decided he could not spare his press secretary from the White House, a decision that no doubt made sense to all parties at the time but later produced confusion and headaches for Early. Others who might ordinarily have traveled with the president included Marvin McIntyre, the appointments secretary, who was too ill even to carry a full load at work, and Pa Watson, who replaced Jimmy Roosevelt in the White House and who helped with presidential appointments. Watson was sick now, too. Instead Roosevelt asked George Durno, who had covered the White House for many years as a reporter for International News Service and now was a captain in the army, to handle the press in North Africa. Early agreed that it would make sense for Durno to pinch-hit for him on this trip. According to Grace Tully, Roosevelt's secretary, Durno sneaked back into Washington, avoiding any of his own press friends, to accompany the presidential party to Morocco. When the censorship on the trip was finally lifted, Durno's dispatches were published in newspapers across the country.[3]

Thus, on the evening of Saturday, January 9, under deepest security, with the names of all the Pullman cars painted out and a group of Filipino mess boys filling in for the regular staff, Roosevelt's train left Washington, heading north toward Hyde Park, in an attempt to hoodwink the press into thinking he was going home. In fact, the train stopped in Baltimore, turned around and traveled south, reaching Miami three days later, at which time Roosevelt and his aides, including Harry Hopkins, Pa Watson (now well enough to travel), and Dr. Ross McIntire, boarded the luxurious Boeing 314 *Dixie Clipper*, operated by Pan American Airways for the navy, and took off for Casablanca, Morocco, situated on the Atlantic Ocean at the northwestern tip of Africa. The president's plane was preceded by another plane and followed by still another serving as escorts. Their route skirted coastlines when possible, even flying inland on occasion in an effort to avoid fire from German submarines in the Caribbean and in the Atlantic off South America, where the planes stopped at Belem, Brazil, to refuel. From there they flew across the Atlantic. On January 14 they arrived in Casablanca, an enthusiastic Roosevelt having suffered only a few minor breathing bouts in the thin air.[4]

Meanwhile, back at the White House, the beleaguered press secretary was left to fend off a bunch of curious reporters who suspected the president had gone somewhere, perhaps overseas. Merriman Smith, the United Press reporter stationed at the White House, said the reporters had heard rumors that president of the United States was traveling halfway around the world, and he complained to Early about the fact that the trip was "completely uncovered by the American press." Early agreed but said there was nothing he could do, since Roosevelt and Churchill had promised each other there would be no reporters on the scene. When the reporters pressed Early for confirmation about Axis broadcasts that Prime Minister Churchill was in North America for another conference, he said, "I don't know that he is and I don't know that he isn't, and if I did know I wouldn't tell you." Amazingly, no one guessed that the two world leaders were secluded in a villa in Morocco for a conference, since they all knew that the last time Roosevelt had been on a plane was when he had flown from Albany to Chicago to accept the Democratic nomination for president, and they knew for certain that he would never sail across the German submarine–infested ocean.[5]

What really confused the press and the public was that on Tuesday, January 19, the White House released a message from Roosevelt ordering striking Pennsylvania coal miners to return to work. This was because soon after Pearl Harbor Early decided, with the president's approval, that for security purposes whenever Roosevelt was away from Washington all stories would be released from the White House. Thus the coal miners story bore a Washington, DC, dateline. Meanwhile, Early's reply to queries about the president's whereabouts went unanswered, and the country's media remained silent, a testament to Early's and Byron Price's continued iron grip on press censorship.[6]

It was not until Price's censorship office sent a memo to newspaper managing editors and broadcasters on January 24 alerting them that dispatches of "unusual importance" would be coming across the Atlantic in a few hours that reporters had a serious clue as to where Roosevelt was. This was Sunday, but the dispatches were to be held for release until Wednesday. The memo said that "it is of the highest importance that no violation of the fixed release date and no disclosure of any kind until the release time arrives."[7]

On Sunday afternoon, January 24, after more than a week of conferring, Roosevelt and Churchill sat on chairs on the lawn of their villa in Casablanca and spoke publicly for the first time since the president had left Washington fifteen days earlier. The two men told about thirty-five reporters and photographers sitting cross-legged like schoolchildren on the grass in front of them that they had now cleared the way for Allied unity and a common strategy on all war fronts. The eventual goal was the enemy's "unconditional surrender." The reporters, however, were not allowed to ask any questions. In a scene reminiscent of a spy film, the correspondents, all accredited to the Allied Headquarters in Tunis in North Africa, suddenly had been notified three days earlier only that they were to board three military transport planes. They then were flown the eight hundred miles to Casablanca. In order for the sudden presence of a large group of reporters who wore the khaki uniforms of the armed forces and who now were hundreds of miles from the war front not to arouse suspicion, their arm bands and insignia signifying their status were removed.[8]

The day after the historic and secretive press conference halfway around the world, reporters converged on Early's office for their morning meeting. Then the delicate dance began. The press secretary knew that the reporters knew, the reporters now had knowledge of the Casablanca meeting, and the reporters knew that he knew. The question was just how much Early actually knew about the president's travels. No doubt he knew more than he had let on to the press, but perhaps even he had been left in the dark on some of the details of the trip. Early opened the press conference with this: "Gentlemen, I heard you were all here, so I thought I would ask you to come in. I asked you to come in just to see you, not to give you any news, because I haven't any."

When they asked him if he expected to have some news soon, he answered, "I don't know how soon. And all that I am talking to you about now is in STRICTEST CONFIDENCE—no part of this is for publication." He went on, "You gentlemen already know—I know that you do—what has, or much of what has been going on." Referring to the delayed publication date of the Casablanca press conference release for the security of the president and the prime minister, Early said, "[B]ecause the time has been extended, there is more anxiety, apprehensiveness and uneasiness—more a state of nerves on the part of the Press than there would be had things gone according to schedule." He asked that they not discuss anything said during this press conference with others who were not present for fear someone "down the line" would not realize it was confidential and publish or broadcast the information. "That has happened, as we all know," he added.

But the immediate problem Early had to tackle was explaining to the assembled reporters, again "in the STRICTEST CONFIDENCE," that a gathering of the White House correspondents that was to be held that Wednesday evening at a local hotel and that Roosevelt had agreed to attend would need to be postponed. He had telegraphed the president to remind him of the event, and Early said the reply was, "Postpone. Sorry cannot give now new date." It was obvious that the White House had expected the president to return after the conference ended. However, the peripatetic Roosevelt had other ideas, leaving Early to stumble his way through an explanation: "Well, that simply means one of two things, or possibly both. The President will not have returned from his trip by Wednesday, or if he has—he does return from his trip by Wednesday, he will not be able to attend your smoker. It may mean one or both, I can't tell you. You know as much as I do." And he probably was correct.

And frustrated: "Now if there is the beginning, or the actual movement home, then above all other times from the standpoint of security and safety, now is the time to be tight. I completely understand the position of you fellows, and I hope that the understanding will be mutual." Early was between a rock and a hard place, and the best he could do was to admit, "I am blind, and I am delighted that I am blind." He even tried handing reporters a crumb: "The President promised me when he left that he would see you when he returned and give it [the story] to you in detail."[9]

It seemed that everyone—the press secretary and the media—was on edge. Radio news commentators were busy making announcements about dramatic and sensational news to come. A slight relaxation of censorship in Washington and London on January 25 permitted the revelation of reports that the Allies were discussing a grand strategy for a smashing blow at Germany.

Early told the reporters, again in strictest confidence, that stories about the conference were written by American and British newspapermen, had passed the American and British censors in Europe, and had come into the United States without further censoring. Early said he did not see the stories until they were published.[10]

What had actually happened to delay Roosevelt's return was that once the conference ended, Roosevelt, who had been relaxed and even playful at times, and Churchill decided to travel to Marrakech to allow the prime minister to paint the exquisite Atlas Mountains. Then they spent a carefree night in a villa before they returned to their respective homelands. Churchill flew directly to London, but Roosevelt made several stops on his trip home. He flew to Liberia to inspect a large detachment of American Negro troops and to lunch with the country's president, Edwin Barclay. His next stop was Natal, Brazil, where he met with President Getulio Vargas to discuss Brazil's safety problems with offshore German submarines.[11]

Censorship regulation made it interesting to follow the published news reports about Roosevelt's trip, always a couple of steps behind his actual movements. For instance, the public learned of his and Churchill's press conference in Casablanca on January 27, three days after it was held, even though reporters had been covering it. The *New*

York Times story about the meeting with the Brazilian president, held on January 28, appeared in the January 30 edition of the newspaper.[12]

On January 27 Early was still grappling with trying to explain Roosevelt's travels to eager reporters: "So, and JUST FOR YOUR GUIDANCE, AND STILL IN THE STRICTEST OF CONFIDENCE TO YOU, I shall be surprised if I see the President this week. Don't make a note of that, please." Considerations of Roosevelt's safety were "paramount," he reminded the reporters. They asked him if he saw any cause for alarm in the fact that the president had not yet returned. With a touch of black humor, Early said, "If I did, I wouldn't see you at all this morning."

But they persisted. Would it be fair, Steve, they said, to ask whether this continued absence is an additional trip or whether it is merely that he is still on his way back? Hesitating briefly, Early said, "So far as I know, it is—so far as I know, and I haven't—I haven't heard anything since yesterday afternoon—it's—it's his return." He ended the exchange with this: "If you think it's worthwhile, I would say something like this, that—" at which point the reporters got out their pencils and began to write. "So far as can be told at the present time, the story is complete. Subsequent chapters undoubtedly will be written as events unfold. That's about all I can say."[13]

Roosevelt was simply being Roosevelt, reveling in the fact that in spite of war raging around the world, he could travel and talk politics and world affairs with heads of state. Did he realize this was making life difficult for his press secretary? Perhaps. Did he care? Probably not. He knew Steve would take care of it.

Roosevelt finally returned home January 31, a Sunday night, and the next morning the famous Steve Early temper began to seep into his press conference. As the reporters crowded into his office, one of them noted that Early had "achieved immortality" on the popular Edgar Bergen radio show the previous night. A joke, something about the "early bird," another reporter said. Early was not amused. "So far as I can find out, this is no time for jokes."

What happened, Early told the reporters confidentially, was that once Roosevelt was back in the White House, he had tried unsuccessfully to persuade him to meet with the press the next morning. But Roosevelt begged off, saying he needed to first meet with the secretary of state, congressional leaders, and others before he could see the reporters. Early said he was hoping the president would meet with them the following morning: "Now I can't tell you that that will be done, but I hope so." They asked if the president was planning a radio talk soon. Early said he did not know, nor did he think anyone else around the White House knew, except of course Roosevelt, and he was not confiding in anyone.[14]

Roosevelt did meet with the radio and print journalists the next day and more or less stuck to an outline Early had prepared for him, including a special thanks to the press and radio people for their "perfect compliance" with censorship regulations. Early also asked Roosevelt to emphasize that there had been continuous communication between the president and Washington throughout the trip. He also provided Roosevelt with travel statistics. So far, the president had traveled 13,122 miles by air, 2,324 by train, and 478 by auto. And he thought the president should give the reporters some human interest stories, such as the trip to Marrakech and that he had been presented with a birthday cake as they flew over Haiti. Considering the strictures of war censorship, the meeting gave reporters enough for page one stories, but little of substance about the meeting in Casablanca.[15]

A week later, Early told the reporters the censorship regulations had been revised to allow announcements of upcoming presidential radio broadcasts to give the day and hour, but not name the place until the very end of the broadcast. This also allowed the print reporters to say where he spoke, but only after the fact. "Previously, you remember, we didn't announce the time. Well, I think that was a mistake," he said.[16]

That winter shards of light broke through the horror of this worldwide war. On January 18, while Roosevelt was in Casablanca, the nine-hundred-day siege of Leningrad ended, a moment in that beautiful old city's history that has continued to haunt its inhabitants. An estimated 642,000 civilians died, most of starvation, before the German blockade could be broken. Britain's Royal Air Force bombers had resumed successful raids on the key German cities of Hamburg and Berlin, and on the other side of the world Allied troops scored their first land victory against the Japanese in New Guinea. Iraq declared war on the Axis at the same time Chile pulled its support from the Axis.[17]

If anyone needed a vacation that winter, it was Early. He told his

February 13 press conference that the president had given him permission to get away for two weeks, adding that his assistant Bill Hassett "will take you on with more mercy and understanding than I, probably. Certainly that would be true if I stayed on feeling like I have lately." They asked where he was going. He told them, "off the record," a quiet, little place on the Gulf of Mexico where he could fish and "get away from the East Coast, the blackouts and the crowds." He let them think it was Corpus Christi, Texas. Early's family remained in Washington.

His destination was in fact Dunedin, Florida, on the Gulf just north of St. Petersburg. Even there he couldn't get away from the reporters. A large photo in the *St. Petersburg Times* on February 27 showed him relaxing at the pool at his hotel, next to a headline that read, "Secretary to F.D.R. Ends Two-Week Visit to Dunedin." To a reporter, he defended censorship, saying that Americans are the best-informed people in the world: "News isn't being supressed—it's being released when the timing is right." He had played golf with his friend Ray Beebe, a Washington attorney, and he took time to inspect a marine base at Dunedin. On his return home, a tanned and rested Early stopped at Camp Lee, Virginia, to witness his son Buddy being inducted into the army.[18]

When he returned from his two-week vacation in Florida, Early told his March 1 press conference that he was rested, but only on the "exterior." Roosevelt had remained in Washington while Early was away, but he spent part of the time laid up with the flu. On March 1, his first press conference after he got back, Early reported that this was the third consecutive day the president had no temperature. "He is going to do what is known in the Army as 'light duty' today," which meant he would remain in his private quarters to meet with his two appointments, his first visitors since he had gotten sick.[19]

It was not long after Early returned to Washington that his daughter, known in the family as "Sis," was hospitalized and underwent surgery to remove a kidney stone. Then Helen Early was felled by the flu, and since the family was temporarily without a cook or a maid, Steve Early came home after work and took on duties as cook and dishwasher. "Life does get terribly complicated at times," Early wrote to his friend Victor Emanuel.[20]

On March 4 Roosevelt and his inner circle at the White House—

Grace Tully, Marvin McIntyre, Pa Watson, and Early—celebrated the tenth anniversary of his first inauguration, gathering around the president's desk for a photo session, Roosevelt insisting he have his cigarette in its holder in his mouth at a jaunty angle. It's a happy-looking group, although a few days earlier the *New York Times* had run two photos of Roosevelt side by side—one from 1933, the other a recent one—showing a president definitely suffering the agonies of war. His cheeks are sunken, his face heavily lined, and the circles under his eyes darker than usual.[21]

It was around this same time that David Brinkley, who was covering his first White House press conference, noticed how old Roosevelt looked. In his book *Washington Goes to War*, Brinkley observed that the face he had seen "a thousand times" in photos in newspapers, magazines, and newsreels was of a "handsome man with well-formed features displaying a smiling, good-natured manner." But the man he saw at this press conference looked old. He described the president's face as "more gray than pink, his hands shook, his eyes were hazy and wandering, his neck drooped in stringy sagging folds accentuated by a shirt collar that must have fit at one time but now was two or three sizes too large."

Brinkley said that in private someone asked Early why the president did not buy new shirts that fit, since the loose collars made him look even more shrunken and drawn. Early replied, "That damned Dutchman is so tight he won't buy new shirts until the old ones are ready to use for cleaning rags." Early was asked what was wrong with Roosevelt. He replied, "He's just tired. Running a war is a hell of a job." Nonetheless, in a letter to Joe Davies in early January that year, Early described Roosevelt as "in magnificent condition. I have never seen him better."[22]

But Roosevelt was not about to hunker down in the White House. In early April he decided it was time for another of his famous cross-country inspection trips via train, a trip that Early described to his son Buddy as "a fairly long, continuously and rapidly moving business trip." This time the White House entourage, which included Early, headed south to visit military bases and factories producing war materials and eventually traveled into northern Mexico for a meeting with Mexican president Manuel Ávila Camacho in Monterrey. Again the trip was not reported on by the media, leaving the president of the

United States off the airwaves and the front pages of the nation's newspapers until the party reached its destination. In all, the trip lasted sixteen days, and, with Early along, there came some light moments, despite the fact he was working "around the clock."[23]

On the evening before the train was to cross into Mexico, Early, Dorothy Brady, who was one of Early's secretaries, and Grace Tully were eating in the dining car together when out of the blue Early asked Miss Brady if she had brought her passport. In a frightened voice, she said, "No, am I supposed to have one? Nobody told me anything about it."

Even though Grace Tully was surprised by Early's question, she knew how he liked to kid his secretary, so she played along, and told Miss Brady she was sorry but apparently in the rush to leave Washington, she had forgotten to mention a passport. When Miss Brady asked her if she had one, Tully said, "Why certainly. We all have them." Miss Brady turned to her boss and asked him if he couldn't do something.

Early thought for a moment, and then told her to get her notebook and he would dictate a telegram to the White House asking someone there to get a passport for her and put it in the next mail pouch. Tully and Early even clued in the telegrapher who was to accept the telegram to tell Miss Brady it was being wired right away. But she was worried that the passport would not arrive in time, so Early suggested she get off the train at the next stop. He would arrange for a car and a Secret Service agent to drive her to where the mail pouch would be delivered by air. They could drive all night, he said. As the evening progressed, so did Miss Brady's anxiety, so Tully insisted they tell her the truth. No one had passports, and they were just teasing her. The next day she still had not recovered from the shock, so when she saw the president, she related the story. Tully says he "howled with laughter and said he wished he could have been there."[24]

The first inkling the general public got of the president's absence from Washington was on April 21, a week after the party left the capital, when the ban on censorship of his trip was temporarily lifted. He already had had met with President Camacho in Monterrey, about two hundred miles southwest of Brownsville, Texas, the previous day, and now the train was moving toward Parris Island, South Carolina, where it would stop to inspect a marine boot camp before making a one-day stopover in Warm Springs, Georgia, and other military bases along the way to Washington. Details and exact dates and times were vague, in keeping with wartime censorship regulations.[25]

Early said later that arrangements remained so secret that the residents of Monterrey did not know until a few hours before he arrived that the president of the United States would be coming to town. When they did find out, the local radio station announced it "with much excitement and gusto," and the newspaper hastily produced an "extra edition." Decorations were put up around town, schools and steel mills were closed, and large posters of Roosevelt were put on display. Early said he had never seen people anywhere give any distinguished visitor such a wholehearted, enthusiastic, noisy welcome. Early left the presidential party soon after the train left Corpus Christi. He drove to New Orleans, where he flew overnight to Washington. Once Roosevelt left Corpus Christi, his travel again became secret, so Early decided he was not needed to deal with the press. "On the other hand, there was real reason that I should rush back to Washington"—to prepare for what he said would be another "secret trip, traveling much greater distances that those I have just concluded."[26]

The "projected new trip" quite possibly was to be a meeting with Joseph Stalin in the early summer somewhere off Alaska or in Iceland to discuss the cross-channel invasion and the Allies' postwar strategy, but the Soviet leader was evasive, like a coy woman playing hard to get who then becomes perplexed, even angry, when the suitor chooses to move on. A determined Roosevelt finally asked his and Early's friend Joseph Davies, the former ambassador to the Soviet Union and a favorite of Stalin's, to go to Moscow to attempt to persuade the leader to agree to a meeting. Maybe in July or August, Stalin replied. The issue remained unresolved until early October, when Roosevelt sent his aging secretary of state, Cordell Hull, to Moscow to plead with Stalin. An agreement was struck, and the resulting conference was held in late November in Tehran, the capital of Persia (now Iran).[27]

With or without Stalin, Roosevelt and his British counterpart would carry on their discussions on how best to proceed with the Allied offensive. So by May 11 that year, reporters were once again hounding Early to comment on published reports that Churchill was due in Washington. Early declined any comment, even "off the record." That was at 10:45 a.m. Then, at 6:45 that evening, Early called the reporters into his office and told them tersely that

Churchill—and his staff of military experts—indeed had arrived in Washington and would again be Roosevelt's guest at the White House "for the duration of his visit." James McGregor Burns decided that the two men met so frequently and in so many venues they were conducting "a kind of traveling strategy conference."[28]

This time the meeting between Roosevelt and Churchill was code named "Trident," and during ten "strenuous days" the two men and their military advisers hammered out plans for a cross-channel invasion of France, settling on May 1, 1944. It was given the code name "Overlord." With the last of the German and Italian troops in North Africa having now surrendered, the immediate focus of the meeting was on an Allied invasion of Sicily, with the intent of eventually knocking Italy out of the war. By the time the conference ended on May 25, the two leaders also agreed to increasing aid to China and stepping up the war against Japan by "island-hopping through the Pacific."[29]

The British prime minister's visits seemed always to mire press secretary Early's office in a bevy of details and frustrations. This time was no different. The morning after Churchill's arrival, Early met with the reporters, who began badgering him for the names of the principal members of Churchill's staff who had traveled to Washington with him. They had wanted them the night before, but Early was unable to supply them. He explained, and this was "off the record," he assured them, that first he had had to get permission from the British Embassy, which in turn told him the names had to be submitted to the prime minister before any release and the prime minister at that moment was in transit to Washington.

By the morning of May 12, Early had the names, and the remainder of his press conference resembled a government spelling bee, with Early reciting names and titles, reporters asking for the spelling, and Early—patiently for him—spelling each name and repeating the title. And, by the way, he said, the president of Czechoslovakian government in exile was arriving that afternoon. So they wanted his name and the correct spelling—E-D-U-A-R-D B-E-N-E-S. Were Roosevelt and Churchill at the Washington Cathedral that morning, one reporter asked? "If the President was at the Cathedral, he has been there since you gentlemen have been in this room," snapped the press secretary. "Now, who exactly is the British minister of defense?"

another asked. "Churchill is Prime Minister and Minister of Defence," answered Early. And so it went.[30]

The next day's press conference brought more questions from the reporters about Churchill, this time about how he traveled to Washington. "Off the record," Early said, despite the fact that some British correspondents had been told by their own government officials that Churchill had crossed the Atlantic on a ship, the prime minister did not want his mode of travel revealed. Then Churchill had a change of mind, and now Early could tell the reporters that he "came by sea." But he could not give them the name of the vessel, the port of entry, or the route followed. The reporters asked if they at least could say Churchill arrived in Washington on a train. "It's obvious you can't bring a big ship into Washington," one quipped.

"Yes, it is. Yes, I should say so. Yes," Early replied. They could say that he arrived in Washington by train. "Yes. That's all right. I don't think that's going to surprise anyone or get a headline," he explained. The reporters continued to pester him for details on with whom Churchill would be meeting. Could Early arrange for the reporters to interview any of these people? What were Churchill and Roosevelt up to that day? Where was the prime minister dining that night?

Early could or would give few answers, and when they inquired about the two men's social plans for the next day, he gave no answer, but cautioned them, "You had better go slow on tomorrow. Better go slow over the weekend. It will be off the record." Anything else? "No. No. Well, that brings you as far up today as I am, fellows."[31]

For the duration of the prime minister's visit, Early's press conferences produced little news. On Saturday, May 22, he greeted the reporters with this: "Gentlemen, I have so little for you this morning I feel like apologizing. There isn't anything here, and won't be over the weekend." A week later, on May 29, Churchill departed, and Early had a lot to tell the reporters at his press conference that morning. Unfortunately for the journalists, most of it was "off the record," or "strictly off the record." He had told the reporters earlier in the week that there would be a joint statement from the two leaders, but a change in plans led to only a brief one from the president, and Early read it to them: "The [recent] conference of the Combined Staffs in Washington has ended in complete agreement on future operations in all theatres of the war."

But they got little information from the statement, and Early said they were forbidden to make any mention of the whereabouts of Churchill, indeed an odd request from a former newsman. But again war censorship regulations must be obeyed, even if the information involved the head of another country. Early told the reporters, "As a matter of fact, your Government would appreciate it if in some manner of writing that is possible and within the borders of truth, the readers of your dispatches should infer from the reading that the Prime Minister is still here. I don't ask you to stretch the truth to the point of deceiving anybody but try your hand at some artistic writing."

The reporters understood the request, but they were not about to accept it without attempting a little verbal subterfuge. They tried reading a cable from London they claimed was addressed to the British United Press Office in New York, saying that the British office had the text of a joint statement from Roosevelt and Churchill, and they just needed a "flash"—the OK—and they would release it. Sorry, said Early, and of course, "off the record, but I am afraid somebody is fishing." He reassured them that any joint statement was "permanently abandoned."

He reminded them that "in times like these there are lots of people who would use us if they could and they try in devious and ingenious ways." So the reporters tried another tack: cooperation. Could the word "recent" be deleted from the president's statement? they asked. Early agreed and left the room briefly to confer with Roosevelt. When he returned, he said, "The President accepts it and asks me to thank you." The word "recent" was deleted from the statement.[32]

Where was Churchill, and why all the secrecy? As soon as the conference ended, he left Washington en route to Gibraltar and Algiers for talks on future Mediterranean plans, a trip that for obvious reasons required the highest security.[33]

That Memorial Day weekend saw the president in Hyde Park, a trip he extended into the following week, leaving Early to once again fend off a cranky press. On June 1 he told the reporters that they could give their editors "a confidential report," which was that Roosevelt would not be holding his regular press conference that afternoon. This information was "not for publication."[34]

In fact, Early said, from this time on, journalists were not allowed to publish or broadcast the fact that the president's press conference was canceled. In the past, this information proved to be a "a complete tip-off to anything and everybody that the President was not in Washington, and then they only have to look for him in one or two other places." That meant, he explained, that such information would be a "confidential note to editors, and not for publication, which I am glad to say the press seems to welcome."[35]

20

MORNINGSIDE DRIVE

When at home, Steve Early was hardly the model of the ever-present dad. Stephen T. Early Jr., known in the family as Buddy, says that when he, his brother, and his sister were growing up, by the time their father returned home in the evening, the children had already eaten dinner. "He'd come in dog tired collapse in a chair usually, and fall asleep before he had supper." His father then would eat, go upstairs, lie down, and fall asleep for the night. "We just didn't have any family life, that was all. That damn job nearly killed any family life."[1]

The Early children may not have adapted well to their father's schedule, but for his wife the long days were nothing out of the ordinary. Early's daughter, Helen Early Elam, explains, "Dad worked odd hours as a reporter and again with Paramount. So mother was used to it when he went to the White House."[2]

In a letter written shortly after Roosevelt died in 1945, Early told his cousin Finks Early, "My life in the past twelve years has just been too hectic. I have not been able to do thousands of things I have wanted to. In fact, I have seen very little of my own family, housed here in Washington. I have only been sleeping there."[3]

In the early spring of 1940, when Early received an invitation from his friend Bernard Baruch for him and Helen to spend a few days at Baruch's vacation home, Hobcaw Barony in South Carolina, Early told Baruch that the president had left Washington and he was holding down the fort, adding that he had no alternative "but to play the role assigned to me—the role of worker-prisoner." He then explained, "My only consolation during the period of confinement is that I have the privileges of a 'trusty.' At least they trust me to dispose of everything possible without referring more than an absolute minimum to them—by mail pouch or by radio."

He said regretfully, "Existing conditions, however, must either tighten the shackles that hold me here or brand me as a traitor." Early still was trying to leave for private employment to earn more money. He told Baruch that maybe the following year would "change many conditions or life. It may even teach the meaning of liberty." It was 1940, and a year later—the year that Early intended to escape—the country was closer to war, and by the end of 1941, Pearl Harbor had been attacked. Early, the good and loyal soldier, remained at his post.[4]

Throughout his twelve years with Roosevelt, Early was forced by virtue of his job to miss dinner at home when big stories were breaking. But sometimes Early did not make it home until late in the evening because of his friendship with a boss who spent his life in a chair and thus found great pleasure in people—and in particular those he knew well, those with whom he felt comfortable, those who laughed at his jokes. And these people tended to be those who worked with him day in and day out at the White House, members of his official "family." In truth, Roosevelt liked nothing more than to gather his staff or inner circle around him at the end of the day for cocktails and talk, a practice he called "The Children's Hour," which began two days after he became president and continued well into the war. A playful Roosevelt would use the buzzer buttons on his desk and one by one summon each member of his inner circle to join him for his famous martinis. Sometimes the conversation was light and joking; other times he took the opportunity to discuss a staff problem.

Some, like Roosevelt's personal secretaries Grace Tully and Missy LeHand, and later Bill Hassett, Early's assistant, were unmarried, while others, like Pa Watson, were married but had no children. Marvin McIntyre's children were grown. Early was not only married but the father of three growing children. Once, when Early's grandson William Elam III met Jimmy Roosevelt, long after both

Steve and FDR had died, Jimmy described the occupants of the White House of his father's day as a big family, each member supporting the others, their private and professional lives intersecting, with few boundaries.[5]

One Saturday evening in March 1940, Early rushed home from work to change his clothes and, leaving Helen at home, hurried back to the White House to accompany the president to the annual White House Correspondents dinner. After dinner they returned to the White House. Early had felt it necessary to be with his friend that evening, since the president had been suffering from a cold and was still running a one-degree fever. Once he deposited Roosevelt at the White House and made sure he would be OK, Early headed off to the Willard Hotel in an attempt to track down a friend who had wanted to meet him there. But their paths did not cross, and late that night a weary Early headed back to the family home on Morningside Drive.[6]

It was not always White House business and socializing that kept Early from his family. There were the trips to Pinehurst, North Carolina, for Attorney General Homer Cummings's annual golf tournaments. Sometimes Early attended—and won enough money to cover his expenses—sometimes he declined, saying he was too busy, which may or may not have been a cover for his budget problems, but probably quite simply it was because he indeed was tied to his desk. After Pearl Harbor he found it more and more difficult to make any personal engagements outside Washington. Even the few he accepted in the city were made on a tentative basis. During the late 1930s and whenever he could break away during the war, he lunched with friends or coworkers, such as Pa Watson, at restaurants near the White House.[7]

How did Helen Early feel about the ringing telephone in the middle of the night, her husband's late hours at the White House, and the days—sometimes weeks—he spent away from Washington? Early once told a radio interviewer who asked this very question, "She's glad that I am able to help the great man who occupies the White House. That's a privilege."[8]

Helen Early was less understanding. She told a reporter in early 1944 that her husband's job had its drawbacks. Because of his late nights at the office, she said, it was "most distracting at dinnertime. We never know whether we are going to have dinner at six o'clock or midnight."

After Pearl Harbor, she said, late-night telephone calls from reporters became so commonplace that the family had to get an unlisted phone number, such a secret that not even the most informed Washington correspondents knew it. But, she sighed, the reporters managed to circumvent this impediment by calling the White House and asking the operator to call Steve at home on their behalf. She admitted, though, that unless the information they were seeking was "highly important," the reporters tended to be considerate of her husband's privacy—or the White House switchboard was being considerate.[9]

When the Early family did get away for a vacation, it often was without the man of the house, or dad would join them for a few days wherever they were staying. When he took a few days for himself—duck hunting, golfing, fishing—it was not unusual for him to be called back to the White House for an emergency. Or too often he would plan the trip, only to have to tell his hosts he could not get away from his desk after all. Of course, once the United States entered the war, vacations, with or without his family, were a rarity.[10]

At the end of his workday, whenever that might be, a White House chauffeured car carried Early north to a relatively new neighborhood of middle- and upper-middle-class houses in the city's Shepard Park section, nestled in the northeast corner of Washington, bordering Maryland on the north and east and the upper reaches of Rock Creek Park on the west.[11]

Shepard Park has been described as "a serene and verdant neighborhood." At the turn of the twenty-first century, it remains an enclave of middle- and upper-middle-class professionals who populate the offices of the District, living in well-kept homes with manicured lawns and street names that reflect the flora of the area: Hemlock, Locust, Geranium, Iris, Juniper, Fern. But in 1864 it was a woods and rolling farm fields where Confederate troops, under the redoubtable Jubal Early—Steve Early's distant relative—gathered to mount an attack on nearby Fort Stevens. After the Civil War, Alexander Robey Shepard, the powerful governor of the Territory of the District of Columbia, purchased some of the land and built a grand Victorian summer home for himself and his wife. Other prosperous businessmen and political leaders of the time followed, finding the area a desirable place to build houses to escape the stifling heat of downtown.

By 1909 Congress saw the neighborhood as an ideal location for a hospital and gave the army funds to build what became the Walter Reed Medical Center, named for the sanitarian and bacteriologist who discovered the cure for yellow fever. It was built at the southeastern edge of what soon became Shepard Park. By 1911 the Shepard estate was sold to an investment company; a series of winding, tree-lined streets were laid out; and homes in colonial and Tudor styles were built, attracting mostly white, Protestant residents whose deeds to their new homes included restrictive covenants that barred "any Negro or colored person or person of Negro blood extraction" along with "Jews and other Semitic people."

The Earlys purchased their home in the early 1930s. It was a modest three-story brick colonial at 7704 Morningside Drive, a street that curves gently through the center of Shepard Park. The neighborhood then was only about twenty years old, but it was considered a most respectable address, a place where a couple could raise a family in a peaceful—and a very white—neighborhood. It was not until the 1950s that Jews slowly began moving there, and by the late 1960s blacks began to buy houses in Shepard Park. Today its homes remain a respectable address for the professionals and their families who are the backbone of the federal government.[12]

On the surface, Early family life seemed more or less normal. The children took in Washington Senators baseball games, but instead of going with dad, a White House car was sent to take them to the ballpark. Sometimes he joined them; often he could not get away from the office. Helen Early Elam says wistfully that her father loved baseball but rarely was able to attend a game, unless it was Opening Day, and then he was working, as part of the presidential party. The Early home had not one but three telephones, two of which the children were forbidden to touch. These were red phones, one located in the den, an addition at the back of the house halfway between the first and second floors, and one on the first floor. Both were connected to the White House switchboard.

While the children were growing up, the Earlys had help: a maid and Steve's chauffeur, who doubled as a handyman for the family. When Helen and the children were on vacation, the household help ensured that the man of the house was cared for.[13]

Sis recalled that her father was helpless in the kitchen, although he could fry a steak. In fact, she said, he would even eat leftover steak for breakfast. He did like vegetables, especially kale, and when the children looked askance at the greens he would ask them to at least try some. When he did manage to be home for more than an overnight sleep, Early worked around the house, like any normal father. He wrote to Helen one time when she was away that he had left the office early, gone home, and washed and painted walls and ceilings: "Much remains to be done with the brush but I think it will all be finished, hard and dry by the time you get home."[14]

The Early family members were dog lovers, and none more than Steve. The family had several dogs, the most famous being Heine, a big brindle-striped boxer, who rode to the White House with his master in a Packard with the seal of the United States of America on its door. On nice days, Early's chauffeur, Frank Mohun, would drive Heine to Rock Creek Park for a long run. The handsome dog had been a gift from James A. Moffett, vice president of Standard Oil and a hunting crony of Early's. Elam recalls that when Heine shook himself, his muzzle spittle would fly everywhere. One time, soon after her mother had wallpaper with a fleur-de-lys design hung on the first floor of their home, Heine decided to give himself a hearty shake and the spittle turned the fleur-de-lys pattern black. "Fortunately, it was washable wallpaper," she says.[15]

Heine quickly became a family favorite. Early called him "a beauty with intelligence and other rare attainments. He is certainly a grand fellow, and, despite the reputation of some of his breed, Heine gets more gentle, more obedient and more companionable as the years pile up." His canine parentage was such that he was registered with the American Kennel Club, and his human "parentage" was nothing to sneeze at. His sire, Blitz V. D. Uhlandshohe, was owned by Moffett; his dam, Blanka V. D. Wolfschluct, belonged to Governor Herbert Lehman of New York.[16]

Heine may have become more gentle as he aged, but apparently the neighborhood air raid warden didn't find the big dog so cordial in February 1942, soon after the country went to war, when the warden, conducting his rounds to make sure the Shepard Park homes had proper protection in the event of an air raid, stopped by the Earlys' house. Heine proved less than friendly, so the warden served notice that if the family preferred to be protected by their pet, he was happy to delete them from his list.[17]

Perhaps serving as the family's "air raid warden" proved too much for Heine. By the summer of 1943, his health began to fail. At first he refused to eat, but the veterinarian said there was nothing organically wrong with him. When Helen, Sis, and Tommy went off on their annual summer vacation to the Adirondack Mountains in New York, Early made sure the family maid took care of the dog when Early was not home, which was often. Then, in August, he had to go to Quebec with Roosevelt for a meeting between the president and Churchill. Rather than take Heine to the kennel, where because of rationing the food would not be too good, Early sent the beloved family pet home with his chauffeur. During the day Mohun brought him back to the Earlys' to keep their maid, Gladys, company; at night he returned to Mohun's. But Heine was throwing up and refusing to eat. Mohun even fed the dog by hand, and Gladys fed him his pills. The vet blamed his illness on a bad throat that he guaranteed would improve when the weather improved and the temperature cooled down.[18]

Early was certain that when the family resumed its normal routine, Heine would recover. "He has been lonesome and I believe lonesomeness is more responsible for his illness than anything else," he told Buddy in a letter. In fact, he was certain that once Tommy returned home, "he will either make Heine over again—into his old self—or help hasten the end for him."[19]

When everyone finally returned home, Heine began to eat. However, Early said, he walked around the house like an old man. They took him back to the vet, who decided his lungs were full of fluid and he had at most a month to live. The family agreed it was time to put their pet to sleep. Early said the household at 7704 Morningside Drive was a very sad home. He told Moffett that he had owned and known many dogs in his life, but none could ever equal Heine. "If there is such a place as a hereafter for our animal friends, Heine today has a seat near the throne in Dog Heaven," he said.[20]

As traumatic as losing Heine was, as the war progressed, the Early family's finances continued to be strained. Early had taken a pay cut to leave Paramount and go to work for Roosevelt when he was elected president, and as the years moved along and the country was at war, he found it progressively more difficult to walk out. What his unqualified loyalty to the Boss, a man he admired and considered a close friend, did was make it impossible for him to leave his post and accept a more lucrative job in the private sector. It also played havoc with his finances. He sometimes referred to this conundrum at his press conferences, and in letters to friends.[21]

It was natural that Steve Early would want the best for his family, but his well-publicized salary of $10,000 as a presidential secretary left the family budget severely strained. By today's measure, that salary would be about $120,000, still not sufficient to fund the kind of lifestyle a prominent Washington official would find himself faced with. Friends sometimes paid for his memberships in clubs, he had several mortgages on his home, and family vacations were at modestly priced resorts on the shore of Maryland or in the Adirondacks, or at the homes of friends.

In addition to caring for his immediate family, as the eldest child in a family of eight, Steve sometimes felt the attendant obligations to help out his extended family whenever he could, despite his own financial problems. His widowed mother required occasional assistance, at various times one or more of his siblings were unemployed or widowed, and his severely crippled younger brother T. J. required special care. Steve even paid for his haircuts. Another brother, Elisha, had been at two years old one of the first infantile paralysis cases and since then could get around only on crutches. As a federal government employee, he sometimes asked Steve to intercede for him or for a friend in securing another job. When his sister Julia's husband, a lawyer in Boston, found himself with little work during the Depression, Steve called on a friend in that city to help out. Early said his brother-in-law's income "puts the family on about a bread and water basis. They need a little meat."[22]

Sometimes his generosity in family affairs became strained. When his brother Felix, who was closest in age to Steve and was a lawyer with the Interstate Commerce Commission, called on his big brother to intercede on his behalf of some unnamed office matter in the middle of the war, Steve was less than amenable and apparently failed to reply. Felix said it caused him some embarrassment in his office, "and, I am frank to confess, some little resentment." He said it was not pleasant to have to tell his boss at the Commerce Commission that his own brother was not returning his telephone calls. "I know yours is an onerous, man-killing task, but I am confident you could find a moment to dictate at least an acknowledgment of my letters," Felix said. Steve replied, "I do the best I can, these days, to attend to the work that properly comes to this office. The matter that you present in behalf of your boss does not come within the scope of the work I am assigned to do over here. As a matter of fact, it has not even the remotest connection with my work. And, there is a great volume of work that belongs to me and to which I give some ten hours each day."[23]

Even his own mother now and again asked for a favor. "My dear Stephen," began a letter dated October 28, 1938. She had two motives for writing to him, she said. The first must have sounded good to his thin pocketbook. He had been sending her $40 a month, which she said has been "so generous," but she realized he had so many expenses now that Buddy was in military school, and she would not mind if he reduced the sum to $25. However, her second motive, she said, was to ask him to find employment for the son of one of her friends. "If this is convenient to you, all right, if not forget it." And like any good mother, she ended the letter by telling him not to work too hard.[24]

Many of the letters between mother and son show a deep warmth and caring. Three days after Pearl Harbor, Ida Early wrote: "My own dear Stephen." She reminded him that he had done so much for her, and she could do so little in return. "I do remember you every day and night in my prayers to God, that he will sustain you in this trying hour, both *spiritually* and *physically*." While Steve had an abiding desire to watch over his family, he exhibited little of his mother's spiritual side. His daughter said she could not recall her father ever attending church services.[25]

Then there was cousin Finks, who lived in Charlottesville, Virginia. He carried on a regular correspondence with Steve, relaying family news and gossip. Nestled in these otherwise innocuous letters sometimes were requests for favors. Could the presidential secretary "facilitate the entry of a friend's daughter into a dietician's program at Walter Reed Hospital? She comes from one of our very best families. She is a fine physical specimen of womanhood." Another time, he wrote: Could Steve help with a claims bill for compensation for an injured friend? And during the Depression he asked: Would it be possible to find Finks's brother-in-law a job at a Civilian Conservation Corps camp? Sometimes Steve was able to help; when he could not, he would send Finks a couple of tickets to an area sporting event, no doubt gifts he himself could not use.[26]

While family members certainly did call on him for help, friends, acquaintances, and even strangers wrote asking for his assistance. Usually the writer was asking for a job for him- or herself, a friend, or a relative. A secretary at the Paramount News office in New York wrote, "Because of your natural and justified influence, I believe that you can assist definitely in helping a situation that has caused me quite some concern during the past few years." Her gentleman friend had been unemployed for several years, and she was certain that Early could help. Or in the case of Alexander Woollcott, the playwright and a former colleague of Early's on *Stars and Stripes*, he wanted good seats for the 1936 presidential inauguration. With most requests, even some from family members, Early replied that he would pass their letter on to the appropriate government agency or individual.[27]

Early himself was not averse to asking his friends for a favor. In 1940, when Buddy had completed his second year at Staunton Military Academy and was sailing as a deck cadet on the SS *Jamaica* that summer, his father asked the governor of the Panama Canal Zone, where the *Jamaica* would be in port, to give Buddy a personal tour of the canal and its operations. In the spring of 1941 Early asked Pa Watson to have the superintendent of Staunton detail Buddy to Roosevelt when he was visiting Woodrow Wilson's birthplace nearby. The request was "gladly complied with."[28]

When his daughter Sis finished her studies at Marjorie Webster Junior College in Washington in the mid-1940s, after Steve had left the White House, she wanted to attend Pratt Institute, a well-known art school in Brooklyn. Apparently there was some problem with her admission, so Dad called on two of his powerful friends in New York: David Sarnoff, chairman of the board of the Radio Corporation of America, which later became NBC, and Anna M. Rosenberg, a Madison Avenue public relations executive and a former policy aide to Roosevelt on defense and labor issues and later an assistant secretary of defense. Sis got in.[29]

During Sis's two years in New York, her "devoted dad" gave her plenty of advice. He worried about whether or not she and her girl-friends would find a nice apartment so she could move out of her temporary quarters in a hotel. He told her not to be concerned about the bill for the room: "I have an idea that will be taken care of, and if you are allowed to pay anything it will be much less than $6.30 a day. If I am wrong in this guess, we will find ways of taking care of it without hurt to anyone." A letter to Sis soon after this alludes to Sarnoff and Victor Emanuel, a wealthy businessman and longtime friend of Early's, either of whom may have been her benefactor. In fact it may have been Victor who had a hand in helping her and her girlfriends find an apartment. In another letter, he reminded her to thank "Uncle" Joe Davies for the monthly checks he was sending her.[30]

When she asked to borrow the family station wagon to haul her belongings home from college for the summer, Dad said he was not worried about her using the wagon, "[b]ut the attendant dangers do worry me—the danger of facing traffic for several hundred miles each way, and in and out of Brooklyn and New York City where truck drivers, taxis and automobile traffic combine to make hazards worse than anywhere else I know in this whole country." Another time when he was in the city on business, he had dinner with Sis and her roommates in their apartment. But when he returned home, he must have decided it needed some minor repairs, so he sent her some money. In another letter, he told her to take care of herself—get plenty of rest and don't lose too much sleep: "You will find life with the other girls in the apartment will have its temptations to stay up late. The social life will rob you of your sleep and there is a bad chance that your school work will take more time than you can give it." And there was this piece of advice from the loving father to his only daughter: "Keep all zippers up."[31]

Later in her life, Sis still had wonderful memories of her father. Unlike Buddy's memories of the absentee father, Sis saw him as "a good father with a good sense of humor," although she said that when he did get angry, his lips disappeared. And angry he got the morning of her wedding. Mrs. Elam said her father began fussing with the flowers, becoming more and more upset about the way they were arranged. She said his famous temper flared for a moment but quickly subsided, an act she attributed to the stress of giving his daughter in marriage. He refused to ever wear white shoes, but when Sis got married in August 1949, he had to wear a white suit, which she reminded him he always did in the summer, but he protested that he would rather go barefoot than wear white shoes. Photos of the wedding show him wearing a white suit, white shoes, and a big grin.[32]

One of the problems that confronted Steve and Helen Early while he was in the White House was that by virtue of his position they frequently were invited to dinner parties and other social events in the capital. Their daughter said that if it had not been for his job, her parents probably would have eschewed much of the capital's social life. This meant proper attire in an era when "going out" translated into dressing up. It also meant reciprocating, whether it was a bridge game with refreshments at their home or gifts to friends—close and not so close—at holidays. A look at Steve Early's check stubs in his files at the Roosevelt Library hint at such expenditures: Cartier playing cards, $24.50 in December 1943, perhaps a Christmas gift for friends like Joe and Marjorie Davies, or maybe for the card games at home with friends, many of them in high places, including the Davies and Dwight and Mamie Eisenhower. Some in Washington believed that Eisenhower's advancement in the army came in part from his friendship with Early, who pushed his name forward to Roosevelt when military appointments were discussed. Early's daughter remembered those bridge and poker games her parents hosted in their modest home on their even more modest budget and the lines of black chauffeured cars that would line up outside.[33]

In the early 1940s, after war rationing was underway, Bernard Baruch threw a lavish party at the posh Carlton Hotel across from the White House. Sixty prominent Washingtonians drank the best French champagne and feasted on an endless flow of caviar and pâté de foie gras, followed by a six-course dinner. Among the elite guests were cabinet officials and their wives, a Vanderbilt, a smattering of movie stars, and Steve and Helen Early. Throughout the war, as heads of state and deposed royalty rolled into the White House for visits—sometimes extended ones—the Earlys were guests at official state dinners as well as less formal meals. There is no record of the attractive, dark-haired Helen Early's clothing expenditures, but no doubt like any housewife, wrestling with rationing and a slim budget during the war, she managed to employ a combination of creativity and thrift. Photos of her in newspapers of the day often showed her in a dark suit or dress, with a good piece of costume jewelry. It may have been the same suit with a change of jewelry.[34]

Early's dilemma was how a White House secretary earning $10,000 a year could ever reciprocate. When Joe Davies returned from one of his trips to Russia, where he was serving as the United States ambassador, he brought his daughter a pale red ruby. She already had one, so he gave it to Helen Early. Another time he brought home a heavy brocaded robe that once had belonged to a Russian Orthodox priest. His wife, Marjorie, the Post cereal heiress, declined it, so it went to Steve and Helen Early to join two Russian oil paintings, earlier gifts from the couple. Although Joe Davies had been friendly with Steve before he married Marjorie, their friendship deepened after the marriage. It could have been coincidental, simply a natural result of their ongoing golf and poker games, but it did not hurt when Davies lobbied for an ambassadorship that his close friend had the ear of the president of the United States every day.[35]

In his letters to Buddy, Early rarely referred to the family's strained finances, but Buddy must have realized the cost of private schooling was not cheap. He may have been surprised when he received a check for his tuition from Davies as a Christmas gift in 1938. With the check was a letter with two challenges from Davies. If Buddy received an average grade of 90 or better in the next semester, Davies would buy him a new suit, "either a dinner coat or a business suit, as you like." If Buddy had a grade average of 85 or better at the end of his time at Staunton, Davies would give him a scholarship to a college of his choice. After the holidays, an apologetic Steve and Buddy each sent Davies a letter explaining that while they appreciated his "great and generous" offer, they would have to return the check. Buddy wrote that as long as his father held his present office, "it would not be altogether right for me, his son, to accept" the check. Buddy told Davies that his father "wants to be able to give me my education. He says it is his duty to me."[36]

Early's penchant for betting on the horses and playing poker may have put small dents in the family budget, although Early's scrapbooks contain numerous memos to and from his poker and golfing friends noting that he had either won money or broken even. Even Roosevelt enjoyed following his betting adventures, especially those at the nearby racetracks. During the war, when everyone, adults and children alike, was using savings to buy War Bonds, Early used his golf skills to raise money for his younger son, Tommy, who was busy collecting junk around the neighborhood to sell so he could get money to buy War Bonds. One afternoon Steve and some of his cronies were playing at the Burning Tree course, and he told them about Tommy's business venture. At lunch one of them got a tip on a horse, so they decided to put their money on it, and if it won, the proceeds would go to Tommy to buy War Bonds. The horse did win, and Tommy's take was $67.50.[37]

Perhaps it was the financial burdens related to the Early family's social life or perhaps it was Steve's late nights working at the White House, but something seemed to be placing a strain on the family. In a letter to Joe Davies in the summer of 1937, Early alluded to "the situation at home," giving no details, but adding, "It eventually must be repaired but there is no haste." This "situation" could have referred to his late nights at the White House away from his wife and family or it could have involved another woman, although that was unlikely—but not out of the question. Power is an aphrodisiac to some women, and Steve Early, although far from handsome, was a powerful man. He also was a devoted family man hamstrung by a tight budget. Only two instances of gossip about Early and other women surfaced in the course of the research for this volume, and both were fairly innocuous.[38]

Raymond Clapper, a White House correspondent until he entered the service after the war started, wrote in his diary in the mid-1930s that very confidentially he was told by another White House reporter covering Roosevelt in Hyde Park that Early had become impressed with a hostess at a the coffee shop in the Nelson House in Poughkeepsie, where Early and the press stayed. They spent some time together, but the reporter assured Clapper that "everything was on the up and up and apparently no funny business." It turned out the hostess was about to lose her job, so kindhearted Steve said he would help her. And he did. He found her a job with Harry Hopkins in the Federal Emergency Relief Administration, and because she had arrived in the capital with no money, Early set about raising money from the White House staff and press corps who knew her when they stayed in the Nelson House to help her buy some furniture. Later they threw a party for her at the home of Charles Hurd, the *New York Times* reporter, and presented her with the furniture.[39]

The other snippet of gossip about Early and another woman, very much secondhand, shows up in *The White House Witness*, a book of memoirs by Jonathan Daniels, who succeeded Early, albeit briefly, before Roosevelt died. The book, petty and often anti-Semitic, is Daniels's version of the wrangling and backbiting among the higher-level members of the White House staff, so the gossip about Early needs to be carefully screened. The story Daniels wrote about came from Bill Hassett, Early's assistant, whom Daniels claimed never particularly liked Early. Hassett, a quiet, acerbic man, no doubt found the press secretary with the roar of a mountain lion a bit too obtrusive for his liking, but publicly the two men seemed friendly enough.

What Hassett told Daniels was that around the time of one of the Quebec conferences in the 1940s, a woman employee in the White House, referred to by Daniels only by her office nickname, "Stinky," asked Early to bring her back a fur coat from Canada. Daniels wrote that Early did indeed send a fur coat in the pouch of papers and documents sent to the White House from Quebec. Considering the constant tenuousness of the Early family budget, it's highly unlikely that Steve purchased the coat for her. She may have given him the money to do so. Daniels claimed that Early was infatuated with Stinky, and that when she was about to have a baby, he became so considerate of her that it became a joke around the White House that he was the father. When she was about to leave to have the baby, Daniels said, Early asked Pa Watson's secretary to hold a baby shower for her, but the secretary is said to have replied that Stinky had no friends to invite. Early did attend the circumcision ceremony, but Daniels said the baby looked so much like his real father that no one could doubt his parentage.[40]

Elam said that later in her life, after Steve had died, Helen, who always handled the money, would talk about the family's finances. She said, "Dad would call from Burning Tree or wherever needing money, and ask my mother, 'Where are we banking now? I've run out of money.'" She said her mother would reply, "Where we've always banked. Riggs." The Riggs National Bank was across the street from the White House.[41]

Reminders of their shaky financial picture came in many forms. For instance, Riggs sent Steve a letter in August 1941 enclosing eight separate extension slips, covering notes signed by him and Helen totaling $7,000. Payment on the extensions, secured by a deed of trust on their home, was due by the following September 26. That same date, their fire insurance policy on the house expired, and they needed to find the funds to pay that bill. In May 1944 a Washington newspaper reported that Early had resigned from Burning Tree, speculating that either the dues were too much for his budget or he was planning to resign and leave Washington. It was the former, coupled with the fact that because of Roosevelt's travels—to his home in Hyde Park and to war conferences—Early had less and less time to spend on the links.[42]

The budget may have been tight, but the Early family benefited in many small ways from Steve's wealthy connections. This was before federal regulations prohibited government employees from accepting gifts from people who would benefit from their influence. The Earlys' dining room table on holidays often was laden with foodstuffs from these friends. John Cowles, president of the *Minneapolis Star Journal* and *Tribune*, contributed a turkey for the Early Thanksgiving dinner during the 1940s. The president of American Airlines, C. R. Smith, sent him a radio for Christmas in 1942, and for Christmas in 1944 Bernard Baruch gave him an 1811 edition of Robert Frankland's *Indispensable Accomplishments*, which Early described as a "very old and rare treasure that could well go into the Library of Congress." On several occasions, Baruch had fresh quail delivered to Early's office. In 1942 Baruch paid to have the rusty galvanized screens on the Earlys' front porch replaced with shiny copper screens, a gift that Early said meant the family "won't be annoyed or bitten by the flies, gnats or mosquitoes this summer." Early once told Baruch, "When and if the day comes—the day when I shall find myself in a position to reciprocate at least some of your many kindnesses—I shall be a very happy person. I realize, of course, that your kindly acts have mounted into what a most confirmed conservative would refer to as a staggering total." Other gifts of food regularly showed up at the Early home at holiday time from Jesse Jones, a wealthy businessman and publisher of the *Houston Chronicle* who served as president of the Reconstruction Finance Corporation in the New Deal and continued to manage the agency during the war when it oversaw procurement of defense supplies.[43]

In October 1943 when Buddy Early, now in the army and training at Camp Croft in South Carolina, was about to be sent overseas, Early's friend Bob Denton knew how much Steve and Helen missed their son. Denton, who had succeeded Early at Paramount News in Washington, invited Steve, Helen, Sis, Steve's sister Mary Holmes, and several other friends to see a Paramount movie production called *Sabotoge*, the story of underground work in Europe. When the movie ended, a picture of General MacArthur came on the screen. A voice said, "No! He is not the greatest soldier in the United States Army."

Then a likeness of General Eisenhower came on the screen, and the voice said, "Neither is Eisenhower the greatest soldier in the United States Army."

To Steve's amazement, the voice said, "His name is Early. He is the greatest soldier in the United States Army." What followed were sequences of Buddy drilling, eating in the mess tent, getting his mail, and doing kitchen duty. It ended with a shot of Steve and Buddy. Denton had sent a camera crew to Camp Croft to make the "short" as a belated birthday present for Early. Buddy came home for Thanksgiving that year, but he never made it for Christmas. His unit was shipped to France.[44]

Early tried to return the favors of his friends, although sometimes he overdid it. Eisenhower's personal naval aide in the war, Harry Butcher, was an old friend of Steve's from Early's days at Paramount and Butcher's at CBS in Washington, and he recalled in his memoirs that one afternoon in March 1943, when Butcher was in Washington on leave, he, Early, and about twenty of their buddies sat down to play poker, a game that continued through dinner and ended about 5:00 a.m. the next morning. Toward the end, someone suggested sending a letter, via Butcher, signed by them all to their friend Ike. Over Butcher's objections, Early took up a collection to buy a gift for the general. It was a handsome Longines gold watch, accompanied by a letter of glowing praise for his work in the war.

A year later, Butcher wrote, Eisenhower was on leave in Washington. He invited the Earlys and several other friends to his apartment for dinner. When Steve learned that the general had a desire for fresh oysters he immediately drove off to a fish market and soon returned with fifty oysters on a tray and several thick steaks. In spite of the war rationing, another friend who had a farm near Washington contributed two chickens, several dozen eggs, and some butter, a real treat.[45]

It was not until he finally left the White House and was working in private industry drawing a commensurate salary that Early could comfortably afford to return the favors and gifts lavished on him by his wealthy friends.

21

EXTRACTING NEWS FROM OYSTERS

Throughout the summer and fall of 1943, Roosevelt was out of the country, on vacation or engaged in parleys on war strategy with world leaders, one of which became a high point of Early's career as the first modern presidential press secretary. But as the year drew to a close, the White House saw the death of two members of FDR's close-knit "family."

By early June 1943 Churchill, having finished for the moment his business with Roosevelt and, to the relief of Early, had gone back to England. The war news coming out of the Pacific and the Far East was at best mildly encouraging. The Allies were on the offensive and believed that eventually they would win, though the effort would continue to prove painful for some time. It seemed Japanese aircraft were attacking everywhere—Guadalcanal, the Aleutian island of Kiska, the Solomon Islands, and elsewhere. On the other side of the world, despite heavy German bombing of Allied targets, as the summer progressed, widening shards of light appeared: Sardinia, Corsica, and Sicily were slowly coming under Allied control, and while Joseph Goebbels, the Nazi propaganda chief, was boasting that Berlin was "free of Jews," US and British bombers were methodically conducting successful raids on strategic German war production plants.[1]

In the middle of June 1943, while Roosevelt was in Hyde Park entertaining, among others, Queen Wilhelmina of the Netherlands, who motored over from her temporary home in nearby Lee, Massachusetts, Early was deliberately misleading the reporters as to the president's whereabouts, explaining that there would be no FDR press conferences for a week. "Just a Shangri-la trip of no consequence at all from the news point of view, all of which I give you OFF THE RECORD, IN CONFIDENCE, AND FOR YOUR OWN GUIDANCE."

He was referring to the president's weekend retreat in Maryland, a two-hour drive from Washington in the cool and secluded Catoctin Hills, away from the oppressive humidity of the capital's summers. If the reporters seemed singularly uninterested in the destination, it was because they knew about Shangri-la. When Roosevelt could not get away to Hyde Park during the war because of fuel rationing or lack of manpower to run the train, this assemblage of simple cabins, once a summer vacation camp for boys and girls and now used as a training camp for the marines, was a place he could escape to, sometimes taking along a few friends or aides. Reporters in Washington knew of its existence, but bound by wartime censorship, most of them kept the secret, except for the occasional newspaper columnist who would mention it or hint at its existence until one day when Early called one of them into his office and blasted him for his indiscretion. Then just to make certain the offending columnist got the point, Early turned him over to a Secret Service agent to have a "friendly" talk with him.[2]

While Roosevelt was entertaining the queen at Hyde Park, Early said he hoped to slip away from the office for a round of golf, "if I can get the clubs on a bus," a reference to the strict gasoline rationing that meant loading his clubs into his car and driving to the golf course was a thing of the past. It is doubtful he managed many rounds of golf in the summer of 1943. News of the war as often as not was released through announcements from Roosevelt when he was in residence. When he was not—and that was more frequent—Early tried to dish out a morsel or two that the reporters could use. Nonetheless, he spent most of his press conferences fobbing off questions on the president's whereabouts and rumors about his activities.[3]

By late July Steve Early was telling his son Buddy, "The news from the East and the South Pacific, also Alaska, is good. The Allies are making excellent progress everywhere and our forces are playing a heroic and courageous role." A month earlier, Allied bombers had attacked Sicily. On July 10, British, American, and Canadian troops invaded the island off the "toe" of Italy; Roosevelt was given the news in the middle of a state dinner at the White House in honor of French general Henri Giraud. On July 16 Roosevelt and Churchill sent a joint message to the people of Italy warning them that if they continued "to tolerate the Fascist regime, which serves the evil power of the Nazis, you must suffer the consequences of your own choice." Three days later Hitler and the Italian leader Mussolini held another of their meetings, their thirteenth. This time the topic was the extent of aid Germany would be willing to give its ally. Although Italy was on the brink of collapse and Mussolini's aides had urged him to disclose this to Hitler, the Italian dictator refused. However, Hitler, afraid that Italy might go over to the Allies, also was clearly aware that continuing to defend Italy against the power of the Allies was a lost cause, and he refused to do so.[4]

A major turning point in the war in Europe came on Sunday, July 25, 1943. Roosevelt was working on an upcoming Fireside Chat with his two principal speechwriters, Sam Rosenman and Robert Sherwood, at Shangri-la. On this hot and humid Washington afternoon, Steve Early was at the White House holding down the fort, catching up on his work and monitoring war news on the tickers in his office and over the radio, when he heard a news flash saying that Mussolini had resigned. He immediately called the president on the direct telephone line to Shrangri-la.

Roosevelt seemed quite surprised, even skeptical, but not tremendously excited about the news. When no one in the White House or at Shangri-la could get confirmation, the president, acting unconcerned, commented, "Oh, we'll find out about it later." The three—Roosevelt, Rosenman, and Sherwood—ate dinner and eventually had a leisurely drive back to Washington. When they got to the White House, the president retired to his study, where he tried to reach Churchill on the telephone. Later that night, he learned that Mussolini had been overthrown by his own generals and politicians. Sherwood was amazed that for five hours the White House lacked the means to learn what had happened, and that what information it did have came from a chance report from Early, who had heard a radio news flash. Sherwood wrote, "One would have thought that during those hours dispatches would have been flashing constantly from and to all directions, even on the radio-equipped Secret Service cars during the drive back to Washington."[5]

Two days after Mussolini's ouster, Early passed along to his son Buddy, training for overseas duty at Fort Benning, Georgia, the following reaction from the White House:

> There is much excitement because of Mussolini's separation from the Government of Italy. We know definitely that he is out and that Fascism is finished. There is a general feeling, although no one knows the facts or the truth of it, that Italy will not last much longer as a nation, even though it continues to fight with the Germans. All manner of stories are coming out of Italy via the press and radio, telling of marching mobs of citizens shouting for peace and for surrender and expressing general dissatisfaction. We will know what all this means in due time. Even the experts hesitate to say when that will be. It is 6:30 by the clock now. The President is just leaving his office for the house. That means we can close up. And that means the end of this. As a matter of fact, I had about reached the point of news exhaustion anyway.[6]

For two months, Early had been trying to catch a few days of vacation away from the smothering heat of Washington. In late June, Joe and Marjorie Davies invited him to spend a few days at their "camp," a magnificent home in the Adirondack Mountains in New York. Two weeks later, Davies was still pressing a busy Early to visit, but he simply could not leave the White House, much as he felt he needed a brief vacation.

Marvin McIntyre, who had been suffering from bouts of tuberculosis and other health problems for several years, had gone to Asheville, North Carolina, for the summer to rest. The city, situated on a plateau between the Blue Ridge and the Great Smoky mountains, was known for its sanitariums, where patients could receive treatment for tuberculosis and other pulmonary diseases. Early told Buddy that Mac was so thin "you could put him in the bore of your rifle barrel, and there would not be enough of him to fill in the rifling grooves. He is a very sick man and while the disease is supposed to have been arrested, I have my doubts as to whether this is true."

Pa Watson was at his home in Charlottesville, Virginia. Then, in early July, Rudolph Forster, the chief clerk of the White House, who had served every president since William McKinley, died of a heart attack. As the chief clerk, he was responsible for seeing that important documents reached the president, whether he was working in the White House or out of the country. Early said Forster, well liked and respected by the rest of the White House staff, had spent the previous day at the office and was getting up in the morning to come to work when he collapsed and died. "We will miss him a lot," Early said. Roosevelt was away in Hyde Park for a few days.

Early remained philosophical about a vacation: "[M]y time for a brief vacation will be coming. I do not know when. Neither do I have any plans." With the death of Forster and Mac's absence no doubt weighing heavily on his mind, he added, "I am in good shape physically and there is no hurry on my part to get away."[7] By July 27 he was telling Buddy that he still had not found "a loophole that will let me jump out of Washington. On the other hand, neither have I given up hope." Joe Davies was still in the Adirondacks and was calling him every Sunday, pressing him to come north for a rest. But a vacation that summer was not in the cards.[8]

By mid-July reporters had been pestering Early to confirm rumors of a Roosevelt vacation, maybe "six days for a rest somewhere." Not the usual weekend away, they explained. His reply? "There are always those rumors, but if there were a trip, I wouldn't tell you except in confidence, and I can tell you, JUST FOR YOUR INFORMATION now, that there is nothing at all definite."[9]

On July 30 the president did depart Washington by way of Hyde Park for a ten-day off-the-record fishing trip on the north shore of Lake Huron in Ontario, near McGregor and Whitefish bays. But this time it was not secrecy but geography that tripped up the curious reporters. Roosevelt had inadvertently told Early he was headed for Lake Ontario. So at his first press conference after Roosevelt returned to the White House, Early read a handwritten announcement from the president that he was fishing on the north shore of Lake Ontario near McGregor and Whitefish bays. One of the reporters said, "Shouldn't that be Lake Huron?" The ever-loyal Early answered, "I thought so when he wrote it, but I didn't check him on it." But a reporter with an even poorer sense of geography piped up, "Whitefish is on Lake Superior, isn't it?" The reporters—at least those who knew where Lake Superior was— laughed. Early decided to check it out officially. "Well, let's look at the map and decide for ourselves." He left the room and returned. It seems the Boss had written Lake Ontario instead of the province of Ontario, and indeed the two bays were on Lake Huron.[10]

Before he left for Canada, Roosevelt had broadcast the Fireside Chat that Sherwood and Rosenman had been preparing when they learned of Mussolini's fall. It was a half-hour radio address to the nation on the progress of a war that at last seemed to be favoring the Allies. He would speak again when he returned, this time about home front issues, because Early believed not only that the president's radio addresses be capped at thirty minutes each, but that to be effective they should be delivered at two-week intervals, a rule Early believed was more in line with the listening habits of the radio audience—many regularly scheduled programs were a half hour in length. He concluded that was "about the limit to keep the attention span of your audience."[11]

At his press conference the day after the radio address, pressed to estimate how many people had tuned in, Early told the reporters to get the exact figures from the Columbia Broadcasting System, which had conducted an audience survey. Then he couldn't resist adding that according to the survey, the president had reached every adult in the United States, even though some of the reporters thought he had done a less than careful job of developing some parts of the talk, such as explaining his plan to give returning war veterans credit allowances to continue their Social Security benefits. To keep the talk to a half hour, Early said, "the speech had to be cut and cut and cut."[12]

As Roosevelt was returning to Hyde Park from fishing in Canada, Churchill was crossing the Atlantic on the liner *Queen Mary* along with his wife; their younger daughter, Mary; and a party of two hundred military and civilian aides. The two men had decided that they should meet again, this time in Quebec City. The need for such a conference arose from the fact that now that Mussolini had been deposed, rumors were flying that Italy's surrender was imminent, leaving its future—as well as Allied operations in the Mediterranean—in question.

Once Roosevelt arrived at Hyde Park, Churchill and Mary left the *Queen Mary* at Halifax, Nova Scotia, and came south to the president's home, where the two men spent three days closeted away laying the groundwork for the conference, code named Quadrant, to be held in Quebec City a week later. It would be the first of two such conferences in the Canadian city. Like this one—the second one, Octagon, in 1944—came on the heels of a successful Allied invasion. As the two leaders discussed strategy, Roosevelt asked Early not to announce the prime minister's presence until after Churchill had departed for Quebec City.[13]

The press had been dropping hints, the White House reporters buzzing for a week before Roosevelt finally announced at his press conference that he would meet with Churchill in Quebec City, but he refused to release a timetable. On Friday, August 13, Early wrote to his son Buddy, still at Fort Benning preparing to be sent to the European front, that the president was getting ready to meet Churchill in Canada. Most of the War Department general staff, he said, already had moved north, adding, "I am hoping that I will not have to go. Nevertheless there is a chance. I will not know definitely until the middle of next week."[14]

The call came the day after Early wrote to Buddy. Perhaps recalling the press problems surrounding the Casablanca conference earlier that year, Roosevelt fired off a telegram to Early telling him that he expected this conference would present an "extremely difficult publicity program." He said, "It would help me a great deal if you would come along with us." Putting aside any hope of a vacation, Early replied succinctly, "OK." Two days later he told his press conference that he had nothing for the reporters, then hinted that Roosevelt had left Hyde Park and had returned to Washington—which he had, but only briefly.[15]

Most of the news about the meeting came out of Quebec, with American newspaper stories carrying a Quebec City dateline. The Canadian press was allowed to write about Churchill's presence in that country and the news, such as it was, that eventually came out of the conferences; Early, hamstrung once again by the US censorship code, was beseeching the White House correspondents to remain "off the record." The reporters knew about the coming Quebec City meeting; they knew that Churchill was in Canada and had just visited Niagara Falls and crossed over to the American side. Did Steve know that story had just been released in Canada and was now coming into newsrooms in the United States via the wire services?

Steve was reaching his boiling point at his August 12 press conference, and not just from the Washington summer steam bath outside. After all, he had promised the Boss he would remain silent.

"Well—and I am OFF THE RECORD with you now—he [Churchill] was on the record in Canada, and so is everybody else, so why he should go entirely off the record when he crosses an imaginary line? He will have to go off the record when he reaches a certain point, but that shouldn't deprive the people of the world from knowing that he is seeing Niagara Falls and probably visiting Buffalo today. But when he leaves there he will be off the record, or in the 'blackout' until he reappears in Canada."16

Two days later Early released a joint statement from Churchill and Roosevelt, the one the two had drafted while they were in Hyde Park. Early was insistent that the logistics involved in the drafting of the statement remain secret—"keep it to yourselves." His reasoning was that since Churchill and Roosevelt's signatures both appeared on the statement, its publication would lead to speculation that the two men had been conferring somewhere in the United States, which, of course, they had.

He could do nothing about rumors that the two men were still conferring in the United States. "If it leads to such speculation, and if there is such writing when this story is prepared for publication, nobody here is going to worry about it, and I have so advised [the Office of] Censorship. I am not going to worry about it, and I told Censorship not to worry about it."17

One newspaper reported that while there were many reasons during those war years why the press should be grateful that Early was handling the news from the White House, one of the most important ones was his refusal to be tempted into either censoring or reading a story in advance of its broadcast or publication. While he remained loyal to the president to the very end, Early remembered those days when he was a reporter and the difficulty the press often had in obtaining information from presidents or their secretaries, and thus he understood the problems these reporters faced.

However, Roosevelt did not remain so calm. On more than one occasion during the war, he insisted that Early, who under trying circumstances sought to remain impartial with reporters and ignore the hostility of antiadministration newspapers, ask FBI head J. Edgar Hoover to look into the publication of possible seditious materials. These were news stories or columns often propagated by isolationist newspapers hostile to the Roosevelt administration and the war, such as the *Chicago Tribune*, owned by Col. Robert McCormick, or his cousin Cissy Patterson's *Washington Times-Herald*. The president hoped he could muzzle such newspapers through indictments brought by the Department of Justice, but they never materialized. And Early, whose history with Roosevelt included numerous showdowns over the president's lack of patience with opposition press, must secretly have been relieved.[18]

On Monday night, August 18, at precisely 8:00, Roosevelt, Early, Harry Hopkins, Grace Tully, Roosevelt's personal physician Dr. Ross McIntire, and a handful of other aides boarded the presidential train for Quebec City on a mission that would place Steve Early at center stage in the ongoing military diplomacy between his Boss and the British prime minister. As the summer light was beginning to fade, the train pulled away from the siding at the Bureau of Engraving and Printing and slowly moved north out of Washington, its destination known only to those on board and to a handful of other highly placed officials who remained behind to run the government.

Twenty-two and a half hours later, the train, a Canadian Pacific that the party had switched to when it crossed into the province of Quebec, pulled into Quebec City, the only walled city north of Mexico and a good choice for a high-level wartime conference. Early and most of the party checked into Le Château Frontenac at the northeast end of the historic city, where it commands views of the St. Lawrence River as it sweeps east toward the Atlantic Ocean. A massive pile of late-eighteenth-century stone resembling a Loire Valley castle, the hotel was built in 1893 to house passengers of the Canadian Pacific Railway. From the beginning it was considered a fine place to stay while touring the battlefields, fortifications, and churches of the city that was founded by a Frenchman, Samuel de Champlain, in 1608 as a base for trade and exploration. In 1759 it fell to the British after a bloody battle between Gen. James Wolfe and the Marquis de Montcalm on the Plains of Abraham, high above the St. Lawrence (Wolfe and Montcalm were both killed in the battle). Almost two hundred years later, the city was perhaps a fitting place for two world leaders to ponder the fate of another bloody war. Early described Quebec to his son as "an ancient and most interesting city." He noted that there was "the old city, called the bottom city, and the new city, atop and dug into the rocky cliffs that rise to heights over the St. Lawrence River."[19]

Churchill, Roosevelt, and a very few of their necessary staff were housed in the Citadel, then the home of the governor general of the province of Quebec, a place the British prime minister declared "in every way delightful, and ideally suited to the purpose" of hammering out future war maneuvers. Today the Citadel is one of two residences of the governor general of Canada. Begun shortly after the War of 1812 under the direction of the Duke of Wellington, who feared another attack by American forces, the star-shaped Citadel is the largest fortification in North America. Set into the Plains of Abraham on a promontory that during those earlier times of war made it an ideal lookout for the enemy arriving on the river, the Citadel is a short walk from Le Château Frontenac.[20]

The evening after their arrival and before they began the serious business of the conference, Churchill, Roosevelt, and Canadian prime minister Mackenzie King hosted a formal dinner at the Citadel for eighteen admirals, including Lord Louis Mountbatten (a cousin of King George VI, a favorite of Roosevelt's, and soon to become the Supreme Commander of Allied Forces in Southeast Asia), American generals, and British field marshals. Early and his British counterpart, Brendan Bracken, were at the table; however, it is certain that Early was focused less on the pomp and circumstance of the evening and more on what he already suspected would be a host of press logistics and problems, the reason Roosevelt had suggested he come along.[21]

When Early arrived in Quebec City, he found forty-eight American reporters and still photographers, many of them the same men and women who covered the White House, waiting for him. Joining them were sixteen British reporters, thirty-five Canadian journalists, five Australians, a Chinese, a French, and a Russian journalist. And all were hungry for news.[22]

So Early fed them, and he tried to feed them well, although not always what they wanted. Even though Roosevelt and Churchill were conferring daily, they refused to allow the reporters inside the Citadel, nor would they talk with them. American journalists complained to Early, but try as he could, he was unable to persuade Roosevelt to be forthcoming with anything of substance. The upshot was that Early was forced to scratch around for scraps of information—color stories on the Citadel, the informal late-night sessions between Churchill and Roosevelt, the arrivals and departures of foreign dignitaries—to feed the hungry press, a move that caused the cynical journalists to applaud him when he walked into his press conference on August 18. These feedbags of nonstories must have worked, because one newspaper complained that the reporters "felt overworked by the flow of news copy that was coming out of the conference, estimated to be about one hundred thousand words a day."[23]

However, Brendan Bracken, the British minister of information, fared far less well with the press. He held his first meeting with reporters at the City Hall on August 19 and opened by reading a statement he had produced. Unfortunately for this former magazine editor turned minister of information, he had never attended one of Steve Early's rough-and-tumble press conferences, which left him totally unprepared for what one Quebec newspaper called "the Washington Wolf Brigade trained on the tough White House course." The *New York Times* wrote that Bracken's "rich voice and clever phrases interested correspondents despite his shortage of information."

While Early watched quietly from a corner of the room, the questions flew hot and fast. When Bracken would come up with a newsy answer, some reporter would propose that it be on the record. Within five minutes, confusion reigned. Nobody knew what was on the record and what was off the record. Finally, one of the reporters read back his notes, with Bracken ruling on various statements as they were read. Yes, that was on the record. No, that statement was not to be printed. Guards stationed at the door kept the reporters from leaving before the press conference ended, and when they did, they charged out the door, armed with their first more or less tangible news story of the conference. The *Quebec Chronicle-Telegraph* said they "thundered down the stairs and across the street to the Clarendon Hotel where they were staying and where a press room had been set up."[24]

The *Montreal Gazette* noted that Bracken, not used to dealing with hordes of nosy newsmen all shouting questions, was relatively ineffectual. The newspaper said it was not until Early, "used to this sort of thing," took over running the press conferences that any satisfactory contact was made between the press and the conference. The paper said that Early "understands the reporters' problem and has energetic and ingenious ways of helping solve it." When he went off the record with the correspondents, Early told them "something really confidential and useful—not a rehash of some old editorials."

The newspaper said that Bracken had "missed the boat with his ill-fated press conference," adding that it had "reached a new low in his barren roster of conferences in Quebec." The *Gazette* described the minister as short and condescending with the reporters and said he "muffed the best chance" that the British government had in a long time to "to tell at least a few things about Britain and the British."[25]

These criticisms of Bracken may have been a bit excessive. Since he had taken over as minister of information in July 1941, he had worked hard to ensure that war news was released to the British media in a timely manner, sometimes to the chagrin of their American counterparts, who were hamstrung by more stringent censorship regulations. Bracken's mentor and friend Churchill had asked his parliamentary secretary to take over the job of overseeing the release of wartime information at a point when the British press was unhappy with the lack of information regarding military campaigns the government was handing out. Bracken had not especially wanted the position, but, according to one biographer, he proved to be "a great success." However, placed side by side with Early in Quebec, Bracken stood no chance with the press, especially the American reporters. To further cement his own relationship with the reporters, Early made it a point to stop by the pressroom in the Clarendon at least once a day.[26]

To summon the reporters to a press conference, Early would ring a historic school bell in the Clarendon Hotel. At about 4:00 a.m. on August 20, probably giddy from late-night carousing, one of the reporters purloined the school bell and ran through the corridors of the hotel frantically ringing it. The *Quebec Chronicle-Telegraph* said that reporters jumped from their beds. Lights went on. Doors opened. Muffled oaths were heard. The excitement lasted about half an hour until the groggy journalists discovered the hoax. At his press conference later that morning, Early disclosed that Roosevelt and Churchill had been talking until 2:30 a.m., leading one reporter to suggest that one of them had rung the bell. Early laughed and agreed that both men had a sense of humor, but neither would go that far.[27]

Early's and Bracken's jobs were made even more difficult because neither Churchill nor Roosevelt was inclined to allow his secretaries to release much information about the progress of the meetings. The *Boston Globe* said the newsmen covering the conference had such problems extracting anything from the two leaders that they began referring to them as "oysters." When Churchill and Roosevelt did hold a joint press conference orchestrated by Early at the end of their meetings, the *Ottawa Evening News* called it "the highlight" of the conference.[28]

In his unpublished dissertation, Steven E. Schoenherr relates an interview he had with William Mylander, the representative at Quebec for the US Office of Censorship. Mylander said Early talked about the difficulty he had getting news for the reporters and how he finally persuaded Roosevelt to hold a press conference on the last day of the meetings. Early told Mylander, "Bill, what the hell are we going to do? All these American reporters as well as the British and Canadian reporters who have been up here, covering this conference, and we haven't been able to tell them a thing. They've been up here trying to suck their fingers and justify their expense accounts. How are we going to wind this thing up?"

When Mylander suggested getting both world leaders together for a press conference, Early pointed out that Churchill never held press conferences at home, and he was wary of holding one in Quebec. Near the end of the war, the *Baltimore Sun* said that Early "worked on" Churchill all evening before the last day of the conference, but the prime minister would not budge. Knowing the president would not meet the press unless Churchill did, too, at about 2:00 a.m. Early tried one last tactic—a bluff. He told Churchill that Roosevelt was going to speak to the reporters at noon the next day. "Will you join him?" he said. Churchill realized it was a challenge he could not turn down, and he grumpily agreed. When the press conference was held the next morning, Churchill was anything but grumpy. Although, he refused to answer any questions (when he did speak, he said it was "off the record"), he was in an impish mood and seemed to enjoy himself. Early, who must have felt sorry for the reporters, who had spent all week in Quebec without getting much news, allowed the American reporters— who, of course, were under no obligation to abide by British censorship rules—to paraphrase Churchill's words for their stories.[29]

The press conference the two leaders held that noon on the terrace of the Citadel elicited little substantive information for the 170 journalists who gathered on the damp ground in a semicircle around them. Perched on the parapet behind them, the mighty St. Lawrence River some three hundred feet below, were Harry Hopkins, British foreign minister Anthony Eden, Bracken, and Early. At one point Churchill warned them to be careful: it was a long fall.

Tumbling into the river was the furthest from Early's mind as he sat there listening to what amounted to banal apologies from Churchill and Roosevelt for having nothing worthwhile to give the reporters. Churchill reminded them that his words were "not for quotation or attribution"; rather, they were "to enable us to exchange greetings [with the press], like at Casablanca." He noted that this was the sixth conference he and Roosevelt had held since the war began, explaining in vague words and phrases the importance of these meetings to the Allies' eventual victory. Early must have breathed somewhat easier when Roosevelt, in his typical fashion, began by apologizing for having no real news, then told the reporters—albeit sketchily—what he and Churchill had discussed: the Mediterranean situation and future invasions in North Africa and Europe, the problems in the Southwest Pacific and China, and their hope for a tripower conference with Stalin. It was not much, but it gave the reporters a morsel of meat, and Early saved face.[30]

Once the press meeting concluded, the presidential party moved west on an overnight train to Ottawa, the Canadian capital, where at 11:00 a.m. on Wednesday Roosevelt spoke on the grounds of the splendid Canadian Parliament Buildings on a hill overlooking the Ottawa River. Early told his son that the American president made a speech to some three hundred thousand Canadians who had assembled there and that he "was most enthusiastically received." The speaker of the Canadian Parliament's House of Commons told the crowd that the people of Canada regarded Roosevelt as their own president, a statement Early believed was "a most courageous thing for a Canadian politician to say," and a statement that he said drew cheers from the audience that morning. The next day, the train carrying the presidential party headed south to Hyde Park, where they were able to get some much-needed—"but not enough"—rest before they went back to Washington. "So here I am on the job again—a little punch drunk," Early told Buddy.[31]

In spite of the tomfoolery and the complaints about "the oysters," Early considered the conference a success, even though he told Buddy soon after he arrived back in Washington, "The decisions made in Quebec by the president, Prime Minister Churchill and the Joint

United States-British Staffs (Army and Navy) cannot be revealed. If they were told now, it would be a plain case of tipping the enemy to the grand strategy and forces that will be used against them." He said that the highest-ranking members of the two staffs—veterans of many war-planning meetings—had told him that they regarded the Quebec meeting "as the most outstanding ever held between the leaders of the two countries." Hyperbole in part these words may have been, but Early assured his son that not only did the Quebec conference make progress "in planning the war and hastening the victory," but the military staffs laid great store in the fact that they got to know one another and to understand each other's "mutuality of interests."

In a letter to the president's daughter, Anna, Early said, "Some day the peoples of the world will learn what the President and the Prime Minister did for them—what tremendous good came to them as a result of friendship, truth, understanding and leadership of these two great men."[32]

Historians have been less than flattering about what the two Allied leaders accomplished, which was very little and may have explained the lack of news for the reporters in Quebec. The two men disagreed on the agenda for Italy: Roosevelt and his military advisers were pushing to limit operations in the Mediterranean and instead expend their energies on a cross-Channel invasion from England to France. On the other hand, Churchill considered a more extensive Italian campaign to weaken the Axis. What Roosevelt really wanted from Churchill, who he felt was stalling, was a renewed commitment to set May 1, 1944, as the date for Operation Overlord, the invasion of Europe. The British leader relented and agreed that the American general Dwight D. Eisenhower would become Supreme Allied Commander for Europe. As a balance, Mountbatten would head operations in Southeast Asia. It was at this Quebec meeting that Roosevelt and Churchill signed a secret agreement to exchange information on atomic energy, the atomic bomb at that time being under construction at Los Alamos, New Mexico.[33]

After the press and the presidential party returned to Washington, a number of reporters and executives from American and Canadian news organizations wrote to Early thanking him for his kindness and assistance at the conference. Schoenherr concluded in his dissertation that the press conference was a success for both the Allied leaders and the press: "It created a sense of unity that hid the deep divisions between the American and British military staffs over the timing of the invasion of France."[34]

Kirk Simpson, a reporter for the United Press, wrote to Early, "I felt that your work at Quebec deserved more commendation that it is ever likely to receive since it saved a very nasty situation. Had there not been some final official word to show allied unity if nothing else, a barrage of rumors of disagreements, clashes and impending bust-ups and the like must have appeared."

Perhaps because of the paucity of news that emanated from the two oysters, twenty-six White House correspondents sent Roosevelt and Early a signed tongue-in-cheek resolution in appreciation of the two men's "conspicuous services" at the conference by having the joint press conference "and thereby justifying our expense accounts." Roosevelt thought it humorous enough to ask Merriman Smith, the United Press White House reporter and the senior officer of the White House Correspondents Association, to read the resolution at his press conference on August 31, and everyone, including the president, enjoyed a hearty laugh—but only briefly.

It was at this press conference that an angry Roosevelt lit out at one of those syndicated columnists he so despised. The president's target was Drew Pearson, based at Cissy Patterson's *Washington Times-Herald*, who the previous day had written that Secretary of State Cordell Hull was "anti-soviet," and wanted "to bleed Russia white." Hull was in the midst of secret and tense negotiations with Stalin to arrange a meeting between the Russian dictator and Roosevelt, and apparently Pearson's vitriolic comments were too much for Roosevelt, who defended his secretary of state and, according to the *New York Times*, "in the strongest possible castigation" called Pearson "a chronic liar."[35]

Another issue that lurked behind the scenes at Quebec—one Roosevelt and Churchill were careful, almost eager, to sidestep—was the continuing plight of the European Jews. James MacGregor Burns thought that Roosevelt truly believed the most effective way to help the Jews was by winning the war as quickly as possible. The issue was so much more complex. Anti-Semitism, while not as rampant and vicious as in prewar Europe, had been a part of the American social fabric for decades. In his book *Israel in the Mind of America*, Peter

Grose says that since the late 1930s Roosevelt had devoted some time to considering the possibilities for resettling Jews and other refugees from the Nazi regime. Burns says that during 1942 the White House began receiving reports "so appalling that administration officials could not believe them and asked representatives abroad to check and verify" them. The reports were of Hitler's "final solution"—to round up all of Europe's Jews and exterminate them. What little substantive information was being published in the United States showed up in the Jewish press, thanks to the Jewish Telegraphic Agency and World-wide News Service. But since the mainstream newspapers in the United States, and in particular the *New York Times*, owned by a Jewish family, were printing very few stories about what we now know as the Holocaust, it is not surprising that those in power in Washington were paying scant attention to the problem.[36]

During the Quebec conference Max Lerner, a prominent American Jew and journalist, sent a telegram to Early asking the president to meet with a delegation from the Emergency Committee to Save the Jewish People of Europe. Early put him off, saying that a meeting in Washington once Roosevelt returned would be more productive. Despite repeated requests for a meeting, it never took place. Then, in early October, a delegation of several hundred rabbis who had come to Washington to plead the cause of the persecuted European Jews signed a petition asking Roosevelt's help in opening Palestine and the Allied nations to the European Jews for resettlement. But the president decided he would not meet with their representatives, and during one of his famous morning meetings in his bedroom he decided to turn the matter over to Marvin McIntyre, after listening to arguments from Sam Rosenman, himself a Jew, who considered this group of rabbis "not representative of the most thoughtful elements in Jewry."

Rosenman said he had tried, obviously without success, to keep "the horde from storming Washington," because, he declared, the leading Jews of his acquaintance opposed the march on the capital. During this bedside meeting, which is recounted in William Hassett's book *Off the Record with FDR*, Rosenman and Roosevelt discussed the possibility of settling the Palestine issue by letting Jews in to the limit that region could support them—and then put a barbed wire fence around the Holy Land, a reference to decades of conflicts between

Jews and Arabs. Rosenman agreed and added that this could work if the fence were a two-way affair to keep the Jews in and the Arabs out. McIntyre agreed to see four members of the rabbi's delegation. If they held out any hope of seeing Roosevelt, they were foiled. On the day of their visit, the president left for an inspection trip to nearby Bolling Air Field in Washington minutes before the rabbis arrived at the White House.[37]

No sooner had Roosevelt and Early returned to the White House from Quebec via Hyde Park than Churchill showed up again to resume discussions on how to persuade Stalin to meet with them, leaving Early to do some fancy footwork explaining—or not—the prime minister's activities. Off the record, he fed the reporters a few scraps, but mostly he asked them not to tell their readers and listeners any of Churchill's plans. Why was he back in Washington? they wanted to know. Was it true that he would soon be going to Massachusetts to accept an honorary degree from Harvard? Yes, Early said, but Churchill wanted no advance publicity on it. Early said he planned to meet with Churchill later in the week to discuss an official announcement.[38]

The portly, cigar-smoking British prime minister continued to fascinate the journalists who covered the White House. After the war, Churchill is to have said, "No lover ever studied the whims of his mistress as I did those of President Roosevelt." And in the tradition of all good journalists, the reporters wanted to know all the details of these clandestine meetings—but, like the trusted servant who quietly enters the chamber of lovers to serve them but never to gather intimate details for sharing, Early could only pass on the most banal of information to the reporters looking for a bigger story.

On September 2 they peppered Early with questions. Exhibiting more patience than the questions probably deserved, Early attempted to give them some answers that they could publish or broadcast. They wanted to know everything: Did the two leaders confer the previous night? Yes, in Roosevelt's study, Early said. What about dinner—formal or informal? Very informal, he replied. When did the two men retire? Roosevelt got to bed at 1:00 a.m., he said. What did they call each other? Frank and Winston? "I don't think they call one another anything. It's just 'Hello, how are you,' and that sort of stuff. I suppose when the occasion is at all formal, or when the President is speaking to others about the Prime Minister, he would call him the Prime Minister."

But what about when they are being informal? "I think they just dispense with names—they just talk to one another." No Winston or Franklin, or anything like that? "I have heard much conversation between the two, and I have never yet heard either one call the other by name, and I have heard each refer to the other." The reporters were still at it when Early called them in to his office later that afternoon to tell them Roosevelt would not be holding his regular press conference the next morning; he would be meeting with Churchill. Did Early have any "tidbits" they could print? No, he did not, and, he said, "The President wouldn't have anything for you, confidentially, if he met with you tomorrow. OFF THE RECORD, he has got some meetings in the morning, and then CONFIDENTIALLY AND OFF THE RECORD, he is getting away from here."[39]

Churchill arrived in Cambridge, Massachusetts, on the morning of September 6, and a short time later he was awarded an honorary doctor of law degree from Harvard at a special convocation. The reporters were told his travel itinerary was secret, but at 11:00 a.m. they were free to announce his arrival. While the prime minister "was in transit," traveling to Boston and returning to Washington that night to continue his meetings with Roosevelt, Early said his movements were "off the record."[40]

Two days later Churchill and Roosevelt were still meeting, their talks focusing on attempts to get Stalin to join them for a conference later in the year, but Early had little news for the reporters. What do you hear from Stalin? they asked him. "I heard nothing," he answered, as always a bit amused at the length the reporters would go to snatch a scrap of news.

Would they be getting a report on the progress of the talks? they asked. Early's reply produced a few chuckles: "A progress report on the Progress? Oh!! No. The President wrote me a little note the other day," and he paused to rummage in the middle drawer of his desk for the note, "in which he said, 'Restraint Pays.'" One of the reporters asked Early if he exercised restraint. "I do," he replied, although it was not clear whether Roosevelt's memo applied to Early's feeding the press as little news as possible or whether it applied to the press secretary's famous temper. Nonetheless, it injected a nice moment of levity and brought an arid press conference to an upbeat end.[41]

If rumors were a staple of the White House press corps

throughout the war, they seemed to be running at warp speed this fall. One morning, around the time the Italian surrender was made public, the reporters told Early there had been a report out of London that Roosevelt had conversed for fifty minutes with Pope Pius XII. A bemused Early looked at the reporters, paused for a moment, and said, "The President and the Pope talked, did they?" A reporter replied, "That's what the (London) newspaper said." Early asked, "In what language?" At that the reporters began laughing. Someone called out, "Latin." Another one suggested that perhaps the telephone operator had served as the interpreter. More laughter. Was Early denying the story? "Never heard of it," he said.

"How the Hell can I deny it, just between us?" he said. The press conference took up other matters, but shortly Early returned to the pope and the president. "Going back again, and I am not saying anything for quotation, and so forth, but FOR YOUR GUIDANCE. I am quite sure the President—the Italian—the Pope doesn't speak English." But the reporters weren't giving up. A chorus of voices responded, "Yes he [Roosevelt] does." Quickly, Early said, "He does, that's right. He does—I remember when he was at Hyde Park."[42] Then, hoping to quash the rumor once and for all, Early told them, "But FOR YOUR GUIDANCE, the President wouldn't have a telephone conversation with anybody over trans-Atlantic or transoceanic lines, seriously. Everybody knows that for security reasons any discussions that are important cannot be held by telephone. You know that." There is no record of Roosevelt and Pope Pius XII ever speaking on the telephone or in person during World War II.[43]

Then came the rumor of an imminent meeting between Roosevelt, Churchill, and Stalin. John Crider, a White House correspondent for the *New York Times*, wrote a story published on November 10 that said the White House was working out details for transporting Roosevelt to such a meeting. Early did not deny that a meeting was in the works. He was concerned about releasing details of the president's travels, wherever they might take him. Crider argued that his story had been vague. "It was a question of whether to write the story vaguely like that and not be scooped by London," he said.

What Crider had written was this: "Moreover, there have been mysterious comings and goings around the White House during the last ten days involving persons who might very well be connected with transportation arrangements for a foreign Presidential trip." Early read this to the reporters and then asked Crider, "What's vague about that?" Early reminded the reporters that he expected "a reasonable degree of security given the President during a travel period by an ally and an allied government." He called this "cooperation and that is a matter of censorship," noting this was the responsibility of Brendan Bracken, the British minister of information, and Byron Price, the head of the US Office of Censorship: "That's what they are working towards, I know." Then he went off the record, saying that there were a number of factors over which the Allied censors have no control: "What are we going to do with the Vichy radio, or the Berlin radio? You can hear them and you pick them up. There are a lot of things we can't control. They belong to the enemy and they are enemy propaganda sounding-out devices, and what have you. All I could suggest to you hereafter on pieces like that [Crider's] is, when you see folks around and begin to add up on a two-and-two-makes-four basis for a piece to protect yourself against a possible scoop from London, to check with the Censor"—which Crider admitted he had not done.

Early would not let it rest. The story had appeared in that morning's edition of the *New York Times* and already he had received some phone calls—"and I am not speaking for anyone in the White House"—protesting the story. "I told them that I wasn't going to protest it. They wanted to. They were agitated and worried and concerned because they have responsibilities that go with transportation." He said they wanted to make an issue of it. When Crider said he knew a lot more than he published, Early said, "I appreciate that, and on the other hand, knowing that is one reason why I am not going to publicly denounce the story."

Reminding them to check stories with the censor and then use caution when they published or broadcast those stories, Early told them about a report he had gotten about Berlin radio reporting an accident on a certain street corner of a certain city in the United States. It gave the names and addresses of the occupants of the car, the license numbers, and the extent of the injuries. He said the announcer told his audience, "We just broadcast this to show you we know what is going on." Early said they checked and found every detail was accurate, "so you don't have to be too definite for these gentlemen."

Turning to Crider, Early said, "I don't think the issues at stake, if something should happen, are worth the news that that space today in your paper gives its readers."

Early knew he was not hiding anything from the reporters. They all knew Roosevelt was about to embark on a trip that would result in a meeting with Churchill and quite probably with Stalin. They just could not publish it. So it was ironic that with all the concern about the "enemy" learning of the president's movements, the only real danger on the trip, which indeed began the following day, came from the United States Navy.[44]

Late on November 11—Armistice Day—Roosevelt, Harry Hopkins, Pa Watson, and several aides sailed down the Potomac River, and at its mouth in the morning dawn they boarded the battleship *Iowa* to cross the Atlantic. Early remained back at the office, quite probably because the Boss may not have expected any "on the record" news to come out of the trip, and because he would be away for five weeks, which was a long time to leave the White House without one of the three secretaries to run the daily show. (McIntyre was back at work, but only part time; Watson was with the president). If it became necessary to release a statement to the press, Hopkins, although ill himself with stomach problems, was Roosevelt's most trusted adviser, and the president thought he could handle the task. The travelers' destination was Cairo, where the president would meet with Chinese generalissimo Chiang Kai-shek, leader of the Chinese nationalist forces, and Churchill before moving on to Tehran, Iran, for a conference with Churchill and Stalin, and then back to Cairo. For all of the preparations to ensure secrecy and safety, on the second day at sea, as Roosevelt looked on, the battleship began conducting a defense drill. Suddenly a torpedo accidentally launched by a destroyer escort exploded in the wake of the *Iowa*—leaving, for just a moment, the life of the president of the United States vulnerable, and not because of any enemy fire.[45]

Roosevelt saw the purpose of the meeting with Chiang as having two goals: to discuss military operations in the Far East and to bring China into the war effort and postwar planning. Churchill had been reluctant to join the two men, fearing that it would take time away from strategy talks he wanted to have with Roosevelt before they met with Stalin the following week. Perhaps to assuage Churchill, Roosevelt hosted a Thanksgiving dinner for the prime minister and his daughter, Sarah. Meanwhile, whether to protect the president's whereabouts or because they believed he was still in Washington, some American newspapers were busy reporting that Roosevelt spent the holiday alone in the White House.[46]

Reporters who came to Cairo were faring no better than their counterparts at home. In fact, they were getting so little news from the conference that at the end of the meetings, forty-three American and British reporters signed a letter to Harry Hopkins expressing "the strongest dissatisfaction with the manner in which we were treated during the present important conferences." They demanded a meeting with Hopkins and asked that they be given information, even if it was "on an off-the-record basis" on what was going on so they could adequately prepare their stories when the censorship ban was lifted. There probably was little Hopkins could or would give the reporters, and anyway, he was no Steve Early. Had Early been there, he would have met with them, perhaps giving them something, or, if not, coaxing them into a more conciliatory mood with a little "off-the-record" or "for your guidance" material. In fact, when he held his press conference on November 22, Early was playing his usual cat-and-mouse game, giving them "in confidence and just for your guidance" information—just enough details about the conferences to keep them pacified.[47]

Left at home to mind the shop while Hopkins, Watson, and the Boss were on the other side of the world, Early had problems of his own. When he became press secretary at the start of Roosevelt's first term, he had decided that only correspondents from daily newspapers would have White House press credentials, meaning they had access to presidential press conferences as well as Early's daily meetings with the reporters. Almost all of them were white males. By the early 1940s a few women showed up at the press conferences, and eventually Early included radio correspondents. However, this still left weekly newspaper reporters on the sidelines, and that included representatives of the Negro press, since almost all the black newspapers in the country were weeklies.

This festering issue came to a head, perhaps coincidentally, shortly after Roosevelt left for the Cairo and Tehran conferences. The National Negro Publishers Association, meeting in Washington, had concerns about the lack of blacks at press conferences and the paucity of Negro subjects in newsreels on coverage of the war. For this latter problem they blamed Elmer Davis, the head of the Office of War Information (OWI), as close to a propaganda agency as the country had during the war. Among its duties was reviewing and approving government-sponsored radio programs and motion pictures, and this often meant altering films and newsreels to conform with America's wartime policies. The black publishers believed that the OWI was deliberately selecting Negro subjects for the newsreels that made them look like "buffoons." So the publishers asked Early if he would meet with them. There was little he could do—or perhaps little he chose to do—to change the OWI's operations at that point, but they hoped he would change the rules on press conference accessibility.

The publishers explained that the *Atlanta Daily World* wanted press credentials for itself and for a small group of black newsmen. Early tap-danced around the problem. According to Betty Houchin Winfield's *FDR and the News Media*, Early managed to extricate himself from the problem by turning the request over to the Congressional Standing Committee of Correspondents, which determined who got press credentials for Congress and the White House. Not until after the war did this committee change its rules. It was another unfortunate example of the Roosevelt administration paying scant attention to the plight of the Negroes in the United States. Had Early felt strongly that they should have press credentials equal to those of the white reporters from the daily newspapers, he had the clout to make it happen.[48]

Early's other big headache came at the end of the Cairo conference, when, on November 30, he took it upon himself to give the White House correspondents a statement from Roosevelt, Churchill, and Chiang at the same time as it was being handed to the American reporters in Cairo. Early said Roosevelt had sent the communiqué to him, but he had failed to give Early any specific release time for the announcement. Both groups of journalists were given strict warnings not to release the contents or to make advance statements to readers or listeners of the pending communiqué until the heads of state had had ample time to leave Cairo for, as Early said, "unannounced destinations."

Then, in typical Early fashion, he took them into his confidence: "Personally, I frankly don't want to get into this picture. It isn't mine. All I am doing here now is trying to perform a service for you, and I think I have got a right to do that, because I can save the transmission of this from Cairo, and the cables and so forth. All the communications will be very heavily loaded [with information], I assume." Just to make sure they understood his position, he asked them not to attribute anything to him or to the White House. At the moment that Early was warning the reporters to abide by the release date, Reuters, the British news agency, and the Soviet government news service Tass were releasing the story to the world. American editors were understandably upset that they had been scooped, and they filed a formal protest with the White House. Elmer Davis in turn protested to Britain's Brendan Bracken. But it was too late, and it was obvious that, as he had done for the Quebec conference, Roosevelt should have insisted that Early accompany him to Cairo to handle the press.[49]

The White House correspondents had respected Early's entreaties, an act he thanked them for at his press conference the next day. He told them he had spent the last day trying to untangle a situation that obviously was frustrating him. He learned that the communiqué was cleared by British censorship, which made him wonder whether the British government had decided to break the embargo date and allow its newspapers and radio to get the statement out first. It was not the first time that British journalists had scooped the American press with a piece of war news. Early reminded the reporters that because the media in the United States were operating under a voluntary censorship plan, he could not take action against them if they ignored a release date. He was right, of course, and he recognized that the press in this country had been most cooperative throughout the war with regard to heeding deadlines and withholding certain kinds of sensitive information from the public. His primary concern, he said, was keeping such information—especially presidential travel arrangements—from the enemy.[50]

By now Roosevelt was in Tehran, which lay south of the base of the Caspian Sea in Iran just beyond the Elbenz Mountains, a city chosen by Stalin, who thought it imperative he be able to maintain secure communication with his armed forces. When the conference, code named Eureka, ended, the three heads of state had agreed to Operation Overlord, a cross-Channel invasion of Europe in May 1944 in conjunction with an invasion of southern France and a Russian drive into Europe from the East. Stalin also formally agreed to enter the war against Japan once Germany was defeated. Again Early met with the reporters, a larger-than-usual gathering all crowded into his office, to release a statement, warning the reporters to heed the release date and time, the following day at 1:00 p.m., when it would be released simultaneously from Tehran by the reporters covering the conference. This time, apparently, all journalists—American and foreign—respected the embargo.[51]

Early told his son Buddy that he was sitting on the lid at the office, a situation that tied him to his desk. Otherwise, he would like to get away: "However, as you well know by now, duty is duty and the calls have to be accepted whether they are welcome or not." Early breathed a sigh of relief when Roosevelt finally returned safely to Washington in mid-December, having been out of the country for five weeks.[52]

While the *Iowa*, carrying the presidential party, was steaming its way back across the Atlantic, the White House inner circle suffered another loss, one that deeply saddened Steve Early. On the morning of December 13, Marvin Hunter McIntyre, Early and Roosevelt's close friend since their days at the Department of the Navy and one of the three original presidential secretaries, died. He had left the White House for the last time three weeks earlier, unable to continue working. Although his death did not come as a shock to his friends and colleagues, his loss was nonetheless sorely felt.

During his first six years at the White House until his health began to fail and Pa Watson took over the job, Mac, as he was affectionately called, served as the presidential appointments secretary, a powerful job, the buffer between the president and the public on matters of official business. When his health allowed, he returned to the White House to handle confidential matters for Roosevelt. He was considered by many in Washington to be one of the few people in the White House who would speak his mind frankly to the Boss, even though what he might have to say could be unpleasant. Mac's interest was politics, not policy, and, in fact, as a conservative Southerner, he seemed almost bemused by the policies of the New Deal. A quiet man with a good sense of humor, Mac displayed great tact as he managed to say no to hundreds of persons who wanted to see Roosevelt during the early days of the New Deal. During one crowded day, a White House telephone operator recalled five hundred incoming calls for him, many handed off to assistants. But Mac himself was known to talk with forty people on the telephone and sixty-one others in person, all before lunch. One of the many obituaries that ran in newspapers around the country said Mac could juggle telephone calls from government officials and interview important visitors, miraculously both at the same time. He was so soft-spoken that he could whisper into the telephone so that the person next to him could not catch a word of what he was saying. The day after Mac died, a somber Early and some of his and Mac's longtime political friends took the overnight train from Washington to Louisville, Kentucky, for the funeral and burial.[53]

On December 16 an exhausted Roosevelt returned to Washington amid rumors put out by the Nazi propaganda machine that his plane had made a forced landing in the Azores because of engine trouble. When reporters queried Early at his press conference the same day the president was en route to the capital, all he would say was, "Happily I can tell you now that he has returned and is safely back in the United States." He refused to allow the reporters to even mention the mode of presidential travel. Oddly, none of Roosevelt's biographers refer to this incident.[54]

Annoyed at the ruckus created by the premature release of news from the Cairo/Tehran conferences by the British and others, Roosevelt told reporters at his first press conference after his return that from then on, there would be no more "hold for release" stories. Early reiterated this policy at his own press conference the next day, explaining that he would get transmitted stories, say, from Cairo, that would be in code, which would be translated in Washington, and the news would be released at the same time it was being given out in Cairo and broadcast or published worldwide, rather than on a "hold-for-release" basis some hours later.

Roosevelt and Early primarily were worried about security. When he traveled during the war, Roosevelt—and Early, if he was along— was careful to orchestrate his meetings with the press or the release of statements with his schedule. For instance, if he were in a foreign city for a few days, nothing could be published while he was still there, only when he had moved on to another city or country. Roosevelt said that when he was in Tehran, Stalin had warned him of a plot against the president's life, so at Stalin's insistence the president moved from the American legation to more secure compound that included the

Russian embassy and the United Kingdom legation where Churchill was staying. Roosevelt told reporters there were "hundreds of German spies in Tehran." He said that at some places he visited, there were so many German planes that he realized it would be like "shooting a duck on the water" if they made him their target.[55]

At his December 17 press conference, Roosevelt said that "Dr. New Deal" was being replaced with "Dr. Win the War." In a scenario that he and Early had cooked up earlier, the president explained to the confused reporters that "Dr. New Deal" had treated the nation for "a grave internal disorder with specific remedies." After the "patient"—the country—recovered, he had "a very bad accident." He said, "on the seventh of December [Pearl Harbor], he was in a pretty bad smashup." So "Dr. New Deal," who knew nothing about legs and arms, called in his partner, "Dr. Win the War," who was an orthopedic surgeon to take over healing the patient.

It became even more confusing. One of the reporters asked him if this meant a fourth-term declaration. Roosevelt replied, "Oh, now, we are not talking about things like that now. You are getting picayune." The reporter said he didn't mean to be "picayune," but he was unclear about the parable. He wondered aloud whether this meant Roosevelt was abandoning the New Deal to Win the War, and then, when the war was won, he would once again focus on the social programs of the New Deal. Or did the president think that the patient was "cured." Not exactly, the president said. The New Deal programs had met the needs of the 1930s, and when the time came, new programs would be required. He refused to elaborate.[56]

Both Early and Roosevelt spent a quiet Christmas that year with their families. However, for the first time the president ordered that none of the gifts for the White House employees should be wrapped. Early told the reporters that Roosevelt decided that this gesture would save two or three barrels of paper that just got wasted. Instead, the presents would be handed out in the cardboard containers they came in. Oh yes, and he didn't want presents that came in for him to be wrapped either, Early said.[57]

On the evening of December 23, a Thursday, Roosevelt boarded the train for Hyde Park. On Christmas Eve he addressed the nation and the armed forces via radio from the cozy library at his home, announcing that Gen. Dwight D. Eisenhower would command the planned Anglo-American assault over the English Channel. No time frame was given, but he told his audience to expect heavy casualties when the invasion did take place.[58]

Early went home to celebrate Christmas with his family. His reprieve was short lived. The president left Hyde Park on the night of December 26 to return to an unusually cold Washington, and the next morning he and his press secretary were in their offices in the White House facing two deepening crises: The nation's railroad unions were threatening to strike, and the steel workers walked off their jobs on Christmas Day because their contracts had expired at midnight. On December 28 Roosevelt ordered Secretary of War Henry Stimson to take over the railroads, and later that day the steel strikers decided to return to work.[59]

The *New York Times* headlines tell the story. On December 24, 1943: "Roosevelt Moves to Take Over the Railroads as 3 Brotherhoods Reject Mediation by Him," and "War Steel Walkout Looms When Pact Expires Tonight." On December 26: "70,000 in 4 States Begin Steel Halt." On December 28: "Army Seizes Railroads on President's Order; Pay Raises to 2 Unions; Steel Men Ordered Back."

It was no wonder that by New Year's Day Roosevelt was in bed with another bout of flu, and Early was left to field questions from reporters eager for regular updates on the president's health, a story that would capture headlines throughout the remainder of the winter and well into the spring. While he continued to play the coy belle of the ball, an ailing Roosevelt secretly was looking toward a fourth term as chief executive. If Steve Early thought he was about to escape from his prison, it would not be a reality anytime soon.[60]

22

"THE GREAT WHITE JAIL"

A weary Early remained harnessed to his desk that winter and into the spring of 1944, while Roosevelt alternately worked late into the night in his office or in the map room to handle political crises, domestic upheavals, and war strategies, or struggled with a series of nagging winter colds and bronchial attacks. Even two week-long visits to his beloved home in Hyde Park did not entirely replenish the president's health, so in early April he took advantage of financier Bernard Baruch's hospitality and spent an off-the-record month at Baruch's plantation, Hobcaw Barony, on the South Carolina coast, leaving Early in what Truman called "the great white jail"—indeed, a bleak White House where he occasionally met the press and attempted to give them scraps of news, even though at times he appeared frustrated by what was less-than-adequate communication with the president. The frustration of that winter and spring, coupled with exhaustion, led him to repeatedly ask the Boss to allow him to resign. But Roosevelt did not want Early to leave because, according to Grace Tully, the president knew how difficult it would be to replace his press secretary, so, she said, he would conveniently forget to reopen any discussions of resignation.

But here was Steve Early, a man heading toward his midfifties with two more children to educate, who had spent the last eleven years working long hours in the most stress-filled job in the White House after that of the president himself. Now it was time to leave, and no doubt he had not felt this strongly since those months in 1936 when he desperately and unsuccessfully sought release from his job. What probably was causing a deepening of his frustration to get out was the suspicion that Roosevelt, his friend and boss for so many years, was planning to run for a fourth term. The Boss, as usual, was playing his cards close to the vest. In a letter to Jimmy Roosevelt, two years after the president's death, Early tried to explain what caused his father to seek a fourth term: "I would not hesitate to bet all the tea in China that he was prompted to run for a fourth term only because his country was at war. He felt, I am very certain, that he could render his greatest service to the nation by keeping the office he had held for the twelve long preceding years. And thank God he did! No one else, in my opinion, could have led this nation, from Pearl Harbor on—and before Pearl Harbor—as he did."[1]

Early went on:

> I think it should be borne in mind that your father concentrated on the war virtually to the complete exclusion of domestic political issues. These, he assigned to others. He put his mind on and gave his heart solely to the winning of the war. He is indeed in a soldier's grave. None can deny this. The reason for a fourth term more than any other consideration, including Dewey, was the war and the all-time suppression of his country's enemy. Had it not been for the war, I do not believe the President would have accepted a fourth-term nomination. With the war on his hands, however, he did the only thing he could—run again and give his all to the winning of the war.[2]

At the same time Early was fobbing off questions about Roosevelt's reelection plans, he was also attempting to minimize the president's winter illnesses to the reporters. One of them, Merriman Smith, the White House correspondent for the United Press, wrote that many people in and out of Washington were forecasting the imminent death of the president. "While the smart boys in 1944 insisted that Mr. Roosevelt was about to die, his doctors insisted he was all right," he said. Rumors were just that, but nonetheless the question that must have preyed on the minds of those who were close to the president was whether his health would indeed allow him to seek that fourth term.[3]

It took the president almost a week to get out of bed after the flu struck him at the end of December, remaining either in his bed or in his study adjoining the bedroom. According to Early, Roosevelt lost ten pounds, and even by mid-January he was "not up to par." Early told reporters, "He has good days and bad days." It's no wonder the rumors were rampant, and they expanded further when, because of the lingering effects of his flu, for the first time Roosevelt chose not to read his annual State of the Union message to Congress in person. (Earlier presidents had chosen to send them to Congress.) A week before he was to speak to Congress, reporters were pestering Early about rumors of Roosevelt's decision not to go to the Capitol. Would he or wouldn't he? they wanted to know. Early had no answer for them. So he waffled: "That takes a lot of strength out of a fellow, but if the progress is such, it will depend." At that same time, Early wrote to Joe Davies, telling him he did not think Roosevelt would have the stamina to make a personal appearance: " [S]tanding and speaking for a half hour or more, I feel would be too much of a physical strain, coming so soon after the flu."[4]

When the day arrived, Roosevelt was still not up to par, so clerks at the Capitol read the message to the jointly assembled members of Congress, and that night from the White House the president gave a half-hour radio address to the nation on the gist of the message, a clever ploy that not only got his thoughts out to a far wider audience than the members of Congress and reporters but allowed the citizens to hear him speak, for the time at least allaying rumors of an ailing chief executive. There is no record of whose idea it was to have Roosevelt take to the airwaves, but it bears Early's imprint.[5]

When Roosevelt finally held his first press conference of 1944, in the late afternoon of Tuesday, January 18, it was shorter than usual, and he engaged in a minimum of bantering with the reporters. Apparently this meeting was the result of a compromise worked out between the Boss and the press secretary. When he was in the White House, Roosevelt normally met with reporters on Tuesday mornings and Friday afternoons, but this week he said he anticipated a lot of appointments on Friday. Early reminded him he had yet to meet the press in 1944. So Roosevelt told him, "Well, I will make a deal with you. If I hold one Tuesday, I have got a busy day Friday, will you let me off Friday?" Early said he told him, "Yes, unless there is a good story." There wasn't any.

Was the president really too busy to meet with reporters that Friday—he did have a full schedule—or did he not want to deal with questions about his health, his reelection plans, and the state of the war? Or was he conserving what energy he had for a trip to Hyde Park? Early told reporters at his own press conference that morning that "OFF THE RECORD you fellows know that the President is leaving today, do you, for his home, and will probably go up there and rest for about a week. That is another reason for no press conference today." It would be "for a rest, and no appointments and no news, or anything else there." Although the press and radio continued to be careful to follow censorship regulations on publishing or broadcasting presidential travels, reporters are notorious gossips, and it would take only a casual slip of the tongue inside the newsroom or even outside to fuel the rumors about his health.[6]

While Roosevelt was resting at Hyde Park, Early stuck his foot in his mouth at one of his own press conferences, but with his usual finesse—and the goodwill of the reporters—he extricated it. Doug Cornell of the Associated Press asked whether or not the United States government had changed its policy and now was releasing stories about atrocities against American soldiers. "Well, I will tell you about it, but let me think for a minute whether I should talk for publication or not. Well, in any event, I will talk, and then we will discuss whether it is for publication or not." Remarkable. Once again, Early was planning to give the press a story and then when he finished he would decide whether or not they could go ahead and publish or broadcast it, something no self-respecting journalist today would allow a politician or his or her aide to get away with—especially not someone in the White House. In the end, he told them that half of the information was "IN CONFIDENCE to you." He added, "I think that is the best way to handle it." The reporters thanked him, saying he had been "very helpful."[7]

What prompted Cornell's question was a headline that morning in the *New York Times* that had run across the top of page one: "5,200 Americans, Many More Filipinos Die of Starvation, Torture After Bataan; Starvation by Japs." In the spring of 1942, when the Japanese made a final push to take over the Bataan Peninsula in the Philippines, about thirty-five thousand American and Filipino troops fell to the Japanese, resulting in the what became known as the "Forced Bataan Death March" from Balanga to San Fernando. It was not until almost two years later that the American public learned of the extent of the horrors of the forced march when the US military decided to release a report on the atrocities.

The government decided to release the report on the atrocities, Early explained, because of the publication—and subsequent syndication in twenty or more newspapers around the country—of a book written by one of the escaped prisoners of war, Lt. Col. William K. Dyess. As long as Dyess was a member of the military, the army forbade him to publish anything about the atrocities and a mercy ship. The *Gripsholm*, with a Swedish crew, was chartered to the US State Department during the war and was used as to get supplies to prisoners of war and as an exchange and repatriation ship. Early said that one of those prisoners was Dyess who first made a report to the government and then wrote a book about the atrocities and the role of the *Gripsholm*, but as long as the ship was on mercy runs the government wanted nothing published about any of it. Then Dyess was killed in a plane accident, so the Joint Chiefs of Staff, after consulation with the British military, decided the story could be told and approved the release of the book.[8]

Early said the decision came after factual reports "had been carefully investigated, authenticated, no hearsay evidence contained in any of them, because we cannot expect to get further relief to our prisoners of war in the hands of the Japanese. I think that's the answer I will give you for publication. I don't mind you fellows knowing personally the whole story as I have given it to you, but for publication purpose I think that's the answer." Then he backtracked. "Does this mean the United States has abandoned hope of getting any more Americans back from the Japanese?" a reporter asked. "We haven't abandoned hope at all, but the ways of getting those fellows out are secret, as you well realize." He added that he was referring to prisoners escaping; exchange arrangements were being handled by the State Department.[9]

Although Early told his press conference on January 28 that nice weather might keep the president in Hyde Park over his birthday the following day, Roosevelt returned to the White House the next morning in time to celebrate his sixty-second birthday with the Cuff Links Gang, now minus Louis Howe, Marvin McIntyre, and Missy LeHand, who was still incapacitated at her home in Massachusetts. About twenty-five guests, including the remaining gang members, along with Pa Watson, Dr. McIntire, and Eleanor, as well as Crown Prince Olaf and Crown Princess Martha of Norway, who were in exile in the United States for most of the war, had an intimate dinner at the White House. As it had been in past years, Roosevelt's birthday was celebrated around Washington, with parties at six hotels to raise money for the National Foundation for Infantile Paralysis.[10]

By the time he held a press conference after he returned from Hyde Park, Roosevelt appeared more relaxed than before his vacation. He joked with reporters, telling them he had been "under the knife" recently at the Naval Hospital in Bethesda, Maryland, for the removal of a wen, or small growth, on the back of his head. It was done under a local anesthetic and he was there for about a half hour, he said. When asked about the surgery, he replied, "Sure, I was under the knife. I am under the knife whenever I cut my fingernails. But actually, I don't know why I should talk about this, it's merely—it might be called—a preventive—that is very often necessary, to use a preventable. I had a pain for—I don't know what?—twenty years or less." Continuing in a light vein, a reporter said, "Did those—Mr. President, did those Naval 'gims'[11] permit you to smoke while they did their hacking?" By then everyone was laughing, and Roosevelt quipped, "No, but I yelled for a cigarette right after it."[12]

The following day, neither Roosevelt nor Early was laughing. Fifteen editors and publishers from the Negro Newspaper Publishers Association had requested a meeting with the president on that Saturday morning. He agreed, somewhat reluctantly. Roughly an hour before they held an off-the-record press conference with Roosevelt, Steve Early had his own morning press conference with the White House press corps—which included no Negroes—and they seemed amused that the president would be meeting with the Negro editors and publishers. Early, no doubt recalling his run-in with the Negro policeman in 1940, was taking the president's meeting seriously, at least publicly. He told his press conference, "They contend they are the opposite numbers of the American Society of Newspaper Editors." The reporters laughed. Early then reminded them that Roosevelt met every year with the American Society of Newspaper Editors, all white, of course. Early called this meeting with the Negro journalists "one hundred percent parity treatment." Then he said, "Now don't go quoting me on this." Again the reporters laughed. He pleaded, "Don't do it now, will you?"[13]

When they met with Roosevelt later that morning, the Negro editors and publishers came armed with a list of grievances, many of which the president managed to sidestep. With Early at his side, Roosevelt seemed almost cheerful as he listened to John Sengstacke, publisher of the *Chicago Defender*, one of the most influential Negro newspapers in the country, read a statement. Mostly they focused on discrimination in jobs, schools, voting, and the armed forces. They pleaded, "This is our country, our native land." They wanted to fight for freedom overseas, to help win the war. But they wanted equality of opportunity. They were "second-class citizens," they said, and reminded the president that this status "violates the Declaration of Independence and the Constitution."

When Sengstacke finished reading, Roosevelt looked at the group and said, "Awfully good statement." But when they asked him if they could come in once a year for an off-the-record meeting, as the American Society of Newspaper Editors did, and suggested the following January 22, 1945, the president was noncommittal. "I'll probably be down in Georgia then," he replied, referring to his home at Warm Springs.

But the Negro journalists were not ready to be dismissed. They presented Roosevelt with what they termed "a pressing question, a grievous and vexing one." When they came home on leave, Negro members of the military were subjected to intimidation by civilian police. "They [the soldiers] think you alone can correct that." The president agreed: "We have got some things to be ashamed of." He thanked the men and as they prepared to leave his office, he told them to arrange with Steve for their next press conference, "maybe in the summer or the fall for the whole association." There is no record of any such meeting between the Negro journalists and Roosevelt.[14]

Two weeks later, to avoid the fallout from what one newspaper termed "the supreme political crisis of his [Roosevelt's] 12 years in the White House," Early and Roosevelt simply chose to avoid the press and go underground. They canceled their press conferences, the president scurried to his home in Hyde Park for a week, and Early hunkered down in his office until the tempest subsided.[15]

It all began with a wartime tax bill recommended by the president that would have raised what then was then the staggering sum of $10.5 billion in new revenue. But the House of Representatives, where tax bills originate, balked, and when the bill was finally passed by the Senate the figure had been reduced to $2.3 billion, far less than Roosevelt had requested. So he decided to veto it. He had his friend former Justice James Byrnes, now head of the Office of War Mobilization, draft what some considered a bitter message that was read to both the House and Senate in which Byrnes called the congressional bill "not a tax bill but a relief bill, providing relief not for the needy, but for the greedy," a phrase that created a political maelstrom leading to the resignation of Sen. Alben Barkley, the Senate majority leader for the last seven years and a longtime supporter of Roosevelt's policies.[16]

Barkley, who later served as Truman's vice president, gave a long speech on the floor of the Senate, analyzing the president's veto points one by one and concluding with his decision to resign the following morning as majority leader. In his autobiography Barkley said it was a decision that left "no joy in my heart." It came down, he said, to a matter of "self-respect." In his biography of Roosevelt, Frank Friedel explains that Barkley was one of several conservative southern Democrats aspiring to the vice presidency, and if Barkley did not back Roosevelt's revenue plan, he probably would forfeit this ambition. If Barkley supported the tax measure, he might have difficulty winning reelection to the Senate in his home state of Kentucky. Barkley chose to fight Roosevelt.[17]

The same day that Senator Barkley was ripping apart the president's tax veto and announcing his intention to resign as Senate leader, Roosevelt arrived in Hyde Park. He was working in his study at his house when he learned of Barkley's speech. His only comment was, "Alben must be suffering from shell shock," as he continued to examine some of his old papers at his desk. Later, with no hint of anger, he said, "It doesn't make sense." But Roosevelt was concerned enough, perhaps about avoiding a split in the Democratic Party with the election on the horizon, to send a long telegram to Barkley via Early, who was at the White House. The president asked his secretary to take the telegram to Barkley's house that evening. He told Early, a longtime personal friend of Barkley's, to ask the senator if Early could release the message from the White House, which he did.

In effect Roosevelt was apologizing to the senator for attacking his integrity and that of the other members of Congress: "Such you must know was not my intention." He pleaded with Barkley to change his mind and return to his post as majority leader, saying, "Certainly, your differing with me does not affect my confidence in your leadership." Barkley said he read the telegram carefully in Early's presence and then the two men quietly discussed the situation for a while, with Early attempting to persuade Barkley to reconsider. The following day, six reporters from the Washington press corps descended, uninvited, on their usual haunt—the Nelson House in Poughkeepsie—demanding that Bill Hassett, who had accompanied Roosevelt to Hyde Park, relay something—anything—from the lips of the president regarding the situation in Washington. But neither FDR nor Hassett would say anything. Hassett reminded them of the wartime censorship code prohibiting him or the president from speaking on the record there, lest their whereabouts become public information, a flimsy excuse, since when it suited his purposes Roosevelt had allowed reporters to quote him when he traveled. But this time it kept the press at bay.[18]

The same day the reporters were busy scratching for information in Poughkeepsie, Barkley agreed to be reelected majority leader, and the House overrode Roosevelt's tax veto; the Senate followed suit the next day, with Barkley joining the majority vote.[19]

The day of Barkley's reelection, Early finally held a press conference in which he explained to the reporters just how the tax bill would affect the president. It seems Roosevelt was cultivating trees at his Hyde Park home and selling some of the oldest and largest for timber for shipbuilding. Some were trees he had known since his childhood, Early said: "He knows them by their first names—on speaking terms with all of them. Don't think he doesn't know his trees up there. He does." In trying to justify the original tax bill, the one Roosevelt proposed, Early said if it had passed, it would have cost him $3,000 a year. Now that his veto had been overridden, it would save him the same amount on taxes, Early said. In other words, he was criticizing the congressional bill for helping the rich, and since they overrode his veto, that bill in effect helped the rich, which included Roosevelt himself.[20]

The next day Early was on the reporters' case about their careless reporting on Roosevelt in Hyde Park that week. The *New York Times* dateline on the story said "With the President," and the story noted that Roosevelt was there because of his health. The *Washington Star* also told readers that the president was out of town "to shake off a recent bout with the flu." Probably Roosevelt had called Early to complain about the onslaught of reporters while he was supposed to be relaxing away from the White House. So an irritated Early barked at the reporters at his press conference, saying "He [the reporter] is not with him. They are miles apart, so to begin with the dateline is erroneous." The *New York Times* reporter was in fact in Poughkeepsie, about eight miles from Hyde Park. And the reporters deserved no "great credit" for going near the president: "They were told in confidence by this office where the President was. They knew, therefore, where to go. They were also told that if the President had any news whatever to give out, it would be given out by this office here in Washington and not by those of the staff who accompanied him." Early went on to remind them that the reporters had gone to Poughkeepsie on their own with the knowledge that no news would be given out there. "Let's not forget that this is war-time and that there are questions of security involved," he said. The *Times* story also had claimed the president "was incommunicado" during the Barkley crisis, a statement that angered Early: "The President is in instantaneous and immediate communication with the White House."

So, what about the president's health? they again asked. "The state of the President's health is as it was when he left here—only for a rest. You saw him at 4:00 o'clock Tuesday afternoon, didn't you? A hundred and fifty or more correspondents saw him at 4:00 o'clock Tuesday afternoon. He left that evening—a couple or so hours later. He is quite all right." Merriman Smith, the White House reporter for the United Press wire service, later wrote that these "off-the-record trips to Hyde Park were perfect rumor breeders, because we [reporters] were rarely allowed to file anything, even after returning to Washington." He concluded that the president did not want anyone outside his official family to know how much time he spent at his family home.[21]

The next day, Saturday, Early again met with the reporters, and, after a night's sleep, his temper seemed under control as he gave them what he called "a good story" on a shortage of trained military per-

sonnel, leading the government to review all occupational defer-
ments, with the goal of making more men available to serve in the
armed forces.[22]

If anyone in Washington needed a ray of sunshine in his life that
winter, it was Steve Early, and it started with an editorial in a small
Southern newspaper and ended with a chuckle at a presidential press
conference.

Some of those close to Roosevelt—including Early, Pa Watson,
and Hopkins—were advising him to dump Vice President Henry Wallace, the somewhat eccentric plant geneticist turned liberal politician
from Iowa, despite the fact he was one of the most popular Democrats
in the country. Considering the president had yet to announce his own
reelection plans, the speculation among those in the White House as
well as many in the media was that he would be seeking a fourth term,
so early in 1944, pundits had any number of suggestions should Roosevelt decide to replace Wallace on the ticket at the Democratic
National Convention the following July. An Associated Press poll of
members of the Democratic National Committee that winter put
Speaker of the House Sam Rayburn, with eighteen votes, at the top of
list of potential vice presidential candidates, followed by Wallace with
fourteen, and then trailing were James Farley and James Byrnes,
leaving twenty-four members who said they had no preference. Senator Harry Truman's name was barely on the radar. Interestingly,
though, some weeks after these poll results appeared, Steve Early's
name came up, if only for a flicker—a kind of brief but funny hiccup.[23]

It seems that Quimbey Melton, the editor of the *Griffin Daily
News* in Georgia and the chair of the Spaulding County Democratic
Executive Committee, decided that the perfect candidate for vice
president of the United States was Early, and he cited four reasons:
Early had been so closely associated with the Roosevelt administration that he knew the program "inside and out," and should anything
happen to the president during his fourth term, Early would be the
right person to carry on the Roosevelt policies. Second—and this
could only come from a Southerner—Early was a descendant (of
sorts) of Confederate general Jubal Early, so he would be acceptable
to the South, "the backbone of the Democratic party." Third, as a veteran of World War I, the press secretary would garner the veterans'
vote. And the final reason, one that some readers might argue with,

was that since Early was a trained newspaperman, he knew the sentiment of the general public.

Newspapers around the country picked up the Melton story and ran with it. The upshot was that Early came in for a lot of ribbing, in particular from Merriman Smith, a bit of a prankster at heart. He promptly appointed himself the "candidate's" manager and, looking for campaign funds, sought out Early's wealthy friend and former ambassador Joe Davies, who was spending the winter with his wealthy wife, Marjorie Meriweather Post, at their estate in Palm Beach. Smith appealed to Davies with a humorous letter:

> The attached clipping [Melton's editorial] should explain why you have been brought into the most burning cause since the Chicago fire.
> The friends of Mr. Early (known hereafter as the Candidate) have emerged from their smoke-filled room long enough to announce your appointment as Chairman of the Candidate's Finance Committee. This was done with his enthusiastic approval and it is, in my capacity as Campaign Manager, that I call upon you to put your able shoulder to the Early wheel lest it gather moss.

Then he listed the "expenses incurred to date": "One hat (thrown in ring), $15. Fee paid two slogan writers who, in less than two hours, came up with 'NO HURLY-BURLY WITH URLY,' and 'THE EARLY WORM SHOULD GET THE BIRD,' $200. Flowers for the Wallace family, $25. Incidentials (explanation furnished only on urgent request), $1,815. We also need money to smother the spreading rumor that the Candidate is a descendant of Gen. Jubal Early, who was a bachelor." Smith added, "2% discount for cash."

Smith even urged Harry Hopkins, who had been ill since the beginning of the year and now was at the Mayo Clinic in Minnesota, to "get on the band wagon." Hopkins declared his "spontaneous support" for Early's candidacy and sent a one-dollar bill, which today is taped in Early's scrapbook for 1944 at the FDR Library in Hyde Park. Keeping in mind Early's penchant for the horses, Hopkins suggested organizing a "Two Dollar Window Group for Early." He had another suggestion for the candidate: "I think the Bible Belt out here would appreciate you more if you would let up a little on the liquor, but even so and nevertheless, you can count on my hearty support."

At Early's press conference on April 4, the reporters were still ribbing him about his "candidacy." Would he care to make a campaign speech? they asked. To much laughter, he declined. Where did he plan to officially begin his campaign? Someone suggested April 13, the opening day at Pimlico, the racetrack in Baltimore. Or maybe at opening day of the Senators baseball team, which would be April 20.

The "candidacy" was dying out a couple of weeks later when a reporter at Roosevelt's press conference, to much laughter, said, "Mr. President, Georgia has come out for Steve Early for Vice President." The president responded, "I saw that. Is he a citizen?" This provoked more laughter. Roosevelt continued, "I know that he's a citizen of somewhere down in the hills back of Charlottesville, but that was before the Civil War and whether he ever got reinstated or not, I don't think so. There isn't anything to show." The reporters were still laughing when Early chimed in, "Paid no taxes to be." The irony was that, as a resident of the District of Columbia, Early could not vote in presidential elections.[24]

What really was on the reporters' minds that spring was the status of a campaign for a fourth term, and indirectly—and sometimes not so indirectly—the state of the president's health. David Brinkley, a young reporter in Washington at that time, wrote that throughout the spring and into the summer, Roosevelt refused to acknowledge whether he would run again. The reporters inquired; the president demurred. Once, when asked about his intentions, he called it "boudoir questions" and said he did not reply to those at his press conferences. Apparently Early found the whole exchange so funny, he had to turn his face to the wall.[25]

But Early was not laughing as reporters continued to bombard him with questions about Roosevelt's health. Most of the time the best he could tell them was that the president was "improving" or "resting" or "doing better," hardly replies to inspire confidence in a nation looking to elect a president in a few months. For instance, on March 14 Early told reporters that the president had awakened that morning with "a stiff neck—a cramped muscle"—a seemingly minor problem—but on March 17 Roosevelt canceled his regular press conference. The reason, according to Early: "The President was up pretty late last night." What was he doing? Early was evasive. It could have been a private social event, or it could have been health related. He wouldn't say.

The reporters were left to speculate. Then, on March 21, Early said Roosevelt was under the weather with a head cold, "sneezing through the night and not resting too well." On March 29 the *Washington Post* reported that Roosevelt had had bronchitis for the last three weeks, resulting in a trip to the Naval Hospital for X-rays. The president had briefly mentioned on his health at his press conference the previous day, saying he had "a touch of bronchitis."[26]

What had happened at the Naval Hospital was that a young navy doctor, Lt. Cdr. Howard G. Bruenn, who was a cardiologist, was called on to examine the president, and it did not take him long to conclude he was a very sick man, "in desperately poor health," with gallstones, a badly enlarged heart, hypertension, hypertensive heart disease, and cardiac failure. But none of that was released to the public. Early never paraded Bruenn before reporters to talk about his findings. In fact, "Roosevelt himself seemed unconcerned."[27]

Finally, at his press conference on April 4, undoubtedly with the presidential seal of approval, Early brought in Dr. Ross T. McIntire, physician to the president for the last twelve years, to give reporters the results of Roosevelt's recent checkup and to assure them—and the country—that the occupant of the White House was indeed healthy enough to lead the country for another four years. Vice Admiral McIntire, surgeon general of the navy, was an ear, nose, and throat specialist about whom Early once said, "Frankly, Ross [McIntire] may not be the world's greatest physician. I do believe he is one of the best administrators." Not unlike Woodrow Wilson's personal physician, Adm. Cary Grayson, who protected the status of Wilson's health from the public after his stroke, here were Early and McIntire doing their best to put a positive spin on an ailing president.

This is what McIntire told the press that April day: Roosevelt's checkup had been "satisfactory," although his recent bout with bronchitis and his busy schedule have not been able "to provide him with enough exercise and sunshine." He concluded with "for a man of 62-plus that we have very little to argue about." His recommendation? A "well-balanced diet" for the president. "We weighed him ten days ago, and he weighed 187-and-a-fraction. But we have put him on a pretty good regime now, and we have decreased his food just a little, so he weighed 184-and-a-half day before yesterday." No mention was made of Bruenn's findings or that the doctors at the Naval Hospital had insisted that Roosevelt immediately begin a program that included digitalis for his heart, less activity, fewer cigarettes every day, ten hours of sleep, rest after meals, a diet low in fats, and mild laxatives to avoid straining.[28]

The journalists' responses to this anemic report were equally anemic. How much swimming is he doing? Can't you make him get more sunshine? No questions about his heart, his blood pressure, or anything else related to the health of a man who had been in a wheelchair for the last three decades and who everyone was assuming would run for reelection. Brinkley called McIntire "more courier than doctor," who "was misleading both the public and the president about the true condition of his patient." Merriman Smith was kinder in his assessment of McIntire: "He was torn between political considerations and his reputation as a physician. To his credit, McIntire never lied about Mr. Roosevelt's condition. He told the truth, but in language that could easily be misleading." But neither Early nor McIntire ever publicly mentioned Bruenn and his findings.[29]

How all of this personally affected Roosevelt's longtime friend and press secretary, one can only speculate, but it could not have come as a complete surprise. You don't know someone intimately for nearly twenty-five years, half that time working next to him daily, and not realize that his health is deteriorating. Grace Tully, Roosevelt's longtime secretary, noticed the changes: "cumulative weariness, the dark circles that never quite faded from under his eyes, the more pronounced shake in his hand as he lit his cigarette, the easy slump that developed in his shoulders as he sat at a desk that was always covered with his work." But she attributed them to the strain of twelve years of the presidency. If Tully saw the changes, then so did Steve Early. Neither wanted to acknowledge that the Boss was dying.[30]

How much of Bruenn's diagnosis was Early privy to? The press secretary stopped keeping a diary just before the war, and he never addressed the events at this time, either in interviews or in letters. McIntire was part of the team of doctors at the Naval Hospital that determined the course of treatment for the president, and he was a part of the White House inner circle, so it is more than likely that he let Early in on the findings. Now this left Early in a quandary. He had always prided himself, as an old reporter, on being up front with the White House press corps, even if it meant giving them details of an event or issue "off the record." But this was different. His boss and friend was obviously very ill, and at the same time was considering a run for reelection. Sharing this kind of information with the press, even in "strictest confidence," was simply more than Steve Early could bring himself to consider.

Early's chief concern always was to ensure the best possible publicity for the president of the United States, and whether in the late spring of 1944 Roosevelt was aware of the intensity of rumors about his ability to carry on for another four years, Early certainly was—and he saw a way to quell some of them.

Quite possibly Early used his friendship with Bernard Baruch to wrangle an invitation for Roosevelt (Eleanor did not accompany him) to spend a month at Baruch's Hobcaw Barony estate in South Carolina, away from the White House fishbowl and the prying press. The president, accompanied by Dr. McIntire, Pa Watson, and two other military aides, left Washington via train on April 9. Surprisingly, he allowed a representative of each of the three wire services to join the party, a move that Merriman Smith attributes to Early's persuasive powers, because Smith said Early was "well aware of the spreading rumors about the president's health." Smith said Early thought that the presence of the wire service reporters in South Carolina would show that the president was healthy enough to travel. However, censorship rules forbade the three reporters from publishing stories on the trip until Roosevelt was back in Washington.[31]

The decision, however, did not sit well with five White House correspondents for the country's largest newspapers, including the *New York Times*, the *New York Herald-Tribune*, and the *Washington Star*. They sent Early a letter signed by all five of them saying their employers asked them to "urgently request" in the event of the president's departure from Washington that they be informed of his whereabouts so they could "stay within reachable distance of him." They claimed they were motivated to send the letter for several reasons. The president's health had not been good in recent months, this was a presidential election year, and it was probably the decisive year in the European war. "If the newspapers are to fulfill their responsibilities to the public, they must do everything possible to cover the President fully at all times, wherever he may be." Their pleas went unheeded.[32]

In fact, for the first time since Pearl Harbor, on the morning after

Roosevelt left Washington, Early was quite open with the reporters at his press conference about the presidential vacation. He did not go so far as to say exactly where the president had gone, but "on the record" he said it was "in the South," and he would be gone at least two weeks and would "devote himself exclusively to relaxation out-of-doors, in fresh air and sunshine."

Then he went "off," to give them a few more details about the president's plans, assuring them Roosevelt would hold no press conferences or "participate in any activity that would under the remotest stretch of the imagination be called news. All of the work he does will be held to a minimum, in order to help him get the most of his time away, and the more rest for him. Any [news about the] work that he does, will be given to you here, and not to the three [reporters] with him."[33]

Hobcaw Barony was twenty-three thousand acres at the edge of Georgetown, South Carolina, between the Atlantic Ocean and Winyah Bay in flat, easygoing plantation country filled with pine, cypress, and moss-hung live oak trees. It was as quiet and secluded a place as an ailing president of the United States could hope for. Baruch had purchased the plantation in 1905, but his graceful red brick Georgian-style house was only a dozen years old. All eight bedrooms had fireplaces, including Roosevelt's, which was on the first floor, making it easy for his wheelchair to navigate the sprawling home. Merriman Smith later reported that, unlike on a previous visit, Roosevelt avoided deep-sea fishing and instead was content to catch catfish off a dock, a humble pastime he once would have scorned.

Smith decided that after a winter of nagging colds and flu, Roosevelt had gone off by himself to "decide whether he could gather enough strength for a fourth-term election campaign." When he arrived at Hobcaw, Smith said, the president "looked ghastly and listless." But the old sailor "perked up" at the smell of the salt air blowing in from the marshes and the bay. Apparently Roosevelt was taking his health seriously, because the following fall he told reporters that before he left for Hobcaw he was smoking two packs of cigarettes a day, and by the time he returned to Washington he was down to less than one pack. The only interruption in his tranquility was word from Washington that Frank Knox, secretary of the navy, had died. Roosevelt did not attend the funeral on May 1, because, as the *New York Times* reported, he "was away in the South for his health." When he returned to Washington a week later, he looked relaxed and tanned, and McIntire told the press, "We gained everything we expected from a four-week rest and I am perfectly satisfied with his physical condition." A more impartial witness, Merriman Smith, decided that the president was "well-tanned but the color was muddy. You could see that he had been in the sun, but the results did not look particularly healthy." His spirits, however, were good.[34]

While Roosevelt was resting and pondering his future in the sea air at Hobcaw, Early managed to escape the "great white jail" for a week of golf with his cronies at Pinehurst, North Carolina. Then it was back to work to face the usual hungry wolves of the press pack—and more questions about Roosevelt's health. On May 10 they asked Early why the president seemed to have no lunch visitors anymore. He told them the doctors didn't want him to: "He is taking it a little easy." As for a fourth term, Roosevelt managed to sidestep all questions at his first press conference after his return from South Carolina. That weekend he and his daughter Anna left for a few days of rest at Shangri-la, but not before he had a nap in the White House and signed some papers. Less than a week later, he was headed to Hyde Park, where he remained for six days, with time to look over the blossoming dogwoods, leisurely read the mail and documents sent up from Washington, and sign papers.[35]

In late May Roosevelt returned to the Naval Hospital for a checkup, and Early asked the reporters not to publish this, cloaking his request this way: "because it would be an announcement of travel." In fact, during the latter part of May, Early's press conferences focused more on jocular banter with the reporters and minor announcements than on subjects of much substance. Horse racing and Early's losing bets consumed more than half of his May 15 meeting with the reporters. On May 26 he and the press men and women joked at length about working conditions, which was an Early ploy to evade answering their questions about either the president's health or rumors he might go to London to meet with de Gaulle and Churchill. The most banal and obvious attempt came on May 31, when Early said he had dug up a letter that he thought might make a good human interest story from someone in Murfreesboro, Tennessee, who said he had heard or read all the speeches made by Roosevelt, Churchill, and "all the foremost speakers, as well as radio and newspaper commentators and writers." Based on all the words used to cover the war, he had come up with those used most often as possible names for the war. The president's favorite was "Tyrants' War." The writer used no first name, only two initials, so Early did not know if the letter came from a man or a woman. It had no street address, and he would not give out the date "because as a matter of fact it's a little old, and it has been here for quite a little while."[36]

What Early also was avoiding during this period was discussion of the progress of the war, and it was because the Allies were making final preparations for the invasion of Normandy, the long-planned and oft-delayed Operation Overlord, which was supposed to begin on June 5 but was postponed for a day by bad weather.[37]

On Tuesday, June 6, as the invasion was getting underway, Early held his press conference an hour earlier than usual, because, he told the reporters, "I know that you are anxious to get anything in the way of news on the invasion." He said the president "had known for some time what the world knows about—the invasion." Roosevelt had begun to receive detailed reports about 11:30 the previous night, so he knew when the first barges started to cross the channel and when they landed. Early said he and Roosevelt were up most of the night, with the president telephoning and receiving calls from the Pentagon. It had been a busy night for both men, because earlier in the evening the president broadcast to the nation news of the Allies' capture of Rome.

As soon as he concluded this press conference, Early said, he planned to ask the radio networks to clear airtime at 10:00 that night for the president to broadcast a prayer, which Roosevelt had written in his room right after he concluded his talk on Rome. But the reporters really wanted to know if the president had gotten any sleep? Yes. For how long? Several hours. Was he up early today? Yes. Unusually early? Yes.

"Now, the fact that the White House was blacked out and you didn't see any lights or signs of activity out here last night meant nothing. The White House didn't black out—we had shades on the windows for a long time, and they were used," Early said, adding, "I've given you as near as I can what went on behind the drawn shades."[38]

Roosevelt held his own press conference later that day, his black Scottie, Fala, in tow, and garnered a record turnout. Despite little sleep the night before, he appeared in fine fettle. He began by asking Early, "Got anything for me?" His press secretary said, "Several suggestions, Mr. President." The reporters laughed when Roosevelt said, "He's always full of suggestions, and he always gets turned down. Doesn't make any difference." In an attempt to appear beleaguered, Early said, "I'm used to it."[39]

The following day, Early brought in McIntire to give the reporters another update on Roosevelt's checkup at the Naval Hospital in late May. Early had actually intended to bring the doctor to his morning press conference, but he said it slipped his mind, so he held a special conference that afternoon. McIntire's report was doublespeak at its finest, and when translated it was that if Roosevelt were not president, and if he spent the rest of his life relaxing, his health probably would improve, or at least not deteriorate. As for the results of his most recent checkup, McIntire said, "I am glad to tell you that everything checked in splendid fashion. In fact, we are well within our normal limits in all respects. That, of course, is a great satisfaction to us all."

What does that mean? one reporter asked. McIntire reiterated, "All of the physical checks are well within normal limits." But what does that mean, sir? another reporter asked, to the amusement of his colleagues. Early fielded this one: "Nothing abnormal."

The reporters remained skeptical, so McIntire continued, "When I say they were within normal limits, we have certain standards, standards that we go by in all of our physical examinations or laboratory examinations or whatnot, and we say that we have limitations for a man who is 20, 30, 40, 50, 60 and so forth; and so I can give you a good report on everything."

Still the reporters weren't satisfied: "Considering his health and general condition?"

"No, not considering his health."

"His age?"

"Yes, for a man of his age."

"A very good report?"

"Excellent, in fact."

The reporters were not about to give up. They tried every which way to get McIntire to state on record that Roosevelt was ailing or at least not in the peak of health. Back and forth they went. Finally one reporter said, "He is in better physical shape than the average man of his age?" McIntire clarified: "Better physical *condition*." The reporter said, "No qualifications?" The doctor replied, "I have no qualifications on that."

The press conference continued with Early aiding and abetting McIntire, making positive statements about the president's health, thus giving the doctor another opportunity to reassure the reporters. One asked, "When you speak about the routine that you have him on now, you are speaking now about reducing the amount of work he is doing?" McIntire replied, "The regularity. That's right—get out, keep away from the daily grind." Early cut in, "Weekends." McIntire said, "You have hit it exactly. That is exactly the thing. Cut down the working hours."

Back and forth they went: McIntire emphasizing Roosevelt's good health, the reporters suspicious. It was, quite simply, complete bull, and the reporters alternately tried playing along and nailing McIntire on semantics. Then he further confused the reporters by going on the record, then going off.

They asked him if the rumor that the president was having "a bit of trouble with his heart" was true. McIntire denied it: "No. I have been very factual with you. I have given the exact—" Early broke in, "I don't think it's a good thing to start denying rumors." He added, "If you do, you just revive them."

McIntire again reassured the reporters that he had given them "the straight dope right through. I haven't varied at all." He said, "The only thing I have not given you are the specific reports on the test of the red corpuscles." A reporter interrupted, "Which we wouldn't want anyway." McIntire answered him, "That's something I have never done, and it would be a very foolish thing to do."

The press conference ended with some joking about Pa Watson's mint juleps, which he claimed were made with eighteen-year-old bourbon, when in fact, Early said, if you went into the kitchen, you would discover he was using four-year old rye. The story provided some humorous fodder for gossip columnists, but on the whole the meeting that day had been a travesty. The doctor knew it. The press secretary knew it. The reporters knew it. Sadly, the reporters did not inform their readers of the travesty. Instead the news of the Normandy invasion took top billing in the media, and in the *New York Times*, for instance, the McIntire-Early press conference was on page 7. By holding the announcement from McIntire until after the invasion, Early well knew the story would be buried, a shrewd public relations move.[40]

The rumors continued. On July 5 the reporters asked Early whether the president was about to undergo another checkup at the Naval Hospital. "Never heard the question," Early replied, and that was the end of that. The truth was that if Roosevelt did have another checkup, it was a precaution before he undertook a several-day meeting with French general Charles de Gaulle in Washington and then set out for a monthlong trip to the West Coast, ostensibly another of his wartime inspections but in reality a campaign jaunt.[41]

First, however, Roosevelt needed all his energy to meet with the difficult Frenchman, a man who was, he told his aide Bill Hassett, "a nut." Although de Gaulle was an important ally, the two men had a continuing difficult relationship, going back to their "awkward encounter" at Casablanca. When de Gaulle did arrive in Washington in early July, Hassett said, Roosevelt refused to treat him as any more than the French brigadier general that he was, even though he claimed to be a major general with precedence over all other French officers. Roosevelt decided that it was a title he probably conferred on himself. Hassett described de Gaulle as having "an air of arrogance bordering on downright insolence, his Cyrano de Bergerac nose high in the air." When de Gaulle's plane was touching down at National Airport on Thursday, July 6, Early appeared unimpressed with the Frenchman's visit as he perfunctorily gave the reporters a rundown on the general's schedule in Washington, which included tea with Roosevelt and members of his cabinet. He would stay at Blair House, the official guesthouse across from the White House, and meet with the president "intermittently" through the weekend.[42]

Steve Early may have concluded that his boss "was prompted to run for a fourth term only because his country was at war," but Merriman Smith came to a somewhat different conclusion: "Mr. Roosevelt did not want to run for a fourth term. Age was beginning to tell on him. He had lost much of his vitality. The specter of illness was increasingly visible. But it [reelection] was a thing he had to do. He was like a fire horse refusing to go to pasture. His love of political warfare, his vanity, and his firm belief that the country needed him got the best of his judgment."[43]

Like the crafty politician that he was, Roosevelt was carefully laying the groundwork for a grand announcement of his intentions. In early June the "greatest amphibious operation in military history" had sent nearly two hundred thousand Allied troops from four thousand ships onto the beaches of Normandy. McIntire seemed to have convinced the public that the president's health was fine or at least good enough to carry out a fourth term. On June 15 Roosevelt announced a proposal for a "fully representative organization," a United Nations of peace-loving countries. Six days later, one thousand Allied bombers, escorted by twelve hundred fighters, staged a massive raid on Berlin. The war in the Pacific was continuing to turn in the Allies' favor, and on July 9 United States forces secured Saipan, an island in the western Pacific.

Two days later, with the convention a mere eight days away, Roosevelt held his regular Tuesday news conference and at long last put the newsmen and women out of their misery and announced his decision—not that most of them doubted what it would be.

First, he engaged in a little Rooseveltian theatrics. Once the reporters were inside his office, he ordered the doors locked and proceeded to read to the two hundred sweating journalists the text of a letter he had received from the chairman of the Democratic National Committee telling him that the results of the state conventions and primaries indicated that he "had more than a clear majority" of delegates committed to him. To build the suspense, he asked the reporters to "wait a minute." He wanted a cigarette. He took out a Camel, which Early lit for him. David Brinkley wrote that a reporter from NBC radio noticed that Roosevelt's hands were trembling as he spoke, and he was scattering ashes all over his desk and on his lap. Yes, the president confirmed, the Democrats were offering him the nomination. Merriman Smith said that with his dramatic voice booming into the domelike ceiling of his office, the president replied that if nominated, he would accept. "If the people elect me, I will serve." But he assured the reporters that because of the war, he would not run "in the usual partisan, political sense." What he really wanted to do, he said, was to not to run again and to return to his home on the Hudson River. Why was he seeking an unprecedented fourth term? "I have as little right to withdraw as the soldier has to leave his post in the line." When he finished, he grinned up at the reporters and told them, "Now, you've got your news—go on and get out."[44]

The next time the president held a press conference was on July 29 at Waikiki in Honolulu, more than a week after the Democrats had met in Chicago and nominated him, in absentia, as their candidate. (The Republicans had chosen New York governor Thomas E. Dewey as their standard bearer at the end of June.) Starting off on what was billed as a nonpartisan trip, much like the "inspection trips" he had undertaken in the fall of previous election years, Roosevelt left Washington on July 13 for an overnight stay at his home in Hyde Park and then embarked by train on an off-the-record trip that took him to the marine base at San Diego, where in a radio address to the nation he accepted the Democratic nomination. From there he boarded the cruiser *Baltimore* and sailed to Hawaii to visit the naval base at Pearl Harbor, his first visit since the Japanese attack in 1941. The party returned by way of Kodiak, Alaska, from where the *Baltimore* cruised down the Inland Passage to Puget Sound and Seattle, where Roosevelt gave the nation a report on his trip and then came back to Washington. In all he was away from the White House for thirty-five days.[45]

Early remained at home "to keep an eye on the convention and other domestic developments." Merriman Smith said he did not fully understand why there was no press secretary on the trip, but Early's absence caused several difficulties. It was hard for the three wire service reporters and the one "pool" radio reporter who were accompanying the president to get any information. Smith said there was "a constantly broiling argument" between the naval aide, Rear Adm. Wilson Brown, and Roosevelt's military aide and friend Pa Watson. While Grace Tully, Roosevelt's private secretary, and his speechwriter Sam Rosenman were along, they were unable to cope with the navy, which Smith said was in control of the trip. One morning, Admiral Brown, who hated civilians, spent some time complaining about the press and telling anyone who would listen why reporters should not be taken on trips of this kind.[46]

Smith said that when the entourage reached San Diego, where the president was to accept the nomination with a radio address, Admiral Brown told the reporters that they must use a Washington dateline on their stories, in a blatant ethical violation of journalistic canon, and that they could say nothing about the president's real whereabouts. Smith said the reporters argued that Roosevelt had been seen by thousands of people on the way to the West Coast, and they refused to go along with the deception.

So Smith went to Grace Tully, who was more or less acting as the presidential press secretary on the trip. Could she intervene with the president? Tully was hesitant, but then she asked herself what Steve would do this instance. "Take the problem to the Boss," she decided. So she told him to stick close to the president's car on the train, and when the door opened she shunted Smith back to Roosevelt's bedroom where he found the Boss in bed, breathing heavily and fighting a cold. But Smith plunged right in with his complaint, to which Roosevelt replied, "Oh damn, that's a lot of nonsense, I say in the first paragraph of my speech that I am speaking from a west coast naval base. Why not use that for a dateline." And they did.[47]

Another moment on the trip west that could have used the deft hand of Steve Early came when, at the conclusion of the formal delivery of his speech in San Diego, Roosevelt, as he often did, reread selected portions of it so still and movie cameramen could take more photos. One of them captured the president with his head bowed over the printed speech, pronouncing a broad vowel, so that at the moment the cameras went to work, his mouth was wide open. Sam Rosenman said the resulting photos showed "a tragic-looking figure; the face appeared to be very emaciated." He said Roosevelt appeared "weary, sick, discouraged and exhausted." Rosenman concluded that if Early had been there, the photo—showing a man "no longer physically or mentally competent to manage his office"—never would have been distributed to the media. Rosenman said he also was sorry Early was not along on this trip because they were "deprived of his sound judgment about the speech." He said Early was always one of the most helpful critics during the final stage of the preparation of a presidential speech. But, Rosenman said, they never showed him the early drafts so Early could honestly tell reporters he did not know what the president would be saying. Besides, the speechwriters wanted to reserve the press secretary's criticism for the nearly finished product.[48]

After Roosevelt returned to Washington, a concerned Early brought in Hollywood film producer Walter Wanger to supervise all still photos of the president. They set aside a room in the White House as a modern Hollywood-style studio with lighting equipment to replace the old floodlights, and the head cameraman from Metro-Goldwyn-Mayer lent his expertise in setting it up. Early's hope was that better lighting would improve the president's looks on movie newsreels. One newspaper said that movie patrons had been complaining about "bad pictures" of the president in the newsreels. Unfortunately for Early, newspapers picked up on this public relations ploy and began running photos of Roosevelt from the 1930s and the present, side by side. The recent pictures showed a decidedly old man, unsmiling, his cheeks sunken, his lips thin and grim. However, when the camera captured him laughing or smiling, he often looked healthy, even carefree and devilish.[49]

The day that Roosevelt and his party departed Washington for the trip west, Early held a press conference and admitted he had slept in that morning because "when the cat's away the mice will play." He said he had nothing for the reporters, but they had a lot of questions for him. For the next two days they pestered him about who Roosevelt's running mate would be. The liberal Wallace simply had made too many enemies within the conservative arm of the Democratic Party. Roosevelt thought that Wallace had "admirable intellectual and moral qualities." As vice president, Wallace was interested in international affairs, pushing for elevation of living standards throughout the world. In 1940 Roosevelt had fought to have Wallace on the ticket as his running mate. By 1944 Roosevelt realized he was not well enough to engage in the political machinations to ensure Wallace a second term as vice president. As he so often did, the president procrastinated on informing Wallace of the need for change and in announcing his choice.[50]

So, here it was a few days before the Democratic convention, and the reporters were asking Early for an update. He could give them none. Early said that he knew nothing about any imminent meetings the president had scheduled with Wallace. The fact is that Early may have known that a meeting of party leaders had huddled at the White House the previous day, but he might not have been told—or he did not want to inquire—that they had selected Senator Harry Truman from Missouri. At any rate, he was not in a position to tell the reporters. The final choice would be resolved on the floor of the convention. Sam Rosenman said that Early never lied to reporters: Although he might decline to answer a question, he never deliberately gave a reporter—even a hostile one—a false lead.[51]

As he had in previous campaigns, Early was working behind the scenes. In early July he sent a list of suggestions to Robert E. Hannegan, chairman of the Democratic National Committee, regarding arrangements and procedures of the convention. He told Hannegan the suggestions were "largely personal," but they no doubt had received Roosevelt's imprimatur. Early said the "tragedy of war—not the convention—is uppermost in the minds of the great majority of the people of the country at this time," so he did not believe the convention should be doing "a lot of rah-rahing, cheering, or flood the nation with a lot of political bunkum disguised as oratory." Early urged Hannegan to use the radio to get out the party's messages. He said he thought that with "properly selected speakers," the convention offered an excellent opportunity to get facts about the war and the home front to the public. He wrote, "I feel very deeply that the convention should be a serious *business* meeting of the Democratic Party—that it *should not be staged as a political show* with the customary old-time props." The real excitement at the convention went on backstage as party leaders maneuvered to ensure that Roosevelt's choice of Truman would be his running mate. The convention delegates nominated Roosevelt on the first ballot, 1,086 votes to 89 for Senator Harry Byrd of Virginia. The "rah-rahing" was kept to a minimum, although Roosevelt addressed the convention via a radio hookup from the West Coast, and when he finished, he received thunderous applause. An unhappy Wallace received at best a lukewarm endorsement from Roosevelt to again be his running mate. In the end, the convention delegates decided on the more moderate senator from Missouri.[52]

On a sad note, it was while Roosevelt was in Hawaii that another member of the close-knit White House staff died. His beloved personal secretary, Missy LeHand, died in a hospital in Chelsea, Massachusetts, near her home in Somerville, after another stroke. She was forty-six years old. Missy had left the White House almost four years earlier when she had a stroke, and she simply never recovered sufficiently to return to Washington. Early told his July 31 press conference "it becomes my sad duty to give you" news of her death that morning. He then read a brief statement from the president in which he praised her "quiet efficiency, which made her a real genius in getting things done." He spent his whole press conference that morning reminiscing about his old friend Missy. Early and Roosevelt had first met Missy when Roosevelt ran for vice president in 1920, and she was Roosevelt's secretary when he was governor of New York and came to the White House with him.[53]

Shortly before Roosevelt left for the West Coast and Hawaii, Early had sent him a brief note telling him he wanted to have "a personal talk" with him on his return. Roosevelt's reply, handwritten on the bottom of Early's typed note, was "Yassir! About Aug. 10—but don't try anything on." This cryptic "conversation" was Early's way of telling the president he wanted to talk about leaving his job and Roosevelt's way of telling his friend not to look for another job before they could talk about it. If the two men discussed this matter soon after Roosevelt returned to Washington, there is no record of it.[54]

But Early was not going anywhere just yet. The Boss had one more conference with Churchill in Quebec City, and then an election to win. Thus, on the heels of the Pacific tour, Roosevelt headed north to Canada, with Early, just recovered from another of his severe sinus attacks, in tow. It was a trip Early told reporters he preferred not to take—again. Before they left Washington, however, there was a flurry of correspondence—letters and memos—circulated among Harry Hopkins, who was convalescing at his home, Roosevelt, Early, and the Canadian prime minister Mackenzie King about the media coverage of the conference. In a memo Hopkins wrote to King, presumably on the advice of Early, Roosevelt said he felt it would be "a great mistake to have newspapermen all over the place and the newspapermen should know that only a communiqué, after the conference, will be issued." The memo further explained that the president was afraid the newspapermen would be demanding press releases every day, something he did not want to bother with. Hopkins and Roosevelt thought that if they made no special arrangements for the press, they would be less likely to come to Quebec.

In the wake of D day, Early recognized that Roosevelt was approaching the conference as strictly a military meeting, and for that reason he doubted there would be much news to release. Nonetheless it still is hard to believe that he would deliberately have chosen to exclude the journalists, but he was battling Hopkins, Roosevelt, and high-level Canadian officials on this one. Early told Lester B. Pearson, then the chargé d'affaires at the Canadian Embassy in Washington and later prime minister, that he wanted a press headquarters set up where the reporters could be called together for press conferences and where US censors, wire facilities, and general information were available to them. He insisted that "everything possible" be done to assure the newspapermen, radio men, and photographers had adequate living quarters and the equipment they needed to get the news out.[55]

In a memo to Pearson, Early argued eloquently, "I need not attempt to tell you what the situation would be if these men got to Quebec and found it impossible to get living accommodations for themselves, impossible to move their stories to their papers, and, on top of that, found that nothing had been done by the Government to help them."

In the end, the reporters, photographers, and radiomen did go to Quebec City, and Early made sure they were allowed access at least to the public rooms in Le Château Frontenac, where the conference was held, although Early warned them there would be little news released.[56]

Still mindful of wartime security, the presidential party, which included Eleanor Roosevelt (who had not accompanied him to previous conferences), Early, Tully, Watson, and McIntire, left Washington on the train on Saturday night, September 9, spending Sunday in Hyde Park. They crossed the Canadian border at 1:00 a.m. Monday and arrived in Quebec City at 8:30 a.m. The staff stayed at Le Château Frontenac, while Roosevelt and Churchill, as they had been at the previous meeting in the city, were quartered in the Citadel.[57]

Once settled in Quebec, Early managed to keep the lid on what could have been a press nightmare. He immediately warned the reporters that because the conference "was purely military" strategy to map final steps in the war and to study postwar problems, there would be little news for them, and he explained that Roosevelt's Pacific tour had indeed been a "necessary preliminary" to the Quebec conference. The more than one hundred newsmen and women managed to take over Le Château Frontenac as their unofficial headquarters, and Early and the Canadian and British press officers held regular press conferences there, a decision the reporters seemed to appreciate. One newspaper predicted that the amount of copy generated would surpass that from the previous Quebec conference.[58]

Once the formal proceedings ended, on September 16, Churchill and Roosevelt met the press on a warm, sunny afternoon on the parapet at the Citadel. As they had at previous Churchill-Roosevelt meetings, reporters sat cross-legged on the floor, like children in a nursery school. Roosevelt's Scottie, Fala, was sprawled at his feet. But reporters were forbidden to ask any questions. They pleaded with Early to at least allow written questions be submitted, but apparently Churchill and Roosevelt were against that. Early did tell the press that he would ask the president if he could be quoted directly in the stories. Roosevelt agreed. As the men spoke, it became clear why they banned reporters' questions. Their report on the meeting was mostly vague and provided no timetables and no details, but the two men did agree the Allies should work as quickly as they could to end the war with Japan. Once the press conference concluded, Roosevelt went back to Hyde Park to await the arrival of Churchill the following day so the two men could continue their discussions. Early returned to the White House.[59]

The remainder of September and October saw the president on the campaign trail, sometimes with Early joining him, but mostly with the press secretary left behind to mind the store. One of the highlights of his campaigning was a whirlwind, one-day tour of the four New York boroughs in late October. Much to the surprise of the reporters covering it, Early told them they could run advance stories and cover the events of the day "on the record," an about-face from the strict wartime security that had enveloped previous presidential travels. In fact, Early told his press conference on October 18, three days before the Saturday visit to New York City, that Roosevelt had "no desire" to invoke the censorship code "to conceal himself on an occasion of this kind." After all, this was a campaign trip, and publicity is the heart and soul of a presidential election. But there were some restrictions, nonetheless: No information was to be released ahead of time regarding when Roosevelt's party, including Early, would leave Washington for New York and when they would arrive there. He stopped short of giving them an itinerary once they reached the city.

The press conference was the usual give-and-take between reporters pressing for even a scrap of information they could print or broadcast and the press secretary, ever mindful of censorship, moving back and forth between "on the record" and "off the record"—and just as often telling them he could not say anything at all. The next day, the reporters told him that newspapers in New York had been told the president's itinerary, but they were confused as to how much they could publish ahead of time. And where exactly was he going anyway?

Early hesitated, "It isn't quite clear to me. I think as soon as the detailed plans and arrangements for the President's visit to New York on Saturday are completed they will be announced to you, and I take it that the announcement is for the purpose of getting it published." This generated laughter among the reporters. Once again, as in past campaigns, Democratic National Headquarters and the White

House were not communicating well, coupled with the sudden relaxation of censorship.[60]

The presidential party, including Early, left Washington by train Friday, October 20, 1944, at 11:00 p.m., arriving at the army supply base at 7:00 the next morning. The day was overcast and drizzly, the tail end of a hurricane that had, according to Bill Hassett, "been creeping up the Atlantic coast." By the time Roosevelt left the train for his tour through four of the boroughs, it was a full-fledged rain, and to increase his visibility among the crowds that lined the route, he rode in a big, open Packard. They stopped off at Ebbets Field, home to the Brooklyn Dodgers, where the president, standing bareheaded and with his navy cape falling from his shoulders in the heavy rain, told the cheering crowd, albeit smaller than hoped for because of the weather, that he often rooted for the Dodgers. This grandstanding, orchestrated to show his detractors that the president was in fine health, led Bill Hassett to write, "Well, the Ebbets Field appearance has made plain, everyday liars out of this species of vermin," referring to those detractors. It was an angry Hassett who wrote those words. He spent half a page in his memoirs denigrating columnists and others who had "carried on unremittingly a whispering campaign, a vendetta" against Roosevelt's health. The ever-loyal Hassett said these detractors had fostered the propaganda that the Boss was old, ill tempered, tired, and worn out. As time proved, they may have been more perceptive than Hassett.[61]

What the public did not see, according to James McGregor Burns, was the rubdown and change of clothes Roosevelt received at a nearby coast guard motor pool before the entourage moved on, the car's top still down, through the boroughs of Queens and the Bronx. Despite the drenching cold rain, by the time they reached Broadway in Manhattan, the crowds were at their thickest, umbrellas and soggy newspapers over their heads, to catch a glimpse of the president of the United States. After a four-hour ride in the open car, the entourage moved on to Mrs. Roosevelt's apartment in Washington Square, where they could change clothes and rest before he gave a speech to the Foreign Policy Association in the ballroom of the grand old Waldorf-Astoria Hotel, an audience Hassett described as mostly elderly men and probably two-thirds Republican.[62]

That night Roosevelt went north to Hyde Park until Monday night, while Early returned to Washington, but only for a few days.

On October 26 they left for a much longer campaign trip, this one taking them first to Wilmington, Delaware, then to Philadelphia, Pittsburgh, through Ohio and Indiana, and to Chicago, where Roosevelt addressed a large crowd at Soldier Field, a crowd that Hassett said numbered about 110,000 with twice that number outside the stadium—the largest crowd ever addressed by a single person. From there, they traveled back across Ohio to Washington, arriving home on Sunday evening, October 29.

The following weekend, just before the election, the president and his staff again left Washington and moved through Connecticut to Boston, making brief stops along the way, a large campaign hurrah. Then it was on to Hyde Park for what now was becoming a familiar scenario to Steve Early.[63]

On Monday the president began his customary tour of his Hudson River neighborhood, what this time he called "a sentimental journey." The following day, he left home shortly after noon, accompanied by Eleanor, one of their grandsons, and his dog, Fala. After a brief stop at the town's elementary school, the party moved on to the Hyde Park Town Hall to vote. At the polling place, he gave his occupation as "tree grower."[64]

The White House staff and the reporters and photographers, as they did when Roosevelt was at his home there, stayed in Nelson House in Poughkeepsie. Merriman Smith called the wait for the election results that evening "loud" but "well-ordered." Before he left Nelson House for Hyde Park, an "expansive" Steve Early ordered drinks for the party, telling the waiters to charge them to the rooms of various reporters. Unfortunately, the next morning, he discovered that with each round of drinks, the reporters had grabbed the checks and signed them "with a flourish—Stephen T. Early, Room 229."[65]

By the time the polls had closed across the country, Roosevelt's dining room table had been cleared of dinner dishes and cutlery, and the president, Early, Sam Rosenman, Henry and Eleanor Morgenthau, close friends of the family, and a few other staff members and friends monitored the Associated Press and United Press teletypes that had been installed in the nearby smoking room. Shortly before midnight, the president appeared on his front porch to acknowledge the Hyde Park villagers, complete with high school band and red flares, who had gathered to wait for the results.

Merriman Smith said he was "shocked" at Roosevelt's physical appearance. With his large wool navy cape wrapped around him and a tweed broad-brimmed hat worn at a "cockeyed angle," Smith said the president looked older than he had ever seen him. When Roosevelt spoke, what he told them was "irrelevant much of the time." He talked about old times, pointing to a tree he used to climb, then about the Connecticut election, in which he hoped Clare Booth Luce, the conservative playwright and wife of *Time* magazine's founder, Henry Luce, would be defeated for Congress. Then, Smith said, he went back into the dining room "to continue his personal computations of the returns." The *Dallas Times-Herald* ran a photo the following day showing a wan but smiling Roosevelt talking to the crowd. However, the following week, *Time* magazine published a photo that captured the president of the United States that night looking old and haggard.[66]

As the state-by-state votes were tabulated by the meticulous Roosevelt, it became apparent that he was winning. At 3:15 a.m., Governor Dewey conceded in a radio speech, and Roosevelt sent him a telegram that read, "I thank you for your statement, which I have heard over the air a few minutes ago." At 3:30, Early telephoned the press at Nelson House and asked Tom Reynolds, White House correspondent for the *Chicago Sun*, to relay his words to the rest of the reporters assembled in the room. He said that contrary to a radio report they had just heard at Hyde Park, the president had not gone to bed. He was still working at his dining room table. At 4:00 a.m. Early's secretary called the press at Nelson House and told them the president had retired at 3:50 a.m., having first sent telegrams not only to Dewey but to Vice President Wallace and Vice President Elect Truman.[67]

Once the Boss had retired, Early returned to Nelson House to celebrate, a bittersweet moment, for he and the president already had secretly agreed that he would leave his position at the White House after the first of the year. Sitting off to the side of the celebration was a group of Washington correspondents drinking away the early morning hours and arguing quietly about the chances of Roosevelt living out a fourth term. Merriman Smith said that those who believed he would "were in a decided minority."[68]

23

To Yalta and Back Again

Three days after his fourth term was secured, in a steady, chilly morning rain, Roosevelt returned to Washington's Union Station to the strains of the district's police band playing "Hail to the Chief," followed by brief welcoming ceremonies and a motorcade of police motorcycles leading a line of limousines to the White House. More than three hundred thousand people, including federal workers and schoolchildren who were given time off, cheered and applauded as the presidential automobile glided by with Roosevelt flanked by an uncomfortable-looking Harry Truman, the newly elected vice president, and Henry Wallace, the reluctant outgoing vice president. Within an hour the Boss was holding a press conference, where a reporter could not resist asking him if he planned to run again in 1948. "That's a question I was asked in 1940, isn't it? It's hoary—absolutely hoary." And that was all they got from him on the topic. Later, he met with his staff and then with the cabinet. It was business as usual.[1]

It must have been most satisfying for the Old Warrior not only to have beaten his younger opponent in the election, but that he had won big: 432 electoral votes to Dewey's 99. And once again, according to his biographer James MacGregor Burns, Roosevelt was victorious in spite of the lack of support from a majority of the country's newspapers. As glorious as that victory must have been to an aging man whose doctors continued to closely monitor his daily activities, he was still just that: an old man—and now he was facing another four years in one of the world's most stressful jobs, his health failing, and he had yet to see the end of a war that was leaving a great deal of the civilized world ravaged.[2]

As he had earlier in the year, Roosevelt continued to remove himself from the White House as often as he felt he reasonably could. He returned to Hyde Park for Thanksgiving, and on his way back stopped in Washington for a Sunday overnight before he went on to Warm Springs, again leaving Early behind to mind the shop. It was cold and rainy much of the time Roosevelt was in Georgia, and he caught a slight cold but was not sick enough to go to bed. After close to three weeks at Warm Springs, the entourage, which had included both presidential physicians, McIntire and Bruenn, left for Washington, returning by way of Camp Lejeune, the North Carolina marine base, for an inspection. The train pulled into Washington on Tuesday, December 19. Four days later it carried the president, members of his family, and a few staffers—but not Early—north to Hyde Park for a Christmas celebration, although by then Bill Hassett thought Roosevelt appeared "tired and weary." When Roosevelt arrived back in Washington on December 30, he had been away from the White House a total of thirty-four days since November 21.[3]

While the Boss was away, his press secretary was becoming the object of press rumors centering on his future. Everybody was speculating, and Early was busy denying or at least sidestepping. *Newsweek* magazine said he had received "a tremendous offer from private industry." The *Washington Times-Herald* said that if Early resigned, he would easily become the highest-paid public relations counsel in the country. The *Washington Post* told its readers that Early might be headed to General Foods, owned by Marjorie Meriweather Post, the wife of Early's good friend Joseph Davies. The *New York Herald-Tribune* said he had been offered a publicity post at NBC. The *New Orleans Item* told its readers that the press secretary had wanted to leave his post for eight years, and now, at the age of fifty-five, he was still earning $10,000 a year—not a lot considering he still had two children to educate and needed to "keep up the necessary front commensurate with an important government position."[4]

At his November 14 press conference, he leveled with the

reporters when one of them asked, "Do you plan to resign?" Reluctantly, and "off the record," he said he had been feeling "an economic pinch that has been getting worse and worse as I have stayed on. I would like to relieve it if I can." Early told the reporters he would not "move on" until he had permission: "That permission I have not yet sought, hence, I have not gotten it. As soon as I do, I will let you know. Meanwhile, I will appreciate it if you will sort of leave it lay." (There is no written record that Early and Roosevelt at this point had discussed his future, but based on what happened in January, by the time Early was telling reporters he had not received permission to leave, a plan for his departure either already was in place, or at least was in the works.)

The following day, the reporters were asking who in the cabinet, if anyone, planned to submit his resignation, as was more or less protocol at the end of a presidential term. Early chastised them, saying that if and when resignations were received, he would let them know, and he encouraged them to refrain from speculation. He said he was including himself in this statement.[5]

Because the president seemed to be away from Washington so often in November and December, Early was forced to remind the reporters of wartime censorship on his travels. On November 27, as Roosevelt was in between his Thanksgiving visit to Hyde Park and his trip to Warm Springs, Early was busy evading details of the itinerary. "Is he leaving soon?" they wanted to know. "Leaving tonight, CONFIDENTIALLY," Early said. And that was all he would say. Sometimes he became downright exasperated and even sarcastic with the reporters, as in the closing minutes of his December 30 press conference when a reporter asked if it was "still off the record" that the president had returned from Hyde Park. Early told him, "Does it mean anything to you? The fact that he is here and has his appointments, and so forth, says that he is back, and shows he is here." But the public did not know he was away, the reporter remonstrated, only to have Early point out, "I am afraid they do, because I noticed two morning papers published Christmas morning said that he was in Hyde Park, which violated the code." He added, "Both of those stories, as I remember them, were written by girl reporters" as if a male reporter would have observed the silence of the code.[6]

The hungry journalists also were curious about a rumor that the president had visited Cordell Hull, his longtime secretary of state, who was ill in the Naval Hospital. Did Steve know if that was true? "Damned if I do. I didn't check. I know he went out the other day, and I told you." Was Hull resigning his post? "I won't say Yes or No." Hull was never a very powerful secretary, in large part because Roosevelt preferred to act as his own secretary of state, and as the war progressed any influence Hull did exert waned. On the day that Early was playing cat and mouse with the reporters, Roosevelt was at the Naval Hospital asking for—and receiving—Hull's resignation. Later that day, shortly before he left for Warm Springs, Roosevelt held a press conference and announced what he called his secretary's "retirement."[7]

One rumor that persisted among the Washington press corps that Early actually wanted to confirm was that the presidential train made regular stops during the latter part of the war to visit Tranquility Farms, the estate of Lucy Mercer Rutherfurd, between Morristown, New Jersey, and the Pennsylvania border. Once Eleanor's personal secretary and then Roosevelt's mistress before he contracted polio, Rutherfurd was now a widow. In recent years she and the president had renewed their friendship, but had kept it secret from Eleanor. When the local newspapers learned of the train stops, they asked Early if they could publish the information, but he told them "in confidence" that the president did not want anything in the press, even though Early figured the details would get into the press eventually and advised the president to let the newspapers run the stories. Roosevelt would not budge.[8]

In spite of his travels between the election and the end of the year, Roosevelt managed to hold six of his own press conferences. They tended to lack substance and were relatively banal and full of rambling reminiscences. He seemed forgetful, frequently turning to Early for a piece of information. Now and again, though, his sharp tongue took aim at someone or something that was annoying him. For instance, on December 22, on a tear about something yet another one of his nemesis columnists had published, he referred to the whole lot of them as "an unnecessary excrescence on our civilization." This was not an especially surprising comment, because throughout his tenure as president Roosevelt had held most columnists in contempt.[9]

The day after he made his disparaging remarks about columnists, Roosevelt left Washington to spend what would be his last Christmas with his family at Hyde Park, where he made his annual Christmas Eve broadcast to the nation. Censorship gave no indication from where he was speaking. The Early family's holiday gathering at their home was far more subdued, since Buddy Early now was on military duty in Europe. Then, two weeks into the new year, with no fanfare, the Bureau of Public Affairs at the War Department—not the White House press secretary—handed out a news release that would mark the beginning of the end of Steve Early's professional association with his old friend the president.[10]

Complaints had been flooding into the War Department about poor press relations and the lack of a timely release of news from the Supreme Headquarters, Allied Expeditionary Forces (SHAEF) at Rheims, France. Reporters were calling the army's censorship methods there "slipshod" and the public affairs officers at SHAEF "blundering" and "stupid." By mid-December, it became apparent that SHAEF was releasing no information to reporters on the carefully coordinated German counteroffensive attacks on the US First and Ninth armies, which took a drubbing in what became known as the Battle of the Bulge. Now, with Roosevelt's blessing, the War Department was sending Early to Europe as a civilian troubleshooter in an attempt to straighten out the problems, to serve in an advisory capacity on general public relations to assure the public would get fuller, more candid, and more timely news from the Western Front. It was about this time that Harry Hopkins once again was in Europe on fact-finding business for Roosevelt when he stopped by SHAEF headquarters and told them that Steve's high standing as a professional newspaperman should produce some good results. Hopkins said reporters in London told him how pleased they were that Early was coming.[11]

The announcement received a lot of press coverage in the United States. The *New York Times* said Early was the ideal person to take on this task: He combined service in the army in World War I, experience with problems in public relations, and the prestige of long association with Roosevelt. In addition, he had made a favorable impression on the American and foreign press at the Quebec conferences, and he was a friend of General Eisenhower, the Supreme Commander of the Allied Forces. Early said he would be a "one-man expedition," a civilian rather than an army lieutenant colonel in the reserves, because he said preferred to not "jump into a uniform and spend a lot of money that I haven't got, and then get out of uniform in sixty days." He had told the president he would be a little better off as a civilian than as a lieutenant colonel saying, "Yes, sir." At his last press conference with reporters before he left for Europe, he shared with them the real reason he would not be jumping into his uniform: He had weighed 132 pounds in 1918; in 1945 he tipped the scales at 167.[12]

The assignment, for which Early obviously was well suited, got him out of the "great white jail," and served as a way for him to gradually ease his way out of the White House and into the private sector job he had desired for so long. The *Houston Chronicle* said that while the trip was necessary to straighten out the publicity problems at SHAEF, it also may have been a gift from Roosevelt to his loyal aide and friend. Roosevelt himself was sentimental about his connection to the Navy Department from his days as an assistant secretary; thus he must have realized how much a trip to the battlefields where he fought as an infantryman in World War I and where his son Buddy now was fighting would tickle the fancy of his press secretary, beneath whose tough exterior lurked a real sentimentalist. The *Washington Star* said it would be "one of the hardest jobs of [Early's] career." And indeed it proved to be just that. But first, he had what became an even more important mission to undertake for the Boss, one that took them halfway around the world to meet with Churchill and Stalin at a little-known city named Yalta.[13]

Slowly, the war had been turning in favor of the Allies, on both the Pacific and the European fronts, and by the end of January 1945, Russian forces had completed their greatest offensive in Poland and East Prussia, which resulted in alleviating pressure on the Western Front by clearing out the German troops. Then the last German troops were removed from the Ardennes bulge; Allied troops were closing in on the mighty Rhine River and were moving forward in France, Belgium, and Holland; and Berlin was under heavy bombing, nearly round-the-clock attacks. Defeat of Hitler's armies appeared to be imminent. In the Pacific the Allies were slowly but steadily eroding the Japanese forces.

Thus, it became of paramount importance that Roosevelt, Churchill, and Stalin hold another conference, the aim of which would be to determine postwar European boundaries, to discuss how to treat Germany, and to grapple with the future of Japanese-occupied East Asia.[14]

Before he could leave Washington for such a conference, Roosevelt had to be sworn in for his fourth term. With the country in the midst of a war, he decided it would be more appropriate to eschew the bells and whistles of a more lavish inaugural and instead have a simple ceremony on the South Portico of the White House. David Brinkley wrote that what Roosevelt did not say was that "he wanted to spare himself a physically taxing ordeal. He simply did not have the strength to endure the traditional four days of ceremony and revelry." Some members of Congress who were unhappy with the scaled-down affair derisively called it "the front-porch inauguration."[15]

In fact, Roosevelt was saving his strength for the imminent conference, which only a handful of close aides were aware of, when at noon on January 20, the first president to be sworn in for a fourth term stood hatless and without his usual heavy navy cape in raw, cold weather, the ground and trees covered with a glistening of overnight snow, while Chief Justice Harlan Fiske Stone administered the oath of office. Hundreds of shivering onlookers stamped their feet to keep warm on the lawn just below the South Portico. His inaugural address lasted about five minutes, followed by a receiving line and buffet luncheon inside the White House. Early saw to it that the ceremony was broadcast live by the three radio networks. The following day the *New York Times* called it "the simplest inauguration on record."[16]

It was while Roosevelt was being sworn in, said his eldest son, Jimmy, that he suffered spasms of chest pain in what probably was a heart attack. It was not the first such episode. Jimmy wrote in a book about his father that Roosevelt had experienced similar severe pain when he was at Camp Pendleton, near San Diego, on his trip to the West Coast the previous summer. Young Roosevelt was temporarily stationed there, and before his father was to review landing exercises, he turned to Jimmy and said he had "horrible pains." He was convinced it was indigestion, not his heart. Jimmy helped him lie on the floor of the railroad car they were in, his eyes closed, his face drawn, and his torso occasionally convulsed with waves of pain that stabbed him. "Never in my life had I felt so alone with him—and so helpless," Jimmy wrote.[17]

So when Jimmy arrived at the White House for the fourth inauguration, he wrote, the first moment he saw his father he realized something was terribly wrong. He looked awful, and regardless of what the doctors had said, Jimmy wrote, "I knew in my heart that his days were numbered." Just before they were to go into a reception in the State Dining Room after the inaugural ceremony, the two men were alone in the Green Room, and the president suffered the same stabbing kind of pain. He said, "Jimmy, I can't take this unless you get me a stiff drink." He added, "You'd better make it straight." Jimmy said that when he handed him the tumbler of whiskey, he drank it as if it were medicine. Jimmy said he had never seen him take a drink in that manner. Then they went into the reception. It was the last time Jimmy saw his father. The previous day, Roosevelt's longtime secretary of labor, Frances Perkins, also was alarmed by his appearance. She wrote that his clothes looked much too big for him, his face looked thin, his color was gray, and his eyes were dull.[18]

Then, two days later, on January 22, under cover of darkness and with no public fanfare, an ailing Roosevelt, Steve Early, Pa Watson, Dr. McIntire, several military aides, and the president's daughter, Anna Roosevelt Boettiger, left Washington by train for the Norfolk Navy Yard in Virginia to board the cruiser *Quincy*. Their destination was Yalta, a resort city on the Black Sea in Soviet Crimea, the choice of Stalin, who refused to leave the USSR. Interestingly, Roosevelt's closest advisers all were against his traveling to Russia, in large part because they did not trust the Russians. It was here that Churchill, Stalin, and Roosevelt would meet to hammer out the fate of postwar Europe. (Harry Hopkins and the new secretary of state, Edward Stettinius, had gone on ahead, making stops along the way to meet with various Allied leaders.) Ironically, the public announcement of what transpired at this conference would prove to be a highlight of Steve Early's career as the presidential press secretary—at the very moment he was quietly planning to leave his friend and Boss.[19]

Bill Hassett wrote that he could think of only one thing as the president set out on this journey: "Having achieved every political ambition a human being could aspire to, there remains only his place in history. That will be determined by the service which he renders to all mankind. So F.D.R. will win his niche or pass into the oblivion which in a quarter of a century has swallowed all of the statesmen of the First World War—in reality only an earlier phase of this struggle." David Brinkley concluded that it was at Yalta that Roosevelt hoped to achieve that niche in history. To do so, he needed his closest and most trustworthy confidants with him.[20]

In an attempt to throw the reporters off the scent, Early had been forced into some fancy footwork the morning of the night the entourage left for Yalta. He told them, OFF THE RECORD, that this would probably be the last press conference he would hold for "at least two months." He said Roosevelt had approved Early's choice of Jonathan Daniels, one of his assistants, to take over his job while he was away. Daniels was the son of Josephus Daniels, the former secretary of the navy when Roosevelt was assistant secretary of the navy.

A reporter for his family's newspaper in Raleigh, North Carolina, and author of a book on the New Deal and the South, Daniels went to Washington after Pearl Harbor as one of a number of anonymous administrative aides to the president, young men attracted to power and eager to undertake small tasks for the White House. Early told the reporters that Daniels would be known for the time being not as acting press secretary but would continue as an administrative assistant to the president. "I would like for you to protect it because it is important. Not important for me. It is for others," Early told them. He asked them to handle Daniels's announcements without any reference to Early. What he was not telling the reporters was that before he undertook his mission to SHAEF, he would be traveling with Roosevelt to the conference at Yalta; thus the need for his subterfuge on the Daniels's appointment. Despite filling the reporters in on a number of high-level government appointments the president had recently made and listing the meetings Roosevelt would be having later that day, Early gave no indication that they were about to embark on one of the most important war conferences of his presidency.[21]

But secrecy in the nation's capital is a relative state. Merriman Smith, the United Press White House reporter, found out in December that a conference was in the works, but there was no indication where it would be held. He learned quite by accident of its location when he was drinking with a "talkative member of our armed forces" at a cocktail party in Washington several weeks before the trip began. The officer suggested Smith bet on "a little Crimean town named Yalta." Because of Stalin's inclusion in the conference and because it was winter, Smith had suspected the meeting might be in the vicinity of the Black Sea, and now he realized Yalta fit the bill perfectly. Of course, then Smith and the reporters for the other two press associations wanted to tag along with the presidential party, and they asked Early about it. He told them it probably was a lost cause. Roosevelt had agreed with Stalin and Churchill to have no reporters from any country there.

Early assured them that he would be traveling to Yalta, and that he would send back to Washington whatever news he could. Perhaps he had argued this issue with Roosevelt, but it probably was hopeless because the decision involved not just the president of the United States, who usually went along with Early's advice on press matters, but also Churchill, who never met with the press, and Stalin, from a country where the "news" came from, well, Stalin himself—when it came at all.

The wire service reporters told Early, "Steve, in all due respect to you, the papers and the radio stations don't want the Big Three [conference] covered by a spokesman for any government. They want their own people to call the shots." Early agreed with the thesis but told them his hands were tied. The three reporters then appealed directly to Roosevelt, but they got nowhere. He had agreed with the other leaders, and he could not—or would not—change the plan. When the president did leave Washington, Smith said, "He could have gone in broad daylight and behind a brass band as far as we were concerned because we knew when he left, where he would depart and where he was going and who was with him. But censorship said no; we couldn't print a line or even speculate." Ironic, Smith said, because even the bus drivers in Washington knew when he left.[22]

On February 2 the USS *Quincy*, carrying the presidential party, arrived at the Mediterranean island of Malta, where its passengers disembarked. The next day they flew to the Saki airfield on the Crimean peninsula, a part of the Soviet Republic of the Ukraine that juts off the northern shore into the Black Sea. It was thought to be too dangerous to bring the *Quincy* into the harbor at Yalta because of the possibility of some remaining German mines. From the airport the Americans were driven the ninety miles over nearly impassable roads to the Lavadia Palace, a fifty-room marble palace that was once a summer home of the Russian Czar Nicholas II, about a mile and a half from the city of Yalta. The city also boasted a number of villas, once vacation homes to the country's royalty and other wealthy citizens, but which, under communism, had been turned into "sanitariums," where high-ranking members of the Communist Party could come for rest and relaxation, often a euphemism for "drying out" from the excesses of vodka. Many of these former villas had been looted and bombed by the Germans during the war.

The ravages of the marauding Germans could not detract from the views from the palace—the soaring, snow-covered Yaila mountains above, the Black Sea below—a scene that must have appealed to both Roosevelt and Churchill based on their reactions to the similarly breathtaking scenery of Casablanca. In his book *Roosevelt and Hopkins*, Robert Sherwood in an understatement calls the accommodations in the palace "unexceptionable." The Very Important Persons, he wrote, had accommodations to themselves. Everyone else had to share, and in the case of sixteen army colonels, they were forced to share one bedroom.[23]

Granted, some of the bedrooms were the size of a skating rink. Roosevelt's suite, once the czar's, consisted of a reception room, a sitting room, a bedroom, and a conference room that had served as a ballroom/banquet hall. On the negative side, before the guests arrived, the building had been crawling with lice and bedbugs and typhus bacilli. Bedding, wall hangings, and anything that might harbor lice, bedbugs, or germs were disinfected. And the plumbing, while fairly new, functioned poorly. When Hopkins was meeting with Churchill in London days before the conference, the prime minister told him, "Ten years of research could not have unearthed a worse place to meet." It was a wonder everyone remained healthy long enough for the long, intense daily meetings and the late evenings of heavy food and alcohol.[24]

Stalin and his party arrived the next morning, Sunday, and after a late-afternoon meeting between Stalin and Roosevelt in a room designated as Roosevelt's study in the palace, they moved downstairs to join Churchill and their respective staffs in the Grand Ballroom for the first formal conference. The meetings continued over the next eight days, with dissension over large and small issues. When they finally concluded, the three world leaders had begun to redraw the boundaries of what would become postwar Europe and had agreed on securing reparations from Germany. Once Germany surrendered, Stalin would send Soviet armed forces to the Far East to assist the Allies in their fight against Japan. Roosevelt succumbed to Stalin's request for seats for the Soviet Republics of the Ukraine and Byelorussia in the General Assembly of the new United Nations.

Harry Hopkins, ill through most of the conference, managed to attend the formal meetings to advise Roosevelt and later said, "We really believed in our hearts that this was the dawn of the new day we had all been praying for and talking about for so many years." Unfortunately, that meeting at Yalta became "the most controversial summit conference in history."[25]

On the day that Roosevelt arrived at Lavadia Palace, the *New York Times* carried a brief story on an inside page with a London dateline saying the conference was reportedly underway, but giving no location. Two days later another small story, this time with a Cairo dateline, informed *Times* readers that the conference was continuing and speculated that Germany was about to make a peace bid to the Allies. Again, no details and no location were published. The following day the story on the conference came with a dateline of Ankara, Turkey, and it said the conference definitely was underway (by now, it was half over), and that "sources in certain circles claim to have a pretty good idea of where the conference is being held. It would be inadvisable for security reasons to pinpoint it at this time." The story said that "Turkish quarters" thought it was being held somewhere in the Black Sea area and quite probably in the Soviet Union. On February 7 a *Times* story out of London confirmed that Churchill was meeting with Stalin and Roosevelt, but there was no hint of where.[26]

Finally the three leaders decided it was time to announce what most of the world now already knew: The conference was in progress. Early sent a two-hundred-word statement to Daniels to that effect, saying only that the conference was underway "somewhere in the Black Sea area." It listed in general terms the issues on the table: joint plans for the occupation of Germany, political and economic problems of liberated Europe, and proposals for a permanent international organization to maintain peace. Early gave Daniels strict instructions not to release it to the press in Washington until 4:30 p.m. the following day, February 7. The statement, approved by the three leaders, left Daniels and Early in a tough spot. Reporters back in Washington wanted to tell their readers and listeners that the "somewhere" was Yalta. But censorship on presidential travels forbade this, and there was nothing either Daniels or Early could do about it. Daniels relayed to Early the pleas of the reporters and their complaints that they were being scooped by the foreign press, which was publishing details of the location. Now Early took the matter into his own hands and somehow must have persuaded Roosevelt to allow the three wire service reporters to join him in the Mediterranean.[27]

Merriman Smith said that two days after the press was allowed to release the brief statement on the conference, Daniels called the three wire service reporters—Smith, Douglas Cornell of the Associated Press, and Robert G. Nixon of International News Service—into his office. Smith said that Daniels's hands trembled as he handed them a message from Early, asking the reporters to come immediately to Casablanca, where they would await orders to join the president's party in Algiers. They were to tell no one about their trip. Smith said they were issued special War Department passes; secret letters from Daniels explaining their mission, to be opened "only in case of something about as drastic as death"; and passports for Jerusalem with stops in Africa and several other countries. Late that afternoon they took off from Washington in an army transport plane.[28]

Meanwhile, the conference had ended, and the president and his party, except for Early and Stettinius, left Lavadia to drive to the airfield at Saki. But at the last minute, Roosevelt changed his mind and asked that they instead drive the eighty miles to Sevastopol so he could visit the USS *Catoctin* to thank the officers and crew for their hard work decontaminating the palace.[29]

Early and the secretary of state remained behind at the palace to fine-tune the final draft of a communiqué of the conference, approved by the three leaders. Early recalled details of his role in the conference in a letter to Stettinius, who was writing a book about Yalta shortly before he died in 1949. Early said he was the one who urged the preparation of data each day so that when the conference reached its final stages, they could produce the American delegates' version of the official communiqué. He said he worked at the British headquarters with Foreign Secretary Anthony Eden and others over the course of several nights so that the American and British delegates could present the Russians with a mutually agreed-upon text for the communiqué, a plan that, he said, "worked most successfully." The upshot was that the Russians accepted the text scarcely without change. Because the communiqué had not been officially transcribed before Roosevelt, Stalin, and Churchill left Yalta that day, Early had each man sign three blank sheets of paper. He said it had been a difficult job phrasing the document, as terms had to be employed that could easily be translated into Russian, Chinese, and French without distortion. Finally, at about 10:00 that night, Early and Stettinius got the communiqué transcribed.

The communiqué then was sent to London, Washington, and Moscow and released simultaneously the next day. This was the best Early could manage to ensure that the citizens of each country received news of the outcome of the conference at the same time. Early joined Roosevelt and the others and spent the night aboard the ship. The communiqué, a detailed account of what happened at the conference within the bounds of military censorship, received high praise from newsmen because of its thoroughness.[30]

One newspaper called it "one of Early's great stories." The genesis of the communiqué came from Early, who realized that when Roosevelt left Yalta, he would be "blacked out" for perhaps ten days or two weeks as he made stops in the Mediterranean area, travel that under the censorship code could not be reported as it was happening. However, Churchill and Stalin were flying back to their respective capitals directly from the conference and immediately would be available to the press. If Roosevelt released only a brief statement that failed to clarify the outcome of the meeting, Early knew it would leave the American press in limbo and at the mercy of the British news agencies, which would get a more comprehensive account from Churchill or his press office.[31]

The following day, the presidential party flew to the US air base at Deversyr, Egypt, and boarded the *Quincy*, anchored nearby in Great Bitter Lake near the Suez Canal. It was here that Roosevelt had historic meetings with three Middle Eastern potentates. While they were still at Yalta, Roosevelt had decided to meet with King Farouk of Egypt, Emperor Haile Selassie of Abyssinia, and King Ibn Saud of Saudi Arabia, a meeting Harry Hopkins said disturbed Churchill, who saw it as "some deep laid plot to undermine the British Empire" in the Middle East. When the three kings did meet Roosevelt on board the *Quincy*, it proved to be none of that; Hopkins called the meetings "a lot of horseplay." James McGregor Burns called the parade of kings in their finery coming aboard the *Quincy* "peacockery." What Roosevelt hoped to accomplish from this charade is unclear, except that at one point he did try to persuade Ibn Saud to admit more Jews into Palestine, but the king said with all seriousness that his subjects did not like Jews. There would be no more Jews allowed into Palestine, he told Roosevelt.[32]

From Great Bitter Lake, the *Quincy* sailed to Alexandria, where Churchill came aboard for lunch. The ship continued to sail through the Mediterranean, and on February 15 it reached Algiers. By this time, Pa Watson had suffered a cerebral hemorrhage and would be dead by the time the *Quincy* arrived home; Harry Hopkins was very ill with stomach pains and would return to the Mayo Clinic when they returned; and Roosevelt, exhausted from the stress of the conference, had less than two months to live. And on top of all this, word reached the ship when it was en route to Algiers that General de Gaulle was refusing to meet with Roosevelt. The haughty and mercurial French general had assured Hopkins that he would like nothing more than to talk with the American president on his way home from Yalta. Now he was reneging, apparently because he did not feel that the Yalta conference had been attentive enough to French postwar demands. Hopkins was upset over this turn of events, and Roosevelt was disappointed that he would not be meeting with de Gaulle. Sam Rosenman, who joined the party in Algiers, said, "All in all, it was a sorry ship."

The death of the genial Watson weighed heavily on the president, who considered Pa one of his closest friends. A jovial, bluff man who enjoyed fishing and hunting, he had been Roosevelt's military aide for twelve years and his appointments secretary for the last five. In recent years, Roosevelt had relied on Watson for his strength, both emotionally and physically. When he left his wheelchair, usually in public, and attempted to "walk," it was Watson who helped him stand and whose arm he held tightly. Watson appeared to be in good health, although he had suffered heart attacks at the Tehran conference and at the Quebec conference in the fall of 1944. In the past, when a member of his inner circle—including his mother—died, Roosevelt refused to show emotion or grieve publicly. When Pa died, he talked with those aboard the *Quincy* about his feelings of sadness, leading them to realize just how fragile he had become.[33]

When the three wire service reporters reached Casablanca late at night on February 11, they did not know the conference had already ended. From then on, their quest to get the Big Story resembled a French farce. They spent three nights in a luxury hotel, waiting for word on where to go next. Then, early on the third day, they were told by senior naval officers they were being flown to a base at Algiers, where they would be met by an army colonel. When they got there the colonel claimed he had no idea why they were there. Eventually they were taken to a hotel in the city. But Merriman Smith said they were worried that the *Quincy* at that moment might be steaming past Algiers and that they were missing their story. The next afternoon, Friday, they were drinking wine at a sidewalk cafe in the city when Sam Rosenman, one of Roosevelt's speechwriters, strolled by. They knew they were in the right place.

By Sunday they had hooked up with Early on board the *Quincy*. Smith said the press secretary ushered them to his cabin and handed Smith six bottles of Johnny Walker Black Label. "Gosh, Steve, this is wonderful. You really are too kind," Smith muttered. Early looked at him and said, "What the hell are you talking about, Smith. I want you to hold those for me while I tie them together. I'm taking them to Paris for Eisenhower." Not only did the reporters not get any good whiskey, they didn't get the story they had traveled halfway around the world in search of. Instead Early showed them a long memorandum, which obviously was the communiqué, and they thanked him, saying, "This will make fine copy, Steve. Worth the trip." Early looked puzzled. "I don't think you understand," he said. "This stuff was sent to the White House today and will be released there. You fellows won't be able to file anything until you return to Washington." The three reporters remained on board the *Quincy*, and during the voyage back to the United States, Roosevelt met twice with them to discuss his impressions of the Lavadia Palace and the town of Yalta. On February 23 he told them Pa Watson had died, but that no announcement would be made until they had returned to Washington.[34]

Early left to undertake his SHAEF mission in Europe. How he felt leaving a ship full of ill friends one can only wonder, but it must have been with a mixture of sadness and relief. The final communiqué of a long and sometimes difficult conference had been dispatched, and he was headed to France, where he would be reunited with both his son Buddy and his good friend Harry Butcher, once the head of Columbia Broadcasting System's Washington Bureau and now a naval aide to General Eisenhower, another old friend of Butcher's and Early's. But more than that, he finally had the monkey called White House off his back. He had every expectation that once he returned to Washington, he would walk out of the "great white jail" and at last earn the money needed to support his family. It did not turn out quite like that.

When Early arrived in Paris and hooked up with Butcher, he was ready to tackle the military's publicity problems, which had been plaguing the more than one thousand accredited correspondents who held identification cards with the special SHAEF stamp. When the military did choose to release news, the reporters, from the pressroom at their hotel, the Scribe in Paris, ensured that it went out over the teletype or the radio wires to their countries around the world. However, the problem was that too frequently the thrice-daily military briefings arranged by SHAEF's public relations staff failed to give the reporters all of the information they wanted, and the reporters were angry about this. Early's job was to attempt to repair this breach.[35]

Early arrived at Orly Airport in Paris from Algiers on February 20 in a C-54 transport plane, bringing with him not only the Johnny Walker for Eisenhower but six bottles of vodka, a gift from Stalin. The whiskey went to the general when they had dinner several nights later. The vodka undoubtedly was doled out as gifts from Early, who preferred bourbon, as he traveled through France. The military had booked Early into the Aga Khan suite at the Ritz Hotel in the heart of Paris, but he took one glance around and decided it was "a very poor address" for him, perhaps because high-ranking German military officials had occupied the once first-class hotel before the Allies liberated Paris from the Nazis. At any rate, he decided to bunk in with Butcher in the far more modest Raphael.

Three nights after Early arrived, he and Butcher joined Eisenhower for dinner at his Paris headquarters, where they shared stories and laughs—Steve told Ike a story about General Patton, who annoyed the War Department with his profane and unusually colorful phrases in his daily situation reports, so the War Department told him to write in less colorful and more official language. He complied, his first report a model of military language—except for the postscript below his signature, which read, "I peed in the Rhine today." For Early the evening meant some warmth in front of a large wood-burning fireplace. It delighted Early, who claimed the Raphael was the coldest place he had ever lived in. Butcher said Early practically sat on Butcher's four-hundred-watt electric heater, which gave out about as much comfort as a flatiron.

Early spent his first few days in Paris observing numerous military briefings, visiting the Communications Center in the Scribe Hotel, where he followed a news story from the time it was filed by a reporter through the copy room, through censorship, and to the commercial transmitter that sent it to New York, a process that took only seventeen minutes from start to receipt in New York—a feat Butcher called "damn good."

Then, on Saturday, February 24, Eisenhower held a press conference for about two hundred reporters at the Scribe Hotel, his first since the previous November and one that had been postponed several times because of calls to the field or lack of timeliness. But now a successful push of the Ninth and First Armies across the Saar and Roer rivers was underway, and Eisenhower wanted to share the news with the reporters. When he finished, Ike called Steve aside and asked what he thought of the press conference. In the hyperbole Early sometimes employed to ingratiate himself with someone he admired, he told the general, "It was the most magnificent performance of any man at a press conference that I have ever seen." He said Eisenhower knew his facts, spoke freely and frankly, and had a sense of humor, poise, and command.[36]

Butcher and Early left Paris the next day: two old friends sharing reminiscences, viewing the ravages of war, eating military grub, and bumping around on rutted roads. In all, they would travel twelve hundred miles through France, Germany, Luxembourg, and Holland. They began their journey by dining with Eisenhower, who had moved from Paris to a château near SHAEF headquarters in Rheims, eighty miles northeast of Paris. The next day they moved east to Verdun, then to the Argonne-Meuse cemetery, where Early found the names of some of his buddies from his old 80th Division in World War I. They spent a night in Luxembourg with about twenty American and British correspondents who were hungry for news about Yalta and the American home front. When Early asked them what they were hearing from their home offices, they replied, "Blivets—nothing but blivets." "What's a blivet?" Early asked. They said, "A blivet is a one-pound bag filled with two pounds of horse manure."[37]

They made a visit to the headquarters of the mercurial General Patton, who was chafing that his troops were not being allowed to finish their final push. He told the two men that one of the finest actions in military history came when the 80th Division recently had crossed the Saar River. This piqued Early's curiosity. The 80th was his division in World War I, and he asked for a guide to take them to the division headquarters at nearby Bitburg, Germany. Butcher wrote in his diary that they talked with some of the officers who crossed the river, a difficult maneuver because the German side was high hills, while the American side was level and wide open. The officers still were not quite sure how they managed the crossing. Butcher noticed that his friend Steve was impressed "that there was some fighting in this war and that all of it had not occurred in World War I." They left the 80th and drove along roads used by Germans in the Battle of the Bulge, an area littered with burned-out German tanks and other detritus of battle.[38]

They spent that night in the small Belgian town of Spa, headquarters of the First Army, where they talked with the few press correspondents who were there, since most had moved forward to cover the First Army's attack on the cathedral city of Cologne on the Rhine River. The next day they drove to Aachen, where they had lunch with the American officers of the military government of the city and ended a long day after driving in heavy rain at the Ninth Army's press camp at Maastricht, Holland. The next day found them back in Belgium in Namur, where they attended a briefing with American bomber pilots just back from missions. They met with General Omar Bradley, who updated them on European war news. Early wanted to get back to the Scribe Hotel in Paris, so they drove all day, stopping briefly at the side of the road, where they shared a lunch of corned beef, the can having been heated on the manifold of the engine en route.[39]

Butcher wrote that the Scribe "was feverish with good news." The Allies now controlled a long stretch of the Rhine River, and American bombers had been busy hitting Tokyo. Early lingered in Paris for a few days. He visited the office of his old army newspaper, *Stars and Stripes*, where the staff received him with great enthusiasm. After they all chatted informally, with Early sitting back reminiscing about his days with the paper, the staff brought out their largest headline, a proof sheet that said: "Early for President." Later Early told Butcher that the visit proved one of the most pleasant parts of his trip. He and Butcher also managed to play some poker with military officers before they drove back to Rheims on March 15 to dine with Eisenhower and to review a parade of paratroopers, where a war correspondent covering the event mistook Early for the mayor of Rheims, which must have given him and Butcher a good laugh. Then it was time to return to Washington.[40]

Early may have enjoyed the social aspects of his trip, but how effective his advice to SHAEF officials was is not clear. His task was one that may have been insurmountable. The report Early filed with the War Department recommended that whenever security required that news be delayed, the reporters would be given sufficient quotable information to write a story so the public would at least be aware of the reasons for the delay. Butcher thought it would greatly help the army's press relations. However, three months later, one newspaper declared that the recommendations had had no visible effect, and the correspondents were still complaining of excessive censorship.[41]

But on March 16, as he was preparing to leave Paris, Early learned that his son Buddy, who was commanding a mortar platoon in Company M of the 259th Infantry of the 65th Division, then northwest of Saarbrucken, Germany, on the eastern border of France, had been wounded in battle. He had been operated on at a field hospital and then, with other wounded men, was evacuated to a hospital near Swindon, England. Within twenty-four hours Harry Butcher had arranged for his friend to see his son, so instead of flying home, a worried Early left Orly Airport for England. When he got there, he found that a bullet had passed through Buddy's left leg just below his knee. Other than being woozy from the medications, Buddy was in good spirits, which greatly reassured his father. Buddy said a small party of Germans had infiltrated the line at night and he and his comrades intercepted them. Fighting broke out. While Buddy got off some hand grenades, he caught a bullet. Early told Butcher that Buddy's biggest concern was how soon he could return to his division.[42]

Early sent Bill Hassett back at the White House a telegram marked "confidential," asking him to inform Helen of their son's injury and to tell her that Buddy was "in excellent condition." She should not worry. He told Hassett to tell her to not make this public until she was given official notification by the War Department. Hassett replied, saying that Helen "understood the situation," and that Early was to tell Buddy that his little brother, Tommy, heard the news, took two hard-boiled eggs with him to keep up his strength, and went fishing. (Six weeks later, Buddy was recovering in a hospital in Richmond, Virginia. His wound healed, but he never returned to his unit.)[43]

Early returned to Paris after he was assured that Buddy would be fine. He remained there for another three days, tying up loose ends from his extensive travels and meetings with military public relations officers, and on March 21 he flew home. While he enjoyed traveling and socializing with his old friend, Butcher probably was not unhappy to put Early on the plane. It seems that, although he had been offered a private office in Paris, Early had refused and instead set up headquarters at a small pine table in Butcher's cramped office. Butcher said both of them had friends coming and going, so they had "practically a continuous bull session."[44]

As he flew across the Atlantic to Washington, Early, not at all a religious man, must have wondered if a guardian angel had placed him a brief plane ride away from his son when he most needed his father. And shortly he would learn that his friend and boss needed him one more time.

24

THEN THERE WAS ONE

When Early arrived back in Washington after the Yalta conference and his work at SHAEF, he had been away from the White House for two months, and a lot had happened. With the death of Pa Watson, Roosevelt was without an appointments secretary. Bill Hassett had been filling the job temporarily, and Jonathan Daniels was attempting to navigate the rough waters of the press office. One of Early's secretaries, Ruthjane Rumelt, wrote to him while he was in France to give him the latest news and gossip from the White House, most notably that they were "anxiously awaiting" his return. She said the press office had been in "a state of confusion" since he left. She sympathized with Early's desire to leave when she wrote, "Certainly you don't deserve to be pulled back here to be tied down to the job of straightening things out again and again and again."[1]

By the time Early was back, Daniels had evidently improved his skills as a press secretary. Because he already had given Early his blessing to leave in June, Roosevelt, with Early's approval, now made Daniels the permanent press secretary. Daniels, who was intimidated by the outspoken and competent Early, was convinced that Early did not really want to leave. Daniels thought that the "truth" about Early's departure was that Roosevelt no longer trusted him and was trying to push him out of the White House because the press secretary had become so well known and his opinions were so highly regarded by those inside and outside government. This is highly dubious speculation from Daniels, who admitted in his memoirs an animosity toward Early for most of the time that he worked for him. Early never—publicly or privately—spoke negatively about Daniels.

The old and ailing president was not keen to see one of his very few remaining close confidants leave his side, so he asked Hassett to return to his job as correspondence secretary, and he turned to Early to fill in as the appointments secretary, a position most recently held by Pa Watson. In a press release handed out on March 24, hours before he was scheduled to leave for four days in Hyde Park, Roosevelt announced that Early had agreed to stay on until June 1, at which time "Steve will be free to enter private employment in accordance with the wishes he has expressed to me." Early said simply, "I'm wide open. I haven't negotiated anything, I haven't accepted anything, and I'm not obligated to anyone."[2]

Once the news broke that Early definitely would be leaving the White House, the letters poured in. His scrapbook for this period is full of messages from friends and journalists. Harold Ickes, secretary of the interior from the beginning of the Roosevelt presidency, wrote: "I do not like the thought of your going." Bert Andrews, White House correspondent for the *New York Herald-Tribune*, said, "Washington won't be the same without you doing business at the old stand." And from Lewis Wood, a *New York Times* reporter in Washington: "I think your loyalty to President Roosevelt, and the work incident to that loyalty, have been magnificent."[3]

Newspapers around the country ran stories about his departure from the press office. The *Tennessean* in Nashville published an editorial that said, "Mr. Early has been the presidential buffer at that sparking point where the capitol newsgatherers meet the nation's most important news source. When the chief executive himself was not available for [an] interview, it has been the press secretary's part to release White House statements, to confirm or deny reports brought to be tested at headquarters, and generally to handle relations of the presidential office with what is undoubtedly the keenest group of inquisitors on earth. Hence, 'Steve Early' has had its place in reams upon reams of copy and has appeared in innumerable dispatches under the Washington dateline."[4]

On March 26, while Roosevelt was still in Hyde Park, Early attended Daniels's morning press conference; rather, he was sitting in his old office clearing out his desk when the newsmen walked in at 10:45. Early looked at Daniels and began to apologize, "I didn't mean to . . ." But the new press secretary, perhaps concerned that the reporters would interpret any other remark as an affront to their old friend, interrupted him: "Keep that seat—keep that seat, Steve." Early continued cleaning out the twelve-year accumulation of papers, knickknacks, photos, and probably an ashtray or two filled with cigarette butts and pipe ashes, along with paraphernalia from his desk, the walls, and his bookshelves. As he worked, he told the reporters, "I am now engaged in the somewhat pleasant but rather dirty task of moving out of here," adding that he was trying to make it "as clean as possible for Mr. Daniels."

Daniels said he not only would try to keep the office clean, but that he and his assistant, Eben Ayers, a former newspaper reporter, "hope very much that we are going to be able to do—to approach doing as good a job as Steve has done; and I am perfectly frank to say that I am as anxious to get into this 'hot seat' as Steve is to get out of it." But Daniels's career as a presidential press secretary would be short lived.[5]

When the president returned from Yalta at the end of February, after more than a month away, Bill Hassett, who had remained in Washington, thought Roosevelt had not looked better in a year. But Grace Tully saw not a president rested from a sea voyage, but "weariness etched deeply in his thinning face." Jonathan Daniels, sitting in Early's office during Yalta, found himself forced to select from the black-and-white photos flown back daily from the conference those that did not make the president "look like an aged, fading, dying man" to release to the press. He found none. Daniels wrote candidly, "I was perhaps guilty, as I have since been charged, of deluding the American people by releasing only the least tragic pictures of the face of Franklin Roosevelt taken there. Those were sad enough." When Roosevelt returned, people spoke openly of his "shocking" appearance and concluded he was seriously failing.[6]

The president's doctor, Ross McIntire, who had been at Yalta, agreed with Grace Tully. Roosevelt was a sick man. When he delivered his report on Yalta to Congress on March 1, McIntire was there.

He wrote in his memoirs that the president's voice sagged, and every now and then he passed his hand over his eyes as if to clear his sight. He asked permission of Congress to sit during his talk, explaining that he would tire himself if he stood with the ten pounds of braces on his legs. David Brinkley, then a young reporter for NBC in the capital, wrote in his book *Washington Goes to War* that it was one of the poorest speeches Roosevelt had ever given. Brinkley said he kept wandering away from the written text and ad-libbing lines that made no sense. His voice was weak and quavering.[7]

As the month of March rolled on, McIntire said, Roosevelt refused to take his afternoon rest, skipped the daily massage of his legs, ate lunch at his desk while he held conferences with visitors, and worked late into the night. When the doctor chastised him, the president told him, "There is a job to be done, and just so much time in which to do it." Then one day at the end of March, Roosevelt announced to that he was going to Warm Springs.[8]

Grace Tully, who spent most days at the president's elbow, said that when he stopped in Washington between Hyde Park and Warm Springs that March, she was startled by the change in his appearance. "I almost burst into tears," she wrote. His face was ashen, with dark shadows under his eyes, his cheeks drawn gauntly. Around this same time, Tully watched patiently as the president attempted to sign some letters, but his hand shook so badly he could not control the pen. Finally, she gently took his arm and told him the task could wait until he was at Warm Springs.[9]

Steve Early never spoke publicly about those last months of the president's life. Did he know of the heart attack episodes about which Jimmy Roosevelt later wrote? Jimmy was in the military service and saw Early perhaps only briefly when he was at the White House for the fourth inauguration and his father's second episode. It is doubtful if either father or son mentioned it to anyone, even to doctors McIntire or Bruenn. Jimmy would not have discussed it without his father's permission, and the president seemed uninterested in his own health.

After a month away from the president, did Early too notice a weary and ailing, now often querulous, Boss? Probably, but he was too busy rearranging his own future to pay much attention. After all, Roosevelt's health had been precarious for well over a year. Jim Bishop wrote that Early and Harry Hopkins and some of the other men close

to the president turned their backs on his deteriorating health, preferring to recall the man they drank cocktails with at the end of the
workday—the man who enjoyed an uproarious game of poker, went
to baseball games in hopes of booing the umpire, and got a kick out
of playing practical jokes. Today we would call that "denial." Steve
Early may have exhibited a "towering temper" on occasion—he may
have roared like a wounded mountain lion when someone crossed his
path—but he was an unusually sensitive and caring man, and it would
have been most unlike him not to be aware of and concerned about
Roosevelt's deteriorating health. However, there was little the president's friends could do to help him if he refused to even pay attention
to the advice of his own doctors.[10]

United Press reporter Merriman Smith said he thought Early was
always honest in what he told the correspondents about the president's health, but as Roosevelt grew older, it seemed Early and the rest
of the staff tried to say less and less about his health. Smith concluded
that in part this was a result of the prevalence of untrue rumors that
circulated about his health, becoming especially virulent during election times.[11]

Would Early have walked out of the White House if he had
known the seriousness of Roosevelt's health? The answer to that is as
complex as their relationship was over the years. On the one hand, he
had spent twelve years as a buffer between a president whose ire often
was directed at a press that was just trying to do its job. For all those
times he was successful in convincing Roosevelt to allow him to give
the reporters the information they desired, he was forced to smooth
things over with angry reporters who had been rebuffed by the president and later take the heat from an angry Roosevelt. As the war progressed, the president became more and more secretive, occasionally
shutting out even those closest to him. It was not that Early would
have chosen to leave his friend at this crucial moment. If indeed he
was in denial over the true state of Roosevelt's health, and it is heavily
documented that Early was in dire need of a larger income, it is reasonable to expect him to seek Roosevelt's approval to leave. And when
given that approval, he would leave.

Between the time Early returned from Europe that March of
1945 and the day Roosevelt left for what would be his last visit to
Warm Springs, they were in the White House at the same time fewer

than three days. When Roosevelt announced he was going to Georgia, what Early did not know was that he would never see his boss and friend alive again. There is no record of what Early actually did as appointments secretary. Because the president was away most of the time, Early probably stopped by the pressroom to chat with the reporters, who were no doubt delighted to banter with the former press secretary. He finished cleaning out his office. He probably peeked over the shoulder of his replacement now and again or handed out some advice, but only when asked. It is likely he had a few long lunches with friends. He may have made it to the racetrack or the golf course, or both. And he made final arrangements for his post–White House employment. Mostly, though, he smiled. A photo of him taken at this time shows him wearing a wide grin. He finally was leaving the pressure-cooker.[12]

What is on record—and what has been recounted in any number of books—is what happened after Roosevelt arrived by train in Warm Springs, Georgia, on that warm and sunny Good Friday afternoon in late March. As he often did when he was planning to be away from the White House for more than a weekend, he took along a fairly sizeable retinue. With him were Bill Hassett; the president's cousins Margaret Suckley and Laura Delano, whose company he always enjoyed; Basil O'Connor, his former law partner and friend; Leighton McCarthy, retiring ambassador to Canada and a trustee of the Warm Springs Foundation; Grace Tully and two other secretaries; Louise Hackmeister and Dewey Long, the White House switchboard operator and the communications officer, respectively; navy lieutenant commander George Fox, the president's masseur and pharmacist; and Dr. Howard Bruenn. (McIntire had remained in Washington to testify before a congressional committee in his capacity as surgeon general.) The three wire service reporters, including Merriman Smith, rode in a separate car on the train, under strict orders from Daniels not to send stories back to their offices unless the president held a press conference or specifically gave them a story.[13]

One evening soon after they arrived, Hassett was walking outside in the warm spring air when he came across Bruenn. He stopped to talk with Bruenn about the president's health. Hassett said, "He is slipping away from us and no earthly power can keep him here." Hassett added that he felt the Boss "was beyond all human resources."

Bruenn reluctantly admitted that Roosevelt's condition was "precarious," but "not hopeless." When their conversation ended, Hassett, a devout Catholic who sometimes could be sentimentally spiritual, said he was convinced "the Boss was leaving us."[14]

Roosevelt had first visited Warm Springs in 1924 when he learned that its warm, rich mineral springs soothed his paralyzed legs. Eventually he bought a modest six-room house, and there, nestled among rolling forests at the southern end of the Appalachian Mountains near the Alabama border, the home became a haven where he could work, relax, and swim in the warm waters. For the next twelve days on what would be his last visit there, Roosevelt alternated between working and resting—sleeping late each morning and taking care only of the most urgent materials that came by air from Washington. On April 5 President Sergio Osmena of the Philippines came to Warm Springs from nearby Fort Benning for lunch and to discuss independence now that it appeared the Japanese were close to being ousted from his country. When their meeting was concluded, the two presidents invited the three wire service reporters into the living room of the small but comfortable Little White House, Roosevelt's home at Warm Springs. Merriman Smith described the president that warm, sunny afternoon as friendly, in an easy mood, but with hands that trembled when he tried to fit a cigarette into his old ivory holder. It was the last press conference he ever held, and Smith wrote that if the three reporters had known that, they would have paid better attention to the smallest details.[15]

The president spoke about his meeting with Osmena and their plans for the United Nations, and especially the United States' use of the islands as military bases to ensure continuing peace in the Pacific. Smith said Roosevelt "coughed lightly at frequent intervals, but he smoked chain fashion." When the conference was over, he joked with the reporters. "Have a cig?" he said, shoving his pack of Camels across the card table toward Smith, who wrote that he was astonished at his use of that slang word, more suitable for flappers and sheikhs in the movies. When Roosevelt tried to remove a cigarette from the pack, his hands shook so badly he could barely get it out. Smith leaned over to light it for him. He declined, saying he had some kitchen matches of his own. Smith said he then seemed to gather all his strength and control to light the cigarette. "It was an intense thing. I wanted not to watch," he recalled.[16]

The president's routine of light work in the morning and rest in the afternoon continued. He was busy making plans to return to Washington on April 18 in time to give a state dinner the following night for the visiting regent of Iraq, and then the next day he would leave for San Francisco to address the opening session of the United Nations, the final details of which had been ironed out at Yalta. Eleanor would accompany him, and they would return via Hyde Park.[17]

News on the war coming in to the Little White House that week was most positive: British and American bombers were continuing a blitz on German cruisers, and the Allies were launching successful raids on the Japanese airfields on Formosa. On April 11 the nearly twenty thousand survivors of Buchenwald concentration camp were liberated. During the two weeks of fighting, Allied forces took three hundred thousand German prisoners.[18]

On Thursday morning, April 12, Steve Early telephoned Bill Hassett to tell him Washington had been fog bound most of the night, so the daily mail pouch had been rushed south by train instead of by air. It would arrive in Atlanta by 9:00 a.m. and would be in Warm Springs two hours later. Oh—and by the way, Early said, let the Boss sleep an extra hour. He probably needed it. Hassett agreed. Meanwhile, Merriman Smith, perhaps to assuage the boredom, a few days earlier had organized a group of friends of Roosevelt's who lived and worked in the area, and they had set about planning a barbecue to be held in the president's honor at 4:00 that afternoon. Hassett told them the president would prefer a pot of Brunswick stew, so they added that to the menu. At the Little White House that Thursday morning, Elizabeth Shoumatoff, an artist and friend of Lucy Mercer Rutherfurd, who had accompanied her friend to Warm Springs, was busy setting up her easel in the living room, despite Hassett's remonstrances that the president was not up to sitting for a portrait. As Shoumatoff measured Roosevelt's facial features, Hassett thought he looked "so fatigued and weary." He decided that he would ask Bruenn "to put an end to this unnecessary hounding of a sick man."[19]

As Shoumatoff worked on the sketch, Roosevelt read some mail that Hassett had given him from the pouch that came in that morning; he signed letters and citations. He inquired about the barbecue. Lunch would be served soon, he was told, but first he decided he would smoke a cigarette and read some more papers. Then, at 1:15

p.m., he lifted his left hand to his temple and immediately dropped it. Quietly, he said, "I have a terrific headache." His body slumped to his left and was motionless. He was still breathing. Shoumatoff ran out the front door and screamed at one of the Secret Service agents standing there, "Call a doctor. Something terrible has happened to the president."

The call went out to find Dr. Bruenn, who was at the swimming pool. Bill Hassett was summoned from his cottage, where he had gone after his lunch. When Hassett got to Roosevelt's cottage, Bruenn was there, and the president had been moved to his bedroom, where he lay on his bed, eyes closed, mouth open and breathing in heavy, noisy gasps: "the awful breathing," Hassett called it. He said he was convinced Roosevelt "was now beyond all earthly help." Bruen telephoned McIntire at the White House, but both men knew there was virtually nothing they could do. McIntire did ask Bruenn to summon Dr. James Paullin, a well-known internist from Atlanta. Paullin drove as fast as he dared. He agreed with Bruenn's diagnosis: There was nothing they could do. Sitting in the living room with Grace Tully and Roosevelt's cousins Laura Delano and Margaret Suckley, Hassett said, he knew when the dreadful breathing stopped that the end had come. At 3:35 p.m., Bruenn pronounced the president of the United States dead. It was 4:35 p.m. Eastern War Time in Washington.[20]

Once he had dealt with the fog-caused delay in getting the mail to Warm Springs, Early spent some time talking with Secretary of State Stettinius, perhaps about their time at Yalta, maybe about Early's job prospects. Then, after lunch, Early headed over to the Washington apartment of Frances Nash Watson, widow of his friend Pa Watson. It is not clear why he went there; however, as he was now sitting in Pa's office as the appointments secretary, it is conceivable that in clearing out he had collected some of Pa's personal belongings and was returning them to his widow. And knowing Steve Early, as a longtime close friend of Pa's, he simply was checking in to make sure she was all right, since the couple had no children. Thus, he was not at the White House when the first call from Dr. Bruenn to Dr. McIntire came in.[21]

Eleanor Roosevelt and her daughter, Anna, were in the White House when the first call from Warm Springs came in. Anna was on her way out to go to the Naval Hospital to visit her son Johnny, who was ill with strep throat. McIntire found her just before she left and said her father had suffered a seizure and she should not be concerned. She went on to the hospital. Laura Delano telephoned Eleanor and said the president had fainted. Only somewhat alarmed at this point, the First Lady summoned McIntire, who told her he was not sure what the problem was, even though he was in constant contact with Bruenn and was aware of the severity of Roosevelt's condition. Eleanor was scheduled to speak at the Sulgrave Club in downtown Washington, and McIntire suggested she keep the engagement. She did.[22]

Merriman Smith was helping put the finishing touches on the barbecue. He had no idea of the drama in progress a few miles away. When 4:00 rolled around and Roosevelt had not arrived, country fiddlers began to play and everyone waited. Smith said that by 4:20, he was a little irritated. He found a Signal Corps sergeant in a nearby barn sitting next to his shortwave portable. Smith asked if the sergeant would contact the Little White House. What he learned was that nothing was moving there: no people coming out, no cars loading up to drive to the barbecue. Smith knew something was wrong. He tracked down a telephone and called Louise Hackmeister, who was in charge of the White House switchboard.

"Hackie, this is Smitty. Why aren't you people on the way? What's holding things up?" Smith wrote that normally Hackie was very level-headed. Today she was shouting, and her voice sounded panicky: "I don't know, Smitty. But Mr. Hassett wants to see you. Get the other two boys [wire service reporters] and go to his cottage as fast as you can." She would say no more. Smith found the reporters and a car and driver to take them down the mountain. He also saw someone who had come for the barbecue who worked for Southern Bell Telephone and Telegraph Company. "Get some circuits lined up to Washington," Smith called to him. As they raced down the narrow, twisting road, the three reporters were sure they knew what was going on: Germany had capitulated.[23]

When Early finally walked into McIntire's office, the doctor was tense. He said he was talking to Bruenn. Then he looked over at Early and said, "Howard [Bruenn] says, 'Hold the phone.' He thinks something has happened in the bedroom. He—" Early could hear a voice interrupt at the other end of the line, and his heart skipped a beat when he saw the look on McIntire's face. "This is the end," the doctor said.[24]

Jonathan Daniels claimed in his diary that Hassett was intimidated by Early and was not especially fond of the teasing, sometimes bordering on the sarcastic, that he sent Hassett's way. But on this day, Hassett in Warm Springs and Early in Washington worked like a precision team. There was a job to do, and they did it. They had to inform the world of the death of the most powerful leader on the planet, a death that hit both men personally as well as professionally. Once Early realized that the president was dead, he instructed McIntire and Hassett to tell no one else until he had broken the news to Mrs. Roosevelt.[25]

Early telephoned Eleanor at the Sulgrave Club and said, "Mrs. Roosevelt, I wish you would come home at once." She did not ask why. She thanked him and immediately returned to the White House. When she arrived, she went to her sitting room and asked Early and McIntire to see her immediately. Steve, whom she had known almost as long as her husband had, looked at her and said, "The President slipped away this afternoon." She told them she must notify her sons, all away in the armed services. Then she told Early, "I am more sorry for the people of the country and the world than I am for us." Early told her he would call Harry Truman to the White House. For the moment, the nation's press could wait.[26]

The vice president was on his way through the Capitol to a private hideaway that House Speaker Sam Rayburn kept on the ground floor, a place where he could meet quietly to conduct informal business away from his office. When he got there, Truman was told he had a call from Steve Early at the White House. Truman fixed himself a drink and then dialed Early. He said Early's voice sounded tense and strange as he told the vice president to come to the White House "as quickly and as quietly" as he could. Truman said later he thought that perhaps the president had returned early from Warm Springs, and he was being summoned to meet with him about something important. He said, "I didn't allow myself to think anything else."[27]

At the White House, as they awaited the arrival of Truman, Early and Mrs. Roosevelt discussed funeral arrangements. She asked Early and McIntire to fly with her that evening to Warm Springs to arrange for the president's body to be returned to Washington the following day.[28]

At the same time, Hassett was informing the three wire reporters that the president was dead. Early left Mrs. Roosevelt and Truman so he could go to his office to let the world in on the death of his friend and boss. Because of wartime censorship, the public was unaware that Roosevelt had been in Warm Springs. Early sat down at his desk, picked up the telephone, and placed a conference call to the Washington bureaus of the three wire services, a call similar to the one he had made just over four years ago when he told them Pearl Harbor had been bombed. The operator at the White House end forgot to tell them who was calling, so when Early got on the line and said, "Flash—The President died this afternoon at—" a telephone operator interrupted, "Do you mean President Roosevelt?" It was a pure Early response. He shouted, "Christ! There's only one President. Of course I mean President Roosevelt." And he calmly continued his announcement. The *Washington News* said this call "revealed Steve at his efficient best."

The newspaper went on to say, "No one will ever know what it cost Steve Early to pick up the telephone and say Flash—The President is dead." At fifty-six, he was the oldest and closest friend of Roosevelt, and, the story said, this was a story Early had not expected he would ever have to handle. The story went on to say that everyone knew how deeply Early "loved the Chief. It would have been understandable if his voice had trembled a little. But it didn't."[29]

There was so much Steve Early had to handle that afternoon that he had little time to stop and grieve. After he summoned Mrs. Roosevelt and Vice President Truman to the White House, after they worked out arrangements for bringing the president's body back to Washington, after he let the world know the Boss was dead, he called Hassett and asked him and Bruenn to select a casket both in keeping with the First Lady's wishes and suitable for the dead commander in chief to make his final ride in back to the capital.[30]

Then, at 6:00 p.m., Early and McIntire held a joint press conference, which the doctor called "a tough one for me to have to give." He gave the reporters a brief summary of the afternoon's events, and still unable—or unwilling—to grasp the president's serious decline in recent months, he said, "This came out of a clear sky." Early gave the doctor about a minute to talk before he took over, presenting a clear and detailed account of what had happened at Warm Springs and in Washington. This press meeting was in sharp contrast to the one Daniels called later that evening, at which he fumbled and hesitated as the reporters peppered him with questions, making it clear that for the most part he had been left out of the loop that day.[31]

Early told the reporters that he, McIntire, and Mrs. Roosevelt would be leaving for Warm Springs by 7:00. Shortly before they left, Early came out of his office and told the reporters that the vice president was with members of the cabinet, and as soon as Chief Justice Stone arrived, he would be sworn in as president. Early's last official announcement to the press in the White House was the following: "When he [Truman] is sworn in, you will be told. And you will be told the second he is sworn in. We expect the Chief Justice to come in to administer the oath." He also ensured that the swearing-in would have maximum press coverage. He asked Truman's permission for news photographers to capture the ceremony. And at 7:05 Eastern War Time that night Vice President Harry Truman was sworn in as the thirty-third president of the United States.[32]

Early, Mrs. Roosevelt, and McIntire flew into a small airport near Columbus, Georgia, and were driven the thirty-five miles north to Warm Springs, arriving around midnight. During the night the president's body was placed aboard the last car—the one where he usually sat—in the twelve-car train at the Warm Springs station, the same train that had brought him and his staff there two weeks earlier. The copper-lined mahogany casket was draped with an American flag, flowers sent by friends were placed around the car, and the shades were left up, a part of Early's plan to ensure that the casket be visible to the grieving crowds he anticipated as the train rolled toward Washington. A military guard of honor representing each of the four branches of the service—army, navy, marines, and coast guard—stood at attention. Early, McIntire, and Bruenn chose to sleep aboard the train that night, a sentimental gesture to be certain, but one they later wished they had forgone, since throughout the night army trucks rumbled into the station and noisily loaded baggage on the train, making it nearly impossible for the three men to get much sleep.[33]

About 10:30 the next morning, the funeral train pulled out of the Warm Springs station to the ringing of church bells and moved slowly toward Washington. At those towns where the train stopped, Early got off and allowed a small delegation to go aboard to place wreaths at the head of the coffin. In towns where the train was not stopping, Early ordered the engineer to slow down so the crowds could see the coffin through the train's window. At night, he ensured that it remained visible by having all the shades on the train drawn except for those in this, the last car. The bright ceiling lights on the raised casket and the military honor guard around it must have been a dramatic sight for the mourners.[34]

As the train rolled along at ten miles an hour toward Washington, it passed through Atlanta, then through western South Carolina and into North Carolina. Merriman Smith's gift for details gave us this description of its passage: "The train passed a cotton field where Negro women were working on spring planting. I looked out and saw four of them kneeling near the edge of the field. Their hands were clasped together and raised in prayerful supplication." He said that at every stop, crowds gathered: Men and women wept openly, church choirs stood by the tracks and sang "Rock of Ages" and "Abide with Me," Boy Scout troops and National Guard units saluted behind lowered flags.

The most impressive moment of the journey, Smith concluded, was when the train passed through a small depot and a handful of Boy Scouts at the front of a group began singing "Onward Christian Soldiers." The adults around them hesitantly joined in, until people for blocks around took up the strains of the song. As their voice grew, he said it was "heartening" to hear the residents of the little town singing "Christianity's wonderful, brave marching song." All night the funeral train moved along, making several stops to change engines and crews. At 6:30 the next morning, the train stopped briefly at Charlottesville, Virginia, a few miles from Early's boyhood home.[35]

At 10:00 a.m., the train pulled into Union Station, where Anna Roosevelt and the wives of her brothers, President and Mrs. Truman, Henry Wallace, and a few old family friends were standing quietly waiting to extend their sympathy to Mrs. Roosevelt. The casket was taken from the train and placed on a black horse-drawn army caisson. Followed by cars carrying the family, along with the staff—Early and Hassett rode in one car—and the three reporters who had come from Warm Springs, the caisson rolled by hundreds of weeping mourners lining the streets of the capital. Merriman Smith said that as the cortege passed the Justice Department building, an old Negro woman broke through the police lines and ran sobbing a few feet into the street, moaning "Lord God, take care of us now."[36]

When the procession reached the White House, the casket was placed in the East Room and the president lay in state, the casket remaining closed. At 4:00 p.m., about two hundred invited guests—

cabinet members; justices of the Supreme Court; Roosevelt's family and his staff; Governor Dewey, his opponent in 1944; and friends such as Bernard Baruch—gathered for a simple funeral service. At 10:00 that night the casket was put back on the train for its last ride, to Hyde Park and his beloved home overlooking the Hudson River. Aboard were most of those who had made the journey from Warm Springs, along with members of the cabinet and their spouses, and other close friends of the late president.

It was now the morning of Sunday, April 15. Bill Hassett wrote in his diary, "F. D. R. came home today." A twenty-one-gun salute echoed and reechoed across the Hudson Valley. With muffled drums, a band played Chopin's "Funeral March." A caisson, drawn by six horses and followed by a seventh horse, boots reversed in its stirrups to symbolize a fallen warrior, bore the casket to the Rose Garden, a modest, secluded plot of land a short distance behind the imposing Roosevelt home. An escort of cadets from West Point stood guard. There the rector of St. James Episcopal Church in Hyde Park, where Roosevelt worshiped when he was home, spoke the committal prayer, and the casket was lowered into the simple grave. Standing behind the Roosevelt family was Steve Early, who chose never to talk about how he felt that day.[37]

25

THE LAST RIDE

The dirt had barely settled on the Old Warrior's grave when it seemed that anyone and everyone who had worked with him began writing their memoirs. Agents and publishers lined up to solicit the manuscripts. Less than a year after the president's death, Ross McIntire had published a book of memories of his twelve years as Roosevelt's personal physician. The book also served as an attempt by the doctor to justify his medical care of the president during his last years and to assuage rumors that Roosevelt had committed suicide or was poisoned. That same year Frances Perkins, the secretary of labor throughout Roosevelt's presidency, rushed out with *The Roosevelt I Knew*. Over the next few years, Harold Ickes, Henry Morgenthau, Bill Hassett, Sam Rosenman, Robert Sherwood, and others wrote detailed books about their experiences with Roosevelt. Even Grace Tully got into the act when she wrote *Franklin Delano Roosevelt, My Boss*.

Some of those closest to him during most or all of his presidency died before they could put pen to paper. Louis Howe's memoirs were left to be "related" by his secretary. Missy LeHand might have written her story, but she too was dead. So was Marvin McIntyre, a former journalist who probably could have told a great story. Harry Hopkins was too busy simply trying to survive to write a book. He died on January 26, 1946. And so it went. Every year, it seemed, someone else who had been a part of the Roosevelt legacy wrote a book. All except Steve Early.

Just twelve days after Roosevelt died, the offers really began pouring in. The first was from Atlantic Monthly Press. Then, on May 1, the William Morris Agency in New York wrote to Early, saying that "one of the leading book publishers" was asking for a book of reminiscences: "The publisher has mentioned that the advance which he would be willing to pay would be extraordinarily high." To both requests, Early replied that at the present time he was not planning to write a book or any articles for magazines or newspapers. His reasons were many, but not the least was his loyalty to his old Boss. "I am one who firmly believes that the confidences and trust received while in public office have no termination date—that they should be kept after one leaves public office as well as during the years he serves, the years he receives the confidence of his Chief," he told another New York book publisher.[1]

A writer by trade, it would have been natural for Early to sit down at the typewriter in his study on Morningside Drive and write a book about his life with Roosevelt. But he chose not to. "To all who have inquired, I have stated my resolve to wait until others—and there are many of them—have finished their respective works," he wrote to an editor in 1947. "Only then can I tell whether the record is fairly reported. Meanwhile, I try to keep an open mind."[2]

Early confided to his friend Joe Davies in 1947:

There are a lot of reasons why I have not written a book or anything. I am told there are now some 17 volumes in the course of preparation. A half dozen or more already have been published. None of these, not even all of them, will silence Westbrook Pegler [the columnist] or others of his ilk. Insofar as Pegler and his sort are concerned, they will continue to denounce and defame our old Chief. Every volume that comes off the presses will give the enemies more ammunition. They will take issue with everything that is written about F.D.R. and it matters not who the author may be. These people will search the pages trying to find something to deny and denounce. The controversy will go on and on as long as they can get something new to shoot at. I am certain, if you or I wrote anything now, the Peglerites would rub their hands in glee—in ghoulish anticipation of the target we would give them. We would encourage them to keep firing. The best way to silence the enemies' guns, assuming the strategy permits the employment of such tactics, is to cut off their supplies, to let them run out of ammunition and to ignore them the meanwhile.[3]

In 1948 Early told FDR's son Jimmy that in the flow of literature being produced about his father's tenure as president, he was reading "some most amazing and unbelievable things" that allegedly occurred when Early and Jimmy worked together in the White House briefly in the late 1930s. "I am tempted to break my resolution and write, but I won't. I have no desire to tell the readers how important I thought I was once upon a time, nor to reveal any of the confidences entrusted to me. I do not believe that the passing of one who shared his secrets with you—who trusted you as a member of the family—gives you the right to sell those secrets now that he has gone. A confidence is a sacred trust not to be violated ever."[4]

The day after Roosevelt's death, Kent Cooper, the executive director of the Associated Press, sent Early a letter offering him a position as a roving reporter with the AP, with no indication of the specific kinds of stories he would cover. Cooper may have had an underlying motive of persuading Early eventually to write a column on his years in the White House, but if so, it was not mentioned in the letter. Cooper reminded Early, the old AP man, that like any other newspaperman, he probably could not "get the whiff of printers' ink out of his nostrils." Early decided that while Cooper was right, such a job was best held by a younger man than he. Early reminded his friend that he was "much older than the fifty six years that have past [*sic*] since I came into the world in '89. In other words, I am more old and worn than the calendar would indicate. Mine has been a fighting life. The work that I have done has been of that nature. And that work has added years the calendar knows nothing about and won't tell. I can feel them."[5]

However, right after Roosevelt died, there was perhaps a more compelling reason why Early shunned the many offers he received to write a book about the Boss: He was busy helping a new president get settled into the White House. On April 21 he was sworn in as a special assistant to Truman, who said he would honor Roosevelt's decision to let Early leave on June 1. An editorial cartoon in the *Washington Star* on April 19 shows Truman at his desk with papers labeled "advice" flying around him and Early standing next to him trying to help organize them. Truman also asked Hassett, Daniels, and Rosenman to stay on to help with the transition.[6]

There was some gossip around the White House as to why Early stayed on, when earlier he had been so eager to leave. Some thought it was because he had not yet secured another job, and with Roosevelt's death his value to any prospective employer ceased. The former was more or less the truth. He was quietly negotiating with the Pullman-Standard Car Manufacturing Company to become a vice president. The latter simply was false. As time would tell, Early's prestige continued at a high level. For now, he would remain at the White House. After all, he was Steve Early. He wanted to help; it was ingrained in him. He also needed to be in familiar surroundings and among colleagues to grieve properly. He had not only lost a boss, he had lost a way of life.[7]

One thing is for certain: When the entourage returned to Washington after Warm Springs, the train rides, and the funeral services, Early was exhausted. Merriman Smith realized he had slept a total of four hours since the night before Roosevelt died. He said that all who had gone through the events in Warm Springs, then Washington, and finally Hyde Park "were red-eyed and their shoulders drooped."[8]

Early wrote little of his feelings about the death of the Boss, but he did attempt to respond to a letter that Eleanor Roosevelt sent to him on April 20. She wrote, "I don't trust myself to say what is in my heart so I write you these few lines. You and I have been 'fellow travelers' since 1920 and you've always been loyal and kind. Franklin loved you and I am deeply grateful to you and have a deep and abiding trust and affection for you." She ended the letter by asking him to keep in touch, "for I shall be wanting to see you whenever you find the time."[9]

To this, Early replied, "For years there have been two I have thought of as the most wonderful women—my Mother and you. This is, I know, a poor way of expressing it. But it is difficult to put into written or spoken words the feelings that have been so long locked deep in my heart. You and the President made me feel almost as one of the family. And that is the way it always will be with me. Please think of me and treat me that way. If I can ever be of service, if you ever want or need me, do let me know. It will be a pleasure, an honor and a privilege." For the next two years, Early and Eleanor occasionally corresponded, apprising each other of such mundane matters as their health and reminiscing about their White House days. She often invited him to visit her in New York City where she now lived; he always replied that his work was keeping him too busy. Once he lectured her about taking some time off from her own work as a delegate to the newly formed United Nations. Another time he sent her flowers for her birthday.[10]

By Monday morning, April 16, 1945, Early was back in the White House ready to serve a new boss, at least temporarily. He and Jonathan Daniels helped a nervous president prepare for his first official meeting with the press. In his memoirs, Truman acknowledged his pleasure—and relief—at having Early, Hassett, Daniels, and Rosenman help him get organized. The following week V. M. Molotov, the Soviet foreign minister, was at the White House, on his way to San Francisco for the United Nations conference. Because Early knew him from his visit in 1942 and because Truman had little knowledge of Soviet affairs, he leaned on Early for advice on how to deal with Molotov and asked him to help with the press coverage.[11]

On Saturday, April 28, Roosevelt's old press secretary had one more meeting with the White House press corps, and it proved to be an unusual one, to say the least. Rumors had been circulating for a week that the war with Germany was about to end. The previous Thursday a news story quoted a congressman who said he had just seen the president and attributed to Truman the belief that the war would end in June. On Saturday the Associated Press office in San Francisco sent an urgent memo over its wire declaring unequivocally that Germany had surrendered and that an official announcement was due momentarily. At the same time Early was cleaning up some work at the White House. He read the AP story on the wire and, assuming the president indeed was about to make an announcement, he called to his office the White House reporters who were still there. Word was flashed to the other White House correspondents, the radio stations, and the National Press Club. Within ten minutes the White House pressroom was crawling with reporters eager to get the big story.

Then someone called out that the president was ready to meet with the reporters. They jumped over chairs, tripped over each other's feet, and skidded down the tiled floors in a mad dash to Truman's office. Once they were all inside, Mr. Truman held a one-minute press conference where he tersely announced, "There is no foundation for the rumor." He said that a short time earlier he had a call from the State Department inquiring about the rumor, so he asked one of his aides, obviously not Early, to call the army's headquarters in Europe, and he learned it was indeed just a rumor. There may be two explanations for the origin of the rumor. One was the fact that Secretary of State Stettinius was in San Francisco at the UN meeting and may have said something that led a reporter to believe there might be a surrender in the offing. The other was that on that same day Benito Mussolini had been caught by Italian partisans as he attempted to flee Italy and had been executed. It is hard to believe that after all those years of carefully confirming information and choosing his words so skillfully, Early would notify the press in this case without sufficient cause. But no one had to wait too long for the real surrender: A week later, on May 7, the German High Command surrendered unconditionally, and it was an Associated Press correspondent, Edward Kennedy, who got the scoop.[12]

It was now mid-May and the press again was speculating about Early's future. The newspapers had him working at a major movie studio as a consultant to advise on the right psychological moment to seek permission from the Roosevelt family to do a movie on the late president's life. Or he would be going to a big public relations outfit in New York. Or—this one proved a bull's-eye—he would become a vice president of Pullman, Inc. and Pullman-Standard Car Manufacturing Company. The latter manufactured equipment for the country's railroads and during the war supplied the government with ordnance, including tanks and ammunition. The former company operated passenger and freight trains.[13]

When Early walked in to the morning conference of presidential aides on May 17, he was greeted with a "Good Morning, Mr. Vice President." Late the previous day, the announcement had been made that Steve Early had a new job and it was not in the White House. He would, however, work out of an office in Washington, where he would oversee business and corporate functions for the giant company. He said his salary would be large enough "to pay off a few mortgages I've acquired." One newspaper speculated that his pay would be $75,000 a year. It was closer to $50,000—a big improvement over the $10,000 he earned as a presidential press secretary and the $12,000 he was currently paid as a special assistant to the president.[14]

Why did he take the Pullman job? A few months later, he answered that question when it was posed by Bob Considine, writing a piece on Early for *Cosmopolitan* magazine. "Because I never had anything to do with the man who offered me the job, and he never had anything to do with me," Early said. This was an odd statement from someone who in the past had been eager to use his friends when he was looking for a job.[15]

Once the White House reporters wrote their stories about Early's new job, the tributes flowed in, mostly in the form of newspaper columns praising his years of service, and saying, as one columnist pointed out, Early had held "one of the most trying jobs in the country." The reporters called him a friend of the American press, noting that for twelve years he had been on twenty-four-hour call to any reporter, "friend or political foe who wanted a fair answer to a fair question." Another reporter wrote that the former press secretary "always talked a first-class news story, with no fumbling for syllables when he speaks, the words marching in an orderly procession as if from a veteran newsman's typewriter."[16]

The accolades, which no doubt pleased Early, culminated in Truman presenting him with the Distinguished Service Medal, the highest noncombat military decoration, normally awarded to members of the armed forces. Truman said he was able to justify awarding the medal because Early was a lieutenant colonel in the army reserve. In reality the medal was given to him in recognition of Early's years of service in the White House.

So at 4:00 p.m. on Thursday, the last day of May, Early was asked to come to the Rose Garden, outside the president's office, and in front of most of the White House staff, Truman made the presentation and read a citation which had been drafted by Early's old friend Sam Rosenman. Early said he was surprised "to the point of being dumbfounded." The citation paid tribute to Early's dedication to Roosevelt, noting that he had remained at his post "at great personal sacrifice and with a fine sense of duty and devotion." It added that he had been "of inestimable help to two Commanders-in-Chief." Referring to his twelve-plus years with Roosevelt, it said that Early was "of great assistance in helping to arouse the Nation in the days of its unpreparedness to a sense of danger which threatened it from aggressions abroad," and added: "In many ways he helped create among his fellow-citizens a sense of great urgency in arming and preparing the United States for war—spiritually and physically; and he was helpful to the leadership of the Nation in building the great military might which is now ours and thereby contributing to the successful prosecution of the war."[17]

In a brief speech, a delighted Early responded, speaking in a soft voice, his sense of humor coming through when he paraphrased Churchill's tribute to the Royal Air Force by telling those gathered in the Rose Garden, "No one ever did so little and received so much." He said it took him two wars to receive this medal and when he did he was not even in uniform. He said that today was his mother's birthday, and he wished she could have been there to see him get the award. Because the presentation was a surprise, no family members were present. Early's daughter said her mother never forgave President Truman for not inviting her.[18]

That same day Truman wrote Early a warm letter expressing his gratitude for the benefit of Early's "innate wisdom and sound judgment." He said, "I am sure that, without you, my task would have been much more difficult." Truman said he knew "from the lips of President Roosevelt" how much he had depended on Early. "Now I know from personal experience how greatly your assistance, cooperation and association can lighten the burdens of high office." Truman told him he was willing to let Early go, "but not without strings." He would be "subject to frequent calls to help me in many ways." Early told Truman, "Please be assured that I shall be happy and proud to be of assistance to you in any way and at any time during the years to come." Little did he know that the president would eventually take him up on his offer.[19]

Early continued to keep in touch with the new president. He sent Truman birthday messages, small gifts, telegrams, and notes. And Truman frequently included Early in his social activities, including poker games, White House dinners, and stag outings at the Jefferson Island Club, the Democratic social club near Annapolis. Early attended these functions when he was not traveling for the Pullman Company. Truman appointed him to the board of visitors of the United States Naval Academy and to the board that made recommendations to the president for Medals of Merit.[20]

However, before he could begin his new job with Pullman and less than two weeks after he walked out of the White House, Early was laid up in the Naval Hospital with an acute attack of bursitis in his left knee. He had been suffering with it for a while, but when the pain became continual and intense, Helen Early called an ambulance to take him to the hospital, where he remained for about a week receiving X-ray treatments to melt the calcium deposits and ease the pain. Early was philosophical about the crimp placed in what was supposed to be a short vacation. In a letter dated June 19 to Early's friend Louis Johnson, Helen Early said, Steve had decided that so many nice things had happened to him lately, that something like this was due to come along. She said that until he went to the hospital, his days had been crowded with business appointments, requests from "the Old Shop" to come there for consultation alternating with innumerable chores performed for "the New Shop" (Pullman).[21]

When he did start his new job, he was without an office, a car, or a secretary—so he worked out of his house. First he began sorting through twelve years' worth of White House files, a prodigious and tedious task in itself. He also was trying to learn about his new job. He told Eleanor Roosevelt in a letter, "No one, I dare say, ever accepted a position and had less time to learn anything about it. I seem to be a stranger, a rookie in the ranks of a new and vast organization largely composed of veterans with long years of experience behind them." He added that those employees he had met had given him a hearty welcome: "They are sympathetic and understanding, not demanding."[22]

He had to purchase a car to replace the official car that had come with his White House positions. Driving the new car required the permission of the Office of Price Administration (OPA) because the country still had wartime gas rationing. In his application to the OPA he explained that while he was working at home, he expected Pullman, which was classified as an industry essential to the war effort, to secure permanent offices in downtown Washington. He would need a car for his daily visits to the office and to the government offices, such as the Pentagon and the Capitol, necessary to his work. He further justified his request by noting that throughout the war, he had been in the habit of picking up pedestrians along his route from home to downtown and back, and he fully expected to continue the practice as long as gas rationing continued.[23]

Pullman found an office for him, the OPA allowed him to get a car, and by fall he was hard at work in his new job. For the next four years he traveled around the country for Pullman, continuing to remain interested in national affairs, acting as a kind of elder statesman. Always a persuasive speaker, he told groups of businessmen that for railroads, innovations were the answer to postwar competition from airlines and buses. He also spoke out about what he saw as the Truman administration's free flow of news to the public and the need for freedom of the press throughout the world. He was a good public relations man for his company, his credibility was excellent with the newsmen covering him, and his name still well known to the public. It even was suggested that he be named commissioner of baseball to succeed the late Kenesaw Mountain Landis, a suggestion that came to naught. Occasionally he spoke publicly about Roosevelt, but always he was circumspect, careful not to reveal any secrets, although he did tell one journalist that if he had completed his fourth term, Roosevelt planned to run a newspaper, probably in New York. Early said he often had heard the president talk about this, and the paper would have been a tabloid format with no editorial page. "He believed that if the people were given the facts, they could draw their own conclusions," Early said.[24]

In 1947 the federal courts decided that Pullman was violating the Sherman Antitrust Act and ordered the company to divest itself of the Pullman Company, which operated passenger and freight railroad cars, leaving it with the Pullman-Standard Car Manufacturing Company. Early was shuttling back and forth on the train between Washington and Pullman's headquarters in Chicago, a two-day trip, once a week for meetings in both cities. As the company's liaison in Washington, he found himself on the front lines of the antitrust action. That June he wrote to Ruthjane Rumelt, his former White House secretary, telling her, "No G-I overseas was infested with cooties and body lice more than I have been with lawyers this week." By 1948 Early said the courts had imposed "severe restrictions" on any possible connection between the two companies, to the point where executives of the car manufacturing company were required to make reservations—and pay for them—on the railway cars the company once owned and operated.[25]

After the first of the year in 1949, his old friend Joe Davies and his wife, Marjorie, invited him and Helen to their palatial Mar-a-Lago mansion in Palm Beach, but Early reluctantly declined, complaining that the latter part of his weekends now were spent traveling to Chicago for early Monday-morning meetings with other Pullman executives. There was, he said, "nothing I dislike more than spending two nights a week on a train shuttling back and forth to Chicago." It seems business was poor, with orders for railroad passenger cars decreasing. "Our freight car production for the past year has been the only thing which has kept us out of the red," he wrote. He added, "If we don't get new orders for freight cars soon our fate will be in the lap of the Gods."[26]

Then, in early April, as Pullman was concluding that orders for rail cars were declining so rapidly that it would have to cut its plant operations by 50 percent as early as June, Harry Truman, having been sworn in in January for his first full term as president, called the fifty-nine-year-old Early back to government service to serve in the newly created post of undersecretary of defense.[27]

The Defense Department itself had only recently come into being as a result of the unification of the armed forces, and it now was in turmoil with the resignation of James V. Forrestal, the first secretary of defense. Forrestal had opposed Truman, who wanted to cut, not increase, defense spending, and finally Forrestal quit, only to commit suicide a month later. As Forrestal's successor Truman appointed the bombastic Louis Johnson, a Virginia lawyer, a former assistant secretary of war, and a close friend of Early's. Johnson, like Truman, believed that military spending had gotten out of hand. Johnson needed an assistant—an undersecretary of defense—and Truman wanted Early to fill the position, a suggestion that satisfied the new secretary. So Early agreed and requested a one-year leave of absence from Pullman. It was granted, and for the second time since Roosevelt had died, Early was working for Truman. The Senate confirmed him unanimously on April 13 for the $10,000 position, the same salary he received when he worked for Roosevelt. A physical examination Early underwent as a condition of his reentry into government service showed that his blood pressure was slightly elevated (140 over 98), but otherwise he was in pretty good health for a man who had spent the last seventeen years in stress-producing jobs.[28]

Early was aboard the aircraft carrier *Midway* off the Virginia Capes as part of a group of businessmen studying problems of the armed services when he learned from a radio broadcast that Truman was tapping him for this post. "I hadn't expected the job and hadn't made any plans for it. I don't particularly want the job, but I'll naturally do my best at it," he said. Early told newsmen he had been given twenty-four hours' warning that Truman was offering him the job. Even Helen Early was surprised to learn her husband had been nominated. For all his reluctance to return to government service, Early was the right man for the job. He had served in the military; he had worked closely with Supreme Headquarters, Allied Expeditionary Forces (SHAEF) in early 1945; and he had the trust of the president. Most important, he was known to be a straight shooter. One newspaper called the appointment "perfect" and said Early "knows his way around the political jungle of Washington and is very pleasant and skillful in his relations with the press."[29]

The main reason Early was given the number-two position at the Pentagon was to straighten out press relations in an attempt to muzzle some of the disputes among the branches of the armed forces that had been making their way into the media. Because he was friends with a number of high-ranking military officials from his days with Roosevelt, and because of his skills as a public relations man, he made inroads into restructuring the press office at the Pentagon to centralize all information to be released to the public. The job also included maintaining contact with officials in other government agencies, members of Congress, representatives of the civilian economy, and the media. In June 1950 Congress created the post of deputy secretary of defense and Early moved into that job, where he occasionally filled in as the secretary when Johnson was out of town. He outranked the army, navy, and air force secretaries and was, in effect, general manager of the military establishment. His salary also increased to $14,500 a year, and a few months later it was increased again, to $20,000.[30]

Thomas K. Finletter, secretary of the air force, later said that Early was frequently called upon in his job as deputy secretary of defense to "serve as a shock absorber between men of firm views and strong convictions." Finletter said, "The strain of that constant mediation of urgent matters was greater than most of his friends knew, but he was one of those all-too-rare Americans who will not resist an invitation to perform public service." Gen. Omar Bradley said he owed a personal debt of gratitude to Early for his advice and support "and for the good judgment he exercised" as undersecretary and then deputy secretary.[31]

By May 1950 Early was planning to return to Pullman, his year's leave having come to an end, but the situation in Korea was heating up and Truman asked him to stay on a bit longer. In late June, what the Pentagon had been fearing and warning Congress about occurred: North Korean troops invaded South Korea. In July, when Early was asked how long the Korean situation might last, he said, "We won't know for a while yet. We don't know whether Korea is a sideshow or the opening scene of the main event." He expected to leave the Pentagon in August, but again Truman asked him to remain on board, this time because, among other things, Louis Johnson, who was under heavy fire for the country's military unpreparedness, had secretly been courting the Republican Party in hopes of securing the nomination for president in the 1952 election. Truman learned of the betrayal that summer, and on September 12 he fired Johnson.[32]

Two weeks before Johnson was dismissed, Early had informed Truman it was time for him to return to Pullman, and Truman reluctantly agreed to accept his resignation. The Pentagon job had been unusually stressful, and Early said his doctor was insisting that he leave. In addition, if he did not return to Pullman soon, his pension and insurance there would lapse.[33]

In submitting his resignation, Early told Truman he had remained longer than he planned because of the Korean situation and would be standing by for government service if and when needed. Truman thanked him, saying, "To you fell the stupendous task in blazing a new trail of government administration in a supremely vital field—that of national defense. You have richly earned the encomium: Well done."[34]

In a letter to his grown sons and daughter, dictated between telephone calls and appointments the day before he departed the government, Early said, "This means that tomorrow will be my last day in government service. I hope that I shall never be called again. The last year and a half has exacted its toll. The old frame has suffered more than it could afford in wear and tear."[35]

After a short vacation with Helen—"a little golf and a lot of rest"—Early returned to his job as vice president of Pullman. In early December Truman called him back to the White House to fill in as press secretary when Charles Ross died suddenly. Truman wanted Early there to oversee press relations when British prime minister Clement Atlee, whom Early knew from wartime meetings with

Churchill, visited Washington that week. Early stayed for less than a week until a new press secretary came on board.[36]

Back at Pullman, a nostalgic Early wrote to his old friend Bernard Baruch, "These are indeed crowded days and life grows increasingly complicated with the passing of each day. I often think of you and the old days and fervently wish that they could return to us once more." Six months later, on Tuesday, August 7, 1951, less than a year after he had left the Pentagon, as he worked at his desk in his Washington office, Early suffered a heart attack. He was taken to George Washington University Hospital in Washington. He appeared to be improving, but three days later, on Friday, Early had another heart attack and died. He was two weeks shy of his sixty-second birthday.[37]

This consummate newsman, a loyal presidential aide and friend, might have been embarrassed, but probably not surprised, at the wide press coverage his death received. He would have appreciated the journalistic reporting that went into the long, detailed obituaries in newspapers throughout the country. To underscore his importance, his death was announced by the White House, little more than seven years after he himself had announced Franklin Roosevelt's death to the world.[38]

As flags fluttered at half-staff on most public buildings in Washington, Early's casket was draped with a flag, as befitted a former soldier. His funeral was the following Tuesday at the National Cathedral, with a host of his friends from government as honorary pallbearers, including Vice President Alben Barkley, Speaker of the House Sam Rayburn, Secretary of Defense George C. Marshall, and Supreme Court Chief Justice Fred M. Vinson. President Truman and Eleanor Roosevelt, as well as many of the journalists who covered the Roosevelt White House, were among the seven hundred people who came to pay their respects. The only member of the immediate Early family not in attendance was his beloved daughter, Sis, who had just given birth to his first grandchild—a boy named William—in St. Louis, Missouri, where she and her husband were living.[39]

Early was eulogized in the House of Representatives by Representative John McCormack of Massachusetts. Condolence letters and telegrams to his widow, Helen, ran into the hundreds. Some were written by people who had only read about Early as FDR's press secretary; others came from prominent Americans, such as J. Edgar Hoover, who sent a kind but formal telegram from San Diego to Mrs.

Early saying he was unable to get away for the funeral but was pleased to be an honorary pallbearer. He expressed his sympathy for her loss and his respect for Early, ending with "The memory of Steve's friendship will live with me forever." It was signed John Edgar Hoover.

Harold Ickes, who considered Steve Early a friend and a loyal and respected press secretary, wrote a two-page letter to Mrs. Early, saying her husband's death "has left me almost speechless." He went on, "I was devoted to him and admired his human qualities and his instinct for leadership." Of Early's relationship with Roosevelt, Ickes said, "I do not believe that President Roosevelt ever had anyone on his staff with such sound judgment as to how the country would feel about some particular act or expression."

Early's death was announced over the Voice of America. David Sarnoff, founder and head of NBC, sent a telegram. Eleanor Roosevelt sent condolences to Mrs. Early in a letter after the funeral and in a telegram: "It was with great sadness that I read of Steve's death. I shall always be grateful for his devotion to my husband."

President Truman called him "honest, honorable, forthright—irascible sometimes but never vindictive and always just—he had vision as well as courage and a rare faculty of seeing all things in due proportion and through to their logical sequence."

According to his wishes, Early was buried in Arlington Cemetery to a nineteen-gun salute on a warm summer day. His grave, at the foot of the Tomb of the Unknown Soldier, rests next to that of George R. Holmes, his favorite brother-in-law, the International News Service Washington bureau chief.[40]

Steve Early came to his job at a time when the country was in the midst of the worst economic depression in its history. On the heels of the Depression came the country's entry into what proved to be the most cataclysmic war in its history. It would have been easy for Early and Roosevelt to simply close their doors and ignore the press, as presidents before them had done. But Early the journalist understood that in times of crisis it is crucial that the public know what is happening. Roosevelt desperately needed the public on his side if his New Deal plans were to be successful. What better way to accomplish both than to use the media?

There are several reasons why Steve Early was effective as the press secretary to a sometimes demanding and mercurial president.

Early was well known in the journalism community, and, more importantly, he understood how the news media worked. Not only had he been a reporter, he had worked in the movie newsreel business, and he had close friends working in the still relatively new medium of radio. In the first week of the presidency, with FDR's blessing, Early told reporters he would have an open-door policy and would hold his own daily press conferences, both of which he continued throughout the Depression and the war. He also made sure that Roosevelt met weekly with reporters when possible. It was critical for the success of Early's open-door policy that both he and the president met regularly with the reporters to ensure that whatever the pressing issue of the moment was, the White House message was transmitted to the public.

Another reason for Early's success as the press secretary was his promise to treat the journalists who covered the White House fairly. He was determined to have no favorites, to release no news scoop to one reporter without releasing it to all the reporters at the same time. For the most part, throughout his twelve years in his job, Early kept his promise. Thus, the convergence of Early and Roosevelt's friendship, Early's successful journalism career, and the opening of the White House to the press on a regular basis led to one of the most effective relationships between the press and the White House in American history. Neither Roosevelt nor Early could have imagined the scope and dominance of the news media in today's society. Nonetheless, their relationship with the news media of their day laid the groundwork for similar relationships between the president and the man or woman he chooses to ensure that his message reaches the public in a timely and cogent manner.

ACKNOWLEDGMENTS

T he idea for this book came from my daughter, Rachel, who was a student in a history and biography course at Mount Holyoke College taught by the Pulitzer Prize–winning biographer Joseph J. Ellis, who has written about John Adams, Thomas Jefferson, and other founding fathers. Dr. Ellis asked the students in the seminar to write a forty-page biography of someone of their choosing. Rachel recalled Steve Early from a history of American journalism class she took with me one summer at the University of Rhode Island when she was in high school. She decided Early would make a fine topic for her paper. She set about searching for information about him, and, other than a short chapter in a book about presidential press secretaries, she found only brief mentions or footnotes concerning him in books about Franklin D. Roosevelt and his presidency. She did manage to unearth enough to write her forty pages, and after Dr. Ellis read her paper, he told her someone should write a biography of Early. She passed his words on to me, and thus I began a decadelong journey.

I took Dr. Ellis's words to heart, and in the summer of 1994 I walked into the FDR Library and announced I planned to write a book about Stephen T. Early. The supervising archivist, Dr. Raymond Teichman, said, "It's about time." Throughout my years of research there, Dr. Teichman, now retired, and the other archivists—notably Dr. Teichman's successor, Bob Clark, and Alycia Vivona—were strong supporters of this project. Mr. Clark called the Early biography "the last important piece of the Roosevelt story that has not been told." My debt of gratitude for their patience, kindness, and continuing friendship made the long summers of research at the library not only productive but enjoyable.

I also found papers relating to Early and his family at the Library of Congress; the Alderman Library at the University of Virginia; the Baker Library at Dartmouth College in Hanover, New Hampshire; the Albermarle County (Virginia) Historical Society; the District of Columbia Office of Records; and the Martin Luther King Library in Washington, DC. Staff at the Truman Library in Independence, Missouri, culled their archives and sent me copies of documents relating to Early's service in the Truman administration. I want to thank Steven Schoenherr, whose dissertation, "Selling the New Deal: Stephen T. Early's Role as Press Secretary," served as a necessary roadmap for some of my research in the early days of this project.

I want to thank Helen Early Elam, Steve Early's daughter, and her son, William Elam, who live in Virginia, for so graciously and eagerly agreeing to share their memories for this book. They really brought Steve Early's story to life. When Mrs. Elam opened her front door to me for the first time in the spring of 1997, it was as if I were meeting her father. The family resemblance was remarkable. Although Will Elam never met his grandfather, he was delighted to learn that someone was writing a book about him. Over the years, he had run across people who had known his grandfather and had listened carefully to their reminiscences, which he shared with me.

Along the way, I received a grant from the Freedom Forum in Washington, DC, and one from the College of Arts and Sciences at the University of Rhode Island, where I am a professor of journalism. These grants helped fund some of my research travels.

While the book idea came from my daughter by way of her professor, the person whom I credit with helping me complete this project is my husband, Leonard I. Levin, a retired editor for the *Providence Journal* and a historian. He read every page as I finished it and had no difficulty telling me when a word was wrong, a paragraph was too long, or vital information was missing. His extensive knowledge of World Wars I and II made him a valuable resource when I was researching and writing chapters dealing with those events. He also joined me several times at the FDR Library, where he patiently copied letters and press conferences to use when I returned home. My daughter Sara, who lives in Seattle, was my long-distance cheerleader for the project. Thank you Sara, and thank you to my friends and colleagues, in particular Dr. Barbara F. Luebke, who probably thought I would never finish this book but nonetheless remained interested and offered words of encouragement when they felt I needed them.

I want to thank Steven L. Mitchell, the editor in chief of Prometheus Books, who understood Early's place in history and agreed to publish this book. His expert editorial guidance was indispensable. Christine Kramer, the production manager for Prometheus Books, showed remarkable patience with my limited technological abilities as we prepared the manuscript for publication. My very special thanks goes to my literary agent, Mike Hamilburg, who believed in the importance of the Early story and, from his office in Los Angeles, worked long and hard to find just the right publisher for the book.

Most of all, I thank Steve Early for having the foresight to carefully preserve his diaries, his letters, and the many, many newspaper clippings, photographs, and other documents, especially during those years he served the Boss in the White House. Nearly everyone who knew Early was dead by the time I began researching this book, so without Early's papers in the Roosevelt Library, I would have found it impossible to construct such a detailed story of his fascinating and historically important life.

Linda Lotridge Levin
Providence, Rhode Island

ENDNOTES

PREFACE

1. Betty Houchin Winfield, *FDR and the News Media* (New York: Columbia University Press, 1994), p. xi.

2. Memo from President Franklin D. Roosevelt to Stephen T. Early (STE), October 24, 1944, STE scrapbook, August 1, 1944–January 20, 1945, FDR Library, Hyde Park, NY.

3. "Early to Daniels," *Nashville Tennessean*, March 31, 1945, STE Scrapbook, January 21, 1945–July 31, 1945.

CHAPTER 1: THE JOURNALIST MEETS THE POLITICIAN

1. Letter from STE to Mrs. R. N. Clark, March 21, 1933, Box 38, STE papers, FDR Library, Hyde Park, NY; letter from STE to Lillian B. Trippe, Washington, DC, November 12, 1940, Box 19, STE papers; R. H. Early, *The Family of Early, which Settled upon the Eastern Shore of Virginia and Its Connection with Other Families* (Lynchburg, VA: Brown-Morrison, 1920), pp. 187–88.

2. Early marriage records, Albermarle County, Virginia; letter from STE to Mrs. Rex K. Early, May 20, 1935, Box 5, STE papers; author interview with Helen Early Elam, April 3, 1997.

3. Author interview with Elam; "Mrs. Roosevelt a Driving Force in New Deal," *Washington Post*, March 4, 1934.

4. Alfred B. Rollins, *Roosevelt and Howe* (New York: Knopf, 1962), p. 437; letter from William Patton Griffith to STE, August 19, 1933, Box 6, STE papers; letter from STE to Griffith, August 23, 1933, Box 6, STE papers.

5. Author interview with Elam.

6. Author interview with Elam; letters from STE to Julia Hennessey (his younger sister), July 2 and 7, 1947, Box 7, STE papers. Letters relate the pulling of strings by Steve that got his brother, T. J., into a Bethesda, Maryland, hospital when it became apparent that their mother was too old to care for him.

7. "President Roosevelt's Right-Hand Men," *Washington Sunday Star*, March 5, 1933, STE scrapbook, March 4, 1933–March 4, 1934, FDR Library, Hyde Park, NY; undated script for STE radio interview, Box 38, STE papers.

8. Letter from STE to Robert W. Summers, Government Printing Office, November 30, 1908; letter from Government Printing Office to STE, December 15, 1908; Form No. 353, Government Printing Office, October 8, 1909. Letters and form are in Box 28, STE papers.

9. Oliver Gramling, *AP: The Story of News* (New York: Farrar and Rinehart, 1940), p. 187.

10. Undated radio interview with Richard Eaton, Box 38, STE Papers.

11. Steven E. Schoenherr, "Stephen T. Early's Role as Press Secretary to Franklin D. Roosevelt" (PhD diss., University of Delaware, 1976), pp. 29, 30; letter from STE to Herbert Bayard Swope, November 5, 1936, Box 19, STE Papers; "Secretary to the President," *St. Louis Post-Dispatch*, July 18, 1937; "Stephen Early: Between the Press and the President," *United States News*, September 3, 1934.

12. Joe Morris, *Deadline Every Minute: The Story of the United Press* (Garden City, NY: Doubleday, 1957), pp. 15–19, 24, 30, 44–45, 50–55.

13. Frank Luther Mott, *American Journalism: A History, 1690–1960* (New York: Macmillan, 1941), p. 603; letter from STE to A. B. Wing, June 17, 1941, Box 22, STE papers.

14. STE draft script for radio interview, circa 1944, Box 38, STE papers.

15. "President Roosevelt's Right-Hand Men."

16. Schoenherr, "Selling the New Deal," p. 13.

17. Kenneth S. Davis, *FDR: The Beckoning of Destiny, 1882–1928: A History* (New York: Putnam, 1972), pp. 275, 276; Frank Burt Freidel, *Franklin D. Roosevelt: The Apprenticeship* (Boston: Little, Brown, 1952), p. 139.

18. Letter from STE to Robert Sherwood, January 16, 1948, Box 17, STE papers; letter from STE to Kent Cooper, March 12, 1940, Box 2, STE papers.

19. Freidel, *Apprenticeship*, p. 157.

20. "Mac and Steve," NBC Radio broadcast transcript, May 15, 1933, Box 38, STE papers.

21. Davis, *Beckoning of Destiny*, p. 284; Freidel, *Apprenticeship*, p. 140; "Mac and Steve"; Mott, *American Journalism*, pp. 554–57; Raymond Clapper, "Cuff Links Club," *Review of Reviews*, April 1935.

22. Clapper, "Cuff Links Club."

23. George Holmes interview with STE on NBC Radio, July 6, 1934; letter from STE to Robert Sherwood, January 16, 1948, Box 17, STE papers; Schoenherr, "Selling the New Deal," p. 32.

24. Davis, *Beckoning of Destiny*, pp. 284, 306, 307.

25. "Stephen Early: Between the Press and the President," *United States News*, September 3, 1934, STE scrapbook, March 4, 1934–March 4, 1935; Freidel, *Apprenticeship*, pp. 158, 160, 168, 221; Davis, *Beckoning of Destiny*, p. 318.

26. Papers of Louis Howe, Box 6, FDR Library; Davis, *Beckoning of Destiny*, pp. 228–29; Freidel, *Apprenticeship*, pp. 25, 227; Schoenherr, "Selling the New Deal," p. 31.

27. "Mac and Steve"; STE press cards, STE scrapbook, 1919–1932.

28. Reporters of the Associated Press, *Breaking News: How the Associated Press Has Covered War, Peace, and Everything Else* (New York: Princeton Architectural Press, 2007), p. 223; Gramling, *AP*, pp. 256–59.

CHAPTER 2: MR. EARLY GOES TO WAR

1. Charles Hurd, *Washington Cavalcade* (New York: E. P. Dutton, 1948), p. 187.

2. Page Smith, *America Enters the World: A People's History of the Progressive Era and World War I* (New York: McGraw-Hill, 1985), pp. 507, 582, 585.

3. Letter from STE to Buddy Early, November 8, 1944, Box 4, STE papers, Hyde Park, NY.

4. "President Roosevelt's Right-Hand Men," *Washington Sunday Star*, March 5, 1933; "Steve Early: White House Spokesman," *Baltimore Sun*, May 23, 1945; Oliver Gramling, *AP: The Story of News* (New York: Farrar and Rinehart, 1940), p. 236.

5. Gramling, *AP*, p. 236.

6. "Stephen Early: Between the Press and the President," *United States News*, September 3, 1934, from STE's official Army Record Book in STE scrapbook, 1919–1927, FDR Library, Hyde Park, NY.

7. Ibid.; letter from STE to Buddy Early, June 29, 1943, Box 4, STE papers.

8. Letter from Sidney Haight to Douglas MacArthur, July 25, 1917, unnumbered STE scrapbook.

9. "Stephen Early: Between the Press and the President"; "President

Roosevelt's Right-Hand Men"; Early's Officer's Record Book, STE scrapbook #1; letter from STE to Buddy Early, June 29, 1943, Box 4, STE papers.

10. Meirion Harries and Susie Harries, *The Last Days of Innocence: America at War, 1917–1918* (New York: Random House, 1997), pp. 132, 134, 137.

11. From STE diary, unnumbered STE scrapbook.

12. Ibid.; Anthony Livesey, *Great Battles of World War I* (New York: Macmillan, 1989), p. 189.

13. From STE diary; Livesey, *Great Battles of World War I*, p. 187.

14. Harries and Harries, *Last Days of Innocence*, p. 353.

15. Author interview with Helen Early Elam, April 3, 1998.

16. Harries and Harries, *Last Days of Innocence*, pp. 356, 357.

17. Livesey, *Great Battles of World War I*, p. 193.

18. The Iron Cross is in STE scrapbook, 1919–1927.

19. Letter from Ted Cogswell to FDR, November 28, 1942, also related by Chief Justice Fred Vinson in a condolence letter to Helen Early after Early's death, August 15, 1951, Box 63, STE papers.

20. The communiqué and Early's note to his mother are in STE scrapbook, 1919–1927.

21. Letter from Nolan to General Burt, May 23, 1919, Box 38, STE papers.

22. "Amazing Adventure of *Stars and Stripes*," Part 1, *Editor & Publisher*, April 23, 1927.

23. Ibid.

24. Ibid.

25. Ibid.; "Amazing Adventures of *Stars and Stripes*," Part 2, *Editor & Publisher*, April 30, 1927.

26. The Providence (RI) Athenaeum has a complete run of *Stars and Stripes* during World War I, and it is from there that the content descriptions were taken for this chapter.

27. Jane Grant, *Ross, the New Yorker and Me* (New York: Reynal, 1968), p. 57.

28. STE memo to FDR, May 30, 1942, Box 17, STE papers; Grant, *Ross*, pp. 57, 58; "Amazing Adventures of *Stars and Stripes*," Part 2. A copy of Ross's letter dated December 17, 1918, to army headquarters citing problems with Viskniskki is in Ross's correspondence folder, 1918–1927, special collections of the Baker Library, Dartmouth College, Hanover, NH.

29. Letter from Early to Samuel Hopkins Adams, April 14, 1944, Box 22, STE papers; Grant, *Ross*, p. 58; "Amazing Adventures *of Stars and Stripes*," Part 2. After the war, Watson joined the staff of the *Baltimore Sun*. In 1942 President Roosevelt asked Early to obtain a run of *Stars and Stripes* during

World War I, and Early replied that because he kept in touch with many of his former colleagues on the newspaper, he would "do my utmost to find 'some kind soul' who possesses one of the few complete files of *Stars and Stripes*—one whose privilege it will be to bequeath his collection to you for keeping in the Hyde Park Library." Memos from FDR to STE and STE to FDR, both dated May 30, 1942, Box 17, STE papers, unnumbered scrapbook. Roosevelt remained in his post as assistant secretary of the navy throughout the war. Twice he traveled to France in his official capacity, once in July and August 1918 and again in January and February 1919. There is no record of a meeting, formal or informal, between Roosevelt and Early. However, it is quite likely that if Early was aware of Roosevelt's presence in Paris, especially while at *Stars and Stripes* in 1919, he sought out his old friend and good source.

30. "Amazing Adventures of *Stars and Stripes*," Part 2.

31. Grant, *Ross*, pp. 20, 22.

32. An account of the trip written by James P. O'Neill, a sergeant in the AEF, appeared in *Gentlemen of the Press*, December 12, 1938, published by the Washington State Press Club, STE scrapbook, 1919–1927.

33. Letter from Ross to Watson, March 26, 1919, Baker Library, Dartmouth College, Hanover, NH.

34. Letter from Nolan to Burt, May 23, 1919; letter from Nolan to STE, June 3, 1919, Box 38, STE papers. Soon after Early became President Roosevelt's press secretary, he was promoted to lieutenant colonel in the Military Intelligence Reserve.

35. Letter from M. Churchill, Brigadier General, Military Intelligence, July 3, 1919, STE scrapbook, 1919–1927.

CHAPTER 3: THE 1920 CAMPAIGN

1. Letter from STE to Buddy Early, November 8, 1944, Box 4, STE papers, FDR Library, Hyde Park, NY.

2. Page Smith, *America Enters the World: A People's History of the Progressive Era and World War I* (New York: McGraw-Hill, 1985), p. 737.

3. "Stephen T. Early," *United States News*, September 3, 1934, STE scrapbook, March 4, 1933–March 4, 1934, FDR Library, Hyde Park, NY.

4. "President Roosevelt's Right-Hand Men," *Washington Sunday Star*, March 5, 1933, STE scrapbook, March 4, 1933–March 4, 1934.

5. Kenneth S. Davis, *FDR: The Beckoning of Destiny, 1882–1828: A History* (New York: Putnam, 1972), pp. 613, 614.

6. Lela Mae Stiles, *The Man behind Roosevelt: The Story of Louis McHenry*

Howe (Cleveland: World Publishing, 1954), p. 68; Stephen T. Early, "The Roosevelt Gang," *Washington Sunday Star*, June 11, 1933.

7. Early, "The Roosevelt Gang." Early may have been at the convention, perhaps as a spectator and probably because he happened to be in that city as part of his Chamber of Commerce travels.

8. Early, "The Roosevelt Gang"; Stiles, *Man behind Roosevelt*, p. 68.

9. Frank Burt Freidel, *Franklin D. Roosevelt: A Rendezvous with Destiny* (Boston: Little, Brown, 1990), p. 617.

10. NBC interview with McIntyre and Early, May 15, 1933, Box 38, STE papers; Freidel, *Rendezvous with Destiny*, p. 617.

11. Letter from FDR to William E. Bailey of Nantucket, MA, July 30, 1920, Box 6, STE papers.

12. Stiles, *Man behind Roosevelt*, p. 67; Davis, *Beckoning of Destiny*, p. 617; G. Jack Gravlee, "Stephen T. Early: The 'Advance Man,'" *Speech Monographs*, March 1963, pp. 42, 47; Freidel, *Rendezvous with Destiny*, p. 79.

13. Davis, *Beckoning of Destiny*, p. 617; FDR Vice Presidential Candidate Papers, FDR Library; correspondence with Louis Howe, Box 6, STE papers, Container 7, FDR Library; Early expense account sheet, Box 6, STE papers.

14. Harold L. Ickes, *The Secret Diary of Harold L. Ickes*, vol. 1: *The First Thousand Days, 1933–1936* (New York: Simon and Schuster, 1953), p. 699; Geoffrey C. Ward, *A First Class Temperament: The Emergence of Franklin Roosevelt* (New York: Harper & Row, 1989), p. 556; Davis, *Beckoning of Destiny*, p. 620; Early, "The Roosevelt Gang"; Donald R. McCoy, *Calvin Coolidge: The Quiet President* (New York: Macmillan, 1967), p. 126.

15. During an investigation of the electoral vote dispute in the 1876 presidential campaign between Republican Rutherford B. Hayes and Democrat Samuel J. Tilden, it was discovered that Tilden's camp had relied on an elaborate code to send telegrams relating to the use of bribery to buy electoral votes. The *New York Tribune* published samples of some of the telegrams asking readers to decode them. Eventually two members of the newspaper's staff succeeded. Charles Richard Williams, *The Life of Rutherford Birchard Hayes, Nineteenth President of the United States*, vol. 2 (Boston: Houghton Mifflin, 1914), pp. 161–64.

16. Gravlee, "The 'Advance Man,'" p. 46; telegram from STE to FDR, August 15, 1920, Box 6, STE papers.

17. Letter from STE to Howe, August 14, 1920, Box 6, STE papers; Freidel, *Rendezvous with Destiny*, p. 80.

18. Stiles, *Man behind Roosevelt*, p. 67.

19. Telegram from STE to FDR, August 15, 1920, Box 6, STE papers.

20. Telegram from STE to McIntyre, August 15, 1920, Box 6, STE papers.

21. Letter from STE to Howe, August 16, 1920, Box 6, STE papers.

22. The Deer Lodge speech story is from Jean Edward Smith, *FDR* (New York: Random House, 2007), p. 182.

23. Telegram from STE to FDR, August 16, 1920, Box 6, STE papers.

24. Letter from STE to McIntyre, August 17, 1920, Box 6, STE papers.

25. Letter from STE to Howe, August 18, 1920, Box 6, STE papers.

26. Letter from STE to FDR, Container 6: 1920 Campaign, FDR papers.

27. Freidel, *Rendezvous with Destiny*, p. 85.

28. *New York Times*, August 9, 1920; quoted in Davis, *Beckoning of Destiny*, p. 621.

29. Freidel, *Rendezvous with Destiny*, pp. 81–82. Freidel says that a comparison of the transcripts of speeches and press releases with newspaper accounts in Republican papers and by the Associated Press during his trip West refute Roosevelt's charge that he was being misquoted.

30. Letter from STE to Howe, September 8, 1920, Box 6, STE papers; Oliver Gramling, *AP: The Story of News* (New York: Farrar and Rinehart, 1940), pp. 264, 288. Coolidge's biographer writes that Coolidge's bit for the campaign "turned out to be less than that of Harding, Cox or Roosevelt." When campaigning in August and September, Coolidge tended to talk to "Yankees in Yankee accents." He spoke mainly in New England, although by October the Republican National Committee had ordered him to make an eight-day tour of the South. He protested, saying he should not remain away from Massachusetts that long, but the committee prevailed. McCoy, *Calvin Coolidge*, pp. 128–29.

31. Letter from STE to Howe, August 22, 1920, Box 6, STE papers.

32. STE expense account, Box 6, STE papers.

33. Letter from Virginia Early to Louis Howe, August 28, 1920, Box 6, STE papers; Stiles, *Man behind Roosevelt*, pp. 69–70.

34. Memo to FDR, September 11, 1920, from McCarthy at FDR Headquarters, Grand Central Palace, New York, Charles McCarthy file, Container 8: FDR Vice President Files, FDR Library.

35. Undated letter from STE to McIntyre, Container 6: 1920 Campaign, FDR papers.

36. Freidel, *Rendezvous with Destiny*, p. 88; Davis, *Beckoning of Destiny*, p. 623.

37. Telegram from STE to FDR, October 15, 1920.

38. Ward, *First Class Temperament*, p. 557.

39. Letter from STE to FDR, November 8, 1920, Box 6, STE papers.

40. Letter from STE to FDR, November 10, 1920, Box 6, STE papers.

41. Early, "The Roosevelt Gang."

42. Invoice from Tiffany & Co. to F. D. Roosevelt, November 30, 1920, STE scrapbook, 1919–1927; Early, "The Roosevelt Gang."

43. NBC radio interview with McIntyre and Early, May 15, 1933.

CHAPTER 4: BACK TO THE ASSOCIATED PRESS

1. Letter from FDR to STE, December 21, 1920; Letter from STE to FDR, December 25, 1920; Container 6: 1920 Campaign, FDR Papers, FDR Library, Hyde Park, NY.

2. Geoffrey C. Ward, *A First Class Temperament: The Emergence of Franklin D. Roosevelt* (New York: Harper & Row, 1989), p. 560.

3. Steven Schoenherr, "Selling the New Deal: Stephen T. Early's Role as Press Secretary to President Franklin D. Roosevelt" (PhD diss., University of Delaware, 1976), p. 36.

4. Oliver Gramling, *AP: The Story of News* (New York: Farrar and Rinehart, 1940), pp. 288, 289.

5. Author interview with Helen Early Elam, April 3, 1998.

6. Kenneth S. Davis, *FDR: The Beckoning of Destiny, 1882–1928: A History* (New York: Putnam, 1972), pp. 637, 638.

7. Ward, *First Class Temperament*, pp. 571, 572; Ward says the three worked in a Navy Department office for the day. Elliott Roosevelt, who edited *F.D.R, His Personal Letters, 1905–1928* (New York: Duell, Sloan, and Pearce, 1948), writes that the statement was written at the Shoreham Hotel in Washington (p. 517).

8. Information on the story of the Newport and Portsmouth investigations and the Senate inquiry came from Ward, *First Class Temperament*, pp. 433–43, 466–69, 487–90, 569–75; Frank Burt Freidel, *Franklin D. Roosevelt: The Ordeal* (Boston: Little, Brown, 1954), pp. 39–50, 96, 97; Garrett D. Byrnes and Charles H. Spilman, *The Providence Journal, 150 Years* (Providence, RI: Providence Journal, 1980); and Roosevelt, *Personal Letters*, pp. 514–22. The *Providence Journal* and its editors' relentless pursuit of the charges against Assistant Secretary Roosevelt had followed him into the 1920 campaign. This resulted in a half-million-dollar libel suit filed shortly before the election by Roosevelt against Rathom. The libel suit was never placed on the calendar in New York State for trial, and Rathom died suddenly in December 1923.

9. Stephen T. Early, "The Roosevelt Gang," *Washington Sunday Star*, July 11, 1933.

10. Ward, *First Class Temperament*, p. 602.

11. Letter from STE to FDR, Box 2: FDR Family, Business and Personal Papers, FDR Library, Hyde Park, NY.

12. Early, "The Roosevelt Gang."

13. "Harding Will Speak Today," *New York Times*, November 11, 1921.

14. Ibid.

15. "Host in Madison Sq. Honors the Dead," *New York Times*, November 12, 1921.

16. "Harding Will Speak Today."

17. Ibid.

18. Service Bulletin of the Associated Press, December 1921, STE scrapbook, 1919–1927, FDR Library, Hyde Park, NY.

19. Gramling, *AP*, p. 298.

20. Schoenherr, "Selling the New Deal," p. 36.

21. Francis Russell, *The Shadow of Blooming Grove: Warren G. Harding in His Times* (New York: McGraw-Hill, 1968), p. 556.

22. STE letter to William L. Pitts, May 10, 1945, Box 29, STE papers. William L. Pitts was a staff man on the *San Francisco Chronicle* when Harding died. Years later, when he was working at the *Detroit Times*, he wrote to Early saying he had "heard hundreds of stories and a thousand alibis for the absence of newspaper men in the hotel" at the time of the president's death. He was now asking Early for the correct version of the events that night. Early sent him a three-page typed reply detailing his role. He concluded the letter with some advice he had been given by Melville Stone, general manager of the Associated Press, when he joined the staff as a young reporter: "Write simply, my son. Write the facts. If given the facts, the American people have sufficient intelligence to draw their own conclusions." Early wrote, "And these are the facts, given to you as a matter of information and guidance, as I remember them." He then told Pitts, "If you use any of this, please do not quote me. I have dictated hurriedly, without notes or records. I have given you only the statements I know to be true."

23. Schoenherr, "Selling the New Deal," p. 35.

24. Samuel Hopkins Adams, *Incredible Era: The Life and Times of Warren Gamaliel Harding* (Boston: Houghton Mifflin, 1939), pp. 336–76.

25. STE scrapbook, 1919–1927.

26. "Showed Improvement on Arrival," *New York Times*, July 30, 1923.

27. STE letter to Pitts, May 10, 1945, Box 29, STE papers.

28. Ibid.

29. Ibid.; Service Bulletin of the Associated Press, October 1923.

30. STE letter to Pitts.

31. Raymond Clapper, "Cuff Links Club," *Review of Reviews*, April 1935.

32. Service Bulletin of the Associated Press, October 1923.

33. Ibid.; *New York Times*, August 4, 1923; telegram from L. C. Probert in Washington to Early and Bartley in San Francisco, August 3, 1923, unnumbered STE scrapbook.

34. Donald R. McCoy, *Calvin Coolidge: The Quiet President* (New York: Macmillan, 1967), pp. 161, 166, 167.

35. "GOP Convention Meets in Cleveland," *Providence Journal*, June 13, 1924.

36. "Bewilderment Hangs Like Storm Cloud Over Democratic Delegates," *Providence Journal*, June 23, 1924.

37. "Wave of Confusion and Disorder Engulfs Democratic Convention." *Providence Journal*, June 26, 1924.

38. Freidel, *Ordeal*, p. 17.

39. "Democrats in Scenes of Wild Disorder Beat Klan Plank by One Vote; Reject Wilsonian League Issue," *Providence Journal*, June 29, 1924.

40. Service Bulletin of the Associated Press, October 1924.

41. Burke Davis, *The Billy Mitchell Affair* (New York: Random House, 1967), pp. 51, 55, 58.

42. Service Bulletin of the Associated Press, January 1926.

43. Gramling, *AP*, pp. 326, 327; Service Bulletin of the Associated Press, October 1926.

44. Schoenherr, "Selling the New Deal," p. 36.

CHAPTER 5: PREPARING FOR THE WHITE HOUSE

1. "S.T. Early Resigns from Staff of A.P.," *Washington Post*, May 24, 1927; letter from STE to Byron Price, May 6, 1927, STE scrapbook, 1919–1932, FDR Library, Hyde Park, NY; Steven Schoenherr, "Selling the New Deal: Stephen T. Early's Role as Press Secretary to President Franklin D. Roosevelt" (PhD diss., University of Delaware, 1976), p. 36; letter from Emanuel Cohen to STE, April 12, 1927; "Steve Early's Qualifications for Defense Undersecretary Are Tops," *Atlanta Journal*, April 12, 1949; letter from Garrison Elliott to STE, STE scrapbook #1, 1919; and "President Roosevelt's Right-Hand Men," *Washington Sunday Star*, March 5, 1933, in STE scrapbook, March 4, 1933–March 4, 1934. According to Early in his 1930 radio address, sometime in the mid-1920s when the Associated Press had assembled the technology to transmit photos over the wires to its member newspapers, it began building its still picture service largely through Paramount and servicing that company with its full leased wire service news dispatches. By 1927 the AP News Photo Service had been established. In the Cohen letter to Early on April 12, 1927, he notes that the Associated Press had just renewed its contract with Paramount News. Quite probably Early had little or nothing to do with the negotiations, since they were probably conducted by the AP management at its New York City headquarters. However, this renewed business arrangement could not have hurt Early's own negotiations for a job with Paramount.

2. STE interview, "The Newsreels," WOR radio, October 15, 1930.

3. Edwin Emery and Michael Emery, *The Press and America: An Interpretive History of the Mass Media*, 5th ed. (Englewood Cliffs, NJ: Prentice-Hall, 1984), pp. 386, 457. Interview with Emanuel Cohen, head of Paramount News, *New York Times*, June 26, 1927.

4. STE interview, "The Newsreels."

5. Ibid.

6. Ibid.

7. "President Roosevelt's Right-Hand Men."

8. Page Smith, *Redeeming the Time: A People's History of the 1920s and the New Deal* (New York: McGraw-Hill, 1987), p. 267.

9. Frank Burt Freidel, *Franklin D. Roosevelt: The Triumph* (Boston: Little, Brown, 1956), p. 14, 30, 31, 40; Alfred B. Rollins, *Roosevelt and Howe* (New York: Knopf, 1962), pp. 260–87.

10. Kenneth S. Davis, *FDR: The Beckoning of Destiny: A History* (New York: Putnam, 1972), pp. 683, 697.

11. Frank Freidel, *Franklin D. Roosevelt: The Ordeal* (Boston: Little, Brown, 1954), p. 267.

12. Freidel, *Ordeal*, pp. 242, 243.

13. Letter from STE to Robert Sherwood, January 16, 1948, Box 17, STE papers, FDR Library, Hyde Park, NY.

14. Schoenherr, "Selling the New Deal," pp. 39–40.

Chapter 6: Launching the Juggernaut

1. Letter from STE to Robert Sherwood, January 16, 1948, Box 17, STE papers, FDR Library, Hyde Park, NY.

2. STE obituary from Associated Press, August 11, 1951, Box 6, STE papers.

3. Ibid.

4. The story about the photograph on the den wall was related by Raymond Clapper in his diary; "Steve Early: White House Spokesman," *Baltimore Sun*, May 23, 1945; James Roosevelt, *My Parents: A Differing View* (Chicago: Playboy Press, 1976), p. 195.

5. "Howe is Chief, M'Intyre and Early Next," unnamed newspaper, STE scrapbook, March 4, 1933–March 4, 1934, FDR Library, Hyde Park, NY; Lela Mae Stiles, *The Man behind Roosevelt: The Story of Louis McHenry Howe* (Cleveland: World Publishing, 1954), p. 239; Roosevelt, *My Parents*, p. 171.

6. Steven Schoenherr, "Selling the New Deal: Stephen T. Early's Role as Press Secretary to President Franklin D. Roosevelt" (PhD diss., University

of Delaware, 1976), p. 42; letter from Sinnett to STE, October 29, 1936, Box 17, STE papers.

7. Roosevelt, *My Parents*, p. 188.

8. Stephen T. Early, "The Roosevelt Gang," *Washington Sunday Star*, June 11, 1933.

9. Alfred B. Rollins, *Roosevelt and Howe* (New York: Knopf, 1962), p. 371; Kenneth S. Davis, *FDR: The New Deal Years, 1933–1937: A History* (New York: Random House, 1986), p. 20.

10. "Mrs. Roosevelt a Driving Force in New Deal," *Washington Post*, March 4, 1934.

11. Frank Luther Mott, *American Journalism* (New York: Macmillan, 1941), pp. 722, 723.

12. Stephen T. Early, "Hobgoblins: 1935 Model," *Redbook*, April 1935.

13. Letter from Raymond Clapper letter to Bob Bender, March 1, 1933, Box 128, Raymond Clapper Papers, Library of Congress; Betty Houchin Winfield, *FDR and the News Media* (New York: Columbia University Press, 1994), p. 29; STE diary, November 12, 1935.

14. Clapper to Bender, March 1, 1933; Early, "Hobgoblins: 1935 Model."

15. Clapper to Bender, March 1, 1933.

16. Ibid.; Winfield, *FDR and the News Media*, pp. 28, 86, 112.

17. Early, "Hobgoblins: 1935 Model."

18. Clapper to Bender, March 1, 1933.

19. Grace G. Tully, *F.D.R., My Boss* (New York: Charles Scribner's Sons, 1949), p. 64.

20. Davis, *New Deal Years*, pp. 33, 34.

21. Schoenherr, "Selling the New Deal," p. 42.

22. Clapper Diary, March 5, 1933, Raymond Clapper Papers; Frank Burt Freidel, *Franklin D. Roosevelt: Launching the New Deal* (Boston: Little, Brown, 1973), p. 216.

23. Davis, *New Deal Years*, p. 35.

24. Schoenherr, "Selling the New Deal," p. 43; Clapper Diary, March 5, 1933.

25. Schoenherr, "Selling the New Deal," pp. 43, 44; Clapper diary, March 6, 1933; Ray Tucker, "Secretary Early Helps Reporters," *New York Herald Tribune*, March 8, 1933, FDR scrapbook #1; press releases, March 5–12, Box 43, STE papers; letter from Bellows to Early, March 6, 1933, OF 136.

26. Tully, *My Boss*, p. 114; "Secretary to the President," *St. Louis Post-Dispatch Sunday Magazine*, July 18, 1937.

27. Schoenherr, "Selling the New Deal," p. 44; press releases, March 7, 1933, Box 44, STE papers.

28. Letter from Clapper to Bender; Tully, *My Boss*, p. 70; Drawing of the West Wing of the White House as it was in 1934, from a schematic that appeared in *Time* magazine, December 17, 1934, and reproduced in the *Washington Post*, February 16, 1998.

29. Author interview with Joseph C. Harsch, September 18, 1996, at Jamestown, RI.

30. Photo in STE scrapbook, March 4, 1933–March 4, 1934.

31. Transcript at FDR Library; Davis, *New Deal Years*, p. 43; Freidel, *Launching the New Deal*, p. 224; Clapper diary, March 8, 1933.

32. Transcript is in STE scrapbook, March 4, 1933–March 4, 1934.

33. Davis, *New Deal Years*, p. 45.

34. Clapper diary, March 8, 1933. "President Meets the Press," *Washington Sunday Star*, March 4, 1934.

35. Roosevelt, *My Parents*, pp. 134, 135; Rollins, *Roosevelt and Howe*, p. 437.

36. Charles Hurd, "President and Press: A Unique Forum," *New York Times Magazine*, June 9, 1935.

37. Bellows letter, Radio Box 1, FDR Library.

38. Leo Rosten, "President Roosevelt and the Washington Correspondents," *Public Opinion Quarterly*, January 1937. Rosten, a freelance writer and scholar, wrote this in 1937 when he was a fellow of the Social Science Research Council in Washington.

CHAPTER 7: THE HONEYMOON

1. Editorial cartoon, *Chicago Daily Times*, February 12, 1935, STE scrapbook, March 4, 1933–March 4, 1934, FDR Library, Hyde Park, NY.

2. Betty Houchin Winfield, *FDR and the News Media* (New York: Columbia University Press, 1994), p. 108.

3. Charles Hurd, *When the New Deal Was Young and Gay* (New York: Hawthorn Books, 1965), p. 248.

4. Steven E. Schoenherr, "Selling the New Deal: Stephen T. Early's Role as Press Secretary to President Franklin D. Roosevelt" (PhD diss., University of Delaware, 1976), pp. 105, 107, 108; "Roosevelt Keeps the Microphone Near at Hand," *New York Times*, March 19, 1933.

5. "Radio in the White House," *Tower Radio*, April 1934.

6. Schoenherr, "Selling the New Deal," p. 109.

7. Ibid., pp. 103, 110; Kenneth S. Davis, *FDR: The New Deal Years, 1933–1937: A History* (New York: Random House, 1986), p. 60. By 1937 there were four radio stations in Washington: WJSV, a CBS station; WMAL and WRC, both NBC stations; and WOL, an independent station.

8. Winfield, *FDR and the News Media*, p. 105. To view the texts of the Fireside Chats, see the FDR Library Web site, http://www.academic.marist.edu/fdr/.

9. Winfield, *FDR and the News Media*, p. 109.

10. "Radio in the White House."

11. Grace Tully, *F.D.R., My Boss* (New York: Charles Scribner's Sons, 1949), p. 100.

12. "Radio in the White House."

13. Winfield, *FDR and the News Media*, p. 108.

14. Ibid., p. 105; "Radio in the White House."

15. Letter from STE to Joseph Davies, December 28, 1940.

16. STE NBC radio interview with Walter Trumbull, September 17, 1933, Box 38, STE Papers.

17. Schoenherr, "Selling the New Deal," pp. 42, 43; STE NBC Radio interview, May 15, 1933, Box 38, STE Papers.

18. "Secretary Early Helps Reporters," *New York World-Telegram*, March 8, 1933, STE scrapbook, March 4, 1933–March 4, 1934.

19. "The White House Revolution Brought about by Roosevelt," *New York Times*, March 19, 1933.

20. Letter from Raymond Clapper to STE, March 18, 1933, Box 2, STE papers.

21. Hurd, *New Deal*, p. 227; Winfield, *FDR and the News Media*, p. 34.

22. Leo Rosten, "President Roosevelt and the Washington Press Corps," *Public Opinion Quarterly*, January 1937.

23. "President Meets the Press," *Washington Sunday Star*, March 4, 1934.

24. Leo E. McGivena, *The News: The First Fifty Years of New York's Picture Newspaper* (New York: News Syndicate, 1969), pp. 298–303.

25. "Capital Stuff," *New York News*, March 20, 1933, STE scrapbook, March 4, 1933–March 4, 1934.

26. "First Lady Makes Luray Caves Visit," *Washington Post*, March 20, 1933; "Mrs. Roosevelt to See Show," unnamed newspaper, March 17, 1933, STE scrapbook, March 4, 1933–March 4, 1934.

27. April 15, 1933, photo from unnamed pictorial section of a Sunday newspaper, STE scrapbook, March 4, 1933–March 4, 1934.

28. Ray Tucker, "People and Politics" column, *Washington News*, June 10, 1933.

29. "Roosevelt and London," *Richmond Times-Dispatch*, June 24, 1933.

30. Frank Burt Freidel, *Franklin D. Roosevelt: A Rendezvous with Destiny* (Boston: Little, Brown, 1990), pp. 116, 117.

31. Photo in STE scrapbook, March 4, 1933–March 4, 1934.

32. Ibid.

33. "Mrs. Roosevelt a Driving Force in New Deal," *Washington Post*,

March 4, 1934; "President Meets the Press," *Washington Sunday Star*, March 4, 1934.

34. "Faith Calls Mrs. Nellie Ross Gracious; That Mr. Stephen T. Early Person Just Grand," *Columbus Journal Dispatch*, no date, STE scrapbook, March 4, 1933–March 4, 1934. But Early did note in his diary on April 9, 1935, that he and Baldwin met that day when she visited the White House.

35. "Stephen T. Early: Roosevelt's Master of Newshawks," *Time*, December 17, 1934.

36. Untitled report, *Washington Star*, November 23, 1933, STE scrapbook, March 4, 1933–March 4, 1934.

37. "Poison Pen Laid to CCC Youth," article in unnamed newspaper, STE scrapbook, March 4, 1933–March 4, 1934; Rosten, "President Roosevelt and the Washington Press Corps."

CHAPTER 8: HOBGOBLINS

1. Untitled articles, *Washington Post*, February 8 and February 13, 1934, STE scrapbook, March 4, 1933–March 4, 1934, FDR Library, Hyde Park, NY.

2. Letter from Elmendorf Carr to STE, February 13, 1934, unnumbered STE scrapbook.

3 Author telephone interview with Helen Early Elam, July 1999. The diaries are in the STE Papers in the FDR Library, Hyde Park, NY.

4. Harold L. Ickes, *The Secret Diary of Harold L. Ickes*, vol. 1: *The First Thousand Days* (New York: Simon and Schuster, 1953), pp. 230–34; STE diary, November 22, 1934. The following year, Moffett and his wife, Kim, gave Early a gold diamond-studded cigarette case for his birthday; STE diary, November 22, 1935.

5. Steven E. Schoenherr, "Selling the New Deal: Stephen T. Early's Role as Press Secretary to Franklin D. Roosevelt" (PhD diss., University of Delaware, 1976), p. 57; Otis L. Graham Jr. and Meghan Robinson Wander, eds., *Franklin D. Roosevelt: His Life and Times: An Encyclopedic View* (Boston: G. K. Hall, 1985), pp. 62–63.

6. STE diary, December 11, 1934.

7. A year later, at Eleanor Roosevelt's request, Early did allow the women who attended Mrs. Roosevelt's press conferences to tour the new White House kitchens; STE diary, November 14, 1935.

8. STE diary, December 27, 1934.

9. Untitled article, *Washington Post*, January 14, 1934, STE scrapbook, March 4, 1933–March 4, 1934.

10. Memo from FDR to STE, September 23, 1935, Box 8, STE papers. The story about Mrs. Howe was in the *Boston Sunday Post*, September 15, 1935.

11. Betty Houchin Winfield, *FDR and the News Media* (New York: Columbia University Press, 1994), p. 79.

12. Schoenherr, "Selling the New Deal," pp. 62–63.

13. Delbert Clark, "Steve Takes Care of It," *New York Times Magazine*, July 27, 1941; Winfield, *FDR and the News Media*, p. 86; Stephen T. Early, "Hobgoblins: 1935 Model," *Redbook*, April 1935.

14. Clark, "Steve Takes Care of It."

15. Early, "Hobgoblins: 1935 Model." He wrote in his diary for January 9 that the article was written in less than a week, as requested by *Redbook*, and Roosevelt looked it over before Early sent it to the magazine. On January 15 Early wrote that he had heard from the editor and "the story pleased him very much." He also noted that he was paid for the article.

16. Winfield, *FDR and the News Media*, p. 94.

17. Early, "Hobgoblins: 1935 Model."

18. "Early Termed Counterpart of Nazi Goebbels," *Chicago Tribune*, October 13, 1934; "It's a Busy Staff That Writes Uncle Sam's Story," *Washington Star*, January 19, 1936.

19. Schoenherr, "Selling the New Deal," p. 74; Winfield, *FDR and the News Media*, pp. 87, 89.

20. Winfield, *FDR and the News Media*, p. 88.

21. Ibid.

22. STE diary, August 4, 1937; Samuel I. Rosenman, *Working with Roosevelt* (New York: Harper, 1952), pp. 155, 217.

23. Schoenherr, "Selling the New Deal," p. 66.

24. Ibid., p. 69.

25. STE diary, August 23 and 24, 1936.

28. Schoenherr, "Selling the New Deal," pp. 74, 75.

29. Clark, "Steve Takes Care of It." The Sullivan column is in STE scrapbook, March 4, 1933–March 4, 1934.

30. STE diary, March 14, 1934.

31. STE diary, May 28, 1934.

32. Page Smith, *Redeeming the Time: A People's History of the 1920s and the New Deal* (New York: McGraw-Hill, 1987), p. 639; Kenneth S. Davis, *FDR: The New Deal Years, 1933–1937: A History* (New York: Random House, 1986), p. 521; Rosenman, *Working with Roosevelt*, p. 111.

CHAPTER 9: ON BEHALF OF THE PRESIDENT

1. STE diary, October 31–November 8, 1935; "Roosevelt Perfects 'Remote Control,'" *New York Times*, November, 24, 1935, STE scrapbook, March 4, 1935–March 4, 1936, FDR Library, Hyde Park, NY.

2. STE diary, April 4, 1934.

3. STE diary, March 26 and 27, 1934.

4. STE diary, March 31 and April 1 and 2, 1934.

5. STE diary, April 1 and 2, 1934.

6. Kenneth S. Davis, *FDR: The New Deal Years, 1933–1937: A History* (New York: Random House, 1986), pp. 367, 368; STE diary, April 3 and 4, 1934.

7. STE diary, April 13, 1934.

8. STE diary, April 14, 1934.

9. STE diary, May 4, 1934.

10. STE diary, May 5, 1934.

11. STE diary, July 1–15, 1934; "Shore Beats Everything," *Asbury Park Press*, July 7, 1934, in STE scrapbook, March 4, 1934–March 4, 1935.

12. STE diary, July 25 and July 28–August 2; STE Diary, August 3, 1934; Davis, *New Deal Years*, pp. 383, 385.

13. STE diary, March 20, 1935.

14. STE diary, March 22 and 26, 1935.

15. STE diary, March 20, 22, 26, and April 6, 1935.

16. STE diary June 28 and 29, 1935.

17. STE diary, July 29–August 4, 1935.

18. Grace Tully, *F.D.R., My Boss* (New York: Charles Scribner's Sons, 1949), p. 87.

19. Ibid.

CHAPTER 10: THE 1936 CAMPAIGN: TO STAY OR LEAVE

1. STE diary, January 3, 1936.

2. STE diary, January 6, 1936.

3. "Washington Merry-Go-Round," *Washington Herald*, February 18, 1936; STE diary, January 7, 1936.

4. STE diary, January 14, 1936.

5. STE diary, March 22 and April 3, 1936.

6. STE diary, April 18, 1936; Alfred B. Rollins, *Roosevelt and Howe* (New York: Knopf, 1962), p. 448.

7. Rollins, *Roosevelt and Howe*, p. 448; untitled article, *New York Herald-Tribune*, March 23, 1936, STE scrapbook, March 4, 1936–January 20, 1937.

8. James A. Farley, *Jim Farley's Story: The Roosevelt Years* (New York: Whittlesey House, 1948), p. 61.

9. Joseph P. Lash, *Eleanor and Franklin: The Story of Their Relationship, Based on Eleanor Roosevelt's Private Papers* (New York: Norton, 1971), p. 435.

10. "FDR Loath to Replace Closest Friend with 'Outsider,'" *Washington Star*, February 26, 1936.

11. Charles Hurd, "The President Holds to His Philosophy," *New York Times*, January 1, 1936; "Washington Merry-Go-Round"; STE diary, February 12, 1936.

12. Graham J. White, *FDR and the Press* (Chicago: University of Chicago Press, 1979), p. 15.

13. STE diary, June 19 and September 21, 1936.

14. Letter from STE to Joseph Davies, August 18, 1936, Box 4, STE papers, FDR Library, Hyde Park, NY.

15. STE diary, March 19, 1936.

16. STE diary, June 8–15, 1936.

17. Untitled article, *Washington Daily News*, August 13, 1936, STE scrapbook, March 4, 1936–January 20, 1937.

18. Steven E. Schoenherr, "Selling the New Deal: Stephen T. Early's Role as Press Secretary to Franklin D. Roosevelt" (PhD diss., University of Delaware, 1976), p. 166.

19. Telegram from FDR to STE, July 28, 1936, Box 23, STE papers; *Liberty* magazine, June 27, 1936; Stephen T. Early, "Below the Belt," *Saturday Evening Post*, June 10, 1939.

20. Letter from Philip Slomovitz to FDR, March 4, 1935, Box 39, STE papers.

21. Letter from FDR to Slomovitz, March 7, *Public Papers and Addresses of FDR* (New York: Random House, 1935), p. 96.

22. Letter from Samuel Dickstein to STE, November 17, 1936; undated and unsigned letter to STE, Box 39, STE papers.

23. Lash, *Eleanor and Franklin*, pp. 446, 448; copy of telegram in STE scrapbook, March 4, 1936–January 20, 1937.

24. Letter from STE to Joseph Davies, August 18, 1936, Box 3, STE papers; memo from Eleanor Roosevelt to STE, July 16, 1936, Box 11, STE papers.

25. Letter from STE to Eleanor Roosevelt, July 20, 1936, Box 11, STE papers.

26. Kenneth S. Davis, *FDR: The New Deal Years, 1933–1937: A History* (New York: Random House, 1986), p. 628.

27. Letter from STE to Eleanor Roosevelt, July 20, 1936, Box 11, STE papers.

28. Schoenherr, "Selling the New Deal," pp. 168, 169.

29. Letter from STE to Eleanor Roosevelt, July 20, 1936, Box 11, STE papers; Schoenherr, "Selling the New Deal," p. 167; Harold L. Ickes, *The Secret Diary of Harold L. Ickes*, vol. 1: *The First Thousand Days, 1933–1936*, (New York: Simon and Schuster, 1953), p. 643.

30. Ickes, *First Thousand Days*, p. 517.

31. Farley, *Jim Farley's Story*, p. 58.

32. Letter from STE to FDR, July 27, 1936, Box 23, STE papers.

33. "Early Holds Key Post with President," *Washington Times*, August 31, 1936.

34. Letter from Marvin McIntyre to David Lawrence, November 11, 1938. PPF 5452: ASNE file, notes that "Steve Early has always acted as liaison between the Society and the President."

35. Leo Rosten, "President Roosevelt and the Washington Correspondents," *Public Opinion Quarterly*, January 1937; Ted Morgan, *FDR: A Biography*, (New York: Simon and Schuster, 1985), pp. 430, 431.

36. STE diary, September 15, 1936.

37. Schoenherr, "Selling the New Deal," p. 175; letter from Carl Byoir to Marvin McIntyre, October 7, 1936, Box 1, STE papers.

38. George Wolfskill and John A. Husdon, *All But the People: Franklin D. Roosevelt and His Critics, 1933–39* (New York: Macmillan, 1969), p. 197.

39. Ibid., pp. 186, 187; Betty Houchin Winfield, *FDR and the News Media* (New York: Columbia University Press, 1994), p. 130.

40. Wolfskill and Hudson, *All But the People*, p. 188.

41. Ibid, pp. 188, 189.

42. Telegram from STE to William Randolph Hearst, October 6, 1934, PPF #62; Wolfskill and Hudson, *All But the People*, p. 191; memo from E. B. Coblentz to Hearst editors and the Universal Service bureaus, PPF #62: August 7, 1935; White House press release, August 15, 1935.

43. Wolfskill and Hudson, *All But the People*, pp. 184, 194; Winfield, *FDR and the News Media*, p. 129.

44. Winfield, *FDR and the News Media*, p. 131; Schoenherr, "Selling the New Deal," p. 176.

45. Letter from STE to Charles Michelson, September 15, 1936, Box 11, STE papers.

46. STE diary, September 29 and October 6, 1936; Schoenherr, "Selling the New Deal," pp. 181–82; STE diary, October 20, 1936.

47. *Literary Digest*, October 1936, STE scrapbook, March 4, 1936–January 20, 1937.

48. Letter from STE to Michelson, October 26, 1936, Box 11, STE papers; Raymond Clapper diary, November 16, 1936, Library of Congress.

49. Wolfskill and Hudson, *All But the People*, p. 187.

50. Clapper diary, November 16, 1936.

51. Letter from STE to Joseph Davies, August 13, 1936, Box 3, STE papers.

52. Paul Mallon, "Behind the News," no publication or date; H. R. Baukhage, "Off the Record," *Cleveland Plain Dealer*, September 8, 1937; "Key Figures of the New Deal Plan to Quit," *Washington Herald*, September 8, 1937; "Stephen Early, Aide to Preseident, May Leave White House," *Chicago Tribune*, November 18, 1936, all in STE scrapbook, March 4, 1936–January 20, 1937.

CHAPTER 11: COURT PACKING AND OTHER PROBLEMS

1. "Features" from the Associated Press Feature Service—Exclusive to Morning Papers, January 21, 1937.

2. STE diary, January 6, 1937; letter from STE to Joseph Davies, January 25, 1937, Box 3, STE papers, FDR Library, Hyde Park, NY; Harold L. Ickes, *The Secret Diary of Harold L. Ickes*, vol. 2: *The Inside Struggle, 1936–1939* (New York: Simon and Schuster, 1954), p. 32; Kenneth S. Davis, *FDR: Into the Storm, 1937–1940: A History* (New York: Random House, 1993), p. 29.

3. Ickes, *Inside Struggle*, pp. 32–33; balance sheet in STE scrapbook, January 21, 1937–January 20, 1938, FDR Library, Hyde Park, NY.

4. STE diary, January 12, 1937; Davis, *Into the Storm*, pp. 35, 36. By the time Congress got around to seriously considering the government reorganization that year, Roosevelt's proposal to expand the membership of the Supreme Court had come before a hostile Congress, and a reorganization plan did not pass until 1939.

5. STE diary, January 12, 1937.

6. Davis, *Into the Storm*, p. 36.

7. STE diary, January 14, 1937.

8. STE diary, January 20, 1937.

9. Ibid.

10. STE diary, January 3, 1937; Davis, *Into the Storm*, p. 8.

11. Letter from STE to Davies, January 25, 1937, Box 3, STE papers; Ickes, *Inside Struggle*, p. 32; Davis, *Into the Storm*, p. 29.

12. STE diary, January 20, 1937.

13. Ibid.

14. Raymond Clapper diary, February 8, 1937, Library of Congress; STE diary, February 5, 1937.

15. STE diary, February 5, 1937; Ickes, *Inside Struggle*, pp. 64–65; Otis L. Graham Jr. and Meghan Robinson Wander, eds., *Franklin D. Roosevelt: His Life and Times: An Encyclopedic View* (Boston: G. K. Hall, 1985), p. 85; Clapper diary, February 8, 1937. For more details on the nuances of Roosevelt's orchestration of the court proposal, see Davis, *Into the Storm*, pp. 38–68.

16. Ickes, *Inside Struggle*, p. 66; STE diary, February 5, 1937.

17. Davis, *Into the Storm*, p. 58.

18. Letter from STE to Davies, February 18, 1937.

19. Ibid.; STE diary, February 18, 1937.

20. Letter from STE to Davies, February 18, 1937; Clapper diary, May 20, 1937.

21. Letter from STE to Davies, July 30, 1937.

22. Ickes, *Inside Struggle*, p. 165.

23. Letter from STE to Davies, July 30, 1937.

24. Clapper diary, May 18, 1937; STE diary, May 20, 1937.

25. Memo from STE to FDR, July 27, 1937; Raymond Clapper, "F. D. Decides against Revival of White House Spokesman," *Washington Daily News*, July 28, 1937.

26. "Roosevelt's Secretaries' Offices Fortified with Special Alarms," *Washington Star*, May 18, 1937, in STE scrapbook, January 21, 1937–January 20, 1938.

27. See Early diary entries for March–May 1937.

28. Davis, *Into the Storm*, p. 106; "Economic Royalists Retain Control of the Spotlight for Roosevelt-Du Pont Wedding," *Washington Herald*, June 20, 1937.

29. Confidential memorandum from STE to FDR, June 21, 1937, Box 23, STE papers; Clapper diary, June 15, 1937; Ickes, *Inside Struggle*, p. 602. When Early said Garner mentioned "relief," he probably was referring to the fact that under the Works Progress Administration (WPA), which Hopkins headed, federal funds were used for the local projects, but the local sponsors contributed on average 22 percent.

30. STE diary, August 12, 1937; "Black Appointment Kept Secret Leaving Early in the Lurch," *Christian Science Monitor*, August 13, 1937; "FDR, Secretary Both Apologize," United Press, both articles in STE scrapbook, January 21, 1937–January 20, 1938.

31. STE diary, August 12, 1937; "Secretary Named in 'Yearbook' Probe," *Madison* (WI) *Journal*, August 13, 1937, STE scrapbook, January 21, 1937–January 20, 1938.

32. Letter from STE to Davies, September 1, 1937.

33. STE diary, September 13, 1937.

34. STE diary, October 14, 1937.

35. STE diary, November 15, 1937.

36. STE diary, November 15, 16, 22, and 27, 1937; STE Diary, December 7 and 9, 1937.

37. STE diary, December 13, 1937; Ickes, *Inside Struggle*, pp. 275, 276.

CHAPTER 12: GOOD FRIENDS AND JOB OFFERS

1. Letter from STE to Joseph Davies, September 1, 1937, Box 3, STE papers, FDR Library, Hyde Park, NY.

2. Letter from STE to Davies, July 30, 1937.

3. Letter from STE to Davies, April 25, 1938.

4. Nancy Rubin Stuart, *American Empress: The Life and Times of Marjorie Merriweather Post* (New York: Villard Books, 1995), p. 206; foreword to Joseph E. Davies, *Mission to Moscow* (New York: Simon and Schuster, 1941); letter from Davies to STE, August 22, 1936; William Wright, *Heiress: The Rich Life of Marjorie Merriweather Post* (Washington, DC: New Republic Books, 1978), p. 122.

5. Letter from Davies to STE, November 26, 1935; STE diary, December 15, 1937; Rubin Stuart, *American Empress*, pp. 216, 217. In *Franklin D. Roosevelt: Launching the New Deal* (Boston: Little, Brown, 1973), Frank Freidel says that Davies himself was a principal donor to FDR's 1932 campaign (p. 137).

6. Letter from STE to Davies, January 3, 1939; author interview with Helen Early Elam, April 3, 1998.

7. Raymond Clapper diary, December 21, 1937; Rubin Stuart, *American Empress*, p. 218; Kenneth S. Davis, *FDR: The New Deal Years, 1933–1937: A History* (New York: Random House, 1986), p. 651.

8. Davies, *Mission to Moscow*, p. xi. Early was in attendance when Davies was sworn in as ambassador on November 23, 1936.

9. Letters from STE to Davies, January 3, 1936, and August 18, 1936; letter from Davies to STE, August 22, 1936.

10. Clapper diary, undated, probably December 1937.

11. Clapper diary, undated; Wright, *Heiress*, p. 131; Rubin Stuart, *American Empress*, p. 218. Early also intervened on Marjorie's behalf when he telephoned his old *Stars and Stripes* buddy, Harold Ross, editor and publisher of the *New Yorker*. The magazine wanted to do a profile on Marjorie, but after the negative publicity about her courtship and marriage to Davies and his appointment as ambassador, she was gun-shy. Early said he told Ross of "my

old friendship for Joe and my more recent affection for you." He also noted that he was asking Ross to give Marjorie "a fair break" on the piece. Letter from STE to Marjorie Davies, November 16, 1938.

12. Wright, *Heiress*, p. 132.

13. Davies, *Mission*, p. 425; letter from STE to Davies, June 1, 1938.

14. Letter from STE to Davies, January 25, 1937.

15. "U.S. Gives President's Son $4,000 Raise," *St. Louis Star-Times*, July 2, 1937.

16. Letter from STE to Davies, June 4, 1937.

17. Letter from STE to Davies, July 6, 1937.

18. Letter from Bernard Baruch to Early, June 10, 1937, Box 1, STE papers.

19. Letter from STE to Davies, July 9, 1937.

20. Otis L. Graham Jr. and Meghan Robinson Wander, eds., *Franklin D. Roosevelt: His Life and Times: An Encyclopedic View* (Boston: G. K. Hall, 1985), p. 23; letters from STE to Baruch, February 18, 1936, and January 27, 1937; letter from Harry Hawes to STE, March 5, 1940, all in Box 3, STE papers.

21. Letter from STE to Davies, September 1, 1937.

22. Ibid.

23. James Roosevelt, *My Parents: A Differing View* (Chicago: Playboy Press, 1976), pp. 68, 131, 230, 231.

24. Kenneth S. Davis, *FDR: Into the Storm, 1937–1940: A History* (New York: Random House, 1993), pp. 299–301; Harold L. Ickes, *The Secret Diary of Harold L. Ickes*, vol. 2: *The Inside Struggle, 1936–1939* (New York: Simon and Schuster, 1954), p. 37; Blanche Wiesen Cook, *Eleanor Roosevelt*, vol. 2: *1933–1938* (New York: Viking, 1999), p. 260.

25. "'My Little Son Jimmy' Is New Deal's Clearing-House," *Washington Post*, October 24, 1937.

26. Ibid; Roosevelt, *My Parents*, p. 248.

27. Author interview with William Elam III, April 3, 1998.

28. See numerous entries in STE diary, 1937; Roosevelt, *My Parents*, p. 109; "Betsy Cushing Whitney Is Dead at 89," *New York Times*, March 26, 1998.

29. Roosevelt, *My Parents*, pp. 248, 249. From the Mayo Clinic, James Roosevelt went to California to recover, accompanied by his nurse at the clinic, whom he later married after he was divorced from Betsy. He later worked in the movie business, served in World War II, and was elected to Congress.

30. Letter from STE to Davies, June 1, 1938.

31. Ibid.

32. Letter from STE to Davies, November 30, 1938.

33. Ibid.

CHAPTER 13: MOVING TOWARD WORLD CHAOS

1. STE diary, January 3, 1938.

2. Harold L. Ickes, *The Secret Diary of Harold L. Ickes*, vol. 2: *The Inside Struggle, 1936–1939* (New York: Simon and Schuster, 1954), pp. 288, 289; STE diary, January 3, 1938.

3. STE diary, January 10, 13, 14, and 15, 1938.

4. STE diary, February 15 and 17, 1938.

5. STE diary, March 19, 1938; letter from STE to Joseph Davies, April 25, 1938, Box 3, STE papers, FDR Library, Hyde Park, NY.

6. STE diary, May 23, 1938. Early's diary entries during the latter part of the decade often make brief mention of these morning meetings.

7. STE diary, March 11, April 19, April 26, and June 20, 1938; letter from STE to Davies, April 25 and June 1, 1938.

8. STE scrapbook, January 21, 1938–January 20, 1939, FDR Library, Hyde Park, NY; letter from STE to Sam Rosenman, February 4, 1938; undated memo by STE.

9. STE diary, May 24, 1938.

10. Ibid.; Grace Tully, *F.D.R., My Boss* (New York: Charles Scribner's Sons, 1949), pp. 185, 186.

11. Early's diaries for 1938 in particular give an excellent idea of the business that the White House inner sanctum conducted day by day.

12. Letter from STE to Davies, June 1, 1938.

13. Letters from STE to Davies, July 7 and August 16, 1938.

14. Letter from STE to Edwin Cox, September 21, 1939, Box 1, STE Papers; Tully, *My Boss*, pp. 204–206.

15. Letter from STE to Davies, August 16, 1938; STE diary, July 9–August 11, 1938; "RITES Too Much for Early, so President Writes News," *Milwaukee Journal*, July 26, 1938, STE scrapbook, January 21, 1938–January 20, 1939. This scrapbook contains numerous articles from newspapers as well as itineraries of the trip.

16. STE diary, August 27, 1938.

17. Letter from STE to Staunton Military Academy, August 23, 1938; letter from STE to Lt. Col. B. M. Creel, Staunton Military Academy, February 4, 1944; letter from STE to Louis Johnson, April 29, 1943, all in Box 4, STE papers.

18. STE diary, September 11–September 15, 1938.

19. Kenneth S. Davis, *FDR: Into the Storm, 1937–1940: A History* (New York: Random House, 1993), p. 310; letter from STE to Davies, September 27, 1938.

20. STE diary, September 22, 1938.

21. STE scrapbook, January 21, 1938–January 20, 1939.

22. STE diary, September 28, 1938.

23. STE diary, January 3, 1939.

24. STE diary, January 12, 1939.

25. STE diary, January 14, 24, and 26, 1939.

26. STE diary, January 26 and February 13, 1939; STE scrapbook, January 21, 1939–August 23, 1939; "Capitol Mourns Holmes' Passing," *San Francisco Examiner*, February 13, 1939; letter from STE to Anna Roosevelt, March 6, 1939, Box 15, Anna Roosevelt Halstead papers, FDR Library; letters from STE to Davies, September 9, 1938, and February 17, 1939.

27. Letter from STE to FDR, STE papers; STE diary, February 15, 1939; letter from STE to Davies, February 17, 1939.

28. STE diary, March 6, 1939. For the ulcer comment, see David McCullough, *Truman* (New York: Simon and Schuster, 1992), p. 829.

29. STE diary, March 9, 14, and 17, 1939; Samuel I. Rosenman, *Working with Roosevelt* (New York: Harper, 1952), p. 524.

30. STE diary, March 23, 1939.

31. Davis, *Into the Storm*, pp. 420–21. (In the endnotes, p. 658, Davis says the account of this phone call is in the "Personal Notes" folder of the Family Correspondence File of the Truman Papers at the Truman Library.)

32. Ibid., pp. 391, 392.

33. STE diary, June 1, 1939.

34. Tully, *My Boss*, p. 314; STE diary, June 8 and 9, 1939. Early's scrapbook, January 21, 1939–August 23, 1939, contains several pages of news clippings and memorabilia from those historic days.

35. STE diary, June 15, 1939.

36. Stephen T. Early, "Below the Belt," *Saturday Evening Post*, June 10, 1939; STE diary, June 19, 1939; clippings of editorials and news stories in STE scrapbook, January 21, 1939–August 23, 1939.

37. Early, "Below the Belt."

38. STE diary, June 21, 1939; and clippings in STE scrapbook, January 21, 1939–August 23, 1939.

39. STE diary, July 11, 13, 25, 26, and 27, and August 11, 1939; letter from STE to Helen Early, July 19, 1939.

40. Letters from STE to Helen Early, July 27 and August 1, 1939.

41. Letter from STE to Davies, August 15, 1939.

42. STE diary, August 24, 1939.

CHAPTER 14: FATAL DAYS IN EUROPE, DECISIONS AT HOME

1. STE diary, August 26–September 1, 1939.
2. STE diary, September 2, 1939.
3. STE diary, September 1, 1939.
4. STE diary, September 2, 1939.
5. STE diary, September 4, 1939; Steven E. Schoenherr, "Selling the New Deal: Stephen T. Early's Role as Press Secretary to Franklin D. Roosevelt" (PhD diss., University of Delaware, 1976), pp. 195, 196.
6. STE diary, September 20, 21, and 22, and October 5 and 19, 1939; Harold L. Ickes, *The Secret Diary of Harold L. Ickes*, vol. 3: *The Lowering Clouds* (New York: Simon and Schuster, 1954), p. 18.
7. Ickes, *Lowering Clouds*, pp. 3, 4; Samuel I. Rosenman, *Working with Roosevelt* (New York: Harper, 1952), p. 3.
8. Letter from STE to Buddy Early, September 27, 1939, Box 4, STE papers, FDR Library, Hyde Park, NY.
9. STE diary October 14, 1939.
10. STE diary, December 14, 1939.
11. STE diary, November 1, 13, and 23–28, 1939; Ickes, *Lowering Clouds*, p. 52.
12. STE diary, November 30, 1939.
13. STE diary, December 4 and 14, 1939.
14. STE diary, November 30 and December 8, 1939.
15. STE diary, December 19, 1939.
16. Kenneth S. Davis, *FDR: Into the Storm, 1937–1940: A History* (New York: Random House, 1993), pp. 537, 538; Rosenman, *Working with Roosevelt*, pp. 191, 192.
17. Davis, *Into the Storm*, p. 544; Doris Kearns Goodwin, *No Ordinary Time: Franklin and Eleanor Roosevelt: The Home Front in World War II* (New York: Simon and Schuster, 1994), pp. 14, 17.
18. "Farley Takes Veiled Slap at Third Term," *New York News*, January 25, 1940, STE scrapbook, January 20 1940–July 31, 1940, FDR Library, Hyde Park, NY.
19. Letter from STE to Davies, September 9, 1938, Box 3, STE papers; letter from STE to James Roosevelt, April 3, 1947, Box 15, STE papers.
20. "Early Rests from Politics," *Miami Herald*, February 9, 1940, STE scrapbook, January 20, 1940–July 31, 1940.
21. "The Cab Driver Said So," *Washington News*, June 7, 1940, STE scrapbook, January 20, 1940–July 31, 1940.
22. STE press conference, June 15, 1940. Chambrun had married the

only daughter of Pierre Laval, who was premier of France in the 1930s and after the fall of France in 1940 became head of the collaborationist Vichy government of France.

23. Ickes, *Lowering Clouds*, p. 95.

24. Joseph P. Lash, *Eleanor and Franklin: The Story of Their Relationship, Based on Eleanor Roosevelt's Private Papers* (New York: Norton, 1971), p. 616.

25. Robert Goralski, *World War II Almanac, 1931–1945: A Political and Military Record* (New York: Putnam, 1981), pp. 114–16.

26. "President Roosevelt Called Two More Emergency Meetings to Draft Big Preparedness Measures Against What the White House Described As a Four-Alarm Fire Sweeping Toward the New World," unnamed wire service dispatch, May 14, 1940, STE scrapbook, January 20, 1940–July 31, 1940.

27. "'Taking It Easy': Seven Days' Work!" *United States News*, March 22, 1940, STE scrapbook, January 20, 1940–July 31, 1940. Also see this scrapbook for other news clippings and Early's press conferences relating to FDR's health that month.

28. Letters from STE to Buddy Early, April 11, 1940, Box 4, STE papers.

29. "Roosevelt Prepares Important Statement," *Washington Post*, June 10, 1940; "Sidelights on Roosevelt's Talk," *Washington Post*, June 11, 1940, STE scrapbook, January 20, 1940–July 31, 1940.

30. Letters from STE to Harold Ross, July 12 and July 16, 1940, Box 16, STE papers; Ickes, *Lowering Clouds*, p. 52.

31. Otis L. Graham Jr. and Meaghan Robinson Wander, eds., *Franklin D. Roosevelt: His Life and Times: an Encyclopedic View* (Boston: G. K. Hall, 1985), pp. 226, 405; Davis, *Into the Storm*, pp. 570–74.

32. Davis, *Into the Storm*, p. 580; Graham and Wander, *Life and Times*, p. 456.

33. Rosenman, *Working with Roosevelt*, p. 203.

34. Grace Tully, *F.D.R., My Boss* (New York: Charles Scribner's Sons, 1949), pp. 235; Davis, *Into the Storm*, p. 589.

35. Tully, *My Boss*, p. 238; James A. Farley, *Jim Farley's Story: The Roosevelt Years* (New York: Whittlesey House, 1948), pp. 247–58, 325.

36. "$4.9 Billion More for Defense," *New York Times*, July 11, 1940; "Roosevelt Draft Started; Rivals Press Campaigns; He Won't Go to Convention," *New York Times*, July 13, 1940; "Overnight Cruise on Potomac," *New York Times*, July 15, 1940.

37. "President Phones Farley in Chicago," *New York Times*, July 16, 1940; "Roosevelt Leaves Third Term to Party; Releases Delegates for a Free Choice; Move to Draft Him is Set for Tonight," *New York Times*, July 17, 1940.

38. "President Explains Why He Had Kept Silence on Third Term," *New York Times*, July 17, 1940; "Nation Will Hear President Tonight," *New York Times*, July 18, 1940; Rosenman, *Working with Roosevelt*, p. 212.

39. "Roosevelt Leaves Third Term to Party; Releases Delegates for a Free Choice; Move to Draft Him is Set for Tonight"; Davis, *Into the Storm*, pp. 601–602; Rosenman, *Working with Roosevelt*, pp. 212–19.

40. STE scrapbook, August 1, 1940–January 20, 1941, includes clippings on this trip: "Democratic Tension Rises as Stephen Early Arrives," *Los Angeles Times*, August 4, 1940; "Stephen Early Tells Broadcasters Radio Is as Free as Press," *Washington Star*, August 4, 1940; "Early Here," *San Francisco News*, August 3, 1940; "Advance Man," *Seattle Star*, August 9, 1940; "Stephen T. Early Passes Here on Eastbound Plane," *Butte Post*, August 9, 1940; "Presidential Aide Goes Through City," *Butte Standard*, August 10, 1940.

41. Ickes, *Lowering Clouds*, p. 351.

42. Stephen T. Early, "Inside the White House with Europe at War," *Cosmopolitan*, Part 1, August 1940, Part 2, September 1940.

43. "FDR to Give '1st Political Talk' Today," *Philadelphia Inquirer*, September 11, 1940.

44. "The Capital Parade," *Washington Star*, October 4, 1940.

CHAPTER 15: THE SLOAN AFFAIR

1. David Brinkley, *Washington Goes to War* (New York: Knopf, 1988), pp. 20–21.

2. "Roosevelt: From Breakfast in Bed to Wisecracks at the Movies, President Retains His Bounce After Eight Years," *Life*, January 20, 1941; Joseph P. Lash, *Eleanor and Franklin: The Story of Their Relationship, Based on Eleanor Roosevelt's Private Papers* (New York: Norton, 1971), p. 522.

3. Blanche Wiesen Cook, *Eleanor Roosevelt*, vol 2: *1933–1938* (New York: Viking, 1999), p. 39; Betty Houchin Winfield, *FDR and the News Media* (New York: Columbia University Press, 1994), p. 56.

4. Lash, *Eleanor and Franklin*, p. 513.

5. Letter from STE to Malvina Thompson, August 5, 1935, Box 24, STE papers, FDR Library, Hyde Park, NY. In *Eleanor and Franklin*, Lash described Walter White as having "blue eyes, fair skin, and blond hair" (p. 522).

6. Letter from Eleanor Roosevelt to STE, August 5, 1935, Box 15, STE papers.

7. Lash, *Eleanor and Franklin*, p. 445.

8. Ibid, p. 530. In *Washington Goes to War*, David Brinkley notes that the New Deal had been little interested in racial issues, such as antilynching leg-

islation, for fear of alienating the Southern Democrats Roosevelt so needed for reelection (p. 78).

9. "Early Admits 'Giving Knee' to Patrolman," *New York Mirror*, October 30, 1940; "Early Admits 'Giving the Knee' to Policeman Who Tried to Bar Him From President's Train," *New York Times*, October 30, 1940; eyewitness accounts from reporters Bruce Pinter, John T. Henry, and Doris Fleeson, STE scrapbook, "Sloan Incident," FDR Library, Hyde Park, NY.

10. "Power Always Corrupts," *New York Mirror*, October 31, 1940; "Association with Gangsters Breeds Gangster Methods," *Call* (Patterson, NJ), October 30, 1940; "Often the Mouthpiece of the Third Term Candidate," *New York Mirror*, October 31, 1940; Harold L. Ickes, *The Secret Diary of Harold L. Ickes*, vol. 3: *The Lowering Clouds, 1939–1941* (New York: Simon and Schuster, 1954), p. 362. The Dewey investigation story was from *New York Age*, November 2, 1940, STE scrapbook, "Sloan Incident"; letter from Eleanor Roosevelt to Mrs. Wender, November 13, 1940, STE scrapbook, "Sloan Incident"; Grace Tully, *F.D.R., My Boss* (New York: Charles Scribner's Sons, 1949), p. 153.

11. "Early Admits 'Giving the Knee' to Policeman Who Tried to Bar Him From President's Train." A copy of the Sloan flyer is in STE scrapbook, "Sloan Incident."

12. "Early Admits 'Giving Knee' to Patrolman," eyewitness accounts by journalists Tom Reynolds and George Durno, and official statement by Early, all in STE scrapbook, "Sloan Incident"; "Nailing a Campaign Lie," *New Republic*, November 25, 1940.

13. Statement is in STE scrapbook, "Sloan Incident."

14. "Nailing a Campaign Lie."

15. Early statement in STE scrapbook, "Sloan Incident."

16. Ickes, *Lowering Clouds*, p. 362; Steven E. Schoenherr, "Selling the New Deal: Stephen T. Early's Role as Press Secretary to Franklin D. Roosevelt" (PhD diss., University of Delaware, 1976), p. 17; memo from STE to William Hassett, November 7, 1940, STE scrapbook, August 1, 1940–January 20, 1941.

17. "White House Corps Defends Early," *Editor & Publisher*, November 16, 1940; STE letter to editors, STE scrapbook, "Sloan Incident"; "Nailing a Campaign Lie."

18. "Early's Temper," *Time*, November 11, 1940.

19. Letter from STE to Samuel I. Rosenman, December 4, 1940, Box 16, STE papers.

20. Letter from James Sloan to STE, November 22, 1940, and letter from STE to Sloan, November 29, 1940, both in STE scrapbook, "Sloan Incident."

21. M. L. Stein, *When Presidents Meet the Press* (New York: Messner, 1969), pp. 88, 89.

22. Robert E. Sherwood, *Roosevelt and Hopkins, An Intimate History* (New York: Harper, 1948), p. 208.

23. Tully, *My Boss*, p. 87.

24. Stein, *When Presidents Meet the Press*, p. 89; Jonathan Daniels, *White House Witness, 1942–1945* (Garden City, NY: Doubleday, 1975), p. 13.

25. "Early's Contribution," *Washington Post*, June 2, 1945.

26. "Cameramen Rebel against Steve Early," *Washington Times-Herald*, September 12, 1940; Winfield, *FDR and the News Media*, p. 113; "Photographers Win Their Argument with Steve Early," *Washington News*, September 14, 1940, STE scrapbook, August 1, 1940–January 20, 1941.

27. "Spokesman Early," *Scranton Tribune*, May 24, 1940.

28. "*Tribune* Scoops World in Story of French Fall," *Chicago Tribune*, June 18, 1940, STE scrapbook, August 1, 1940–January 20, 1941.

29. Brinkley, *Washington Goes to War*, pp. 175, 186; "'Steve' Early, One-time Reporter, Plays New and Difficult Role As Spokesman for the President," *St. Louis Post-Dispatch*, November 19, 1939.

30. "People of the Week," *United States News*, December 6, 1940, STE scrapbook, August 1, 1940–January 20, 1941.

31. James Roosevelt, *My Parents: A Differing View* (Chicago: Playboy Press, 1976), p. 187; Hugh Gregory Gallagher, *FDR's Splendid Deception* (New York: Dodd, Mead, 1985), pp. 94–95.

32. Memo from STE to Dr. Ross McIntire, August 13, 1937, Box 11, STE papers; Schoenherr, "Selling the New Deal," pp. 145, 156.

33. Schoenherr, "Selling the New Deal," p. 147.

34. J. B. West, *Upstairs at the White House: My Life with the First Ladies* (New York: Coward, McCann & Geoghegan, 1973), p. 17.

35. Gallagher, *Splendid Deception*, p. 94.

36. Schoenherr, "Selling the New Deal," p. 148. Recently, the FDR Library placed on its Web site (www.fdrlibrary.marist.edu/) photos that show Roosevelt standing, such as when he voted in Hyde Park and when he greeted a dignitary. However, if you look closely, you will see that he always is holding on to someone with one hand and leaning on his cane with the other.

37. Schoenherr, "Selling the New Deal," p. 157; author interview with Helen Early Elam, April 3, 1998.

38. Roosevelt, *My Parents*, p. 83.

CHAPTER 16: "JUST BETWEEN US 'GIRLS'"

1. Delbert Clark, "Steve Takes Care of It," *New York Times Magazine*, July 27, 1941; "People of the Week," *United States News*, December 6, 1940.

2. "Steve Early Speaks for F.R.," *St. Paul Pioneer Press*, January 19, 1941; Steven E. Schoenherr, "Selling the New Deal: Stephen T. Early's Role as Press Secretary to Franklin D. Roosevelt" (PhD diss., University of Delaware, 1976), pp. 191–95.

3. "'Steve' Early, Onetime Reporter, Plays New and Difficult Role as Spokesman for the President," *St. Louis Post-Dispatch*, November 19, 1939.

4. John Gunther, *Roosevelt in Retrospect* (London: Hamish Hamilton, 1950), p. 49; Walter Trohan, "A Great American Passes," *Carbuilder*, October 1951, Box 63, STE papers, FDR Library, Hyde Park, NY. "'Steve' Early, One-time Reporter, Plays New and Difficult Role as Spokesman for the President."

5. "The Life of Early in Brief," *Carbuilder*, October 1951, Box 63, STE papers.

6. FDR press conference, March 10, 1942; "President Has Early Rewrite Landis' Polysyllabic Order," *Washington Star*, March 11, 1942, STE scrapbook, January 21, 1942–July 31, 1942, FDR Library, Hyde Park, NY.

7. "President Tardy, Blames Early's Cheap Clock," *Washington Star*, March 7, 1941; "F.D.R.'s No. 1 Buffer," *Look*, March 11, 1941.

8. "The Life of Early in Brief"; Jonathan Daniels, *White House Witness, 1942–1945* (Garden City, NY: Doubleday, 1975), p. 142.

9. William D. Hassett, *Off the Record with F.D.R., 1942–1945* (New Brunswick, NJ: Rutgers University Press, 1958), p. ix.

10. Early's vital statistics from a memo from Ruthjane Rumelt, his secretary, to Atlas Sport Shop, Washington, DC, November 15, 1943, Box 28, STE papers. The description of Early is taken from "Columnist Visits Secretary Early," *Akron Beacon-Journal*, April 5, 1940, STE scrapbook, January 20, 1940–July 31, 1940; from S. J. Woolf, "Up the Ladder with F.D.R.," *New York Times Magazine*, August 27, 1939; from his daughter Helen Early Elam in interviews with the author; from Clark, "Steve Takes Care of It"; from Grace Tully, *F.D.R., My Boss* (New York: Charles Scribner's Sons, 1949), p. 293; and from "How Steve Early Told Press of Hawaii Attack," *Philadelphia Inquirer*, December 14, 1941. The "hard boiled" description is from David McCullough, *Truman* (New York: Simon and Schuster, 1992), p. 363; letter from STE to Joseph Davies, July 7, 1938, Box 3, STE papers.

11. "Roosevelt Aide," *Philadelphia Bulletin*, undated, STE scrapbook, August 1, 1940–January 20, 1941.

12. "President, 3 Aides Felled by Colds," *New York Times*, January 28, 1941; STE press conference, January 29, 1941.

13. "The Presidency," *Time*, March 31, 1941; Robert H. Jackson, *That Man, An Insider's Portrait of Franklin D. Roosevelt*, (New York: Oxford University Press, 2003), p. 148.

14. "Columnist Visits Secretary Early"; "'Steve' Early, Onetime Reporter, Plays New and Difficult Role as Spokesman for the President."

15. STE press conference, May 6, 1941, Box 40, STE papers; "'Steve' Early, Onetime Reporter, Plays New and Difficult Role As Spokesman for the President."

16. STE press conference, May 7, 1941, Box 40, STE papers.

17. STE press conference, May 8, 1941, Box 40, STE papers.

18. STE press conference, May 9, 1941, Box 40, STE papers.

19. STE press conferences, May 10, 12, and 13, 1941, Box 40, STE papers.

20. Kenneth S. Davis, *FDR: The War President, 1940–1943: A History* (New York: Random House, 2000), p. 154.

21. FDR press conference, May 16, 1941.

22. "Tired President Still Declines to Delegate Power," AP story in *Topeka Journal*, May 8, 1941.

23. "Soldier-Columnist Loses Commission," *Washington News*, April 30, 1941; "One Man's Opinion," *Washington News*, May 2, 1941.

24. "Early Wonders If Lindbergh Will Return Nazi Decoration," *Washington Star*, April 29, 1941.

25. Memo from STE to FDR, May 24, 1941, STE scrapbook, January 21, 1941–July 31, 1941; "4-Ex-Foes Support F.D. in Word-War on War," *Washington News*, May 29, 1941.

26. "President Catches Cold; Cancels All Engagements," *Washington Star*, June 13, 1941.

27. "Roosevelt Off on Secret Yacht Trip," *New York Herald-Tribune*, August 3, 1941.

28. Memo from STE to FDR, August 7, 1941, STE scrapbook, August 1, 1941–January 20, 1942.

29. Radiogram from STE to FDR, August 13, 1941, STE scrapbook, August 1, 1941–January 20, 1942.

30. Tully, *My Boss*, p. 152; radiogram from STE to FDR, August 14, 1941, STE scrapbook, August 1, 1941–January 20, 1942.

31. Telegram from FDR to STE, August 15, 1941, STE scrapbook, August 1, 1941–January 20, 1942.

32. Untitled story, *St. Paul Pioneer Press*, August 16, 1941, STE scrapbook, August 1, 1941–January 20, 1942; "F.D.R. Joins Churchill in Peace Aims," *New York Daily News*, August 15, 1941.

33. "F.D.R. Lifts Iceland Ban for Newsmen," *New York Daily News*, August 26, 1941.

34. STE press conference, August 27, 1941.

35. Davis, *War President*, pp. 282, 283; STE press conference, September 15, 1941; memo in STE scrapbook, August 1, 1941–January 20, 1942.

36. "Annulment Is Requested by Early's Niece," *New York Mirror*, September 16, 1941.

37. STE memo in STE scrapbook, August 1, 1941–January 20, 1942.

38. "Little Old New York," *New York News*, November 15, 1941; STE and FDR telegrams, STE scrapbook, August 1, 1941–January 20, 1942.

39. "Messages to President Show 10 to 1 Agreement," *New York Herald-Tribune*, September 13, 1941.

40. Davis, *War President*, pp. 283–85.

41. "Jews and F.D. Leading Us to War—Lindbergh," *Washington News*, September 12, 1941; "Assail Lindbergh for Iowa Speech," *New York Times*, September 13, 1941.

42. STE press conference, November 19, 1941.

43. STE press conference, November 22, 1941.

44. "Roosevelt Hurries Back in Crisis," *New York Times*, December 1, 1941; Tully, *My Boss*, pp. 249–50; Robert Goralski, *World War II Almanac 1931–1945: A Political and Military Record* (New York: Putnam, 1981), pp. 176, 183.

45. "Source of War Plan Story to be Probed, Early Says," *Washington Star*, December 4, 1941; Davis, *War President*, p. 336; "U.S.A. Probes Disclosure of Army's Secrets," *P.M.*, December 5, 1941.

46. Davis, *War President*, p. 336.

47. STE press conference, December 6, 1941.

CHAPTER 17: PEARL HARBOR

1. "Winter and War Full on the Capital," *New York Times*, December 8, 1941; STE talk at 1949–1950 Harlan Fiske Stone Memorial Lecture at Amherst, December 7, 1949, Box 61, STE papers, FDR Library, Hyde Park, NY; STE scrapbook, August 1, 1941–January 20, 1942, FDR Library, Hyde Park, NY; transcript of radio interview by Richard Eaton with STE, "Behind the White House," *News Digest*, June 1944; "War Brings a Tense Day to White House Press Room," *Washington Post*, December 8, 1941; Robert Goralski, *World War II Almanac, 1931–1945: A Political and Military Record* (New York: Putnam, 1981), pp. 186–87.

2. STE talk at Amherst; Grace Tully, *F.D.R., My Boss* (New York: Charles Scribner's Sons, 1949), p. 254.

3. Tully, *My Boss*, p. 254; "War Brings a Tense Day to White House Press Room"; "White House Staff Leaps into Action," *New York Times*, December 8, 1941; Steven E. Schoenherr, "Selling the New Deal: Stephen T. Early's Role as Press Secretary to Franklin D. Roosevelt" (PhD diss., University of Delaware, 1976), p. 190; James MacGregor Burns, *Roosevelt: The Soldier of Freedom, 1940–1945* (New York: Harcourt Brace Jovanovich, 1970), p. 163; STE press conference, 3:10 p.m., December 7, 1941.

4. STE press conferences, 3:15 p.m. and 3:20 p.m., December 7, 1941.

5. STE press conferences, 4:00 p.m. and 4:10 p.m., December 7, 1941.

6. "War Brings a Tense Day to White House Press Room"; "White House Staff Leaps into Action."

7. STE press conference, 4:30 p.m., December 7, 1941; "The News Comes to America: Scenes in Times Square, at the Navy Yard and at White House," *New York Times*, December 8, 1941; Burns, *Soldier of Freedom*, p. 165; "War Brings a Tense Day to White House Press Room." In *My Boss*, Grace Tully says it was not long before Washington correspondents for publications from the Axis countries were rounded up and placed in custody (p. 260).

8. STE press conference, 4:30 p.m., December 7, 1941.

9. STE press conference, 5:55 p.m., December 7, 1941; Schoenherr, "Selling the New Deal," p. 190.

10. Burns, *Soldier of Freedom*, p. 171.

11. Tully, *My Boss*, p. 259; A. Merriman Smith, *Thank You, Mr. President: A White House Notebook* (New York: Harper & Brothers, 1946), p. 119.

12. Tully, *My Boss*, p. 260; STE press conference, December 8, 1941.

13. Kenneth S. Davis, *FDR: The War President, 1940–1943: A History* (New York: Random House, 2000), p. 341; Otis L. Graham Jr. and Meghan Robinson Wander, eds., *Franklin D. Roosevelt: His Life and Times: An Encyclopedic View* (Boston: G. K. Hall, 1985), p. 318.

14. Tully, *My Boss*, p. 260.

15. STE telephone memo, December 8, 1941.

16. "Capital Swings into War Stride," *New York Times*, December 9, 1941; Davis, *War President*, pp. 342, 343.

17. STE press conference, December 8, 1941; "Army, Navy Order Wide Censorship," *New York Times*, December 8, 1941.

18. David Brinkley, *Washington Goes to War* (New York: Knopf, 1988), p. 93.

19. Thomas Parrish, ed., *Simon and Schuster Encyclopedia of World War II* (New York: Simon and Schuster, 1978), p. 168.

20. STE press conference, December 9, 1941.

21. Davis, *War President*, p. 349.

22. STE press conference, December 10, 1941; Davis, *War President*, p. 352.

23. STE press conference, December 11, 1941; Brinkley, *Washington Goes to War*, p. 201.

24. STE press release, December 13, 1941.

25. STE press conference, December 15, 1941.

26. William David Sloan and James D. Startt, *The Media in America: A History* (Northport, AL: Vision Press, 1999), p. 422; Frank Luther Mott, American Journalism (New York: Macmillan, 1941), p. 627.

27. STE press conference, February 20, 1942.

28. Stephen T. Early, "No Iron Heel Here—Your Press Is Free," *Philadelphia Inquirer*, June 15, 1941.

29. FDR press conference, December 9, 1941; "Censorship Rules Set by President," *New York Times*, December 10, 1941.

30. Oliver Gramling, *AP: The Story of News* (New York: Farrar and Rinehart, 1940), p. 419; "President Appoints Byron Price to Direct Wartime Censorship," *New York Times*, December 17, 1941; letter from STE to Kent Cooper, December 31, 1941, Box 2, STE papers; letter from STE to Byron Price, Box 2, STE papers.

31. Mott, *American Journalism*, p. 762; STE press conference, December 17, 1941.

32. Letter to STE from Delbert Clark, *New York Times* White House reporter, December 18, 1941, STE scrapbook, August 1, 1941–January 20, 1942; "Steve Knows a Story," *Decatur Herald and Review*, December 25, 1941; letter from STE to Cooper, December 31, 1941.

33. STE press conference, December 20, 1941; David Stafford, *Roosevelt and Churchill: Men of Secrets* (Woodstock, NY: Overlook Press, 2000), p. 123.

34. Davis, *War President*, pp. 365, 366; STE press conference, December 23, 1941; photo of Churchill and Roosevelt, *New York Times*, December 23, 1941, p. 1.

35. STE press conference, December 22, 1941.

36. STE press conference, 10:40 a.m., December 23, 1941.

37. STE press conference, 12:30 p.m., December 23, 1941.

38. Memo from STE to William Hassett, December 23, 1941, Box 7, STE papers; Davis, *War President*, p. 367.

39. Burns, *Soldier of Freedom*, p. 178; Davis, *War President*, p. 368.

40. Davis, *War President*, p. 368; STE press conference, December 26, 1941.

41. STE press conference, December 26, 1941.

42. Ibid.

43. Burns, *Soldier of Freedom*, p. 178; Tully, *My Boss*, p. 261.

44. STE press conference, December 29, 1941.

45. STE press conference, December 31, 1941; Burns, *Soldier of Freedom*, pp. 184, 185.

46. STE press conference, January 3, 1942.

CHAPTER 18: "SERVE IN SILENCE"

1. "White House Press Conferences Drying Up as News Sources," *Philadelphia Bulletin*, January 28, 1942.

2. Ibid.; STE press conference, January 7, 1942; William D. Hassett, *Off the Record with F.D.R., 1942–1945* (New Brunswick, NJ: Rutgers University Press, 1958), p. vii.

3. "Behind the White House," *Newsdigest*, June, 1944; STE press conference, May 23, 1942.

4. "Behind the White House."

5. Robert E. Sherwood, *Roosevelt and Hopkins, An Intimate History* (New York: Harper, 1948), p. 207; Robert C. Withers, *The President Travels by Train* (Lynchburg, VA: TLC Publishing, 1995), p. 151.

6. "OPA Bans New Autos, May Commandeer Old Cars," *New York Times*, January 3, 1942.

7. James MacGregor Burns, *Roosevelt: The Soldier of Freedom, 1940–1945* (New York: Harcourt Brace Jovanovich, 1970), pp. 213, 214.

8. STE press conference, January 16, 1942.

9. STE press conference, February 2, 1942

10. Untitled article in untitled magazine, January 19, 1942, STE scrapbook, August 1, 1941–January 20, 1942, FDR Library, Hyde Park, NY; and STE press conference, March 30, 1942.

11. STE press conference, January 6, 1942; Steven E. Schoenherr, "Selling the New Deal: Stephen T. Early's Role as Press Secretary to Franklin D. Roosevelt" (PhD diss., University of Delaware, 1976), p. 205.

12. Burns, *Soldier of Freedom*, p. 198; Sherwood, *Roosevelt and Hopkins*, p. 444; for the personal relationship of the two men, see Hassett, *Off the Record*, p. 67.

13. STE press conference, January 7, 1942.

14. Grace Tully, *F.D.R., My Boss* (New York: Charles Scribner's Sons, 1949), p. 268; STE press conference, January 7, 1942.

15. STE press conference, January 7, 1942.

16. Kenneth S. Davis, *FDR: The War President, 1940–1943: A History* (New York: Random House, 2000), p. 401; STE press conference, January 17, 1942.

17. Burns, *Soldier of Freedom*, p. 198.

18. STE press conference, January 19, 1942.

19. STE press conference, January 26, 1942.

20. STE press conference, January 27, 1942.

21. STE press conference, February 2, 1942.

22. STE press conference, February 7, 1942.

23. "President Kept to Rooms by Coed," *Washington Post*, February 20, 1942; untitled newspaper article in STE scrapbook, January 21, 1942–July 31, 1942.

24. See FDR Library Web site for complete set of Fireside Chats, www.fdrlibrary.marist.edu/firesi90.html; also Schoenherr, "Selling the New Deal," p. 216.

25. McIntyre press conference, March 3, 1942; Hassett, *Off the Record*, p. xiii; Hassett press conference, March 9, 1942.

26. Tully, *My Boss*, p. 271; Davis, *War President*, p. 128; Hassett, *Off the Record*, pp. xii, xiii.

27. STE press conference, March 26, 1942.

28. Ibid.

29. STE press conferences, March 18 and April 11, 1942.

30. STE press conference, April 4, 1942.

31. A. Merriman Smith, *Thank You, Mr. President: A White House Notebook* (New York: Harper & Brothers, 1946), pp. 2, 10.

32. Schoenherr, "Selling the New Deal," p. 212; STE press conference, April 17, 1942; "Press Rumors on News Irks White House," *Washington Times-Herald*, April 18, 1942.

33. Hassett, *Off the Record*, pp. 36–41; Smith, *Thank You*, p. 58.

34. STE press conference, May 23, 1942.

35. Davis, *War President*, pp. 493, 494; STE press conference, May 23, 1942.

36. STE press conference, May 23, 1942; Smith, *Thank You*, p. 129.

37. Davis, *War President*, pp. 494, 495; Burns, *Soldier of Freedom*, p. 232; STE press conference, June 2, 1942; Smith, *Thank You*, p. 130; Sherwood, *Roosevelt and Hopkins*, p. 568.

38. STE press conference, June 2, 1942

39. "Churchill Here for Talks on Second Front," *New York Times*, June 19, 1942; Burns, *Soldier of Freedom*, p. 235; STE press conference, June 19, 1942.

40. "Behind the White House."

41. "Have You Heard," *Life*, July 13, 1942.

42. "Roosevelt Accused of 'Rumor Factory' Talk," *Jackson (MS) Clarion-Ledger*, March 23, 1942.

43. "Roosevelt Bares Visit to His Hyde Park Home," *Philadelphia Inquirer*, September 16, 1942.

44. STE press conference, August 22, 1942; "Leak Charge Arouses White House," *Washington Post*, August 21, 1942.

45. Letter from William Stanley to FDR, May 11, 1942, STE scrapbook, January 21, 1942–July 31, 1942.

46. Letter from FDR to Stanley, May 20, 1942. See newspaper clippings, photos, and a copy of the speech in STE scrapbook, January 21, 1942–July 31, 1942.

47. Sherwood, *Roosevelt and Hopkins*, pp. 606, 607; clippings and itinerary in STE scrapbook, January 21, 1942–July 31, 1942; Harry C. Butcher, *My Three Years with Eisenhower: The Personal Diary of Captain Harry C. Butcher, USNR, Naval Aide to General Eisenhower, 1942 to 1945* (New York: Simon and Schuster, 1946), pp. 23–32.

48. STE press conference, July 16, 1942.

49. "Steve Early, 53, Today Learns Relaxation from Roosevelt," *Washington Evening Star*, August 27, 1942; "Memo from the *Tribune*'s Washington Bureau," *Minneapolis Tribune*, September 14, 1942; "Washington Wire," *Pittsburgh Post-Gazette*, September 18, 1942.

50. Burns, *Soldier of Freedom*, p. 268.

51. Betty Houchin Winfield, *FDR and the News Media* (New York: Columbia University Press, 1994), pp. 202, 203.

52. Smith, *Thank You*, pp. 49–54.

53. Davis, *War President*, p. 611, 612; David Brinkley, *Washington Goes to War* (New York: Knopf, 1988), p. 106.

54. Davis, *War President*, p. 612; Smith, *Thank You*, p. 49.

55. FDR press conference, October 2, 1942; Brinkley, *Washington Goes to War*, p. 170.

56. "35 News Writers Protest to F.D.R. on Censored Trip," *Philadelphia Record*, October 2, 1942; "35 News Writers Send Protest to Roosevelt," *New York Herald Tribune*, October 2, 1942; "Banned From Trip, Reporters Protest," *New York Times*, October 2, 1942; "Censorship Fast Closing in at Washington, Bars Much News Not of Aid to Enemy," *St. Louis Post-Dispatch*, October 2, 1942, all in STE scrapbook, August 1, 1942–January 20, 1943. See also Smith, *Thank You*, p. 56.

57. Memo from FDR to STE, October 24, 1944, Box 24, STE papers, FDR Library, Hyde Park, NY.

58. Raymond Clapper papers, Library of Congress.

59. "Roosevelt Calls Step 'Effective Second-Front Assistance,'" *Baltimore Sun*, November 8, 1942; Robert Goralski, *World War II Almanac, 1931–1945: A Political and Military Record* (New York: Putnam, 1981), p. 243.

60. Hassett, *Off the Record*, p. 141; FDR press conference, December 1, 1942.

61. Hassett, *Off the Record*, pp. 139–49.

62. STE press conference, December 31, 1942; FDR press conference, January 1, 1943.

63. STE press conference, January 12, 1943.

CHAPTER 19: "THE TRAVELINGEST PRESIDENT"

1. "Darlan Shot Dead by Frenchman in Algiers; President Asks Swift Justice in 'Cowardly' Darlan Killing," *New York Times*, December 25, 1942; Samuel I. Rosenman, *Working with Roosevelt* (New York: Da Capo Press, 1972), pp. 369, 500; William D. Hassett, *Off the Record with F.D.R.*, *1942–1945* (New Brunswick, NJ: Rutgers University Press, 1958), p. 150; John Gunther, *Roosevelt in Retrospect* (London: Hamish Hamilton, 1950), p. 152.

2. "A Close-Up View of the War," *United States News*, February 5, 1943; Gunther, *Roosevelt in Retrospect*, p. 152; FDR press conference, February 2, 1943; "Roosevelt Sets Travel Records," *New York Times*, January 27, 1943; STE press conference, February 1, 1943.

3. Grace Tully, *F.D.R., My Boss* (New York: Charles Scribner's Sons, 1949), pp. 208, 209; "Roosevelt Stops Off in Brazil after Short Visit to Liberia," *New York Times*, January 29, 1943.

4. Tully, *My Boss*, pp. 209, 210; Raymond W. Copson, "Summit at Casablanca," *American History*, April 2002; Gunther, *Roosevelt in Retrospect*, pp. 153, 154.

5. "Capital Guesses," AP press release, STE scrapbook #15, January 21, 1943–July 31, 1943, FDR Library, Hyde Park, NY; A. Merriman Smith, *Thank You, Mr. President: A White House Notebook* (New York: Harper & Brothers, 1946), p. 57.

6. "Roosevelt Orders Miners to Pits or Face War Action; Some Unions Still Defiant," *New York Times*, January 20, 1943; Steven E. Schoenherr, "Selling the New Deal: Stephen T. Early's Role as Press Secretary to Franklin D. Roosevelt" (PhD diss., University of Delaware, 1976), p. 215.

7. Memo from the Office of Censorship in a folder marked "Confidential" in STE scrapbook #15.

8. "Roosevelt, Churchill Map 1943 War Strategy at Ten-Day Conference Held in Casablanca; Giraud and De Gaulle Present, Argue on Aims," *New York Times*, January 27, 1943; "Baudry Was Killed on Way to Parley," *New York Times*, January 27, 1943.

9. STE press conference, January 25, 1943.

10. Ibid.

11. James MacGregor Burns, *Roosevelt: The Soldier of Freedom, 1940–*

1945 (New York: Harcourt Brace Jovanovich, 1970), p. 322; "Roosevelt Stops off in Brazil after Short Visit to Liberia; Russians March on Junctions," *New York Times*, January 29, 1943; "Roosevelt, Vargas Affirm Aim to Make Atlantic Safe for All; Russians Rout 7 Reich Divisions," *New York Times*, January 30, 1943.

12. "Roosevelt Stops Off in Brazil After Short Visit to Liberia; Russians March on Junctions"; "Roosevelt, Vargas Affirm Aim to Make Atlantic Safe for All; Russians Rout 7 Reich Divisions."

13. STE press conference, January 27, 1943.

14. STE press conference, February 1, 1943.

15. Outline and memo in STE scrapbook #15; FDR press conference, February 2, 1943.

16. STE press conference, February 11, 1943.

17. David M. Glantz, *The Battle for Leningrad: 1941–1944* (Lawrence: University Press of Kansas, 2002), p. 547; also from author's visits to Leningrad, St. Petersburg, 1990–1998.

18. Memo regarding dates and place of vacation, in STE scrapbook #15; "Secretary to F.D.R. Ends Two-Week Visit to Dunedin," *St. Petersburg Times*, February 27, 1943.

19. STE press conference, March 1, 1943.

20. Letter from STE to Buddy Early, March 10, 1943, Box 4, STE papers, FDR Library, Hyde Park, NY; letter from STE to Victor Emanuel, March 6, 1943, Box 4, STE papers.

21. Photos in STE scrapbook #15; "The President Today and Ten Years Ago," *New York Times*, January 31, 1943.

22. David Brinkley, *Washington Goes to War* (New York: Knopf, 1988), pp. 252, 253; letter from STE to Joseph Davies, January 1, 1943, Box 3, STE papers.

23. Letter from STE to Buddy Early, April 12, 1943, Box 4, STE papers; "President Stirred by Visits to Camps," *New York Times*, April 19, 1943; "Roosevelt on Tour, Visits Mexican President; They Pledge Fight for 'Good Neighbor World,'" *New York Times*, April 21, 1943.

24. Doris Kearns Goodwin, *No Ordinary Time: Franklin and Eleanor Roosevelt: The Home Front in World War II* (New York: Simon and Schuster, 1994), p. 426; Hassett, *Off the Record*, p. 168; Tully, *My Boss*, pp. 207–208.

25. "President Stirred by Visits to Camps"; "Roosevelt on Tour, Visits Mexican President; They Pledge Fight for 'Good Neighbor World.'"

26. Letter from STE to Buddy Early, April 22, 1943, Box 4, STE papers.

27. Burns, *Soldier of Freedom*, p. 368; Frank Freidel, *Franklin D. Roosevelt: A Rendezvous with Destiny* (Boston: Little, Brown, 1990), pp. 474–76.

28. STE press conference, 10:42 a.m., May 11, 1943; STE press confer-

ence, 6:47 p.m., May 11, 1943; "Churchill Arrives for Talks with Roosevelt," *New York Times*, May 12, 1943; Burns, *Soldier of Freedom*, p. 389.

29. David Stafford, *Roosevelt and Churchill: Men of Secrets* (Woodstock, NY: Overlook Press, 2000), p. 222–23; Freidel, *Rendezvous*, p. 468; Robert Goralski, *World War II Almanac, 1931–1945: A Political and Military Record* (New York: Putnam, 1981), p. 267.

30. STE press conference, May 12, 1943.

31. STE press conference, May 13, 1943.

32. STE press conference, May 27, 1943.

33. Stafford, *Roosevelt and Churchill*, p. 223.

34. Hassett, *Off the Record*, pp. 170, 174; STE press conference, June 1, 1943.

35. STE press conference, June 1, 1943.

CHAPTER 20: MORNINGSIDE DRIVE

1. Steven E. Schoenherr, "Selling the New Deal: Stephen T. Early's Role as Press Secretary to Franklin D. Roosevelt" (PhD diss., University of Delaware, 1976), pp. 45, 46.

2. Author interview with Helen Early Elam, April 3, 1998.

3. Letter from STE to Finks Early, March 27, 1945, Box 5, STE papers, FDR Library, Hyde Park, NY.

4. Letter from STE to Bernard Baruch, February 15, 1940, Box 1, STE papers.

5. Hugh Gregory Gallagher, *FDR's Splendid Deception* (New York: Dodd, Mead, 1985), p. 125; Eleanor Roosevelt, *Mother and Daughter, The Letters of Eleanor and Anna Roosevelt*, ed. Bernard Asbell (New York: Fromm International, 1988), p. 97; author interview with Elam, April 3, 1998; and Grace Tully, *F.D.R., My Boss* (New York: Charles Scribner's Sons, 1949), pp. 23, 71–73.

6. Letter from STE to James A. Moffett, March 18, 1940, Box 12, STE papers.

7. See the letters from STE to Hearst executive Joseph V. Connolly, April 22, 1942, and March 17, 1944, Box 2, STE papers; and Early's diaries throughout the 1930s for records of his lunches.

8. Script for a radio interview by Richard Eaton with STE, undated, Box 31, STE papers.

9. "Wife of Presidential Secretary Visitor Here," *Columbus (GA) Enquirer*, January 17, 1944.

10. See Early's diaries and letters to family and friends for details.

11. Author interview with Elam, April 3, 1998.

12. Kathryn Schneider Smith, ed., *Washington at Home, An Illustrated History of Neighborhoods in the Nation's Capital* (Northridge, CA: Windsor Publications, 1988). The information on Shepard Park was from the chapter by the late Marvin Caplan, a longtime resident of the neighborhood.

13. Letter from STE to Helen Early, August 16, 1941, Box 5, STE papers.

14. Author interview with Elam, April 3, 1998; letter from STE to Helen Early, August 7, 1946, Box 5, STE papers.

15. Author interview with Elam, April, 3, 1998; letter from STE to Mary Catherine Holmes, August 15, 1937, Box 7, STE papers; letter from STE to Moffett, April 29, 1943, Box 12, STE papers.

16. Letters from STE to Moffett, April 29, 1943, and December 18, 1940, Box 12, STE papers.

17. "Sideglances in Washington: Early Dog Acts as Warden," *Christian Science Monitor*, February 10, 1942.

18. Letter from STE to Moffett, September 22, 1943, Box 12, STE papers; letter from Ruthjane Rumelt letter to Helen Early, August 18, 1943, Box 4, STE papers.

19. Letter from STE to Buddy Early, August 31, 1943, Box 5, STE papers.

20. Letter from STE to Moffett, September 22, 1943, Box 12, STE papers.

21. Harold L. Ickes, *The Secret Diary of Harold L. Ickes*, vol. 1: *The First Thousand Days, 1933–1936* (New York: Simon and Schuster, 1953), p. 405.

22. Letters from STE to various family members are in Boxes 4 and 5 of the STE papers at the FDR Library. Letters reading T. J. and the haircuts were from Ruthjane Rumelt, Early's secretary, to Thomas J. Early Jr., July 8, 1942, and STE to T. J. Early, November 18, 1937. The letter regarding his brother-in-law was from STE to John A. Sargent, November 15, 1938, all in Box 5, STE papers.

23. Letters from Felix Early to STE, June 9 and 15, 1942; letter from STE to Felix Early, June 16, 1942, all in Box 5, STE papers.

24. Letter from Ida Early to STE, October 28, 1938, Box 5, STE papers.

25. Letter from Ida Early to STE, December 10, 1941, Box 5, STE papers; author interview with Elam, April, 3, 1998.

26. A collection of letters between Finks Early and Steve Early are in Box 5, STE papers.

27. Numerous letters asking for Early's help are in various boxes of Early's papers at the FDR Library. The letter from Marie Smith, Paramount, to STE is in Box 18; the Wolcott letter to STE is in Box 22.

28. Letter from STE to Col. Glen E. Edgerton, governor of the Panama Canal Zone, July 23, 1940; telegrams from Pa Watson to Col. Walter McCabe, superintendent of Staunton Military Academy, April 29, 1941, all in Box 4, STE papers.

29. Letter from STE to Anna Rosenberg, September 30, 1946, Box 5, STE papers; letter from STE to David Sarnoff, September 30, 1946, Box 5, STE papers.

30. Letters from STE to Helen "Sis" Early, September 26, 1946, October 7, 1946, and March 13, 1947, all in Box 5, STE papers.

31. Letters from STE to Helen "Sis" Early, May 5, 1947, November 22, 1946, and October 7, 1946, all in Box 5, STE papers; author interview with Elam, April 3, 1998.

32. Author interview with Elam, April 3, 1998.

33. A small collection of Early's personal checkbooks and deposit slips from 1940 to 1946 are in Box 26 in the STE papers; Jonathan Daniels, *White House Witness, 1942–1945* (Garden City, NY: Doubleday, 1975), p. 12; author interview with Elam, April 3, 1998.

34. "These Charming People," undated Igor Cassini column, *Washington Herald*, STE scrapbook, January 21, 1941–July 31, 1941, FDR Library, Hyde Park, NY.

35. Author interview with Elam, April 3, 1998; letter from STE to Davies, September 27, 1938, Box 3, STE papers.

36. Letter from Davies to Buddy Early, December 1, 1938; letter from STE to Davies, January 3, 1939; letter from Buddy Early to Davies, January 3, 1939, all in Box 5, STE papers.

37. Letter from STE to Helen Early, August 16, 1941, Box 5, STE papers.

38. Letter from STE to Davies, July 30, 1937, Box 3, STE papers.

39. Raymond Clapper diaries, Box 128, Clapper Papers, Library of Congress.

40. Daniels, *White House Witness*, p. 268.

41. Author interview with Elam, April 3, 1998.

42. Letter from Riggs National Bank to STE, August 7, 1941, Box 19, STE papers; "These Charming People," *Washington Times-Herald*, May 28, 1944.

43. See thank-you letters from STE to John Cowles, November 26, 1941; November 9, 1942; November 6, 1943; and November 24, 1944, Box 2, STE papers; letters from STE to Bernard Baruch, February 2, 1942; December 29, 1944; May 12, 1941; and March 6, 1940, Box 1, STE papers.

44. Letter from STE to Buddy Early, September 17, 1943, Box 5, STE papers.

45. Harry C. Butcher, *My Three Years with Eisenhower: The Personal Diary of Captain Harry C. Butcher, USNR, Naval Aide to General Eisenhower, 1942 to 1945* (New York: Simon and Schuster, 1946), p. 466.

CHAPTER 21: EXTRACTING NEWS FROM OYSTERS

1. Robert Goralski, *World War II Almanac, 1931–1945: A Political and Military Record* (New York: Putnam, 1981), pp. 267–77.

2. STE press conference, June 17, 1943; Wiliam D. Hassett, *Off the Record with F.D.R., 1942–1945* (New Brunswick, NJ: Rutgers University Press, 1950), p. 174; Samuel I. Rosenman, *Working with Roosevelt* (New York: Da Capo Press, 1972), pp. 349–50; A. Merriman Smith, *Thank You, Mr. President: A White House Notebook* (New York: Harper & Brothers, 1946), pp. 123, 126–27.

3. STE press conference, June 17, 1943; see also STE press conferences for June and July 1943.

4. Letter from STE to Buddy Early, July 27, 1943; Goralski, *World War II Almanac*, p. 272; Frank Burt Freidel, *Franklin D. Roosevelt: A Rendezvous with Destiny* (Boston: Little, Brown, 1990), p. 469.

5. Rosenman, *Working with Roosevelt*, pp. 349, 350; James MacGregor Burns, *Roosevelt: The Soldier of Freedom, 1940–1945* (New York: Harcourt Brace Jovanovich, 1970), p. 383; Goralski, *World War II Almanac*, p. 273; and Robert E. Sherwood, *Roosevelt and Hopkins, An Intimate History* (New York: Harper, 1948), p. 742.

6. Letter from STE to Buddy Early, July 27, 1943, Box 4, STE papers, FDR Library, Hyde Park, NY.

7. Letter from STE to Buddy Early, July 19, 1943; Hassett, *Off the Record*, p. 189.

8. Letter from STE to Buddy Early, July 27, 1943, Box 4, STE papers.

9. STE press conference, July 14, 1943.

10. STE press conference, August 9, 1943; "Roosevelt Makes a Slip of Geography," *New York Times*, August 10, 1943; FDR handwritten memo, August 9, 1943, STE scrapbook, August 1, 1943–January 20, 1944, FDR Library, Hyde Park, NY.

11. Hassett, *Off the Record*, pp. 194–95; letter from STE to Buddy Early, July, 27, 1943; FDR Fireside Chat, July 28, 1943; STE press conference, July 29, 1943.

12. STE press conference, July 29, 1943.

13. "Roosevelt and Churchill Confer: Meet in U.S. on Way to Quebec," *New York Times*, August 15, 1943; "Churchill Is Back in Quebec after His Visit to Hyde Park," *New York Times*, August 16, 1943; Burns, *Soldier of Freedom*, p. 392; memo from FDR to Early, August 15, 1943, STE scrapbook, August 1, 1943–January 20, 1944.

14. "Talks to Be Anglo-American, Roosevelt Asserts in Capital," *New*

York Times, August 11, 1943; letter from STE to Buddy Early, August 13, 1943, Box 4, STE papers.

15. Betty Houchin Winfield, *FDR and the News Media* (New York: Columbia University Press, 1994), p. 204; telegram from FDR to STE, August 14, 1943; telegram from STE to FDR, August 14, 1943, STE scrapbook, August 1, 1943–January 20, 1944; STE press conference, August 16, 1943.

16. "Roosevelt to Go to Quebec for Parley," *New York Times*, August 12, 1943; "Churchill Crossed into U.S., Stops Off at Niagara Falls," *New York Times*, August 13, 1943; STE press conference, August 12, 1943.

17. STE press conference, August 14, 1943.

18. "3 Roosevelt Aides to Go Overseas," *Baltimore Sun*, January 26, 1945; "The FBI, the Roosevelt Adminstration, and the 'Subversive' Press," *Journalism History* 19, no. 1 (Spring 1993); letters from STE to J. Edgar Hoover, December 11 and 12, 1941, and letter from Hoover STE, December 12, 1941, Box 29, STE papers.

19. "Roosevelt Arrives in Quebec for Conference," *New York Times*, August 18, 1943. Itinerary of this trip is in STE scrapbook, August 1, 1943–January 20, 1944; letter from STE to Buddy Early, August 31, 1943, Box 4, STE papers.

20. Richard Alexander Hough, *Mountbatten* (New York: Random House, 1981), p. 163.

21. Early's invitation to the dinner and a seating chart for the guests is in STE scrapbook, August 1, 1943–January 20, 1944; Hough, *Mountbatten*, pp. 162, 164.

22. Itinerary of the trip, STE scrapbook, August 1, 1943–January 20, 1944; "Newsmen of Six Nations in City for Conference," *Quebec Chronicle-Telegraph*, August 18, 1943; "Roosevelt Expected Soon," *Montreal Sun*, August 17, 1943.

23. "Bracken Proves Good Copy for Correspondents," *Quebec Chronicle-Telegraph*, August 20, 1943; Steve E. Schoenherr, "Selling the New Deal: Stephen T. Early's Role as Press Secretary to President Franklin D. Roosevelt" (PhD diss., University of Delaware, 1976), p. 207.

24. "War for Total Defeat of Axis Mapped by Roosevelt, Churchill," *New York Times*, August 20, 1943; "Bracken Proves Good Copy for Correspondents."

25. "A Reporter's Advice to Brendan Bracken," *Montreal Gazette*, August 24, 1943; "Brendan Bracken and Others," *Montreal Gazette*, August 24, 1943.

26. Charles Edward Lysaght, "Brendan Bracken: The Fantasist Whose Dreams Came True," lecture at Churchill College, Cambridge, May 9, 2002; "Reporter's Advice to Brendan Bracken."

27. "Revelling Newsman Wakes Conferees from Slumber with Famed School Bell," *Quebec Chronicle-Telegraph*, August 21, 1943.

28. "Round About with M. E. Hennessy," *Boston Globe*, undated, STE scrapbook, August 1, 1943–January 20, 1944; "Press Conference Quebec Highlight for the Newsmen," *Ottawa Evening Citizen*, August 25, 1943.

29. Schoenherr, "Selling the New Deal," p. 208; see letter from STE to Harry Butcher, Frank Page folder, Box 13, STE papers; "Round About with M.E. Hennessy"; "Steve Early: White House Spokesman for a Dozen Years," *Baltimore Sun*, May 23, 1945; "Press Conference Quebec Highlight for the Newsmen," *Ottawa Evening Citizen*, August 25, 1943.

30. Roosevelt-Churchill joint press conference, Quebec City, August 24, 1944, STE scrapbook, August 1, 1943–January 20, 1944.

31. Letter from STE to Buddy Early, August 31, 1943, Box 4, STE papers.

32. Ibid.; letter from STE to Anna Roosevelt, September 7, 1943, Box 15, Anna Roosevelt Halstead papers, FDR Library.

33. Otis L. Graham Jr. and Meghan Robinson Wander, eds., *Franklin D. Roosevelt: His Life and Times: An Encyclopedic View* (Boston: G. K. Hall, 1985), pp. 15, 340–41; David Stafford, *Roosevelt and Churchill: Men of Secrets* (Woodstock, NY: Overlook Press, 2000), p. 236.

34. "Roosevelt Blast at Pearson as 'Liar' Climaxes Longtime Feud with Press," *Newsweek*, September 13, 1943; Schoenherr, "Selling the New Deal," p. 208.

35. "Roosevelt Blast at Pearson as 'Liar' Climaxes Longtime Feud with Press"; "President Brands Columnist a Liar," *New York Times*, September 1, 1943.

36. Burns, *Soldier of Freedom*, pp. 395, 397; Peter Grose, *Israel in the Mind of America* (New York: Knopf, 1983), p. 130; Linda Lotridge Levin, "The Rhode Island Jewish Press in the Twentieth Century," *Rhode Island Jewish Historical Notes*, November 1987, pp. 26–36.

37. Hassett, *Off the Record*, pp. 209–10. Two years earlier, when the producers of a Jewish rally at Madison Square Garden had asked for a brief statement of encouragement from the president, a request that went through Early, who apparently talked it over with Roosevelt, the two men, who considered Jews among their closest friends, decided not to issue one. Roosevelt never considered himself an anti-Semite, and indeed his administration included more Jews than any preceding one. His most prominent Jewish appointee was his longtime friend and Hyde Park neighbor Henry Morgenthau, the secretary of the treasury. Numerous articles and books, including David S. Wyman, *The Abandonment of the Jews: America and the Holocaust, 1941–1945* (New York: Pantheon, 1984), have documented the apparent apathy of the Roosevelt administration, in particular the Department of State, in dealing in a timely manner with the issue of the extermination of the Jews in Europe.

38. "Churchill Renews Roosevelt Parley," *New York Times*, September 2, 1943; STE press conference, August 30, 1943.

39. Stafford, *Roosevelt and Churchill*, p. xxiii; STE press conferences, 10:35 a.m. and 5:25 p.m., September 2 and 3, 1943; letter from STE to Anna Roosevelt, September 7, 1943, Box 15, Anna Roosevelt Halstead papers, FDR Library.

40. STE press conference, September 6, 1943.

41. STE press conference, September 8, 1943.

42. As a young man, Roosevelt had studied French, German, Greek, and Latin, and probably knew a few Italian words.

43. STE press conference, September 9, 1943.

44. "Early Roosevelt-Stalin Meeting Seen in Activities in Washington," *New York Times*, November 10, 1943; STE press conference, November 10, 1943.

45. Burns, *Soldier of Freedom*, p. 402; Robert Sherwood, *Roosevelt and Hopkins, An Intimate History* (New York: Harper, 1948), pp. 767–68.

46. Graham and Wander, *Life and Times*, pp. 50–51; "FDR Sits Very Much Alone at End of White House Day," *New York Evening Post*, November 22, 1943.

47. Sherwood, *Roosevelt and Hopkins*, p. 775.

48. "Negro Publishers Plan Greater News Coverage," *People's Voice*, November 20, 1943; Winfield, *FDR and the News Media*, p. 56.

49. STE press conference, November 30, 1943; "Censorship Merry Go-Round Breaks Down: British Call 'Sphinx' Secrecy 'Incredible Farce,'" *New York Sun*, December 2, 1943; "Davis Hunts '50–50 Break,'" *Washington Times-Herald*, December 5, 1943.

50. STE press conference, December 1, 1943.

51. STE press conference, December 5, 1943.

52. Letter from STE to Buddy Early, November 29, 1943, Box 4, STE papers; STE press conference, December 16, 1943.

53. STE press conference, December 13, 1943; "Marvin McIntyre, Presidential Secretary Since 1933, Dies," *Washington Star*, Decmber 13, 1943; "Marvin M'Intyre Is Dead in Capital," *New York Times*, December 14, 1943; "Marvin McIntyre Dead: Close Friend of F.D," *Washington News*, December 13, 1943; Rosenman, *Working with Roosevelt*, p. 411; STE press conference, December 14, 1943; "Marvin H. McIntyre Buried; Frank Walker, Stephen Early Attend," *Louisville Courier Journal*, December 16, 1943.

54. "Nazis Say Roosevelt's Plane Was Forced Down," *New York Sun*, December 16, 1943; STE press conference, December 16, 1943.

55. FDR press conference, December 17, 1943; STE press conference, December 18, 1943; "Censorship Office Eases Curbs on War News of Press and Radio," *New York Times*, December 11, 1943.

56. FDR press conference, December 17, 1943; Geoffrey C. Ward, ed., *Closest Companion, The Unknown Story of the Intimate Friendship between*

Franklin Roosevelt and Margaret Suckley (Boston: Houghton Mifflin, 1995), p. 265; Burns, *Soldier of Freedom*, pp. 423–24.

57. STE press conference, December 22, 1943.

58. Hassett, *Off the Record*, pp. 222–23.

59. "Roosevelt Moves to Take Over the Railroads as 3 Brotherhoods Reject Mediation by Him" and "War Steel Walkout Looms When Pack Expires Tonight," *New York Times*, December 24, 1943; "70,000 in 4 States Begin Steel Halt; Spread Indicated," *New York Times*, December 26, 1943; "Army Seizes Railroads on President's Order; Pay Raises to 2 Unions; Steel Men Ordered Back," *New York Times*, December 28, 1943.

60. STE press conference, January 1, 1944.

CHAPTER 22: "THE GREAT WHITE JAIL"

1. STE press conferences for that winter and spring; "Roosevelt Reports on Health; Has Had Bronchitis for 3 Weeks," *Washington Post*, March 29, 1944; "Here's How President Looked to Reporters," *New York World-Telegram*, May 10, 1944; "Truman Wrote of '48 Offer to Eisenhower," *New York Times*, July 11, 2003; Grace Tully, *F.D.R., My Boss* (New York: Charles Scribner's Sons, 1949), p. 184. In 1944 Roosevelt was away from Washington approximately 163 days, based on William D. Hassett, *Off the Record with F.D.R., 1942–1945* (New Brunswick, NJ: Rutgers University Press, 1958). By comparison, in 2003, a year in which American troops were engaged in a war in Iraq, President George W. Bush was away from the capital for about 196 days. The difference was that more than half of the days Bush was away were one-day flights to a city or military camp in the United States. On the other hand, Roosevelt flew only when he was forced to cross the Atlantic. His travels at home were via train. Sources for the statistics on Bush were Edward Bell, Boston bureau chief for the Associated Press, and Sandy Johnson, Washington, DC, bureau chief for the Associated Press.

2. STE letter to James Roosevelt, April 3, 1947, Box 15, STE papers, FDR Library, Hyde Park, NY.

3. A. Merriman Smith, *Thank You, Mr. President: A White House Notebook* (New York: Harper & Brothers, 1946), p. 133.

4. STE press conferences, January 3, 7, and 17, 1944; letter from STE to Joseph E. Davies, January 8, 1944, Box 3, STE papers.

5. "Returned Congress Won't Hear Roosevelt in Person," *Washington News*, January 10, 1944.

6. FDR press and radio conference #930, January 18, 1944; STE press conference, January 21, 1944.

7. STE press conference, January 28, 1944.

8. Robert Goralski, *World War II Almanac, 1931–1945: A Political and Military Record* (New York: Putnam, 1981), pp. 211, 302.

9. STE press conference, January 28, 1944.

10. Ibid.; "Annual Cuff Links Dinner Held by Roosevelts at White House," *Baltimore Sun*, January 30, 1944; "Dances, Gayety Mark President's Birthday," *Washington Post*, January 30, 1944.

11. The reporter could have been abbreviating the expression gimlet or gimlet-eyed, which can mean someone who is keen-eyed or sharp-sighted.

12. FDR press conference, February 4, 1944.

13. James MacGregor Burns, *Roosevelt: The Soldier of Freedom, 1940–1945* (New York: Harcourt Brace Jovanovich, 1970), p. 463; STE press conference, February 5, 1944.

14. Ibid.; Lee Finkle, *Forum for Protest: The Black Press During World War II* (Rutherford, NJ: Fairleigh Dickinson University Press, 1975), p. 89. According to Finkle, there were one hundred and forty-three Negro newspapers in thirty-two states and the District of Columbia during World War II, with an average weekly circulation of about 1.6 million (p. 52).

15. "White House Becomes Sphinx in News Desert," *New York News*, February 25, 1944.

16. Samuel I. Rosenman, *Working with Roosevelt* (New York: Harper, 1972), p. 429.

17. Alben W. Barkley, *That Reminds Me* (Garden City, NY: Doubleday, 1954), pp. 169–82; Frank Freidel, *Franklin D. Roosevelt: A Rendezvous with Destiny* (Boston: Little, Brown, 1990), pp. 501–502.

18. Hassett, *Off the Record*, pp. 235–36; Rosenman, *Working with Roosevelt*, p. 431; Barkley, *That Reminds Me*, pp. 177–80; "Barkley Quits Senate Post Over Tax Veto" and "Barkley Won Post by Roosevelt Aid," *New York Times*, February 24, 1944; STE press conference, February 24, 1944; "President Holds Aloof from Press," *New York Times*, February 25, 1944.

19. "Senate Re-elects Barkley; House Overrides Roosevelt Tax Veto, 299–95," *New York Times*, February 25, 1944; "Taxes Voted Law by 72–14 in the Senate," *New York Times*, February 26, 1944.

20. STE press conference, February 24, 1944.

21. "President Holds Aloof from Press"; "President, Out of City, Resting from Recent Influenza Attack," *Washington Star*, February 25, 1944; STE press conference, February 25, 1944; Smith, *Thank You*, p. 58.

22. STE press conference, February 26, 1944.

23. Burns, *Soldier of Freedom*, p. 503; David McCullough, *Truman* (New York: Simon and Schuster, 1992), pp. 292, 295; "Rayburn Tops List for Wallace Post in Committee Poll," *New York Times*, January 24, 1944.

24. "Good Evening," editorial in the *Griffin (GA) Daily News*, March 22,

1944; "Georgia Editor Proposes Early as Vice President," *Washington Star*, March 23, 1944; letter from Harry Hopkins to STE, March 28, 1944, Box 26, STE papers; STE press conference, April 4, 1944; FDR press conference, March 28, 1944. Harry Hopkins, the president's closest policy aide and, as Roosevelt's enemies claimed, the president's Svengali, fell ill on New Year's Day 1944. He was in several hospitals for chronic digestive problems that spring and did not return to the White House full time until late summer. Robert E. Sherwood, *Roosevelt and Hopkins, An Intimate History* (New York: Harper, 1948), pp. 804, 809.

25. David Brinkley, *Washington Goes to War* (New York: Knopf, 1988), p. 254; "F.D.R. and Early Enjoy Laughs Over Third Term," *Philadelphia Inquirer*, June 15, 1944.

26. STE press conferences, March 14, 17, and 21, 1944; "Roosevelt Reports on Health; Has Had Bronchitis for 3 Weeks," *Washington Post*, March 29, 1944; FDR press conference, March 28, 1944.

27. Brinkley, *Washington Goes to War*, p. 261; Burns, *Soldier of Freedom*, pp. 448–49.

28. STE press conference, April 4, 1944. The quote about McIntire was in a letter from STE to Frank Walker, September 20, 1946, Box 12, STE papers.

29. Brinkley, *Washington Goes to War*, p. 261; Smith, *Thank You*, pp. 134–35.

30. Tully, *My Boss*, pp. 273–74.

31. Smith, *Thank You*, pp. 58–59.

32. Letter to STE from five White House correspondents, March 31, 1944, Box 21, STE papers.

33. "Here's How the President Looked to Reporters," *New York World-Telegram*, May 10, 1944; STE press conference, April 10, 1944.

34. Smith, *Thank You*, pp. 135–41; "President Returns from Month's Rest on Baruch Estate" and "Roosevelt Rested at Quiet Manor," *New York Times*, May 8, 1944; FDR press conference, November 27, 1944; "Final Tribute Paid to Secretary Knox," *New York Times*, May 2, 1944.

35. Tom Blake (STE's assistant) press conference, April 26, 1944, Box 42, STE papers; letter from STE to Pvt. Joseph Rumelt, April 19, 1944, Box 16, STE papers; STE press conference, May 10, 1944; Hassett, *Off the Record*, pp. 243–47.

36. STE press conferences, May 15, 25, 26, and 31, 1944.

37. "Allied Armies Land In France In the Harve-Cherbourg Area; Great Invasion Is Underway," *New York Times*, June 6, 1944; "Hitler's Sea Wall Is Breached, Invaders Fighting Way Inland; New Allied Landings Are Made," *New York Times*, June 7, 1944.

38. STE press conference, June 6, 1944.

39. FDR press conference, June 6, 1944.

40. STE press conference, June 8, 1944; Leonard Lyons, "Off

Broadway's Bulletin Board," *Washington Post*, June 14, 1944; "President's Health 'Excellent,' McIntire Reports," *New York Times*, June 9, 1944.

41. STE press conferences, June 15 and July 5, 1944.

42. STE press conference, July 6, 1944; Burns, *Soldier of Freedom*, p. 480; Hassett, *Off the Record*, pp. 257, 259.

43. Letter from STE to James Roosevelt, April 3, 1947, Box 15, STE papers; Smith, *Thank You*, p. 145.

44. FDR press conference, July 11, 1944; Brinkley, *Washington Goes to War*, pp. 256–57; Smith, *Thank You*, pp. 145–46.

45. FDR press conference, July 29, 1944; Hassett, *Off the Record*, pp. 263–65; Smith, *Thank You*, p. 151.

46. Smith, *Thank You*, pp. 146–47.

47. Tully, *My Boss*, pp. 271–72; Smith, *Thank You*, p. 148.

48. Rosenman, *Working with Roosevelt*, p. 453.

49. Examples of photos from a folder in Box 33, STE papers, marked "Pictures of the President Good and Bad Used in 1944," include "Better Photos of President" in *New York World-Telegram*, November 1, 1944; *Syracuse Post-Standard*, October 20, 1944; *Time*, October 30, 1944; and *Spokane Spokesman-Review*, October 7, 1944.

50. Rosenman, *Working with Roosevelt*, pp. 453–54; Freidel, *Rendezvous with Destiny*, pp. 530–31; Otis L. Graham Jr. and Meghan Robinson Wander, eds., *Franklin D. Roosevelt: His Life and Times: An Encyclopedic View* (Boston: G. K. Hall, 1985), pp. 442–43.

51. STE press conferences, July 13 and 14, 1944.

52. Letter from STE to Robert E. Hannegan, July 3, 1944, Box 17, STE papers; Jim Bishop, *FDR's Last Year, April 1944–April 1945* (New York: William Morrow, 1974), pp. 106–109.

53. STE press conference, July 31, 1944.

54. Memo from STE to Roosevelt, with Roosevelt reply written on it, July 13, 1944, STE scrapbook, January 21, 1944–July 31, 1944, FDR Library, Hyde Park, NY.

55. STE press conference, August 29, 1944; Tom Blake press conference, August 24, 1944; STE press conference, August 28, 1944; memo marked "Personal and Secret" from Harry Hopkins to Mackenzie King, August 31, 1944, and letter from Lester B. Pearson to Hopkins, September 3, 1944, both in STE scrapbook, August 1, 1944–January 20, 1945.

56. Letter from A. D. Dunton to STE, September 3, 1944; letter from STE to Pearson, September 6, 1944, both in STE scrapbook, August 1, 1944–January 20, 1945.

57. Itinerary in STE scrapbook, August 1, 1944–January 20, 1945.

58. "Allied Chieftains Meet Informally at Railway Siding Prior to Confer-

ence Which Is Expected to Map Final Steps of War and Study Postwar Problems," *Christian Science Monitor*, September 11, 1944; "Stephen Early Hints Little News Expected," *Quebec Chronicle-Telegraph*, September 11, 1944; "Washington Memo," *New York Evening Post*, September 16, 1944; "Over 100 Newsmen at Quebec Parley," *Montreal Gazette*, September 11, 1944.

59. "F.D.R. and Churchill to Meet Mute Press," *New York Daily News*, September 16, 1944; "Quebec Parley Talk with Press Held at Citadel," *New York Herald-Tribune*, September 17, 1944; Hassett, *Off the Record*, pp. 271–72.

60. STE press conferences, October 18 and 19, 1944.

61. "President Discards Censorship to Make Public Campaign Tour," *Buffalo Evening News*, October 20, 1944; Burns, *Soldier of Freedom*, p. 525; Hassett, *Off the Record*, pp. 278–79.

62. Burns, *Soldier of Freedom*, pp. 525–26; "F.D.R. Starts 4-Borough Tour, Hailed by Cheering Crowds," *New York Evening Post*, October 21, 1944; Hassett, *Off the Record*, pp. 279–80.

63. Itineraries of the Philadelphia to Chicago and the Boston trips are in STE scrapbook, August 1, 1944–January 20, 1945.

64. Hassett, *Off the Record*, pp. 292–93.

65. Smith, *Thank You*, p. 158.

66. Ibid., pp. 158–59; untitled article in *Dallas Times-Herald*, November 8, 1944; untitled article in *Time*, November 20, 1944.

67. "Returns Keep President Up Late; Dewey Takes Defeat with a Smile," *Washington Star*, November 8, 1944; Hassett, *Off the Record*, p. 294; transcript of telephone call from STE to Nelson House, November 8, 1944, and transcript of telephone call from Ruthjane Rumelt to Nelson House, November 8, 1944, STE scrapbook, August 1, 1944–January 20, 1945.

68. Smith, *Thank You*, p. 159.

CHAPTER 23: TO YALTA AND BACK AGAIN

1. William D. Hassett, *Off the Record with F.D.R., 1942–1945* (New Brunswick, NJ: Rutgers University Press, 1950), pp. 295–96; James MacGregor Burns, *Roosevelt, The Soldier of Freedom, 1940–1945* (New York: Harcourt Brace Jovanovich, 1970), p. 532; David Brinkley, *Washington Goes to War* (New York: Knopf, 1988), p. 264; FDR press conference, November 10, 1944.

2. Burns, *Soldier of Freedom*, pp. 532–33.

3. Bill Hassett's *Off the Record* gives an excellent day-by-day account of most of Roosevelt's travels from January 1942 until his death. The quote on the president's appearance at Christmas is from p. 307.

4. "Broadway" column, *Washington Times-Herald*, November 10, 1944; "National Notes," *Newsweek*, November 13, 1944; "Early May Not Quit White House Post," *Detroit Free Press*, November 19, 1944; "Loose-Leaf Notebook," *Washington Post*, November 23, 1944; "Broadway" column, *Herald-Tribune*, December 22, 1944; "Early Resignation Rumors," *New Orleans Item*, January 13, 1945.

5. STE press conferences, November 14 and 15, 1944.

6. STE press conferences, November 27 and 30, 1944.

7. STE press conference, November 27, 1944; FDR press conference, November 27, 1944.

8. Memo from STE to Hassett, September 1, 1944, and memo from STE to Tom Blake, September 14, 1944, both in Box 33, STE papers, FDR Library, Hyde Park, NY. In his book *FDR's Last Year, April 1944–April 1945* (New York: William Morrow, 1974), Jim Bishop says that it was not until the day after her husband died that Eleanor Roosevelt learned from one of his cousins that he had been seeing Lucy Mercer Rutherford in recent years, at her home and in the White House when Eleanor was out of town, thus breaking a promise that Franklin made to Eleanor years earlier when he ended his romance with the then Lucy Mercer that he would never see her again. Bishop also says that Early and others close to Roosevelt in the White House knew of his relationship with Mrs. Rutherfurd (p. 635).

9. See FDR press conferences, November 14, 17, 21, and 27, and December 19 and 22, 1944. The comment about columnists was from the December 22 conference.

10. Hassett, *Off the Record*, p. 307; letter from STE to Buddy Early, December 28, 1944, Box 4, STE papers; "Early Will Advise SHAEF on Publicity," *New York Times*, January 14, 1944.

11. "Early's Trip Recalls 'Muffing' of SHAEF News," *Washington Times-Herald*, January 13, 1945; "Slipshod Censorship Methods," *Durham (NC) Herald-Sun*, January 28, 1945; Steven Schoenherr, "Selling the New Deal: Stephen T. Early's Role as Press Secretary to President Franklin D. Roosevelt" (PhD diss., University of Delaware, 1976), p. 211; Robert Goralski, *World War II Almanac 1931–1945: A Political and Military Record* (New York: Putnam, 1981), p. 365; Harry C. Butcher, *My Three Years with Eisenhower: The Personal Diary of Captain Harry C. Butcher, USNR, Naval Aide to General Eisenhower, 1942 to 1945* (New York: Simon and Schuster, 1946), p. 751.

12. "Early's Mission to Europe Covers War-News Reports," *Christian Science Monitor*, January 15, 1945; "Expert on the Job," *Philadelphia Record*, January 15, 1945; "Early Will Advise SHAEF on Publicity," *New York Times*, January 14, 1944; STE press conference, January 22, 1945.

13. "Army Public Relations," *Houston Chronicle*, May 29, 1945; "Early's

Task Abroad to Be One of Hardest Jobs of His Career," *Washington Star*, January 14, 1945.

14. Goralski, *World War II Almanac*, pp. 372–76.

15. Brinkley, *Washington Goes to War*, p. 263; "Housekeeper Vetoes Roosevelt on Menu," *New York Times*, January 20, 1945.

16. Grace Tully, *F.D.R., My Boss* (New York: Charles Scribner's Sons, 1949), p. 251; Hassett, *Off the Record*, pp. 312–13; "6,000 Attend Simple Inaugural," *New York Evening Post*, January 20, 1945; "Roosevelt Sworn in for Fourth Term; Extends Good Neighbor Policy to World," *New York Times*, January 21, 1945. Roosevelt's biographer, James MacGregor Burns, in *Soldier of Freedom*, concluded that Roosevelt preferred a more simple inaugural ceremony as a cost-cutting measure. The Senate had appropriated $25,000, but Roosevelt felt he could do it for less than $2,000 (p. 562).

17. James Roosevelt, *Affectionately, F.D.R.* (New York: Harcourt, Brace, 1959), p. 351.

18. Ibid., pp. 354–55; Frances Perkins, *The Roosevelt I Knew* (New York: Viking, 1946), p. 391.

19. Hassett, *Off the Record*, pp. 313–14; Robert E. Sherwood, *Roosevelt and Hopkins, An Intimate History* (New York: Harper, 1948), p. 845; "Steve Early: White House Spokesman for a Dozen Years," *Baltimore Sun*, May 23, 1945. During the last seventeen months of the president's life, his daughter, Anna, whose husband, John Boettiger, was in the army, and her two children lived in the White House (Roosevelt, *Affectionately, F.D.R.*, p. 348).

20. Hassett, *Off the Record*, p. 314; and Brinkley, *Washington Goes to War*, p. 265.

21. STE press conference, January 22, 1945; Jonathan Daniels, *White House Witness, 1942–1945* (Garden City, NY: Doubleday, 1975), pp. x–xi.

22. A. Merriman Smith, *Thank You, Mr. President: A White House Notebook* (New York: Harper & Brothers, 1946), pp. 162–63; and Samuel I. Rosenman, *Working with Roosevelt* (New York: Harper & Brothers, 1972), p. 521.

23. Sherwood, *Roosevelt and Hopkins*, p. 850.

24. Itinerary of the Yalta trip is in STE scrapbook, January 21, 1945–July 31, 1945; along with a memo "Notes on the Crimea," prepared by the US Embassy in Moscow. The description of the villas and the destruction came from FDR press conference, February 19, 1944; Burns, *Soldier of Freedom*, p. 564; Ross T. McIntire, *White House Physician* (New York: G. P. Putnam's Sons, 1946), pp. 213, 214–15, 227.

25. Sherwood, *Roosevelt and Hopkins*, pp. 851, 870; Otis L. Graham Jr. and Meghan Robinson Wander, eds., *Franklin D. Roosevelt: His Life and Times: An Encyclopedic View* (Boston: G. K. Hall, 1985), p. 469.

26. *New York Times* stories: "Peace Seen as Big 3 Issue; Parley Reported

Underway" (London dateline), February 2, 1945; "German Peace Bid to Big 3 Rumored" (Cairo dateline), February 4, 1945; "Belief Grows Big 3 Meet in Russia; Soviet Pacific Role Held on Agenda" (Ankara dateline), February 5, 1945; "Big 3 Parley Is On, Citrine Asserts" (London dateline), February 7, 1945.

27. The statement with a handwritten note on it saying Churchill, Stalin, and Roosevelt approved it is in STE scrapbook, January 21, 1945–July 31, 1945, FDR Library, Hyde Park, NY. The wire service reporters' problem comes from Smith, *Thank You*, p. 166. Also see "Big 3 Set Final Steps to Crush Germany," *New York Times*, February 8, 1945.

28. Smith, *Thank You*, pp. 166, 167.

29. McIntire, *White House Physician*, p. 226; Yalta itinerary, STE scrapbook, January 21, 1945–July 31, 1945.

30. McIntire, *White House Physician*, p. 226; Yalta itinerary, STE scrapbook, January 21, 1945–July 31, 1945; Jim Bishop, *F.D.R.'s Last Year* (New York: William Morrow, 1974), pp. 430–31; letter from STE to Edward R. Stettinius Jr., March 17, 1949, Box 17, STE papers; "Text of Big Three Announcement on the Crimea Conference," *New York Times*, February 13, 1945.

31. See Yalta itinerary, STE scrapbook, January 21, 1945–July 31, 1945; "Capitol Stuff," *Washington Times-Herald*, February 14, 1945; Sherwood, *Roosevelt and Hopkins*, p. 873; "Tribute to Steve," *Washington News*, February 15, 1945.

32. Sherwood, *Roosevelt and Hopkins*, pp. 871–72; Burns, *Soldier of Freedom*, p. 578.

33. From the itinerary in STE scrapbook, January 21, 1945–July 31, 1945; "Gen. Watson Dead; Roosevelt's Aide," *New York Times*, February 28, 1945; Sherwood, *Roosevelt and Hopkins*, pp. 861, 874; Bishop, *F.D.R.'s Last Year*, p. 450; Rosenman, *Working with Roosevelt*, p. 522. For Pa Watson's death and its effect on Roosevelt, see John Gunther, *Roosevelt in Retrospect* (London: Hamish Hamilton, 1950), p. 397; Hassett, *Off the Record*, p. 316; Sherwood, *Roosevelt and Hopkins*, p. 874.

34. Smith, *Thank You*, pp. 167–72; Yalta itinerary, STE scrapbook, January 21, 1945–July 31, 1945; FDR press conferences on board the USS *Quincy*, February 19 and 23, 1945.

35. Harry C. Butcher, *My Three Years with Eisenhower: The Personal Diary of Captain Harry C. Butcher, USNR, Naval Aide to General Eisenhower, 1942 to 1945* (New York: Simon and Schuster, 1946), pp. 744–45.

36. Ibid., pp. 761, 762–63.

37. Itinerary of the trip in STE scrapbook, January 21, 1945–July 31, 1945; Butcher, *My Three Years with Eisenhower*, p. 765.

38. Itinerary in STE scrapbook, January 21, 1945–July 31, 1945; Butcher, *My Three Years with Eisenhower*, pp. 765, 766.

39. Itinerary in STE scrapbook. January 21, 1945–July 31, 1945; Butcher, *My Three Years with Eisenhower*, pp. 765–67.

40. Goralski, *World War II Almanac*, pp. 385, 386; Butcher, *My Three Years with Eisenhower*, pp. 768, 776; "Press Conference," *Carbuilder*, October 1951.

41. Butcher, *My Three Years with Eisenhower*, p. 776; "Stimson Declares Germany Is Beaten," *New York Times*, March 30, 1945; "Army Public Relations," *Houston Chronicle*, May 29, 1945.

42. Butcher, *My Three Years with Eisenhower*, p. 775; letter from STE to Maj. Gen. S. E. Reinhardt, April 19, 1945, Box 4 (Buddy Early File), STE papers; notes on itinerary of Early's trip to Europe, STE scrapbook, January 21, 1945–July 31, 1945.

43. Butcher, *My Three Years with Eisenhower*, p. 775; telegram from STE to Hassett, March 19, 1945, and Hassett telegram to STE, March 19, 1945, both in STE scrapbook, January 21, 1945–July 31, 1945; Hassett, *Off the Record*, p. 325; itinerary of Early's trip, STE scrapbook, January 21, 1945–July 31, 1945; letter from Maj. Gen. John Stoner to STE, April 19, 1945, Box 4 (Buddy Early file), STE papers.

44. Butcher, *My Three Years with Eisenhower*, pp. 774–75.

CHAPTER 24: AND THEN THERE WAS ONE

1. Letter from Ruthjane Rumelt to STE, March 12, 1945, Box 16, STE papers, FDR Library, Hyde Park, NY.

2. Jonathan Daniels, *White House Witness, 1942–1945* (Garden City, NY: Doubleday, 1975), p. 275; letter from STE to Robert Sherwood, January 16, 1948, and FDR press release, both in STE scrapbook, January 21, 1945–July 31, 1945, FDR Library, Hyde Park, NY; "White House Faces Showdown with Press on News Coverage," *Washington Times-Herald*, February 1, 1945. This news story said that Daniels, "the tubby bespeckled son of former Navy Secretary Josephus Daniels," refused to give out any information on almost anything at his first press conference. Speculations about Daniels are in Eben A. Ayers, *Truman in the White House, The Diary of Eben A. Ayers* (Columbia: University of Missouri Press, 1991), pp. 3, 36–37. "Changes White House Jobs," *Kansas City Star*, March 26, 1945; "Early Looking for a Job," *New York Evening Post*, March 26, 1945; "Early Bows Out, Daniels Steps In," *New York World-Telegram*, March 26, 1945, all in STE scrapbook January 21 ,1945–July 31, 1945.

3. Letter from Harold Ickes to STE, March 25, 1945; letter from Bert Andrews to STE, April 4, 1945; letter from Lewis Wood to STE, March 27, 1945, all in STE scrapbook, January 21, 1945–July 31, 1945.

4. "Early to Daniels," *Nashville Tennesean*, March 31, 1945.

5. Daniels press conference, March 26, 1945, Box 42, STE papers.

6. Grace Tully, *F.D.R., My Boss* (New York: Charles Scribner's Sons, 1949), pp. 354, 455; William D. Hassett, *Off the Record with F.D.R., 1942– 1945* (New Brunswick, NJ: Rutgers University Press, 1950), p. 318; Frances Perkins, *The Roosevelt I Knew* (New York: Viking, 1946), p. 395; David Brinkley, *Washington Goes to War* (New York: Knopf, 1988), p. 265; Daniels, *White House Witness*, p. 3.

7. Ross T. McIntire, *White House Physician* (New York: G. P. Putnam's Sons, 1946), p. 236; Brinkley, *Washington Goes to War*, pp. 265, 266–67.

8. McIntire, *White House Physician*, p. 236; Tully, *My Boss*, p. 355.

9. Jim Bishop, *FDR's Last Year, April 1944–April 1945* (New York: William Morrow, 1974), pp. 158, 481, 520; and Tully, *My Boss*, p. 357.

10. Bishop, *FDR's Last Year*, p. 481.

11. A. Merriman Smith, *Thank You, Mr. President: A White House Notebook* (New York: Harper & Brothers, 1946), pp. 199–200.

12. Photo is with a story, "Early Looking for a Job," *New York Evening Post*, March 26, 1945, STE scrapbook, January 21, 1945–July 31, 1945.

13. Hassett, *Off the Record*, p. 327; Tully, *My Boss*, pp. 358–59; Bishop, *FDR's Last Year*, pp. 526–27.

14. Bishop, *FDR's Last Year*, p. 532; Hassett, *Off the Record*, p. 328.

15. Hassett, *Off the Record*, p. 330; Smith, *Thank You*, pp. 183–84.

16. Smith, *Thank You*, pp. 185–86.

17. Hassett, *Off the Record*, p. 332.

18. Robert Goralski, *World War II Almanac, 1931–1945: A Political and Military Record* (New York: Putnam, 1981), pp. 394–95.

19. Bishop, *FDR's Last Year*, p. 569; James MacGregor Burns, *Roosevelt: The Soldier of Freedom, 1940–1945* (New York: Harcourt Brace Jovanovich, 1970), pp. 599–600; Hassett, *Off the Record*, pp. 332–34.

20. Bishop, *FDR's Last Year*, pp. 580–81; Burns, *Soldier of Freedom*, p. 600; Smith, *Thank You*, p. 188; Hassett, *Off the Record*, pp. 334–37.

21. Hassett, *Off the Record*, p. 337.

22. Bishop, *FDR's Last Year*, pp. 526, 585–86; Hassett, *Off the Record*, p. 337.

23. Smith, *Thank You*, pp. 179–81.

24. "Steve," *Cosmopolitan*, January 1946.

25. Hassett, *Off the Record*, p. 337; Tully, *My Boss*, p. 363.

26. Bishop, *FDR's Last Year*, pp. 592, 596; STE press conference, April 12, 1945. Several years after the president's death, Eleanor Roosevelt said she never remembered saying those words, "I am more sorry. . . ." Early, the public relations man, could have thought she said them or wished she had, and thus the oft-repeated quote was released by the White House. From Eleanor Roosevelt, *Mother and Daughter, The Letters of Eleanor and Anna Roo-*

sevelt, ed. Bernard Asbell (New York: Fromm International, 1988), pp. 185–86.

27. David McCullough, *Truman* (New York: Simon and Schuster, 1992), p. 342.

28. Hassett, *Off the Record*, p. 338; STE press conference, April 12, 1945.

29. "Tragic Message Stunned Whole of America," *London Daily Telegraph*, April 13, 1945; Smith, *Thank You*, p. 364; Bishop, *FDR's Last Year*, pp. 598–99; "Steve Early Flashed Story He Hoped Never to Cover," *Washington News*, April 13, 1945.

30. Bishop, *FDR's Last Year*, p. 611.

31. STE and Daniels press conferences, April 12, 1945.

32. STE brief meeting with the press at 6:30 p.m., April 12, 1945; and Bishop, *FDR's Last Year*, p. 609.

33. Tully, *My Boss*, pp. 369–70; Eleanor Roosevelt, *This I Remember* (New York: Harper, 1949), p. 345; Smith, *Thank You*, p. 189; Hassett, *Off the Record*, p. 339; Bishop, *FDR's Last Year*, p. 621.

34. Bishop, *FDR's Last Year*, pp. 194–95.

35. Ibid., p. 624; Smith, *Thank You*, pp. 195–96.

36. Smith, *Thank You*, p. 197; "Many Weep Openly as Caisson Carrying Roosevelt Goes By," *Washington Star*, April 15, 1945.

37. Hassett, *Off the Record*, p. 343; Burns, *Soldier of Freedom*, p. 612; Bishop, *FDR's Last Year*, p. 666; Smith, *Thank You*, p. 205; "Humble and Great Grieve at Funeral," *Illinois State Journal and Register*, April 15, 1945.

CHAPTER 25: THE LAST RIDE

1. Letter from STE to Stanley Salman, Atlantic Monthly Press, Boston, April 27, 1945; letter from STE to Lowell Brentano, Coward McCann, Inc., New York, January 18, 1946, Box 21, STE papers, FDR Library, Hyde Park, NY.

2. Letter from STE to Elizabeth Phinney, Current Books, Inc., New York, June 17, 1947, Box 21, STE papers.

3. Letter from STE to Joseph Davies, February 17, 1947, Box 3, STE papers.

4. Letter from STE to Jimmy Roosevelt, June 8, 1948, Box 15, STE papers.

5. Letter from Kent Cooper to STE, April 13 and 19, 1945, Box 2, STE papers.

6. "Early an Aide to Truman," *New York Times*, April 22, 1945; editorial cartoon, *Washington Star*, April 19, 1945; "Trenchant and Witty in First

Press Parley," *New York Journal and American*, April 17, 1945, STE scrapbook, January 21, 1945–July 31, 1945, FDR Library, Hyde Park, NY.

7. Eben A. Ayers, *Truman in the White House: The Diary of Eben A. Ayers* (Columbia: University of Missouri Press, 1991), p. 13.

8. A. Merriman Smith, *Thank You, Mr. President: A White House Notebook* (New York: Harper & Brothers, 1946), p. 208.

9. Letter from Eleanor Roosevelt to STE, April 20, 1945, Box 34, STE papers.

10. Letter from STE to Eleanor Roosevelt, April 26, 1945, Box 34, STE papers; see other correspondence between STE and Eleanor Roosevelt in this file.

11. Harry S. Truman, *Memoirs*, vol 1: *Year of Decisions* (New York: Doubleday, 1955), pp. 48, 60; Smith, *Thank You*, p. 211; David McCullough, *Truman* (New York: Simon and Schuster, 1992), pp. 355, 375; Ayers, *Truman in the White House*, pp. 10, 13.

12. "President Calm as He Kills Rumor," *Washington Post*, April 29, 1945; Robert Goralski, *World War II Almanac, 1931–1945: A Political and Military Record* (New York: Putnam, 1981), pp. 400–401, 404–405.

13. "Here Is Chicago," *Chic News*, April 25, 1945; "Personnel, Late but Ample," *Time*, May 28, 1945; appendix G to Early's Application for Supplemental and Occupational Mileage Ration, Office of Price Administration, June 1945, Box 53, STE papers.

14. Ayers, *Truman in the White House*, pp. 22–23; "Early Takes Post Here as Vice President of Pullman Company," *Washington Star*, May 17, 1945; "Big Salary for Early," *Zanesville (OH) Times Recorder*, May 29, 1945; letter from Harry S. Truman to STE, April 21, 1945, Official File, Harry S. Truman papers, Truman Library.

15. "Steve," *Cosmopolitan*, January 1946.

16. "Steve Early: White House Spokesman for a Dozen Years," *Baltimore Sun*, May 23, 1945; "They Were Three—Louis, Mac, Steve—During Comet Career of Their Chief; Today There's Only One, Soon to End Longest Run as White House Secretary," *Washington Post*, April 1, 1945.

17. "Early Gets a DSM for Public Service," *New York Times*, June 1, 1945; letter from STE to Eleanor Roosevelt, June 25, 1945, Box 34, STE papers; Ayers, *Truman in the White House*, pp. 37–38. The proclamation, dated May 31, 1945, is in Harry S. Truman papers.

18. "Truman Confers Medal on Early," *Philadelphia Inquirer*, June 1, 1945; author interview with Helen Early Elam, April 3, 1998.

19. Letter from Truman to STE, May 31, 1945; letter from STE to Truman, May 28, 1945, both in Harry S. Truman papers.

20. Birthday letter from STE to Truman, May 12, 1947; reply from

Truman to STE, May 12, 1947; reply from Truman to STE's Christmas gift of a small silver match box, December 24, 1946; reply from Truman to STE for a French canteen, December 26, 1947; reply from Truman to STE telegram, March 7, 1947; see Ayers, *Truman in the White House*, pp. 32, 42, 43, 134, 165–66 for accounts of poker games; letter from Truman to STE regarding appointment to medals board, October 4, 1945; letter from STE to Truman regarding STE resignation from Naval Academy board, all in Harry S. Truman papers. "Truman Relaxes at Stag Outing," *Washington Times-Herald*, September 23, 1945; "Truman Initiates His New Yacht," *Washington Times-Herald*, December 3, 1945.

21. Letter from Helen Early to Louis Johnson, June 19, 1945, and letter from STE to Johnson, June 23 and 25, 1945, all in Box 8, STE papers.

22. Letter from STE to Eleanor Roosevelt, June 25, 1945, Box 34, STE papers.

23. Early's Application for Supplemental and Occupational Mileage Ration, Office of Price Administration, June 1945.

24. "Early Asserts Railroad Innovations Are Answer to Postwar Competition from Air and Bus Lines," *Advertising Club Weekly*, August 6, 1945; "Truman to Aid Press Abroad, Early Says," *St. Louis Post-Dispatch*, July 31, 1945; "Why Not 'Steve' Early?" *Johnstown* (PA) *Democrat*, February 22, 1945; "Early Asserts Roosevelt Planned to Publish a Newspaper," *New York Herald-Tribune*, August 20, 1945.

25. Letter from STE to Ruthjane Rumelt, June 25, 1947, Box 16, STE papers; letter from STE to James Roosevelt, June 8, 1948, Box 15, STE papers.

26. Letters from STE to Joseph Davies, February 14 and 24, 1949, both in Box 3, STE papers.

27. Letter from STE to Davies, March 3, 1949, Box 3, STE papers.

28. For an account of Truman and Forrestal's relationship, Forrestal's suicide, and Johnson's appointment, see McCullough, *Truman*, pp. 736–41. "Stephen T. Early Is Nominated as Under Secretary of Defense," *New York Herald-Tribune*, April 8, 1949; "Early Confirmed for Defense Post," *Washington Post*, April 14, 1949. Early's medical report is in his Department of Defense files, Box 57, STE papers.

29. "Stephen T. Early Is Nominated as Under Secretary of Defense," *New York Herald-Tribune*, April 8, 1949; "Nomination a Surprise, Says Early," *Washington Post*, April 4, 1949; "Defense Problems—II," *New York Times*, April 15, 1949.

30. "Steve Early's Job Is to Muzzle the Loud-Mouth Brass in Pentagon," *Washington Daily News*, April 8, 1949; "Early Quits as Top Aide to Johnson," *Washington Evening Star*, September 12, 1950; "Early Steps Down as Defense

Deputy," *New York Times*, September 13, 1950; "Steve Early, Aide to Roosevelt, Former Defense Official, Dies," *Washington Star*, August 11, 1951. Early's personnel forms for the two salaries are in his Department of Defense files, Box 57, STE papers.

31. Comments from Finletter and Bradley are part of a series of eulogies for Early in *Carbuilder*, October 1951.

32. "Early to Leave Post with Defense Department," *New York Herald-Tribune*, May 11, 1950; "Robert S. Allen's Roundup," *New York Post*, July 9, 1950; "Early to Keep U.S. Job," *Morning Kansas City Star*, July 18, 1950; Ayers, *Truman in the White House*, p. 361; Robert J. Donovan, *Tumultuous Years: The Presidency of Harry S. Truman, 1949–1953* (New York: Norton, 1982), p. 266.

33. "Early Quits as Top Aide to Johnson."

34. Letter from STE to Truman, September 1, 1950, and letter from Truman to STE, September 12, 1950, both in STE scrapbook, April 1949–September 1950.

35. Letters from STE to Buddy Early, Helen "Sis" Early, and Thomas Early, September 28, 1950, Box 55, STE papers.

36. Ibid.; Ayers, *Truman in the White House*, pp. 386–87.

37. Letter from STE to Bernard Baruch, January 5, 1951, Box 1, STE papers; "Stephen T. Early Dies in Capital, 61," *New York Times*, August 12, 1951.

38. "Steve Early, Ex-Aide to Presidents, Dies," *Washington Post*, August 12, 1951.

39. Author interview with Elam, April 3, 1998; "Truman Attends Funeral of Early," *New York Times*, August 15, 1951. Helen Wrenn Early, Steve Early's widow, died in July 1978, at the age of eighty-three, in a nursing home in Alexandria, Virginia, where she had resided for five years after suffering a stroke; "Helen Wrenn Early" (obituary), *Washington Post*, July 20, 1978.

40. Obituaries and letters about Early's death are in Box 63, STE papers.

INDEX

about FDR having a mistress, 399

about FDR involved in Lindbergh baby kidnapping, 199

about FDR's having Jewish ancestry, 146–47, 199

about FDR's health, 133, 166, 199, 219, 241–42, 364–65, 375–78, 382–84

about government payments to FDR's mother, 146

on job offers for Early, 435

during World War II, 285–86, 290–91, 352–53

    about Churchill and FDR meetings, 341

    about war with Germany ending, 436

    after Pearl Harbor attack, 262

    on closing the Panama Canal, 240

    created by FDR, 291

    forced landing in Azores, 360

    Life photo essay on wartime rumors, 290

    off-the-record trips to Hyde Park, 372

    plot against FDR's life, 360–61

Rutherfurd, Lucy Mercer, 399, 424

Sabotage (movie), 332

St. Louis Dispatch (newspaper), 154, 235

St. Paul (Minnesota) *Pioneer Press* (newspaper), 234

St. Petersburg Times (newspaper), 309

San Francisco News (newspaper), 218

Sanger, Margaret, 65

Saratoga Sun (newspaper), 25

Sarnoff, David, 16, 179, 257, 326, 327, 446

Saturday Evening Post (magazine), 199–200

Schall, Thomas D., 127

Schechter brothers, 129–30

Schenck, Joseph M., 118

Schoenherr, Steven E., 127, 146, 156, 232, 283, 346, 348–49

Schulman, Sammy, 233

scotus. *See* Supreme Court of the United States

Scripps, E. W., 22–24

Seattle Post-Intelligencer (newspaper), 53, 54

Seattle Times (newspaper), 53, 54

secrecy. *See* censorship of the press

"Secretariat, The." *See* Early, Stephen Tyree; Howe, Louis; McIntyre, Marvin "Mac"

Securities and Exchange Commission, 169, 180

Selassie, Haile, 409

self-censorship, 264, 265–66, 284–85, 358

"Selling the New Deal: Stephen T. Early's Role as Press Secretary to President Franklin D. Roosevelt" (unpublished dissertation of Schoenherr), 127, 232, 283

Senate

    Early providing AP coverage of, 62–85

    investigation of FDR as assistant secretary of the navy, 66–69

Sengstacke, John, 369

Sequoia (houseboat), 112

"Serve in Silence." *See* censorship of the press

SHAEF. *See* Supreme Headquarters, Allied Expeditionary Forces

Shangri-la (weekend retreat in Maryland), 335–36, 380

    See also travels of FDR

Shepard, Alexander Robey, 320

Sherman Antitrust Act, 441

Sherwood, Robert E., 288

    clearing speeches of federal officials, 281

    memoirs relating to FDR, 406, 432

    speechwriter for FDR, 120, 227, 273, 276, 336, 339

Shoumatoff, Elizabeth, 424–25